THE BIRDWATCHER'S
YEARBOOK 2011

Designed and published by
Hilary Cromack

Edited by
David Cromack

BUCKINGHAM PRESS LTD

In association with

SWAROVSKI
OPTIK

Published in 2013 by
Buckingham Press Ltd
55 Thorpe Park Road, Peterborough
Cambridgeshire PE3 6LJ
United Kingdom

01733 561 739
e-mail: admin@buckinghampress.com
www.buckinghampress.co.uk

© Buckingham Press Ltd 2013

ISBN 978-0-9569876-6-2
ISSN 0144-364 X

Cover image: Smew by Jackie Garner.
Jackie Garner can be reached at The Old Cider House Studio, Humphries End, Randwick, Stroud, Glos GL6 6EW; 01453 847 420; (M)07800 804 847.
e-mail: artist@jackiegarner.co.uk
www.jackiegarner.co.uk

Black and white images: by Steve Cale.
Steve Cale can be reached at 10 Fairview Drive, Colkirk, Norfolk NR21 7NT.
Tel: 01328 862 265; (M)07866 263 673; e-mail : steveshrike@aol.com
www.steve-cale-artist.co.uk

Printed and bound in Great Britain by
Berforts Information Press, Oxford UK.

CONTENTS

PREFACE — 5

FEATURES — 7
The Great Fen — 8
Ornithological News Headlines — 11
Mapping a Positive Future for Birds — 17
Best Bird Books of the Year — 21

BIRDWATCHER'S DIARY — 27
Events guide for 2014 includes bird fairs, conferences and
other key UK events, plus some international conferences — 28
Day-by-day diary, plus blank sheets for
recording your birding outings — 30
Year planner for 2015 — 54

LOG CHARTS — 55
Guide to using the log charts — 56
Full log charts for BOU-approved British List — 58
Log charts for British dragonflies — 86
Log chart for British butterflies — 87

ART, PHOTOGRAPHY AND LECTURERS — 89
Art galleries — 90
Artists, birds and wildlife — 90
Photographers, birds and wildlife — 92
Lecturers, a nationwide guide and BTO talks listing — 94

TRADE DIRECTORY — 103
Bird garden suppliers — 104
Bird magazines — 105
Book publishers — 105
Book sellers — 107
Clothing suppliers — 108
Equipment suppliers and services — 108
Holiday companies — 109
Optical dealers — 113
Optical manufacturers and importers — 115
Optical repairs and servicing — 116

BIRD RESERVES AND OBSERVATORIES — 117
With county maps in colour and an updated listing of sites.

ENGLAND
Central England — 118
Eastern England — 140
Northern England — 158

CONTENTS

South East England 179
South West England 196

SCOTLAND
Border Counties 208
Central Scotland 210
Eastern Scotland 215
Highlands & Islands 219

WALES
Eastern Wales 223
Northern Wales 225
Southern Wales 228
Western Wales 230

COUNTY DIRECTORY 233
Under each county heading you will find:
Bird atlases/avifaunas; bird recorders; bird reports; BTO
regional representatives; clubs and societies; ringing groups;
RSPB local groups; wildlife hospitals and county Wildlife Trusts.

England 234
Scotland 271
Wales 279
Isle of Man 283
Channel Islands 284
Northern Ireland 285
Republic of Ireland 286

NATIONAL DIRECTORY 287
National organisations 288
National projects 301

INTERNATIONAL DIRECTORY 305
International organisations 306
Special interest organisations 312

QUICK REFERENCE SECTION 313
Tide tables 2014-15 314
Sunrise and sunset times 2014 320
Sea Areas 322
Schedule 1 species 323
Birdwatchers and twitchers take note!
— the dangers of ticks (the insect variety) when out birdwatching 323
National and regional birdlines 325

INDEX TO RESERVES AND OBSERVATORIES 326

PREFACE

FINDING new customers during a long drawn-out economic recession is the holy grail for any company, so I'm delighted to report around 15% of purchasers of the 2013 edition of *The Birdwatcher's Yearbook* were first time buyers.

Naturally we hope they will join our 'regulars' who appreciate the benefits of having all the relevant information for their hobby checked and printed in one volume. While it is perfectly possible to gather information from the internet, many on-line surfers find the process can be a frustrating and long-winded affair.

The Birdwatchers' Yearbook should be a one-stop solution to all your information needs, but if there are extra features you'd like to see added, please do not hesitate to make contact.

One well-established section of the *Yearbook* is the guide to nature reserves, and I've spent a considerable amount of time reviewing which sites to include in this edition. While I've added several new sites to ensure we include places that consistently deliver great birding experiences, I'd welcome nominations for other sites that you can recommend.

As Buckingham Press is based in Peterborough, I take a particular interest in the Great Fen project which is seeking to re-create the ancient wetland which once ranged over a vast area to the south of our city. It is one of the nation's most exciting conservation projects and I'm delighted to have Jon Smith bring our readers up to date with what is happening with the project in the Features section.

Conscious that *The Yearbook* is a journal of record, I've again asked Richard Facey to summarise some of the most important ornithological happenings of the past 12 months and Gordon Hamlett selects the pick of natural history and bird books published in recent months. To complete our major features, the BTO's Graham Appleton provides a behind-the-scenes look at the work that went into producing *Bird Atlas 2007-2011*, together with some of the amazing findings it has uncovered.

I'd like to end by thanking all the club secretaries, county recorders and myriad other contributors who take the time and trouble to update the information each year — without their willing assistance, this unique publishing venture simply would not be possible.

David Cromack (EDITOR)

A MESSAGE FROM THE SPONSORS
OF THIS BOOK

WELCOME to the 34th edition of *The Birdwatcher's Yearbook*, which over the course of its history has played a vitally important role in providing comprehensive and verified printed information on the birding scene in Britain. It is a publication which Swarovski has been pleased to sponsor since 2002.

Inside this issue, you will be able to read special features on two important projects that are destined to benefit birdlife in this country for many years to come – the Great Fen habitat restoration project and the publication of *Bird Atlas 2007-2011*.

The latter, which brings together data from countless bird surveys carried out by thousands of volunteers, has been a tremendous undertaking and can be considered a Domesday Book of the nation's current birdlife. More importantly, its findings will inform the decision-makers who must plan effective conservation measures going forward. I urge you to read both articles as an uplifting antidote to the many doom-and-gloom stories which populate the national press on a regular basis.

Ever since Swarovski launched its binoculars and telescopes into the birding market it has made a commitment to identify and support worthwhile conservation projects around the globe – from establishing a nature reserve on a Polish island to funding research into the endangered Sociable Plover.

As the chairwoman of Swarovski Optik's executive board, Carina Schiestl-Swarovski said: *"Our aim is always to work with nature and the environment, because this forms the basis for the use of our products. Biodiversity and wildlife conservation are important in their own right, but they also help our customers to enjoy breathtaking, unforgettable visual experiences."*

I'm sure you'll find the contents of this *Yearbook* will help you get more out of your hobby. For instance, why not spread your wings and visit a different nature reserve? Inside you'll find details of almost 400 key sites and if you are heading to the coast then the tide table calculator is an invaluable aid to being in situ at the best time.

Contact details for local bird clubs and RSPB members groups offer the opportunity to meet up with like-minded people in your area and the checklists of birds, butterflies and dragonflies are once again in place to help you keep track of what you've seen.

Put the *Birdwatcher's Yearbook* to the test and I'm sure you'll discover it can enhance your experiences in 2014. Happy birdwatching.

Peter Antoniou
Country Manager, UK & Republic of Ireland,
Swarovski Optik UK

SWAROVSKI
OPTIK

FEATURES

Alan Williams

Common Crane is just one of the many bird species destined to benefit from the Great Fen's habitat restoration programme.

The Great Fen — 8
Ornithological News Headlines — 11
Mapping a Positive Future for Birds — 17
Best Bird Books of the Year — 21

THE GREAT FEN –
WATCH THIS (HUGE) SPACE!

Jon Smith of the Wildlife Trust for Bedfordshire, Cambridgeshire and Northamptonshire explains why birdwatchers might want to keep their binoculars trained on a massive area of developing wetland and grassland between Peterborough and Huntingdon.

I WAS DELIGHTED to become Great Fen restoration officer for the Wildlife Trust in 2011. Here was my chance to be part of possibly the biggest and most ambitious habitat restoration project in Europe; be part of something that would change the way we conduct nature conservation in the UK; and last but not least help to create some fantastic places for wildlife.

I already knew the two surviving fragments of original fen at Woodwalton and Holme, which are now at the heart of Great Fen area. It had always felt awe-inspiring to be in parts of Woodwalton Fen that had stayed unchanged for centuries – a really rare thing with wetland habitats. But these isolated relics and their fragile wildlife needed to become part of a much bigger area of habitat if they were to survive in the long term, which is how the idea for a huge landscape-scale approach to habitat protection began to take shape in the late 1990s.

This 'big idea' was beyond creating another nature reserve. It was to re-create thousands of acres of an astonishing range of wildlife habitats – reedbed, meres, ponds, fen, wet and dry meadows, woodland, mire and heath – working all the while to balance the needs of, and provide benefit for, local people, farmers and businesses. It also encompassed providing facilities for the anticipated visitors who would be ultimately attracted by the nature and beauty of 14 square miles of such an amazing restored landscape.

Since the project got underway in 2001 with the creation of a partnership to steer all the practical, economic and social decisions needed, the progress has been faster than anyone could have dared hope for. This is down to the help of so many local people, businesses, Trust supporters and funders.

The biggest boost of all came in 2008 when the Heritage Lottery Fund awarded its largest ever grant for an environmental project of £7.2 million to the Great Fen. Thanks to this and other generous support, over half of the land in the Great Fen has already been bought by the partners.

Great Fen Facts

IN THE 1800s Bitterns were so common around Whittlesea Mere that punt-gunners could 'dispatch several with one shot'. Savi's Warblers bred regularly and Montagu's Harriers were common.

KING JOHN used to visit regularly to hunt Common Cranes in the Middle Ages – they had disappeared by the 17th Century.

THE GREAT FEN – WATCH THIS (HUGE) SPACE!

By autumn 2013 more than 3,000 acres (1,196 hectares) will be undergoing restoration and being managed for nature conservation. Add in Holme and Woodwalton Fens and you have a staggering total of 3,754 acres (1,521 hectares) of land now being managed for nature – which is over 41% of the whole project area.

Particularly exciting at the moment is the re-creation of a

This artist's impressions of Rymes Reedbed depicts the wildlife-friendly scene as it will be in a few years' time, if the Great Fen restoration goes according to plan. Opposite, an aerial photograph shows the farmland as it looks today.
John Walsom / copyright Wildlife Trust BCN

spectacular new reedbed, with pools and wet grassland – the size of Woodwalton Fen – on the edge of the former Whittlesea Mere. The Mere was once the largest lake in England outside the Lake District, but was lost to drainage in 1851.

Under restoration now from arable fields, the new Rymes Reedbed will provide a home for Bitterns, Yellow Wagtails, Grasshopper Warblers, Bearded Tits, Cuckoos and Cranes, not to mention otters and water voles. An elevated hide has been created so you can watch the restoration work as it happens – and watch the wildlife as it starts to return.

Looking at the potential range of bird species that could take up home across the Great Fen, the future is incredibly exciting. With such a variety of habitat on offer the sky's the limit. Large areas of the project are focused around a variety of wetland habitats and all the birds and other wildlife that go with them.

Species such and Lapwing, Redshank and Snipe should become commonplace and species such as Bittern and Crane could return. Add in the other areas being created in the wider Fenland basin and I can envisage this part of the country becoming the future 'go to' destination for birdwatchers in England.

Great Fen Facts

LAPWING and Snipe now breed at Darlow's and Middle Farm, while Cranes and Avocets have recently been seen in the Great Fen. It is hoped that they will breed along with Spoonbills one day.

WHOOPER and Bewick's Swans have been seen in recent winters in areas being restored.

BITTERNS and Bearded Tits are sometimes seen in the reedbeds, with Quail, Grey Partridge, Grasshopper Warbler, Corn Bunting, Yellow Wagtail and Linnet regularly reported.

ALL BUT FOUR of the British raptors can be seen during the course of a year. Marsh Harrier, Buzzards, Red Kite and Peregrine are regular, with Merlin and Hen Harrier appearing in greater numbers during the winter. Hobbies may be seen at Woodwalton Fen in the summer.

ALL species of British owl can be found in the Great Fen though Short-eared Owls only occur in winter.

THE GREAT FEN – WATCH THIS (HUGE) SPACE!

Restoring a large-scale wetland environment gives us hope that the large copper butterfly, which went extinct in Britain in 1851 as a result of habitat loss, could be reintroduced at some point in the near future.

Away from the wetland areas on the 'fenland rises' there will be drier areas, where in time species-rich grasslands and meadows will develop. These will produce a wealth of insects and with some careful management the chance for farmland and other song birds to thrive. Species such as Corncrake will hopefully be heard along with many of our declining songbirds such as Corn Bunting, Linnet, Skylark and many others.

As restoration extends the area of reedbeds within the Great Fen, sightings of Bitterns are expected to becoming increasingly common. Photograph by Tony Bates

Great Fen numbers

- **302** wonderful volunteers have helped with the work since 2008.
- **99%** of wetlands have been lost from the Fens since 1600.
- **1,360** plant and animal species have been recorded on land restored so far. Bird species recorded on these areas have increased from 57 in 2007 to 71 in 2011
- **70** kilometres of ditches have been re-profiled to make them more wildlife friendly.

The Wildlife Trust has recently been given an exciting chance to restore another 182 hectares of the highest priority land in the Great Fen which will not only be transformed in to valuable wetland habitat in its own right but will enable the re-wetting of other areas of land, speeding up restoration to wildlife rich habitat. This could begin as early as 2014 and the Wildlife Trust is running a major appeal to help the multi-million pound costs of this new scheme (more on this at www.wildlifebcn.org).

For lots more about the Great Fen including wildlife sightings, work in progress and the growing number of sites to visit in the area go to greatfen.org.uk

The support team

This birdwatching hotspot in the making would not be possible without the incredible support of over 1,500 individual donors and grant funders. Not to mention the volunteers and staff from the partner organisations who are: Environment Agency; Huntingdonshire District Council; Middle Level Commissioners; Natural England; Wildlife Trust for Bedfordshire, Cambridgeshire and Northamptonshire.

Did you know?

- Woodwalton Fen is one of Britain's oldest nature reserves.
- 'Celebrity' support for the project has come from Sir John Major, Stephen Fry, HRH the Prince of Wales and Nigel Marven.
- 9,100 acres of wildlife habitat will be restored in the Great Fen – an area the size of Peterborough.
- Holme Fen is the largest birch woodland in lowland Britain.
- Water voles, in serious decline across the UK, are increasing their numbers in the Great Fen.
- Eels were once so common in the Fens they were used as payment for rent.
- Beavers were found in the Fens for thousands of years.

NEWS HEADLINES FROM THE BIRD WORLD

Richard Facey brings you a selection of significant news stories about wild birds from Britain and further afield.

On the track of avian mysteries

TRACKING BIRDS with cutting-edge technology is in vogue and while the BTO's Cuckoo project has rightly accrued much press coverage, other projects should prove equally rewarding.

In 2013 an international team from the Wildfowl & Wetlands Trust (WWT) and the Bulgarian Society for the Protection of Birds (BSPB), fitted satellite tags to 11 Red-breasted Geese, a species at the centre of an ornithological mystery.

Just over a decade ago more than 50,000 individuals disappeared from their traditional wintering grounds along the Black Sea coast. Since then co-ordinated international counts have failed to locate the missing geese and conservationists don't know if these birds have been permanently lost due to hunting, changes in agriculture or development, or have just moved their wintering grounds to an unknown location.

The satellite tags will allow the species' epic 6,000km migration to their breeding grounds in Arctic Russia to be tracked, providing invaluable data for the future conservation of the species.

Meanwhile, GPS tracking of Taiga Bean Goose by WWT on behalf of Scottish Natural Heritage has revealed the migration patterns of Scotland's only flock. Once common, declines over the last century mean that only a single flock of around 250 birds spends its winter on the Slamannan plateau near Falkirk. This is a trend mirrored across Europe where the species has declined from approximately 100,000 geese in 1995 to no more than 65,000 by 2009.

Six geese fitted with GPS tags on the Slamannan plateau during the 2012/13 were tracked as they moved within Scotland before heading across the North Sea. The geese then spent a few weeks in late March feeding 40km north-east of Oslo, Norway before travelling a

Anger over ban veto

THE WELSH Government angered conservationists in 2013 by deciding not to introduce a statutory ban on hunting White-fronted Geese in Wales. Though a voluntary ban remains in place on the Dyfi Estuary, its Welsh stronghold, it is still legal to hunt the goose elsewhere – making Wales the only UK country where it is not protected by law.

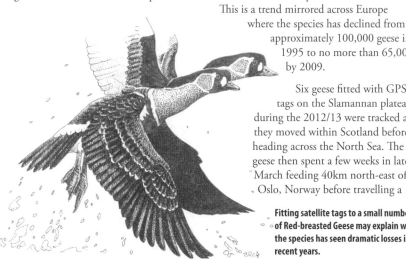

Fitting satellite tags to a small number of Red-breasted Geese may explain why the species has seen dramatic losses in recent years.

Boost for wild parrot numbers

TWO parrot species with perilously low wild populations had a boost in 2013. Numbering just 110 to 130, the Blue-throated Macaw is a Critically Endangered species. However, in early 2013 a pioneering move was made to save the species as part of a decade-long project led by the World Parrot Trust. Six macaws were transferred from their home in Paradise Park, Cornwall, to Bolivia for release into the wild.

Meanwhile the Scarlet Macaw made a comeback to the jungles of Palenque National Park, Mexico, when 60 birds were released. The species has been absent from the area for more than 70 years, and is believed to be extinct in 95% of its former range in Mexico. The pioneering party was bred by the Excaret ecopark which will supply 60 birds a year for release up to 2015.

further 200km to Dalarna County in west Sweden, where they are believed to be breeding.

Tracking technology has also been used to solve another ornithological mystery – the whereabouts of the breeding grounds of the New Zealand Storm-Petrel. Believed extinct until its rediscovery in 2003, the species' breeding territories have never been found since it was first recorded in the 1800s.

However, a team of scientists caught 24 birds at seas before attaching 1g radio transmitters and used these to track them to three islands; Poor Knights, Mokohinau and Little Barrier. Scientists camping on the latter, a mere 50km from Auckland City, used signals from the transmitters to confirm the petrels were breeding in the island's forest.

Meanwhile 20,000 images, captured by ten camera-carrying Gannets revealed some interesting foraging habits. Gannets, particularly male birds, have a liking for fishing boat discards, so the EU's decision to phase out the dumping of unwanted fish overboard may have a impact on the species in future.

Putting down a welcome mat for new species

A NEW STUDY published in 2013 presented clear-cut evidence of the benefits of nature reserves and other protected areas. Work by the University of York and the RSPB shows that as well as being vital for the conservation of wildlife, protected sites offer a welcome mat for those species colonising or recolonising our shores as a result of global environmental change.

The team looked at the extent to which new wetland colonists rely on protected areas to establish populations. Since the 1960s, eight new species have established a permanent breeding presence in the UK and six of these have been wetland species. These six – Mediterranean Gull (in 1968), Goldeneye (1970), Cetti's Warbler (1973), Whooper Swan (1978), Common Crane (1981) and Little Egret (1996) – all chose Sites of Special Scientific Interest (SSSI) on which to set up base camp.

From here they established population centres, allowing the colony to grow large enough to expand into suitable habitat outside the protected site. In total, of 20 wetland species, including those above and others that have not yet established a permanent population, 18 first bred on protected sites.

In 2012 the first two pairs of Great White Egrets ever to breed in the UK chose protected sites, while Little Bitterns again bred at the RSPB's Ham Wall reserve (Somerset) in 2013, where they have been suspected of breeding since 2010.

NEWS HEADLINES FROM THE BIRD WORLD

Last year the first Crane eggs laid in the west of Britain in more than 400 years were in a nest in WWT Slimbridge, Gloucestershire. It also marked the first known egg laid as a result of the Great Crane Project release scheme. Sadly, though one egg hatched, the chick perished one or two days later.

However RSPB Scotland was pleased to announce the first successful breeding of Common Crane in the country since the 16th Century in 2012 and 2013, though the exact breeding location is unknown.

Little Bitterns have benefited from lack of disturbance and good habitat conditions to breed successfully on a British nature reserve since 2010.

Night Parrot finally comes in from the dark

AUSTRALIA'S most secretive bird, the Night Parrot (*Pezoporous occidentalis*) has not been seen flying in the wild for so long that news of its 're-discovery' was bound to cause some excitement.

Queensland naturalist John Young presented still photographs and six seconds of video footage of the bird in its habitat of thick spinifex to an invited audience at Queensland Museum in July 2013. The images are part of a collection of 600 photographs taken at a secret site in south-west Queensland.

The images and video, including calls, are the first ever of live Night Parrots and the first real glimpses of the species' behaviour and ecology. However, Mr Young has come in for criticism because he won't reveal the location of his site and won't allow his sound recording to be used by scientists trying to locate other populations of the parrot.

Dipper eggs aid river pollution checks

THE RIVERS of South Wales, which 50 years ago were among the most polluted in Europe, have gone through major clean-ups and are now rich in wildlife. One species to benefit is the Dipper (*Cinculus cinculus*), which can now be found flying alongside the Millennium

Heronries Census 86 years old

LAUNCHED in 1928 through *British Birds* journal, the Heronries Census celebrated its 86th birthday in 2013. The BTO's annual count of apparently occupied Grey Heron nests means it is the longest running annual survey on a breeding bird. Since its inception, other species have colonised the UK with Little Egret, Spoonbill and Cattle Egret all featuring in survey returns.

Stadium in Cardiff, as well as along more rural stretches.

In view of the general improvement in urban water quality, there was a surprise when a team of scientists, led by Cardiff University, examined the levels of pollutants in the eggs of Dippers from 33 Welsh rivers. They found that eggs of the urban site nesters contained some pollutants at levels, on average, more than four times greater than in nearby rural rivers. In some cases the were the highest ever levels found in songbirds.

Work to reduce pollution in rivers located in urban areas of Wales has not been as successful as first thought – a fact uncovered by testing the eggs of Dippers.

The pollutants included polychlorinated biphenyls (PCBs) and polybrominated diphenyl ethers (PBDEs), which can take decades to break down. Despite being banned, PCBs were found in increased concentrations in urban rivers compared to 20 years ago. Such high levels cause developmental problems in young birds and there is some evidence that productivity is being hampered, though the exact cause is not known.

As these chemicals can also affect humans, the Dipper could become the "canary in the coal mine" for water companies and environmental regulators. The study's authors point out that testing blood or egg samples provides information on the real level of exposure to pollutants, and could become a useful addition to the current methods used to test and monitor water quality.

Asia produces two new bird species

NOT EVERYONE is able to discover a new species to science just half an hour from their front door in a capital city of 1.5 million people. Simon Mahood is the exception.

He and his colleagues discovered a new species of tailorbird in Phnom Penh, the capital city of Cambodia and named it the Cambodian Tailorbird (*Orthotomus chaktomuk*). It is a wren-sized grey bird with a rufous cap and black throat and is one of two tailorbirds found exclusively in the country.

It was discovered during routine monitoring for avian influenza. Initially misidentified, the bird's true identity was realised in 2013. Among the places it was found was a flooded construction site, though the species typically inhabits dense, humid lowland scrub in Phnom Penh and the surrounding floodplain.

Only tiny areas of the species' habitat remain within Phnom Penh and the tailorbird is in decline outside the city; as a result the species has been recommended for classification as Near Threatened under the IUCN's Red List.

Another species announced in 2013 has also been hiding in plain sight. Since 1896, when seven specimens were collected, the Indonesian island of Lombok has long been known to be the home of a scops owl, but the species was wrongly identified as the widespread Moluccan Scops Owl (*Otus magicus*).

After being misidentified for more than 100 years, the Rinjani Scops Owl was finally acknowledged as a distinct species by two separate ornithologists.

It was not until two researchers, operating on different parts of the island, discovered within days of arriving something that had gone unnoticed in the preceding 100 years – the Molunccan Scops Owls on Lombok just did not sound right.

Further investigation revealed it to be a previously unknown species, now named the Rinjani Scops Owl (*Otus jolandae*). The species is locally common and occurs within Gunung Rinjani National Park and is Lombok's first endemic bird species.

Where have all the birds gone?

HABITAT LOSS has been a major factor in the decline of many British bird species, but it appears the weather is playing an increasingly important role. Authors of *The State of the UK's Birds 2012* estimate that the UK has lost in the region of 44 million nesting birds since 1966, or more graphically, that's one nesting pair a minute.

Wrens have suffered badly because of cold winters – since 2000 the UK has lost an average of 835 Wrens a day due to cold weather, but happily it remains our most common and widespread bird. The situation looks bleaker for Hen Harriers and Turtle Doves, the two big losers in the UK conservation stakes in 2013.

England's two known pairs of Hen Harrier both failed to fledge young, the worst

NEWS HEADLINES FROM THE BIRD WORLD

performance since 1960s, but the Turtle Dove is having a bad time across the entire UK. The Breeding Bird Survey Report 2012 reveals a loss of 85% of the population, one of the largest declines of species covered by the survey since 1995.

In complete contrast, Collared Doves are thriving and now number close to one million pairs in Britain. BBS 2012 shows other species are doing well; 43 species have increased significantly since the start of the survey. Though these include non natives such as the Ring-necked Parakeet, which has seen more than a 1,000% increase, it includes conservation successes such as Red Kite which is up by 676%.

Tree Sparrow, a personal favourite, also goes from strength to strength showing a 113% increase between 1995 and 2012; though this should be read in the context of its historical declines. It is encouraging to read that species such as Bittern, Corncrake and Nightjar have all shown significant growth in their populations.

Amid much doom and gloom, the continued rise of Britain's Red Kite population is to be welcomed.

It started with a letter

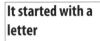

In 1933 a group of birdwatchers wrote to *The Times* to announce the formation of the British Trust for Ornithology – 80 years later the BTO boasts 100 staff and up to 60,000 volunteers contributing to its myriad surveys. The original letter and more can be found here www.bto.org/news-events/news/2013-07/it-started-letter

---

Key contributors

GRAHAM APPLETON
A trained bird ringer and bird survey enthusiast, Graham is Director of Communications at the British Trust for Ornithology, overseeing the funding of research and surveys and looking after members and volunteers. He's authored three children's books and been closely involved in *Bird Atlas 2007-2011*, the subject of his article on page??

STEVE CALE
A busy professional wildlife artist based in Norfolk, Steve runs painting courses, gives lectures to bird clubs and art societies and hosts birdwatching tours to Turkey and Northern Cyprus. Too see examples of his work, visit: www.steve-cale.co.uk

RICHARD FACEY
Regular contributor Richard is an ecologist, currently working as a conservation officer for Natural Resources Wales. He's an active member of Cardiff Bird Ringers and has served as a trustee for the Welsh Ornithological Society since 2011.

JACKIE GARNER
Working at Nature In Art Museum fired Jackie's love of wildlife and she's now been painting birds and other creatures for more than 30 years. Since establishing her new studio in Gloucestershire, she has expanded her range of wildlife paintings, cards and puzzles and more recently has completed work on *The Wildlife Artist's Handbook*. To se more of her work, visit: www.jackiegarner.co.uk

GORDON HAMLETT
A repected book reviewer and author of the acclaimed *Best Birdwatching Sites: Scottish Highlands*, Gordon has been busy working on an expanded 2nd edition, which is due to be published in 2013. In addition, he has continued working as a freelance contributor to *Bird Watching* magazine.

JON SMITH
A wildlife enthusiast from his childhood, Jon works for the Bedfordshire, Cambrdgeshire and Northamptonshire Wildlife Trust as a restoration officer for the Great Fen project and provides an entertaining account of this impressive habitat restoration scheme.

MAPPING A POSITIVE FUTURE FOR BRITAIN'S BIRDS

We have all read that *Bird Atlas 2007–11* will set the conservation agenda for birds for the next 20 years but how will the information collected by 40,000 birdwatchers be used? BTO's Graham Appleton supplies some of the answers.

Bird Atlas 2007-11
The breeding and wintering birds of Britain and Ireland

Dawn Balmer, Simon Gillings, Brian Caffrey, Bob Swann, Iain Downie & Rob Fuller

DID YOU KNOW that Green Woodpeckers are disappearing from western Wales, that Garden Warblers and Goldfinches are continuing to expand into Scotland and that Great Spotted Woodpeckers now breed in Ireland? On the downside, that there is only one 10-km square south and east of London which still holds breeding Willow Tits.

This is all new information, summarised for nearly 300 species in the newly-published *Bird Atlas 2007–11*. Behind each story lie questions relating to the way our county bird lists are changing. What do the declines in south and east England tell us about the pressures facing the habitats upon which birds depend, how is changing climate affecting where species can winter or breed, and what do differing fortunes in uplands and lowlands tell us about changing land-use practices?

For Dawn Balmer and Simon Gillings, respectively leading on survey organisation and analysis for *Bird Atlas 2007–11*, the last two years of the Atlas project were tough. Having worked very hard to make sure that the fieldwork period was successfully organised – which it certainly was – a huge amount of effort went into encouraging teams of regional validators to complete validation.

They also had to work with NGOs and agencies to bring together data-sets on species for which special surveys had been organised during the

Buying the atlas will not only support BTO's ongoing research work, but enable every reader to get a much more accurate picture of how relatively common species, such as Nuthatch, are faring in different parts of the country. Photograph by Alan Williams

MAPPING A POSITIVE FUTURE FOR BRITAIN'S BIRDS

Checking the data

The information that went into Bird Atlas 2007–11 is robust and reliable. For all bird records submitted via the website, there was built-in, online validation at the data entry stage, to flag up unusual species, high counts and unusual dates. This alerted the volunteer to the fact that he or she had entered something unusual, giving the opportunity to delete, change or confirm the record.

A 'Review and Validation Module' allowed teams of volunteer Validators, involving Regional Organisers and local bird clubs and bird recorders, to validate every record received either online or by paper. This module allowed 600 data validators to drill down on records for their region, either by species, 10-km square, tetrad or the records of individual surveyors. The validation of bird records was of utmost importance; a considerable amount of time was spent by local experts, checking records and contacting volunteers for verification.

Atlas period. The data sets were not finally closed until the spring of 2013, though the writing of species accounts and chapters had been underway for some time.

A local dimension

A significant amount of support has been given to local atlas projects. At the heart of the relationship are shared data, collected using the system developed for *Bird Atlas 2007–11* and kept open for an extra 30 months to facilitate the completion of local projects. Dawn Balmer and Simon Gillings have produced tailor-made maps, contributed to local conferences and assisted with analyses. Early planning of the project enabled the parallel development of 43 local atlas projects, encouraging the collection of more data at finer resolutions.

Publication of some of the local atlases is already at an advanced stage. Early examples include the already-published Buckinghamshire, Bute and Avon Atlases, the Herts Bird Club county-wide on-line data resource http://www.hertsatlas.org.uk/ and the CD of maps sold by Sussex Ornithological Society, while in parallel working on a new book of the county's avifauna.

Using the information

The aim of *Bird Atlas 2007–11* was to produce maps of distribution and relative abundance for all bird species breeding and wintering in Britain and Ireland, to highlight areas of particular importance for each individual bird species. In addition it assesses changes in bird distributions since previous breeding atlases in 1970 and 1990, and since the last winter atlas of the early 1980s.

When reading the new book, each of us will have species that we want to check first. There are questions to ask too:
• Have we seen a halt to the continuing contraction of ranges of species linked with arable farmland?
• How widespread are declines of woodland species?
• Are changes in numbers for summer migrants reflected in the distribution maps?
• Have species such as Nuthatch continued to expand their ranges and are there different patterns in different parts of Britain and Ireland?

To find out the answers, start reading chapter six of the Atlas! The Atlas highlights new patterns for individual species that are not well-covered in other long-term surveys, several of which are biodiversity action plan (BAP) and candidate BAP species.

MAPPING A POSITIVE FUTURE FOR BRITAIN'S BIRDS

Researchers interested in a particular species can use Atlas data to measure abundance changes. For instance, we know, from the BTO/JNCC/RSPB Breeding Bird Survey, that Kestrel numbers have declined by 17% since 1995 but we have no separate figures for Wales, Northern Ireland or two of the nine regions of England. Comparing the abundance data for the 1988–91 and 2008–11 breeding seasons shows intriguing patterns for Britain and Ireland. Why are there increases in the eastern and southern Midlands of England, when the main picture is one of widespread decline across Britain? Photograph by Bill Coster

While the authors were still writing the book, provisional atlas data were already being used by conservation scientists looking to undertake fieldwork (e.g. on Lesser Spotted Woodpecker), designing surveys (e.g. Nightingale), putting together population figures (Avian Population Estimates Panel), refining farm subsidy systems and tackling planning issues. There will be many more examples in the next few years.

When several species are looked at together, as families, habitat specialists (e.g. upland species, woodland species) or species sharing other traits (e.g. migrants) then patterns are starting to emerge, as you will read in Chapter 6 of the new book. The stories might not be as simple as 20 years ago, when the focus was predominantly on range contractions and declines in farmland birds, but they will have major relevance to conservation planning and future research.

For the first time, researchers will be able to use measures of abundance to explore the possible causes of change more deeply than has been possible thus far. Potentially there is even more to be gained by combining atlas data with other volunteer-based information on productivity and survival in different parts of a species' range. Where a species is spreading, or conversely contracting, is this driven by processes operating at the edge or core of the range? What can Atlas data tell us about the relative importance to birds of the many different changes occurring to habitats, land-use and weather?

The coming decades will see more land released for building, a focus on food and energy security, and almost certainly the further expansion of non-native species – can Atlas data help to inform us of the likely implications for our native bird life?

Bird Atlas 2007–11 has provided rich veins of data to mine. Though the BTO has research plans of its own, we shall look to build partnerships with universities and other organisations, so that wider use can be made of the records that have been so readily provided by an estimated 40,000 birdwatchers.

We are particularly keen to work with academic researchers who have access to funding, so that we can make the best return on the £1.5 million investment that the BTO and its supporters have made in the data-collection and collation processes.

Productive partnerships

The book celebrating *Bird Atlas 2007-11* has been ten years in the making; starting in 2004, with discussions between BTO and its traditional atlas partners, BirdWatch Ireland and the Scottish Ornithologists' Club. From the outset, Bird Atlas 2007–11 was destined to set the agenda for ornithological conservation in Britain and Ireland for the next 20 years. For the survey part of the project, the BTO took the lead within the UK and BirdWatch Ireland undertook complementary work within the Republic.

Though the BTO received excellent help from a small number of Trusts, particularly the Garfield Weston Foundation, the Esmée Fairbairn Foundation, the J & J R Wilson Trust and the AEB Trust, from businesses and from its members

The intensification of agriculture has had a well documented impact on farmland species such as Corn Bunting — the new Atlas will tell us if declines have continued.
Photograph by Alan Williams

and supporters, the project made a dent in reserves that became significant during a period of economic recession.

BirdWatch Ireland made similarly significant investments in the project, with support from the National Parks & Wildlife Service, the Heritage Council, the Environment & Heritage Service (Northern Ireland) and the Environmental Protection Agency. We are grateful to everyone who has supported the Atlas project and promise to try to make the best possible use of the data you have collected and the money you have provided.

BEST BIRD BOOKS OF THE YEAR

Readers looking for more than another standard fieldguide or avifauna have been spoilt for choice in the past 12 months. Reviewer Gordon Hamlett picks out some titles well worth seeking out...

IT HAS BEEN a fabulous year for natural history publishing. Traditionally, bird titles would fall into one of three categories: fieldguides, where-to-watch guides and avifaunas, but with most of those jigsaws having been completed, publishers have been forced to look elsewhere for inspiration. The result is an eclectic mix of titles where there is something to appeal to all tastes.

The major new technological development has come from Helm. Their wonderful range of fieldguides has been supplemented by enhanced e-book editions, complete with the birds' calls, ideal if you are visiting a country for the first time. Discussion on the internet has ranged as to which is the worst disaster; dropping a traditional paper book in a river, or dropping an e-book reader on a rock...

Strigiophiles, or owl lovers if you prefer, have been well served, with three first class volumes for their delectation. *Owls of the World: A Photographic Guide* (Mikkola, Helm, 512pp hb, ISBN 978-1-4081-3028-5 £35) has a plethora of colour pictures of every known species, together with introductory chapters on biology etc.

Owls (Taylor, Bloomsbury, 224pp hb, ISBN 978-1-4081-5553-0, £25) concentrates more on behaviour, coupled with detailed accounts for all the northern hemisphere species. For a phenomenally detailed account of just one species, you can't go wrong with *The Snowy Owl* (Potapov and Sale, Poyser, 304pp hb ISBN 978-0-7136-8817-7 £50) which covers everything from bribing huskies to finding nests, through to the owl's relationships with man.

EXERCISING THE GREY MATTER

Some books are for entertainment, others for reference. But there is a third category which can loosely be described as books that make you think. *Feral* by environmentalist George Monbiot (Allen Lane, hb 320pp, ISBN 978-1-846-14748-7, £20) argues the case for reintroducing different species from wolf and lynx downwards. Bird species considered include Dalmatian Pelicans, Eagle Owls and White Storks.

We get so used to getting our news and views fed to us by government conservation bodies, wildlife charities or professional ornithologists, that it easy to forget that not everyone shares the same opinions.

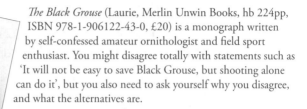

The Black Grouse (Laurie, Merlin Unwin Books, hb 224pp, ISBN 978-1-906122-43-0, £20) is a monograph written by self-confessed amateur ornithologist and field sport enthusiast. You might disagree totally with statements such as 'It will not be easy to save Black Grouse, but shooting alone can do it', but you also need to ask yourself why you disagree, and what the alternatives are.

Mark Avery spent 25 years working for the RSPB, finishing up as Conservation Director. *Fighting for Birds* (Pelagic Publishing, 324pp, pb, ISBN 978-1-907807-29-9 £12.99) is a wonderful romp through his career, explaining why the RSPB campaigned as it did. You may agree or not with his views (mostly agree), but Mark never pulls his punches and you'll never be anything less than royally entertained.

STORY-TELLING PAR EXCELLENCE

For men of a certain age, a book that combines a prisoner-of-war story with birdwatching has got to be the ultimate fantasy. *Birds in a Cage* (Niemann, Short Books, hb 312pp, ISBN 978-1-78072-093-7, £20, also available in pb) tells the story of men who used birdwatching as a means of getting through their time in captivity. Their collective post-war achievements helped to define British ornithology for decades to come. Highly recommended.

Bryan Bland is a brilliant raconteur and tour guide leader. Who else would try to engineer a temporary ceasefire in a war so that his group could see a key species? *The Profit of Birding* (New Holland hb 352pp ISBN 978-1-78009-124-2) brings together some of those stories combined with large chunks of history and music thrown in too. My only disappointment is that some of the trip reports get a bit 'samey'.

Looking for the Goshawk (Jameson, Bloomsbury, hb 368pp ISBN 978-1-4081-6487-7 £18.99) is a beautifully written account of one man's search for this elusive hunter. If you are looking for a little light reading before bedtime, then *Birduder 344* (Sawyer, Brambleby Books, pb 320pp ISBN 978-1-908241-09-2 £12.99), and *Scilly Birding* (Davey, Brambleby Books, 184pp ISBN 978-1-908241-17-7 £8.99) will put a smile on your face and evoke memories we can all relate to.

VARIED MONOGRAPHS TO ENJOY

This year's crop of monographs range from the quirky to scholarly.

BEST BIRD BOOKS OF THE YEAR

Ostrich (Williams, Reaktion Books, pb 184pp ISBN 978-1-78023-039-9, £9.99) is the latest title in an excellent on-going series that looks at the history of a creature and its relationship with man over the centuries.

The Rutland Water Ospreys (Mackrill et al, Bloomsbury, hb 160pp, ISBN 978-1-4081-7414-2 £20) tells the story of the bird's successful reintroduction to the Midlands. Two more titles have been released in the New Naturalist series: *Partridges* (Potts, Collins, pb 466pp, ISBN 978-0-00-741871-8, £30) and *Terns* (Cabot and Nisbet, Collins, pb 462pp ISBN 978-0-00-741248-8, £35) are self-recommending if you are particularly interested in these groups of birds. Hardback versions of both titles are also available.

The Mandarin Duck (Lever, Poyser, hb 192pp ISBN 978-1-4081-4963-8, £49.99) makes clear that despite popular belief, the colourful member of the wildfowl world isn't more abundant in Britain in its native Far East. Poyser monographs have a deserved reputation for excellence and this book easily maintains the standard.

CELEBRATING BIRDS AND HABITATS IN BRITAIN

Having mentioned the dearth of traditional titles, *Birds of the Heart of England* (ed Easterbrook, Liverpool University Press, hb 202pp, ISBN 978-1-84631-885-6, £24.99) is an avifauna, unusually, not devoted to a particular county, but centred around the town of Banbury instead.

The Ancient Pinewoods of Scotland (Bain, Sandstone Press, hb 224pp, ISBN 978-1908737-25-0, £24.99) is an unusual site guide because it concentrates on habitat rather than wildlife. Here you get details on the remaining pockets of Caledonian forests, important for the likes of iconic species such as Capercaillie, Scottish Crossbill and Crested Tit. What really strikes you is just how little of this once mighty forest remains.

Ostensibly a coffee table photographic guide, what sets *Birds Through Irish Eyes* (McGeehan and Wylie, Collins Press, hb 328pp, ISBN 978-1-84889-162-3, £34.99) apart, is the fabulous descriptions of the birds. These range from the simple 'black and buttercup bill' of a Whooper Swan to '…uncannily reminiscent of the sound of dental amalgam being crimped into a tooth', describing the call of a Sandwich Tern.

BEST BIRD BOOKS OF THE YEAR

SUPERB IMAGES ABOUND

Fans of great bird photography should check out two books from New Holland: *Fascinating Birds* (Varesvuo, hb 160pp, ISBN 978-1-78009-178-5, £20) and *Penguins – Close Encounters* (Tipling hb 160pp, ISBN 978-1-78009-247-8, £20). They're both good enough to make you sell all your camera equipment straight away.

Drawn from Paradise (Attenborough and Fuller, Collins, hb 254pp, ISBN 978-0-00-748761-5, £30) surveys the discovery of this extraordinary family through the first drawings and paintings of the various Birds of Paradise species. A glorious mix of history and art.

Langford Press, a small independent publisher, continues to produce eye-catching titles in its Wildlife Art Series which features some of Britain's leading bird artists. Solway-based John Threlfall follows up his first book on estuaries with *Drawn To The Edge* (hb 190pp, ISBN 978-1-904078-38-8, £38), which examines a broader range of coastal habitats, all lavishly illustrated with his distinctively bold paintings.

It neatly complements *Jewels Beyond The Plough* (Jefferson, Davis, Langford Press, hb 168pp, ISBN 978-1-904078-41-8, £38), which celebrates Britain's wildflower grasslands. Informed text is provided by Richard Jefferson, Natural England's senior grassland specialist, but every page is enhanced by John Davis' evocative watercolours of plants, bugs, birds and mammals.

The story underpinning *Troubled Waters* (Pearson, Langford Press, hb 136pp, ISBN 978-1-904078-48-7, £38) concerns a conservation horror story – the huge loss of albatrosses and other seabirds snared on fishing hooks. Artist Bruce Pearson pledged himself to raising awareness of the issues and his enthusiastic text and wonderfully varied artwork achieve their aim splendidly.

John Busby, one of the founding members of the modern British bird art movement, is an appropriate author to launch Langford Press' new Wildlife Art Techniques series. As the title *Looking At Birds* (Busby, Langford Press, pb 98pp, ISBN 978-1-904078-55-5, £15) suggests, John advocates working from life to understand how birds move and he provides many sketches to get his points across.

BEST BIRD BOOKS OF THE YEAR

John, a great seabird enthusiast, provides illustrations for *On The Rocks* (Nelson, Busby, Langford Press, pb 292pp, ISBN 978-1-904078-56-2, £20) in which Brian Nelson, director of the Scottish Seabird Centre, recounts his most memorable encounters with birds and islands over a 60-year period.

Extinct Boids (Steadman, Bloomsbury, hb 240pp, ISBN 978-1-4081-7862-1, £35) is a real Marmite book. You will either love it or hate it; there is no middle ground. Ralph Steadman's cartoon style is well known and here he turns his attention to a variety of extinct species. Just to keep you on your toes, he throws in several imaginary creatures too. Count me as a fan but I can accept that purists will be offended.

Most birdwatchers are concerned with the outward appearance of birds, but artist Katrina Van Grouw has gone beneath the feathers to create a unique book about bird anatomy. *The Unfeathered Bird* (Princeton Press, hb 288pp, ISBN 978-0-691-15134-2, £40) shows off Katrina's exceptional drawing skills to perfection, but I would recommend that buyers of the book pay equal attention to her writing, which belies the depth of research with language that is always accessible to the non-expert reader.

Her husband Hein, a qualified taxidermist, also deserves plaudits for assembling the skeletons in life-like poses (a wing-drying Cormorant for instance) – no mean feat when you consider more than 200 specimens from around the globe were involved.

EXAMINING MAN'S IMPACT ON BIRDLIFE

My final two choices complement each other in a strange sort of way. *Silent Spring Revisited* (Jameson, Bloomsbury, pb 288pp, ISBN 978-1-4081-9407-2, £9.99) looks at how man affected his environment in the five decades since Rachel Carson's seminal *Silent Spring*. Topics include seabirds being washed up after oil spillages at sea, buying land for Cirl Buntings, shifts in Corncrake and Red-backed Shrike populations and Peregrines moving into urban environments.

Mankind has interacted with birds for thousands of years, not just in matters involving the environment. *Birds and People* (Cocker, Jonathan Cape, hb 592pp, ISBN 978-0-224-08174-0, £40) looks at every bird family on the planet, exploring those relationships.

Profusely illustrated by David Tipling's photos and written by the author of the wonderful *Birds Britannica*, this book has the amazing ability to wreak havoc with Einstein's theories of relativity. You pick it up to look at one particular entry. Something else catches your eye and suddenly a few hours have mysteriously disappeared.

How can you resist something that ranges from subjects as diverse as the place of the Goldfinch in Renaissance Art, the use of chicken soup as the Jews' panacea for curing all known ills, plovers and weather prediction, and feather boas as worn by the likes of Marlene Dietrich and Kylie Minogue?

This book is an absolute joy from beginning to end. The only downside is that it is large format and way too heavy to take to bed with you. Caveat emptor too. There is another book with the same title still available. If you take steps to make sure that it is the Cocker volume you get; you won't regret it.

All the above titles are recommended, but the three books that I have enjoyed most throughout the year are:-

BIRDS AND PEOPLE

BIRDS IN A CAGE

FIGHTING FOR BIRDS

Kitty the Toon
The World's First Inland Colony

Text by John Miles
Artwork by Barry Robson

FOR YOUNGER READERS

BOOKS that encourage children to take a greater interest in the natural world should be widely applauded, so look out for these titles. In *Kitty The Toon* (Miles, Robson, Langford Press, hb 32pp, ISBN 978-1-904078-53-1, £7), former RSPB warden John Miles and illustrator Barry Robson tell a fact-based tale of how a young Kittiwake grows up along the River Tyne.

Two other books in the Myweebooks series are aimed at younger readers. Both *How Very Nice* (Hb 28pp £6) and *After That He Ate Them* (Hb, 24pp £7.50) are written and illustrated in charming fashion by Leon Hills in association with the Amphibian and Reptile Conservation organisation and feature a hungry frog and the creatures that make up his diet! Entertaining and educational too.

BY LEON HILLS

DIARY 2014

David Cromack

Art enthusiasts can catch up with the Society of Wildlife Artists' latest work at the Birdfair each August or the group's annual exhibition in London in the autumn.

Events guide for 2014   28

Day-by-day diary for 2014   30

Year planner for 2015   54

EVENTS DIARY 2014

While every effort has been made to check the accuracy of these entries, the publishers advise making contact with the event organisers to ensure there are no late changes. TBA = To Be Announced (for those dates not settled before the *Yearbook* went to press).

JANUARY

4: 4th Global Bird Watchers Conference
Dhordo, Kutch, Gujarat, India
Contact: info@gbwc.org or www.gbwc.org

20 to Feb 14: Big Schools Birdwatch
UK-wide event to get children interested in wild birds.
Contact: www.rspb.org./schoolswatch for events in your area

25-26: Big Garden Birdwatch
UK-wide survey of garden birds
Contact: www.rspb.org.uk/birdwatch

FEBRUARY

2: World Wetlands Day
Various 'Wetlands and Agriculture' events around the globe celebrating the International Year of Family Farming.
Contact: www.ramsar.org

19-22: Pacific Seabird Group AGM
Centennial Hall, Juneau, Alaska.
Contact: www.pacificseabirdgroup.org

28 to March 2: BTO Bird Survey Techniques residential course
Juniper Hall Field Studies Council, Dorking, Surrey.
Contact: anne.cotton@bto.org

MARCH

22: SOC/BTO Scottish Birdwatchers' Conference
Aberdeenshire.
Contact: www.the-soc.org.uk

22: Bird of Prey Conservation Conference
Essex Birdwatching Society, Writtle College, Lordship Campus CM1 3RR.
Contact: www.ebws.org.uk

APRIL

1-3: BOU annual spring conference
Ecology and Conservation of Birds in Alpine and Upland Habitats
Gilbert Murray Conference Suite, University of Leicester, Oadby campus.
Contact: www.bou.org.uk

12: African Bird Club AGM,
Full programme of talks on research and conservation work in Africa.
Flett Theatre, Natural History Museum, Cromwell Road, London SW7 5BD.
Contact: info@africanbirdclub.org or www.africanbirdclub.org

11-13: RSPB Members' Weekend
University of York.
Contact: www.rspb.org.uk

4-6: BTO bird survey techniques residential course.
Dale Fort Field Studies Council, Haverfordwest.
Contact: anne.cotton@bto.org

11-13: BTO bird survey techniques residential course.
Derrygonnelly Field Studies Council, Co Fermanagh.
Contact: anne.cotton@bto.org

22-26: American Birding Association Convention
To raise awareness and money to support hawk research. Corpus Christi, Texas.
Contact: events@aba.org

MAY

2-4: BTO bird survey techniques residential course
How Hill Trust, Ludham, Norfolk.
Contact: anne.cotton@bto.org

3: Go Green Fair
Promoting recycling, nature conservation and energy-reduction. BTO among the stall-holders.
Mell Square, Solihull.
Contact: www.solihullfaithsforum.org

9-11: BTO bird survey techniques residential course
The Kingcombe Centre, Dorchester, Dorset.
Contact: anne.cotton@bto.org

9-11: BTO bird survey techniques residential course/ Bird ID course
Malham Tarn Field Studies Council, North Yorkshire.
Contact: anne.cotton@bto.org

10-11: Scottish Birdfair
More than 110 exhibitors and varied events programme at Hopetoun House, Edinburgh.

EVENTS DIARY 2014

Contact: stacey.maden@rspb.org.uk or visit www.scottishbirdfair.org.uk

17-18: Norfolk Bird Fair
For birdwatchers, photographers, wildlife enthusiasts and families. Mannington Hall, near Aylsham, Norfolk.
Contact: birdfairnorfolk@yahoo.com or 01603 219 119.

23-25: BTO bird survey techniques residential course
Lagganlia Centre for Outdoor Learning, Kingussie, Highlands.
Contact: anne.cotton@bto.org

25: Neotropical Bird Club general meeting
AGM, plus talks, quizzes and book sales at Cley Village Hall, Norfolk. Starts 10.30am.
Contact: d.j.fisher@ntlworld.com or secretary@neotropicalbirdclub.org.uk

JUNE

30-June 1: BTO Bird survey techniques residential course
Rhyd-y-Creuau Field Studies Centre, Betws-y-Coed, Gwynedd.
Contact: anne.cotton@bto.org

JULY

6: AGM of OSME (Ornithological Society of the Middle east, Caucasus and Central Asia).
Doors open 10am. Non-members welcome for five talks on the region's birds.
The Nunnery, Thetford, Norfolk.
Contact: secretary@osme.org or 01545 571 022.

21-25: 26th International Congress for Conservation Biology
Baltimore, Maryland.

18-August 3: National Exhibition of Wildlife Art
Preview evening July 17.
Gordale Nursery, Burton, The Wirral.
Contact: newa@mtuffrey.freeserve.co.uk or visit www.newa-uk.com

AUGUST

8-10: RSPB Big Wild Sleepout
Camping event for people to raise money for wildlife.
Contact: www.rspb.org.uk/thingstodo/sleepout/

18-24: 26th International Ornithological Congress
Discussing various aspects of avian biology.

Ikebukuro Campus, Rikkyo University, Tokyo, Japan.
Contact: http://ioc26.jp/index.html

15-17: British Birdwatching Fair
Egleton Nature Reserve, Rutland Water, Rutland.
Contact: callen@birdfair.org.uk or visit www.birdfair.org.uk

SEPTEMBER

5-7: BTO bird ID course
The Kingcombe Centre, Dorchester, Dorset.
Contact: anne.cotton@bto.org

24-27: Annual meeting of American Ornithologists Union
(held jointly with Cooper OS and Society of Canadian Ornithologists).
YMCA of the Rockies, Estes Park Centre, Colorado.
Contact: www.aou.org

OCTOBER

Date to be advised
The Natural Eye - Annual Exhibition Society of Wildlife Artists
Mall Galleries, Pall Mall, London.
Contact: www.swla.co.uk

25: RSPB Members' Day and AGM
International Conference Centre, Birmingham
Visit www.rspb.org.uk

26-28: BTO bird ID residential course
How Hill Trust, Ludham, Norfolk
Contact: anne.cotton@bto.org

NOVEMBER

5-8: 24-29: Waterbird Society's 38th annual meeting
La Paz, Mexico.
Contact: www.waterbirds.org

8: Welsh Ornithological Society Annual Conference.
Venue in North Wales to be advised at later date.
Contact: www.birdsinwales.org.uk

DECEMBER

5-7: BTO Annual Conference
Hayes Conference Centre, Swanwick, Derbyshire.
Contact: info@bto.org

29

DIARY – JANUARY 2014

1	Wed	New Year holiday
2	Thu	Holiday (Scotland)
3	Fri	
4	Sat	
5	Sun	
6	Mon	
7	Tue	
8	Wed	
9	Thu	
10	Fri	
11	Sat	
12	Sun	
13	Mon	
14	Tue	
15	Wed	
16	Thu	
17	Fri	
18	Sat	
19	Sun	
20	Mon	
21	Tue	
22	Wed	
23	Thu	
24	Fri	
25	Sat	
26	Sun	
27	Mon	
28	Tue	
29	Wed	
30	Thu	
31	Fri	

DIARY – FEBRUARY 2014

1	Sat	
2	Sun	
3	Mon	
4	Tue	
5	Wed	
6	Thu	
7	Fri	
8	Sat	
9	Sun	
10	Mon	
11	Tue	
12	Wed	
13	Thu	
14	Fri	
15	Sat	
16	Sun	
17	Mon	
18	Tue	
19	Wed	
20	Thu	
21	Fri	
22	Sat	
23	Sun	
24	Mon	
25	Tue	
26	Wed	
27	Thu	
28	Fri	

DIARY – MARCH 2014

1	Sat	
2	Sun	
3	Mon	
4	Tue	
5	Wed	
6	Thu	
7	Fri	
8	Sat	
9	Sun	
10	Mon	
11	Tue	
12	Wed	
13	Thu	
14	Fri	
15	Sat	
16	Sun	
17	Mon	St Patrick's Day
18	Tue	
19	Wed	
20	Thu	
21	Fri	
22	Sat	
23	Sun	
24	Mon	
25	Tue	
26	Wed	
27	Thu	
28	Fri	
29	Sat	
30	Sun	British Summertime begins – Mothering Sunday
31	Mon	

1	Tue	
2	Wed	
3	Thu	
4	Fri	
5	Sat	
6	Sun	
7	Mon	
8	Tue	
9	Wed	
10	Thu	
11	Fri	
12	Sat	
13	Sun	
14	Mon	
15	Tue	
16	Wed	
17	Thu	
18	Fri	Good Friday
19	Sat	
20	Sun	Easter Day
21	Mon	Easter Monday
22	Tue	
23	Wed	
24	Thu	
25	Fri	
26	Sat	
27	Sun	
28	Mon	
29	Tues	
30	Wed	

DIARY – MAY 2014

1	Thu	
2	Fri	
3	Sat	
4	Sun	
5	Mon	May Day
6	Tue	
7	Wed	
8	Thu	
9	Fri	
10	Sat	
11	Sun	
12	Mon	
13	Tue	
14	Wed	
15	Thu	
16	Fri	
17	Sat	
18	Sun	
19	Mon	
20	Tue	
21	Wed	
22	Thu	
23	Fri	
24	Sat	
25	Sun	
26	Mon	Spring Bank Holiday
27	Tue	
28	Wed	
29	Thu	
30	Fri	
31	Sat	

DIARY – JUNE 2014

1	Sun	
2	Mon	
3	Tue	
4	Wed	
5	Thu	
6	Fri	
7	Sat	
8	Sun	
9	Mon	
10	Tue	
11	Wed	
12	Thu	
13	Fri	
14	Sat	
15	Sun	
16	Mon	
17	Tue	
18	Wed	
19	Thu	
20	Fri	
21	Sat	
22	Sun	
23	Mon	
24	Tue	
25	Wed	
26	Thu	
27	Fri	
28	Sat	
29	Sun	
30	Mon	

DIARY – JULY 2014

1	Tue	
2	Wed	
3	Thu	
4	Fri	
5	Sat	
6	Sun	
7	Mon	
8	Tue	
9	Wed	
10	Thu	
11	Fri	
12	Sat	
13	Sun	
14	Mon	
15	Tue	
16	Wed	
17	Thu	
18	Fri	
19	Sat	
20	Sun	
21	Mon	
22	Tue	
23	Wed	
24	Thu	
25	Fri	
26	Sat	
27	Sun	
28	Mon	
29	Tue	
30	Wed	
31	Thu	

DIARY – AUGUST 2014

1	Fri	
2	Sat	
3	Sun	
4	Mon	
5	Tue	
6	Wed	
7	Thu	
8	Fri	
9	Sat	
10	Sun	
11	Mon	
12	Tue	
13	Wed	
14	Thu	
15	Fri	
16	Sat	
17	Sun	
18	Mon	
19	Tue	
20	Wed	
21	Thu	
22	Fri	
23	Sat	
24	Sun	
25	Mon	Summer Bank Holiday
26	Tue	
27	Wed	
28	Thu	
29	Fri	
30	Sat	
31	Sun	

DIARY – SEPTEMBER 2014

1	Mon	
2	Tue	
3	Wed	
4	Thu	
5	Fri	
6	Sat	
7	Sun	
8	Mon	
9	Tue	
10	Wed	
11	Thu	
12	Fri	
13	Sat	
14	Sun	
15	Mon	
16	Tue	
17	Wed	
18	Thu	
19	Fri	
20	Sat	
21	Sun	
22	Mon	
23	Tue	
24	Wed	
25	Thu	
26	Fri	
27	Sat	
28	Sun	
29	Mon	
30	Tue	

1	Wed	
2	Thu	
3	Fri	
4	Sat	
5	Sun	
6	Mon	
7	Tue	
8	Wed	
9	Thu	
10	Fri	
11	Sat	
12	Sun	
13	Mon	
14	Tue	
15	Wed	
16	Thu	
17	Fri	
18	Sat	
19	Sun	
20	Mon	
21	Tue	
22	Wed	
23	Thu	
24	Fri	
25	Sat	
26	Sun	British Summertime ends
27	Mon	
28	Tue	
29	Wed	
30	Thu	
31	Fri	

DIARY – NOVEMBER 2014

1	Sat	
2	Sun	
3	Mon	
4	Tue	
5	Wed	
6	Thu	
7	Fri	
8	Sat	
9	Sun	Remembrance Sunday
10	Mon	
11	Tue	
12	Wed	
13	Thu	
14	Fri	
15	Sat	
16	Sun	
17	Mon	
18	Tue	
19	Wed	
20	Thu	
21	Fri	
22	Sat	
23	Sun	
24	Mon	
25	Tue	
26	Wed	
27	Thu	
28	Fri	
29	Sat	
30	Sun	

DIARY – DECEMBER 2014

1	Mon	
2	Tue	
3	Wed	
4	Thu	
5	Fri	
6	Sat	
7	Sun	
8	Mon	
9	Tue	
10	Wed	
11	Thu	
12	Fri	
13	Sat	
14	Sun	
15	Mon	
16	Tue	
17	Wed	
18	Thu	
19	Fri	
20	Sat	
21	Sun	
22	Mon	
23	Tue	
24	Wed	
25	Thu	Christmas Day
26	Fri	Boxing Day
27	Sat	
28	Sun	
29	Mon	
30	Tues	
31	Wed	

DIARY 2014

YEAR PLANNER 2015

January
February
March
April
May
June
July
August
September
October
November
December

LOG CHARTS

David Cromack

Added to the British List as an introduced species, Egyptian Geese are proving adept at surviving in the British climate and feral populations are now well established in various parts of the country.

Guide to using the log charts   56

Full log charts for BOU-approved British List   58

Log charts for British dragonflies   86

Log charts for British butterflies   87

A CHECKLIST OF BIRDS

Based on the British List formulated by the British Ornithologists' Union

MANY READERS have asked why our Checklist of Birds keeps changing from year to year. It is based on the official British List maintained by The British Ornithologists' Union (BOU) which sits in judgement on which birds you can count on your lists, and which you can't. They do this in two ways:

1): If someone claims to have seen a species never recorded in Britain, a panel of experts (the BOU Rarities Committee) assesses the record, making sure that the identification of the bird was proved beyond all possible doubt. Then the bird's credentials are also assessed, to determine whether it was a genuine vagrant, rather than one that had just hopped over the fence from the nearest zoo or aviary.

Only if the bird passes every single strenuous test does it get accepted onto the list....a process that may take many years. Similarly, historical records are reassessed in the light of advances in identification skills.

2): The BOU also takes advice from taxonomists on the need to split or lump together sub-species. The current trend towards splitting is usually driven by DNA evidence suggesting that a particular sub-species is sufficiently different to warrant full species status.

Since the publication of the last Birdwatcher's Yearbook, the following decisions have been reached regarding species on the list:
● Capercaillie reassigned to Category C3 because the indigenous population became extinct prior to January 1, 1800.
● Madeiran Storm Petrel removed from list.
● Scopoli's Shearwater added to the list.

As a result of these changes, the official British list now stands at 596 species, made up of 578 species in Category A, eight in Category B and ten in Category C. See below for a full description of what the different categories mean.

In addition, there have been a few minor tweaks to the order of some species such as the auks being moved forward to now sit between skuas and terns and gulls being located after terns. For a full discussion of these changes, go to the BOU's website, **www.bou.org.uk**. In this edition, species in Category C (introduced species) have been sub-divided into six separate categories (see below).

SPECIES, CATEGORIES, CODES – YOUR GUIDE TO GET THE BEST USE FROM THE CHECKLIST

Species categories (column 1)

The following categories are those assigned by the British Ornithologists' Union.

A - Species recorded in an apparently natural state at least once since January 1, 1950.

B - Species recorded in an apparently natural state at least once between January 1, 1800 and December 31,1949, but not subsequently.

C - Species that, though introduced, now derive from the resulting self-sustaining populations: **C1** (*Naturalized introduced species*) Species that have occurred only as a result of introduction, e.g. Egyptian Goose; **C2** (*Naturalized established species*) – Species resulting from introduction by Man, but which also occur in an apparently natural state, e.g. Greylag Goose; **C3** (*Naturalized re-established species*) Species successfully re-established by Man in areas of former occurrence, e.g. Red Kite; **C4** (*Naturalized feral species*) Domesticated species established in the wild, e.g. Rock Pigeon (Dove)/Feral Pigeon; **C5** (*Vagrant naturalized species*) Species from established naturalized populations abroad. There are currently no species in category C5; **C6** (*Former naturalized species*) Species formerly in C1

whose naturalized populations are either no longer self-sustaining or are considered extinct, e.g. Lady Amherst's Pheasant.

D - Species where there is reasonable doubt that they have ever occurred in a natural state. Species placed solely in Category D form no part of the British List, and are not included in the species totals.

E - Species that have been recorded as introductions, human-assisted transportees or escapees from captivity, and whose breeding populations (if any) are thought not to be self-sustaining. Species in Category E that have bred in the wild in Britain are designated as E*. Category E species form no part of the British List (unless already included within Categories A, B or C).

A species is usually placed in only one category, but some are placed in multiple categories, for example, those species occurring in Category A which now have naturalised populations (e.g. Red Kite).

The British List comprises only those species in Categories A, B and C.

LOG CHARTS

Species list (column 2)

The *Yearbook* Checklist includes all species from categories A, B and C on the British List, based on the latest BOU listing. Selected species included in categories D and E are listed separately at the end of the log chart.

Vagrants which are not on the British List, but which may have occurred in other parts of the British Isles, are not included. Readers who wish to record such species may use the extra rows provided on the last page. In this connection it should be noted that separate lists exist for

Northern Ireland (kept by the Northern Ireland Birdwatchers' Association) and the Isle of Man (kept by the Manx Ornithological Society), and that Irish records are assessed by the Irish Rare Birds Committee.

The commoner species in the log charts are indicated by the * symbol to help make record-keeping easier.

The species names are those most widely used in the current fieldguides and each is followed by its scientific name, printed in italics.

Life list (column 3)

Ticks made in the 'Life List' column suffice for keeping a running personal total of species. However, added benefit can be obtained by replacing ticks with a note of the year of first occurrence. To take an example: one's first-ever Marsh Sandpiper, seen on April 14, 2013, would be logged with '13' in the Life List and '14' in the April column (as well as a tick in the 2013 column). As Life List entries are carried forward annually, in years to come it would be a simple matter to relocate this record.

First and last dates of migrants

Arrivals of migrants can be recorded by inserting dates instead of ticks in the relevant month columns. For example, a Common Sandpiper on March 11 would be recorded by inserting '11' against Common Sandpiper in the March column. The same applies to departures, though dates of last sightings can only be entered at the end of the year after checking one's field notebook.

Unheaded columns

The three unheaded columns on the right of the December column of each chart are for special (personal) use. This may be, for example, to cater for a second holiday, a particular county or a 'local patch'. Another use could be to indicate species on, for example, the Northern Ireland List or the Isle of Man List.

BTO species codes (column 23)

British Trust for Ornithology two-letter species codes are shown in brackets in the fourth column from the right. Readers should refer to the BTO if more codes are needed.

Rare breeding birds (column 24)

Species monitored by the Rare Breeding Birds

Panel (see National Directory) comprise all those on Schedule 1 of the Wildlife and Countryside Act 1981 (see Quick Reference) together with all escaped or introduced species breeding in small numbers. The following annotations in the charts (third column from the right) reflect the **RBBP's categories:**
A) Rare Breeding Birds in UK (Regular Breeders); B) Rare Breeding Birds in UK (Occasional Breeders); C) Rare Breeding Birds in UK (Potential Breeders); D) Rare Non-native Breeding Birds in UK (Regular Breeders); E) Rare Non-native Breeding Birds in UK (Occasional Breeders); F) Rare Non-native Breeding Birds in UK (Potential Breeders).

Rarities (column 25)

Rarities are indicated by a capital letter 'R' in the column headed BBRC (British Birds Rarities Committee).

EURING species numbers (column 26)

EURING databanks collect copies of recovery records from ringing schemes throughout Europe and the official species numbers are given in the last column. As they are taken from the full Holarctic bird list there are many apparent gaps. It is important that these are not filled arbitrarily by observers wishing to record species not listed in the charts, as this would compromise the integrity of the scheme.

Similarly, the addition of a further digit to indicate sub-species is to be avoided, since EURING has already assigned numbers for this purpose. The numbering follows the Voous order of species so some species are now out of sequence following the re-ordering of the British List. For full details, visit: www.euring.org

SWANS, GEESE, DUCKS

BOU	Name	Scientific name	Life list	2014 list	24 hr	Garden	Holiday	Jan	Feb	Mar	Apr	May	Jun	Jul	Aug	Sep	Oct	Nov	Dec	BTO	RBBP	BBRC	EU No
*AC2	Mute Swan	Cygnus olor																		MS			0152
*AE	Bewick's Swan	Cygnus columbianus																		BS	C		0153
AE	Whooper Swan	Cygnus cygnus																		WS	A		0154
*AE	Bean Goose	Anser fabalis																		BE	E		0157
*AE	Pink-footed Goose	Anser brachyrhynchus																		PG	E		0158
*AE	White-fronted Goose	Anser albifrons																		WG	E		0159
AE	Lesser White-fronted Goose	Anser erythropus																		LC	F	R	0160
AC2C4E	Greylag Goose	Anser anser																		GJ			0161
AC2E	Snow Goose	Anser caerulescens																		SJ	D		0163
AC2E	Canada Goose	Branta canadensis																		CG			0166
AC2E	Barnacle Goose	Branta leucopsis																		BY	D		0167
*AE	Brent Goose	Branta bernicla																		BG			0168
AE	Red-breasted Goose	Branta ruficollis																		EB	E	R	0169
C1E	Egyptian Goose	Alopochen aegyptiaca																		EG	D		0170
BDE	Ruddy Shelduck	Tadorna ferruginea																		UD	D		0171
*A	Shelduck	Tadorna tadorna																		SU			0173
C1E	Mandarin Duck	Aix galericulata																		MN			0178
AE	Wigeon	Anas penelope																		WN	A		0179
AE	American Wigeon	Anas americana																		AW			0180
*AC	Gadwall	Anas strepera																		GA			0182
*AE	Baikal Teal	Anas formosa																				R	1830
*A	Teal	Anas crecca																		T			0184
A	Green-winged Teal	Anas carolinensis																			C		1842
AC2C4E	Mallard	Anas platyrhynchos																		MA			0186
	Sub total																						

58

LOG CHARTS

BOU	DUCKS Cont		Life list	2014 list	24 hr	Garden	Holiday	Jan	Feb	Mar	Apr	May	Jun	Jul	Aug	Sep	Oct	Nov	Dec		BTO	RBBP	BBRC	EU No
A	Black Duck	Anas rubripes																			BD	B	R	0187
*AE	Pintail	Anas acuta																			PT	A		0189
*A	Garganey	Anas querquedula																			GY	A		0191
AE	Blue-winged Teal	Anas discors																			TB	E	R	0192
*A	Shoveler	Anas clypeata																			SV	A		0194
AC2E	Red-crested Pochard	Netta rufina																			RQ	D	R	0196
AE	Canvasback	Aythya valisineria																					R	0197
AE	Pochard	Aythya ferina																			PO	A		0198
AE	Redhead	Aythya americana																			AZ		R	0199
A	Ring-necked Duck	Aythya collaris																			NG	B		0200
AE	Ferruginous Duck	Aythya nyroca																			FD	B		0202
*A	Tufted Duck	Aythya fuligula																			TU			0203
*A	Scaup	Aythya marila																			SP	B		0204
*A	Lesser Scaup	Aythya affinis																			AY		R	0205
*A	Eider	Somateria mollissima																			E			0206
*A	King Eider	Somateria spectabilis																			KE	C	R	0207
A	Steller's Eider	Polysticta stelleri																			ES		R	0209
A	Harlequin Duck	Histrionicus histrionicus																			HQ		R	0211
*A	Long-tailed Duck	Clangula hyemalis																			LN	C		0212
*A	Common Scoter	Melanitta nigra																			CX	A		0213
A	Black Scoter	Melanitta americana																					R	2132
*A	Surf Scoter	Melanitta perspicillata																			FS		R	0214
A	Velvet Scoter	Melanitta fusca																			VS	C		0215
AE	Bufflehead	Bucephala albeola																			VH		R	0216
	Sub total																							

BOU	DUCKS, GAMEBIRDS, DIVERS, ALBATROSS		Life list	2014 list	24 hr	Garden	Holiday	Jan	Feb	Mar	Apr	May	Jun	Jul	Aug	Sep	Oct	Nov	Dec		BTO	RBBP	BBRC	EU No
A	Barrow's Goldeneye	Bucephala islandica																					R	0217
AE	Goldeneye	Bucephala clangula																			GN	A		0218
A	Hooded Merganser	Lophodytes cucullatus																					R	2190
*A	Smew	Mergellus albellus																			SY	C		0220
*A	Red-breasted Merganser	Mergus serrator																			RM			0221
*A	Goosander	Mergus merganser																			GD			0223
C1E	Ruddy Duck	Oxyura jamaicensis																			BY	D		0225
*A	Red Grouse	Lagopus lagopus																			RG			0329
*A	Ptarmigan	Lagopus muta																			PM			0330
*AE	Black Grouse	Tetrao tetrix																			BK			0332
*BC3	Capercaillie	Tetrao urogallus																			CP	A		0335
*A	Quail	Coturnix																			Q	A		0370
C1E	Red-legged Partridge	Alectoris rufa																			RL			0358
AC2E	Grey Partridge	Perdix perdix																			P			0367
C1E	Pheasant	Phasianus colchicus																			PH			0394
C6E	Lady Amherst's Pheasant	Chrysolophus amherstiae																			LM	D		0397
C1E	Golden Pheasant	Chrysolophus pictus																			GF	D		0396
*A	Red-throated Diver	Gavia stellata																			RH	A		0002
*A	Black-throated Diver	Gavia arctica																			BV	A		0003
A	Pacific Diver	Gavia pacifica																					R	0033
*A	Great Northern Diver	Gavia immer																			ND	C		0004
A	White-billed Diver	Gavia adamsii																			IW	C		0005
A	Black-browed Albatross	Thalassarche melanophris																			AA	C	R	0014
A	Yellow-nosed Albatross	Thalassarche chlororhynchos																					R	0150
	Sub total																							

FULMAR, PETRELS, SHEARWATERS, CORMORANTS, FRIGATEBIRDS, BITTERNS

BOU	Species	Scientific name	Life list	2014 list	24 hr	Garden	Holiday	Jan	Feb	Mar	Apr	May	Jun	Jul	Aug	Sep	Oct	Nov	Dec	BTO	RBBP	BBRC	EU No
*A	Fulmar	Fulmarus glacialis																		F			0020
A	Fea's Petrel	Pterodroma feae																				R	0026
A	Capped Petrel	Pterodroma hasitata																				R	0029
A	Cory's Shearwater	Calonectris borealis																		CQ			0036
A	Scopoli's Shearwater	Calonectris diomedea																					
*A	Great Shearwater	Puffinus gravis																		GQ			0040
*A	Sooty Shearwater	Puffinus griseus																		OT			0043
A	Manx Shearwater	Puffinus puffinus																		MX			0046
A	Balearic Shearwater	Puffinus mauretanicus																					0046
A	Macaronesian Shearwater	Puffinus baroli																			C	R	0048
*A	Wilson's Petrel	Oceanites oceanicus																					0050
B	White-faced Petrel	Pelagodroma marina																				R	0051
*A	Storm Petrel	Hydrobates pelagicus																		TM			0052
*A	Leach's Petrel	Oceanodroma leucorhoa																		TL			0055
A	Swinhoe's Petrel	Oceanodroma monorhis																				R	0056
A	Red-billed Tropicbird	Phaethon aethereus																				R	0064
*A	Gannet	Morus bassanus																		GX			0071
*A	Cormorant	Phalacrocorax carbo																		CA			0072
A	Double-crested Cormorant	Phalacrocorax auritus																				R	0078
*A	Shag	Phalacrocorax aristotelis																		SA			0080
A	Ascension Frigatebird	Fregata aquila																				R	0093
A	Magnificent Frigatebird	Fregata magnificens																				R	0095
*A	Bittern	Botaurus stellaris																		BI	A		0095
A	American Bittern	Botaurus lentiginosus																		AM		R	0096
	Sub total																						

61

BITTERNS, HERONS, STORKS, SPOONBILL, GREBES, RAPTORS

BOU	Name	Scientific name	Life list	2014 list	24 hr	Garden	Holiday	Jan	Feb	Mar	Apr	May	Jun	Jul	Aug	Sep	Oct	Nov	Dec	BTO	RBBP	BBRC	EU No
A	Little Bittern	Ixobrychus minutus																		LL	B	R	0098
AE*	Night Heron	Nycticorax nycticorax																		NT	E		0104
A	Green Heron	Butorides virescens																		HR		R	0107
A	Squacco Heron	Ardeola ralloides																		QH	B	R	0108
AE	Cattle Egret	Bubulcus ibis																		EC			0111
A	Snowy Egret	Egretta thula																				R	0115
*A	Little Egret	Egretta garzetta																		ET	A		0119
A	Great White Egret	Ardea alba																		HW	C		0121
A	Grey Heron	Ardea cinerea																		H			0122
A	Great Blue Heron	Ardea herodias																				R	1230
A	Purple Heron	Ardea purpurea																		UR	B		0124
AE	Black Stork	Ciconia nigra																		OS		R	0131
AE	White Stork	Ciconia ciconia																		OR	C		0134
AE	Glossy Ibis	Plegadis falcinellus																		IB		R	0136
*AE	Spoonbill	Platalea leucorodia																		NB	A		0144
A	Pied-billed Grebe	Podilymbus podiceps																		PJ	B	R	0006
*A	Little Grebe	Tachybaptus ruficollis																		LG			0007
*A	Great Crested Grebe	Podiceps cristatus																		GG			0009
*A	Red-necked Grebe	Podiceps grisegena																		RX	B		0010
*A	Slavonian Grebe	Podiceps auritus																		SZ	A		0011
*A	Black-necked Grebe	Podiceps nigricollis																		BN	A		0012
*A	Honey-buzzard	Pernis apivorus																		HZ	A		0231
AE	Black Kite	Milvus migrans																		KB	B		0238
AC3E	Red Kite	Milvus milvus																		KT	A		0239
	Sub total																						

BOU	RAPTORS Cont		Life list	2014 list	24 hr	Garden	Holiday	Jan	Feb	Mar	Apr	May	Jun	Jul	Aug	Sep	Oct	Nov	Dec	BTO	RBBP	BBRC	EU No
*AC3E	White-tailed Eagle	Haliaeetus albicilla																		WE	A		0243
BDE	Egyptian Vulture	Neophron percnopterus																				R	0247
A	Short-toed Eagle	Circaetus gallicus																				R	0256
*A	Marsh Harrier	Circus aeruginosus																		MR	A		0260
*A	Hen Harrier	Circus cyaneus																		HH	A		0261
A	Pallid Harrier	Circus macrourus																			C	R	0262
*A	Montagu's Harrier	Circus pygargus																		MO	A		0263
AC3E	Goshawk	Accipiter gentilis																		GI	A		0267
*A	Sparrowhawk	Accipiter nisus																		SH			0269
AE	Buzzard	Buteo buteo																		BZ			0287
*AE	Rough-legged Buzzard	Buteo lagopus																		RF	C		0290
B	Greater Spotted Eagle	Aquila clanga																				R	0293
*AE	Golden Eagle	Aquila chrysaetos																		EA	A		0296
AE	Osprey	Pandion haliaetus																		OP	A		0301
A	Lesser Kestrel	Falco naumanni																				R	0303
*A	Kestrel	Falco tinnunculus																		K			0304
AE	American Kestrel	Falco sparverius																				R	0305
*A	Red-footed Falcon	Falco vespertinus																		FV			0307
A	Amur Falcon	Falco amurensis																				R	3080
*A	Merlin	Falco columbarius																		ML	A		0309
*A	Hobby	Falco subbuteo																		HY	A		0310
A	Eleonora's Falcon	Falco eleonorae																					0311
*AE	Gyrfalcon	Falco rusticolus																		YF	C	R	0318
*AE	Peregrine	Falco peregrinus																		PE	A		0320
	Sub total																						

CRAKES, GALLINULES, CRANES, BUSTARDS AND WADERS

BOU	Species	Scientific name	Life list	2014 list	24 hr	Garden	Holiday	Jan	Feb	Mar	Apr	May	Jun	Jul	Aug	Sep	Oct	Nov	Dec				BTO	RBBP	BBRC	EU No
*A	Water Rail	Rallus aquaticus																					WA	A		0407
*A	Spotted Crake	Porzana porzana																					AK	A		0408
A	Sora	Porzana carolina																							R	0409
A	Little Crake	Porzana parva																					JC		R	0410
A	Baillon's Crake	Porzana pusilla																					VC	C	R	0411
AE	Corncrake	Crex crex																					CE	A		0421
*A	Moorhen	Gallinula chloropus																					MH			0424
A	Allen's Gallinule	Porphyrio alleni																							R	0425
A	Purple Gallinule	Porphyrio martinica																							R	0426
*A	Coot	Fulica atra																						CO			0429
A	American Coot	Fulica americana																							R	0430
*A	Crane	Grus grus																						AN	A		0433
A	Sandhill Crane	Grus canadensis																							R	0436
A	Little Bustard	Tetrax tetrax																							R	0442
A	Macqueen's Bustard	Chlamydotis macqueenii																							R	0444
AE*	Great Bustard	Otis tarda																					US	B	R	0446
*A	Stone-curlew	Burhinus oedicnemus																					TN	A		0459
*A	Black-winged Stilt	Himantopus himantopus																					IT	B	R	0455
*A	Avocet	Recurvirostra avosetta																					AV	A		0456
*A	Oystercatcher	Haematopus ostralegus																					OC			0450
A	American Golden Plover	Pluvialis dominica																					ID			0484
A	Pacific Golden Plover	Pluvialis fulva																					IF		R	0484
*A	Golden Plover	Pluvialis apricaria																					GP			0485
*A	Grey Plover	Pluvialis squatarola																					GV			0486
	Sub total																									

WADERS Cont

BOU	Species	Scientific name	Life list	2014 list	24 hr	Garden	Holiday	Jan	Feb	Mar	Apr	May	Jun	Jul	Aug	Sep	Oct	Nov	Dec	BTO	RBBP	BBRC	EU No
A	Sociable Plover	*Vanellus gregarius*																		IP		R	0491
A	White-tailed Plover	*Vanellus leucurus*																				R	0492
*A	Lapwing	*Vanellus vanellus*																		L			0493
*A	Little Ringed Plover	*Charadrius dubius*																		LP	A		0469
*A	Ringed Plover	*Charadrius hiaticula*																		RP			0470
A	Semipalmated Plover	*Charadrius semipalmatus*																		TV		R	0471
A	Killdeer	*Charadrius vociferus*																		KL	C	R	0474
A	Kentish Plover	*Charadrius alexandrinus*																		KP	B		0477
A	Lesser Sand Plover	*Charadrius mongolus*																				R	0478
A	Greater Sand Plover	*Charadrius leschenaultii*																				R	0479
A	Caspian Plover	*Charadrius asiaticus*																				R	0480
*A	Dotterel	*Charadrius morinellus*																		DO	A		0482
A	Upland Sandpiper	*Bartramia longicauda*																				R	0544
A	Little Whimbrel	*Numenius minutus*																		UP		R	0536
B	Eskimo Curlew	*Numenius borealis*																				R	0537
A	Hudsonian Whimbrel	*Numenius hudsonicus*																				R	
*A	Whimbrel	*Numenius phaeopus*																		WM	A		0538
A	Slender-billed Curlew	*Numenius tenuirostris*																				R	0540
*A	Curlew	*Numenius arquata*																		CU			0541
*A	Black-tailed Godwit	*Limosa limosa*																		BW	A		0532
A	Hudsonian Godwit	*Limosa haemastica*																		HU		R	0533
*A	Bar-tailed Godwit	*Limosa lapponica*																		BA	C		0534
*A	Turnstone	*Arenaria interpres*																		TT	C		0561
A	Great Knot	*Calidris tenuirostris*																		KO		R	0495
	Sub total																						

65

WADERS Cont

BOU	Species	Scientific name	Life list	2014 list	24 hr	Garden	Holiday	Jan	Feb	Mar	Apr	May	Jun	Jul	Aug	Sep	Oct	Nov	Dec	BTO	RBBP	BBRC	EU No
*A	Knot	Calidris canutus																		KN			0496
*A	Ruff	Calidris pugnax																		RU	A		0517
A	Sharp-tailed Sandpiper	Calidris acuminata																		VV		R	0508
A	Broad-billed Sandpiper	Calidris falcinellus																		OA	C	R	0514
*A	Curlew Sandpiper	Calidris ferruginea																		CV			0509
A	Stilt Sandpiper	Calidris himantopus																				R	5150
A	Red-necked Stint	Calidris ruficollis																				R	0500
A	Long-toed Stint	Calidris subminuta																				R	0503
*A	Temminck's Stint	Calidris temminckii																		TK	B		0502
*A	Sanderling	Calidris alba																		SS	C		0497
*A	Dunlin	Calidris alpina																		DN			0512
*A	Purple Sandpiper	Calidris maritima																		PS	A		0510
A	Baird's Sandpiper	Calidris bairdii																		BP		R	0506
*A	Little Stint	Calidris minuta																		LX			0501
A	White-rumped Sandpiper	Calidris fuscicollis																		WU			0505
A	Least Sandpiper	Calidris minutilla																		EP		R	0504
A	Buff-breasted Sandpiper	Calidris subruficollis																		BQ	C		0516
A	Pectoral Sandpiper	Calidris melanotos																		PP	C		0507
A	Western Sandpiper	Calidris mauri																		ER		R	0499
A	Semipalmated Sandpiper	Calidris pusilla																		PZ		R	0498
A	Wilson's Phalarope	Phalaropus tricolor																		WF		R	0563
*A	Red-necked Phalarope	Phalaropus lobatus																		NK	A		0564
*A	Grey Phalarope	Phalaropus fulicarius																		PL			0565
A	Terek Sandpiper	Xenus cinereus																		TR		R	0555
	Sub total																						

BOU	WADERS Cont, PRATINCOLES AND SKUA		Life list	2014 list	24 hr	Garden	Holiday	Jan	Feb	Mar	Apr	May	Jun	Jul	Aug	Sep	Oct	Nov	Dec	BTO	RBBP	BBRC	EU No
*A	Common Sandpiper	Actitis hypoleucos																		CS			0556
A	Spotted Sandpiper	Actitis macularius																		PQ	B	R	0557
*A	Green Sandpiper	Tringa ochropus																		GE	A		0553
A	Solitary Sandpiper	Tringa solitaria																		I		R	0552
A	Grey-tailed Tattler	Tringa brevipes																		YT		R	0558
*A	Spotted Redshank	Tringa erythropus																		DR			0545
A	Greater Yellowlegs	Tringa melanoleuca																		LZ		R	0550
*A	Greenshank	Tringa nebularia																		GK	A		0548
A	Lesser Yellowlegs	Tringa flavipes																		LY		R	0551
*A	Marsh Sandpiper	Tringa stagnatilis																		MD		R	0547
*A	Wood Sandpiper	Tringa glareola																		OD	A		0554
*A	Redshank	Tringa totanus																		RK			0546
*A	Jack Snipe	Lymnocryptes minimus																		JS	C		0518
A	Short-billed Dowitcher	Limnodromus griseus																				R	0526
A	Long-billed Dowitcher	Limnodromus scolopaceus																		LD		R	0527
*A	Woodcock	Scolopax rusticola																		WK			0529
*A	Snipe	Gallinago gallinago																		SN			0519
A	Wilson's Snipe	Gallinago delicata																				R	5192
A	Great Snipe	Gallinago media																		DS	C	R	0520
A	Collared Pratincole	Glareola pratincola																				R	0465
A	Oriental Pratincole	Glareola maldivarum																		GM		R	0466
A	Black-winged Pratincole	Glareola nordmanni																		KW		R	0467
A	Cream-coloured Courser	Cursorius cursor																				R	0464
*A	Pomarine Skua	Stercorarius pomarinus																		PK			0566
	Sub total																						

SKUAS Cont. AUKS AND TERNS

BOU	Species	Scientific name	Life list	2014 list	24 hr	Garden	Holiday	Jan	Feb	Mar	Apr	May	Jun	Jul	Aug	Sep	Oct	Nov	Dec			BTO	RBBP	BBRC	EU No
*A	Arctic Skua	Stercorarius parasiticus																				AC	A		0567
*A	Long-tailed Skua	Stercorarius longicaudus																				OG			0568
*A	Great Skua	Stercorarius skua																				NX			0569
A	Tufted Puffin	Fratercula cirrhata																						R	
*A	Puffin	Fratercula arctica																				PU		R	0654
A	Long-billed Murrelet	Brachyramphus perdix																						R	6412
*A	Black Guillemot	Cepphus grylle																				TY			0638
A	Ancient Murrelet	Synthliboramphus antiquus																						R	0645
*A	Razorbill	Alca torda																				RA			0636
B	Great Auk (extinct)	Pinguinus impennis																							
*A	Little Auk	Alle alle																				LK			0647
*A	Guillemot	Uria aalge																				GU			0634
A	Brunnich's Guillemot	Uria lomvia																				TZ		R	0635
A	Aleutian Tern	Onychoprion aleuticus																						R	0617
A	Sooty Tern	Onychoprion fuscatus																						R	0623
A	Bridled Tern	Onychoprion anaethetus																						R	0622
*A	Little Tern	Sternula albifrons																				AF	A		0624
A	Gull-billed Tern	Gelochelidon nilotica																				TG	B	R	0605
A	Caspian Tern	Hydroprogne caspia																				CJ		R	0606
*A	Whiskered Tern	Chlidonias hybrida																				WD		R	0626
*A	Black Tern	Chlidonias niger																				BJ	C		0627
*A	White-winged Black Tern	Chlidonias leucopterus																				WJ			0628
A	Cabot's Tern	Sterna acuflavida																						R	
*A	Sandwich Tern	Sterna sandvicensis																				TE			0611
	Sub total																								

68

LOG CHARTS

BOU	TERNS Cont, GULLS		Life list	2014 list	24 hr	Garden	Holiday	Jan	Feb	Mar	Apr	May	Jun	Jul	Aug	Sep	Oct	Nov	Dec		BTO	RBBP	BBRC	EU No
A	Royal Tern	Sterna maxima																			QT		R	0607
A	Lesser Crested Tern	Sterna bengalensis																			TF	B	R	0609
A	Forster's Tern	Sterna forsteri																			FO		R	0618
*A	Common Tern	Sterna hirundo																			CN			0615
*A	Roseate Tern	Sterna dougallii																			RS	A		0614
*A	Arctic Tern	Sterna paradisaea																			AE			0616
*A	Ivory Gull	Pagophila eburnea																			IV		R	0604
*A	Sabine's Gull	Xema sabini																			AB			0579
*A	Kittiwake	Rissa tridactyla																			KI			0602
A	Slender-billed Gull	Chroicocephalus genei																			EI	C	R	0585
A	Bonaparte's Gull	Chroicocephalus philadelphia																			ON		R	0581
*A	Black-headed Gull	Chroicocephalus ridibundus																			BH			0582
*A	Little Gull	Hydrocoloeus minutus																			LU	B		0578
A	Ross's Gull	Rhodostethia rosea																			QG		R	0601
*A	Laughing Gull	Larus atricilla																			LF		R	0576
A	Franklin's Gull	Larus pipixcan																			FG		R	0577
*A	Mediterranean Gull	Larus melanocephalus																			MU	A		0575
A	Audouin's Gull	Larus audouinii																					R	0589
B	Great Black-headed Gull	Larus ichthyaetus																					R	0573
*A	Common Gull	Larus canus																			CM			0590
*A	Ring-billed Gull	Larus delawarensis																			IN	B		0588
*A	Lesser Black-backed Gull	Larus fuscus																			LB			0591
*A	Herring Gull	Larus argentatus																			HG			0592
A	Yellow-legged Gull	Larus michahellis																				A		5927
	Sub total																							

69

GULLS Cont. DOVES, CUCKOOS AND OWLS

BOU			Life list	2014 list	24 hr	Garden	Holiday	Jan	Feb	Mar	Apr	May	Jun	Jul	Aug	Sep	Oct	Nov	Dec		BTO	RBBP	BBRC	EU No
A	Caspian Gull	*Larus cachinnans*																						5927
A	American Herring Gull	*Larus smithsonianus*																					R	26632
*A	Iceland Gull	*Larus glaucoides*																			IG			0598
A	Glaucous-winged Gull	*Larus glaucescens*																					R	5960
*A	Glaucous Gull	*Larus hyperboreus*																			GZ	B		0599
*A	Great Black-backed Gull	*Larus marinus*																			GB			0600
A	Pallas's Sandgrouse	*Syrrhaptes paradoxus*																					R	0663
AC4E	Rock Dove / Feral Pigeon	*Columba livia*																			DV			0665
*A	Stock Dove	*Columba oenas*																			SD			0668
*A	Woodpigeon	*Columba palumbus*																			WP			0670
*A	Collared Dove	*Streptopelia decaocto*																			CD			0684
*A	Turtle Dove	*Streptopelia turtur*																			TD			0687
A	Rufous Turtle Dove	*Streptopelia orientalis*																					R	0689
A	Mourning Dove	*Zenaida macroura*																					R	0695
C1E	Ring-necked Parakeet	*Psittacula krameri*																			RI			0712
A	Great Spotted Cuckoo	*Clamator glandarius*																			UK		R	0716
*A	Cuckoo	*Cuculus canorus*																			CK			0724
A	Black-billed Cuckoo	*Coccyzus erythropthalmus*																					R	0727
A	Yellow-billed Cuckoo	*Coccyzus americanus*																					R	0728
AE	Barn Owl	*Tyto alba*																			BO			0735
A	Scops Owl	*Otus scops*																				C	R	0739
*A	Snowy Owl	*Bubo scandiacus*																			SO	B	R	0749
A	Hawk Owl	*Surnia ulula*																					R	0750
*A	Little Owl	*Athene noctua*																			LO			0757
	Sub total																							

70

BOU — OWLS Cont. NIGHTJARS, SWIFTS, KINGFISHERS, BEE-EATERS AND WOODPECKERS

BOU			Life list	2014 list	24 hr	Garden	Holiday	Jan	Feb	Mar	Apr	May	Jun	Jul	Aug	Sep	Oct	Nov	Dec	BTO	RBBP	BBRC	EU No
*A	Tawny Owl	*Strix aluco*																		TO			0761
*A	Long-eared Owl	*Asio otus*																		LE	A		0767
*A	Short-eared Owl	*Asio flammeus*																		SE	A		0768
A	Tengmalm's Owl	*Aegolius funereus*																				R	0770
*A	Nightjar	*Caprimulgus europaeus*																		NJ			0778
B	Red-necked Nightjar	*Caprimulgus ruficollis*																				R	0779
A	Egyptian Nightjar	*Caprimulgus aegyptius*																				R	0781
A	Common Nighthawk	*Chordeiles minor*																				R	0786
A	Chimney Swift	*Chaetura pelagica*																				R	0790
A	Needle-tailed Swift	*Hirundapus caudacutus*																		NI		R	0792
*A	Swift	*Apus apus*																		SI			0795
A	Pallid Swift	*Apus pallidus*																			C	R	0796
A	Pacific Swift	*Apus pacificus*																				R	0797
A	Alpine Swift	*Apus melba*																		AI			0798
A	Little Swift	*Apus affinis*																				R	0800
*A	Kingfisher	*Alcedo atthis*																		KF			0831
A	Belted Kingfisher	*Megaceryle alcyon*																				R	0834
A	Blue-cheeked Bee-eater	*Merops persicus*																				R	0839
*A	Bee-eater	*Merops apiaster*																		MZ	B		0840
A	Roller	*Coracias garrulus*																				R	0841
*A	Hoopoe	*Upupa epops*																		HP	B		0846
*A	Wryneck	*Jynx torquilla*																		WY	A		0848
*A	Green Woodpecker	*Picus viridis*																		G			0856
A	Yellow-bellied Sapsucker	*Sphyrapicus varius*																				R	0872
	Sub total																						

BOU	WOODPECKERS Cont., VIREOS, SHRIKES AND CORVIDS	Life list	2014 list	24 hr	Garden	Holiday	Jan	Feb	Mar	Apr	May	Jun	Jul	Aug	Sep	Oct	Nov	Dec		BTO	RBBP	BBRC	EU No
*A	Great Spotted Woodpecker *Dendrocopos major*																			GS			0876
*A	Lesser Spotted Woodpecker *Dendrocopos minor*																			LS	A		0887
A	Eastern Phoebe *Sayornis phoebe*																					R	0909
A	Yellow-throated Vireo *Vireo flavifrons*																					R	1628
A	Philadelphia Vireo *Vireo philadelphicus*																			EV		R	1631
A	Red-eyed Vireo *Vireo olivaceus*																					R	1633
*A	Golden Oriole *Oriolus oriolus*																			OL	A		1508
A	Brown Shrike *Lanius cristatus*																					R	1513
A	Isabelline Shrike *Lanius isabellinus*																			IL		R	1514
*A	Red-backed Shrike *Lanius collurio*																			ED	A		1515
A	Long-tailed Shrike *Lanius schach*																					R	1517
*A	Lesser Grey Shrike *Lanius minor*																					R	1519
*A	Great Grey Shrike *Lanius excubitor*																			SR	C		1520
A	Southern Grey Shrike *Lanius meridionalis*																					R	1520
A	Woodchat Shrike *Lanius senator*																			OO			1523
A	Masked Shrike *Lanius nubicus*																					R	1524
AE	Chough *Pyrrhocorax pyrrhocorax*																			CF			1559
*A	Magpie *Pica pica*																			MG	A		1549
*A	Jay *Garrulus glandarius*																			J			1539
A	Nutcracker *Nucifraga caryocatactes*																			NC		R	1557
*A	Jackdaw *Corvus monedula*																			JD			1560
*A	Rook *Corvus frugilegus*																			RO			1563
*A	Carrion Crow *Corvus corone*																			C			1567
*A	Hooded Crow *Corvus cornix*																						1567
	Sub total																						

'CRESTS', TITS, LARKS, MARTINS AND SWALLOWS

BOU	English name	Scientific name	Life list	2014 list	24 hr	Garden	Holiday	Jan	Feb	Mar	Apr	May	Jun	Jul	Aug	Sep	Oct	Nov	Dec			BTO	RBBP	BBRC	EU NO
*A	Raven	Corvus corax																				RN			1572
*A	Goldcrest	Regulus regulus																				GC			1314
*A	Firecrest	Regulus ignicapilla																				FC	A		1315
A	Penduline Tit	Remiz pendulinus																				DT	C	R	1490
*A	Blue Tit	Cyanistes caeruleus																				BT			1462
*A	Great Tit	Parus major																				GT			1464
*A	Crested Tit	Lophophanes cristatus																				CI			1454
*A	Coal Tit	Periparus ater																				CT			1461
*A	Willow Tit	Poecile montana																				WT	A		1442
*A	Marsh Tit	Poecile palustris																				MT			1440
*A	Bearded Tit	Panurus biarmicus																				BR	A		1364
A	Calandra Lark	Melanocorypha calandra																						R	0961
A	Bimaculated Lark	Melanocorypha bimaculata																						R	0962
A	White-winged Lark	Melanocorypha leucoptera																						R	0965
A	Black Lark	Melanocorypha yeltoniensis																						R	0966
A	Short-toed Lark	Calandrella brachydactyla																							0968
A	Lesser Short-toed Lark	Calandrella rufescens																						R	0970
AE	Crested Lark	Galerida cristata																						R	0972
*A	Woodlark	Lullula arborea																				WL	A		0974
*A	Skylark	Alauda arvensis																				S			0976
*A	Shore Lark	Eremophila alpestris																				SX	B		0978
*A	Sand Martin	Riparia riparia																				SM			0981
A	Tree Swallow	Tachycineta bicolor																						R	0983
A	Purple Martin	Progne subis																						R	0989
	Sub total																								

73

BOU	SWALLOWS Cont, WARBLERS		Life list	2014 list	24 hr	Garden	Holiday	Jan	Feb	Mar	Apr	May	Jun	Jul	Aug	Sep	Oct	Nov	Dec		BTO	RBBP	BBRC	EU No
A	Crag Martin	Ptyonoprogne rupestris																			SL		R	0991
*A	Swallow	Hirundo rustica																						0992
*A	House Martin	Delichon urbicum																			HM			1001
A	Red-rumped Swallow	Cecropis daurica																			VR	C		0995
A	Cliff Swallow	Petrochelidon pyrrhonota																					R	0998
*A	Cetti's Warbler	Cettia cetti																			CW	A		1220
*A	Long-tailed Tit	Aegithalos caudatus																			LT			1437
A	Eastern Crowned Warbler	Phylloscopus coronatus																					R	12860
A	Green Warbler	Phylloscopus nitidus																			NP	C	R	12910
A	Greenish Warbler	Phylloscopus trochiloides																						1293
A	Arctic Warbler	Phylloscopus borealis																			AP		R	1295
A	Pallas's Warbler	Phylloscopus proregulus																			PA			1298
*A	Yellow-browed Warbler	Phylloscopus inornatus																			YB			1300
A	Hume's Warbler	Phylloscopus humei																					R	1300
A	Radde's Warbler	Phylloscopus schwarzi																						1301
A	Dusky Warbler	Phylloscopus fuscatus																			UY			1303
*A	Western Bonelli's Warbler	Phylloscopus bonelli																			IW		R	1307
A	Eastern Bonelli's Warbler	Phylloscopus orientalis																					R	1307
*A	Wood Warbler	Phylloscopus sibilatrix																			WO			1308
*A	Chiffchaff	Phylloscopus collybita																			CC			1311
A	Iberian Chiffchaff	Phylloscopus ibericus																				C	R	1311
*A	Willow Warbler	Phylloscopus trochilus																			WW			1312
*A	Blackcap	Sylvia atricapilla																			BC			1277
*A	Garden Warbler	Sylvia borin																			GW			1276
	Sub total																							

WARBLERS Cont

BOU	Name	Life list	2014 list	24 hr	Garden	Holiday	Jan	Feb	Mar	Apr	May	Jun	Jul	Aug	Sep	Oct	Nov	Dec	BTO	RBBP	BBRC	EU No
A	Barred Warbler *Sylvia nisoria*																		RR			1273
*A	Lesser Whitethroat *Sylvia curruca*																		LW			1274
A	Orphean Warbler *Sylvia hortensis*																			C	R	1272
A	Desert Warbler *Sylvia nana*																			C	R	1270
*A	Whitethroat *Sylvia communis*																		WH			1275
A	Spectacled Warbler *Sylvia conspicillata*																			C	R	1264
*A	Dartford Warbler *Sylvia undata*																		DW	A		1262
A	Marmora's Warbler *Sylvia sarda*																		MM	C	R	1261
A	Rüppell's Warbler *Sylvia rueppelli*																				R	1269
A	Subalpine Warbler *Sylvia cantillans*																			C		1265
A	Sardinian Warbler *Sylvia melanocephala*																			C	R	1267
A	Pallas's Grasshopper Warbler *Locustella certhiola*																				R	1233
A	Lanceolated Warbler *Locustella lanceolata*																				R	1235
*A	Grasshopper Warbler *Locustella naevia*																		GH			1236
A	River Warbler *Locustella fluviatilis*																		VW	C	R	1237
A	Savi's Warbler *Locustella luscinioides*																		VI	A	R	1238
A	Thick-billed Warbler *Iduna aedon*																				R	1254
A	Booted Warbler *Iduna caligata*																			C	R	1256
A	Sykes's Warbler *Iduna rama*																				R	12562
A	Eastern Olivaceous Warbler *Iduna pallida*																				R	1255
A	Olive-tree Warbler *Hippolais olivetorum*																				R	12580
*A	Icterine Warbler *Hippolais icterina*																		IC	B		1259
*A	Melodious Warbler *Hippolais polyglotta*																		ME	C		1260
A	Aquatic Warbler *Acrocephalus paludicola*																		AQ			1242
	Sub total																					

75

WARBLERS Cont, WAXWNGS, NUTHATCHES, TREECREEPERS AND THRUSHES

BOU	Name	Scientific	Life list	2014 list	24 hr	Garden	Holiday	Jan	Feb	Mar	Apr	May	Jun	Jul	Aug	Sep	Oct	Nov	Dec	BTO	RBBP	BBRC	EU No
*A	Sedge Warbler	Acrocephalus schoenobaenus																		SW			1243
A	Paddyfield Warbler	Acrocephalus agricola																		PY		R	1247
A	Blyth's Reed Warbler	Acrocephalus dumetorum																			C	R	1248
*A	Marsh Warbler	Acrocephalus palustris																		MW	A		1250
*A	Reed Warbler	Acrocephalus scirpaceus																		RW			1251
A	Great Reed Warbler	Acrocephalus arundinaceus																		QW	C	R	1253
A	Fan-tailed Warbler	Cisticola juncidis																				R	1226
A	Cedar Waxwing	Bombycilla cedrorum																				R	1046
*AE	Waxwing	Bombycilla garrulus																		WX	C		1048
A	Wallcreeper	Tichodroma muraria																				R	1482
A	Red-breasted Nuthatch	Sitta canadensis																				R	1472
*A	Nuthatch	Sitta europaea																		NH			1479
*A	Treecreeper	Certhia familiaris																		TC			1486
A	Short-toed Treecreeper	Certhia brachydactyla																		TH	C	R	1487
*A	Wren	Troglodytes troglodytes																		WR			1066
AE	Northern Mockingbird	Mimus polyglottos																				R	1067
A	Brown Thrasher	Toxostoma rufum																				R	1069
A	Grey Catbird	Dumetella carolinensis																				R	1080
*A	Starling	Sturnus vulgaris																		SG			1582
A	Rose-coloured Starling	Pastor roseus																		OE			1594
*A	Dipper	Cinclus cinclus																		DI			1050
A	White's Thrush	Zoothera dauma																				R	1170
A	Varied Thrush	Ixoreus naevius																		VT		R	1172
A	Wood Thrush	Hylocichla mustelina																				R	1175
	Sub total																						

THRUSHES Cont, CHATS, FLYCATCHERS, ROBINS

BOU	Species	Scientific name	Life list	2014 list	24 hr	Garden	Holiday	Jan	Feb	Mar	Apr	May	Jun	Jul	Aug	Sep	Oct	Nov	Dec	BTO	RBBP	BBRC	EU No
A	Hermit Thrush	Catharus guttatus																				R	1176
AE	Swainson's Thrush	Catharus ustulatus																				R	1177
A	Grey-cheeked Thrush	Catharus minimus																				R	1178
A	Veery	Catharus fuscescens																				R	1179
A	Siberian Thrush	Geokichla sibirica																				R	1171
*A	Ring Ouzel	Turdus torquatus																		RZ			1186
*A	Blackbird	Turdus merula																		B			1187
A	Eyebrowed Thrush	Turdus obscurus																				R	1195
A	Dusky Thrush	Turdus eunomus																				R	1196
A	Naumann's Thrush	Turdus naumanni																				R	11960
A	Black-throated Thrush	Turdus atrogularis																				R	1197
A	Red-throated Thrush	Turdus ruficollis																				R	11970
*A	Fieldfare	Turdus pilaris																		FF	A		1198
*A	Song Thrush	Turdus philomelos																		ST			1200
*A	Redwing	Turdus iliacus																		RE	A		1201
*A	Mistle Thrush	Turdus viscivorus																		M			1202
AE	American Robin	Turdus migratorius																		AR		R	1203
A	Rufous Bush Chat	Cercotrichas galactotes																				R	1095
A	Brown Flycatcher	Muscicapa dauurica																				R	
*A	Spotted Flycatcher	Muscicapa striata																					1335
*A	Robin	Erithacus rubecula																		R			1099
A	Siberian Blue Robin	Larvivora cyane																				R	1112
A	Rufous-tailed Robin	Larvivora sibilans																				R	1102
A	White-throated Robin	Irania gutturalis																				R	1117
	Sub total																						

77

BOU	FLYCATCHERS Cont, CHATS, WHEATEARS		Life list	2014 list	24 hr	Garden	Holiday	Jan	Feb	Mar	Apr	May	Jun	Jul	Aug	Sep	Oct	Nov	Dec	BTO	RBBP	BBRC	EU No
A	Thrush Nightingale	Luscinia luscinia																		FN	C	R	1103
*A	Nightingale	Luscinia megarhynchos																		N			1104
A	Bluethroat	Luscinia svecica																		BU	B		1106
A	Siberian Rubythroat	Calliope calliope																				R	1105
AE	Red-flanked Bluetail	Tarsiger cyanurus																				R	1113
*A	Red-breasted Flycatcher	Ficedula parva																		FY			1343
A	Taiga Flycatcher	Ficedula albicilla																				R	1343
A	Collared Flycatcher	Ficedula albicollis																				R	1348
*A	Pied Flycatcher	Ficedula hypoleuca																		PF			1349
*A	Black Redstart	Phoenicurus ochruros																		BX	A		1121
*A	Redstart	Phoenicurus phoenicurus																		RT			1122
A	Moussier's Redstart	Phoenicurus moussieri																				R	1127
A	Rock Thrush	Monticola saxatilis																		OH		R	1162
AE	Blue Rock Thrush	Monticola solitarius																				R	1166
*A	Whinchat	Saxicola rubetra																		WC			1137
A	Siberian Stonechat	Saxicola maurus																				R	
*A	Stonechat	Saxicola rubicola																		SC			1139
A	Isabelline Wheatear	Oenanthe isabellina																				R	1144
*A	Wheatear	Oenanthe oenanthe																		W			1146
A	Pied Wheatear	Oenanthe pleschanka																		PI		R	1147
A	Black-eared Wheatear	Oenanthe hispanica																				R	1148
A	Desert Wheatear	Oenanthe deserti																				R	1149
A	White-crowned Black Wheatear	Oenanthe leucopyga																				R	1157
*A	Dunnock	Prunella modularis																		D			1084
	Sub total																						

SPARROWS, WAGTAILS, PIPITS AND FINCHES

BOU	Species	Scientific	Life list	2014 list	24 hr	Garden	Holiday	Jan	Feb	Mar	Apr	May	Jun	Jul	Aug	Sep	Oct	Nov	Dec	BTO	RBBP	BBRC	EU No
A	Alpine Accentor	Prunella collaris																				R	1094
*A	House Sparrow	Passer domesticus																		HS			1591
A	Spanish Sparrow	Passer hispaniolensis																				R	1592
*A	Tree Sparrow	Passer montanus																		TS			1598
A	Rock Sparrow	Petronia petronia																				R	1604
*A	Yellow Wagtail	Motacilla flava																		YW			1017
A	Citrine Wagtail	Motacilla citreola																			C	R	1018
*A	Grey Wagtail	Motacilla cinerea																		GL			1019
*A	Pied Wagtail	Motacilla alba																		PW			1020
A	Richard's Pipit	Anthus richardi																		PR			1002
A	Blyth's Pipit	Anthus godlewskii																				R	1004
A	Tawny Pipit	Anthus campestris																		TI			1005
A	Olive-backed Pipit	Anthus hodgsoni																		OV		R	1008
*A	Tree Pipit	Anthus trivialis																		TP			1009
A	Pechora Pipit	Anthus gustavi																				R	1010
*A	Meadow Pipit	Anthus pratensis																		MP			1011
A	Red-throated Pipit	Anthus cervinus																		VP			1012
*A	Rock Pipit	Anthus petrosus																		RC			1014
*A	Water Pipit	Anthus spinoletta																		WI			1014
A	Buff-bellied Pipit	Anthus rubescens																				R	1014
*AE	Chaffinch	Fringilla coelebs																		CH			1636
*A	Brambling	Fringilla montifringilla																		BL	B		1638
*AE	Greenfinch	Chloris chloris																		GR			1649
*A	Serin	Serinus serinus																		NS	B		1640
	Sub total																						

79

FINCHES AND NEW WORLD BUNTINGS

BOU		Scientific name	Life list	2014 list	24 hr	Garden	Holiday	Jan	Feb	Mar	Apr	May	Jun	Jul	Aug	Sep	Oct	Nov	Dec	BTO	RBBP	BBRC	EU No
A	Citril Finch	Carduelis citrinella																				R	
*A	Goldfinch	Carduelis carduelis																		GO			1653
*A	Siskin	Carduelis spinus																		SK			1654
*A	Linnet	Carduelis cannabina																		LI			1660
*A	Twite	Carduelis flavirostris																		TW			1662
*A	Lesser Redpoll	Carduelis cabaret																		LR			1663
*A	Mealy Redpoll	Carduelis flammea																			A		1663
A	Arctic Redpoll	Carduelis hornemanni																		AL			1664
*A	Two-barred Crossbill	Loxia leucoptera																		PD		R	1665
*A	Common Crossbill	Loxia curvirostra																		CR			1666
*A	Scottish Crossbill	Loxia scotica																		CY			1667
*A	Parrot Crossbill	Loxia pytyopsittacus																		PC	A		1668
AE	Trumpeter Finch	Bucanetes githagineus																				R	1676
*A	Common Rosefinch	Carpodacus erythrinus																		SQ	B		1679
AE	Pine Grosbeak	Pinicola enucleator																				R	1699
*A	Bullfinch	Pyrrhula pyrrhula																		BF			1710
*A	Hawfinch	Coccothraustes coccothraustes																		HF	A		1717
A	Evening Grosbeak	Hesperiphona vespertina																				R	1718
*A	Snow Bunting	Plectrophenax nivalis																		SB	A		1850
A	Lapland Bunting	Calcarius lapponicus																		LA	B		1847
A	Summer Tanager	Piranga rubra																				R	1786
A	Scarlet Tanager	Piranga olivacea																				R	1788
A	Rose-breasted Grosbeak	Pheucticus ludovicianus																				R	1887
AE	Indigo Bunting	Passerina cyanea																				R	1892
	Sub total																						

80

BOU	NEW WORLD SPARROWS AND BUNTINGS		Life list	2014 list	24 hr	Garden	Holiday	Jan	Feb	Mar	Apr	May	Jun	Jul	Aug	Sep	Oct	Nov	Dec	BTO	RBBP	BBRC	EU No
A	Eastern Towhee	Pipilo erythrophthalmus																				R	1798
A	Lark Sparrow	Chondestes grammacus																				R	1824
A	Savannah Sparrow	Passerculus sandwichensis																				R	1826
AE	Song Sparrow	Melospiza melodia																				R	1835
AE	White-crowned Sparrow	Zonotrichia leucophrys																				R	1839
AE	White-throated Sparrow	Zonotrichia albicollis																				R	1840
AE	Dark-eyed Junco	Junco hyemalis																		JU		R	1842
AE	Black-faced Bunting	Emberiza spodocephala																				R	1853
A	Pine Bunting	Emberiza leucocephalos																		EL		R	1856
*A	Yellowhammer	Emberiza citrinella																		Y			1857
*A	Cirl Bunting	Emberiza cirlus																		CL	A		1958
A	Rock Bunting	Emberiza cia																				R	1860
A	Ortolan Bunting	Emberiza hortulana																		OB			1866
A	Cretzschmar's Bunting	Emberiza caesia																				R	1868
A	Yellow-browed Bunting	Emberiza chrysophrys																				R	1871
A	Rustic Bunting	Emberiza rustica																					1873
A	Chestnut-eared Bunting	Emberiza fucata																		LJ		R	1869
A	Little Bunting	Emberiza pusilla																					1874
A	Yellow-breasted Bunting	Emberiza aureola																			C	R	1876
*A	Reed Bunting	Emberiza schoeniclus																		RB			1877
A	Pallas's Reed Bunting	Emberiza pallasi																				R	1878
AE	Black-headed Bunting	Emberiza melanocephala																				R	1881
*A	Corn Bunting	Emberiza calandra																		CB			1882
A	Bobolink	Dolichonyx oryzivorus																				R	1897
	Sub total																						

81

NEW WORLD WARBLERS

BOU	NEW WORLD WARBLERS		Life list	2014 list	24 hr	Garden	Holiday	Jan	Feb	Mar	Apr	May	Jun	Jul	Aug	Sep	Oct	Nov	Dec	BTO	RBBP	BBRC	EU No
A	Brown-headed Cowbird	*Molothrus ater*																				R	1899
AE	Baltimore Oriole	*Icterus galbula*																				R	1918
A	Ovenbird	*Seiurus aurocapilla*																				R	1756
A	Northern Waterthrush	*Parkesia noveboracensis*																				R	1757
A	Golden-winged Warbler	*Vermivora chrysoptera*																				R	1722
A	Black-and-white Warbler	*Mniotilta varia*																				R	1720
A	Tennessee Warbler	*Oreothlypis peregrina*																				R	1724
A	Common Yellowthroat	*Geothlypis trichas*																				R	1762
A	Hooded Warbler	*Setophaga citrina*																				R	1771
AE	American Redstart	*Setophaga ruticilla*																		AD		R	1755
A	Cape May Warbler	*Setophaga tigrina*																				R	1749
AE	Northern Parula	*Setophaga americana*																				R	1732
A	Magnolia Warbler	*Setophaga magnolia*																				R	1750
A	Bay-breasted Warbler	*Setophaga castanea*																				R	1754
A	Blackburnian Warbler	*Setophaga fusca*																				R	1747
A	Yellow Warbler	*Setophaga petechia*																				R	1733
A	Chestnut-sided Warbler	*Setophaga pensylvanica*																				R	1734
AE	Blackpoll Warbler	*Setophaga striata*																				R	1753
A	Yellow-rumped Warbler	*Setophaga coronata*																				R	1751
A	Wilson's Warbler	*Cardellina pusilla*																				R	1772
	Sub total																						

CATEGORY D & E SPECIES, PLUS SELECTED EUROPEAN SPECIES

BOU	Species	(Scientific name)	Life list	2014 list	24 hr	Garden	Holiday	Jan	Feb	Mar	Apr	May	Jun	Jul	Aug	Sep	Oct	Nov	Dec				BTO	RBBP	BBRC	EU No
D	Ross's Goose	Anser rossii																								R	0181
D	Falcated Duck	A. falcata																					FT		R	0183
D	Baikal Teal	A. formosa																					IK		R	0195
D	Marbled Duck	Marmaronetta angustirostris																								0226
EU	White-headed Duck	Oxyura leucocephala																					WQ			0357
EU	Rock Partridge	Alectoris graeca																								0359
EU	Barbary Partridge	A. barbara																								0082
EU	Pygmy Cormorant	P. pygmeus																					YP		R	0088
D	Great White Pelican	Pelecanus onocrotalus																								0089
EU	Dalmatian Pelican	P. crispus																								
D	Greater Flamingo	Phoenicopterus roseus																					FL		R	0147
EU	Black-winged Kite	Elanus caeruleus																								0235
D	Bald Eagle	H. leucocephalus																							R	0244
EU	Lammergeier	Gypaetus barbatus																								0246
D	Black Vulture	Aegypius monachus																							R	0255
EU	Levant Sparrowhawk	A. brevipes																								0273
EU	Long-legged Buzzard	B. rufinus																								0288
EU	Lesser Spotted Eagle	Aquila pomarina																								0292
EU	Imperial Eagle	A. heliaca																								0295
EU	Booted Eagle	Hieraaetus pennatus																								0298
EU	Bonelli's Eagle	H. fasciatus																								0299
EU	Lanner Falcon	Falco biarmicus																					FB			0314
D	Saker Falcon	F. cherrug																					JF		R	0316
EU	Andalusian Hemipode	Turnix sylvatica																								0400
	Sub total																									

83

BOU	CATEGORY D & E SPECIES, PLUS SELECTED EUROPEAN SPECIES		Life list	2014 list	24 hr	Garden	Holiday	Jan	Feb	Mar	Apr	May	Jun	Jul	Aug	Sep	Oct	Nov	Dec	BTO	RBBP	BBRC	EU No
EU	Purple Gallinule	Porphyrio porphyrio																					0427
EL	Crested Coot	F. cristata																					0431
EU	Spur-winged Plover	Hoplopterus spinosus																		UW			0487
EU	Black-bellied Sandgrouse	Pterocles orientalis																					0661
EU	Pin-tailed Sandgrouse	P. alchata																					0662
EU	Eagle Owl	Bubo bubo																		EO	bD		0744
EU	Pygmy Owl	Glaucidium passerinum																					0751
EU	Ural Owl	S. uralensis																					0765
EU	Great Grey Owl	S. nebulosa																					0766
EL	White-rumped Swift	Apus caffer																					0799
EU	Grey-headed Woodpecker	Picus canus																					0855
EU	Black Woodpecker	Dryocopus martius																					0863
EU	Syrian Woodpecker	D. syriacus																					0878
EU	Middle Spotted Woodpecker	D. medius																					0883
EU	White-backed Woodpecker	D. leucotos																					0884
EU	Three-toed Woodpecker	Picoides tridactylus																					0898
EU	Dupont's Lark	Chersophilus duponti																					0959
EU	Thekla Lark	G. theklae																					0973
EU	Black Wheatear	Oenanthe leucura																				R	1158
EU	Cyprus Warbler	S. melanothorax																					1268
D	Mugimaki Flycatcher	F. mugimaki																				R	1344
EU	Semi-collared Flycatcher	F. semitorquata																					1347
EU	Sombre Tit	P. lugubris																					1441
EU	Siberian Tit	P. cinctus																					1448
	Sub total																						

LOG CHARTS

BOU	CATEGORY D & E SPECIES, PLUS SELECTED EUROPEAN SPECIES		Life list	2014 list	24 hr	Garden	Holiday	Jan	Feb	Mar	Apr	May	Jun	Jul	Aug	Sep	Oct	Nov	Dec				BTO	RBBP	BBRC	EU No
EU	Krüper's Nuthatch	Sitta krueperi																								1469
EU	Corsican Nuthatch	S. whiteheadi																								1470
EU	Rock Nuthatch	S. neumayer																								1481
EU	Siberian Jay	Perisoreus infaustus																								1543
EU	Azure-winged Magpie	Cyanopica cyana																								1547
EU	Alpine Chough	Pyrrhocorax graculus																								1558
D	Daurian Starling	Sturnus sturninus																							R	1579
EU	Spotless Starling	S. unicolor																								1583
D	Snow Finch	Montifringilla nivalis																							R	1611
D	Palm Warbler	D. palmarum																							R	1752
D	Yellow-headed Blackbird	Xanthocephalus xanthocephalus																								1911
EU	Cinereous Bunting	E. cinerea																								1865
D	Chestnut Bunting	E. rutila																							R	1875
D	Red-headed Bunting	E. bruniceps																								1880
D	Blue Grosbeak	Guiraca caerulea																							R	1891
	Sub total																									

85

BRITISH DRAGONFLY LIST

SPECIES	2014 list	Life list
DAMSELFLIES		
Calopterygidae (Demoiselles)		
Banded Demoiselle		
Beautiful Demoiselle		
Coenagrionidae (Blue, blue-tailed & red damselflies)		
Small Red Damselfly		
Northern Damselfly		
Irish Damselfly		
Southern Damselfly		
Azure Damselfly		
Variable Damselfly		
Dainty Damselfly		
Common Blue Damselfly		
Red-eyed Damselfly		
Small Red-eyed Damselfly		
Blue-tailed Damselfly		
Scarce Blue-tailed Damselfly		
Large Red Damselfly		
Lestidae (Emerald damselflies)		
Southern Emerald Damselfly		
Scarce Emerald Damselfly		
Emerald Damselfly		
Willow Emerald Damselfly		
Winter Damselfly		
Platycnemididae (White-legged damselflies)		
White-legged Damselfly		
DRAGONFLIES		
Aeshnidae (Hawkers and Emperors)		
Southern Migrant Hawker		
Azure Hawker		
Southern Hawker		
Brown Hawker		
Norfolk Hawker		

SPECIES	2014 list	Life list
Common Hawker		
Migrant Hawker		
Vagrant Emperor		
Emperor Dragonfly		
Lesser Emperor		
Hairy Dragonfly		
Cordulegastridae (Golden-ringed Dragonflies)		
Golden-ringed Dragonfly		
Corduliidae (Emerald dragonflies)		
Downy Emerald		
Orange-spotted Emerald		
Northern Emerald		
Brilliant Emerald		
Gomphidae (Club-tailed Dragonflies)		
Common Club-tail		
Libellulidae (Chasers, Skimmers and Darters)		
Scarlet Darter		
White-faced Darter		
Broad-bodied Chaser		
Scarce Chaser		
Four-spotted Chaser		
Black-tailed Skimmer		
Keeled Skimmer		
Wandering Glider		
Black Darter		
Vagrant Darter		
Yellow-winged Darter		
Red-veined Darter		
Banded Darter		
Ruddy Darter		
Common Darter		
TOTAL		

BRITISH BUTTERFLY LIST

SPECIES	2014 list	Life list
Hesperiidae - Skippers		
Chequered Skipper		
Lulworth Skipper		
Essex Skipper		
Small Skipper		
Silver-spotted Skipper		
Large Skipper		
Grizzled Skipper		
Dingy Skipper		
Papilionidae		
Swallowtail		
Pieridae - The Whites		
Wood White		
Clouded Yellow		
Brimstone		
Large White		
Small White		
Green-veined White		
Orange Tip		
Lycaenidae - Hairstreaks, Coppers and Blues		
Green Hairstreak		
Brown Hairstreak		
Purple Hairstreak		
White-letter Hairstreak		
Black Hairstreak		
Large Copper		
Small Copper		
Small Blue		
Silver-studded Blue		
Northern Brown Argus		
Brown Argus		
Common Blue		
Chalkhill Blue		
Adonis Blue		
Holly Blue		

SPECIES	2014 list	Life list
Large Blue		
Riodinidae - Metalmarks		
Duke of Burgundy		
Nymphalidae - Vanessids, Emperors and Fritillaries		
White Admiral		
Purple Emperor		
Painted Lady		
Small Tortoiseshell		
Red Admiral		
Peacock		
Comma		
Small Pearl-bordered Fritillary		
Pearl-bordered Fritillary		
High Brown Fritillary		
Dark Green Fritillary		
Silver-washed Fritillary		
Marsh Fritillary		
Glanville Fritillary		
Heath Fritillary		
Camberwell Beauty		
Queen of Spain Fritillary		
Satyridae - The Browns		
Speckled Wood		
Wall		
Scotch Argus		
Mountain Ringlet		
Gate Keeper		
Marbled White		
Grayling		
Meadow Brown		
Ringlet		
Small Heath		
Large Heath		
TOTAL		

Best Birdwatching Sites

The trusted name for accurate, accessible site information

Best Birdwatching Sites in Norfolk (3rd Edition) by Neil Glenn. Features 85 locations, all of which have been completely updated and includes nine new sites. 272pp. **Price: £17.95.**

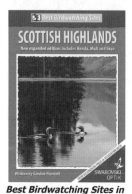

Best Birdwatching Sites in the Scottish Highlands (2nd Edition) by Gordon Hamlett. New, expanded edition features 26 birding routes from John O'Groats to Pitlochry and includes the islands of Handa, Mull and Skye. **Price: £17.95**

Best Birdwatching Sites: North-East England by Brian Unwin. Features 17 birding sites in Cleveland; 37 sites in Co Durham and 42 sites in Northumberland. 308 pp. **Price £17.95**

Best Birdwatching Sites: The Solway by John Miles. Features 76 birding sites in Cumbria and 84 in Dumfries & Galloway. 260 pp. **Price £17.50**

Best Birdwatching Sites: Dorset by Neil Gartshore. Features 65 reserves and birding areas, including a full range of habitats from heathland to coastal sites. 248 pp. **Price £17.95**

Best Birdwatching Sites in Cornwall & Scilly by Sara McMahon and Nigel Hudson. Features 52 mainland sites, plus seven routes around the key islands of Scilly. 208pp. **Price: £17.50 15.00**

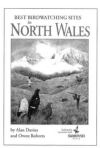

Best Birdwatching Sites in North Wales by Alan Davies and Owen Roberts. Features 58 major sites in Gwynedd and Clwyd, plus 11 smaller birding spots around Wrexham. 192pp. **Price: £15.95**

For details of latest special offers on our books please contact Buckingham Press, 55 Thorpe Park Road, Peterborough PE3 6LJ. 01733 561 739; or visit www.buckinghampress.co.uk (see entry on page 109).

88

DIRECTORY OF ARTISTS, PHOTOGRAPHERS AND LECTURERS

David Cromack

The colourful birds of North America, such as this Great Horned Owl, feature in several of the talks on offer from speakers in the Directory of Lecturers.

Art Galleries	90
Artists	90
Photographers	92
Lecturers	94

DIRECTORY OF
WILDLIFE ART GALLERIES

BIRDSCAPES GALLERY
Offers top quality bird art all year round, plus
landscapes and other wildlife originals, sculptures,
prints, wildlife art books and cards. More than
50 regular artists, including SWLA members, are
represented, with new exhibitions each month.
Opening times: Mon-Sat, (10am-5pm), Sunday,
(10am-4pm). The gallery may be closed for part of
the day before a new exhibition.
Address: The BIRDscapes Gallery, Manor Farm Barns,
Glandford, Holt, Norfolk. NR25 7JP. 01263 741 742;
e-mail: art@birdscapes.co.uk
www.birdscapesgallery.co.uk

NATURE IN ART
The world's first museum dedicated exclusively to
art inspired by nature. The collection spans 1,500
years, covers 60 countries and includes work by
Tunnicliffe, Harrison, Thorburn, Scott and other bird
artists. See work being created by artists in residence
(see website for dates), plus a vibrant exhibitions
programme. Sculpture garden, coffee shop, gift shop
and children's activity areas.
Opening times: 10am-5pm (Tuesday to Sunday and
bank holidays). Admission £5.25 (adults), £4.75
(concessions), £15 (family), under-8s free.
Address: Wallsworth Hall, Twigworth, Gloucester
GL2 9PA (two miles N of city on A38). 01452 731 422.
e-mail: enquiries@nature-in-art.org.uk
www.nature-in-art.org.uk

THE WILDLIFE ART GALLERY
Opened in 1988 as a specialist in 20th Century and
contemporary wildlife art. It exhibits work by many
of the leading European wildlife artists, both painters
and sculptors, and has published several wildlife
books.
Opening times: Mon-Sat (10am-4.30pm) and Sun
(2pm-4.30pm).
Address: 98/99 High Street, Lavenham, Suffolk CO10
9PZ; 01787 248 562; (Fax) 01787 247 356.
E-mail: info@wildlifeartgallery.com
www.wildlifeartgallery.com

DIRECTORY OF
WILDLIFE ARTISTS

ALLEN, Richard
Watercolour paintings, sketches and illustrations of
birds, wildlife, flowers and landscapes, mainly based
on extensive field sketching. Book work includes:
Sunbirds (Helm) and *Guide to Birds of SE Asia* (New
Holland). Also stamp designs for The Solomons,
Ascencion Island and Kiribati and in RSPB *Birds*
magazine.
Artwork for sale: Watercolour paintings, limited
edition prints, original cover paintings from *Birding
World* and header illustrations from *British Birds*.
See website for details.
Address: 34 Parkwood Avenue, Wivenhoe, Essex,
CO7 9AN; 01206 826 753.
E-mail: richard@richardallen31.wanadoo.co.uk
www.richardallenillustrator.com

DAVIS, John
Paintings and illustrations of many wildlife subjects
and landscapes. Published work includes a new
book from Langford Press: *Beyond the Plough*,
illustrations for the new Buckingham Press title:
Best Birdwatching Sites: Dorset, regular illustrations
for RSPB's *Birdlife Magazine*. Member of SWLA since
1987 and exhibits at their annual exhibition at the
Mall Galleries.
Formats: Paints in oils, acrylics and watercolour.

Artwork for sale: Commissions accepted.
Address: 6 Redmoor, Birdham, West Sussex
PO20 7HS; 01243 512 351;
e-mail: johndavis.wildlife@tiscali.co.uk

DEMAIN, Michael
Started painting in 1992, turning professional
in 1998. In his spare time he helps the RSPB,
monitoring breeding raptors in the Bowland Fells.
Artwork for sale: A selection of acrylic and oil
paintings and limited edition prints.
Exhibitions for 2014: Bird Fair at Rutland Water,
NEWA.
Address: 175 Richmond Road, Accrington, Lancs BB5
0JB; 01254 237 378;
e-mail: mdemainwildart@aol.com
www.michaeldemainwildlifeart.co.uk

GARNER, Jackie FRSA
Professional wildlife artist & illustrator. Author of
The Wildlife Artist's Handbook. Cover illustrator
for the *Birdwatcher's Yearbook 2014*. Specialises in
original paintings based on field sketches. Aigas Field
Centre tutor.
Formats: Acrylics, watercolours, sketches,
illustrations.
Exhibitions for 2014: Group exhibitions (SWLA,
NEWA etc). See website for details.

DIRECTORY OF WILDLIFE ARTISTS

Artwork for sale: Originals, limited edition prints, cards, puzzles. See website for latest availability. Commissions accepted.
Address: The Old Cider House Studio, Humphries End, Randwick, Stroud, Glos GL6 6EW; 01453 847 420; (M) 07800 804 847.
e-mail: artist@jackiegarner.co.uk
www.jackiegarner.co.uk

GRIFFITHS, Ian
Birds and their habitat is the main subject matter for Griff's paintings. Having lived throughout the UK and travelled widely around the world, he has a wealth of field experience to draw upon. In 2011 he was a winner in the *BBC Wildlife* artist of the year competition and runner-up in 2012.
Subjects: Mainly birds in various mediums.
Exhibitions for 2014: His own studio/gallery.
Artwork for sale: Commissions considered and through his website.
Address: Griff's wildlife studio, Creftow, 6 Church Street, Helston, Cornwall TR13 8TG; 07971 678 464.
e-mail: mail@artbygriff.com www.artbygriff.com

LEAHY, Ernest
Original watercolours and drawings of Western Palearctic birds, wildlife and country scenes. Also paints British mammals and butterflies. Illustrations for many publications including Poysers. Commissions accepted and enquiries welcome. See website for available artwork.
Formats: Wide range of framed and unframed originals available. E-mail for details of current work available and for quotations on commissioned work.
Artwork for sale: See www.flickr.com/photos/ernsbirdart for latest work.
Address: 32 Ben Austins, Redbourn, Herts, AL3 7DR; 01582 793 144; e-mail: ernest.leahy@ntlworld.com www.flickr.com/photos/ernsbirdart

MILLER, David
Based in West Wales, David is best known for his underwater paintings of game, sea and coarse fish and he has provided images for the UK rod licence over the past few years. He also specialises in sea-birds and waders and regularly exhibits at both the British Birdfair and BIRDscapes Gallery, Glandford, Norfolk.
Subjects: British fish, coastal birds and wildlife mostly in oils. Some mixed media.
Exhibitions for 2014: Visit David's website for events and exhibitions.
Artwork for sale: A selection of original oils and prints of British wildlife, fish and birds are available to buy on the website. Commissions available.
Address: Nyth-Gwdi-Hw, New Mill, St Clears, Carmarthenshire SA33 4HY; 01994 453 545; (M)07900 825 404; e-mail: david@davidmillerart.co.uk
www.davidmillerart.co.uk

ROSE, Chris
Originals in oils and acrylics of birds and animals in landscapes. Particular interest in painting water and its myriad effects. Limited edition reproductions available. Art book, *In a Natural Light - the Wildlife Art of Chris Rose* published 2005. Illustrated many books including *Grebes of the World* (publ.2002) and *Handbook to the Birds of the World*.
Artwork for sale: Original drawings and paintings, linocuts, illustrations, limited edition reproductions, postcards.
Address: 6 Whitelee Cottages, Newtown St Boswells, Melrose, Scotland TD6 0SH; (Tel/Fax)01835 822 547.
e-mail: chris@chrisrose-artist.co.uk
www.chrisrose-artist.co.uk

THRELFALL, John
Member of the Society of Wildlife Artists. Swarovski/ *Birdwatch* Bird Artist of the Year 2007. Award-winner at the NEWA 2001, 2004, 2006 exhibitions. BIRDscapes Gallery Award 2007.
Formats: Paintings in oils, pastel and acrylic.
Artwork for sale: Contact artist.
Exhibitions for 2014: McGill Duncan Gallery, King Street, Castle Douglas, Dumfries and Galloway, 15th Feb to 29th March. Spring Fling Open Studios, Dumfries and Galloway, 24th to 26th May. Scottish Ornithologists Club, Waterston House Aberlady, East Lothian, 25th July to 17th Sept. The British Birdfair, Art Marquee, Rutland 15th to 17th Aug. The Society of Wildlife Artists, Mall Galleries, London, November. Birdscapes Gallery, Glandford, North Norfolk, November.
Address: Saltflats Cottage, Rockcliffe, Dalbeattie, Kirkcudbrightshire DG5 4QQ; 01556 630 262.
e-mail: john@johnthrelfall.co.uk
www.johnthrelfall.co.uk
Facebook: JohnThrelfallWildlifeArt

WARREN, Michael
Member of Society of Wildlife Artists (treasurer). President of Nottinghamshire Birdwatchers. His latest book *American Birding Sketchbook* was published by Langford Press in 2012.
Exhibitions for 2014: Will exhibit at Rutland Birdfair in August, and Society of Wildlife Artists in October — See website for more information during year.
Artwork for sale: Original watercolour paintings of birds, all based on field observations. Books, calendars, cards and commissions welcomed.
Address: The Laurels, The Green, Winthorpe, Nottinghamshire, NG24 2NR; 01636 673 554.
e-mail: mike.warren@tiscali.co.uk
www.mikewarren.co.uk

DIRECTORY OF WILDLIFE PHOTOGRAPHERS

ALMOND, Jim
Bird Photographer with additional interest
in Butterflies and Odonata
Subjects: All UK birds, special interest in wild
Peregrines. See website for main interests, gallery
and portfolio.
Products and services: Images for publication,
lectures and workshops / individual tuition available.
Vast library of images. Available for commissions,
lectures and tours. Competitive terms for larger
projects.
Address: 5 Coolock Close, St Peters Park, Shrewsbury
SY3 9QD; 07940 678 719;
e-mail: almond.jim@virgin.net
Website: http://shropshirebirder.co.uk/

BASTON, Bill
Photographer, lecturer.
Subjects: East Anglian rarities and common birds,
Mediterranean birds and landscapes, UK wildlife
and landscapes, Northern Greece & Western Turkey,
Spain, Goa, General wildlife photography, The
Gambia, Northern India (birds and tigers), Costa Rica,
North East India and the Himalayan foothills, Western
Australia, Morocco.
Products and services: Prints, slides, digital,
mounted/unmounted.
Address: 86 George Street, Hadleigh, Ipswich, IP7
5BU; 01473 827 062; www.billbaston.com
e-mail: billbaston@btinternet.com

BEJARANO, Santiago
An Ecuadorean naturalist and wildlife photographer
who worked in the Galapagos for almost two decades,
with a great depth of knowledge and unique insight
into these remarkable islands and their wildlife.
Subjects: Flora and fauna of Galapagos Islands and
birds of Ecuador.
Products and services: Prints and posters of the
wildlife of the Galapagos Islands and birds of Ecuador.
Introductory classes to wildlife photography, including
digital and basic Photoshop® techniques.
Address: 25 Trinity Lane, Beverley, East Yorkshire
HU17 0DY; 01482 872 716; www.thinkgalapagos.com
e-mail: info@thinkgalapagos.com

BELL, Graham
Professional ornithologist, photographer, author,
cruise lecturer worldwide.
Subjects: Birds, animals, flowers, landscapes, all
seven continents, from Arctic to Antarctic.....
Products and services: Original slides for sale, £2
each. Lecture: 'Taking Better Photos'.
Address: Ros View, South Yearle, Wooler,
Northumberland, NE71 6RB; 01668 281310.
e-mail: seabirdsdgb@hotmail.com

BROOKS, Richard
Wildlife photographer, writer, lecturer, birding guide.
Subjects: Owls (Barn especially), raptors, Kingfisher
and a variety of European birds (Lemnos and Lesvos
especially) and landscapes.
Products and services: Guided birding and wildlife
photography in Norfolk, by arrangement. Mounted
and unmounted computer prints (6x4, A3+ size),
framed pictures, A5 greetings cards, surplus slides for
sale. Norfolk bird calendar available (see website).
Address: 24 Croxton Hamlet, Fulmodeston,
Fakenham, Norfolk, NR21 0NP; 01328 878 632.
e-mail: email@richard-brooks.co.uk
(or r.brooks662@btinternet.com)
www.richard-brooks.co.uk

BUCKINGHAM, John
Worldwide bird and wildlife photographer
Subjects: Huge range of birds, botany and wildlife
in UK and Europe, plus great coverage from Africa,
Americas, Australia and worldwide..
Products and services: Original slides for lectures
and personal use.
Address: 3 Cardinal Close, Tonbridge, Kent, TN9 2EN;
(Tel/fax) 01732 354 970.
e-mail: john.birdtalk@btinternet.com

DUGGAN, Glenn
Specialist in tropical birding
Subjects: Tropical birds, Trogons, Tanagers, Birds of
Paradise.
Address: 25 Hampton Grove, Fareham, Hampshire,
PO15 5NL; 01329 845 976, (M)07771 605 320.
e-mail: glenn.m.duggan@ntlworld.com
www.birdlectures.com

GALVIN, Chris
A birding photographer with passion for birds for
more than 30 years.
Subjects: Birds.
Products and services: Images for publication,
prints, mounted prints, commissions considered.
Address: 17 Henley Road, Allerton, Liverpool,
Merseyside L18 2DN; 07802 428 385 or 0151 729 0123.
e-mail: chris@chrisgalvinphoto.com
www.chrisgalvinphoto.com

GROVE, Ashley
Professional photographer, Tour Leader, Lecturer and
runs Photography Workshops. References on request
if required.
Tours: Ashley arranges and leads very reasonably
priced tours for wildlife photographers and
birdwatchers. He has led tours to The Gambia since
2011 and other destinations are opening up during
2014/15 including a challenging two week tour to
Trinidad & Tobago to photograph Hummingbirds and
many other resident beauties. Visit Ashley's website
for more information on the tours and to see a

DIRECTORY OF WILDLIFE PHOTOGRAPHERS

selection of images he has gathered on his trips.
Address: 16, Lint Meadow, Wythall, Worcestershire
B47 5PH; 07704 189 835;
e-mail: birdergrove@gmail.com
www.vp.ashleygrovewildimages.co.uk/lectures.php

LANE, Mike
Wildlife photographer and lecturer.
Subjects: Birds and wildlife from around the world,
also landscapes and the environment.
Products and services: Website with instantly
downloadable online pictures. Talks and workshops.
Address: 36 Berkeley Road, Shirley, Solihull, West
Midlands B90 2HS; 0121 744 7988; (M)07766 418 013;
e-mail: mikelane@nature-photography.co.uk
www.nature-photography.co.uk

LENTON, Graham
PhD Ornithology/Ecology. Former lecturer at Oxford
University and Oxford Brookes University. Lifetime
photographer of wildlife, with publications of articles
and photographs of birds and wildlife.
Subjects: Worldwide birds, mammals of Africa,
wildlife, worldwide travel.
Products and services: Photos available for sale or
reproduction.
Address: The Old School, 25A Standlake Road,
Ducklington, Witney, Oxon OX29 7UR; 01993 899 033.
e-mail: grahamlenton@btopenworld.com
www.gml-art.co.uk

LINGARD, David
Wildlife photographer, retired from RAF, now UK
delegate to LIPU (BirdLife in Italy).
Subjects: Birds and views of places visited around
the world.
Products and services: 35mm transparencies (last
Century) but now, exclusively digital images.
Address: Fernwood, Doddington Road, Whisby, Lincs
LN6 9BX; 01522 689 030.
e-mail: mail@lipu-uk.org - www.lipu-uk.org

NASON, Rebecca
UK, Shetland- based bird and wildlife photographer
and tour Leader.
Subjects: Wildlife Photography. Specializing in birds,
from common to rare!
Products and services: Large image stock library.
Professionally printed high quality images available,
various sizes, limited editions, mounts and frames
from 6 x 4 to A1+.
Large Aluminium prints also available for a modern,
clean, artistic look for the home or office.
Popular wildlife greeting card and postcard range
(trade prices for larger stockists). Commissions
undertaken.
Bespoke Shetland & Fair Isle birding & bird
photography tours available & a NEW Shetland B&B
opening in 2014 . . . .please email me for details.
Address: Ortolan House, 14 Law Lane, Lerwick,
Shetland, Shetland Islands ZE1 0EA; 07919 256 386.
e-mail: rebecca@rebeccanason.com
www.rebeccanason.com

NEWTON, Ian
Photographer (ARPS) and lecturer, Chairman York
Ornithological Club.
Subjects: Mainly birds and other wildlife of North,
Central and South America, Europe and UK.
Products and services: Prints, canvas & board
mounted images etc.
Address: 5 Fairfields Drive, Skelton, York YO30 1YP ;
01904 471 446; (M)07976 849 832;
e-mail: iannewton@acsemail.co.uk
www.iannewtonphotography.com

PARKER, Susan and Allan ARPS
Professional photographers (ASPphoto - Images of
Nature) lecturers and tutors.
Subjects: Birds plus other flora and fauna from the
UK, Spain, Lesvos, Cyprus, Florida and Texas.
Products and services: 35mm and digital images,
mounted digital images, greetings cards and digital
images on CD/DVD for reproduction (high quality
scans up to A3+).
Address: Windhover Barn, 51b Kiveton Lane, Todwick,
Sheffield, South Yorkshire, S26 1HJ; 01909 770 238;
e-mail: aspphoto@btinternet.com

PETTIT, Brian
Wildlife consultant and photographer.
Subjects: Wide-ranging bird, mammal, plant and
landscape subjects from UK and overseas.
Products and services: Mounted and unmounted
prints of standard sizes, but call to discuss any special
requirements. *Wildlife Photography On a Budget* book
available from the website. Brian also escorts tours to
Zimbabwe designed to appeal to photographers and
non-photographers alike.
Address: 18 Okeford Road, Broadstone, Poole, Dorset
BH18 8PA; 07979 056 144;
e-mail: wildlifepics@ntlworld.com
www.naturepicturesworldwide.com

READ, Mike
Photographer (wildlife and landscapes), tour leader,
writer.
Subjects: Birds, mammals, plants, landscapes, and
some insects. UK, France, USA, Ecuador (including
Galapagos) plus many more. Behaviour, action,
portraits, artistic pictures available for publication.
More than 100,000 images in stock.
Products and services: Extensive stock photo library.
Canvas and giclee prints, greetings cards, books.
Address: Claremont, Redwood Close, Ringwood,
Hampshire, BH24 1PR; 01425 475 008.
e-mail: mike@mikeread.co.uk - www.mikeread.co.uk

SMART, Oliver
Photographer, lecturer and ornithologist.
Subjects: All wildlife subjects, UK based, also Alaska,
Canada, Cuba, Ethiopia, Europe, Madagascar and the
Seychelles.
Products and services: Acrylic prints, bean bags,
canvas prints, desk calendars, digital image library,
digital slideshow lectures, greeting cards, mounted

prints (to A2 size), photographic workshops and puzzles.
Address: 78 Aspen Park Road, Weston-Super-Mare, Somerset BS22 8ER; (M)07802 417 810.
e-mail: oliver@smartimages.co.uk
www.smartimages.co.uk

OFFORD, Keith
Photographer, writer, tour leader, conservationist.
Subjects: Birds, other wildlife and scenery of UK, Europe, USA, Africa, Costa Rica, Australia, India.
Products and services: Conventional prints, greetings cards, framed pictures.
Address: Yew Tree Farmhouse, Craignant, Selattyn, Nr Oswestry, Shropshire, SY10 7NP; 01691 718 740;
e-mail: keith.offord@virgin.net
www.keithofford.co.uk

SWASH, Andy and Gill
Professional wildlife photographers, tour leaders and authors.
Subjects: Birds, mammals, general wildlife and landscapes from all continents; extensive photographic library of over 250,000 high quality images, including more than 3,500 bird species.
Products and services: Images for publication and lectures. High resolution images on CD/DVD.

Conventional and digital prints, unmounted, mounted or framed. Greetings cards.
Address: Stretton Lodge, 9 Birch Grove, West Hill, Ottery St Mary, Devon, EX11 1XP; 01404 815 383, (M)07760 188 594;
e-mail: swash@worldwildlifeimages.com
www.worldwildlifeimages.com

TYLER, John
Subjects: Plants, fungi, insects and other invertebrates.
Products and services: Images for sale.
Address: 5 Woodfield, Lacey Green, Buckinghamshire, HP27 0QQ; 07814 392 335; www.johntyler.co.uk
e-mail: johnclarketyler@gmail.com

WARD, Chris
Lecturer, N Bucks RSPB Local Group Leader.
Subjects: Primarily birds (and some other wildlife) and landscapes from UK and worldwide (Spain, Mallorca, Romania, Cyprus, Oman, Americas, Africa).
Products and services: Digital images and prints on request.
Address: 41 William Smith Close, Woolstone, Milton Keynes, MK15 0AN; 01908 669 448.
e-mail: cwphotography@hotmail.com
www.cwardphotography.co.uk

DIRECTORY OF LECTURERS

ALMOND, Jim
Photographer and very active birder. Experienced lecturer.
Subjects: See website for full descriptive details and titles. Wild Peregrines, Birding in Shropshire / Venus Pool, Out and About in the UK (year listing), North Norfolk, Bird and Nature Photography, Bird identification plus other wildlife including butterflies and dragonflies. All talks are digitally presented in an entertaining style with audio-visual finale. I can cater for all levels of interest.
Fees: £75 for standard lecture plus fuel at 30p per mile. **Limits:** None. **Time limitations:** None
Address: 5 Coolock Close, St Peters Park, Shrewsbury SY3 9QD; 07940 678 719.
e-mail: almond.jim@virgin.net
Website: http://shropshirebirder.co.uk/

BAINES, Richard
Director for Yorkshire Coast Nature. Professional ecologist and birder, Conservation Officer for Flamborough Bird Observatory.
Subjects: Flamborough Headland, Rarities on the Great White Cape; Birds and Environmental Stewardship on Flamborough Headland.

Fees: Flexible. **Limits:** None. **Time limitations:** None.
Contact: 01262 851 999;
e-mail: richard.baines@yorkshirecoastnature.co.uk
www.yorkshirecoastnature.co.uk

BASTON, Bill
Photographer, lecturer.
Subjects: East Anglian rarities and common birds, Mediterranean birds and landscapes, Northern Greece & Western Turkey, Spain, Goa, General wildlife photography, The Gambia, Northern India (birds and tigers), Costa Rica, North East India and the Himalayan foothills, Western Australia, Morocco.
Fees: Negotiable. **Limits:** Preferably within East Anglia.
Address: 86 George Street, Hadleigh, Ipswich, IP7 5BU; 01473 827 062; www.billbaston.com
e-mail: billbaston@btinternet.com

BEJARANO, Santiago
An Ecuadorean naturalist and wildlife photographer who worked in the Galapagos for over a decade, with a great depth of knowledge and unique insight into these remarkable islands and their wildlife.

DIRECTORY OF LECTURERS

Subjects: 'Galapagos Islands', 'Birds of Galapagos', 'Ecuador — Land of Mega Diversity', 'Hummingbirds'. Fees: £40.00. Limits: None. Time limitations: None. Address: 25 Trinity Lane, Beverley, East Yorkshire HU17 0DY; 01482 872 716; www.thinkgalapagos.com e-mail: info@thinkgalapagos.com www.thinkgalapagos.com

BELL, Graham
Cruise lecturer worldwide, photographer, author, former BBRC member.
Subjects: Arctic, Antarctic, Siberia, Australia, Iceland, Seychelles, UK — identification, behaviour, seabirds, garden birds, entertaining bird sound imitations, birds in myth and fact, bird names, taking better photos, etc.
Fees: £20 plus travel and B&B if required.
Limits: None. Time limitations: None.
Address: Ros View, South Yearle, Wooler, Northumberland, NE71 6RB; 01668 281310.
e-mail: seabirdsdgb@hotmail.com

BOND, Terry
Ex-Company Chairman, International consultant, Bank director. Conference speaker worldwide, photographer, group field leader, lecturer on birds for more than thirty years.
Subjects: 6 talks - including Scilly Isles, Southern Europe, North America, Scandinavia, 'Birdwatching Identification - a New Approach' (an audience participation evening).
Fees: By arrangement (usually only expenses).
Limits: Most of UK. Time limitations: Evenings.
Address: 3 Lapwing Crescent, Chippenham, Wiltshire, SN14 6YF; 01249 462 674.
e-mail: terryebond@btopenworld.com

BOWDEN, Paul
Birdwatcher and nature photographer (Video, HD-Video and DSLR photos of birds and other wildlife) for 30+ years (serious amateur). Founder member and current Chairman of Glamorgan Wildlife Photographic Club (see website). Member of local bird and nature clubs, RSPB and WWT. Lectures to local clubs and nature groups but can travel anywhere in UK.
Subjects: Birds of Europe (Austria, Bulgaria, Estonia, Finland, Germany, Greece, Hungary, Italy, Portugal, Spain, Sweden & UK), Egypt, Libya, Oman, Azerbaijan, Panama, USA (9 States: AZ, CA, FL, HI, IL, MO, OR, TX, WA), Canada, Hong Kong, Japan and Australia. Also Butterflies and Dragonflies of UK, Europe and Overseas. Presentations as Video, HD Video and/or Powerpoint.
Fees: Lecture fee of £55 plus reasonable travelling expenses (plus overnight accommodation where necessary for longer trips). Limits: None, but longer trips may require overnight stay. Time limitations: None. Lecture anytime by arrangement.
Address: 4 Patmore Close, Gwaelod-y-Garth, Cardiff, CF15 9SU; 029 2081 3044.
e-mail: bowden_pe@hotmail.com
www.glamorganwildlifephotoclub.org.uk

BROOKS, Richard
Wildlife photographer, writer, lecturer, birding guide.
Subjects: Over a dozen talks - including Lemnos, Lesvos, Evros Delta, Kerkini, Spain, Israel, Canaries, Oman, plus E.Anglia, Wales, Scotland and Western Isles (Uist, Mull and Islay).
Fees: £80 plus petrol. Limits: None if accom provided. Time limitations: None.
Address: 24 Croxton Hamlet, Fulmodeston, Fakenham, Norfolk, NR21 0NP; 01328 878 632.
e-mail: email@richard-brooks.co.uk
(or r.brooks662@btinternet.com)
www.richard-brooks.co.uk

BUCKINGHAM, John
Long-standing and popular lecturer, photographer, tour leader.
Subjects: 60+ titles covering birds, wildlife, botany, ecology and habitats in UK, Europe, Africa, Australia, Indian sub-continent, North-South and Central America including favourites such as 'How Birds Work', 'The Natural History of Birds' and 'Wonders of Bird Migration'.
Fees: £90 plus expenses. Limits: None. Time limitations: None.
Address: 3 Cardinal Close, Tonbridge, Kent, TN9 2EN; (Tel/fax) 01732 354 970.
e-mail: john.birdtalk@btinternet.com

CARTY, Peter
National Trust's Countryside, Parkland and Garden Manager in South Shropshire. A warden for 26 years, from the Sefton Coast in Merseyside to the Seychelles. A keen birder and observer of plants, reptiles, amphibians, dragonflies, butterflies and mammals. He has led tours to Bulgaria.
Subjects: Various talks on birds, natural history and conservation in Bulgaria.
Fees: £50 (negotiable) plus travel expenses.
Limits: Two hours from Bishop's Castle in Shropshire, eg North and South Wales, Manchester, Liverpool, Birmingham and Bristol areas.
Time limitations: None.
Address: Sefton, Harley Jenkins Street, Bishop's Castle, Shropshire SY9 5AH; 01588 638 664.
e-mail: peter@carty.org.uk

CLEAVE, Andrew MBE
Wildlife photographer, author, lecturer and tour leader
Subjects: More than 30 talks (including India, Galapagos, Iceland, Mediterranean birds and wildlife, Lundy, Shetland, Ancient Woodlands, Dormice and Seashore). Full list available.
Fees: £65 plus petrol. Limits: Approx. 60 mls without o.n accom. Time limitations: Afternoons and evenings, not school holidays.
Address: 31 Petersfield Close, Chineham, Basingstoke, Hampshire, RG24 8WP; 01256 320 050.
e-mail: andrew@bramleyfrith.co.uk

DIRECTORY OF LECTURERS

COUZENS, Dominic
Full-time birdwatcher, tour leader (UK and overseas), writer and lecturer.
Subjects: The Secret Lives of Garden Birds', 'Birds Behaving Badly - the trials and tribulations of birds through the year', 'Have Wings Will Travel' -the marvel of bird migration, 'Vive la Difference' - a comparison of British birds with those across the Channel, 'My Family and 50 Other Animals' - a year spent trying to show 2 young children 50 species of mammals in Britain, 'Birding a Local Patch', Mammal Watching in Britain, Puffins Near and Far, Encounters with Remarkable Birds, Europe's Top 10 Birding Sites.
Fees: £80 plus travel. **Limits:** London and south.
Time limitations: None.
Address: 3 Clifton Gardens, Ferndown, Dorset, BH22 9BE; (Tel/fax) 01202 874 330; www.birdwords.co.uk
e-mail: dominic.couzens@btinternet.com

CROMACK, David
Professional journalist, currently President of Peterborough Bird Club.
Subjects: Subjects: 1) Bird Magazines and the Art of Bird Photography; 2) Wild West Birding (Arizona and California); 3) World Class Bird Images (International Wildbird Photographer competitions); 4) More World Class Bird Images; 5) Asia's Teardrop - Birding in Sri Lanka; 6) Bird Artists of the Modern Era. Leaflet available on request. In preparation, 'America's Serengeti — wildlife of Yellowstone'.
Fees: £75 plus travel expenses (30p per mile). **Limits:** 150 miles from Peterborough. **Times:** All requests considered.
Address: 55 Thorpe Park Road, Peterborough PE3 6LJ. 01733 566 815; (Fax) 01733 561 739;
e-mail: d.cromack@btinternet.com

CROUCHER, Roy
Lecturer, Former RSPB staff member, former local authority ecologist.
Subjects: 'The wildlife of northern France', 'Managing the countryside for wildlife'.
Fees: £60, plus the cost of petrol from Leicester (return) at £15 per 100 miles. **Limits:** Anywhere in mainland Britain. **Time limitations:** November and December.
Address: Place de L'Eglise, 53700, Averton, France; 0033 243 00 6969.
e-mail: nfwt@online.fr - website: nfwt.online.fr

DAVIES, Alan & MILLER, Ruth
Alan and Ruth both worked for the RSPB before giving up their jobs to travel the world, setting a new bird-ing world record for the most bird species recorded in a single year: 4,341 species. They now run The Biggest Twitch, their own birdwatching tour and talks company. They are based in North Wales but run tours throughout the UK and beyond.
Subjects: 'The Biggest Twitch', around the world in 4,000 birds; the entertaining warts-and-all story of their big birding year; Also a range of illustrated talks each covering birding in a different region including the UK, Europe, South America, North America, Ethiopia, Southern Africa, Australia, and India. We are continuously adding to our range of talks.
Fees: £60 for the talk plus the cost of fuel used on the return journey. **Limits:** None, though overnight accommodation needed for talks too far from North Wales to return the same evening. **Time limitations:** Very flexible all year, please e-mail to check availability.
Address: 12 Ormeside Court, 19 Church Walks, Llandudno Ll30 2HG; 01492 872 407;
e-mail: info@thebiggesttwitch.com
www.thebiggesttwitch.com

DUGGAN, Glenn
Ex-Commander Royal Navy, tour leader, researcher.
Subjects: Over 10 different talks including, the rare and extinct birds of the world, birds of paradise and bower birds, Trogons and Tanagers, history of bird art (caveman to present day), modern day bird artists (includes voting for the audience's favourite artist), famous Victorian bird artists (John Gould, John James Audubon, Lear), scientific voyages of discovery. For something different how about two different talks of 45 minutes duration each in one evening to provide variety to your members?
Fees: £70 plus reasonable mileage expenses. **Limits:** none with o.n accom. **Time limitations:** None.
Address: 25 Hampton Grove, Fareham, Hampshire, PO15 5NL; 01329 845 976, (M)07771 605 320.
e-mail: glenn.m.duggan@ntlworld.com
www.birdlectures.com

ELSOM, Stuart, LRPS
Tour leader, ecologist and wildlife photographer with Royal Photographic Society distinction.
Subjects: Currently offers around a dozen talks covering a wide range of birding destinations across 6 continents.
Fees: £70 and 40p per mile travel expenses. **Limits:** Willing to travel up to 100 miles. **Time limitations:** Daytime and evening. Travelling for approx 4 months per year normally with several weeks in between, so reasonable notice (6+ months) required when booking talks.
Address: 117 Andrew Road, St Neots, Cambs, PE19 2PP; e-mail: stuartelsom@btinternet.com
www.stuartelsom.co.uk Facebook:
www.facebook.com/stu.elsom

EYRE, John
Author, photographer, ornithological consultant and ex-chairman Hampshire Ornithological Society.
Subjects: Many talks covering birding around the world (Europe, Africa, Asia, Australasia and the Americas), plus special Hampshire subjects. Examples include: 'New Zealand - Seabird Feast, Land Bird Famine', 'California Birds - Sea, Sage and Spotted Owls', 'Gilbert White's Birds' and 'The Secret Lives of Heathland Birds'. Several others so please call or e-mail to discuss options.

DIRECTORY OF LECTURERS

Fees: £70 plus travel. **Limits:** Any location negotiable. **Time limitations:** None. **Address:** 3 Dunmow Hill, Fleet, Hampshire, GU51 3AN; 01252 677 850. e-mail: John.Eyre@ntlworld.com

GALLOP, Brian
Speaker, photographer, tour leader.
Subjects: 35 talks covering UK, Africa, India, Galapagos, South America and Europe – All natural history subjects. Made-to-measure talks available on request. 24hr emergency service.
Fees: £50 plus travel expenses. **Limits:** None – o.n acc. if over 100 mls. **Time limitations:** None.
Address: 13 Orchard Drive, Tonbridge, Kent, TN10 4LT; 01732 361892.
e-mail: brian_gallop@hotmail.co.uk

GALVIN, Chris
A birding photographer with passion for birds for more than 30 years.
Subjects: 'Northwest Year', 'Around the World in 80 Birds', 'Bee-eaters & Kingfishers: an intro to the Birds of Goa', 'Birding by Camera', 'Birding on the Doorstep'.
Fees: £80- £140 depending on distance travelled. **Limits:** 125 miles radius from home.
Address: 17 Henley Road, Allerton, Liverpool, Merseyside L18 2DN; 07802 428 385 or 0151 729 0123.
e-mail: chris@chrisgalvinphoto.com
www.chrisgalvinphoto.com

GARNER, David
Wildlife photographer.
Subjects: 20 live talks and audio-visual shows on all aspects of wildlife in UK and some parts of Europe - list available.
Fees: £45.00 plus 30p per mile. **Limits:** None. **Time limitations:** None.
Address: 73 Needingworth Road, St Ives, Cambridgeshire, PE27 5JY; (H)01480 463194; (W)01480 463194.
e-mail: david@hushwings.co.uk
www.hushwings.co.uk

GARNER, Jackie, FRSA
Professional wildlife artist, author & illustrator of *The Wildlife Artist's Handbook*.
Subjects: Birds/Nature in Art, Focus on the Falklands, Wildlife of Ancient Egypt, Wildlife Artist's World, The Making of a Wildlife Art Book.
Fees: £100 + expenses.
Distance limits: None. **Time limits:** None.
Address: The Old Cider House Studio, Humphries End, Randwick, Stroud, Glos GL6 6EW; 01453 847 420; (M)07800 804 847.
e-mail: artist@jackiegarner.co.uk
www.jackiegarner.co.uk

GARTSHORE, Neil
23-years working in nature conservation (National Trust, South Africa, RSPB) now a freelance contractor, writer, lecturer, tour guide and natural history book seller.
Subjects: Various talks including South Africa; Sub-Antarctic Prince Edward Islands; Japan; Farne Islands; Heathlands; and Poole Harbour.
Fees: Negotiable. **Limits:** Anything considered. **Time limitations:** Flexible.
Address: Moor Edge, 2 Bere Road, Wareham, Dorset BH20 4DD; 01929 552 560.
e-mail: neilgartshore@btinternet.com

GLENN, Neil
Author of *Best Birdwatching Sites in Norfolk*; regular contributor to *Bird Watching* magazine; bird tour leader for Avian Adventures.
Subjects: Wildlife of the Lower Rio Grande Valley, Texas. Birding the Arctic Circle. Moroccan Spice: From The Sahara to The Atlas Mountains. More to follow!
Fees: Negotiable. **Limits:** None.
Time limitations: Any day.
Address: 13 Gladstone Avenue, Gotham, Nottingham NG11 0HN; 0115 983 0946.
e-mail: n.glenn@ntlworld.com

GREATOREX-DAVIES, Nick
Retired. Formerly an entomologist from 1974 to 2009 at the Centre for Ecology and Hydrology, Monks Wood, Cambridgeshire. Co-ordinator of the UK's Butterfly Monitoring Scheme from 1995 to 2007. A keen general interest in natural history but specialist in British Lepidoptera and European butterflies. Has led butterfly and moth tours to Bulgaria since 2003.
Subjects: Talk on Bulgaria's butterflies and their conservation. Also a variety of talks on British butterflies and moths.
Fees: £30 (negotiable) plus travel expenses. **Limits:** Up to 300 miles round trip from Huntingdon but may on occasions be willing to travel further. **Time limitations:** None.
Address: 28 Old Pound Close, Hemingford Grey, Huntingdon, PE28 9DY; 01480 301 685
e-mail: nickgdlepman@googlemail.com

GROVE, Ashley
Professional photographer, with a specialism in wildlife images. References on request if required.
Subjects: 1)'Shetland to Scilly; Birds of the British Isles', 2) 'Jewels of the Gambia, Kingfishers, Bee-eaters & Rollers', 3) 'Great British Birds', 4) 'Lammergeiers of the Spanish Pyrenees'. 5) 'Trinidad & Tobago, Home of the Hummingbird' 6) 'A Beginners Guide to Birdwatching'. More talks under construction.
Fees: £80 plus 25p per mile expenses (this may be negotiable if you are able to recommend a nearby group to speak to on an adjacent evening). **Limits:** None, within reason. **Time limitations:** None.
Address: 16, Lint Meadow, Wythall, Worcestershire B47 5PH; 07704 189 835.
e-mail: birdergrove@gmail.com
www.vp.ashleygrovewildimages.co.uk/lectures.php

DIRECTORY OF LECTURERS

HAAR, Ronnie
Birdwatcher, musician, lecturer.
Subjects: 'Songs about Birds', celebrating British birds in song. Live performance of species-specific songs, with quiz, projection of artwork and lyrics; entertaining and educational, usually accompanied by professional female singer Louise Sofield. 20% of CD sales donated to your group or to 'Save the Albatross Campaign.'
Fees: £50 plus petrol. **Limits:** SE England
Address: 93 Colfe Road, London SE23 2EX. 0208 699 9394; e-mail: haarhaar@hotmail.com
www.themusicalbirder.com

HAMMOND, Nicholas
Lecturer, author, former RSPB and Wildlife Trust staffer.
Subjects: More than 30 topics covering Art and Wildlife, History and Wildlife, Wildlife and Conservation. Popular topics include Modern Wildlife Painting, Hippos and Hoopoes, The Great Fen, Birds through Other People's Eyes. E-mail for full list of subjects.
Fees: From £75 plus travel expenses.
Limits: 120 miles from Sandy.
Address: 30 Ivel Road, Sandy, Beds SG19 1BA; 01767 680 504; e-mail: n.hammond4@ntlworld.com

LANE, Mike
Wildlife photographer and lecturer.
Subjects: Many talks from the UK and abroad.
Fees: Negotiable. **Limits:** None.
Time limitations: None.
Address: 36 Berkeley Road, Shirley, Solihull, West Midlands B90 2HS; 0121 744 7988; (M)07766 418 013; e-mail: mikelane@nature-photography.co.uk
www.nature-photography.co.uk

LENTON, Graham
PhD Ornithology/Ecology. Former lecturer at Oxford University and Oxford Brookes University. Lifetime photographer of wildlife - publications of articles and photographs of birds and wildlife.
Subjects: Barn Owls of Malaysia and Rat Control; Birds of the Seychelles; Wildlife and Birds of Antarctica; Birds of New Zealand; Birds of Namibia; Two Islands (Handa & The Farnes); An Arctic Journey; Svalbard; Gorilla in my midst — a Ugandan Odyssey; Barn Owls — past, present and their future; Wildlife of Madagascar — a genetic melting pot.
Fees: £65. **Limits:** Preferably within 60mls.
Time limitations: 60 to 90 minute talks.
Address: The Old School, 25A Standlake Road, Ducklington, Witney, Oxon OX29 7UR; 01993 899 033. e-mail: grahamlenton@btopenworld.com
www.gml-art.co.uk

LINGARD, David
Photographer, retired from RAF, now UK delegate to LIPU (BirdLife in Italy).
Subjects: Choice of talks on birding but primarily on birdwatching in Italy and the work of LIPU.
Fees: Donation to LIPU, plus petrol costs. **Limits:** None. **Time limitations:** None.
Address: Fernwood, Doddington Road, Whisby, Lincs LN6 9BX; 01522 689 030; e-mail: mail@lipu-uk.org
www.lipu-uk.org

LOVELL, Stephen
Naturalist, RSPB lecturer, photographer, adult education teacher.
Subjects: Talks available on several European destinations including Lesvos, Majorca, Extremadura and Britain. Other talks available on a wide variety of destinations to include Costa Rica, Trinidad and Tobago, Nepal, Sri Lanka, Southern India, New Zealand, Austrailia, Tanzania and St Lucia. I also have a wide variety of talks on the topic to encourage Wildlife into our Gardens and generic ornithological topics such as migration etc.
Fees: £50 to £90 plus travel or overnight accommodation. **Limits:** 130 miles from Lincoln.
Time limitations: None.
Address: 6 Abingdon Close, Doddington Park, Lincoln LN6 3UH; 01522 689 456; (M)07957 618 684.
e-mail: stephenlovell58@btinternet.com
www.stevelovellgreenspaces.co.uk

MAYER, Edward
Founder of "London's Swifts" and "Swift Conservation".
Subjects: Swifts and their Conservation; Biodiversity Strategies and Techniques for the Built Environment; presentations and training for enthusiasts, ornithologists, architects, developers, town planners and biodiversity officers.
Fees: £60 upwards depending on type and length of talk, or collection/donation, plus travel expenses.
Limits: UK/EC (further by special arrangement).
Address: 28 Yale Court, Honeybourne Road, London NW6 1JG; 020 7794 2098.
e-mail: mail@swift-conservation.org
www.swift-conservation.org

MEREDITH, Stuart
Former RSPB and WWT employee who is now a tour guide and proprietor of Ribble Bird Tours.
Subjects: Currently offers around a dozen different talks covering birding destinations in the UK & abroad, as well as general interest areas.
Fees: £60 plus travel expenses. **Limits:** Mainly North West England, within 100 miles of Fylde Coast, but will consider further afield.
Time limitations: Anytime of day.
Address: 01253 312 043; www.ribblebirdtours.co.uk
e-mail: smrbt@blueyonder.co.uk

MILES, John
Former warden for RSPB Geltsdale in Cumbria, tour guide, consultant and author of *Best Birdwatching Sites: The Solway, Hadrian's Birds, Exploring Lakeland Wildlife, Pharoah's Birds, Hadrian's Wildlife* and magazine articles. Series of children's books with first out in November 2012 - *Kitty the Toon* followed by *Screamer the Swift* [September 2013] and *Horus the Peregrine* [December 2013].

DIRECTORY OF LECTURERS

Subjects: 1) 'The Solway' covers birding throughout the whole of Cumbria and Dumfries & Galloway; 2) 'Hadrian's Wildlife' examines the habitats along Hadrian's Wall from Cumbria to Tyne & Wear and the history of birds back to Roman times. 3) 'Death on the Nile' looks at the history of birds from Ancient Egypt to present time birds while cruising the Nile. **Fees:** Prices on request. **Limits:** Anywhere in UK, w/o overnight accommodation.
Time limitations: Evenings best.
Address: Jockey Shield, Castle Carrock, Carlisle, Cumbria CA4 9NF; 01228 670 205;
e-mail: jmiles3@toucansurf.com

MUDDEMAN, John & VILLA, Santiago
Tour leaders, photographers and author (JM)
Subjects: Talks on the different principal bird and wildlife watching destinations in Spain, inc. Extremadura, Doñana, Strait of Gibraltar, Pyrenees, Picos de Europa, Somiedo (Brown Bears+), Andújar (Iberian Lynx+), etc.
Fees: Negotiable. **Limits:** As travel to UK required, please consult for options. **Time limitations:** Talk duration usually 60-90 minutes.
Contact: (0034) 649 608 747;
e-mail: john@iberianwildlife.com
www.iberianwildlife.com

NEWTON, Ian
Photographer (ARPS) and lecturer, Chairman York Ornithological Club.
Subjects: 14 talks, all digital, mainly birds and other wildlife of North, Central and South America, Europe and UK.
Fees: £60 plus petrol. **Limits:** None. **Time limitations:** None.
Address: 5 Fairfields Drive, Skelton, York YO30 1YP ; 01904 471 446; (M)07976 849 832;
e-mail: iannewton@acsemail.co.uk
www.iannewtonphotography.com

OFFORD, Keith
Photographer, writer, tour leader, conservationist.
Subjects: 16 talks covering raptors, flight, uplands, gardens, migration, woodland wildlife, Australia, Southern USA, Gambia, Spain, Iceland, Costa Rica, Namibia, Western Cape.
Fees: £100 plus travel. **Limits:** none.
Time limitations: Sept - April.
Address: Yew Tree Farmhouse, Craignant, Selattyn, Nr Oswestry, Shropshire, SY10 7NP; 01691 718 740;
e-mail: keith.offord@virgin.net
www.keithofford.co.uk

PARKER, Susan and Allan, ARPS
Professional photographers, (ASPphoto – Images of Nature), lecturers and tutors.
Subjects: 16 plus slide and digital talks on birds and natural history, natural history photography – countries include UK, USA (Texas, Florida), Spain, Greece, Cyprus.
Fees: On application. **Limits:** Any distance with o.n accom or up to 120 mls without.

Time limitations: None.
Address: Windhover Barn, 51b Kiveton Lane, Todwick, Sheffield, South Yorkshire, S26 1HJ; 01909 770238.
e-mail: aspphoto@btinternet.com

PEARSON, Mark
Tour leader Yorkshire Coast Nature. Professional ornithologist, birder.
Subjects: The joys of patch birding – from urban London to an east coast observatory; Greyhounds and Bluebirds - backpacker-birding the USA.
Fees: Flexible. **Limits:** None.
Time limitations: None.
Contact: 01262 851 999;
e-mail: mark.pearson@yorkshirecoastnature.co.uk
www.yorkshirecoastnature.co.uk

PETTIT, Brian
Wildlife Consultant and photographer.
Subjects: Fully illustrated multi-media presentations featuring a wide range of talks on wildlife from UK and worldwide, incorporating plants, invertebrates, reptiles, mammals, birds and wildlife photography. Full list on website or on application.
Fees: From £60 (4:3) and £100 (16:9 widescreen) for single club meetings, to £250 for major fundraising events. We have all our own equipment including screens and sound system. **Limits:** Anwhere worldwide. **Time limitations:** Talk season from 1st Oct to 31st March.
Address: 18 Okeford Road, Broadstone, Poole, Dorset BH18 8PA; 07979 056 144.
e-mail: wildlifepics@ntlworld.com
www.naturepicturesworldwide.com

PICKERING, Pollyanna
Wildlife Artist, conservationist.
Subjects: 12 talks available on a variety of subjects, from running a wildlife sanctuary in Derbyshire to travelling into remote areas to paint endangered species in their natural habitat. Details of individual talks on request.
Fees: £125.00 plus travelling expenses. **Limits:** None.
Time limitations: Evening talks only.
Address: Brookvale House, Oaker, Matlock, Derbyshire DE4 2JJ; 01629 55 851.
e-mail: annalouise@talktalk.net
www.pollyannapickering.co.uk

RACE, Steve
Director for Yorkshire Coast Nature, Professional wildlife photographer, birder, website manager for Scarborough Birders.
Subjects: Life on the Ledge-Seabirds of Bempton Cliffs; Yorkshire Coast Nature-Wildlife Photography from the Yorkshire Coast.
Fees: Flexible. **Limits:** None.
Time limitations: None.
Address: 01262 851 999;
e-mail: steve.race@yorkshirecoastnature.co.uk
www.yorkshirecoastnature.co.uk

DIRECTORY OF LECTURERS

READ, Mike
Photographer, tour leader, writer.
Subjects: 12 talks featuring British and foreign subjects (list available on receipt of sae or see website).
Fees: £70 plus travel. **Limits:** 100 mls from Ringwood.
Time limitations: Talks available 1st Sept to 31st March each winter.
Address: Claremont, Redwood Close, Ringwood, Hampshire, BH24 1PR; 01425 475 008.
e-mail: mike@mikeread.co.uk www.mikeread.co.uk

REDMAN, Nigel
Tour leader, publisher and author.
Subjects: Mostly birds, including Ethiopia, Somaliland, the Horn of Africa, Morocco, Russia (and former Soviet Union), the Caucasus, and Kenya.
Fees: Negotiable. **Limits:** None (but overnight accommodation may be required).
Time limitations: None.
Address: Moons Hill Cottage, Moons Hill, Ninfield, East Sussex TN33 9LH; 01424 893 023; 07734 886 515.
e-mail: nigel.redman@bloomsbury.com

SCOTT, Ann
Retired. Formerly Senior Wildlife Adviser for RSPB. Tour leader, lecturer and teacher of ornithology.
Subjects: Various talks on UK and abroad - please ask for list. A number of talks on Bulgaria and its wildlife.
Fees: £50 plus expenses (negotiable).
Distance limitation: Normally 2 hours drive from Huntingdon but willing to discuss.
Time limitations: Any month from Mid-March to Mid-November.
Address: 17, Springfield Close, Buckden, Huntingdon, Cambs. PE19 5UR; 01480 811 848.
e-mail: abscott@buckdencambs.co.uk

SMART, Oliver
Photographer, lecturer and ornithologist.
Subjects: 1) 'Exploring Ethiopia'; 2) 'Butterfly Britain'; 3) 'From 60 Degrees North'; 4) 'Cameras and Creatures, from Cumbria to Canada'; 5) 'Cuba: A Flicker of Interest'; 6) 'Birds of Lesvos'; 7) 'RAW Nature: Images Uncovered'; 8) 'Grizzly Bears of Alaska'.
Fees: £80 plus 25p per mile plus £10 per hour above two hours total travel time. **Limits:** None and can also provide own accommodation.
Time limitations: None.
Address: 78 Aspen Park Road, Weston-Super-Mare, Somerset BS22 8ER; (M)07802 417 810.
e-mail: oliver@smartimages.co.uk
www.smartimages.co.uk

SWASH, Andy
Professional wildlife photographer, tour leader, lecturer and author.
Subjects: The World's Rarest Birds, Beautiful Birds, and tales from travels in search of little-known birds around the world, including the Andamans, Australia, Brazil, Ecuador, Ethiopia, Galápagos, México, Peru, Southern Africa, Sri Lanka, Tanzania, and various birding hotspots in the USA.
Fees: £100 plus travel. **Limits:** None. **Time limitations:** Evenings preferred.
Address: Stretton Lodge, 9 Birch Grove, West Hill, Ottery St Mary, Devon, EX11 1XP; 01404 815 383, (M)07760 188 594. www.worldwildlifeimages.com
e-mail: swash@worldwildlifeimages.com

TODD, Ralph
Lecturer & photographer, former tour leader and course tutor.
Subjects: 10 talks incl. 'Galapagos Wildlife', 'On the Trail of the Crane - parts 1 and 2', 'Polar Odyssey', 'Operation Osprey', 'Natural Wonders and Wildlife of Iceland', 'Man and Birds-Travels through Time', 'A Summer in Northern Landscapes', 'Where Yeehaa meets Ole', 'Birds in the Land of Disney', 'Antarctic Adventure', 'Wildlife of Pyrenees and Lesvos'.
Fees: £75 plus expenses. **Limits:** None. **Time limitations:** Anytime - also short notice.
Address: 9 Horsham Road, Bexleyheath, Kent, DA6 7HU; (Tel/fax)01322 528 335.
e-mail: rbtodd@btinternet.com

TYLER, John
Wildlife walks and talks.
Subjects: Life in a Nutshell (The world of small things); The Island of Crabs; Volcanoes and Dragons; Changing Wildlife of the Chilterns; The Ridgeway; The Glow-worm; The World of Fungi; Making Space for Wildlife.
Fees: £60 plus 50p per mile. **Limits:** 25 mile radius from Princes Risborough, Bucks.
Time limitations: None.
Address: 5 Woodfield, Lacey Green, Buckinghamshire, HP27 0QQ; 07814 392 335.
e-mail: johnclarketyler@gmail.com
www.johntyler.co.uk

WARD, Chris
Photographer, N Bucks RSPB Local Group Leader.
Subjects: 20+ talks on UK and worldwide topics (Spain, Mallorca, Romania, Cyprus, Oman, Americas, Africa) – primarily birds, some other wildlife.
Fees: £50 plus petrol @30p/mile. **Limits:** 120 miles.
Time limitations: None. Short notice possible..
Address: 41 William Smith Close, Woolstone, Milton Keynes, MK15 0AN; 01908 669 448.
e-mail: cwphotography@hotmail.com
www.cwardphotography.co.uk

WREN, Graham J, ARPS
Wildlife photographer, lecturer, tour guide.
Subjects: 25 talks featuring birds – UK 'Breeding Birds of Southern Britain' and 'Northern Britain', including habitats, also Scandinavia. Nest-boxes (new), the environment, wildlife of Kenya. Detailed information package supplied on request.
Fees: £50-80 plus petrol. **Limits:** None.
Time limitations: None.
Address: The Kiln House, Great Doward, Whitchurch, Ross-on-Wye, Herefordshire, HR9 6DU; 01600 890 488.
e-mail: susanjhampshire@aol.com

BTO SPEAKERS

This directory has been compiled to help Bird Clubs and similar organisations in finding speakers for their indoor meetings. Each entry consists of an individual speaker, a list of talks/ lectures available, details of fees and expenses required and travel distance limitations. If you are interested in any of the speakers, please contact Ieuan Evans (ieuan.evans@bto.org) or Ellen Walford (ellen.walford@bto.org) directly. Alternatively, contact BTO: 01842 750 050. Members of the BTO/ Bird Clubs Partnership have a 25% discount.

Appleton, Graham (Director of Communications)
Subjects: Atlas 2007 – 11; Flyway to Iceland; Time to Fly – Bird Migration; Tracking African Migrants
Fees: £40 Negotiable. Distance: Dependent on expenses.

Austin, Dr Graham (Senior Research Ecologist, Wetland & Marine Research)
Subjects: Wetland Bird Survey.
Fees: £40. Distance: Travel by agreement.

Baillie, Dr Stephen (Science Director Modelling & Demography)
Subjects: BirdTrack; Population Monitoring.
Fees: £40. Distance: Travel by agreement.

Baker, Jeff (Head of Marketing)
Subjects: Little Brown Jobs – Warblers & How to Identify Them; The Work of the BTO; Garden Birds & Feeding.
Fees: £40. Distance: Dependent on expenses.

Balmer, Dawn (Atlas Co-ordinator)
Subjects: Bird Atlas 2007 - 11.
Fees: £40. Distance: 100 mile radius of Thetford.

Barimore, Carl (Nest Records Organiser)
Subjects: Nest Records Scheme.
Fees: £40. Distance: By agreement.

Blackburn, Jez (Licensing and Sales Manager)
Subjects: Demography Team Bird Moult (suitable for ringers); Ringing for Conservation; Sule Skerry Seabirds. Fees: £40 (£70 for private talks). Distance: East Anglia.

Bray, James (Fieldwork & Training Coordinator BTO Scotland)
Subjects: The Work of BTO Scotland; BTO Atlas 2007-11; BBS, Birdtrack & other BTO surveys in Scotland; Garden BirdWatch.
Fees: £40. Distance: By agreement.

Clark, Jacquie (Head of Demography Team & Head of Ringing Scheme)
Subjects: Waders & Severe Weather; Ringing for Conservation; Why Ring Birds?
Fees: £40. Distance: 100 mile radius of Thetford.

Clark, Dr Nigel (Head of Projects Development Department)
Subjects: Waders, Man & Estuaries; What hope for the Spoon-billed Sandpiper?
Fees: £40. Distance: 100 mile radius of Thetford.

Conway, Greg (Research Ecologist, Land-use Research)
Subjects: Nightjars; Woodlarks; Dartford Warblers; Wintering Warblers in the UK; Firecrests.
Fees: £40. Distance: 100 mile radius of Thetford.

Dadam, Dr Daria (Reseach Ecologist Demography)
Subjects: Bird Disease.
Fees: Negotiable. Distance: By agreement.

Fuller, Prof Rob (Director of Science)
Subjects: Changing Times for Woodland Birds.
Fees: £40. Distance: Anywhere.

Gillings, Dr Simon (Senior Research Ecologist Land Use Research)
Subjects: Atlas 2007 – 11; Winter Golden Plovers & Lapwings; Waders; Knot Migration; Winter Farmland Birds. Fees: £40. Distance: Negotiable.

Gough, Su (Editor, BTO News & Training Officer)
Subjects: The Work of the BTO; Urban Birds. Private talks: Wildlife of Canada; Wildlife of Southwestern USA; Wildlife of European Mountains; Wildlife of Texas; Wildlife of the Middle East.
Fees: £40. Distance: Negotiable.

Henderson, Dr Ian (Senior Research Ecologist International Research)
Subjects: Arable Farming and Birds.
Fees: £40. Distance: By agreement.

Johnson, Dr Alison (Ecological Statistician, Population Ecology & Modelling)
Subjects: Climate Change and Birds.
Fees: £40. Distance: East Anglia

Lack, Dr Peter (Information Services Manager)
Private talks: Palearctic Migrants in Africa; On Foot in Rwanda and Zambia; Ecology in East African Savannahs; General Natural History of Eastern Africa.
Fees: Negotiable. Distance: 60 miles of Bury St Edmunds.

Marchant, John (Projects Co-ordinator Monitoring)
Subjects: Monitoring Heronries: Nine Decades of Monitoring; Waterways Bird & Breeding Bird Surveys.
Fees: £40. Distance: By agreement.

Moran, Nick (BirdTrack Organiser)
Subjects: Mapping migration with BirdTrack; Hard weather effects on birds; Birds and birding in Arabia (private talk).
Fees: £40. Distance: By agreement.

Musgrove, Dr Andy (Head of Monitoring)
Subjects: The Wetland Bird Survey; Little Egrets in the UK. Fees: £40. Distance: By agreement.

Newson, Dr Stuart (Senior Research Ecologist' Population Ecology & Modelling)
Subjects: Tree nesting Cormorants.
Fees: £40. Distance: By agreement.

101

Noble, Dr David (Principal Ecologist, Monitoring)
Subjects: Developing Bird Indicators; Population Trends. Fees: £40. Distance: By agreement.

Pearce-Higgins, Dr James (Principal Ecologist, Climate Change)
Subjects: Birds and climate change; Upland birds; A year in the life of a Golden Plover. Fees: £40. Distance: By agreement.

Risely, Kate (Breeding Bird Survey National Organiser)
Subjects: BTO/JNCC/RSPB Breeding Birds Survey. Fees: £40. Distance: By agreement.

Robinson, Dr Rob (Principal Ecologist, Modelling & Demography)
Subjects: Farming & Birds; Conservation Value of Ringing. Fees: £40. Distance: By agreement.

Ross-Smith, Dr Viola (Research Ecologist, Wetland & Marine)
Subjects: Gulls, seabirds, tracking studies. Fees: £40. Distance: By agreement.

Simm, Clare (GBW Development Officer)
Subjects: Are Gardens Good for Birds or Birdwatchers? Fees: £40. Distance: 50 mile radius of Thetford.

Siriwardena, Dr Gavin (Head of Land-Use Research)
Subjects: Research Farmland Birds (General); Marsh & Willow Tits; Quantifying Migratory Strategies; Winter Feeding of Farmland Birds. Fees: £40. Distance: Negotiable.

Standiffe, Paul (Press Officer)
Subjects: Atlas 2007-11; Homes to Let – Nestboxes; Birds, Birders and the Work of the BTO; Tracking African Migrants Fees: £40. Distance: Negotiable.

Toms, Mike (Head of Garden Ecology Team)
Subjects: Are Gardens Good for Birds or Birdwatchers? Fees: £40. Distance: 50 mile radius of Thetford.

Wernham, Dr Chris (Senior Research Ecologist BTO Scotland)
Subjects: The Work of BTO Scotland; Breeding Bird Survey in Scotland; BirdTrack in Scotland. Fees: £40. Distance: Travel Scotland and NE England.

Wright, Dr Lucy (Research Ecologist, Wetland and Marine Research)
Subjects: Non-native Waterbirds in Eurasia & Africa. Fees: £40. Distance: By agreement.

ID Insights Pocket Cards

British Birds
113 common but tricky-to-identify species. Illustrated by Dave Nurney with ID tips from top writer Dominic Couzens. Ten cards.

British Dragonflies
Expert illustrator Dan Powell covers 51 species of dragonflies and damselflies, together with details of habitats, distribution and main flight times, on 13 cards.

British Garden Birds
Perfect for beginners, children and casual birdwatchers. Covers 65 species on 11 cards and feature artwork and ID advice from Dan and Rosie Powell.

Butterflies of Great Britain
Life-size artwork of 58 species on 12 cards. Rosie Powell illustrates male and female, plus wing patterns for each species. Also habitats, distribution and main flight times.

TRADE DIRECTORY

David Cromack

Spectacular scenery like this river valley in the Spanish Pyrenees, adds to the magic of a birding holiday overseas and a number of tour companies offer trips to exciting destinations in this region.

Bird garden suppliers	104	Holiday companies	109
Bird magazines	105	Optical dealers	113
Book publishers	105	Optical importers and manufacturers	115
Book sellers	107		
Clothing suppliers	108	Optical repairs and servicing	116
Equipment suppliers and services	108		

BIRD GARDEN SUPPLIERS

BIRD GARDEN SUPPLIERS

ARK WILDLIFE LTD

Company ethos: The garden wildlife company. Friendly, knowledgeable staff, great service, FREE next day delivery, on-line and 50-page full colour mail order catalogue.

Key product lines: Carefully selected fresh, natural bird and wildlife food, habitats, accessories and garden wildlife seeds.

Other services: Mail order company, 24-hour shopping on-line, with free next day delivery. Phone for a free catalogue.

Opening times: Mon - Fri (9am-5.30pm). Out of hours answer phone service.

Address: Dog Kennel Farm, Charlton Road, Hitchin, Hertfordshire SG5 2AB. 0800 085 4865; (fax) 01462 420 022; e-mail: office@arkwildlife.co.uk www.arkwildlife.co.uk

BAMFORDS TOP FLIGHT

Company ethos: Family owned manufacturing company providing good

quality bird foods via a network of UK stockists or mail order. RSPB Corporate Member, B.T.O. Business Ally, Petcare Trust Member.

Key product lines: A range of wild bird mixtures containing the unique 'Pro-tec Health Aid', developed by Bamfords, to protect and promote the welfare of wild birds. Vast array of other foods and seeds for birds.

Other services: Trade suppliers of bulk and pre-packed bird and petfoods. Custom packing/own label if required.

New for 2014: Robin & Small Bird Mix; a highly nutritious combination of soft grains and bite-size pieces which are the perfect attractant for Robins, Wrens and many other small birds.

Opening times: Mon - Fri 8.00 - 5.30pm; Sat 8.00 – 12.00 noon; (Sunday 10.00 – 12.00 noon, Mill Shop only).

Address: Globe Mill, Midge Hall, Leyland, Lancashire PR26 6TN; 01772 456 300; (fax) 01772 456 302. e-mail: sales@bamfords.co.uk www.bamfords.co.uk

CJ WILDBIRD FOODS LTD

Company ethos: CJ Wildlife is Europe's leading garden wildlife specialists and aims to make significant, recognisable contributions to the protection and welfare of wild birds and other wildlife. Our ornithologists and wildlife advisors

undertake research projects to ensure we are continually producing high quality products that meet the needs of the wildlife for which they are intended.

Key product lines: High quality bird feeders, bird food, nest boxes, wildlife-friendly plants, bird tables and accessories, along with a broad range of wildlife care products, all at great value prices. Products are available via website or by mail order from our free catalogue.

Other services: Next day delivery to most of UK, free on orders over £50. Our comprehensive online shop also has additional useful advice on caring for wildlife or if you prefer we can send you a free catalogue containing a wide range of products. A 10% discount is offered on purchases collected from our warehouse in Shropshire (excluding books, optics and multimedia). CJ Wildlife products are also stocked in selected supermarkets, garden centres and pet shops.

New for 2014: We are continuously adding new products to the range. Visit the website, or follow us on Twitter and Facebook for the latest products, news and offers.

Opening times: Call centre (Freephone 0800 731 2820) Monday to Friday (9am-5pm), Saturday (9am-12pm). Online ordering 24hrs.

Address: The Rea, Upton Magna, Shrewsbury, Shropshire SY4 4UR; 0800 731 2820; (fax) 01743 709 504; e-mail: sales@birdfood.co.uk www.birdfood.co.uk

SOAR MILLS SEED

Company ethos: Third generation, independently-owned mail order company, providing foods for wild birds and wildlife, sourcing raw materials, where possible, from

local growers employing eco-friendly practices.

Key product lines: Top quality bird foods, feeders and habitats which help promote the welfare and protection of wild birds and wildlife in general.

Other services: Vast array of bird feeders for peanuts and seed, plus other wildlife foods, all of which can be ordered via a secure on-line website. Send for free catalogue.

New for 2014: Bird foods in a handy 12.75kg bag. No VAT and great value.

Opening times: Telesales (freephone) 8.00 - 5.30pm (order before midday for next day delivery). Answer phone outside these hours. On-line ordering and fax, 24 hours.

Address: Foodforbirds, Leyland, PR26 6TN; (Freephone)0800 043 9022; (Fax)01772 456 302. e-mail: sales@foodforbirds.co.uk www.foodforbirds.co.uk

BIRD MAGAZINES AND BOOK PUBLISHERS

BIRDING WORLD
Type of publication: The cutting edge monthly journal for keen birders, lavishly illustrated with colour photographs throughout. Emphasis is on rare and scarce British and European bird news and advances in identification and taxonomy, as well as overseas birding. Monthly, available only on subscription.
Other services: Own on-line bird and wildlife bookshop, Books for Birders, www.birdingworld.co.uk has huge stocks and offers very prompt, friendly and helpful service.
Editor: Steve Gantlett.
Contact: Birding World, Sea Lawn, Coast Road, Cley-next-the-Sea, Norfolk NR25 7RZ; 01263 741 139; e-mail: steve@birdingworld.co.uk
www.birdingworld.co.uk

BIRDWATCH
Type of publication: A monthly magazine available either by subscription, in newsagents, WH Smith, and selected supermarkets, plus also available as a digital magazine via the Birdwatch app on iTunes or Android. Containing informative features each month on birding ID, the latest reports, optics reviews, birding around the world and more, this is the UK's number one monthly magazine for keen birders.
Other services: The Birdwatch Bookshop, free e-newsletter, reader holidays and more can be found at www.birdwatch.co.uk
Editor: Dominic Mitchell.
Contact: Birdwatch Magazine, Warners Group Publications, The Chocolate Factory, 5 Clarendon Road, London N22 6XJ; 020 8881 0550.
E-mail: editorial@birdwatch.co.uk
www.birdwatch.co.uk

BIRD WATCHING (BAUER MEDIA)
Type of publication: A4 magazine (116 to 124pp) published 13 times a year. Available on subscription and at newstand. Contents include latest bird sightings, news, reviews, site guides and ID advice for birdwatchers of all abilities.
Other services: Website, Facebook and Twitter pages, Bookshop (run through WildSounds (www.wildsounds.com), regular Readers' Holidays through Heatherlea, Avian Adventures and The Grant Arms.
Editor: Matt Merritt.
Contact: Bird Watching (editorial or advertising), Media House, Lynch Wood, Peterborough PE2 6EA; 01733 468 536;
e-mail: birdwatching@bauermedia.co.uk
www.birdwatching.co.uk

BRITISH BIRDS
Company ethos: British Birds is the birdwatchers' journal of record, publishing ground-breaking articles on (e.g.) identification, distribution, migration, conservation and taxonomy. British Birds is published by BB 2000 Ltd, which is wholly owned by a charitable trust; all profits generated by the journal support worthwhile conservation and research projects.
Type of publication: Subscription-only monthly journal. Annually also publishes the reports of the British Birds Rarities Committee and the UK Rare Breeding Birds Panel.
Other services: British Birds' 100+ year archive can be accessed free of charge on www.britishbirds.co.uk, with the most recent material available exclusively to subscribers.
Editor: Roger Riddington.
Contact: British Birds, 4 Harlequin Gardens, St Leonards-on-Sea, East Sussex TN37 7PF; 01424 755 155; e-mail: subscriptions@britishbirds.co.uk
www.britishbirds.co.uk

BUCKINGHAM PRESS LTD
Imprints: Single imprint company – publishers of *The Birdwatcher's Yearbook* since 1981, *Who's Who in Ornithology* (1997), *Best Birdwatching Sites* series covering North-East England, Norfolk, Highlands of Scotland, Solway (Cumbria and Dumfries & Galloway), North Wales, Cornwall & Scilly. Plus sets of identification cards for British birds, garden birds, dragonflies and butterflies.
New for 2014: *Best Birdwatching Sites: Yorkshire; Best Birdwatching Sites: Scottish Highlands (2nd edition)*, including Handa, Mull and Skye.
Address: 55 Thorpe Park Road, Peterborough, PE3 6LJ, 01733 561 739.
e-mail: admin@buckinghampress.com
www.buckinghampress.co.uk

BLOOMSBURY PUBLISHING (incorporating Christopher Helm Publishers, T & Ad Poyser and New Holland Publishers)
Imprints: *Christopher Helm:* the leading publisher of ornithology books in the world; includes many field guides, identification guides, family guides, county and country avifaunas, the *Birds of Africa* series, and a *Where to Watch Birds* series.
T & AD Poyser: an acclaimed series of respected ornithology monographs. **Bloomsbury Publishing:** publisher of definitive natural history books including the monumental *Mammals of Africa*. **RSPB:** publishing partners for a wide range of nature books.
New Holland: a newly acquired list of acclaimed natural history books.
New for 2014: *Woodpeckers of the World* by Gerard Gorman, *Birds of London* by Andrew Self, *Lost Animals* by Errol Fuller, *The Helm Guide to Bird Identification* by Keith Vinicombe, Alan Harris and Laurel Tucker, *Tales of Remarkable Birds* by Dominic Couzens, *Grouse of the World* by Richard Sale and

Roald Potapov, *Invasive Plants and Animals of Britain* by Olaf Booy, Max Wade and Helen Roy, *Birds of Western Africa 2nd edition* by Nik Borrow and Ron Demey, *Message from Martha* by Mark Avery, *A History of Birdwatching in 100 Objects* by David Callahan and Dominic Mitchell, *National Birds* by Ron Toft.
Address: 50 Bedford Square, London, WC1B 3DP; 020 7631 5600; (fax) 020 7631 5800;
e-mail: nigel.redman@bloomsbury.com
www.bloomsbury.com/naturalhistory

HARPER COLLINS PUBLISHERS

Imprints: William Collins Natural History – the leading publisher of fieldguides to the natural world. **Collins New Naturalist Series** – the encyclopaedic reference for all areas of British natural history. **HarperCollins** – publisher of the best illustrated books and more.
New for 2014: *New Naturalist Owls* by Mike Toms (January 2014); *Collecting the New Naturalists* by Tim Bernhard and Timothy Loe (February 2014); *Collins British Wild Flower Guide* by David Streeter, illustrated by Christina Hart-Davies, Audrey Hardcastle, Felicity Cole and Lizzie Harper (April 2014); *Collins British Tree Guide* by Owen Johnson and David More (April 2014); *Collins British Butterfly Guide* by Tom Tolman, illustrated by Richard Lewington (April 2014); *New Naturalist Brecon Beacons* by Jonathan Mullard (May 2014); *Life of a Chalkstream* by Simon Cooper (May 2014); *Pests, Diseases and Disorders of Garden Plants*, updated 4th edition by Prof Stefan Buczacki and Keith Harris (June 2014); *New Naturalist Nature in Towns and Cities* by David Goode (September 2014); *Human Universe* by Professor Brian Cox and Andrew Cohen (September 2014); *Collins Field Guide - Birds of India* by Norman Arlott (October 2014).
Address: 77-85 Fulham Palace Rd, Hammersmith, London, W6 8JB; 020 8741 7070;
e-mail: julia.koppitz@harpercollins.co.uk
www.harpercollins.co.uk www.newnaturalists.com
www.williamcollinsbooks.com

PRINCETON/WILDGUIDES LTD

Imprints: WILDGuides: natural history fieldguides covering Britain's wildlife: butterflies, dragonflies, reptiles and amphibians, orchids, arable plants and plant galls.
OCEANGuides: Identification guides to marine wildlife covering Antarctic, Atlantic and Pacific oceans.
Destination Guides: Lavishly illustrated visitor guides to Galapagos, Seychelles, South Georgia, Falklands.
Crossbill Guides: Regional

WILD*Guides*

guides to the top wildlife destinations in Europe covering Spain, France, Poland, Hungary and Finland.
Recently published: *Britain's Freshwater Fishes, Britain's Hoverflies, Britain's Day-flying Moths, The World's Rarest Birds, England's Rare Mosses and Liverworts, The Crossley ID Guide to Britain and Ireland.*
New for 2014: *A Field Guide to the Larger Mammals of Tanzania, A Sparrowhawk's Lament, Britain's Dragonflies Ed 3, Birds of the Serengeti, Animals of the Serengeti, Birds of Kenya's Rift Valley.*
Address: Princeton University Press, c/o John Wiley & Sons Ltd, New Era estate, Oldlands Way, Bognor Regis, West Sussex PO22 9NQ; 0800 243 407.
e-mail: (for orders): cs-books@wiley.com
www.press.princeton.edu/wildguides

THE LANGFORD PRESS

Imprints: Wildlife Art Series (WAS): Showcasing the best in contemporary wildlife art in large format hardback books.
Wildlife Art Techniques (WAT): As well as showing wildlife art, this series gives the reader insights into how the finished piece of art is created. Available as both hard and paper backs.
Wildlife and People (WAP): Gives insight into fieldwork and results of those who spend a great deal of time studying birds in depth.
Myweebooks: Providing younger readers with easy-to-understand facts about wildlife (all titles well illustrated and many contain learning games).
New for 2014: *Wildlife Art Series:* Top bird artists and authors concentrate on the finding of new birds for their GB lists in *Rare Birds*; *Lines from Nature* by John Busby; *The Art of Bird Carving* by two masters of the craft, Mike Wood and Keith Royle. Lisa Hooper's book about her print-making will follow. Please check website for news of other titles in the pipeline.
Wildlife Art Techniques: A new book delving into print-making techniques for beginners and more experienced image-makers.
Wildlife and People: New titles on Harriers, Honey Buzzards, Red Kites and Short-eared Owls, plus a tribute to field naturalist Derek Ratcliffe.
Myweebooks: Screamer The Swift, and a range of titles covering the ecology and concerns of bird species.
Address: 10 New Road, Langtoft, Peterborough PE6 9LE; e-mail: sales@langford-press.co.uk
www.langford-press.co.uk

THE SOUND APPROACH

Company ethos: An independent publishing company committed to turning bird-watchers into bird-listeners. We publish high quality books by talented authors and aim to change people's perception of the world of birdsong. We hope our books provide readers with the tools for understanding the birds heard in the field and encourage them to start recording for themselves.
Imprints: Founder Mark Constantine launched the company with *The Sound Approach To Birding* and

BOOK SELLERS

followed with *Petrels Night And Day* by Magnus Robb and *Birding From The Hip* by Anthony McGeehan.
New for 2014: *Undiscovered Owls* by Magnus Robb and the Sound Approach
Address: 12 Market Street, Poole, Dorset BH15 1NF; 01202 641 004; e-mail: info@soundapproach.co.uk www.soundapproach.co.uk

BOOK SELLERS

CALLUNA BOOKS

Company ethos: We specialise in buying and selling out of print natural history titles, with an emphasis on quality stock at competitive prices.
Key subjects: Birds, mammals, flora, invertebrates in the UK and worldwide, including the Poyser and New Naturalist series, and general natural history, conservation and countryside titles including some reports and journals. Stock of 2,500+ titles maintained.
Other services: Catalogues issued (usually 3 p.a.). We exhibit at some events including The Bird Fair. Wants lists welcomed – no obligation to buy.
Opening times: Mail order but viewing by appointment possible.
Address: Moor Edge, 2 Bere Road, Wareham, Dorset BH20 4DD;01929 552 560.
e-mail: enquiries@callunabooks.co.uk
www.callunabooks.co.uk

NHBS – everything for wildlife, science & environment

Company ethos: To contribute to the discovery, understanding and conservation of biodiversity and natural ecosystems.
Key subjects: Ecology and conservation books and equipment: natural history, birding, zoology, botany, entomology; bat detectors, field kit, photography, sampling, tracking etc.
Other services: Search and browse our full online catalogue of more than 110,000 products (www.nhbs.com).
Opening times: Mon-Fri (8.30am-5pm), for customer service. Browse or order anytime at www.nhbs.com
Address: 2-3 Wills Road, Totnes, Devon TQ9 5XN; 01803 865 913; e-mail: customer.services@nhbs.co.uk www.nhbs.com

PICTURE BOOK

Company ethos: Picture Book is a general bookshop specialising in bird books and local history.
Key subjects: Birdwatching, natural history, local history. Churnet Valley publish local history and Arnold Bennett titles in paperback and hardback with introductions by the Arnold Bennett Society.

Other services: Amazon mail order, new and secondhand books.
Opening times: The shop is open to the public Tuesday to Saturday 10am - 4.30pm. Best to phone to check if travelling any distance.
Address: Picture Book, 6 Stanley Street, Leek, ST13 5HG; 01538 399 033 and 01538 384 337; (fax) 01538 399 696; e-mail: info@leekbooks.co.uk www.leekbooks.co.uk

SECOND NATURE

Company ethos: Buying and selling out-of-print/ secondhand/antiquarian books on natural history, topography and travel.
Key subjects: Birds, mammals, flowers and all other aspects of natural history.
Other services; Exhibits at bird/wildlife fairs.
New for 2014: A comprehensive website – www.secondnaturebooks.com
Opening times: Mail order only.
Address: Knapton Book Barn, Back Lane, Knapton, York YO26 6QJ; 01904 795 489.
e-mail: SecondnatureYork@aol.com
www.secondnaturebooks.com

SUBBUTEO NATURAL HISTORY BOOKS

Company ethos: Specialisation and careful selection has enhanced our reputation for supplying and publishing natural history books, DVDs, travel and fieldguides for those who enjoy birdwatching and the natural world, while providing a fast, knowledgeable and efficient service.
Key subjects: Ornithology (UK, Europe & worldwide), mammals, reptiles & amphibians, aquatic fauna, butterflies & moths, plants & fungi, natural history, ecology & environmental science, wildlife art & photography.
Other services: Comprehensive online bookstore, gift wrap service, booklist service, worldwide book sourcing. Online ordering, with free delivery on orders over £50 (in-print titles & UK titles only), free catalogue, updates and monthly e-newsletter. Subbuteo Natural History Books is a division of CJ WildBird Foods Ltd.
New for 2014: Continuously adding new titles to our extensive range – call for a catalogue, visit the website or visit us in Shropshire. You can now find us on Twitter and Facebook for the latest news and offers.
Opening times: Call 01743 709 420 Monday to Friday (9am-5pm). Saturday (9am-12pm). Online ordering 24 hrs.
Address: The Rea, Upton Magna, Shrewsbury, Shropshire SY4 4UR; 01743 709 420; (fax) 01743 709 504; e-mail: info@wildlifebooks.com www.wildlifebooks.com

CLOTHING AND EQUIPMENT SUPPLIERS

WILDSOUNDS

Company ethos: Species Champion for the endangered Spoonbill Sandpiper. Corporate sponsor of Norfolk Wildlife Trust. Donates a significant portion of profits to bird conservation and is committed to sound environmental practices. Operates the *Bird Watching* magazine bookshop.

Key product lines: Bird and other wildlife books, including wildlife art and photography, at discounted prices. Publisher of *Birding in Eastern Europe* by Gerard Gorman, *Garden Bird Sounds* by Geoff Sample and *Bird Songs and Calls of Britain & Europe* by Jean C Roche. Attends all major Bird Fairs and many local events.

New for 2014: Expanded range of products and new product lines – see the enhanced and improved website.

Office opening times: Weekdays (9.30am-5pm). Shop 24/7 on www.wildsounds.com

Address: Cross Street, Salthouse, Norfolk NR25 7XH; 01263 741 100; e-mail: sales@wildsounds.com www.wildsounds.com

CLOTHING SUPPLIERS

COUNTRY INNOVATION

Company ethos: Specialists in high performance clothing, footwear and accessories specifically for the birdwatching market. Friendly advice by well trained staff. Total customer satisfaction.

Key product lines: Full range of outdoor wear: jackets, fleeces, trousers, travel clothing, Ventile garments, Brasher footwear, Tilley hats, bags and accessories. Ladies fit available.

Other services: Retail shop, mail order sales and online sales at www.countryinnovation.co.uk. Check website for appearances at shows and events.

New for 2014: New Raptor Waistcoat - made from a very tough hardwearing fabric with loads of useful pockets. New Linnet Jacket and Smock – waterproof yet packable and comfortable to wear.

Opening times; Tues-Fri (9am-5pm), Sat (10am-2pm).

Address: 1 Broad Street, Congresbury, North Somerset BS49 5DG; 01934 877 333..

e-mail: sales@countryinnovation.com www.countryinnovation.com

PARÁMO DIRECTIONAL CLOTHING SYSTEMS

Company ethos: Innovators of technical mountain, birding and travel clothing using revolutionary and long-lasting Nikwax fabrics and functional design to provide quiet performance and comfort for all outdoor enthusiasts, professionals & fieldworkers. Ethical manufacture.

Key product lines: Waterproof jackets and trousers, technical baselayers, insulating

overlayers and ultra-cooling travel wear. Of especial note: Halcon, Pájaro and Alondra birdwatching jackets and Pájaro waterproof trousers, Halcon Waistcoat and Halcon Traveller, plus Andy Rouse Limited Edition Aspira Smock, Cascada Trousers, Grid Baselayer and Katmai Shirt.

Other services: Repair, service & recycling of Páramo garments; online sales at www.naturallyparamo.co.uk

New for 2014: Ladies' Alondra Jacket – seven carefully sited pockets. Generous length for protection, with flattering lines. Every Alondra Jacket sold plants a sapling in the Scottish Highlands with Trees for Life.

Opening times; For independent retailers, consult our website or ring 01892 786 444 for stockist list and catalogue pack. Páramo London Store, 29 Henrietta Street, WC2E 8NA. Open 10.30am - 7pm (Mon - Fri), 11am- 5pm (Sat) and 11am – 4pm (Sun). Páramo Wadhurst Village Shop, 1 Central Parade, High Street, Wadhurst, TN5 6AL. Open 9am - 5.30pm (Mon-Sat) and at other times for groups by appointment.

Address: Unit F, Durgates Industrial Estates, Wadhurst, East Sussex TN5 6DF; 01892 786 444. e-mail: info@paramo.co.uk www.paramo.co.uk

EQUIPMENT SUPPLIERS

BIRD IMAGES

Company ethos: High quality products at affordable prices.

Key product lines: Bird DVDs. A range of titles including identification guides and innovative guides to birdwatching places in the UK and overseas.

New for 2014: *Birdwatching at RSPB Titchwell Marsh.* A birdwatching year at this hugely popular reserve.

Opening times: Telephone first.

Address: 28 Carousel Walk, Sherburn in Elmet, North Yorkshire LS25 6LP; 01977 684 666.

e-mail: paul@birdvideodvd.com www.birdvideodvd.com

BIRDGUIDES LTD

Company ethos: Better birding through technology. The number one birder's website.

Key product lines: Software and video guides to birds and insects. Rare bird news services via web, apps, e-mail and sms.

Address: BirdGuides Ltd, Warners Group Publications, The Chocolate Factory, 5 Clarendon Road, London N22 6XJ; Order line: (freephone) 0800 919 391; e-mail: contact@birdguides.com www.birdguides.com

BIRDGUIDES

BLUEBIRD TECHNOLOGY

Company ethos: Bluebird Technology focuses on creating quality wildlife recording software products for all birders to enjoy. All of our software is really easy to use; you don't have to be a computer or database geek to use it.

Key product lines: Bird Journal for Windows, iPhone/iPad and Android.

New for 2014: Bird Journal for Android.

Opening times: Lines are open 9am-5pm (UK time), Monday to Friday, except national holidays. Calls charged at local rate.

Address: Bluebird Technology, 1 Turnbridge Court, Cambridge, CB24 4GH; 0845 094 6012.

e-mail: mail@bluebirdtechnology.com
www.bluebirdtechnology.com

Follow us on Twitter: http://twitter.com/Bluebird_Tech/ FaceBook: http://www.facebook.com/BluebirdTechnology/

THE ONE STOP NATURE SHOP

Company ethos: To bring together all aspects of watching wildlife in one unique and exciting shop. Friendly advice and a commitment to quality service.

Key product lines: Binoculars, telescopes, microscopes (traditional and USB), magnifiers, books, bird feeders and food, entomological supplies, laboratory equipment.

New for 2014: The revolutionary Newton research grade portable microscope.

Opening times: Every day except Dec 25. 10am – 5pm.

Address: The One Stop Nature Shop, Dalegate Market, Burnham Deepdale, Norfolk PE31 8FB; 01485 211 223; e-mail: sales@onestopnature.co.uk
www.onestopnature.co.uk

WILDLIFE WATCHING SUPPLIES

Company ethos: To bring together a comprehensive range of materials, clothing and equipment to make it easier and more comfortable for you to blend in with the environment. Quick and friendly service.

Key product lines: Hides, camouflage, bean bags, lens and camera covers, scope covers, clothing etc.

Opening times: Mon to Fri (9am-5pm), mail order. Visitors by appointment.

Address: Wildlife Watching Supplies, Tiverton Way, Tiverton Business Park, Tiverton, Devon EX16 6TG; +44 (0)1884 254 191; Fax: +44 (0)1884 250 460.

e-mail: enquiries@wildlifewatchingsupplies.co.uk
www.wildlifewatchingsupplies.co.uk

HOLIDAY COMPANIES

AVIAN ADVENTURES

Company ethos: Celebrating 21 years of providing first class, value-for-money tours, escorted by friendly, experienced professional leaders at a fairly relaxed pace. Financial protection - ATOL 3367.

Types of tours: Birdwatching, birds and wildlife photography and wildlife safaris, all suitable for both the first-time and the more experienced traveller.

Destinations: 50 tours worldwide.

New for 2014: Ecuador; Falklands & Chile; Guatemala; Birds & Wine in South Africa's Western Cape. Plus new photographic tours to Botswana, Spain and Yellowstone National Park, USA.

Brochure from: 49 Sandy Road, Norton, Stourbridge, DY8 3AJ; 01384 372 013; (Fax)01384 441 340.

e-mail: avianadventures@btinternet.com
www.avianadventures.co.uk

BIRDFINDERS

Company ethos: Top-value birding tours to see all specialities/endemics of a country/area, using leading UK and local guides. ATOL 5406.

Types of tours: Birdwatching holidays for all abilities.

Destinations: Nearly 80 tours in UK, Europe, Africa, Asia, Australasia, North, Central and South America and Antarctica.

New for 2014: France (south and Corsica), Honduras, India (north), Morocco (Buttonquail), Philippines, Spain (Tarifa migration) and Uzbekistan.

Brochure from: Vaughan Ashby, Westbank, Cheselbourne, Dorset DT2 7NW.01258 839 066 (office open seven days a week (8am-8pm); e-mail: birdfinders@aol.co.uk
www.birdfinders.co.uk

Birdfinders

BIRDWATCHING BREAKS

Company ethos: Overseas breaks and Black Isle Birding: watching birds in their natural habitat and putting money into the local economy.

Types of tours: Birding tours for all abilities to little-known destinations, plus more traditional areas, using local guides in addition to our own. No more than 8 clients per tour, to give the best views of birds and wildlife. We also specialise in Northern Scotland including the Highlands and Islands under the Black Isle Birding banner. Many of our tours are suitable for photography.

Destinations: Australia, Belarus, Canada, Cambodia & Vietnam, Chile, Cyprus, Ethiopia, France, Ghana, Hungary, India, Israel, Jamaica, Japan, Lesser Antilles, Malaysia, Russia, Senegal, Seychelles, Uganda, USA and numerous in Scotland. Some tours are regularly featured, while others are old favourites re-introduced for this year.

New for 2014: Benin, Tunisia & Algeria, China (Tibet), Australia (Darwin to Adelaide via Alice Springs), Bolivia. Mexico (Oaxaca).

Brochure from: Birdwatching Breaks, Cygnus House, Gordon's Mill, Balblair, Ross-shire IV7 8LQ; 01381 610 495; e-mail: enquiries@birdwatchingbreaks.com or markfinn55@btinternet.com
www.birdwatchingbreaks.com

BIRD WATCHING & WILDLIFE CLUB

Company ethos: To provide birdwatchers with high quality, reasonably priced accommodation, enabling them to experience the abundance of wildlife in the Highlands area.

Types of tours: Based at the 3-star, 50-bedroom Grant Arms Hotel, the BWWC provides information and advice on wildlife sites nearby, plus a programme of events (guided trips can also be arranged), helping guests to make the most of their holiday while remaining free to create their own itinerary.

Destinations: Cairngorms, Speyside and North-East Scotland.

Brochure from: Grant Arms Hotel, 25 The Square, Grantown-on-Spey, Highlands PH26 3HF; 01479 872 526; e-mail: bookings@bwwc.co.uk www.bwwc.co.uk

BRITISH-BULGARIAN FRIENDSHIP SOCIETY

Company ethos: To introduce people to the beauty of Bulgarian wildlife at exceptional value prices with expert leaders. ATOL 4465.

Types of tours: Birdwatching tours in winter, spring and autumn, also early summer and midsummer butterfly tours. Group size 12-14 persons. Tailor-made tours on any subject for individuals or groups of any size.

Destinations: Specialists to Bulgaria, over 35 years experience.

New for 2014: Spring birdwatching tour in Bulgaria, Macedonia and Greece. Free society membership for 2014 with all B-BS tour bookings.

Brochure from: Balkania Travel Ltd, Avanta Harrow, 79 College Road, Harrow, Middlesex, HA1 1BD.020 7536 9400; e-mail: ognian@balkaniatravel.com or annie.kay@btinternet.com www.bbfs.org.uk

CLASSIC JOURNEYS

Company ethos: Professional and friendly company, providing well organised and enjoyable walking, wildlife and photography holidays.

Types of tours: Walking holidays, plus wildlife and photography holidays.

Destinations: Antarctica, The Arctic, Brazil, Bhutan, Borneo, Canada, Ecuador & Galapagos, India, Morocco, Myanmar (Burma), Nepal, Peru, Sri Lanka, Tanzania and Tibet.

New for 2014: Cambodia, Myanmar (Burma).

Opening times: Mon-Fri (9:30am - 3pm).

Further Information: www.classicjourneys.co.uk 01773 873 497; e-mail: info@classicjourneys.co.uk

EXPERIENCE NATURE

Company ethos: To exceed the expectations of wildlife watchers and photographers, by providing tailor-made itineraries to suit each of these interests separately.

Types of tours: Each of the destinations below has a purpose-built tour for photographers and one for wildlife watchers. Our watchers get to see a great selection of wildlife specific to their chosen destination and take time to enjoy the highlights of the tour, rather than being rushed along in a bid to add the next tick. For the photographers even more time is allocated to ensure ample opportunity to get stunning images of the headline species.

Each tour includes local guides who know the areas we visit and the associated wildlife well, along with a UK representative to help with identification and to offer advice to photographers where needed. The safety, comfort and happiness of each of our clients is the ultimate aim for each tour and to go about this with minimum disturbance to the environment is of paramount importance.

Destinations: The Gambia, Trinidad & Tobago, Spain & France.

Brochure from: Experience Nature, 16 Lint Meadow, Wythall, Worcestershire B47 5PH. 07704 189 835. E-mail - info@experiencenature.co.uk

GLENLOY WILDLIFE

Company ethos: We offer guided exploration of the stunning West Coast of Scotland, based from beautiful Glen Loy near Fort William in a former hunting lodge with views over the Nevis Range. The

glen contains Red Deer, Eagles, Otter and Chequered Skippers with Pine Martens visiting the Lodge each evening.

Types of tours: We visit a variety of habitats by minibus and by foot. Suitable for anyone who can walk 3-4 miles.

Destinations: We explore the region of Lochaber, including the Great Glen, Ardnamurchan peninsula and the Small Isles.

Further information from: Jon Mercer, Glenloy Lodge Guest House, Banavie, Nr Fort William PH33 7PD; 01397 712 700 or 07817 443 370. e-mail: info@glenloylodge.co.uk www.glenloylodge.co.uk www.glenloy-wildlife.org.uk

HEATHERLEA

Company ethos: Scotland's premier birding and wildlife holiday operator. Exciting holidays to see all the birds of Scotland and selected overseas destinations. Experienced guides with a wealth of experience, small groups and our own comfortable award-winning hotel.

Types of tours: Birdwatching and wildlife watching tours.

Destinations: Scottish Highlands, including holidays from our base in Nethybridge, plus Outer Hebrides,

Orkney, Shetlands and more. Overseas destinations throughout the world include Costa Rica, the Pyrenees, Lesvos, Nepal and Trinidad.
New for 2014: New short breaks in Scotland, new Hebridean itineraries, also Ireland, Cuba, Texas, Panama and more.
Brochure from: The Mountview Hotel, Nethybridge, Inverness-shire PH25 3EB; 01479 821 248; (Fax)01479 821 515; e-mail: info@heatherlea.co.uk
www.heatherlea.co.uk – twitter@heatherleabirds

IBERIAN WILDLIFE TOURS
Company ethos: Highly experienced bilingual guides offer top quality, low impact small group tours to help visitors observe and appreciate Spain's enormous wealth of wildlife.
Types of tours: Tailor-made and fixed itinerary trips, from half and full-day local trips up to 15 days for longer excursions. For individuals, couples and groups (max. 14 clients with two guides). Birds, wildflowers, mammals, butterflies, dragonflies, reptiles and amphibians.
Destinations: Throughout Spain, but principally Madrid and surrounds, Extremadura & Gredos, Picos de Europa, Pyrenees and Andújar (Iberian lynx +).
Information from: John Muddeman, Teresa Farino and Mike Lockwood, Calle Alcocer 1 1-C, Fresnedillas de la Oliva, 28214 Madrid, Spain; (0034) 649 608 747.
e-mail: john@iberianwildlife.com
www.iberianwildlife.com

JULIAN SYKES WILDLIFE HOLIDAYS
Company ethos: Smaller groups - bigger experiences.
Types of tours: From the beginner to the keenest watcher, our tailor-made tours, holidays and short breaks feature all types of wildlife with an emphasis on various species. We keep it interesting, informative and fun!
Destinations: Spain (Extremadura, Pyrenees, Picos de Europa, Iberian lynx, Cantabrian bear, Iberian wolf and wild cat), plus India (Tigers & Taj Mahal), Jordan (Petra & Wildlife), Southern Turkey, India (Asiatic lion and much more), SE Australia (Birds and mammals).
Information from: Julian Sykes or Jane Lees, Avinguda Font d'en Carros, 16, Oliva 46780, Valencia, Spain (0034 687 567 286 or 630 603 753.
e-mail: info@juliansykeswildlife.com
www.juliansykeswildlife.com

NORTH WEST BIRDS
Company ethos: Friendly, relaxed and unhurried but targetted to scarce local birds.
Types of tours: Very small groups (up to four) based on large family home in South Lakes with good home cooking. Short breaks with birding in local area. Butterflies in season.

Destinations: Local to Northwest England: Lancashire, Morecambe Bay and Lake District.
Brochure from: Mike Robinson, Barn Close, Beetham, Cumbria LA7 7AL; (Tel/fax)015395 63191.
e-mail: mike@nwbirds.co.uk www.nwbirds.co.uk

NORTHERN FRANCE WILDLIFE TOURS
Company ethos: Friendly personal attention, including meals by a qualified chef (Shirley). Normally a maximum of four in a group, but other arrangements can be made. Totally flexible approach.
Types of tours: Beginners to experienced birders. Local birds include Black Woodpecker, Bluethroat, Melodious Warbler.
Destinations: Brittany, Normandy and Pays de la Loire.
Brochure from: Place de L'Eglise, 53700, Averton, France; 0033 243 006 969; e-mail: nfwt@online.fr
Website: nfwt.online.fr

ORIOLE BIRDING

Company ethos: Enhancing your ID skills and enjoyment of birding with small group tours. ATOL protected 6839.
Types of tours: Norfolk and South Wales birding tours year-round, covering all the best sites and species, plus a selection of Britain's best destinations. Also a comprehensive range of international holidays and pelagics. We also specialise in bug watching tours in the UK covering Norfolk and the New Forest.
Destinations: Norfolk, South Wales, Solway, Speyside, Cornwall, Isles of Scilly pelagics, North-east England, Shetland, County Wexford, Mull and Iona, Extremadura, Romania, South Africa, The Gambia, Israel, Finland, Lesvos, Turkey, Morocco, Poland, Holland, Panama, Lake Kerkini.
New for 2014: Cuba, Gibraltar and Northern Morocco, Kalahari, Latvia, Sicily, Western Isles, Isles of Scilly in autumn.
Brochure from: Oriole Birding, 8 Newcastle Hill, Bridgend CF31 4EY; 01656 711 152.
e-mail: info@oriolebirding.com
www.oriolebirding.com

ORNITHOLIDAYS
Company ethos: Oldest bird tour company in the world (established 1965). Friendly and fun holidays led by full-time tour leaders. ATOL no 0743.
Types of tours: Escorted birdwatching, photographic and natural history tours.
Destinations: Worldwide including Trinidad and Tobago, Chile, Cuba, Bhutan, Taiwan, Sri Lanka, South Africa, Iceland, Spitsbergen and Antarctica.
New for 2014: Mongolia, Kuwait, St Lucia, Italy (Po Delta and Sicily) and USA (New England).
Brochure from: 29 Straight Mile, Romsey, Hampshire SO51 9BB; 01794 519 445.
e-mail: info@ornitholidays.co.uk
www.ornitholidays.co.uk

HOLIDAY COMPANIES

ROMNEY MARSH BIRDWATCHING BREAKS

Company ethos: To pass on an appreciation of the wildlife of Romney Marsh in a family friendly atmosphere.
Types of tours: Fully inclusive 3 or 5 day Birdwatching Breaks based at our cottage in Lydd-on-Sea. Also, one day birdwatching and historical tours around Romney Marsh.
Destinations: Romney Marsh, including Dungeness and Rye Harbour, and elsewhere across Kent and Sussex.
New for 2014: Day trips to northern France.
Brochure from: Paul Trodd, Plovers, 1 Toby Road, Lydd-on-Sea, Romney Marsh, Kent TN29 9PG; 01797 366935 & 07920 197535..
E-mail: troddy@plovers.co.uk
www. plovers.co.uk

SPAINBIRDS NATURE TOURS

Company ethos: A registered travel agent legally able to offer ground packages with a small team of highly experienced, resident, long-standing bilingual guides to ensure high quality, low-impact, small-group experiences.

Types of tours: Mainly birdwatching and photography tours. Tailor-made and more fixed itinerary trips, from half-day local trips up to 15 days for longer excursions. For individuals, couples or groups of all knowledge levels; max. 14 clients with 2 guides. Birds, mammals, butterflies, dragonflies, etc.
Destinations: Throughout Spain; principally Madrid, La Mancha, Andújar (Iberian lynx+), Strait of Gibraltar, Doñana, Extremadura & Gredos, Picos de Europa & Pyrenees.
Brochure from: Santi VillaC/Nogal, 7 – 1°B, Guadalix de la Sierra, 28794 Madrid,Spain; (+34) 687 83 77 19.
e-mail: info@spainbirds.com
www.spainbirds.com

SPEYSIDE WILDLIFE

Company ethos: Fun-filled wildlife experiences with expert guides, where you are always treated as an individual, not one of a crowd.
Types of tours: Fully-inclusive bird and mammal watching holidays, in small groups, with like-minded guests, around Scotland and overseas (ATOL no 4259). Also tailor-made trips to suit your wishes, for individuals, couples and groups, plus day guiding and dusk watches in the Cairngorms National Park.

SPEYSIDE WILDLIFE *international.*

Destinations: Speyside in the Cairngorms National Park and around Scotland and its islands; England; Mainland Europe; Scandinavia and the Arctic; North, Central and South America; Asia.
New for 2014: The Forest of Dean, Islay and Knapdale, The Farne Islands, Hungary in summer, Spitsbergen, Slovakia, New York City, Alaska and the Pribilofs, Peru and Machu Picchu, Sri Lanka, California and Patagonia.
Brochure from: Wester Camerorie, Ballieward, Grantown-on-Spey, Cairngorms National Park, Highlands, Scotland PH26 3PR: (Tel/fax) +44 (0) 1479 812 498;
e-mail: enquiries@speysidewildlife.co.uk
www.speysidewildlife.co.uk, Twitter:@ SpeyWildlife www.facebook.com/speysidewildlife

SUNBIRD

Company ethos: Enjoyable birdwatching tours led by professional leaders. ATOL no 3003.
Types of tours: Birdwatching.
Destinations: Worldwide.
New for 2014: Spain Lynx tour, Ecuador, Cuba, Panama, Belarus, Turkey, several destination in North America, Philippines, Brazil Photo tour, Argentina.
Brochure from: 26B The Market Square, Potton, Sandy, Bedfordshire SG19 2NP; 01767 262 522; (fax) 01767 262 916; e-mail: sunbird@sunbirdtours.co.uk
www.sunbirdtours.co.uk check new destinations.

THE BIGGEST TWITCH BIRDWATCHING TRIPS

Company ethos: We run relaxed-paced birdwatching tours and daytrips with both Alan Davies and Ruth Miller to provide expert, professional guiding by two world record-breaking birders. We only take small groups to ensure that everyone has the best possible experience and personal attention.
Types of tours: Small group birdwatching daytrips, weekends and longer breaks; set departures and custom tours tailored just to suit you.
Destinations: North Wales: as the author of *Best Birdwatching Sites in North Wales*, nobody knows the best places to find birds better than Alan; Norfolk; Suffolk; Scottish Highlands and islands; Spain including Catalonia and Extremadura; Finland and Norway.
New for 2014: Portugal; Estonia.
Brochure from: info@thebiggesttwitch.com; visit www.thebiggesttwitch.com for information

THE DORSET BIRDING AND WILDLIFE EXPERIENCE

Company ethos: To provide a local knowledge and an expertise of Dorset's birds and wildlife, catering for all levels of experience and tailor-made to your requirements.
Types of tours: A guiding service for individuals and groups aimed at providing an experience of Dorset's birds, wildlife and landscapes. Although there is a particular emphasis on birds, all species groups are covered. Bookings taken for half-days, full-days, weekends or longer. We can also provide a guiding and accommodation package.
Destinations: Dorset.
Brochure from: Moor Edge, 2 Bere Road, Wareham, Dorset BH20 4DD; 01929 552 560.
e-mail: enquiries@dorsetbirdingandwildlife.co.uk
www.dorsetbirdingandwildlife.co.uk

HOLIDAY COMPANIES AND OPTICAL DEALERS

THINKGALAPAGOS

Company ethos: Specialists in the Galapagos Islands, great value, expert guides and personal attention to ensure a once-in-a-lifetime adventure travel experience.
Types of tours: Friendly and relaxed holidays that are educationally orientated for people with a keen interest in wildlife and photography. Suitable for both the first-time and more experienced traveller.
Destinations: Galapagos and mainland Ecuador.
Brochure from: Rachel Dex, 25 Trinity Lane, Beverley, East Yorkshire HU17 0DY; 01482 872 716.
E-mail: info@thinkgalapagos.com
www.thinkgalapagos.com

WILD INSIGHTS

Company ethos: Friendly, no-rush tours designed to savour, understand and enjoy birds and wildlife. Emphasis on quality and no intentional disturbance of wildlife. ATOL no 5429 (in association with Wildwings).
Types of tours: Skills-building UK courses, UK identification workshops plus a range of overseas tours.
Destinations: Various UK locations, plus selected destinations throughout Europe, USA, Central America, Africa, Asia.
New for 2015: Sri Lanka.
Calender brochure from: Yew Tree Farmhouse, Craignant, Selattyn, Oswestry, Salop SY10 7NP. (Tel/fax) 01691 718 740; e-mail: keith.offord@virgin.net
www.wildinsights.co.uk

YORKSHIRE COAST NATURE

Company ethos: Yorkshire Coast Nature is dedicated to providing unforgettable wildlife experiences in one of England's most beautiful, inspiring regions. At YCN we make it a policy to help the wildlife and places which give us so much enjoyment. We allocate significant company resources to local and national conservation projects.
Types of tours: Nature Tours from Snakes and Badgers to Honey Buzzards and rare bird finding on the glorious east coast of Yorkshire
Destinations: Yorkshire Coast and beyond.
New for 2014: North Yorkshire nature safaris in forest and moorland, Seabird Spectacular on Flamborough Headland, Migration Discovery Days at Spurn NNR.
Address: 5 Coastguard Cottages, Lighthouse Road, Flamborough, YO15 1AW. 01262 851 999; e-mail: info@yorkshirecoastnature.co.uk
www.yorkshirecoastnature.co.uk

BIRDNET OPTICS LTD

Company ethos: To provide the birdwatcher with the best value for money on optics, books and outdoor clothing.
Viewing facilities: Clear views to distant hills for comparison of optics at long range and wide variety of textures and edges for clarity and resolution comparison.

BINOCULARS, TELESCOPES & BOOKS

Optical stock: Most leading binocular and telescope ranges stocked. If we do not have it in stock, we will endeavour to get it for you.
Non-optical stock: Books incl. New Naturalist Series and Poysers, videos, CDs, audio tapes, tripods, hide clamps, accessories and clothing.
Opening times: Mon-Sat (9:30am-5:30pm). Sundays, see website for details.
Address: 5 Trenchard Drive, Buxton, Derbyshire SK17 9JY; 01298 71 844; e-mail: paulflint@birdnet.co.uk
www.birdnet.co.uk

THE BIRDERS STORE

Company ethos: A leading specialist retailer of quality optical products and accessories at competitive prices for birders worldwide. Operated by birders for birders.
Optical stock: Extensive range of binoculars, monoculars and telescopes in stock. Swarovski Premier Dealer. Zeiss Optics Partner. Vortex Prime Dealer. Also Barr & Stroud, Hawke, Kite, Kowa, Minox, Opticron and many other leading brands stocked, along with a selection of used optics. Viewing area adjacent to the shop.
Non-optical stock: Tripods, monopods, Skua cases, Tilley Hats, Country Innovation clothing etc. Also an extensive range of birding books and DVDs in stock.
New for 2014: Minox BL HD binoculars, Swarovski SLC and CL Pocket binoculars, Zeiss Terra ED binoculars.
Opening times: Tues to Sat (9am-4.30pm).
Address: 7 King Charles Place, St John's, Worcester, Worcestershire WR2 5AJ; 01905 312 877.
www.birders-store.co.uk

CLIFTON CAMERAS

Company ethos: Optical specialists for binoculars and spotting scopes based near Slimbridge Wetland Centre in Gloucestershire. Main sponsors of the Dursley Birdwatching Society.
Optical stock: All top brands stocked. Nikon Premier Dealer, Swarovski Premier Dealer, Zeiss Centre Partner and Leica Premier Dealer.

TRADE DIRECTORY

113

cliftoncameras.co.uk

Non-optical stock: Professional camera supplier, Canon, Nikon, Pentax, Sigma and Gitzo Tripods to name a few. Viewing area adjacent to the shop.
New products to try: Zeiss Terra ED and Victory HT binoculars, Swarovski CL Compact Binoculars and Leica M.
Opening times: Mon-Sat (9am-5.30pm).
Address: 28 Parsonage Street, Dursley, Gloucestershire GL11 4AA; 01453 548 128.
e-mail: sales@cliftoncameras.co.uk
www.cliftoncameras.co.uk

FOCUS OPTICS

Company ethos: Friendly, expert service. Top quality instruments. No 'grey imports'.
Viewing facilities: Our own pool and nature reserve with feeding stations.
Optical stock: Full range of leading makes of binoculars and telescopes.
Non-optical stock: Waterproof clothing, fleeces, walking boots and shoes, bird food and feeders. Books, videos, walking poles.
Opening times: Mon-Sat (9am-5pm). Some Bank-holidays.
Address: Church Lane, Corley, Coventry, CV7 8BA; 01676 540 501/542 476; (Fax) 01676 540 930.
e mail: enquiries@focusoptics.eu www.focusoptics.eu

IN-FOCUS

Company ethos: The binocular and telescope specialists, offering customers informed advice at birdwatching venues throughout the country. Leading sponsor of the British Birdwatchng Fair.
Viewing facilities: Available at all shops (contact your local outlet), or at field events (10am-4pm) at bird reserves (see *Bird Watching* magazine or website www.at-infocus.co.uk for calendar)
Optical stock: Many leading makes of binoculars and telescopes, plus own-brand Delta range of binoculars and tripods.
Non-optical stock: Wide range of tripods, clamps and other accessories. Repair service available.
Opening times: These can vary, so please contact local shop or website before travelling.

BRANCHES:
Gloucestershire: The Wildfowl and Wetlands Trust, Slimbridge, Gloucestershire GL2 7BT.
Tel: 01453 890 978.

Hertfordshire: Willows Farm Village, Coursers Road, London Colney, Hertfordshire AL2 1BB.
Tel: 01727 827 799.

Lancashire: The Wildfowl and Wetlands Trust, Martin Mere, Burscough, Ormskirk, Lancashire L40 0TA.
Tel: 01704 897 020.

London, South West: The Wildfowl and Wetlands Trust, London Wetland Centre, Queen Elizabeth's Walk, Barnes, London SW13 9WT.
Tel: 020 8409 4433.

Norfolk: Main Street, Titchwell, Nr. King's Lynn, Norfolk PE31 8BB
Tel: 01485 210 101.

Rutland: Anglian Water Birdwatching Centre, Egleton Reserve, Rutland Water, Rutland LE15 8BT
Tel: 01572 770 656.

Yorkshire: Westleigh House Office Estate, Wakefield Road, Denby Dale, West Yorkshire HD8 8QJ
Tel: 01484 864 729.

LONDON CAMERA EXCHANGE

Company ethos: To employ knowledgeable staff to supply good quality optical equipment at a competitive price.
Viewing facilities: In shop and at local shows. Contact local branch for details of local events or check adverts in monthly birding magazines.
Optical stock: All leading makes of binoculars and scopes.
Non-optical stock: All main brands of photo, digital and video equipment.
Opening times: Most branches open 9am to 5.30pm.

BRANCHES
Bath: 13 Cheap Street, Bath, Avon, BA1 1NB; 01225 462 234.

Bristol: 53 The Horsefair, Bristol BS1 3JP;01179 276 185.

Cheltenham: 10-12 The Promenade, Cheltenham, GL50 1LR; 01242 519 851.

Chester: 9 Bridge Street Row, CH1 1NW; 01244 326 531.

Chesterfield: 1A South Street, Chesterfield, Derbyshire, S40 1QZ; 01246 211 891.

Chew Valley: Lakeside Optics, Chew Valley Tea Shop, near Bristol; 01275 332 042.

Colchester: 12 Led Lane, Colchester, Essex CO1 1LS; 01206 573 444.

Derby: 17 Sadler Gate, Derby, Derbyshire, DE1 3NH; 01332 348 644.

Exeter: 174 Fore Street, Exeter, Devon, EX4 3AX; 01392 279 024/438 167.

Fareham: 135 West Street, Fareham, Hampshire, PO16 0DU; 01329 236 441.

Gloucester: 12 Southgate Street, Gloucester, GL1 2DH: 01452 304 513.

Guildford: 8/9 Tunsgate, Guildford, Surrey, GU1 2DH; 01483 504 040.

Leamington: 4c Lunn Poly House, Clarendon Avenue, Royal Leamington Spa CV32 5PP; 01926 886 166.

Lincoln: 6 Silver Street, Lincoln, LN2 1DY; 01522 514 131.

Lincoln: 155 High Street, Lincoln, LN5 7AA; 01522 528 577.

London, Strand: 98 The Strand, London, WC2R 0AG; 020 7379 0200.

Manchester: 37 Parker Street, Picadilly, M1 4AJ; 0161 236 5819.

Norwich: 12 Timber Hill, Norwich, Norfolk NR1 3LB; 01603 612 537.

Nottingham: 7 Pelham Street, Nottingham, NG1 2EH; 0115 941 7486.

Plymouth: 10 Frankfort Gate, Plymouth, Devon, PL1 1QD; 01752 668 894.

Portsmouth: 40 Kingswell Path, Cascados, Portsmouth, PO1 4RR; 023 9283 9933.

Reading: 7 Station Road, Reading, Berkshire, RG1 1LG; 0118 959 2149.

Salisbury: 6 Queen Street, Salisbury, Wiltshire, SP1 1EY; 01722 335 436.

Southampton: 10 High Street, Southampton, Hampshire, SO14 2DH; 02380 221 597.

Southampton: 11 Civic Centre Road, Southampton SO14 7FJ; 02380 331 720.

Taunton: 6 North Street, Taunton, Somerset, TA1 1LH; 01823 259 955.

Winchester: 15 The Square, Winchester, Hampshire, SO23 9ES; 01962 866 203.

Worcester: 8 Pump Street, Worcester WR1 2QT; 01905 22314.

WILKINSON CAMERAS
Company ethos: The widest range of photographic and birdwatching equipment available at competitive prices at all times.
Viewing facilities: Optical field days at selected nature reserves in northern England. See website for details of photographic courses and other events.
Optical stock: Binoculars from Canon, Celestron, Hawke, Leica, Nikon, Swarovski. Spotting scopes from Celestron, Hawke, Leica, Nikon, Swarovski.
Non-optical stock: Wide range of bags, tripods, digital cameras, lenses and video equipment.
Opening times: Branches open Monday to Saturday (9am-5:30pm), Sunday (11am-4pm) - Preston, Carlisle & Warrington only; e-mail: sales@wilkinson.co.uk
www.wilkinson.co.uk

Wilkinson
Cameras
www.wilkinson.co.uk

BRANCHES
Blackburn: 42 Northgate, Blackburn, Lancs BB2 1JL: 01254 581 272; (Fax) 01254 695 867; e-mail: preston@wilkinson.co.uk

Burnley: 95 James Street, Burnley, Lancs BB11 1PY; 01282 424 524; (Fax) 01282 831 722; e-mail: preston@wilkinson.co.uk

Bury: 61 The Rock, Bury, Greater Manchester BL9 0NB; 01617 643 402; (Fax) 01617 615 086; e-mail: preston@wilkinson.co.uk

Carlisle: 13 Grapes Lane, Carlisle, Cumbria CA3 8NQ; 01228 538 583; (Fax) 01228 514 699. e-mail: preston@wilkinson.co.uk

Kendal: 19A The Westmorland Centre, Kendal, Cumbria LA9 4AB; 01539 735 055; (Fax) 01539 734 929; e-mail: preston@wilkinson.co.uk

Lancaster: 6 James Street, Lancaster, Lancs LA1 1UP; 01524 380 510; (Fax) 01524 380 512. e-mail: preston@wilkinson.co.uk

Liverpool: 51 Lord Street, Liverpool L2 6PB; 0151 255 0345; e-mail: liverpool@wilkinson.co.uk

Preston: 27 Friargate, Preston, Lancs PR1 2NQ; 01772 556 250; (Fax) 01772 259 435; e-mail: preston@wilkinson.co.uk

Southport: 38 Eastbank Street, Southport, Merseyside, PR8 1ET. 01704 534 534; (Fax) 01704 501 546; e-mail: southport@wilkinson.co.uk

Warrington: 10 The Mall, The Golden Square, Warrington WA1 1QE. 01925 638 290; e-mail: warrington@wilkinson.co.uk

OPTICAL IMPORTERS AND MANUFACTURERS

CARL ZEISS LTD
Company ethos: World renowned, high quality performance and innovative optical products.
Product lines: Victory HT, Conquest HD, Terra ED binoculars, Victory and Classic compacts and Victory Diascope T FL telescopes.
Address: 509 Coldhams Lane, Cambridge, Cambs CB1 3JS; 01223 401 525.
e-mail: christine.karn@zeiss.co.uk
www.zeiss.co.uk/sportsoptics

DEBEN GROUP INDUSTRIES
Company ethos: We design Hawke Sport Optics as a quantity range of binoculars and spotting scopes, which in turn offer excellent value for money. We have various market leaders within the range and will continue to create a simple but very popular range.
Product lines: Hawke Sport Optics consists of the following families: New Panorama ED, New Sapphire ED, Frontier ED, Endurance PC and the much-loved Nature-Trek range. The full range offers compacts, mid-size and full size binoculars from £50 - £600, plus spotting scopes (from £100 - £1300) which also includes models with double ED glass. A range of trap cameras for filming wildlife now

OPTICAL IMPORTERS AND MANUFACTURERS

has an 8M HD model with colour screen.
New for 2014: New Endurance PC compacts, plus entry-level Prostalk nature camera which is now a 5M camera system at £130. Deben now distributes the Olight professional torch range, which offers extreme performance, quantity and toughness. Known for their huge beam throws and lumen levels, they are ideal for nocturnal wildlife watching with the addition of a red filter.
Address: Avocet House, Wilford Bridge Road, Melton, Woodbridge, Suffolk IP12 1RB; 01394 387 762 .
e-mail: salesl@deben.com
www.hawkeoptics.com www.olight.co.uk

INTRO 2020 LTD
Company ethos: Experienced importer of photo and optical products.

Product lines: Steiner binoculars, Tamron lenses, Crumpler bags, Tamrac bags, Velbon tripods, Slik tripods, Hoya and Cokin filters, Optech straps. Plus many other photographic accessories.
Address: Unit 1, Priors Way, Maidenhead, Berkshire SL6 2HP; 01628 674 411; (fax) 01628 771 055.
e-mail: sales@intro2020.co.uk
www.intro2020.co.uk, www.cokin.co.uk, www.lensbaby.co.uk, www.lenspens.co.uk, www.optechusa.co.uk, www.phottix.co.uk, www.sliktripod.co.uk, www.steiner-binoculars.co.uk, www.tamrac.co.uk, www.tamron.co.uk, www.velbon.co.uk

NEWPRO UK LTD
Company ethos: Vortex, a very well-established and respected brand name with new company technology and a value/features/ quality attitude coupled with superb customer service.
Product lines: Vortex binoculars, scopes and monoculars – all with an unlimited lifetime warranty. ROR (Residual Oil Remover) optics cleaner. PhoneSkope smartphone and iPhone adapters for just about every 'scope on the market as well as many binoculars, microscopes and astronomy telescopes for phonescoping still images and video.
New for 2014: Vortex 'Razor' 50mm HD and Vortex 'Razor' 65mm HD 'scopes.
Opening times: Mon-Fri (8.30am-5pm) plus many outdoor events.
Address: Old Sawmills Road, Faringdon, Oxon SN7 7DS; 01367 242 411; (fax) 01367 241 124.
e-mail: sales@newprouk.co.uk www.newprouk.co.uk
www.vortexoptics.co.uk www.phonescope.co.uk

OPTICRON
Company ethos: To deliver the best solution to wildlife enthusiasts irrespective of age, budget or

experience by providing the very best mix of quality, choice and value, backed up with exceptional customer service.
Product lines: Opticron binoculars, monoculars, telescopes, tripods, telephotography/digi-scoping equipment and accessories.
New for 2014: MM3 50 ED Travelscopes. For more information visit: www.opticron.co.uk/Pages/npn.htm
Address: Unit 21, Titan Court, Laporte Way, Luton LU4 8EF; 01582 726 522; (fax) 01582 273 559.
e-mail: sales@opticron.co.uk
www.opticron.co.uk

SWAROVSKI OPTIK
Company ethos: Swarovski Optik is committed to supporting international conservation projects to ensure the survival of some of the world's most endangered species and also supports the Society of Wildlife Artists' annual competition. Our wish is to reveal the beauty of the world 'with the eyes of a hawk and to constantly improve what is good with innovative products.
Product lines: ATX/STX Modular Telescope System, ATS/STS Observation Telescopes, photographic accessories and tripods. EL50, 42 and 32 Swarovision, CL Companion x 30 binoculars.
New from Sept 2013: CL Pockets 8 x 25 and 10 x 25 and new SLC 42 and 56 binoculars.
Address: Unit 11, Tarbot House, Perrywood Business Park, Salfords, Surrey RH1 5JQ; 01737 856 812; (fax) 01737 856 885; e-mail: info@swarovski.com

OPTICAL REPAIRS AND SERVICING

OPTREP OPTICAL REPAIRS

Company ethos: To give a speedy, economical and effective repair service.
Key services: Servicing and repair of binoculars, telescopes etc. Conversant with the special needs of birdwatchers.
Opening times: Mon-Thu (9am-5pm), Fri (9am-2pm)
Address: 16 Wheatfield Road, Selsey, West Sussex PO20 0NY; 01243 601 365.
e-mail: info@opticalrepairs.com
www.opticalrepairs.com

116

NATURE RESERVES AND OBSERVATORIES

Golden Plovers swirl above one of the hides at the RSPB's Frampton Marsh reserve on the Lincolnshire side of the Wash.

ALL ENTRIES in the Reserves Directory are listed on a regional basis. This has been the standard practice for Scotland and Wales in recent editions, whereas the English counties have been listed alphabetically, but it is felt that grouping counties into regions will be more helpful to our readers.

This year we have made every effort to include postcodes for sites, to aid sat-nav users. We hope this proves helpful but welcome reader feedback on any way we can improve this section of the *Yearbook*.

Please e-mail your comments to the Editor David Cromack at: d.cromack@btinternet.com

ENGLAND		SCOTLAND		WALES	
Central England	118	Border Counties	208	Eastern Wales	223
Eastern England	140	Central Scotland	210	Northern Wales	225
Northern England	158	Eastern Scotland	215	Southern Wales	228
South East England	179	Highlands & Islands	219	Western Wales	230
South West England	196				

Central England

Derbyshire, Gloucestershire, Leicestershire & Rutland, Lincolnshire, Northamptonshire, Nottinghamshire, Oxfordshire, Shropshire, Stafford-shire, Warwickshire, West Midlands, Worcestershire

Derbyshire

WITH 75% of the county's population living in towns, Derbyshire can offer birdwatchers many square miles of open countryside, including a large part of the Peak District National Park. Other attractions include Carsington Water, Willington, Ogston Reservoir and Foremark Reservoir which attract huge gull roosts in winter. Valleys, such as those in the Peak District, attract Redstarts, Pied Flycatchers and Wood Warblers.

1. CARR VALE NATURE RESERVE

Derbyshire Wildlife Trust.
Location: Sat nav: S44 6JX. SK 459 701. 1km W of Bolsover on A632 to Chesterfield. Turn L at roundabout (follow brown tourist signs) into Riverside Way. Use County Council's Stockley Trail car park at end of road.
Access: Open all year. Follow footpath (waymarked) around Peter Fidler reserve. Dogs only on leads.
Facilities: Car park, coach parking on approach road, good disabled access, paths, viewing platforms.

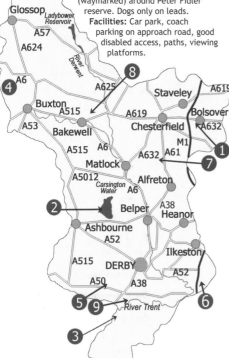

Public transport: Stagecoach services from Chesterfield (Stephenson Place) pass close to the reserve: Mon to Sat - 83 serves Villas Road, 81, 82, 82A and 83 serve the roundabout on A632. Sun - 81A, 82A serve roundabout on A632.
Habitat: Lakes, wader flashes, reedbed, sewage farm, scrub, arable fields.
Key birds: Up to 150 species seen annually. *Winter:* Large numbers of wildfowl including flocks of Wigeon and Teal, also wintering flocks of finches and buntings, Water Rail. Large skeins of geese fly over in early and late winter. *Spring/autumn:* Migrants include Swallows, pipits and thrushes. In September Swallows gather in the marsh, in a gigantic roost of between 10-12,000 birds. They usually attract Hobbies. *Early summer:* Breeding birds, including Reed and Sedge Warblers, Whitethroat, Yellowhammer, Moorhen and Gadwall, plus Skylark. Long list of rarities.
Other notable fauna: Dragonflies, mammals (hare, water vole, harvest mouse, water shrew).
Contact: Derbyshire Wildlife Trust, 01773 881 188; e-mail: enquiries@derbyshirewt.co.uk
www.derbyshirewildlifetrust.org.uk

2. CARSINGTON WATER

Severn Trent Water/RSPB
Location: Sat nav: DE6 1ST. SK 241 515 (for visitor centre and main facilities). Off B5035 Ashbourne to Wirksworth road.
Access: Open all year except Dec 25. Car parks open 7am to sunset (Apr – end Oct) and 7.30am to sunset in winter. Charges at main car park, but Sheepwash car park is free. Good access for wheelchairs. Mobility scooters for hire.
Facilities: Visitor centre with exhibition, restaurant, four shops (inc RSPB), play area and toilets. Four bird hides and three car parks.
Public transport: TM Travel operates service 411 from Matlock and Ashbourne. Call TM on 01142 633 890.
Habitat: Open water, islands, mixed woodland, scrub and grasslands, small reedbed.
Key birds: More than 215 bird species recorded. *Winter:* Wildfowl and a large gull roost plus possibility of divers and rare grebes. *Spring:* Good spring passage including Yellow and White Wagtails, Whimbrel, Black and Arctic Terns. *Summer:* Warblers and breeding waders. *All year:* Tree Sparrows and Willow Tits.
Other notable flora and fauna: Species-rich hay meadows, ancient woodlands with bluebells, three species of orchid, five species of bat, 21 species of butterfly and water vole.
Contact: Carsington Water Visitor Centre, 01629 540 696; e-mail: carsington.water@rspb.org.uk
www.carsingtonbirdclub.co.uk

NATURE RESERVES - CENTRAL ENGLAND

3. DRAKELOW NATURE RESERVE

E-ON, leased to Derbyshire Wildlife Trust.
Location: Sat nav: DE14 3FG. SK 223 204 (OS Landranger 128, Explorer 245). Drakelow Power Station on the outskirts of Branston, one mile NE of Walton-on-Trent, off A38, S of Burton-on-Trent.
Access: Dawn to dusk for Wildlife Trust permit-holders only (plus up to two guests). Dogs on leads.
Facilities: Five hides, car park inside former power station grounds. Nesting platforms for Ospreys erected.
Public transport: None.
Habitat: Disused flooded gravel pits with wooded islands, riverside meadows and reedbeds.
Key birds: *Summer:* Breeding Reed and Sedge Warblers. Water Rail, Hobby. *Winter:* Wildfowl (Goldeneye, Gadwall, Smew), Merlin, Peregrine. Rarities include Great White and Little Egrets, Bittern, Spotted Crake, Ring-necked Duck and American Wigeon.
Other notable flora and fauna: Good for common species of dragonflies and butterflies.
Contact: Trust HQ, 01773 881 188;
e-mail: enquiries@derbyshirewt.co.uk

4. GOYT VALLEY

Forestry Commission.
Location: Sat nav: SK17 6SX (Errwood Hall car park, SK 011 748) for woodland species, Derbyshire Bridge (SK 018 716) for moorland birds. From Buxton take A5004 (Manchester Road), then bear left on Goyt's Lane to Errwood Hall.
Access: Open all year. Footpath between Errwood Hall and Goyt's Clough Quarry. Use Old Coach Road for walk between Derbyshire Bridge and Burbage.
Facilities: Toilets at Derbyshire Bridge, Goyt's Clough Quarry and Bonsal Cob. Several picnic sites.
Public transport: Bowers bus services along A5004.
Habitat: Conifer woodland, moorland, River Goyt and two reservoirs.
Key birds: *Spring/summer:* Breeding Wood Warbler, Pied and Spotted Flycatchers, Tree Pipit, Redstart and Cuckoo, plus common woodland species. Long-eared Owls and Goshawks also present. Grey Wagtail and Dipper on river and Common Sandpiper on Errwood Reservoir. Ring Ouzel, Red Grouse, Curlew and Whinchat breed on moorland stretches.
Contact: Forestry Commission 0117 906 6000;
e-mail: fe.england@forestry.gsi.gov.uk

5. HILTON GRAVEL PITS

Derbyshire Wildlife Trust.
Location: Sat nav: DE65 5FN (Willowpit Lane). SK 249 315. From Derby, take A516 from Mickleover W past Etwall onto A50 junction at Hilton. Turn R at first island onto Willowpit Lane. Turn L next to a large white house and park next to the gate. Follow track along S side of the pools.
Access: Open all year. Main path and viewing screen suitable for wheelchair users. Dogs on leads only on main perimeter track.

Facilities: Tracks, boardwalks, viewing screens, bench.
Public transport: Local Trent Barton Villager V1 & V2 bus services from Derby to Burton-on-Trent and Arriva X50 bus service from Derby to Stoke-on-Trent.
Habitat: Ponds, lakes, scrub, woodland, fen.
Key birds: *Spring/summer:* Great Crested Grebe, Common Tern, warblers. *Winter:* Wildfowl, Siskin, Goldcrest. *All year:* All three woodpeckers, Kingfisher, tits inc possible Willow Tit, Tawny Owl, Bullfinch.
Other notable flora and fauna: Dragonflies (15 species inc emperor, ruddy darter and red-eyed damselfly), great crested newt, orchids, black poplar.
Contact: Trust HQ, 01773 881 188;
e-mail: enquiries@derbyshirewt.co.uk

6. OGSTON RESERVOIR

Severn Trent Water/Ogston Bird Club
Location: Sat nav: DE55 6FN. SK 371 603. From Matlock, take A615 E to B6014, just after Tansley. From A61 (Alfreton to Chesterfield road), at the White Bear PH, Stretton turn onto B6014 towards Tansley, cross the railway, take to left fork in the road and continue over the hill, the reservoir on L after the hill.
Access: View from roads, car parks or the public hide. Suitable for smaller coaches. Heronry in nearby Ogston Carr Wood (private property) viewable from road, W of reservoir. Ogston Bird Club organises monthly guided walks (see website for details).
Facilities: Three car parks (no charges). Toilets now closed. Ogston BC members-only hide and public hide both wheelchair-accessible. Information pack provided to all new bird club members.
Public transport: Hulleys 63 bus service (Chesterfield to Clay Cross) and 64 service (Clay Cross to Matlock) both serves N end of reservoir (not Sundays).
Habitat: Open water, pasture, mixed woodland.
Key birds: All three woodpeckers, Little and Tawny Owls, Kingfisher, Grey Wagtail, warblers. Passage raptors (inc. Osprey), terns and waders. *Winter:* Gull roost attracts thousands of birds, inc regular Glaucous and Iceland Gulls. Top inland site for Bonaparte's Gull and also attracts Caspian/ Herring Gull complex. Good numbers of wildfowl, tit and finch flocks.
Contact: Peter Birley, Secretary, Ogston Bird Club, 35 Rosemary Drive, Alvaston, Derby DE24 0TA. 01332 753 078; peter.birley@sky.com; www.ogstonbirdclub.co.uk

7. PADLEY GORGE

The National Trust (East Midlands).
Location: Sat nav: S11 7TZ (Longshaw visitor centre). From Sheffield, head SW on A625. After eight miles, turn L on B6521 to Nether Padley. Grindleford Station is just off B6521 (NW of Nether Padley) and one mile NE of Grindleford village.
Access: All year, dawn to dusk. Not suitable for disabled people or those unused to steep climbs. Some of the paths are rocky. Dogs on leads only.
Facilities: Café, shop and toilets (inc disabled) at Longshaw visitor centre. RADAR key needed for Hollin Bank, Hathersage toilets.

Public transport: Bus: from Sheffield to Bakewell stops at Grindleford/Nether Padley. Tel: 01709 566 000. Train: from Sheffield to Manchester Piccadilly stops at Grindleford Station. Tel: 0161 228 2141.
Habitat: Steep-sided valley containing largest area of sessile oak woodland in south Pennines.
Key birds: *Summer:* Pied Flycatcher, Spotted Flycatcher, Redstart, Wheatear, Whinchat, Wood Warbler, Tree Pipit.
Contact: National Trust, High Peak Estate Office, 01433 670 368. www.nationaltrust.org.uk

8. WILLINGTON GRAVEL PITS
Derbyshire Wildlife Trust
Location: Sat nav: DE65 6BX (Repton Road). SK 285 274. From A50 'Toyota Island' head towards Willington and Repton. Go through village towards Repton. Just before bridge over River Trent, turn R onto un-made track (Meadow Lane). Park here and walk along lane.

Access: Access only along Meadow Lane to viewing platforms all year. No access on site. Steps prevent wheelchair access to platforms.
Facilities: Viewing platforms and benches. Limited parking in lane.
Public transport: Local trains stop at Willington, local Trent Barton Villager V3 bus service from Derby to Burton-on-Trent.
Habitat: Open water, reedbed, shingle island, grassland.
Key birds: *Summer:* Breeding Lapwing, other waders, Common Tern, raptors, including Peregrine, Kestrel, Hobby and Sparrowhawk, Sand Martin, wildfowl. *Winter:* Waders and large flocks of wildfowl including Wigeon, Teal, Pochard and Shoveler. *Passage:* Large numbers of Curlew in spring, up to 20 species of waders in spring/autumn.
Other notable flora and fauna: Short-leaved water starwort. Several species of dragonfly, plus occasional otter signs, fox and other mammals.
Contact: Trust HQ, 01773 881 188.

Gloucestershire

STRADDLING the mighty Severn estuary and river, Gloucestershire can boast a world-famous wetland site in the form of Slimbridge, but on the other side of the river, the Forest of Dean is one of the best places in Britain to see good numbers of Goshawks displaying in February and March. The county Wildlife Trust manages more than 60 nature reserves.

1. COOMBE HILL CANAL & MEADOWS
Gloucestershire Wildlife Trust
Location: Sat nav: GL19 4BB. SO 887 272. SSSI midway between Gloucester and Tewkesbury off the A38 at Coombe Hill. Take minor road by Swan Inn where A38 meets A4019.
Access: Open at all times. Main canalside path (one mile) is also used by horse riders so can be rutted and muddy. Can flood after heavy rain. Wheelchair access not possible. Dogs only on leads.
Facilities: Hard-surface parking for six vehicles. Two hides overlook the wetland.
Habitat: Wetland, disused canal, hedgerows and adjoining 200 acres of meadows and former farmland.
Key birds: Common wildfowl, Kingfisher, plus waders such as Greenshank, Ringed Plover and Snipe and birds of prey such as Peregrine, Hen Harrier and Goshawk. Warblers and other migrants in summer.
Contact: Trust HQ, 01452 383 333;
e-mail: info@gloucestershirewildlifetrust.co.uk
www.gloucestershirewildlifetrust.co.uk

2. HIGHNAM WOODS
RSPB (South West England Office).
Location: Sat nav: GL2 8AA. SO 778 190. Sign-posted on A40 three miles W of Gloucester.

Access: Open at all times, no permit required. The nature trails can be very muddy. Some limited wheelchair access. Dogs allowed on leads. Groups should book ahead.
Facilities: One nature trail (approx 1.5 miles).
Public transport: Contact Traveline (public transport information) on 0871 2002 233 between 7am-10pm each day.
Habitat: Ancient woodland in the Severn Vale with areas of coppice and scrub.
Key birds: *Spring/summer:* The reserve has about 12 pairs of breeding Nightingales, plus common migrant warblers and Spotted Flycatcher. Resident birds include all three woodpeckers, Marsh Tit, Buzzard and Sparrowhawk. Ravens are frequently seen. *Winter:* Feeding site near car park good for woodland birds.
Other notable flora and fauna: Tintern spurge in late June-early July. White-letter hairstreak and white admiral butterflies seen annually.
Contact: The Site Manager, 01594 562 852; e-mail: highnam.woods@rspb.org.uk; www.rspb.org.uk

3. NAGSHEAD
RSPB (South West England Office).
Location: Sat nav: GL15 4JQ. SO 606 085. In Forest of Dean, N of Lydney. Signed immediately W of Parkend village on B4431 road to Coleford.
Access: Reserve open at all times, no permit required. Information centre (with toilets) open 10am to 4pm at weekends between Easter and August Bank Holiday. The reserve is hilly but there is limited wheelchair access. Dogs on leads during bird nesting season and under close control at other times.
Facilities: Two nature trails (one mile and 2.25 miles). Information centre, with toilet facilities (including disabled), open at weekends mid-Apr to end Aug.
Public transport: Buses run from Lydney Bus Station

(circular), to the stop along B4431 signposted to Coleford. Contact Traveline (0871 2002 233).
Habitat: Much of the reserve is 200-year-old oak plantations, grazed in some areas by sheep. The rest of the reserve is a mixture of open areas and conifer/mixed woodland.
Key birds: *Spring:* Pied Flycatcher, Wood Warbler and commoner warblers, Redstart. *Summer:* Nightjar. *Winter:* Siskin, Crossbill in some years. *All year:* Buzzard, Raven, Hawfinch, Woodcock, all three woodpeckers.
Other notable fauna: Golden-ringed dragonfly seen annually. Silver-washed and small pearl-bordered fritillaries and white admiral butterflies present.
Contact: The Site Manager, 01594 562 852; e-mail: nagshead@rspb.org.uk

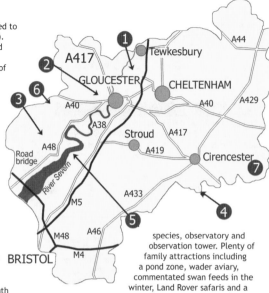

4. SHORNCOTE REEDBED

Cotswold Water Park Society.
Location: Sat nav: GL7 5US (South Cerney car park). Lakes 84 and 85, Cotswold Water Park. From A419 Cirencester to Swindon road, take B4696 towards Cotswold Water Park West. Turn R at crossroads towards South Cerney. Follow road through village and park in playing fields car park after sharp R bend (SU 044 970). Take footpath through playing fields, cross road and continue on path through reedbeds to small lakes and hides.
Access: Open at all times, most paths firm and flat so suitable for wheelchairs.
Facilities: Toilets, refreshments, car parking and information available from nearby Keynes Country Park. Two hides.
Public transport: Bus: from Kemble, Cheltenham, Cirencester and Swindon. 08457 090 899. Train: Kemble station four miles. 08457 484 950.
Habitat: Lakes with reedbed, marsh, ditches, islands and loafing areas.
Key birds: *Winter:* Common wildfowl, Smew, Peregrine, Merlin, Bittern, Stonechat. *Summer:* Breeding ducks, Little Grebe, warblers, Hobby, Snipe, Sand Martin, Reed Bunting.
Other notable flora and fauna: Otter, water vole, several species of dragonfly and damselfly.
Contact: Cotswold Water Park Soc, 01793 752 413.

5. SLIMBRIDGE

The Wildfowl & Wetlands Trust.
Location: Sat nav: GL2 7BS. SO 723 048. On banks of River Severn, S of Gloucester. Signposted from M5 (exit 13 or 14).
Access: Open daily (9am-5.30pm or 5pm in winter) except Dec 25. Last entry 30 mins before closing. Wheelchair hire (book beforehand) – all paths wheelchair accessible. Free parking. Admission charges for non-WWT members. Assistance dogs only.
Facilities: Restaurant, gift shop, gallery, cinema, discovery centre. Outdoor facilities inc 15 hides, tropical house, worldwide collection of wildfowl

species, observatory and observation tower. Plenty of family attractions including a pond zone, wader aviary, commentated swan feeds in the winter, Land Rover safaris and a canoe safari trail. Binoculars for hire.
Public transport: Request bus service – contact www.stroud.gov.uk. Nearest train station at Cam and Dursley (4 miles).
Habitat: Reedbed, saltmarsh, freshwater pools, mudflats and wet grassland.
Key birds: More than 200 species each year. *Winter:* Between 30,000 to 40,000 wildfowl esp. Bewick's Swan, White-fronted Goose, Wigeon, Teal, Pintail. Waders inc Lapwing, Golden Plover, Spotted Redshank and Little Stint. Often there are large roosts of Starlings and gulls. *Breeding:* Kingfisher, Lapwing, Redshank, Oystercatcher, Common Tern, Reed Bunting and a good range of warblers. *Passage:* Waders, terns and gulls, inc Mediterranean and Yellow-legged Gulls. Yellow Wagtail and large passerine movements. Hobbies now reach double figures and good list of rarities.
Other notable flora and fauna: Brown hare, otter, polecat and water vole. Scarce chaser and hairy dragonfly among 22 recorded species.
Contact: Marketing Manager, 01453 891 900; e-mail: info.slimbridge@wwt.org.uk

6. SYMONDS YAT

RSPB/Forestry Commission England.
Location: Sat nav: HR9 6JL. SO 563 160. Hill-top site on the edge of Forest of Dean, three miles N of Coleford on B4432, signposted from Forest Enterprise car park. Also signposted from A40, S of Ross-on-Wye.
Access: Open at all times. RSPB Information Officer on site daily, April to August.
Facilities: Car park (fee payable), toilets with adapted facilities for disabled visitors, picnic area, drinks and light snacks. Environmental education programmes available.

Public transport: Very limited.
Habitat: Cliff above the River Wye and woodland.
Key birds: *Summer*: Peregrine, Buzzard, Goshawk, Raven and woodland species. Telescope is set up daily by RSPB volunteers to watch the Peregrines on the nest (April to August).
Contact: RSPB, 01594 562 852.

7. WHELFORD POOLS

Gloucestershire Wildlife Trust
Location: Sat nav: GL7 4EH. SU 174 995. Lakes lying in eastern section of Cotswold Water Park between Fairford and Lechlade, from minor road south of A417.
Access: Open at all times. Dogs must be on leads.
Facilities: Car park for 12 vehicles (one designated

for disabled). Two bird hides.
Public transport: Cycle path from Lechlade.
Habitat: Former gravel pit workings now reverted to nature – part of a SSSI. Two large lakes, plus three smaller pools for dragonflies.
Key birds: Wintering wildfowl inc Wigeon, Pochard and Tufted Ducks, plus occasional Bittern sightings. *Spring/summer*: Common Tern, Kingfisher and Nightingale, plus breeding Sedge Warbler, Reed Bunting and Great Crested Grebe. Artificial nesting bank for Sand Martins. Waders on passage.
Other notable flora and fauna: County's only site for pea mussel. Emperor, migrant hawker, blacked-tailed skimmer and red-eyed damselfly all breed.
Contact: Reserve manager (GWT) 01452 383 333; e-mail: info@gloucestershirewildlifetrust.co.uk

Leicestershire and Rutland

AN INLAND COUNTY better known for fox hunting than its birding potential, Leicestershire can boast 31 Wildlife Trust reserves with a broad range of habitats. However, it is the adjoining county of Rutland that holds the jewel in the crown — Rutland Water with its breeding Ospreys, huge numbers of wildfowl, and good selection of passage waders — while nearby Eyebrook Reservoir is excellent for Smew, sizeable Golden Plover flocks and roosting gulls in winter.

EYEBROOK RESERVOIR

Corby & District Water Co.
Location: Sat nav: LE15 9JG. SP 853 964. Reservoir built 1940. S of Uppingham, from unclassified road W of A6003 at Stoke Dry.
Access: Access to 150 acres of private grounds granted to members of Leics and Rutland OS and Rutland NHS. All visitors should sign in at fishing lodge. Organised groups should contact Andy Miller on 01536 772 930. Otherwise view from roadside lay-bys.
Facilities: SSSI since 1956. Three bird hides. Fishing season March - Nov. Toilets and visitor centre at fishing lodge.
Public transport: None.
Habitat: Open water, plantations and pasture.
Key birds: *Summer*: Good populations of breeding birds, sightings of Ospreys and Red Kite. Passage waders and Black Tern. *Winter*: Wildfowl (inc. Goldeneye, Goosander, Smew) and waders. Tree Sparrow and Yellowhammer at feeding station, also Barn and Short-eared Owl can be seen hunting at dusk near Great Easton village (close to recycling centre).
Other notable flora and fauna: Otter, muntjac deer, red darter, demoiselles and blue damselfly, scalloped hazel and riband wave moths.
Contact: Andy Miller, Fishery Estate Manager, 01536 772 930; e-mail: fishing.lodge@tatsteel.com
www.eyebrook.com

NARBOROUGH BOG

Leics and Rutland Wildlife Trust.
Location: Sat nav: LE19 2DB. SP 549 979. Reserve lies between River Soar and M1, 8km S of Leicester. From city, turn L off B4114 just before going under motorway, follow track to sports club. Park near club house and walk across recreation ground to reserve entrance.
Access: Open at all times, please keep to paths. Not suitable for wheelchairs. Dogs on short leads only.
Facilities: None. Small bus/coach could park in sports field car park.
Public transport: Narborough train station. Buses X5, 140 to Narborough then 1km walk. Contact Traveline for more information on 0871 200 22 33.
Habitat: Peat bog SSSI (the only substantial deposit in Leicestershire), wet woodland, reedbed, dense scrub and fen meadow.
Key birds: More than 130 species of birds recorded including all three species of woodpeckers, six species of tit, Tawny Owl, Sparrowhawk and Kingfisher.
Other notable flora and fauna: Good range of butterflies including common blue, meadow brown, large and small skippers, small heath and gatekeeper. Banded demoiselles, also good for moths and beetles. Harvest mice and water voles recorded, also breeding grass snakes. Meadow saxifrage, common meadow-rue and marsh thistle.
Contact: Trust HQ, 0116 272 0444; e-mail: info@lrwt.org.uk

RUTLAND WATER

Location: Two nature reserves — 1: Egleton Reserve (Sat nav: LE15 8BP. SK 878 075: from Egleton village off A6003 or A606 S of Oakham. Hosts British Birdwatching Fair every August. 2: Lyndon Reserve SK 894 058: south shore E of Manton village off A6003 S of Oakham. Follow 'nature reserve' signs to car park.
Access: 1: Open daily 9am-5pm, (4pm Nov to Jan).

2: Open winter (Sat, Sun 10am-4pm), Summer daily (9am-5pm). Day permits available for both. Reduced admission for disabled and carers. Closed Dec 25 and 26. Badger-watching hide can be booked from mid-April to July.

Facilities: 1: Birdwatching Centre has toilets and disabled access, mobility scooter for hire, conference facilities. 27 hides - disabled access possible to 20 hides. Nine new lagoons planned. 2: Interpretive centre toilets, including disabled, paths, use of a mobility scooter. Seven hides, four accessible to wheelchairs.Trail leaflet.

Public transport: None.

Habitat: Ramsar designated reservoir, lagoons, scrapes, woods, meadows, plantations, reedbeds.

Key birds: *Spring/autumn*: Outstanding wader passage, with up to 28 species recorded. Also wide range of harriers, owls, passerine flocks, terns (Black, Arctic, breeding Common, occasional Little and Sandwich). *Winter*: Up to 28 species of wildfowl (inc internationally important numbers of Gadwall and Shoveler). Also Goldeneye, Smew, Goosander, rare grebes, all divers, Ruff. *Summer*: Ospreys among 70 breeding species.

Other notable flora and fauna: Otter, badger, fox, weasel, stoat. Up to 20 species of dragon and damselflies and 24 butterfly species.

Contact: Tim Appleton, 01572 770 651; www.rutlandwater.org.uk www.ospreys.org.uk

SENCE VALLEY FOREST PARK

Forestry Commission

Location: Sat nav: LE67 6NW. SK 400 115. Within The National Forest. 10 NW of Leicester and two miles SW of Coalville, between Ibstock and Ravenstone. The car park is signed from A447 N of Ibstock.

Access: Open all year: 8am to 7pm (April 1 to Sept 30; 9am to 4pm rest of year. (precise times on noticeboard). Lower car park (2.2m height barrier) gives easy access to wheelchair-friendly surfaced paths. Week's notice required for coach or minibuses visits.

Facilities: Two car parks, toilets (including disabled and baby-changing facilities), information and recent sightings boards, hide, all-abilities surfaced trails.

Public transport: None.

Habitat: New forest (native broadleaf, mixed and pine), rough grassland, wildflower meadow, pools, wader scrape, River Sence.

Key birds: *Spring/summer*: Artificial Sand Martin nesting wall, Wheatear, Whinchat, Redstart, Common and Green Sandpiper, Ringed and Little Ringed Plovers, Redshank. Dunlin and Greenshank frequent, possible Wood Sandpiper. Reed Bunting, Meadow Pipit, Skylark, Linnet, Yellow Wagtail. Possible Quail. Kestrel and Barn Owl occasionally. *Winter*: Stonechat, Redpoll, Short-eared Owl, Goosander and Wigeon possible.

Contact: Forestry Commission, 01283 551 211; e-mail: enquiries@nationalforest.org www.nationalforest.org

SWITHLAND RESERVOIR

Severn Trent Water

Location: Sat nav: LE7 7SB. SK 558 140. Lies south of Quorn, east of A6 (Leicester to Loughborough road). Use minor road between Swithland and Rothley for southern section. For northern section take Kinchley Lane along eastern shore to the dam.

Access: No access to the water's edge– view from public roads.

Facilities: None.

Public transport: None.

Habitat: Large reservoir (mile long) divided by Great Central Railway line. Small area of woodland (Buddon Wood).

Key birds: Good numbers of common wildfowl are regular, but the site has produced sightings of seaduck such as Common Scoter, Scaup and Long-tailed Duck. Black-necked Grebe seen in late summer/autumn, while Mediterranean Gulls are seen annually. High water levels curb wader sightings, but Kingfishers are regular and Ravens are seen daily. All three woodpeckers are in Buddon Wood, along with a range of woodland species. It is the county's best site for wintering Peregrines. Also Buzzards, Sparrowhawks and Hobbies (summer). Good track record of rarities in recent years.

Other notable flora and fauna: Buddon Wood along Kinchley Lane is good for purple hairstreak butterflies and orange underwing moths – look for the latter around silver birch.

WATERMEAD COUNTRY PARK

Leics County Council/Leicester City Council

Location: LE7 1PD. SK 613 111. Located off Wanlip Road, Syston, six miles north of Leicester city centre.

Access: Open from 7am all year. Closing times vary from 4pm (Dec-Jan) to 8pm (May-Aug). Reedbed Nature Reserve open 9am to 4pm. North entrance in Wanlip Road gives access to four parking areas. Southern entrance is in Alderton Close, Thurmaston. Car parking fees. Wheelchair access on 9km of surfaced tracks. RADAR key needed by mobility scooter riders to negotiate kissing gates on perimeter track.

Facilities: Four bird hides in nature reserve area. Heronry hide now closed. Toilets, inc disabled. Sand Martin nesting wall.

Public transport: Buses on the 5/5A/6 route from Leicester to Syston/East Goscote/Melton buses every few minutes in the daytime to/from Leicester and up to 3 buses an hour on Sundays. Get off at Alderton Close.

Habitat: River Soar and Grand Union Canal, plus 12 lakes and pools, wildflower meadow, woodland and reedbeds (one of largest in Midlands). Park stretches nearly two miles in length. Wanlip Meadows can be viewed from Plover Hide.

Key birds: 200 species recorded, including common wildfowl, Little Egret, Kingfisher, Water Rail, Cetti's Warbler. *Winter*: Bittern, Caspian Gull, Yellow-legged Gull and Scandinavian thrushes. *Passage*: Garganey

123

and Black Terns. Wanlip Meadows very good for waders, including Little Ringed Plover, and is the county's best site for Temminck's Stint.
Other notable flora and fauna: Otters now regular,

but elusive. Emperor and other dragonfly species.
Contact: Tel: 0116 305 5000 (8.30am - 5pm Mon - Thu, 8.30am - 4.30pm Fri); e-mail: countryparks@ leics.gov.uk (week days only).

Lincolnshire

THIS large rural county sits between two major bird-friendly estuaries — the Humber and the Wash — and boasts a good number of coastal sites such as Frieston Shore and Gibraltar Point which are attractive to migrants and wintering wildfowl. Agriculture dominates inland, but there are reservoirs which can produce interesting birds. Lincoln Cathedral, one high point in a very flat county has attracted breeding Peregrines.

1. ALKBOROUGH FLATS

North Lincs Council
Location: Sat nav: DN15 9JJ. SE 880 218 (Julian's Bower maze) at Alkborough village. Follow Back Street past church to Prospect Lane. Located on S bank of Humber where it meets the Rivers Trent and Ouse.
Access: Open at all times. Limited access for disabled visitors.
Facilities: Four bird hides, including 5m tower hide at eastern end of site. Wheelchair-friendly footpaths.
Public transport: Bus service to Alkborough from Scunthorpe. Contact Traveline on 0871 200 2233.
Habitat: 440 hectares of tidal mudflats and wet grassland created by breaching the river defences to protect homes from flooding.
Key birds: 197 species recorded. Lying on a key migration route, the sites attracts geese and ducks in large numbers, and Long-billed Dowitcher, Lesser Yellowlegs and Marsh Sandpiper recently brought the site's wader total to 40 species. *Winter:* Huge flocks of Lapwings (10,000 regularly) and Golden Plover (up to 12,000 in the wider area), plus Marsh Harrier, Hen Harrier, Peregrine and Merlin.   lowhammer, Linnet, Water Pipit and Grey Wagtail, while a large flock of Barnacle Geese can be seen at nearby Whitton Sands. *Summer:* Marsh Harriers have attempted to breed and Hobbies attack flocks of Sand Martins in Aug/Sept.
Other notable flora and fauna: Roe deer, badger, brown hare, noctule bat. Wall brown among a range of butterflies and black-tailed skimmer among the dragonflies.
Contact: Site manager Anna Moody 01724 721 269; e-mail: anna.moody@northlincs.gov.uk
Alkborough Flats Project: http://www.northlincs.gov.uk/leisure/tourism/brigg-tourist-information-centre/

2. DONNA NOOK

Lincolnshire Wildlife Trust.
Location: Sat nav: LN11 7PB. TF 422 998. Several access points off the main A1031 coastal road with parking facilities at Stonebridge (TF 422 998),

Howden's Pullover (TF 449 952), Sea Lane, Saltfleet (TF 456 944) and Saltfleet Haven (TF 4679 35).
Access: Donna Nook beach is closed on weekdays as this is an active bombing range, but dunes remain open. Dogs on leads. Some disabled access.
Facilities: No toilets or visitor centre.
Habitat: Dunes, slacks and intertidal areas, seashore, mudflats, sandflats.
Key birds: *Summer:* Little Tern, Ringed Plover, Oystercatcher. *Winter:* Brent Goose, Shelduck, Twite, Lapland Bunting, Shore Lark, Linnet.
Other notable flora and fauna: The reserve has one of the largest and most accessible breeding colonies of grey seals in the UK. Other mammals include fox, badger, stoat and weasel and three species of shrew have been identified. Common lizard.
Contact: Lincolnshire Wildlife Trust, 01507 526 667; e-mail: info@lincstrust.co.uk; www.lincstrust.org.uk

3. EPWORTH TURBARY

Lincolnshire Wildlife Trust.
Location: Sat nav: DN9 1EA. SE 758 036. SW of Scunthorpe. Take A18 W from Scunthorpe then A161 S to Epworth. Turn R on High Street, and head towards Wroot. The entrance is near bridge over Skyer's Drain. Park inside gate, which should be kept closed, or on verge adjoining reserve. Park well away from corner.
Access: Open at all times. Keep to waymarked paths and use hides when viewing open area to avoid disturbing birds on the ponds.
Facilities: Car park, way-marked trail, two hides.
Habitat: One of the few relics of raised bog in Lincolnshire. Though extensively dug for peat in the past, areas of active sphagnum bog still exist. Areas of reed swamp and mixed fen vegetation, also considerable area of birch woodland of varying ages.
Key birds: *Spring/summer:* Breeding birds include Tree Pipit, warblers, finches, Green and Great Spotted Woodpeckers and Woodcock. Greenshank, Green Sandpiper and Little Grebe are attracted to the wet area. Around Steve's Pond, occasional Hobby and Marsh Harrier, plus Teal, Little Grebe, Tree Pipit, Sparrowhawk and Buzzard. Willow Tit, Long-tailed Tit, Reed Bunting and Willow Warbler in the woodland areas. Occasionally Corn Buntings on the adjoining farmland. *Autumn/winter:* Large flocks of Rooks, Crows and Jackdaws roost in reserve. At Pantry's Pond in winter occasional Hen Harrier. Other birds include Yellowhammer, Linnet, Jay and Magpie. Sometimes in winter Long-eared Owls can be observed roosting close to the path.
Other notable flora and fauna: 11 species of breeding dragonflies and damselflies recorded. Wood tiger moth is well established. Plants include sneezewort, yellow and purple loosestrife, meadow-

rue, and devil's-bit scabious.
Contact: Lincolnshire Wildlife Trust, 01507 526 667; e-mail: info@lincstrust.co.uk ww.lincstrust.org.uk

4. FRAMPTON MARSH

RSPB (Eastern England Office).
Location: Sat nav: PE20 1BA. TF 356 392. Four miles SE of Boston. From A16 follow signs to Frampton then Frampton Marsh.
Access: Visitor Centre open 10am to 4pm each day (Oct-Mar) except Dec 25, 10am to 4pm weekdays, 10am to 5pm weekends (Apr-Sept). Footpaths and hides open at all times. Visitor Centre (including toilets), footpaths and hides all suitable for wheelchairs.
Facilities: Visitor Centre with hot drinks and snacks, three hides, footpaths, benches, viewpoints, 50-space car park (three for disabled visitors), binocular hire, bicycle rack, free information leaflets and events programmes.
Public transport: None.
Habitat: Saltmarsh, wet grassland, freshwater scrapes and developing reedbed.
Key birds: *Summer:* Breeding Redshank, Avocet, Lapwing, Skylark, Little Ringed Plover, Ringed Plover, Sand Martin and several species of ducks plus passage waders (inc Greenshank, Curlew Sandpiper, Wood Sandpiper, Little and Temminck's Stints, Ruff and Black-tailed Godwit), Marsh Harrier and Hobby. *Winter:* Hen Harrier, Short-eared Owl, Merlin, dark-bellied Brent Goose, Twite, Golden Plover, Lapland Bunting.
Other notable flora and fauna: Water vole, stoat. Dragonflies inc emperor, hawkers, chasers and darters. Common butterflies plus wall brown, painted lady and speckled wood. Scarce pug, star wort and crescent striped moths on saltmarsh. Important brackish water flora and fauna includes nationally scarce spiral tassleweed and several rare beetles.
Contact: Reserve Manager, 01205 724 678; e-mail: lincolnshirewashreserves@rspb.org.uk

5. FREISTON SHORE

RSPB (Eastern England Office).
Location: Sat nav: PE22 0LZ. TF 398 425. Four miles E of Boston. From A52 at Haltoft End follow signs to Freiston Shore.
Access: Open at all times, free.
Facilities: Footpaths, two car parks, bird hide, wetland trail. Free information leaflets on site, guided walks programme. Bicycle rack, benches, viewpoints, seawatching shelter, viewing screen and viewing platform.
Public transport: None.
Habitat: Saltmarsh, saline lagoon, mudflats, wet grassland.
Key birds: *Summer:* Breeding waders including Avocet, Ringed Plover and Oystercatcher, Common Tern, Corn Bunting and Tree Sparrow. *Winter:* Twite, dark-bellied Brent Goose, wildfowl, waders, Short-

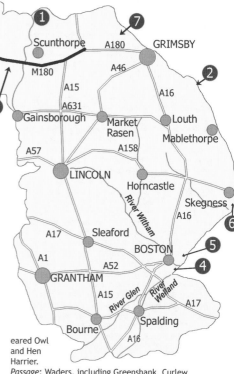

eared Owl and Hen Harrier.
Passage: Waders, including Greenshank, Curlew Sandpiper and Little Stint. *Autumn:* Occasional seabirds including Arctic and Great Skuas.
Other notable flora and fauna: Water vole, muntjac and roe deer, stoat. Dragonflies inc emperor, hawkers, chasers and darters. Common butterflies plus wall brown, painted lady and speckled wood. Scarce pug, star wort and crescent striped moths on saltmarsh. Important lagoon invertebrates and plants.
Contact: As Frampton Marsh

6. GIBRALTAR POINT NNR & BIRD OBSERVATORY

Lincolnshire Wildlife Trust.
Location: Sat nav: PE24 4SU. TF 556 580. Three miles S of Skegness on the N edge of The Wash. Signposted from Skegness town centre.
Access: Reserve open dawn-dusk all year. Charges for car parking. Free admission to reserve, visitor centre and toilets. Some access restrictions to sensitive sites at S end, open access to N. Dogs on leads at all times — no dogs on beach during summer. Visitor centre and toilets suitable for wheelchairs, as well as network of surfaced foot paths. Bird observatory and four hides suitable for wheelchairs. Day visit groups must be booked in advance. Access for coaches. Contact The Wash Study Centre for residential or day visits.
Facilities: Visitor centre and café open 10am to 4pm (Apr-end Oct), 11am to 3pm weekdays, 11am to 4pm

weekends (Nov-end Mar). Site also location of Wash Study Centre and Bird Observatory. Field centre is an ideal base for birdwatching/natural history groups in spring, summer and autumn. Toilets open daily. Footpaths bisect all major habitats. Public hides overlook freshwater and brackish lagoons. Wash viewpoint overlooks saltmarsh and mudflats.

Public transport: Bus service from Skegness runs occasionally but summer service only. Otherwise taxi/car from Skegness. Cycle route from Skegness.

Habitat: Sand dune grassland and scrub, saltmarshes and mudflats, freshwater marsh and lagoons.

Key birds: Large scale visible migration during spring and autumn passage. Internationally important populations of non-breeding waders between Jul-Mar (peak Sep/Oct). Winter flocks of Brent Geese, Shelduck and Wigeon on flats and marshes with Hen Harrier, Merlin and Short-eared Owl often present. Red-throated Divers offshore, (peak Feb). A colony of Little Tern and Ringed Plover in summer. More than 100 species can be seen in a day during May and Sept. Good passage of autumn seabirds in northerly winds.

Other notable flora and fauna: Patches of pyramidal orchids. Grey and common seal colonies, with porpoises offshore in most months. Butterflies include brown argus and green hairstreak.

Contact: Reserve and wildlife: Kev Wilson. Visit bookings: Jill Hardy, Sykes Farm, Gibraltar Point Nature Reserve, Gibraltar Road, Skegness, Lincs PE24 4SU. 01754 898 057; e-mail: kwilson@linwtrust.co.uk or gibadmin@lincstrust.co.uk www.lincstrust.org.uk GibraltarPointBIrdObservatory.blogspot.com

7. KILLINGHOLME HAVEN PITS

Lincolnshire Wildlife Trust.

Location: Sat nav: DN40 3LX. TA 165 199 NW of Grimsby. Take A180 W, then A1173 towards Immingham. Turn L at roundabout and continue to A160. Turn L then R onto Eastfield road. Turn R onto Chase Hill road then L onto Haven road. The reserve is situated to the S of Haven Road on the approach to North Killingholme Haven.

Access: Park carefully on the road. No general access to the reserve, but adequate viewing points are available from the public road and bank-top footpath.

Facilities: None. **Habitat:** Marsh/wetland.

Key birds: Diving ducks, such as Pochard, Tufted Duck and, occasionally, Scaup. Breeding species include Little Grebe, and Reed, Sedge, Willow and Grasshopper Warblers. The two large shallow pits are of the greatest importance for birds, particularly for migrant waders in spring and autumn. Spotted Redshank, Dunlin, Greenshank, Common Sandpiper, Little Ringed Plover, Ruff and Black-tailed Godwit, the latter often in large numbers, are regular visitors. Long list of scarce and rare species, including Spoonbill, Avocet, Little Egret, Little and Temminck's Stints, Red-necked Phalarope, and Curlew, Pectoral, Baird's and White-rumped Sandpipers.

Contact: Lincolnshire Wildlife Trust, 01507 526 667; e-mail: info@lincstrust.co.uk

Northamptonshire

RED KITES were re-introduced in the area north-east of Corby and they, along with Buzzards, are thriving and spreading out. Blatherwycke Lake is good for Mandarins, while Thrapston and Ditchford gravel pits, Pitsford and Hollowell reservoirs are good for a range of wildfowl, especially in winter. Harrington airfield can hold good numbers of wintering Short-eared Owls and other raptors.

1. DITCHFORD LAKES

Beds, Cambs, Northants Wildlife Trust.
Beds, Cambs & Northants Wildlife Trust.

Location: Sat nav: NN8 1RL. SP 930 678. From Wellingborough, take A45 towards Rushden and Higham Ferrers. Take exit marked A5001 to Rushden. Turn L at roundabout onto Ditchford Road towards Irthlingborough/Ditchford. 500 m on R is small car park.

Access: Rough grass paths, flat overall. Some areas soft and muddy especially in winter. Grazing animals at certain times of the year. Dogs on leads.

Facilities: Car park (height restrictions).

Public transport: None.

Habitat: Part of the upper Nene valley floodplain — a complex of old gravel pits, grassland, lakes

surrounded by mature scrub.

Key birds: *Winter*: Common Sandpiper, Snipe, Teal, Wigeon, Gadwall, Tufted Duck. *Spring*: Redshank, Oystercatcher, Cetti's Warbler, Little Grebe, Grey Heron. *Summer*: Reed Warbler, Sedge Warbler, Swift, House Martin. *Autumn*: Snipe, Great Crested Grebe, Moorhen, Coot, Grey Heron.

Other notable flora and fauna: Hairy dragonfly, grass snake, otter. Plants include marsh woundwort, dropwort, great burnet.

Contact: Reserves Manager, 01604 405 285; e-mail: northamptonshire@wildlifebcn.org

2. PITSFORD WATER

Anglian Water/BCN Wildlife Trust.

Location: Sat nav: NN6 9SJ. SP 786 700. Five miles N of Northampton. From A43 take turn to Holcot and Brixworth. From A508 take turn to Brixworth and Holcot.

Access: Reserve (N of causeway) open all year to permit holders. Day permits available at fishing lodge, open mid-Mar to mid-Nov from 8am-dusk. Winter opening times variable, check in advance. No dogs. Disabled access from Lodge to first hide.

Facilities: Toilets available in Lodge, 15 miles of paths, nine bird hides, car parking.

Habitat: Open water (up to 120 ha), marginal

vegetation and reed grasses, wet woodland, grassland and mixed woodland (40 ha).
Key birds: Typically 165-170 species per year with a total list of 253 species. *Summer:* Breeding warblers, terns, grebes, herons. *Autumn:* Waders if water levels suitable. *Winter:* Up to 10,000 wildfowl, feeding station with Tree Sparrow and occasional Corn Bunting.
Other notable flora and fauna: 32 butterfly species, 392 macro moths, 21 dragonfly species (including damselflies), 377 species of flora and 105 bryophytes, 404 fungi species.
Contact: Sarah Gibbs, Pitsford Water Lodge, Brixworth Road, Holcot, Northampton, NN6 9SJ. 01604 780 148; e-mail: pitsford@wildlifebcn.org

3. STANWICK LAKES

Rockingham Forest Trust/ East Northants Council
Location: Sat nav: NN9 6GY. SP 967 715. Entrance off the A45, eight miles N of Wellingborough.
Access: Open 7am to 9pm (March to Oct); 7am to 5pm (Nov to Feb). Visitor centre open 10am to 5pm (sometimes later in summer). Closed Dec 25. Charges for car and coach parking. Disability scooter available for hire.
Facilities: All paths, visitor centre, gift shop, toilets and bird hide are wheelchair accessible.
Habitat: 750-acre countryside park includes Ramsar-designated wetland on site of former quarry, part of Nene Valley Special Protection Area. Includes reedbeds, hedgerows and grazed areas.
Key birds: Resident Little Egret, Kingfisher, Green and Great Spotted Woodpeckers, Grey Wagtail, Cetti's Warbler and Barn Owl. *Autumn/winter:* Wildfowl Pintail, Goldeneye and Goosander. Bittern, Redpoll and Siskin. *Spring/summer:* Waders inc Oystercatcher (breeding), Little Ringed Plover, Greenshank and Green Sandpiper. Hobby, Yellow Wagtail, hirundines and migrant warblers.
Other notable fauna: Otter, grass snake, 150 moth species, dragonflies.
Contact: Rockingham Forest Trust. 01933 625 522; e-mail: info@rftrust.org.uk

4. SUMMER LEYS LNR

Location: Sat nav: NN29 7TQ. SP 885 634. Off Hardwater Road, Great Doddington, three miles from Wellingborough, accessible from A45 and A509.
Access: Open 24 hours a day, 365 days a year, no permits required. Dogs on leadss. 40 space car park, small tarmaced circular route suitable for wheelchairs.
Facilities: Three hides, one feeding station. No toilets, nearest are at Irchester Country Park on A509 towards Wellingborough.
Public transport: Nearest main station is Wellingborough. No direct bus service, though buses run regularly to Great Doddington and Wollaston, both about a mile away. Tel: 01604

670 060 (24 hrs) for copies of timetables.
Habitat: Scrape, two ponds, lake, scrub, flood meadows, hedgerow.
Key birds: *All year:* Tree Sparrow. *Spring/summer:* Common Tern, Black-headed Gull, Ringed and Little Ringed Plover, Redshank and Oystercatcher all breed. Whimbrel, Turnstone, Common Sandpiper on passage. *Winter:* Large numbers of common wildfowl, plus Lapwing, Golden Plover and Ruff.
Other notable flora and fauna: 16 species of dragonfly recorded, including hairy dragonfly (check Marigold Pond). Common blue and brown argus butterflies on grassland.
Contact: Northant office, 01604 405 285; e-mail: northamptonshire@wildlifebcn.org

5. THRAPSTON GRAVEL PITS & TITCHMARSH LNR

Natural England/BCN Wildlife Trust.
Location: Sat nav: NN14 3EN (Lowick Road car park). TL 004 803. Seven miles E of Kettering. From A14 take A605 N. For Titchmarsh turn L at Thorpe Waterville, continue towards Aldwincle. Take first L after church (Lowick Lane) and continue to small car park on L. Take footpath to reserve.
Access: As well as the Aldwincle access point, there is a public footpath from lay-by on A605 N of Thrapston. Muddy conditions after heavy rain.
Facilities: Six hides.
Public transport: Bus service to Thrapston.
Habitat: Alder/birch/willow wood; old duck decoy; series of water-filled gravel pits.
Key birds: *Summer:* Breeding Grey Heron (no access to heronry), Common Tern, Little Ringed Plover; warblers. Migrants, inc. Red-necked and Slavonian Grebes, Hobby, Bittern and Marsh Harrier recorded. *Winter:* Good range of wildfowl inc nationally important numbers of

Gadwall, Wigeon and Goosander and gulls. Waders on passage.

Other notable flora and fauna: Banded demoiselle, red-eyed damselfly, brown, southern and migrant hawker dragonflies.

Contact: Northants office 01604 405 285; e-mail: northamptonshire@wildlifebcn.org

6. TOP LODGE-FINESHADE WOOD

RSPB/Forestry Commission
Location: Sat nav: NN17 3BB. SP 978 983. Off the A43 between Stamford and Corby. Follow brown tourist signs to Top Lodge Fineshade Woods.
Access: Fully accessible visitor centre (10am – 5pm summer: closes 4pm winter), open daily except Christmas Day. Caravan Club site open Mar-Nov (please see CC website for details). Smelter's Walk is an all-ability trail leading to the hide.
Facilities: Two pay-and-display car parks. Visitor centre with live footage of Red Kite nests in season,

toilets, Top Lodge Café, guided walks and events throughout the year. Wildlife hide in wood. Three way-marked walking trails (one is for all abilities, two are surfaced), 1 horse trail, 1 family cycle trail, dedicated coach and horse box parking.
Public transport: None.
Habitat: Ancient woodland, coniferous woodland, beech woodland, open areas, small pond.
Key birds: Centre of Northants' Red Kite reintroduction scheme. A wide range of birds of mixed woodlands. *All year:* Red Kite, Great Spotted Woodpecker, Goshawk, Nuthatch, Crossbill, Marsh Tit, Willow Tit. *Summer:* Turtle Dove, warblers. *Winter:* Hawfinch.
Other notable flora and fauna: Adder, grass snake, slow worm, common lizard. Fallow deer, badger. Orchids including greater butterfly, early purple and common spotted, other flora of ancient woodland.
Contact: Forestry Commission, Top Lodge, 01780 444 920; e-mail: northants@forestry.gsi.gov.uk
www.forestry.gov.uk/toplodge

Nottinghamshire

GRAVEL PITS are the dominant birding habitat in Nottinghamshire, though remnant pockets of heathland still hold iconic species such as Nightjar and Woodlark. The most recently developed gravel pit sites are the Idle Valley NR (formerly known as Lound) and the RSPB's new reserve at Langford Lowfields, near Newark. A raptor watchpoint at Welbeck can produce sightings of Honey Buzzard, Goshawk and Osprey and you can try for Hawfinches in winter in Clumber Park.

1. ATTENBOROUGH NATURE RESERVE

Location: Sat nav: NG9 6DY. Nottingham alongside River Trent. Sign-posted from A6005 between Beeston and Long Eaton.
Access: Open all year (am to 5pm (6pm on bank holidays and weekends). Dogs on leads (guide dogs only in visitor centre). Paths suitable for disabled access. Coaches by prior appointment. Car park charge.
Facilities: Education and visitor centre with café and shop, all accessible to wheelchair users. Nature trail (leaflet from Notts WT), one hide.
Public transport: Railway station at Attenborough – reserve is five mins walk away, visitor centre a further 10 minutes. Trent Barton Indigo bus service between Nottingham Broadmarsh and Derby bus station runs regularly throughout day. Alight at Chilwell Retail Park and walk 500m along Barton Lane.
Habitat: Disused, flooded gravel workings with associated marginal and wetland vegetation.
Key birds: *Spring/summer:* Breeding Common Tern (40-plus pairs), Reed Warbler, Black Tern regular (bred once). *Winter:* Wildfowl, plus Bittern, Grey Heron colony, adjacent Cormorant roost.

Other notable flora and fauna: Smooth newt, dragonflies including four-spotted chaser and migrant hawker.
Contact: Attenborough Nature Centre, 01159 721 777; www.attenboroughnaturecentre.co.uk
e-mail: enquiries@attenboroughnaturecentre.co.uk

2. BESTHORPE NATURE RESERVE

Nottinghamshire Wildlife Trust.
Location: Sat nav: NG23 7HL. SK 817 640 and SK813 646 (access points north and south of Trent Lane). Take A1133 N of Newark. Turn into Trent Lane S of Besthorpe village, reserve entrances second turn on L and R turn at end of lane (at River Trent).
Access: Open access to a hide, several screens (one in south section with disabled access from car park). No access to SSSI meadows. Limited access to areas grazed with sheep. Dogs on leads.
Facilities: No toilets (pubs etc in Besthorpe village), two hides in southern section, paths, nature trail (northern part), several screens.
Public transport: Buses (numbers 22, 67, 68, 6, S7L) run by Marshalls, Lincs, Road Car and Travel Wright along A1133 to Besthorpe village (0.75 mile away). Tel: 0115 924 0000 or 01777 710 550 for information.
Habitat: Former gravel workings with islands, SSSI neutral grasslands, hedges, reedbed, etc.
Key birds: *Spring/summer:* Breeding Grey Heron, Cormorant, Little Ringed Plover, Common Tern, Kingfisher, Grasshopper Warbler. *Winter:* Large numbers of ducks (Pochard, Tufted Duck, Pintail, Wigeon) and Peregrine. Recent re-profiling of water margins has increased the numbers of visiting waders.
Other notable flora and fauna: Meadows home to a nationally rare plant community.
Contact: Notts Wildlife Trust, 01159 588 242; e-mail: info@nottswt.co.uk

NATURE RESERVES - CENTRAL ENGLAND

3. COLWICK COUNTRY PARK

Nottingham City Council.
Location: Sat nav: NG4 2DW. SK 610 395. Access from Mile End Road, off A612 two miles E of Nottingham city centre. Adjacent to park-and-ride car park.
Access: Open at all times, but no vehicle access after dusk or before 7am. Best parking is in Colwick Hall access road from the racecourse.
Facilities: Nature trails. Sightings log book in Fishing Lodge.
Public transport: Nottingham City Transport Buses: Number 44 from stop Q3 on Queens Street (outside the Post Office); Park and Ride Service: Citylink2 from stop CL2 on Lower Parliament Street (outside Victoria Centre).
Habitat: Lakes, pools, woodlands, grasslands, new plantations, River Trent.
Key birds: *Summer:* 64 breeding species recorded, inc warblers and Common Tern (15+ pairs). Good track record for rarities. *Winter:* Wildfowl (high concentrations of Goldeneye) and gulls. In nature reserve look for Lesser Spotted Woodpecker, Water Rail and Kingfisher. Passage migrants inc Stonechat and Whinchat.
Other notable flora and fauna: Pool designated a SSSI for its 14 species of breeding dragonfly. Purple and white letter hairstreak butterflies.
Contact: Head Ranger, The Fishing Lodge, Colwick, Country Park, River Road, Colwick, Nottingham NG4 2DW. 01159 870 785; www.nottinghamcity.gov.uk

4. IDLE VALLEY (SUTTON & LOUND GRAVEL PITS)

Nottinghamshire Wildlife Trust/Tarmac/Private.
Location: Sat nav: DN22 8SG. SK 690 856. S end of reserve is 0.5 mile N of Retford off A638 to Barnby Moor, via entrance to Tarmac. Rural Learning Centre is on R.
Access: Open all year. Keep to walkways and public rights of way. Parking for reserve in first parking bay (large car park is for Learning Centre only). Footpath at S end is wheelchair accessible.
Facilities: Learning Centre reception and toilets open (10am- 4pm) all year. Refreshments (vending machine) available Mon-Sun (10am- 4pm). Idle Valley Café open Sundays (11.30am-3.30pm). Six viewing screens, two overlooking Chainbridge NR Scrape, two at Neatholme Scrape and single screens at Neatholme Fen and Neatholme Pit. Two hides in Chainbridge Wood.
Public transport: Buses from Doncaster, Gainsborough and Worksop to Retford (Bus station) then on local Stagecoach service 27 via Lound Village crossroads (Chainbridge Lane).
Habitat: Former sand and gravel quarries, restored gravel workings, conservation grazed areas, woodland, reedbed, river valley, farmland, scrub, willow plantations, open water.
Key birds: 251 species recorded. *Summer:* Gulls, terns, wildfowl and waders. Passage waders, terns, passerines and raptors. *Winter:* Wildfowl, gulls, raptors. Good site for rarities, which have included

Broad-billed Sandpiper, Great White Egret, Baird's Sandpiper and Steppe Grey Shrike in recent times.
Contacts: Lound Bird Club, Gary Hobson (chairman), 01924 384 419; e-mail: loundbirdclub@btinternet.com James Simpson (NWT Reserve Officer), Idle Valley Rural Learning Centre, Great North Road, Retford. DN22 8RQ; e-mail: jsimpson@nottswt.co.uk

5. LANGFORD LOWLANDS

RSPB Midlands Office
Location: Sat nav: NG23 7RF. SK 821 601. Lies NE of Newark-on-Trent. From A1 take A46 (signposted to Lincoln) and then turn onto A1133 (to Collingham). After two miles turn left on Tarmac access road (signposted Langford Quarry). Park in Tarmac car park.
Access: No access to main working quarry, except for working parties and guided group walks (see RSPB website for dates). View from public footpath around perimeter (mostly not suitable for disabled visitors, except for resurfaced section from new car park on NE boundary).
Facilities: Viewing screen overlooking reedbed. No toilets except for work party volunteers.
Public transport: Newark-Collingham buses will stop near to footpath if requested.
Habitat: RSPB is working with Tarmac to create the East Midland's largest reedbed (currently 30 ha) at this sand and gravel quarry site. Mature woodland, lake and shallow pools.
Key birds: Winter months generate large waterfowl numbers, Starling roosts, and five owl species. Bittern also

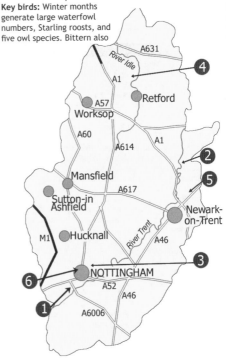

recorded. Summer months include regionally important numbers of Reed and Sedge Warblers, numerous Cuckoos, Marsh Harriers, Hobbies, hirundines and breeding Avocets.
Other notable flora and fauna: Badgers. More than 18 species of butterflies.
Contact: Call RSPB on 01636 893 611 to book group visits or enquire about work parties.

6. WOLLATON HALL & DEER PARK

Wollaton Hall.
Location: Sat nav: NG8 2AE. Situated N of A52, Derby road, approx three miles W of Nottingham City Centre.
Access: Open all year from 8am (weekdays), 9am (weekends and bank hols). Free admission to hall and park, but parking charges apply.
Facilities: Pay/display car parks. Some restricted

access (deer), leaflet about park's birdlife at the hall's main entrance. Two walk routes (1 and 3 miles).
Public transport: Trent Buses: No (2) and Nottingham City Transport: No 30 to entrance, 35 and 36 along Derby Road running approx every 15 mins.
Habitat: Lake, small reedbed, woodland.
Key birds: *All year:* Main woodland species present, with good numbers of Nuthatch, Treecreeper and all three woodpeckers. *Summer:* Commoner warblers, incl Reed Warbler, Hobby, hirundine species, Spotted Flycatcher. Hobbies hunt the hirundines. *Winter:* Pochard, Gadwall, Wigeon, Goosander, occasional Smew and Goldeneye. Flocks of Siskin and Redpoll, often feeding by the lake, Redwing and occasional Fieldfare. Large corvid roost.
Contact: Wollaton Hall 01159 153 900; e-mail: wollaton@ncmg.org.uk
www.wollatonhall.org.uk

Oxfordshire

A LAND-LOCKED, largely agricultural county, Oxfordshire has two outstanding birding locations: Farmoor reservoir for passage migrants, wintering wildfowl and rarities and Otmoor, where wet meadows and reedbeds are being developed by the RSPB to benefit breeding waders such as Redshank, Snipe and Lapwing in spring and Hobbies in summer. Wildfowl numbers increase in winter and Hen Harriers, Merlins, Peregrines and Short-eared Owls hunt.

1. ASTON ROWANT NNR

Natural England.
Location: Sat nav: HP14 3YL (for Beacon Hill car park). SU 731 966. From the M40 Lewknor interchange at J6, travel NE for a short distance and turn R onto A40. After 1.5 miles at the top of hill, turn R and R again into a narrow, metalled lane. Drive to car park, which is signposted from the A40.
Access: Open all year. Some wheelchair access at Cowleaze Wood, please contact Reserve Manager for more information.
Facilities: On-site parking at Beacon Hill and Cowleaze Wood, viewpoint, seats, interpretation panels.
Public transport: Red Rose buses between High Wycombe and Oxford stop at both Stokenchurch and Lambert Arms, Aston Rowant. Stagecoach Oxford Tube buses stop at Lewknor village, a short walk from reserve.
Habitat: Chalk grassland, chalk scrub, beech woodland.
Key birds: *Spring/summer:* Blackcap, other warblers, Turtle Dove. Passage birds inc Ring Ouzel, Wheatear and Stonechat. *Winter:* Brambling, Siskin, winter thrushes. *All year:* Red Kite, Buzzard, Sparrowhawk, Woodcock, Tawny Owl, Green and

Great Spotted Woodpeckers, Skylark, Meadow Pipit, Marsh Tit.
Other notable flora and fauna: Rich chalk grassland flora, including Chiltern gentian clustered bellflower, frog, bee, pyramidal and fragrant orchids. Good range of less common butterflies, inc silver-spotted,

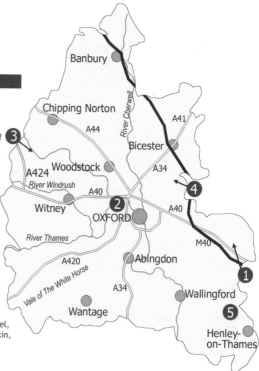

dingy and grizzled skippers, chalkhill blue, adonis blue, green hairstreak and green fritillary.
Contact: Natural England, Aston Rowant NNR, 01844 351 833; e-mail: enquiries@naturalengland.org.uk

2. FARMOOR RESERVOIR

Thames Water/ Environment Agency
Location: Sat nav: OX2 9NT. SP 452 061. Lies W of Oxford between A 40 and A420. Widely sign-posted by brown tourist signs. At mini-roundabout in Farmoor village, turn left and look for car park at Gate 3 (half mile distance).
Access: One-day permits (£1) or year-long permits (£10). Free car parking at Gate 3 for permit holders. Key for Pinkhill hide can be bought at gatehouse. No walking permitted between reservoir and Shrike Meadows to prevent disturbance to birds.
Facilities: Car park off B4017. Bird hide at Pinkhill Reserve, west of reservoir.
Public transport: Frequent Stagecoach 100 buses between Oxford and Witney stop in Farmoor village (half-mile walk to Gate 3).
Habitat: The county's largest body of fresh water contained in two concrete basins separated by a causeway. Shallow pools in Pinkhill Reserve. Reedbed, wet grassland and pools in the small Shrike Meadow and Buckthorne Meadow reserves.
Key birds: Attractive to passage migrants such as White and Yellow Wagtails, Wheatear, Black Tern, Little Gull, Dunlin and Little Stint, plus a long history of rarities. *Winter:* Wildfowl, grebes, divers and gulls. Snipe and Water Rail at Pinkhill. *Summer:* Breeding Little Ringed plover, Common Tern and Black-headed Gull. Large numbers of hirundines, Hobby, Cuckoo.
Other notable fauna: Dragonflies, aquatic life-forms.
Contact: Warden's lodge: 01865 863 033.

3. FOXHOLES RESERVE

Berks, Bucks & Oxon Wildlife Trust.
Location: Sat nav: OX7 6RW. SP 254 206. Travelling north on A424 from Burford, take right to Bruern. Continue past staggered crossroads towards Bruern for two miles then past right turn to Shipton-under-Wychwood. Park in lay-by after 200m and walk 600m down pot-holed track to reserve entrance. 4x4 vehicles can drive track to surfaced car park.
Access: Open all year. Please keep to the paths.
Facilities: Car park. Footpaths can be very muddy.
Public transport: None.
Habitat: Broad-leaved Woodland, and grassland.
Key birds: *Spring/summer:* Spotted Flycatcher, Marsh Tit and warblers. *Winter:* Redwing, Fieldfare, Woodcock. *All year:* Raven, Tawny Owl, Little Owl, all three woodpeckers, common woodland species.
Other notable flora and fauna: Fantastic show of bluebells in May. Autumn fungi. Silver-washed fritillary butterfly among 23 species recorded.
Contact: Berks, Bucks & Oxon Wildlife Trust, 01865 77 5476; e-mail: wendytobbitt@bbowt.org.uk

4. OTMOOR NATURE RESERVE

RSPB (Central England Office).
Location: Sat nav: OX3 9TD (Otmoor Lane). SP 570 126. Car park seven miles NE of Oxford city centre. From J8 of M40, take A40 W to Wheatley, then B4027. Take turn to Horton-cum-Studley, then first L to Beckley. After 0.67 miles turn R (before the Abingdon Arms public house). After 200 yards, turn L into Otmoor Lane. Reserve car park is at the end of the lane (approx one mile).
Access: Open dawn-dusk. No permits or fees. No dogs allowed on the reserve visitor trail (except public rights of way). In wet conditions, the visitor route can be muddy and wellingtons are essential.
Facilities: Limited. Small car park with cycle racks, visitor trail (3 mile round trip) and two screened viewpoints. The reserve is not accessible by coach and is unsuitable for large groups.
Public transport: None.
Habitat: Wet grassland, reedbed, open water.
Key birds: *Summer:* Breeding birds include Cetti's and Grasshopper Warblers, Lapwing, Redshank, Curlew, Snipe, Yellow Wagtail, Shoveler, Gadwall, Pochard, Tufted Duck, Little and Great Crested Grebes. Hobby breeds locally. *Winter:* Wigeon, Teal, Shoveler, Pintail, Gadwall, Pochard, Tufted Duck, Lapwing, Golden Plover, Hen Harrier, Peregrine, Merlin. *Autumn/spring passage:* Marsh Harrier, Short-eared Owl, Greenshank, Green Sandpiper, Common Sandpiper, Spotted Redshank and occasional Black Tern.
Contact: RSPB, c/o Folly Farm, Common Road, Bexley, OX3 9YR. 01865 351 163.

5. WARBURG RESERVE

Berks, Bucks & Oxon Wildlife Trust.
Location: Sat nav: RG9 6BL. SU 717 879. Leave Henley-on-Thames NW on A4130. Turn R at end of Fair Mile onto B480. Take L fork in Middle Assendon. After 1 mile, follow road round to R at grassy triangle, car park is on R after 1 mile.
Access: Open all year — visitor centre opens 9am-5pm. Please keep dogs on a lead. In some areas, only guide dogs allowed.
Facilities: Visitor Centre, toilets, car park, two hides, one with disabled access, nature trail, leaflets. Visitors with disabilities and groups should contact the warden before visits. Car park not suitable for coaches, only mini-buses.
Habitat: Scrub, mixed woodland, chalk grassland, ponds.
Key birds: *Spring/summer:* Whitethroat, Lesser Whitethroat. *All year:* Sparrowhawk, Red Kite, Treecreeper, Nuthatch, Tawny Owl and Lesser Spotted Woodpecker. *Winter:* Redpoll, Siskin, sometimes Crossbill, Woodcock.
Other notable flora and fauna: Good for orchids (15 species), butterflies (inc purple hairstreak and silver-washed fritillary) and common deer species.
Contact: Warburg Reserve, 01491 642 001; e-mail: wendytobbitt@bbowt.org.uk

Shropshire

AN EXTENSIVE county lying along the Welsh border, Shropshire's habitats range from upland moorland with its Red Grouse and Ring Ouzels to fertile lowland valleys, extensive farmland and mixed woodland. The cluster of waters near Ellesmere attract winter wildfowl and gulls while Venus Pools, Wood Lane and Chelmarsh are the county's chief wader-watching sites.

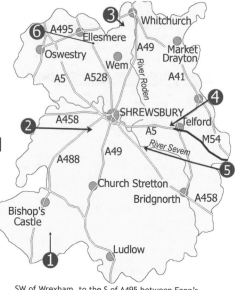

1 CLUNTON COPPICE

Shropshire Wildlife Trust.
Location: Sat nav: SY7 0HL. SO 342 806. From Craven Arms, take B4368 to Clunton village, go straight over bridge and up the hill to small car park just before reserve sign.
Access: Open at all times. Access along road and public rights of way only.
Facilities: Limited parking in small quarry entrance on R, or opposite The Crown pub.
Public transport: Buses between Craven Arms and Clun stop at Clunton. Steep one mile walk to reserve.
Habitat: One of the county's largest sessile oak woods. Good for ferns, mosses and fungi.
Key birds: Great Spotted Woodpecker, Buzzard and Raven regular. *Spring/summer*: Wide range of woodland birds, inc. Redstart, Wood Warbler, Spotted and Pied Flycatchers, Woodcock.
Other notable flora: Hairy woodrush and bromerape, sessile oak woodland plants, bluebell, bilberry.
Contact: Trust HQ, 01743 284 280.
www.shropshirewildlifetrust.org.uk

2. EARLS HILL

Shropshire Wildlife Trust
Location: Sat nav: SY5 0UH. SJ 409 048. Near Minsterley, SW of Shrewsbury. Turn off A488 at Pontesford along lane by Rea Valley Tractors. Car park 700 yards further on.
Access: Follow green route for easier walking. Purple route leads to summit. Car park at entrance.
Facilities: None.
Public transport: Buses to Bishops Castle and Minsterley stop at Pontesford.
Habitat: Steep-sided volcanic hill, scree slopes and crags, topped by Iron Age fort. Ancient woodland on eastern slopes.
Key birds: *Spring*: Migrants species such as Redstart, Pied Flycatcher and warblers. Dipper and Grey Wagtail on stream. Green Woodpecker common on open grassland.
Other notable flora and fauna: Dormouse. More than 30 species of butterfly recorded, yellow meadow ant. Spring ephemerals on anthills.
Contact: Trust HQ, 01743 284 280;

3. FENN'S WHIXALL AND BETTISFIELD MOSSES NNR

Natural England (North Mercia Team).
Location: Sat nav: SY13 3NY (Fenn's Bank).
Located four miles SW of Whitchurch, ten miles SW of Wrexham, to the S of A495 between Fenn's Bank, Whixall and Bettisfield. Roadside parking at entrances, car parks at Morris's Bridge, Roundthorn Bridge, World's End and a large car park at Manor House. Disabled access by prior arrangement along the railway line.
Access: Permit required except on Mosses Trail routes.
Facilities: Panels at all main entrances to the site, and leaflets are available when permits are applied for. Three interlinking Mosses Trails explore the NNR and canal from Morris's and Roundthorn bridges.
Public transport: Bus passes nearby. Railway two miles away.
Habitat: 2,000 acres of raised peatland meres and mosses.
Key birds: *Spring/summer*: Breeding Teal, Mallard, Nightjar, Hobby, Curlew, Tree Sparrow. Hobbies hunt here. *All year*: Kingfisher, Skylark, Linnet. *Winter*: Short-eared Owl.
Other notable flora and fauna: Water vole, brown hare, polecat, adder, 2,000 species of moth, 27 species of butterfly, nationally important for dragonflies, inc white-faced darter and yellow-spot chaser.
Contact: Natural England, Attingham Park, 01743 282 000; e-mail: north.mercia@natural-england.org.uk

4. PRIORSLEE LAKE

Severn Trent Water/Friends of Priorslee Lake
Location: Sat nav: TF2 9CQ. SJ 725 094. Located in Telford between M54 and A5. Leave M54 going north (B5060) at junction 4 and park in lay-by (100 yards from J4) overlooking the lake. Alternatively park carefully without blocking gates by the Waters Sports Association entrance gate at the end of Teece Drive, Priorslee, Telford

Access: Open at all times. Footpath around lake but can be muddy when wet.
Facilities: None.
Public transport: No. 24 bus from Telford town centre bus station, 3 miles from site, goes via train station, 2 miles.
Habitat: A man-made balancing lake, surrounded by woodland, rough grassland and three reedbeds on northern side.
Key birds: More than 155 species recorded. *Winter:* A nearby landfill site makes Priorslee Lake a magnet for gulls and as well as the common species, the site has a good track record for Yellow-legged, Caspian and white-winged gulls. Check the wildfowl for less common species such as Goosander and Pintail. Bittern and Snipe have been recorded in the reedbed areas. Finches, tits (including Willow), Redpoll, Siskin in woodland. *Summer:* Warblers, including Reed and Sedge Warbler.
Other notable flora and fauna: Wide range of butterflies, dragonflies and other insects. Southern marsh, bee and common spotted orchids.
Contact: Richard Camp, FoPL Co-ordinator, 01952 247 783; e-mail: mail@richardcamp.co.uk.
Friends Website: www.priorslee.org.uk

5. VENUS POOL

Shropshire Ornithological Society.
Location: Sat nav: SY5 6JT. SJ 548 062. 6 miles SE of Shrewsbury in angle formed by A458 and minor road leading S to Pitchford. Entrance is half a mile along minor road which leaves A458 half a mile (0.8 km) SE of Cross Houses.
Access: Public access to much of site, including four hides. Please keep to footpaths shown on notice boards at both entrances. Wheelchair-friendly paths to two public hides and Lena's Hide overlooking feeding station. Dogs not allowed.
Facilities: Car park with height barrier. Five hides (two for SOS members only). Information boards.
Public transport: Shrewsbury-Bridgnorth buses stop at Cross Houses, which is one mile walk from Venus Pool, partly along busy main road.
Habitat: Approx 27 hectares site. Pool, several islands, open shoreline, marshy grassland, hedgerows, scrub and woodland. Species-rich meadows, field growing bird-friendly crops.
Key birds: Noted for wintering wildfowl and passage waders, plus occasional county rarities, including Black-necked Grebe, Purple Heron, Spoonbill, Red Kite and Woodlark. *All year:* Common ducks and waterfowl, passerines, including Tree Sparrow. *April-June:* Passage waders include Curlew, Ringed Plover, Dunlin, Redshank, Green and Common Sandpipers, and both godwits. Passage Black Tern. Breeding Oystercatcher, Little Ringed Plover, Lapwing, warblers, hirundines. *July-September:* Wader passage can include Little Stint, Greenshank, Green, Wood, Curlew and Common Sandpipers, and possible rarities. *October-March:* Occasional wintering Bittern, Tundra and Whooper Swans (both scarce). Geese include occasional White-fronted. Ducks include Wigeon, Teal, Pintail, Shoveler, Pochard, Goosander (up to 50 in evening roosts) and occasional Goldeneye. Water Rail, vagrant raptors and owls, winter thrushes and large passerine flocks including Lesser Redpoll, Linnet, Tree Sparrow, Reed Bunting and Yellowhammer.
Contact: www.shropshirebirds.com/venus_pool/venuspool.htm

6. WOOD LANE

Shropshire Wildlife Trust.
Location: Sat nav: SY12 0HY. SJ 424 328. Turn off A528 at Spunhill, 1 mile SE of Ellesmere. Car park is three quarter miles down on R.
Access: Open at all times. Visit Trust website to apply on-line for permit to use hides. Reserve accessible to people of all abilities.
Facilities: Car parks signposted. Hides (permit only).
Habitat: Gravel pit restored by Tudor Griffiths.
Key birds: 168 species recorded since 1999. *Summer:* 168 species recorded since 1999. Breeding Sand Martin, Lapwing, Little Ringed Plover, Yellowhammer and Tree Sparrow. Osprey platforms erected to tempt over-flying birds. Popular staging post for waders (inc. Redshank, Greenshank, Ruff, Dunlin, Little Stint, Green and Wood Sandpiper). *Winter:* Large flocks of Lapwing, plus Curlew and common wildfowl.
Other notable fauna: Good range of dragonflies.
Contact: Trust HQ, 01743 284 280.

Staffordshire

OUTSIDE its urban areas, the county can offer Red Grouse on the northern moors, as well as Lesser Spotted Woodpeckers, Pied Flycatchers and other songbirds at RSPB Coombes Valley. Cannock Chase is good for Nightjars, Woodlark and Goshawk, and often has wintering Great Grey Shrikes. Belvide, Blithfield and Croxall Lakes are the best reservoirs to work for wintering birds.

1. BELVIDE

British Waterways Board and West Midland Bird Club.
Location: Sat nav: ST19 9LX. SJ 870 099. Entrance and car park on Shutt Green Lane, Brewood, seven miles NW of Wolverhampton.
Access: Access only by permit from the West Midland Bird Club (free for members, otherwise £20).
Facilities: Five hides (3 with wheelchair access), hard surface paths. Parking for 25-30 cars (lock combination issued to permit holders).
Public transport: Wolverhampton buses (3 and 877) and Walsall service (6) all stop at Kiddermore Green (eight minute walk to reserve).
Habitat: Reservoir with marsh, reedbeds, woodland and scrub.
Key birds: Wintering wildfowl, inc Great Northern Diver, Bewick's Swan and Goosander. Winter gull roost sometimes includes Glaucous or Iceland Gulls.

Breeding and passage waders (up to 12 species in a day when conditions are right) and terns. Warblers breed in reedbeds and hedgerows. Recent scarcities include Sabine's Gull, White-winged and Whiskered Tern and Yellow-browed Warbler.
Other notable fauna: Dragon and damselflies.
Contact: Permit Secretary, 147 World's End Lane, Quinton, Birmingham B32 1JX. E-mail:permits@westmidlandbirdclub.com. For other info: belvide@westmidlandbirdclub.com
www.westmidlandbirdclub.com/belvide

2. BLITHFIELD RESERVOIR

South Staffs Water/West Midland Bird Club
Location: Sat nav: WS15 3NJ. SK 058 237. View from causeway on B5013 (Rugeley/Uttoxeter). Close to village of Abbots Bromley. Look for signposts to Blithfield Education Centre.
Access: For members of WMBC only or one-off group permit. Further details from secretary@westmidlandbirdclub.com.
Facilities: Free car park, toilets. Walk 1 has partial wheelchair access.
Public transport: None. **Habitat:** Large reservoir.
Key birds: More than 250 species recorded. *Winter:* Good populations of wildfowl (inc. Bewick's Swan, Goosander, Goldeneye), large gull roost (can inc. Glaucous, Iceland, Mediterrean and Caspian). Passage terns (Common, Arctic, Black) and waders, esp. in autumn (Little Stint, Curlew Sandpiper, Spotted Redshank regular).
Contact: WMBC Secretary: e-mail:secretary@westmidlandbirdclub.com

3. COOMBES VALLEY

RSPB (Midlands Regional Office).
Location: Sat nav: ST13 7EU. SK 005 530. Three miles E of Leek. From Leek take A523 towards Ashbourne. After Bradnop, turn R on minor road (cross a railway line) to Apesford and follow signs to reserve.
Access: Open daily 9am to 9pm or dusk (except Dec 25), no charge. Free parking. Coach groups welcome by prior arrangement. No dogs allowed. Most trails unsuitable for disabled visitors.
Facilities: Information centre (closes at 5pm), toilets and hot drinks. Two nature trails with eight benches.
Public transport: 108 bus from Leek to Ashbourne, twice daily stops 1.2 miles from reserve, walk towards Ashbourne then take first R, cross railway and continue to reserve.
Habitat: Steep-sided valley with sessile oak woodland, unimproved pasture and meadow.
Key birds: *Spring:* Displaying Woodcock, drumming Great Spotted Woodpeckers and common woodland species are joined by migrant Pied and Spotted Flycatchers, Redstarts, Tree Pipits and Wood Warbler. *Jan-Mar:* Displaying birds of prey. *Autumn/winter:* Lesser Redpoll, Siskin, winter thrushes.
Other notable flora and fauna: Bluebells, various butterflies.
Contact: Reserve warden. 01538 384 017: e-mail: coombes.valley@rspb.org.uk

4. CROXALL LAKES

Staffordshire Wildlife Trust
Location: Sat nav: WS13 8QX. SK 190 139. From Lichfield head N on A38, following signs for National Memorial Arboretum. At NMA entrance, continue over river bridge and turn left on second track into car park.
Access: Open at all times, except to restricted areas. Surfaced access to track to hide overlooking main lake. Wheelchair ramps for both hides but woodland path is uneven. Kissing gate at entrance wide enough for wheelchairs. Restricted areas for dog walkers.
Facilities: Small car park, two bird hides.
Public transport: Bus services from Lichfield to Alrewas (1.2 miles from reserve).
Habitat: Two large lakes formed from gravel pits at the junction of Rivers Tame, Trent and Mease, plus shallow pools, wader scrapes and reedbeds.
Key birds: *Winter:* Substantial numbers of wildfowl, inc Wigeon, Teal, Goldeneye, Shoveler and occasional Smew. Between Nov and Jan, Short-eared Owls hunt over rough ground. *Spring/summer:* Nesting species include grebes, plus waders such as Redshank, Oystercatcher, Ringed Plover and Lapwing. Other species on passage.
Other notable flora and fauna: Otters, water voles and harvest mice all present but dragonflies will be easier to see.
Contact: Trust HQ 01889 880 100; e-mail:info@staffs-wildlife.org.uk

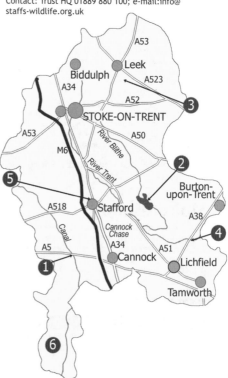

NATURE RESERVES - CENTRAL ENGLAND

5. DOXEY MARSHES

Staffordshire Wildlife Trust.
Location: Sat nav: ST16 1PU. SJ 903 250. On W side of Stafford town centre, just off A513 (Eccleshall Road) from Junction 14 on the M6. Parking by play park at end of Wootton Drive/ Creswell Farm Drive.
Access: Open at all times. Most of site accessible by wheelchair. Dogs on leads in sensitive areas.
Facilities: One hide, three viewing platforms.
Public transport: Buses and trains to Stafford town centre, walk upstream from Sainsbury's supermarket along River Sow to reserve entrance.
Habitat: Designated SSSI for wet meadow habitats. Marsh, pools, reedbeds, hedgerows, reed sweet-grass swamp
Key birds: More than 200 species (80 breeding) recorded. *Spring/summer:* Breeding Lapwing, Redshank, Little Ringed Plover, Oystercatcher, Shelduck, warblers, Skylark, Water Rail. *Autumn/ Winter:* Snipe, Jack Snipe, Goosander, other wildfowl, Passage waders, vagrants
Other notable flora and fauna: Otter, harvest mouse, water shrew, noctule bat, musk beetle, reed-sweet grass.
Contact: Staffordshire Wildlife Trust, 01889 880 100; e-mail:info@staffs-wildlife.org.uk

6. HIGHGATE COMMON

Staffordshire Wildlife Trust.
Location: Sat nav: DY7 5BS (Highgate Road). SO 836 895. From A449 at Himley take B4176 towards Bridgnorth. After approx 1 mile, turn left at traffic lights onto Wombourne Rd, signposted towards Swindon. Continue through Swindon, along Chasepool Rd. At the T Junction turn R onto Camp Hill Road. About 1 mile after Camp Farm, take 1st L then R at the T junction onto Highgate Rd. Take 1st entrance on R.
Access: Several car parks, network of paths.
Facilities: Public toilets at Warden's Office (restricted opening hours).
Public transport: None.
Habitat: Lowland heath with broadleaf woodland.
Key birds: Cuckoo, Green Woodpecker, Stonechat, Tree Pipit, Skylark, Yellowhammer.
Other notable flora and fauna: More than 5,000 species of insect recorded, including several red data book species of bee and wasp, also glow worm and common lizard.
Contact: Trust HQ, 01889 880 100.

Warwickshire & West Midlands

FOR A COUNTY so far from the sea, Warwickshire's river valleys and gravelpits are crucially important for breeding and passage birds. Tame Valley sites such as Kingsbury, Ladywalk and the Sandwell reserves attract passage waders while Brandon Marsh, HQ for the local Wildlife Trust, is important for breeding Cetti's and Grasshopper Warblers. The Trust manages 56 nature reserves.

1. BRANDON MARSH

Warwickshire Wildlife Trust.
Location: Sat nav: CV3 3GW. SP 386 762. Three miles SE of Coventry, 200 yards SE of A45/A46 junction (Tollbar End). Turn E off A45 (just after Texaco garage) into Brandon Lane. Reserve entrance signposted 1.25 miles in R.
Access: Open weekdays (9am-4.30pm), weekends (10am-4pm). Entrance charge currently £2.50 (free to Wildlife Trust members). Wheelchair access to nature trail and Wright hide. No dogs. Parking for 2 coaches.
Facilities: Visitor centre, toilets, tea-room (open daily 10am-3pm weekdays, 10am-4pm weekends), nature trail, seven hides.
Public transport: Bus service from Coventry to Tollbar End then 1.25 mile walk. Tel Travel West Midlands 02476 817 032 for bus times.
Habitat: Ten pools, together with marsh, reedbeds, willow carr, scrub and small mixed woodland in 260 acres, designated SSSI in 1972.
Key birds: More than 230 species recorded. *Spring/ summer:* Garden and Grasshopper Warblers, Whitethroat, Lesser Whitethroat, Hobby, Little Ringed Plover, Whinchat, Wheatear. *Autumn/winter:* Bittern (last three winters), Dunlin, Ruff, Snipe, Greenshank, Green and Common Sandpipers, Wigeon, Shoveler, Pochard, Goldeneye, Siskin, Redpoll. *All year:* Cetti's Warbler, Kingfisher, Water Rail, Gadwall, Little Grebe, Buzzard.
Other notable flora and fauna: More than 20 species of butterfly and 18 species of dragonfly recorded. Almost 500 plants species listed on www.brandonbirding.co.uk
Contact: Visitor centre hotline 02476 308 999; e-mail: enquiries@wkwt.org.uk

2. COOMBE COUNTRY PARK

Coventry City Council
Location: Sat nav: CV3 2AB. SP 402 795. At Binley, five miles E of Coventry centre, on B4027 Coventry to Brinklow road.
Access: Park open every day, 7.30am to dusk. Entry by foot is free. Pay-and-display parking. Paths mainly hard surfaces accessible for wheelchairs. Manual wheelchairs can be hired for a £5 returnable deposit.
Facilities: Information centre, toilets, disabled, café, bird hide, gift shop, picnic benches and wildflower meadow (March to September).
Public transport: By rail: To Coventry City Centre, 20 minute bus journey to park. By bus: No 585 Mike de Courcey Travel (for timetable ring 024 7630 2656).
Habitat: Parkland, lake, woodland and formal gardens.
Key birds: Large heronry, plus many Cormorants.

135

Lesser Spotted Woodpecker and Marsh Tit top the list of woodland species.
Other notable flora and fauna: More than 250 species of plant, including lesser celandine, foxglove, bluebell, red campion and herb robert. Mammals include wood mouse and muntjac deer.
Contact: Coombe Country Park, 02476 453 720; e-mail: Coombe.countrypark@coventry.gov.uk

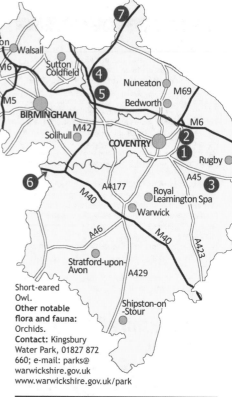

3. DRAYCOTE WATER

Severn Trent Water
Location: Sat nav: CV23 8AB. SP 460 700. Reservoir and 20-acre country park situated near Dunchurch, 3.5 miles SW of Rugby off the A426.
Access: Open all year, except Dec 25. Access to reservoir on foot or bicycle only. Cars must stop at pay-and-display car park. Disabled parking in top car park. Paths good for wheelchairs. Dogs only in Country Park.
Facilities: Newly-refurbished visitor centre, with toilets. Five mile road surrounding reservoir. One bird hide.
Habitat: Very large storage reservoir, surrounded by grassland and wooded areas.
Key birds: *Winter:* A wide range of common wildfowl species, plus regular sightings of less common species such as Smew, Black-necked Grebe and Scaup. Gull roost can number in excess of 50,000 birds, with white-winged gulls seen regularly. *Spring and autumn:* Birds on passage include waders, Black and Arctic Terns and Ospreys. Farm and woodland species in surrounding countryside all year round.
Contact: Draycote Water, Kites Hardwick, Warwickshire CV23 8AB. 01788 811 107; e-mail: visitor.sites@severntrent.co.uk.

4. KINGSBURY WATER PARK

Warwickshire County Council.
Location: Sat nav: B76 0DY. SP 203 960. Signposted `Water Park' from J9 M42 and A4097 NE of Birmingham.
Access: Open all year except Dec 25 (generally 8am to dusk). Pay on entry car park.
Facilities: Four hides, two with wheelchair access overlooking Cliff Pool nature reserve. Miles of flat surfaced footpaths, loan scheme for mobility scooters. Cafes, Information Centre with gift shop (open 9.30am to 4.30pm weekdays; 9am to 5pm weekends and bank holidays).
Public transport: Call for advice.
Habitat: Open water; numerous small pools, some with gravel islands; gravel pits; silt beds with reedmace, reed, willow and alder; rough areas and grassland.
Key birds: 230 species recorded. *Summer:* Breeding warblers (nine species), Little Ringed Plover, Great Crested and Little Grebes. Shoveler, Shelduck and a thriving Common Tern colony. Passage Ospreys, Hobbies, waders (esp. spring). *Winter:* Wildfowl,

Short-eared Owl.
Other notable flora and fauna: Orchids.
Contact: Kingsbury Water Park, 01827 872 660; e-mail: parks@warwickshire.gov.uk
www.warwickshire.gov.uk/park

5. LADYWALK RESERVE

CEGB/West Midland Bird Club
Location: Sat nav: B46 2BS. SP 212 917. Former site of Hams Hall power station, situated in Tame Valley ten miles from Birmingham city centre. From junction 9 of M42, head south on A446 to Hams Hall Distribution Centre. Follow Faraday Avenue to reserve. WMBC members can use secure car park near to Sainsbury's warehouse.
Access: Enter site by footbridge. Reserve open only to WMBC members, but other groups can organise visits with club sec. Non-members can observe site from public footpaths east of River Tame. No easy access on site for disabled visitors. Display permits on dashboard if using secure car park. Dogs not allowed.
Facilities: Six bird hides, including elevated River Walk Hide. Other screens for close-up viewing. Circular footpath (1.6 miles).
Public transport: Buses for Birmingham Airport (17 and 717 from Nuneaton) and 777 (from Coleshill) stop in Faraday Avenue.
Habitat: 125 acres of floodland, reedbed and woodland within a loop of The River Tame.
Key birds: More than 200 species recorded. *Winter:* Hundreds of wildfowl, inc Wigeon, Teal, Shoveler, Goldeneye and Goosander. Water Rail and Woodcock

regular and lots of small bird activity at the feeding stations. Up to four Bitterns in recent years, plus Siskin, Redpoll and winter thrushes. *Spring/summer:* Passage waders inc Greenshank, Curlew, godwits and plovers, plus many hirundines and other migrants. **Other notable flora and fauna:** Five species or orchid, including the county's only known colony of marsh hellibore. Also locally rare yellow bird's nest. Butterflies are plentiful and 16 species of dragonfly recorded.
Contact: WMBC permit secretary: Barbara Oakley, 147 Worlds End Lane, Quinton, Birmingham B32 1JX. E-mail: permits@westmidlandbirdclub.com

6. LICKEY HILLS COUNTRY PARK

Location: Sat nav: B45 8ER. At Rednal, 11 miles SW of Birmingham City Centre. Leave M42 at J1 or M5 at J4.
Access: Open all year, (10am-7pm in summer; 10am-4.30pm in winter). Land-Rover tours can be arranged for less able visitors.
Facilities: Car park, visitor centre with wheelchair pathway with viewing gallery, picnic site, toilets, café, shop.
Public transport: Bus: West Midlands 62 Rednal (20 mins uphill walk to visitor centre). Rail: Barnt Green (25 mins walk through woods to the centre).
Habitat: Hills covered with mixed deciduous woodland, conifer plantations and heathland.
Key birds: *Spring/summer:* Warblers, Tree Pipit, Redstart. *Winter:* Redwing, Fieldfare. *All year:* Common woodland species.
Other notable flora and fauna: Badger, deer species, 380 flowering plants.
Contact: The Visitor Centre, Lickey Hills Country Park, 01214 477 106;
e-mail: lickey.hills@birmingham.gov.uk

7. MIDDLETON LAKES

RSPB (Midlands Regional Office)
Location: Sat nav: B78 2AE. SP 192 967. Reserve lies in the Tame Valley, S of Tamworth, next to Middleton Hall. Leave M42 at J9 onto A446, then A4091 and finally into Bodymoor Heath Road.
Access: Open dawn till dusk daily. Surfaced path from car park to Middleton Hall and heronry. Other paths are unsurfaced but generally flat. Playmeadow Trail has wheelchair access for part of the route. Car parking for 30 and bike racks on site. Dogs allowed on leads in parts of the site.
Facilities: Three viewing platforms and a viewing screen. A hide will be constructed soon. Four trails, ranging from 500m to 3km in length.
Public transport: No local bus service. Wilnecote train station is 2.5 miles from the reserve.
Habitat: This former quarry now boasts lakes, reedbeds, meadows and woodland areas.
Key birds: *All year:* Barn Owls are regularly seen and Cetti's Warbler frequently heard. *Spring/summer:* 100-strong heronry, plus common migrant warblers, Lapwing, hirundines and woodland species. *Winter:* Lesser Spotted and Great Spotted Woodpeckers and Willow Tit on the feeders, plus peak numbers of

wildfowl and waders. Raptors include Hen and Marsh Harriers, Merlin, Peregrine and Short-eared Owl.
Other notable wildlife: Bluebells and spring flowers, grass snake, common butterflies and moths.
Contact: Call reserve on 01827 259 454;
e-mail: middletonlakes@rspb.org.uk

8. ROUGH WOOD CHASE LNR

Walsall Metropolitan Borough Council
Location: Sat nav: WV12 5NH. SJ 984 007. Reserve composed of six sites on W edge of Walsall Borough. From M6 (Jt 10) head for Willenhall and A462. Turn right into Bloxwich Road North and right again into Hunts Lane. Car park on bend.
Access: Open all year.
Facilities: Circular nature trail linking all sites.
Public transport: WMT bus 341 from Walsall.
Habitat: 70 acres of oakwood, significant for West Midlands. Sneyd reservoir, meadows, ponds, pools, marsh and scrubland.
Key birds: Great Crested and Little Grebes on pools in the north end of Chase. Breeding Jay and Sparrowhawk. Common woodland species all year and warblers in summer.
Other notable flora and fauna: Great crested and smooth newts, water vole, various dragonfly species, purple hairstreak, brimstone and small heath butterflies.
Contact: Walsall Countryside Services, Walsall MBC, 01922 4589 813:
e-mail: countrysideservices@walsall.gov.uk

9. SANDWELL VALLEY COUNTRY PARK

Sandwell Metropolitan Borough Council.
Location: Sat nav: B71 4BG (Salter's Lane). Entrances at SP 012 918 and SP 028 992. Located approx. 1 mile NE of West Bromwich town centre. Main entrance off Salters Lane or Forge Lane.
Access: Car parks open 8am to sunset. Wheelchair access to Priory Woods LNR, Forge Mill Lake LNR and other parts of the country park.
Facilities: 1,700 acre site. Visitor centre, toilets, café at Sandwell Park Farm (10am-4.30pm). Good footpaths around LNRs and much of the country park. Coach parking by appointment. Also 20 acre RSPB reserve (see below).
Public transport: West Bromwich bus station and central metro stop. (Traveline 0871 200 2233).
Habitat: Pools, woodlands, grasslands, including three local nature reserves.
Key birds: Wintering wildfowl including regular flock of Goosander, small heronry. *All year:* Grey Heron, Great Crested Grebe, Lapwing, Reed Bunting, Great Spotted and Green Woodpeckers, Sparrowhawk, Kestrel. *Spring:* Little Ringed Plover, Oystercatcher, up to 8 species of warbler breeding, passage migrants. *Autumn:* Passage migrants. *Winter:* Goosander, Shoveler, Teal, Wigeon, Snipe.
Other notable flora and fauna: Common spotted and southern marsh orchid. Ringlet butterfly. Water vole, weasel.

Contact: Senior Countryside Ranger, Sandwell Park Farm, 01215 530 220 or 2147.

10. SANDWELL VALLEY RSPB

RSPB (Midlands Regional Office).
Location: Sat nav: B43 5AG. SP 035 928. Great Barr, Birmingham. Follow signs S from M6 J7 via A34. Take R at 1st junction onto A4041. Take 4th L onto Hamstead Road (B4167), then R at 1st mini roundabout onto Tanhouse Avenue.
Access: 800 metres of paths accessible to assisted and powered wheelchairs with some gradients (please ring centre for further information). Dogs on leads. Car parks closed on Mon and Tues.
Facilities: Visitor centre unavailable following fire – toilets, refreshments and car parking at Forge Mill Farm (15 minute walk). Viewing screens. Phone centre for details on coach parking. Lakeside hide

and car park are open (10.30am-1pm Tue-Fri), (10.30am-3.30pm Sat-Sun), at other times the reserve is open to pedestrians. More facilities are being added.
Public transport: Bus: 16 from Corporation Street (Stand CJ), Birmingham City Centre (ask for Tanhouse Avenue). Train: Hamstead Station, then 16 bus for one mile towards West Bromwich from Hamstead (ask for Tanhouse Avenue).
Habitat: Open water, wet grassland, reedbed, dry grassland and scrub.
Key birds: *Summer:* Lapwing, Little Ringed Plover, Reed Warbler, Whitethroat, Sedge Warbler, Willow Tit. *Passage:* Sandpipers, Yellow Wagtail, chats, Common Tern. *Winter:* Water Rail, Snipe, Jack Snipe, Goosander, Bullfinch, woodpeckers and wildfowl.
Contact: Sandwell Valley RSPB Reserve, 0121 357 7395; e-mail: sandwellvalley@rspb.org.uk

Worcestershire

THE LARGELY rural county has only one sizeable reservoir – Bittell – but there are excellent wetlands to explore at Upton Warren and Bredon's Hardwick. For the widest range of woodland species, the best area is the Wyre Forest west of Kidderminster, but the Wildlife Trust owns or manages 70 reserves covering a wide range of habitats.

1. KNAPP & PAPERMILL

Worcestershire Wildlife Trust.
Location: Sat nav: WR6 5HR. Take A4103 SW from Worcester; R at Bransford roundabout then L towards Suckley and reserve is approx three miles (do not turn off for Alfrick). Park at Bridges Stone lay-by (SO 751 522), cross road and follow path to the Knapp House.
Access: Open daily. Large parties should contact Warden in advance. Paths steep and uneven.
Facilities: Nature trail, small visitor centre with toilets, wildlife garden, Kingfisher viewing screen.
Public transport: None.
Habitat: Broadleaved woodland, unimproved grassland, fast stream, old orchard in Leigh Brook Valley.
Key birds: *Summer:* Breeding Grey Wagtail and Dipper, Nuthatch and common woodland species, Kingfisher, Spotted Flycatcher (nests in warden's garden), all three woodpeckers. Buzzard, Sparrowhawk and Redstart also occur.
Other notable flora and fauna: Otters have returned recently. Good numbers of dragonflies and butterflies (30 species recorded) on all three meadows include holly blue, purple hairstreak and white admiral. Bluebells, green-winged and spotted orchids.
Contact: The Warden, Knapp and Papermill reserve, The Knapp, Alfrick WR6 5HR. 01905 754 919; enquiries@worcestershirewildlifetrust.org

2. MALVERN HILLS

Malvern Hills Conservators
Location: Sat nav: WR13 6HR (British Camp car park). SO 756 402. An eight-mile-long range of hills and commons lying S and W of Great Malvern, covering approx 3,000 acres. Best birding areas include Castlemorton Common and Midsummer Hill.
Access: Open all year. Charge for car parks is £2 per day or £25 for year-long permit.
Facilities: Public toilets with disabled access opposite British Camp car park (A449 Worcester Road). Two easy-access trails at Earnslaw (400 metres long) and Blackhill (200 metres long).
Habitats: Grassland on hilltops, mixed woodland, scrub, quarries, small reservoirs and lakes.
Key birds: Raptors include Buzzard, Sparrowhawk, Peregrine and Hobby. Ravens nest in quarries and spring passage migrants include Wheatear, Ring Ouzel (best in Happy Valley between Worcestershire Beacon and North Hill) and more rarely, Dotterel. Autumn sees a good range of migrants heading south. Wooded areas hold all the expected common species, plus breeding warblers and flycatchers, all three woodpeckers and Tree Pipits on woodland edges. A few Nightingales hang on in areas of dense scrub, which also hold chats, pipits and Linnets. A winter highlight is Snow Bunting on the highest hills.
Other notable flora and fauna: Lesser horseshoe and barbastelle bats, polecat, 25 species of butterfly recorded, inc high brown fritillary. Broad range of plants include blinks, crosswort and common spotted orchid.
Contact: Malvern Hills Conservators, Manor House, Grange Road, Malvern WR14 3EY. Tel: 01684 892 002; e-mail: conservators@malvernhills.org.uk

3. TIDDESLEY WOOD NATURE RESERVE

Worcestershire Wildlife Trust.
Location: Sat nav: WR10 2AD. SO 929 462. Take B4084 from Pershore towards Worcester. Turn L towards

NATURE RESERVES - CENTRAL ENGLAND

Besford and Croome near town boundary just before the summit of the hill. Entrance is on L after about 0.75 miles.
Access: Open all year except Dec 25. Cycles and horses only allowed on the bridleway. Dogs on leads. Avoid military firing range in SW corner of wood, marked by red flags. Do not enter NE plot, which is private property. Main ride stoney, with some potholes. Small pathways difficult if wet. Coach parking by appointment.
Facilities: Information board. Circular trail around small pathways. Car park off B4084 (signposted to Besford and Croome).
Public transport: First Midland Red services.
Habitat: Ancient woodland, conifers.
Key birds: *All year:* Coal Tit, Goldcrest, Sparrowhawk, Willow Tit, Marsh Tit. *Spring:* Chiffchaff, Blackcap, Cuckoo. *Winter:* Redwing, Fieldfare.
Other notable flora and fauna: Dragonflies including club-tailed and white-legged damselflies. Good for butterflies, including white admiral, peacock and gatekeeper. Important invertebrates include nationally rare noble chafer beetle which has been recorded here for many years.
Contact: Trust HQ, 01905 754 919: e-mail: enquiries@worcestershirewildlifetrust.org

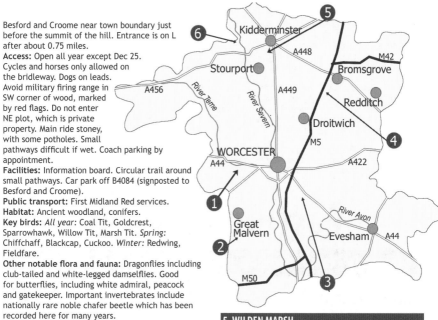

4. UPTON WARREN

Worcestershire Wildlife Trust.
Location: Sat nav: B61 7EX. SO 936 677. Two miles S of Bromsgrove on A38. Leave M5 at junction 5 and head N on A38.
Access: Christopher Cadbury Wetland Reserve consists of Moors Pools (freshwater) and Flashes Pools (saline). Always open except Dec 25. Free for Trust members, or £3 day permit from Trust centre at Smite, education centre or volunteers on site. Disabled access to hides at Moors Pools only by prior arrangement. No dogs.
Facilities: Seven hides, maps at entrances, paths can be very muddy. Coach parking at sailing centre by previous booking.
Public transport: Birmingham/Worcester buses pass reserve entrance.
Habitat: Fresh and saline pools with muddy islands, some woodland and scrub.
Key birds: *Winter:* Wildfowl. *Spring/autumn:* Passage waders. *Summer:* Breeding Avocet, Redshank, Little Ringed Plover, Oystercatcher, Common Tern, Sedge, Reed, Grasshopper and Cetti's Warblers. Hobby nearby.
Other notable flora and fauna: Saltmarsh plants, dragonflies.
Contact: A F Jacobs, 3 The Beeches, Upton Warren, Bromsgrove, Worcs B61 7EL. 01527 861 370.

5. WILDEN MARSH

Worcestershire Wildlife Trust.
Location: Sat nav: DY13 9JT. SO 825 730 and SO 829 735. S of Kidderminster. Take A449 S from Kidderminster. At junction with A442 go straight across roundabout into Wilden Lane, a very busy road with few parking spaces, so park carefully. There are gated entrances off Wilden Lane.
Access: Gated entrances are open at all times. Permit needed for more northerly part of site. This reserve is complex and new visitors should consult a map. Secure cattle gates at all times. Beware boggy areas, steep banks by the River Stour and deep ditches.
Facilities: None. Limited parking on Wilden Lane.
Public transport: Nearest bus stop at Wilden, half mile from reserve.
Habitat: Dry and marshy fields with small alder and willow woods, reedbeds and many drainage ditches.
Key birds: 192 bird species have been recorded since 1968 and about 70 breed, including Yellow Wagtail, nine species of warblers and Redshank. Wintering area for Water Pipits, though numbers have declined recently.
Other notable fauna: Plants include southern marsh orchids, marsh cinquefoil, marsh arrow-grass, marsh pennywort and lesser water parsnip.
Contact: Trust HQ, 01905 754 919; e-mail: enquiries@worcestershirewildlifetrust.org

6. WYRE FOREST NNR

Natural England/Worcs Wildlife Trust.
Location: Sat nav: DY12 3AA (Fred Dale car park). SO

750 760. 0.5 miles NW of Bewdley (on the A456) and 4.5 miles W of Kidderminster.
Access: Observe reserve signs and keep to paths. Forestry Commission visitor centre at Callow Hill. Fred Dale Reserve is reached by footpath W of B4194 (parking at SO 776 763).
Facilities: Toilets and refreshments (with disabled access) at Wyre Forest Visitor Centre (near the Discovery Centre). Several waymarked trails in (some suitable for wheelchair users) as well as regular guided walks, also family cycle routes through the reserve.
Public transport: The nearest train station is in Kidderminster. Local bus services between Bewdley and Kidderminster are provided by First Group (0871 200 2233).

Habitat: Oak forest, conifer areas, birch heath, lowland grassland, stream.
Key birds: Breeding birds include Redstart, Pied Flycatcher, Wood Warbler, Buzzard and Raven, with Dipper, Grey Wagtail and Kingfisher found on the larger streams.
Other notable flora and fauna: Mammals include, fallow, roe and muntjac deer, polecat, otter and mink, yellow neck mouse, dormouse, voles and water shrew. Several bat species including pipistrelle and Daubenton's. Important site for invertebrates including England's largest colony of pearl-bordered fritillary butterflies.
Contact: Wyre Forest NNR, Natural England Office, Lodge Hill Farm, Dowles Brook, Bewdley DY12 2LY. 01299 400 686.

Eastern England

Bedfordshire, Cambridgeshire, Essex, Hertfordshire, Norfolk, Suffolk

Bedfordshire

THOUGH one of England's smallest counties, Bedfordshire is not devoid of birding interest. Blows Down is one of the best southern sites in to see Ring Ouzels on spring passage. Intense observer coverage at the RSPB's HQ at The Lodge, Sandy, has produced a series of excellent records. Exploring Country Parks such as Priory and Harold-Odell is best early in the morning before the dog-walkers are out.

1. BLOW'S DOWN

Beds, Cambs & Northants Wildlife Trust.
Location: Sat nav: LU5 4AR. TL 033 216. On the outskirts of Dunstable. Take A5065 from W of Luton, cross M1, take first exit at roundabout, park with care on verge. Can also walk half mile from Dunstable centre to W entrance at Half Moon Lane off A5.
Access: Open all year, not suitable for wheelchairs due to steep slopes.
Facilities: None. Park on road verge. Public transport: None.
Habitat: SSSI, chalk downland, scrub and grassland, that is a traditional resting place for incoming spring migrants.
Key birds: *Winter:* Lapwing, Meadow Pipit, Skylark. *Spring/autumn:* Ring Ouzel, Wheatear, Whinchat, Black Redstart, Stonechat, Willow Warbler.
Other notable flora and fauna: Chalkhill blue, brown argus and marbled white butterflies. Plants include small scabious, burnet-saxifrage, squinancywort, great pignut, common spotted and bee orchids.
Contact: Trust Bedfordshire office HQ, 01234 364 213, 01954 713 500; e-mail: bedfordshire@wildlifebcnp.org www.wildlifebcn.org

2. FLITWICK MOOR

BLocation: TL 046 354. E of Flitwick. From Flitwick town centre (Tesco roundabout) on A5120, cross railway bridge, R at roundabout, immediately L into

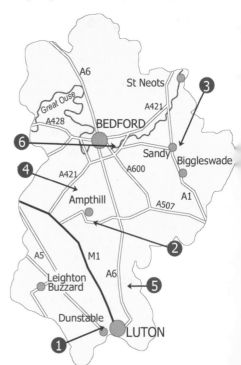

140

King's Road. After 500m, L into Moulden Road towards A507. After quarter mile R at Folly Farm, follow track to small car park. Also footpath to reserve from Moor Lane.
Access: Open all year.
Facilities: Car park. Please stick to public paths.
Public transport: Frequent buses (United Counties) from Bedford and Luton to Flitwick, or take train to Flitwick and then three-quarter mile walk.
Habitat: SSSI. Important wetland for the area, blend of fen, meadow, wet woodland and fragile peaty soil. Supports mosses ferns and flowers.
Key birds: *Winter*: Siskin, Water Rail, Great Spotted Woodpecker. *Spring*: Lesser Spotted Woodpecker, Willow Warbler, Blackcap. *Summer*: Water Rail, Grasshopper and Garden Warblers, Cuckoo. *Autumn*: Brambling.
Other notable flora and fauna: Good variety of butterflies and dragonflies, plus chimney sweeper moth and conehead bush cricket. Plants include nine species of sphagnum moss, marsh pennywort, black knapweed, water figwort plus fly agaric and yellow brain fungus in autumn.
Contact: Reserves manager 01234 364 213; e-mail: bedfordshire@wildlifebcn.org

3. THE LODGE

RSPB (Central England Office).
Location: Sat nav: SG19 2DL. TL 191 485. Reserve lies 1 mile E of Sandy, sign-posted from the B1042 road to Potton.
Access: Reserve is open daily 7am-9pm (or sunset when earlier); shop 9am-5pm weekdays, 10am-5pm weekends and bank hols. Non-members: £4 per motor vehicle. Dogs only allowed on bridleway.
Facilities: Five miles of nature trails. One bridleway (half mile) and gardens are wheelchair/pushchair accessible. One hide (wheelchair accessible), 50 yards from car park. Coach parking at weekends by arrangement. Refreshments at shop. Toilets (in disabled).
Public transport: Buses to Sandy Market Square from Bedford, infrequent service. One mile walk or cycle from centre of Sandy or half mile from Sandy railway station, in part along trail through heathland restoration.
Habitat: This 180-hectare reserve is a mixture of woodland, heathland and acid grassland and includes the formal gardens of the RSPB's UK headquarters. New land being restored to heathland.
Key birds: *Spring/summer*: Hobby, Spotted Flycatcher, breeding common woodland species and warblers. *All year*: Woodpeckers, woodland birds. *Winter*: Winter thrushes, woodland birds.
Other notable flora and fauna: Natterjack toads, rare heathland insects. Particularly good site for fungi, and lichens. Garden pools are good for dragonflies.
Contact: RSPB The Lodge Shop 01767 680 541; e-mail: thelodgereserve@rspb.org.uk

4. MARSTON VALE MILLENIUM COUNTRY PARK

Marston Vale Trust.
Location: Sat nav: MK43 0PR. TL 004 417. SW of Bedford off A421 at Marston Moretaine. Only five mins from J13 of M1 along A421 towards Bedford.
Access: View Stewartby Lake at any time. Park and forest centre open summer 10am to 6pm, winter 10am to 5pm. Forest Centre and car park closed Dec 25/26 and Jan 1. No dogs in wetlands. Entry charge for wetland reserve. Main 8km trail surfaced for wheelchair and pushchair access. All-terrain wheelchair available for free loan. Coach parking available.
Facilities: Cafe bar, gift shop, art gallery, exhibition. Free parking. The 2km wetland trail is a level path with a compacted, loose stone surface inc two hand gates with top latches.
Public transport: Trains to Millbrook and Stewartby station, 20 minute walk to Forest Centre.
Habitat: Stewartby Lake covers 610 acres and attracts birds when smaller waters are frozen. Freshwater marsh (man-made), reedbed, woodland, hawthorn scrub and grassland.
Key birds: *Winter*: Iceland and Glaucous Gulls (regular), plus Caspian and Mediterranean Gulls in gull roost, wildfowl, Great Crested Grebe. Rarer species can include all three divers and Scaup. *Spring*: Passage waders and terns (Black Tern, Arctic Tern), Garganey. *Summer*: Nine species of breeding warblers, Hobby, Turtle Dove, Nightingale, Bearded Tit. *Autumn*: Passage waders and terns. *Rarities*: White-winged Black Tern, Laughing Gull, divers, Manx Shearwater, Bittern.
Other notable flora and fauna: Dingy and grizzled skipper butterflies, excellent for dragonflies. Also otter and brown hare, plus bee and pyramidal orchids and stoneworts.
Contact: Forest Centre, 01234 767 037; e-mail: info@marstonvale.org; www.marstonvale.org

5. PEGSDON HILL RESERVE

Beds, Cambs & Northants Wildlife Trust.
Location: TL 120 295. 5 miles W of Hitchin. Take B655 from Hitchin towards Barton-le-Clay. Turn R at Pegsdon then immediately L and park in lay-by. Reserve entrance across B655 via footpath.
Access: Open all year. Dropping off point for coaches only.
Facilities: None.
Public transport: Luton to Henlow buses (United Counties) stop at Pegsdon.
Habitat: Chalk grassland, scrub and woodland.
Key birds: *Winter*: Brambling, Stonechat, winter thrushes, raptors including Buzzard. *Spring*: Wheatear, Ring Ouzel, Tree Pipit, Yellowhammer. *Summer*: Turtle Dove, Grey Partridge, Lapwing, Skylark.
Other notable flora and fauna: Dark green fritillary, dingy and grizzled skippers, chalkhill blue, brown argus and small heath butterflies. Glow worms. Plants

include pasqueflower in spring, fragrant and common spotted orchids.
Contact: Bedfordshire office 01234 364 213; e-mail: bedfordshire@wildlifebcn.org www.wildlifebcn.org

6. PRIORY COUNTRY PARK

Bedford Borough Council.
Location: Sat nav: MK41 9TR. TL 071 495. 1.5 miles SE from Bedford town centre. Signposted from A4280 and A421. Entry point to new 'River Valley Park'
Access: Park and hides open at all times. No access to fenced/gated plantations.
Facilities: Toilets and visitor centre open daytime, all-year-round disabled access on new path around lake. Hides, nature trails, labyrinth, cycle hire, Premier Inn for meals, accommodation.
Public transport: Stagecoach (01604 676 060) 'Blue Solo 4' every 20 mins. Mon-Sat. Alight 1st stop Riverfield Drive (200 m). Rail station at Bedford (approx 2.5 miles)
Habitat: Lakes, reedbeds, scrub and woodland,

meadows adjoining Great Ouse.
Key birds: 212 species recorded. Good numbers/variety of winter wildfowl, varied mix of spring passage species, with breeding warblers and woodpeckers, augmented by feeding terns, hirundines and raptors lakeside. *Winter*: Grebes, Pochard, Shoveler, Gadwall, Merlin, Water Rail, gulls, thrushes, Chiffchaff, corvids, buntings. *Passage*: Raptors, waders, terns, pipits. *Summer*: Hobby, Turtle Dove, Swift, hirundines, *acrocephalus* and *sylvia* warblers. *All year*: Cormorant, Little Egret, Heron, Stock Dove, woodpeckers, Kingfisher, Grey Wagtail, Treecreeper, Goldfinch, Bullfinch.
Other notable flora and fauna: 23 species of dragonfly, incl small red-eyed damsel and hairy hawker. 20 species of butterfly. Large plant list. Fox, muntjac and otter.
Contact: Jon Bishop, Wardens Office, Visitor Centre, Priory CP, Barkers Lane, Bedford, MK41 9SH. 01234 211 182.

Cambridgeshire

THE NENE and Ouse Washes are superb for wintering wildfowl, owls and raptors, with the former also offering the chance of Cranes, breeding Black-tailed Godwits, Spotted Crakes plus introduced Corncrakes in summer. Grafham Water attracts plenty of scarce species, while Paxton Pits is probably the best place in the country to actually see Nightingales.

1. FEN DRAYTON

RSPB (Eastern England Office).
Location: TL 352 680. NW of Cambridge. Leave A14 at Junction 28; follow signs to Swavesey. Turn L in Boxworth End (signed to Fen Drayton). Turn R onto minor road (signed to Swavesey), then L into entrance to Fen Drayton Lakes. Follow signs to car park.
Access: Open at all times. Dogs are only allowed on public footpaths and bridleways. Disabled birders can get car access to one viewing screen.
Facilities: Rights of way around lakes and two open access fields. Information boards give access details. Free trail guides and events leaflets are available from the Elney car park.
Public transport: Cambridgeshire Guided Bus service between Huntingdon and Cambridge (runs every ten mins) has a request stop in the reserve.
Habitat: A complex of lakes (former gravel workings) and traditional riverside meadows next to the River Great Ouse.
Key birds: At least 213 species have been recorded in the area with some 65 species being regular breeders, including Common Tern. Hobby, waders on passage. Rarities include Great White Egret, Purple Heron, Glossy Ibis, Common Crane, Red-Footed Falcon, Honey Buzzard and Whiskered Tern. Bitterns

are now a regular sight, with Holywell Lake and Elney Lake being the favoured sites. *Winter*: Nationally important numbers of Gadwall and Coot.
Other notable fauna: Good site for butterflies, dragonflies and mammals.
Contact: Fen Drayton, 01954 233 260; e-mail: fendraytonlakes@rspb.org.uk

2. FERRY MEADOWS COUNTRY PARK

Nene Park Trust.
Location: Sat nav: PE2 6YT. TL 145 975. Three miles W of Peterborough and two miles E of A1. On all major routes into city, follow brown tourist signs for Nene Park or country park symbol. Also signed on Oundle Road (A605).
Access: Open all year, 7am to dusk (summer), 8am until sunset in winter. Electric scooters and wheelchair available for loan – call to book in advance. Coach parking free at all times. Car parking charge (£4) applies at weekends and Bank Holidays between March - Oct.
Facilities: Car park, visitor centre (opens 10am), toilets (inc disabled), café, two wheelchair-accessible hides in nature reserve area. Hard surface paths in park's central areas, but steep slopes in Bluebell Wood.
Public transport: Stagecoach X14 stops on A605 by Notcutts Nursery. Half mile walk to park entrance. Tel. Traveline 0870 6082 608 or www.traveline.org.uk
Habitat: Lakes, meadows, scrub, broadleaved woodland and small wetland nature reserve.
Key birds: *All year*: Good selection of woodland and water birds, Kingfisher.
Spring: Terns, waders, Yellow Wagtail. *Winter*: Grebes, Siskin, Redpoll, Water Rail, occasional Hawfinch.
Other notable flora and fauna: Bluebell, wood anemone, wild garlic in woodland.

NATURE RESERVES - EASTERN ENGLAND

Contact: Visitor Services Officer, Nene Park Trust, 01733 234 443; www.nene-park-trust.org.uk
e-mail: visitor.services@ neneparktrust.org.uk

3. FOWLMERE

RSPB (Eastern England Office).
Location: Sat nav: SG8 6EZ. TL 406 461. 7 miles S of Cambridge. From A10, turn towards Fowlmere at Fowlmere-Shepreth crossroads (no RSPB sign); after 1 mile, turn R by cemetery (RSPB sign); after another 0.6 mile, turn L into reserve.
Access: Access at all times along marked trail. Dogs only on private track on eastern boundary.
Facilities: 1.5 miles of trails. Three hides, visitor centre and toilets. Space for one coach, prior booking essential. Wheelchair access to one hide, toilet and some of the trails.
Public transport: Shepreth railway station 2 miles. By bus: Dunsbridge Turnpike (outside Country Homes & Gardens), 1 mile. Walk towards Melbourn; after 300 m, cross road and turn left on to single track road to Fowlmere (beware of traffic); after 0.75 mile (1.2 km), turn right into reserve (RSPB sign).
Habitat: Reedbeds, meres, woodland, scrub.
Key birds: *Spring/summer*: Little Grebe, Turtle Dove, ten breeding warblers. *All year*: Water Rail, Kingfisher, Reed Bunting. *Autumn*: Yellowhammer, Corn Bunting. *Winter*: Snipe, Water Rail, raptors.
Other notable flora and fauna: Healthy population of water shrews and otters. 18 species of dragonfly.
Contact: Fowlmere, 01763 208 978;
e-mail:fowlmere@rspb.org.uk

4. GRAFHAM WATER

Beds, Cambs & Northants Wildlife Trust.
Location: Sat nav: PE28 0DW (West Perry car park). TL 143 671. Follow signs for Grafham Water from A1 at Buckden or A14 at Ellington. Follow B661 road towards Perry and Staughtons to West Perry. As you leave village, Anglian Water's Mander car park is signposted on R. Car parking charges apply.
Access: Open all year. Dogs barred in wildlife garden only, on leads elsewhere. Car parking £2 for day ticket.
Facilities: Five bird hides in nature reserve, two in bird sanctuary area. Two in wildlife garden accessible to wheelchairs. Cycle track through reserve also accessible to wheelchairs. Visitor centre with restaurant, shop and toilets. Disabled parking. Use Plummer car park for lagoons and Marlow car park for dam area (good for waders and vagrants).
Public transport: None.
Habitat: Open water, settlement lagoons ranging from reedbeds, open water, wet mud and willow carr, ancient and plantation woodland, scrub, species rich grassland.
Key birds: *Resident*: Common woodland birds, wildfowl. *Winter*: Waders including Common Sandpiper and Dunlin, Great Crested Grebe, Wildfowl

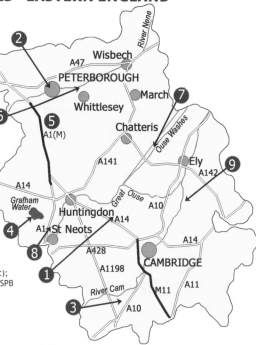

including large flocks of common species, plus Shelduck, Goldeneye, Goosander and Smew, gulls (can be up to 30,000 roosting in mid-winter). *Spring/summer*: Breeding Nightingale, Reed, Willow and Sedge Warblers, Common and Black Terns. *Autumn*: Passage waders. *Rarities*: Have included Wilson's Phalarope (2007), Ring-necked Duck, Great Northern Diver, Glaucous, Iceland and Mediterranean Gulls.
Other notable flora and fauna: Bee,common spotted and early purple orchids, common twayblade (in woods), cowslip. Common blue and marbled white butterflies, dragonflies including broad-bodied chaser, voles, grass snakes.
Contact: The Warden, Grafham Water Nature Reserve, 01480 811 075; grafham@wildlifebcn.org

5. THE GREAT FEN

BCN Wildlife Trust/Natural England/Environment Agency/Hunts District Council
Location: Sat nav: PE26 2RS. TL 245 848 (Ramsey Heights), plus Holme Fen NNR and Woodwalton NNR (Chapel Road, Ramsey Heights), south of Peterborough, lying between the A1 in the west and Ramsey. B660 runs through the centre of Great Fen.
Access: Open access at all times to three visitor sites with views over farmland linking the reserves. Eventually Great Fen will occupy 9,000 acres. No dogs allowed. Wheelchair access difficult on grassy rides.
Facilities: Countryside Centre at Ramsey Heights site. Three elevated bird hides at Woodwalton reached via steps. One bird hide at Holme Fen. Grassed paths

NATURE RESERVES - EASTERN ENGLAND

at Woodwalton and Holme Fens. New Decoy visitor information point.
Public transport: Limited bus service between Peterborough and Ramsey stops at end of Chapel Road, half mile from Countryside Centre.
Habitat: Pools formed from clay pits at Ramsey Heights; extensive birch forest (largest in lowland Britain) and reedbed at Holme Fen; mixed woodland, open waters, fen and grassland at Woodwalton.
Key birds: Wide variety of common wildfowl, plus Kingfisher, Grey Heron, Bittern and wintering Goosander on meres. Hen Harriers visit in winter while Marsh Harriers breed in reedbed, along with Bearded Tit and Cetti's Warbler. Common Crane observed in recent years. Wet meadows at Darlow's Farm attractive to breeding Lapwing, Snipe and Redshank and wintering Whooper and Bewick's Swans.
Other notable flora and fauna: Great Crested Newt and rare beetles at Ramsey Heights; otter, hare, deer species, water vole; scarce chaser dragonfly, small copper and white admiral butterflies. Wide variety of bog and heath plants.
Contact: Great Fen Team - 01487 710 420: e-mail: info@greatfen.org; www.greatfen.org.uk

6. NENE WASHES

RSPB (Eastern England Office).
Location: Sat nav: PE7 2DD. TL 318 991. Reserve is 8 miles E of Peterborough, and NE of Whittlesey. Car park at end of Eldernell Lane, off A605 east of Coates. There is currently no signposting to reserve.
Access: Open at all times along South Barrier Bank, accessed at Eldernell. Group visits along central path by arrangement. No access to fields or for wheelchairs along bank.
Facilities: Small car park — one coach max — at end of Eldernell Lane. No toilets or hide. Nene Valley Way path offers elevated views over reserve.
Public transport: Stagecoach Bus runs on A605, alight at Coates, walk down Eldernell Lane. 01733 554 575.
Habitat: Wet grassland with ditches. Often flooded.
Key birds: *Spring/early summer:* Corncrake release scheme. Breeding waders (inc Black-tailed Godwit and Snipe), duck (inc Garganey), Marsh Harrier, Hobby and Tree Sparrow. *Winter:* Waterfowl in large numbers (inc Bewick's Swan, Pintail, Shoveler), Barn and Short-eared Owls, Hen Harrier, Common Crane.
Other notable flora and fauna: Water vole, otter, water violet, flowering rush and fringe water lily.
Contact: Charlie Kitchin, RSPB Nene Washes, 21a East Delph, Whittlesey, Cambs PE7 1RH. 01733 205 140.

7. OUSE WASHES

RSPB (Eastern England Office).
Location: Sat nav: PE15 0NF. TL 471 860. Between Chatteris and March on A141, take B1093 to Manea. Reserve signposted from Manea. Reserve office and visitor centre located off Welches Dam
Access: Access from visitor centre (open 9am-5pm daily except Dec 25/26). Welches Dam to public hides approached by marked paths behind boundary bank. No charge. Dogs on leads. Disabled access to Welches

Dam hide, 350 yards from car park. Groups welcome, but large coaches (36+ seats) cannot traverse final bend to reserve.
Facilities: Car park (inc 2 disabled bays) and toilets. Space for up to two small coaches. Visitor centre unmanned but next to reserve office. Ten hides overlooking the reserve: nearest 350 yards from visitor centre (with disabled access) up to 1.8 miles from visitor centre. Boardwalk over pond — good for dragonflies in summer.
Public transport: None to reserve entrance. Buses and trains stop at Manea — three miles from reserve.
Habitat: Lowland wet grassland — seasonally flooded. Open pool systems in front of some hides, particularly Stockdale's hide.
Key birds: *Summer:* Around 70 species breed including Black-tailed Godwit, Lapwing, Redshank, Snipe, Shoveler, Gadwall, Garganey and Spotted Crake. Also Hobby and Marsh Harrier. *Autumn:* Passage waders including Wood and Green Sandpipers, Spotted Redshank, Greenshank, Little Stint, plus terns and Marsh and Hen Harriers. *Winter:* Large number of wildfowl (up to 100,000 birds) including Bewick's and Whooper Swans, Wigeon, Teal, Shoveler, Pintail, Pochard.
Other notable flora and fauna: Good range of dragonflies, butterflies and fenland flora.
Contact: Site Manager, Ouse Washes Reserve, 01354 680 212; e-mail: ouse.washes@rspb.org.uk

8. PAXTON PITS NATURE RESERVE

Huntingdonshire District Council.
Location: Sat nav PE19 6ET. TL 196 629. Access from A1 at Little Paxton, two miles N of St Neots. Reserve signposted from edge of Little Paxton.
Access: Free entry. Open 24 hours. Visitors' centre open 7 days a week. Dogs allowed under control. Heron trail suitable for wheelchairs during summer. Coaches and group visits by arrangement.
Facilities: Visitors' centre sells books, bird feeders and seed etc, plus light refreshments. Leaflets for reserve can also be purchased. Toilets (including disabled) are available when the visitors' centre is open. Two bird hides (always open), marked nature trails.
Public transport: Buses run from St Neots and Huntingdon to Little Paxton (enquiries 0845 045 5200). The nearest train station is St Neots (enquiries 0845 748 4950).
Habitat: Grassland, scrub, lakes. Site being expanded over the next 10 years, to include extensive reedbed.
Key birds: *Spring/summer:* Nightingale, Kingfisher, Common Tern, Sparrowhawk, Hobby, Grasshopper, Sedge and Reed Warblers, Lesser Whitethroat. Large Cormorant colony. *Winter:* Smew, Goldeneye, Goosander, Gadwall, Pochard.
Other notable flora and fauna: Wildflowers, butterflies (27 species recorded) and dragonflies (21 species regularly seen) are in abundance. Along the meadow trail there are common spotted orchids. Bee orchids are found around the car park. Otters are known to use the reserve.

Contact: The Rangers, Paxton Pits Nature Reseve, High Street, Little Paxton, St Neots, Cambs PE19 6ET. 01480 406 795; www.paxton-pits.org.uk e-mail: paxtonpits@huntingdonshire.gov.uk

9. WICKEN FEN NNR

The National Trust.
Location: Sat nav: CB7 5XP (Lode Lane, Ely). TL 563 705. Lies 17 miles NE of Cambridge and ten miles S of Ely. From A10 drive E along A1123.
Access: Reserve open daily except Dec 25. Entry fee for non-members of NT. Visitor centre and shop open daily (10am to 5pm). Weds to Sun Nov - Feb. Boardwalk suitable for wheelchairs, with 2 hides. Disabled toilet.
Facilities: Toilets, visitor centre, café, nine wildlife hides (two equipped for wheelchairs), boardwalk, footpaths, cycle route (NCN Route 11 passes through

reserve) , coach and disabled parking. Dragonfly Centre open weekends during the summer months.
Public transport: No buses to Wicken.
Habitat: A wetland of international importance, includes open fen, cut hay fields, sedge beds, grazing marsh, partially flooded wet grassland, reedbed, scrub, woodland.
Key birds: *Spring:* Passage waders and passerines. *Summer:* Marsh Harriers, Hobbies, waders and warblers. *Winter:* Wildfowl, Hen Harriers roost on Sedge Fen, Marsh Harrier, Barn and Short-eared Owls, Bittern, Black-tailed Godwit, Cetti's Warbler.
Other notable flora and fauna: More than 8,000 species recorded: 21 species of dragonfly/damselfly, 27 species of butterfly and 1,000-plus species of moth. Water vole, otter.
Contact: The Warden, Wicken Fen, 01353 720 274; e-mail: wickenfen@nationaltrust.org.uk www.wicken.org.uk

Essex

ESSEX Wildlife Trust manages 87 nature reserves of varied habitats throughout this huge county. As well as woodland at Epping Forest, the reservoirs at Abberton and Hanningfield, plus coastal marshes such as Rainham Marshes RSPB and Old Hall Marshes RSPB, are all rich in birds. Try the migration hotspots at the Naze, a bird observatory at Bradwell and even seawatching along the Thames off Southend Pier.

1. ABBERTON RESERVOIR

Essex Wildlife Trust.
Location: Sat nav: CO2 0EU. TL 962 177. Six miles SW of Colchester on B1026 (Colchester - Maldon). Follow signs from Layer-de-la-Haye or Great Wigborough.
Access: Open daily (9am-5pm) except Dec 25/26.

Good viewing where roads cross reservoir. Electric wheelchair for hire.
Facilities: New visitor centre includes toilets, viewing verandah, light refreshments and gift shop. Nature trails with panoramic views, two bird hides overlook water, one more in woodland. Ample parking, including disabled and coaches.
Habitat: 60 acres on edge of expanding 1,200-acre reservoir. Concrete edges being replaced by wader-friendly muddy margins.
Key birds: *Winter:* Nationally important for Coot, Mallard, Teal, Wigeon, Shoveler, Gadwall, Pochard, Tufted Duck, Goldeneye, Smew, Bittern and Goosander regular. Golden Plover flocks on surrounding fields. Passage waders, terns, birds of prey. *Summer:* Tree-nesting Cormorant colony; raft-nesting Common Tern. Hobby, Yellow Wagtail, warblers, Nightingale, Turtle Dove, Skylark, Corn Bunting. *Autumn:* Red-crested Pochard, waders.
Other notable flora and fauna: Dragonflies including broad-bodied chaser, small red-eyed damselfly, butterflies including green and purple hairstreak, roesel's bush-cricket. Brown hare.
Contact: Centre Manager, Essex Wildlife Trust, Church Road, Layer-de-la-Haye, Colchester. 01206 738 172; e-mail:abberton@essexwt. org.uk

2. ABBOTT'S HALL FARM

Essex Wildlife Trust.
Location: Sat nav: CO5 7RZ. TL 963 145. On Blackwater estuary, seven miles SW from Colchester. Turn E off B1026 (Colchester-Maldon road) towards Peldon. Entrance is 0.5 mile on R.
Access: Weekdays (9am-5pm). Two hides with wheelchair ramps. Dogs only in designated area. Wildlife Trust HQ. Working farm so please take care.

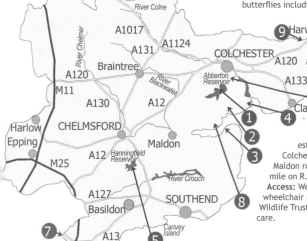

NATURE RESERVES - EASTERN ENGLAND

Facilities: Toilets, three hides, guided walks, fact-sheets, information boards. Many footpaths through active farmland areas.
Public transport: None.
Habitat: Saltmarsh, saline lagoons, grazing marsh, farmland, woodland, freshwater lakes and ponds with Ramsar, SPA and SAC designations.
Key birds: *Winter*: Waders and wildfowl, large roost of Little Egrets. Passage migrants and summer warblers. Skylark, Grey Partridge, Corn Bunting and other farmland species
Other notable flora and fauna: Range of butterflies, reptiles, newts and water vole.
Contact: Trust HQ, 01621 862 960; e-mail: admin@essexwt.org.uk

3. BRADWELL BIRD OBSERVATORY
Essex Birdwatching Society.
Location: Sat nav: CM0 7PN. TM035 085. 100 yards S of St Peter's Chapel, Bradwell-on-Sea. Mouth of Blackwater estuary, between Maldon and Foulness.
Access: Open all year.
Facilities: Accommodation for eight in hut; two rooms each with four bunks; blankets, cutlery, etc. supplied.
Habitat: Mudflats, saltmarsh.
Key birds: *Winter*: Wildfowl (inc. Brent Geese, Red-throated Diver, Red-breasted Merganser), large numbers of waders; small numbers of Twite, Snow Bunting and occasional Shore Lark on beaches, also Hen Harrier, Merlin and Peregrine. Good passage of migrants usual in spring and autumn. *Summer*: Small breeding population of terns and other estuarine species.
Other notable flora and fauna: A variety of dragonflies inc hairy dragonfly and scarce emerald damselfly.
Contact: Graham Smith, 48 The Meads, Ingatestone, Essex CM4 0AE. 01277 354 034.

4. FINGRINGHOE WICK
Essex Wildlife Trust.
Location: Sat nav: C05 7DN. TM 048 193. The reserve is signposted from B1025 to Mersea Island, five miles S of Colchester.
Access: Open Tuesday to Sunday all year, except Dec 25/26. (9am to 5pm). Entry by suggested donation: adult £2, child £1 and family £5. Dogs on leads limited to dog walk area.
Facilities: Visitor centre: toilets inc: baby changing facilities, easy access toilet. One wheelchair is available. Gift shop, light refreshments, optics, observation room with displays, observatory, car park, Reserve: seven bird hides, nature trails.
Public transport: None.
Habitat: Old gravel pit, large lake, many ponds, sallow/birch thickets, young scrub, reedbeds, saltmarsh, gorse heathland.
Key birds: Up to 200 species recorded. *Autumn/winter*: Brent Goose, waders, Hen Harrier, Little Egret. *Spring*: 30 male Nightingales. Good variety of warblers in scrub, thickets, reedbeds and Turtle Dove,

Green/Great Spotted Woodpeckers. *Winter*: Little Grebe, Mute Swan, Teal, Wigeon, Shoveler, Gadwall on lake.
Other notable flora and fauna: Swathes of sea lavender in summer among 350 plants on site. Numerous dragonfly and butterfly species.
Contact: Louise Beary, Fingringhoe Wick Visitor Centre, 01206 729 678; www.essexwt.org.uk e-mail: louiseb@essexwt.org.uk

5. HANNINGFIELD RESERVOIR
Essex Wildlife Trust
Location: Sat nav: CM11 1WT. TQ 725 971. Three miles N of Wickford. Exit off Southend Road (Old A130) at Rettendon onto South Hanningfield Road. Follow this for two miles until reaching the T-junction with Hawkswood Road. Turn R and the entrance to the visitor centre and reserve is one mile on the R.
Access: Open daily (9am-5pm) except Dec 25/26. Voluntary entrance donation. Disabled parking, toilets, adapted hide. No dogs. No cycling.
Facilities: Visitor centre, gift shop, optics, refreshments, toilets, four bird hides, nature trails, picnic area, coach parking, education room.
Public transport: Chelmsford to Wickford bus no 14 to Downham village and walk half mile down Crowsheath Lane.
Habitat: Mixed woodland (110 acres) with grassy glades and rides, adjoining 870-acre Hanningfield Reservoir, designated an SSSI due to its high numbers of wildfowl.
Key birds: *Spring*: Good numbers and mix of woodland warblers. *Summer*: Vast numbers of Swifts, Swallows and martins feeding over the water. Hobby and Osprey. *Winter*: Good numbers and mix of waterfowl. Large gull roost.
Other notable flora and fauna: Spectacular displays of bluebells in spring. Damselflies and dragonflies around the ponds. Grass snakes and common lizards sometimes bask in summer.
Contact: Hanningfield Reservoir Visitor Centre, 01268 711 001; www.essexwt.org.uk

6. OLD HALL MARSHES
RSPB (Eastern England Office).
Location: Sat nav: CM9 8TP. TL 959 122. Overlooks River Blackwater, SW of Colchester. From the A12 take the B1023, via Tiptree to Tolleshunt D'Arcy. Turn L at village maypole then R into Chapel Road (back road to Tollesbury). After approx 1 mile (1.6 km), turn L into Old Hall Lane. Continue up Old Hall Lane, through iron gates, then follow signs straight ahead to car park.
Access: Car park by permit only (free in advance from e-mail address below). Open 9am-9pm or dusk. No wheelchair access or facilities. No coaches. Assistance dogs only.
Facilities: Two trails — one of three miles and one of 6.5 miles. Viewing screens overlooking saline lagoon area at E end of reserve. No visitor centre or toilets.
Public transport: Limited bus service to Tollesbury (one mile). Train to Kelvedon followed by bus to

Tollesbury or cycle.

Habitat: Coastal grazing marsh, reedbed, open water, saline lagoon, saltmarsh and mudflat.

Key birds: *Summer:* Breeding Avocet, Redshank, Lapwing, Pochard, Shoveler, Gadwall, Marsh Harrier and Barn Owl. *Winter:* Large assemblies of wintering wildfowl: Brent Goose, Wigeon, Teal, Shoveler, Goldeneye, Red-breasted Merganser, all the expected waders, Hen Harrier, Merlin, Short-eared Owl and Twite. *Passage:* All expected waders plus Spotted Redshank, Green Sandpiper and Whimbrel. Yellow Wagtail, Whinchat and Wheatear.

Other notable fauna: Brown hare, water vole, hairy dragonfly, scarce emerald damselfly, ground lackey moth, cream spot tiger, white letter hairstreak.

Contact: Site Manager, 01621 869 015. e-mail: oldhallmarshes@rspb.org.uk

7. RAINHAM MARSHES

RSPB (Eastern England office)

Location: Sat nav: RM19 1SZ. TQ 552 792. Off New Tank Hill Road (A1090) in Purfleet, just off the A1306 between Rainham and Lakeside. This is accessible from the Aveley, Wennington and Purfleet junction off A13 and junction 30/31 of M25.

Access: Open Nov 1-Mar 31 (9.30am-4.30pm). April 1 – Oct 31 (9.30am-5pm). Closed Dec 25/26. Entry fee for non-RSPB members. Guided walks – check RSPB website for details. Approx 2.5 miles of boardwalks suitable for wheelchairs and pushchairs.

Facilities: Visitor centre, disabled toilets, car park on site, picnic area, shop, refreshments available. Three bird hides. Entry charges for non-RSPB members.

Public transport: Route 44 (Ensignbus – 01708 865 656) runs daily between Grays and Lakeside via Purfleet. Nearest train station is Purfleet. Reserve is a 15 min walk.

Habitat: Former MoD shooting range, largest remaining area of lowland wetland along the Thames.

Key birds: *Spring:* Marsh Harrier, Hobby, Wheatear, hirundines and other migrants. *Summer/autumn:* Many waders, including Black-tailed Godwit, Whimbrel, Greenshank, Snipe, Lapwing, Avocet. Yellow-legged Gull. Hunting Merlin and Peregrine. *Winter:* Waders, wildfowl, Water Pipit, Short-eared Owl, Little Egret and Penduline Tit most winters.

Other notable flora and fauna: 21 species of dragonfly, including hairy hawker, scarce emerald and small red-eyed damselfly. Marsh frog, water vole, water shrew, fox, stoat, weasel, 32 species of butterfly, and 13 species of orthoptera. Deadly nightshade, flowering rush.

Contact: The Warden, The Visitor Centre, 01708 899 840; www.rspb.org.uk/rainham

8. THURROCK THAMESIDE NATURE PARK

Essex Wildlife Trust/ Cory Environmental Trust

Location: Sat nav: SS17 0RN. TQ 698 806. From Basildon head SW on A13 towards Stanford-le-Hope. Take A1014 exit and follow signs for Walton Hall Farm Museum. Past the museum entrance turn right into

Mucking Wharf Road and take single lane entrance road to visitor centre.

Access: Free access daily (9am to 5pm) except Dec 25/26. Good access for wheelchair users to visitor centre, toilet and paths. Dogs must be on leads.

Facilities: Visitor centre with rooftop viewing platform, café, gift shop, toilets (inc disabled). Bird hide overlooks mudflats.

Public transport: No trains or buses within three miles of reserve.

Habitat: Reclaimed landfill site covering 120 acres overlooking Mucking Flats SSSI and the Ramsar-designated Thames estuary. Features saltmarsh, grassland, woodland, ponds and reedbed.

Key birds: Internationally important numbers of Ringed Plover and Avocet and nationally significant numbers of Grey Plover, Dunlin Redshank and godwits. Also look for wildfowl, Kingfisher, Barn Owl, Reed Bunting, Bearded Tit, Cetti's Warbler and Skylark.

Other notable flora and fauna: Water vole, harvest mouse, shrill carder bee, great crested newt, adder.

Contact: Nature Park 01261 862 960; e-mail: admin@essexwt.org.uk

9. TOLLESBURY WICK MARSHES

Essex Wildlife Trust.

Location: Sat nav: CM9 8RJ. TL 970 104. On Blackwater Estuary eight miles E of Maldon. Follow B1023 to Tollesbury via Tiptree, leaving A12 at Kelvedon. Then follow Woodrolfe Road S towards the marina. Use small public car park at Woodrolfe Green (TL 964 107), 500m before reserve entrance on sea wall. Car park suitable for mini-buses and small coaches.

Access: Open all times along exposed sea wall footpath. Motorised wheelchair access possible to Block House Bay.

Facilities: Bird hide. Public toilets at Woodrolfe Green car park.

Public transport: Hedingham bus services run to Tollesbury from Maldon, Colchester and Witham – call 01621 869 214 for information.

Habitat: Estuary with fringing saltmarsh and mudflats with some shingle. Extensive freshwater grazing marsh, brackish borrowdyke and small reedbeds.

Key birds: *Winter:* Large numbers of wintering wildfowl and waders, particularly Brent Geese and Wigeon, Lapwing and Golden Plover. Short-eared Owl, Hen Harrier and, increasingly, Marsh Harrier. *Summer:* Breeding Avocet, Redshank, Lapwing, Little Tern, Reed and Sedge Warblers, Reed Bunting, Barn Owl. *Passage:* Whimbrel, Spotted Redshank, Green Sandpiper.

Other notable flora and fauna: Plants include spiny restharrow, grass vetchling, yellow horned-poppy, slender hare's-ear. Hairy dragonfly, Roesel's and great green bush-crickets. Hares and occasional common seals can be seen from the sea wall.

Contact: Reserve Manager 01621 868 628. www.essexwt.org.uk

10. WRABNESS NATURE RESERVE AND MARSH

Essex Wildlife Trust
Location: Sat nav: CO11 2TD. TM 167 315. Lies of southern bank of Stour estuary. From B1352 between Bradfield and Wrabness turn down Whitesheaf Lane to reach reserve. Car park is on left just beyond railway bridge.
Access: Open all year. Hard-surfaced path around site suitable for wheelchairs.
Facilities: Car park, footpath, bird hide.
Public transport: Wrabness railway station is a mile walk from reserve on public footpath. Bus service from Colchester to Harwich runs along the B1352.

Habitat: 60-acre site of grazed grassland and open scrub overlooking wader and wildlfowl feeding grounds in Jacques Bay.
Key birds: *Winter:* Internationally important species such as Brent Goose, Shelduck, Wigeon, Pintail, Black-tailed Godwit, Grey Plover, Dunlin, Turnstone and Curlew. Short-eared and Barn Owls hunt over grassland. *Spring/summer:* Nightingale, Whitethroat, Turtle Dove, Bullfinch, Yellowhammer.
Other notable flora and fauna: Wildflowers, plus good range of butterflies and dragonflies.
Contact: Essex Wildlife Trust 01621 862 960; e-mail: admin@essexwt.org.uk; www.essexwt.org.uk

Hertfordshire

WITH more than 40 nature reserves under its control, the Herts & Middlesex Wildlife Trust can offer residents of the urbanised Home Counties a welcome taste of the countryside. Gravel pits such as those at Amwell and Tring are the best places to watch for birds, the latter holding a special place in the history of British birding as the site where Little Ringed Plovers first bred in this country.

1. AMWELL NATURE RESERVE

Herts Wildlife Trust.
Location: Sat nav: SG12 8LT. TL 376 127. In Lee Valley near Ware. From A10, leave at junction signposted A414 to Harlow. At first roundabout, take B181 to St Margarets and Stanstead Abbotts. On entering St Margarets, just before railway, turn L on Amwell Lane. Reserve is on the R (signposted).
Access: Open all year. Dragonfly Trail open May-Sept.
Facilities: Three hides, several viewing areas and Dragonfly Trail boardwalk.
Public transport: St Mary's Church, Hoddesdon Road, St Margarets (310, 311, C4) 5 minute walk from railway station. Rail: St Margarets (0.75 miles). From station walk E along B181 to towpath of River Lee Navigation, then walk N for 0.5 miles to reserve.
Habitat: Disused gravel pit with reedbeds and woodland.
Key birds: *Spring/summer:* Ringed Plover, Little Ringed Plover. *Winter:* Smew, other ducks, Bittern. In process of becoming SSSI for wintering Gadwall and Shoveler.
Other notable fauna: Best county site for dragonflies (19 species recorded), otter, nationally scarce marsh dock, plus early and southern marsh orchids.
Contact: Trust HQ, 01727 858 901; e-mail: info@hmwt.org; www.hertswildlifetrust.org.uk

2. KINGS MEAD

Herts & Middlesex Wildlife Trust /various owners.
Location: TL 352 141. From Ware head SE on A1170 High Street, turn R into Burgage Lane shortly after Ware Museum. Park in public car park. From here pedestrian access is via the River Lee — go over the bridge, turn R and walk 250 yards. Turn L into the reserve.
Access: Open all year.
Facilities: None.
Public transport: Bus stops on Hertford Road (A119). Trains to Ware station (five minute walk to reserve).
Habitat: Largest remaining area of grazed riverside flood meadow in Hertfordshire.
Key birds: 119 species recorded. *Summer:* Skylark, Reed Warbler, Reed Bunting, seven species of breeding warblers, Yellow Wagtail. *Winter/spring:* Gadwall, Shoveler, Wigeon, Teal, Snipe, gulls, waders.

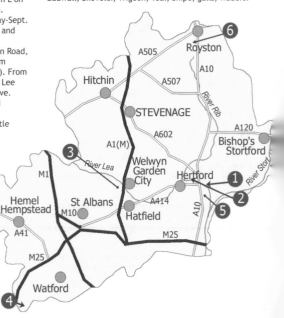

Other notable flora and fauna: 265 species of wildflower, 18 species of dragonfly. Significant population of short-winged conehead.
Contact: Herts & Middlesex Wildlife Trust, 01727 858 901. e-mail: info@hmwt.org

3. LEMSFORD SPRINGS

Herts & Middlesex Wildlife Trust.
Location: Sat nav: AL8 7TN. TL 222 123. Lies 1.5 miles W of Welwyn Garden City town centre, off roundabout leading to Lemsford village on B197, W of A1(M). Park in cul-de-sac next to reserve entrance.
Access: Access, via key, by arrangement with warden. Open at all times, unless work parties or group visits in progress. Keep to paths. Dogs on leads. 150m earth path to hide. Wheelchair access ramp to hide. Coaches welcome and room to park on road, but limit of 30 persons.
Facilities: Two hides, classroom, chemical toilet, paths and bridges. Circular walk.
Public transport: Bus: The Sun Inn, Lemsford Village (36, 61). Nearest railway station Welwyn Garden City (25 minute walk).
Habitat: Former water-cress beds, open shallow lagoons. Stretch of the River Lea, marsh, hedgerows. Nine acres.
Key birds: *Spring/summer*: Breeding warblers, Grey Wagtail, Kestrel, Green Woodpecker. *Autumn/winter*: Green Sandpiper, Water Rail, Snipe, Siskin, Little Egret, occasional Jack Snipe. *All year*: Mandarin Duck, Kingfisher, Grey Heron, Sparrowhawk.
Other notable flora and fauna: Muntjac, fox and stoat. Common butterflies and damselflies in summer.
Contact: Barry Trevis, Warden, 11 Lemsford Village, Welwyn Garden City, Herts, AL8 7TN. 01707 335 517; e-mail: info@hmwt.org; www.hertswildlifetrust.org.uk

4. MAPLE LODGE

Thames Water/Maple Lodge Conservation Society
Location: Sat nav: WD3 9SF. TQ 036 925. South of Rickmansworth, close to village of Maple Cross. From M25 junction 17 turn L at traffic lights. Drive down Maple Lodge Close and park in social club car park.
Access: Restricted to members of MLCS. Visits by non-members and groups can be arranged in advance. Site can be boggy — please keep to designated paths.
Facilities: Information centre, toilets. Ten bird hides — two wheelchair-friendly. Winter feeding stations.
Public transport: Bus services are available from Rickmansworth train station to Maple Cross.
Habitat: A man-made wetland habitat formed from two gravel pits and a sludge settlement area. Two lakes and a reedbed. Mixed broadleaf plantation on eastern side.
Key birds: Wildfowl throughout year, numbers building in winter. All three woodpeckers, plus variety of finches, thrushes and woodland species. Nesting species include Kingfisher, Tawny Owl and migrant warblers. Snipe, Green and Common Sandpipers on passage. Birds of prey including Sparrowhawk, Hobby,

Red Kite and Common Buzzard.
Other notable flora and fauna: 250 species of moth recorded, plus many butterflies and aquatic insects. 125 species of wildflower recorded. Seven of the nine bat species found in Herts recorded.
Contact: Chairman Keith Pursall, 07850 535 986; e-mail: keith.pursall@ntlworld.com www.maplelodge.org

5. RYE MEADS

RSPB/Hertfordshire & Middlesex Wildlife Trust.
Location: SG12 8JS. TL 389 103. Take Hoddesdon turn off A10 and follow brown duck signs. Near Rye House railway station.
Access: Open every day 10am-5pm (or dusk if earlier), except Dec 25/26. Gates are locked when the reserve is closed.
Facilities: Disabled access and toilets. Drinks machine, staffed reception, classrooms, picnic area, car park, bird feeding area. Nature trails, 10 hides. RSPB reserve has close-circuit TV on Kingfisher and Common Tern nests in summer. Car parking charge for non members.
Public transport: Rail (Rye House) 370 metres, bus (310) stops 600 metres from entrance.
Habitat: Marsh, willow scrub, pools, scrapes, lagoons and reedbed.
Key birds: *Summer*: Breeding Water Rail, Tufted Duck, Gadwall, Common Tern, Kestrel, Kingfisher, Little Ringed Plover, nine species of warblers. *Winter*: Bittern, Shoveler, Water Rail, Teal, Snipe, Jack Snipe, Redpoll and Siskin. *Autumn*: Birds on passage including Green Sandpipers, Teal and Snipe, plus occasional rarities.
Other notable flora and fauna: Fen vegetation, invertebrates and reptiles.
Contact: RSPB Rye Meads Visitor Centre, 01992 708 383; e-mail: rye.meads@rspb.org.uk

6. THERFIELD HEATH LNR

Therfield Regulation Trust.
Location: Sat nav: SG8 9NT. TL 335 400. Common land SSSI lies west and south of Royston and is accessed from A505 (Baldock Road).
Access: Open at all times.
Facilities: Open downland walks, gold course and sorts fields.
Public transport: Royston railway station a two minute walk from heath.
Habitat: Natural chalk/grass downland.
Key birds: Noted stop-off site for migrants such as Ring Ouzel and Wheatear. *Spring/summer*: Breeding Skylark, Meadow Pipit, Willow Warbler, Whitethroat, Lesser Whitethroat and Grey Partridge. Good selection of raptors seen regularly.
Other notable flora and fauna: 26 species of butterfly recorded, inc increasingly rare chalkhill blue. Several orchid species, plus pasque flower and wide variety of chalk grassland flowers.
Contact: Therfield Regulation Trust; e-mail: clerk.conservators.therfield@gmail.com

7. TRING RESERVOIRS

All four reservoirs - British Waterways/H&M Wildlife Trust/Friends of Tring Res. WTW lagoon - Thames Water/FoTR.

Location: Sat nav: HP23 4NW (Wilstone Res. SP 905 134). Other reservoirs SP 920 135. WTW Lagoon SP 923 134 adjacent to Marsworth Res. Reservoirs 1.5 miles due N of Tring, all accessible from B489 which crosses A41 Aston Clinton by-pass. NB: exit from by-pass only Southbound.

Access: Reservoirs open at all times. WTW Lagoon and hide open at all times (by permit from FoTR). Coaches can only drop off and pick up, for advice contact FoTR. Wilstone Res. has restricted height access of 2.1 metres. Disabled access available for Startops and Marsworth Reservoirs from car park, as well as FoTR Lagoon Hide.

Facilities: Café and pubs adjacent to Startops Res. car park, safe parking for cycles. Wilstone Res: Pub 0.5 mile away in village. Cafe and farm shop 0.25 mile from car park. Hides on all reservoirs.

Public transport: Buses from Aylesbury and Tring including a weekend service, tel. 0871 200 2233. Tring Station is 2.5 miles away via canal towpath.

Habitat: Four reservoirs with surrounding woodland, scrub and meadows. Two of the reservoirs have extensive reedbeds. WTW Lagoon with islands and dragonfly scrape, surrounding hedgerows and scrub.

Key birds: *Spring/summer*: Breeding water birds Common Terns and heronry. Regular Hobby, Black Terns and Red Kite, warblers including Cetti's. Occasional Marsh Harrier, Osprey. *Autumn/winter passage*: Waders, occasional White-winged Black Tern. *Winter*: Gull roost, large wildfowl flocks, bunting roosts, Bittern.

Other notable flora and fauna: Black poplar trees, some locally rare plants in damp areas. 18 species of dragonfly include black-tailed skimmer, ruddy darter and emerald damselfly. Holly blue and speckled wood butterflies. Chinese water deer, daubenton's, natterer's and both pipistrelle bats.

Contact: Herts & Middsx Wildlife Trust (www.hertswildlifetrust.org.uk) Friends of Tring Reservoir (www.fotr.org.uk).

Norfolk

ITS EAST COAST location and largely unspoilt coastline ensures Norfolk's reputation as our finest birding county. Whatever the season you can be guaranteed a wide variety of birds, including many vagrants, out-and-out rarities and thousands of over-wintering geese, ducks and waders. This survey details a small selection of popular sites, but the revised 3rd edition of *Best Birdwatching Sites: Norfolk* spotlights more than 85 valuable birding locations.

1. CLEY MARSHES NNR

Norfolk Wildlife Trust

Location: Sat nav: NR25 7SA. TG 054 441. Situated four miles N of Holt on A149 coast road, half a mile E of Cley-next-the-Sea. Visitor centre and car park on inland side of road.

Access: Open every day, except Dec 25 as follows: Mar-Oct inc. (10am-5pm). Nov-Feb inc. (10am-4.30pm). The café closes 30 minutes before the centre. Free admission to visitor centre but reserve fee is £5 with Gift Aid (£4.50 without). NWT members and children are free. No dogs.

Facilities: Environmentally-friendly visitor centre (wheelchair accessible) incorporates an observation area, interactive interpretation, including remote controllable wildlife camera, café and sales area. Five hides (three with excellent wheelchair access). Audio trail. Wildlife detective bumbags for children, free to hire. Boardwalk and information boards. Reserve leaflet. Regular events.

Public transport: Coasthopper bus service stops outside, every two hours. Connections for train and bus services at Sheringham. Special discounts to visitors arriving by bus. Call 01603 223 800 for info.

Habitat: Reedbeds, salt and freshwater marshes, scrapes and shingle ridge with international reputation as one of the finest birdwatching sites in Britain.

Key birds: Bittern, Avocet, Marsh Harrier, Spoonbill, Bearded Tit and large numbers of wildfowl, including Wigeon, Teal, Pintail and Brent Goose. Migrating waders such as Ruff and Temminck's Stint. Many rarities.

Contact: NWT Cley Marshes Visitor Centre, 01263 740 008; e-mail: cleyvisitorcentrestaff@ norfolkwildlifetrust.org.uk www.norfolkwildlifetrust.org.uk

2. HICKLING BROAD NNR

Norfolk Wildlife Trust

Location: Sat nav: NR12 0BW. TG 428 222. Approx four miles SE of Stalham, just off A149 Yarmouth Road. From Hickling village, follow brown badger tourist signs into Stubb Road at the Greyhound Inn. Follow Stubb Road for another mile and turn R at the end for nature reserve.

Access: Reserve open all year (dawn to dusk). Visitor centre open Easter to Oct (10am-5pm daily. Cost: adults £4.50 (with Gift Aid), children under 16 and NWT members free. Dogs only allowed on Weaver's Way footpath.

Facilities: Visitor centre, boardwalk trail through reedbeds to open water, birdwatching hides, wildlife gift shop, refreshments, picnic site, toilets, coach parking, car parking, disabled access to broad, boardwalk and toilets. Groups welcome. Water trail boat trips mid-May to mid-Sept (additional charge — booking essential).

Public transport: Morning bus service only Mon-

Fri from Norwich (Neaves Coaches) Cromer to North Walsham (Sanders). Buses stop in Hickling village, a 25 minute walk away.
Habitat: Hickling is the largest, wildest Norfolk Broad with reedbeds, grazing marshes and wide open skies.
Key birds: Marsh Harrier, Bittern, warblers. From October to March the raptor roost at Stubb Mill, provides excellent views of raptors flying in to roost. Likely birds include Marsh and Hen Harriers, Merlin, Crane and Pink-footed Goose.
Autumn/winter: Shoveler, Teal and Goldeneye. *All year:* Bittern, Pochard, Water Rail, Cetti's Warbler, Bearded Tit.
Other notable flora and fauna: Swallowtail butterfly, Norfolk hawker dragonfly, marsh orchid.
Contact: Hickling Broad Visitor Centre, 01692 598 276; e-mail: info@norfolkwildlifetrust.org.uk www.norfolkwildlifetrust.org.uk

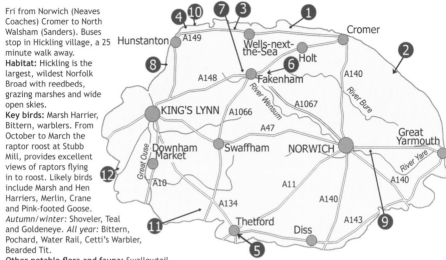

3. HOLKHAM NNR

Natural England (Norfolk and Suffolk Team).
Location: Sat nav: NR23 1RJ. TF 890 450. Three miles W of Wells on A149. From Holkham village turn down Lady Ann's Drive (opposite entrance to Holkham Hall) to park. More parking at end of Wells Beach Road in Wells.
Access: Access unrestricted, but keep to paths and off grazing marshes and farmland. Pay-and-display parking.
Facilities: Two hides. Disabled access.
Public transport: Coasthopper bus service every 30 mins in summer. Norbic Norfolk bus information line 0845 3006 116.
Habitat: Sandflats, dunes, marshes, pinewoods.
Key birds: *Passage:* Migrants, including Yellow Wagtail, Wheatear and many unusual species.
Winter: Wildfowl, inc. Brent, Pink-footed and White-fronted Geese and Shelduck. Shorelark, Twite and Snow Bunting. *Summer:* Breeding Little Tern, Snipe, Oystercatcher and Ringed Plover. *All year:* Marsh Harrier, Grey Heron, Lapwing, Barn Owl, Kestrel.
Other notable flora and fauna: Seablite bushes, attractive to incoming migrant birds, sea aster and sea lavender.
Contact: Sarah Henderson, Hill Farm Offices, Main Road, Holkham, Wells-next-the-Sea, NR23 1AB. 01328 800 730; e-mail: s.henderson@holkham.co.uk

4. HOLME OBSERVATORY

Norfolk Ornithologists' Association (NOA).
Location: Sat nav: PE36 6LQ. TF 717 450. E of

Hunstanton, signposted from A149. Access from Broadwater Road, Holme. Reserve and visitors centre are beyond the White House at the end of the track.
Access: Open daily to members dawn to dusk; non-members (9am-5pm) by permit from the Observatory. Parties by prior arrangement. Dogs on leads.
Facilities: Accredited Bird Observatory operating all year for bird ringing, MV moth trapping and other scientific monitoring. Visitor centre, car park and several hides (seawatch hide reserved for NOA members), together with access to beach and coastal path.
Public transport: Coastal bus service (Hunstanton to Sheringham) roughly every 30 mins in summer. Phone Norfolk Green Bus, 01553 776 980.
Habitat: In ten acres of diverse habitat: sand dunes, Corsican pines, scrub and reed-fringed lagoon make this a migration hotspot.
Key birds: Species list over 320. Ringed species over 150. Recent rarities have included Red Kite, Common Crane, Osprey, Red-flanked Bluetail, Yellow-browed, Pallas's, Arctic and Barred Warblers.
Other notable flora and fauna: Moth trap run March 1 to Oct 31 migrant moths and butterflies recorded yearly.
Contact: Sophie Barker, Holme Bird Observatory, Broadwater Road, Holme, Hunstanton, Norfolk PE36 6LQ. 01485 525 406; e-mail: info@noa.org.uk www.noa.org.uk

5. NUNNERY LAKES

British Trust for Ornithology.
Location: TL 873 815. On the S edge of Thetford, adjacent to the BTO's headquarters at The Nunnery. Main access point is via Nun's Bridges car park, across pedestrian bridge at TL 874 821.
Access: Open dawn to dusk. Public access along permissive paths. Keep dogs on leads at all times. Call

reception in advance to arrange wheelchair access to the lakes and hide.

Facilities: Waymarked paths, information panels, bird hide, boardwalk through wet woodland. Pre-booked coaches can park in grounds.

Public transport: Thetford railway station approx 1 mile (0845 7484 950). Thetford bus terminal approx 0.5 mile (0870 6082 608).

Habitat: Flood meadows, scrape, flooded gravel pits, scrub and woodland.

Key birds: Wide range of species present throughout the year including Grey Heron, Egyptian Goose, Kingfisher, Green Woodpecker. *Spring*: Passage waders, hirundines, Swift, passerines. *Summer*: Warblers, Cuckoo, Oystercatcher, Lapwing, Hobby. *Winter*: Goosander, Teal, Water Rail, Snipe, Siskin.

Other notable flora and fauna: Otter, brown hare, muntjac, grass snake, common lizard. Emperor dragonfly, red-eyed damselfly. Speckled wood and orange tip butterflies. Mossy stonecrop.

Contact: Chris Gregory, The British Trust for Ornithology, The Nunnery, Thetford, Norfolk, IP24 2PU. 01842 750 050; e-mail: chris.gregory@bto.org www.bto.org

6. PENSTHORPE RESERVE AND GARDENS

Private ownership / Pensthorpe Conservation Trust.

Location: Sat nav: NR21 0LN. TG 950 295. Take A1067 Norwich road E from Fakenham. After 1 mile look for signs for Pensthorpe Nature Reserve & Gardens. Look for brown tourist signs from all major roads.

Access: Open all year except Dec 25/26 from 10am (closes 5pm between March 1 and Dec 31; 4pm rest of year). Wheelchair-friendly route to hides overlooking wader scrape. Paths are firm, but those S of River Wensum can be muddy. Toilets for disabled at cafe and main toilet block. Designated Blue Badge parking. Admission charges (see website).

Facilities: Café open from 9am. Shop sells bird food, nest boxes, natural history books and optical equipment.

Public transport: Bus stops at top of drive; Norfolk Green's X29 (hourly service between Norwich and Fakenham). The X10 connects to King's Lynn; the 'Coast Hopper' service links Fakenham to the north Norfolk coast.

Habitat: Woodland, farmland, the River Wensum, eight large lakes, gardens and wildflower meadows.

Key birds: *Spring/summer*: Little Ringed Plover, Lapwing, Oystercatcher and Redshank breed, with Green Sandpipers and other waders on migration. Common warblers plus smaller numbers of Garden Warbler. Linnets nest in the gorse. Hobbies hunt in summer, while Buzzards, Kestrels, Sparrowhawks and Barn Owls all breed. Marsh Harriers breed nearby. *Winter*: Large flocks of Wigeon and Teal, plus Shoveler and Gadwall. Birds of prey inc. Buzzard, Marsh Harrier and Peregrine. Bittern is regularly seen. The woodland and its feeders attract finches in winter including Brambling, Nuthatch and Treecreeper.

Other notable flora and fauna: 21 species of butterfly and 19 species of dragonfly. Southern marsh

and common spotted orchid.

Contact: Pensthorpe Nature Reserve and Gardens, Fakenham Norfolk NR21 0LN. 01328 851 465. e-mail: info@pensthorpe.com www.pensthorpe.com

7. SCULTHORPE MOOR

Hawk and Owl Trust.

Location: Sat nav: NR21 9GN. TF 900 305. In Wensum Valley, just W of Fakenham, on A148 to King's Lynn. Nature reserve sign-posted opposite village of Sculthorpe. Follow Turf Moor Road to Visitor Centre.

Access: Open Tue-Sun plus Bank Holiday Mondays (except Dec 25). April to September: Tues-Wed (8am-6pm), Thur-Sun (8am-dusk). October to March: Tues-Sun (8am-4pm). £3 suggested donation for adult visitors. Guide dogs only.

Facilities: Visitor centre open 9am-5pm (4pm in winter) Tuesday to Sunday, with adapted toilets, hot drinks, interpretive displays and live CCTV coverage from around the reserve. Reserve and 2 hides accessible to wheelchairs and buggies via a mile of boardwalk. Bark chipping path to other hides. Coach parking available.

Public transport: Norfolk Green (01553 776 980 www. norfolkgreen.co.uk) bus X8 Fakenham to King's Lynn stops at end of Turf Moor Road. Sustrans no.1 cycle route runs within 200 metres of Turf Moor Road. Bike racks on site.

Habitat: Wetland reserve, fen containing saw sedge (a European priority habitat), reedbed, wet woodland, pools, ditches and riverbank.

Key birds: More than 80 species recorded, including breeding Marsh Harrier, Barn Owl and Tawny Owl, visiting Buzzard, Goshawk, Hobby, Kestrel, Osprey, Sparrowhawk, also Water Rail, Kingfisher, Marsh Tit, Lesser Spotted Woodpecker and Willow Tit and Golden Pheasant.

Other notable flora and fauna: Otter, water vole, roe deer, 19 species of dragonfly/damselfly, butterflies including white admiral, glow-worms.

Contact: The Hawk and Owl Trust, Turf Moor Road, Sculthorpe, Fakenham NR21 9GN. 01328 856 788; e-mail: leanne.thomas@hawkandowl.org

8. SNETTISHAM

RSPB (Eastern England Office).

Location: Sat nav: PE31 7PS. TF 651 330. Car park two miles along Beach Road, signposted off A149 S of Hunstanton, opposite Snettisham village.

Access: Open at all times. Dogs on leads. Two hides suitable for wheelchairs. Disabled access is across a private road, so please phone office for permit and directions. Coaches — book in advance so height barrier can be removed.

Facilities: Four birdwatching hides, connected by reserve footpath. No toilets on site. Closest hide 1 mile from car park. Three signposted nature trails. Nearest public toilets 100 metres W of reserve car park (april to Oct only).

Public transport: Nearest over two miles away.

Habitat: Intertidal mudflats, saltmarsh, shingle

beach, brackish lagoons, and unimproved grassland/scrub. Highest tides best for good views of waders.
Key birds: *Autumn/winter/spring:* Waders (particularly Knot, Bar and Black-tailed Godwits, Dunlin, Grey Plover), wildfowl (particularly Pink-footed and Brent Geese, Wigeon, Gadwall, Goldeneye), Peregrine, Hen Harrier, Merlin, owls. Migrants in season. *Summer:* Breeding Mediterranean Gull, Ringed Plover, Redshank, Avocet, Common Tern. Marsh Harrier regular.
Other notable flora and fauna: Yellow horned poppies and other shingle flora along the beach.
Contact: RSPB, Barn A, Home Farm Barns, Common Road, Snettisham, King's Lynn, Norfolk PE31 7PD. 01485 542 689; e-mail: snettisham@rspb.org.uk www.rspb.org.uk

9. STRUMPSHAW FEN

RSPB (Eastern England Office).
Location: Sat nav: NR13 4HS. TG 341 065. Seven miles ESE of Norwich. Follow signposts. Entrance across level-crossing from car park, reached by turning sharp R and R again into Low Road from Brundall, off A47 to Great Yarmouth.
Access: Open dawn-dusk. RSPB members free, adults £3.50, children £1.50, family £7. Guide dogs only. Limited wheelchair access – please phone for advice.
Facilities: Toilets, reception hide and two other hides, two walks, five miles of trails.
Public transport: Brundall train station about one mile from reserve. Bus 17A from Norwich stops 0.5 mile from reserve – First Buses (0845 602 0121).
Habitat: Reedbed and reedfen, wet grassland and woodland.
Key birds: *Summer:* Bittern, Little Egret, Bearded Tit, Marsh Harrier, Hobby, Kingfisher, Cetti's Warbler and other reedbed birds. *Winter:* Bittern, wildfowl, Marsh and Hen Harrier.
Other notable flora and fauna: Rich fen flora: six species of orchid, inc marsh helleborine and narrow-leaved marsh orchid. Otter, Chinese water deer and water vole. Swallowtail, white admiral and small heath butterflies, Norfolk hawker, scarce chaser and variable damselfly among 20 dragonfly species.
Contact: Tim Strudwick, Staithe Cottage, Low Road, Strumpshaw, Norwich, Norfolk NR13 4HS. 01603 715 191; e-mail: strumpshaw@rspb.org.uk

10. TITCHWELL MARSH

RSPB (Eastern England Office).
Location: Sat nav: PE31 8BB. TF 750 438. E of Hunstanton, signposted off A149.
Access: Reserve and hides open at all times. Wheelchairs available (no charge). All paths and trails suitable for wheelchairs. Coach parking – pre-booking essential. Car park fee for non-RSPB members.
Facilities: Visitor centre, shop with large selection of optics, birdfood and books, open every day 9.30am-5pm (Nov to Feb, 9.30-4pm). Cafe open 9.30am-4.30pm every day (Nov-mid Feb, 9.30-4pm). Visitor centre and tearoom closed Dec 25/26.

Public transport: Phone Traveline East Anglia on 0871 200 22 33 for times of Coasthopper buses.
Habitat: Freshwater reedbed and fresh water lagoons, extensive salt marsh, dunes, sandy beach with associated exposed peat beds.
Key birds: Diverse range of breeding reedbed and wetland birds with good numbers of passage waders during late summer/autumn. *Spring/summer:* Breeding Avocet, Bearded Tit, Bittern, Marsh Harrier, Reed Sedge and Cetti's Warbler, Redshank, Ringed Plover and Common Tern. *Summer/autumn:* Passage waders including Knot, Wood and Green Sandpiper, Little Stint, Spotted Redshank, Curlew Sandpiper and many more. *Winter:* Brent Goose, Hen/Marsh Harrier roost, Snow Bunting. Offshore Common and Velvet Scoter, Long-tailed Duck, Great Northern and Red-throated Divers.
Other notable flora and fauna: 25 species of butterfly, including all the common species plus Essex skipper and annual clouded yellow. 21 species of dragonfly, including small red-eyed damselfly. Good diversity of saltmarsh plants including shrubby sea-blite and three species of sea lavender.
Contact: Centre Manager, 01485 210 779; e-mail: titchwell@rspb.org.uk

11. WEETING HEATH

Norfolk Wildlife Trust.
Location: TL 756 881. Weeting Heath is signposted from the Weeting-Hockwold road, two miles W of Weeting near to Brandon in Suffolk. Nature reserve can be reached via B1112 at Hockwold or B1106 at Weeting.
Access: Open daily from Apr-Sep. Cost: £4.00 with gift aid, £3.50 without, children free. NWT members free. Disabled access to visitor centre and hides.
Facilities: Visitor centre open daily Apr-Aug, birdwatching hides, wildlife gift shop, refreshments, toilets, coach parking, car park, groups welcome (book first).
Public transport: Train services to Brandon and bus connections (limited) from Brandon High Street.
Habitat: Breckland, grass heath.
Key birds: Stone Curlew, migrant passerines, Wood Lark, Spotted Flycatcher.
Contact: *In season:* The Summer Warden, Weeting Heath, Hockwold Road, Weeting, Brandon, Norfolk. *Out of season:* Darrell Stevens, Norfolk Wildlife Trust, Bewick House, 22 Thorpe Road, Norwich NR1 1RY. 01603 625 540; www.norfolkwildlifetrust.org.uk e-mail: DarrellS@norfolkwildlifetrust.org.uk

12. WELNEY

The Wildfowl & Wetlands Trust.
Location: Sat nav: PE14 9TN. TL 546 944. Ten miles N of Ely, signposted from A10 and A1101.
Access: Open daily except Dec 25. Open Nov to Feb (Mon-Wed 10am to 5pm, Thurs-Sun 10am to 8pm); Mar to Oct (Mon-Sun 9.30am to 5pm). Free admission to WWT members. Wheelchair accessible. Access roads and paths to remote hides may be flooded

check before visiting.

Facilities: Visitor centre (wheelchair-friendly). Cafe opening times: Winter: Mon to Fri 10am to 4.30pm; Sat & Sun 10am to 6.15pm. Summer: 10am to 4.30pm daily (changing to 10am - 4pm daily from April 1). Large, heated observatory, additional 5 hides. Free parking and coach parking. Blue Badge parking, wheelchairs for hire (1 electric scooter and 2 manual chairs), lifts, disabled toilets, ramps.

Public transport: None.

Habitat: 1,000 acres of washland reserve, spring damp meadows, winter wildfowl marsh (SPA, Ramsar site, SSSI, SAC). Additional 200 acres of recently created wetland habitat next to visitor centre.

Key birds: Large numbers of wintering wildfowl are replaced by breeding waders, terns and warblers. *Winter:* Bewick's and Whooper Swans, wintering wildfowl e.g. Wigeon. *Spring/summer:* Common Tern, Avocet, Lapwing, Black-tailed Godwit, House Martin, occasional rarities.

Other notable flora and fauna: Purple loosestrife, meadow rue, mixed grasses. Dragonflies include scarce chaser, emperor, banded demoiselle, small red-eyed damselfly. Approx. 400 species of moth including goat moth. Butterflies include brown argus.

Contact: WWT Welney, 01353 860 711; e-mail: info. welney@wwt.org.uk www.wwt.org.uk/visit/welney/plan-your-visit/

Suffolk

SUFFOLK hosts more Breckland sites than neighbouring Norfolk and there are other inland locations good for birds among the Wildlife Trust's 52 reserves. However, it is the coastal hotspots such as Minsmere, Landguard Bird Observatory, Walberswick and Dunwich Heath that tend to get most attention from visiting birders.

1. BENACRE BROAD NNR

Natural England (Suffolk team)

Location: Sat nav: NR34 7JW (Covehithe). TM 528 827. On coast S of Kessingland. From A12 take minor road to Covehithe at Wrentham. Park near Covehithe church.

Access: Open at all times on permissive paths. Clifftop from Covehithe unstable – walk with care. If sea has breached sandbar it is not possible to reach bird hide from the north. Telescope needed for best views. Dogs on lead.

Facilities: Elevated bird hide on southern edge of Broad.

Public transport: None.

Habitat: Coastline, saline lagoons, reedbeds,

woodland, heathland.

Key birds: 100 species of breeding bird, inc Marsh Harrier, Bearded Tits, Water Rail and wildfowl. Bittern breeds irregularly. Woodlark, Hobby and Wheatear breed on heathland areas and Little Terns fish off the coast. *Winter:* Shorelark possible on cliff-top areas, winter thrushes.

Other notable flora and fauna: Lagoon shrimp, starlet sea-anemone, yellow-horned poppy, grey hair grass.

Contact: Natural England, 110 Northgate Street, Bury St Edmunds IP33 1HP; e-mail: enquiries.east@ naturalengland.org.uk

2. BOYTON MARSHES

RSPB (Eastern England Office).

Location: Sat nav: IP12 3LR. TM 387 475. Approx. seven miles E of Woodbridge. Follow B1084 to Butley. Turn R and follow to Capel St. Andrew before turning L towards Boyton village. Approximately 0.25 mile before village, bear L down concrete track on sharp right-hand turn.

Access: Open at all times. Entrance free but donations welcome. Public footpath on site not suited to wheelchair use. Dogs only on public footpaths.

Facilities: Car park too small for coaches. No toilets or hides.

Public transport: Route 160 Ipswich-Bealings-Woodbridge-Orford (stopping at Boyton village). Reserve is located 0.5 mile NE of village.

Habitat: 57 ha of coastal grazing marsh and saltmarsh on the lower Alde-Orr estuary.

Key birds: *Spring:* Breeding waders and wildfowl, such as Lapwing,

LOWESTOFT
A144
Diss
A143
Southwold
Newmarket
Bury St Edmunds
Saxmundham
A14
Stowmarket
River Debden
Aldeburgh
River Alde
A134
Woodbridge
A12
River Gipping
Orford Ness
Sudbury
IPSWICH
A12
River Orwell
A1071
Felixstowe

Avocet, Shoveler and Gadwall. Spring migrants inc Yellow Wagtail and Whitethroat. Barn and Little Owls. *Autumn:* Wintering wildfowl such as Teal and Wigeon. Migrating waders inc Whimbrel, Black-tailed Godwit and Greenshank. *Winter:* Wintering wildfowl and wading birds, including Wigeon, Teal, Curlew, Dunlin and Redshank.
Other notable flora and fauna: Grassland butterflies such as skippers, wall and meadow browns and dragonflies.
Contact: RSPB Havergate, 01394 450 732. www.rspb.org.uk/reserves/guide/b/boytonmarshes/ e-mail: havergate.island@rspb.org.uk

3. CARLTON MARSHES

Suffolk Wildlife Trust.
Location: TM 508 920. SW of Lowestoft, at W end of Oulton Broad. Take A146 towards Beccles and turn R after Tesco garage.
Access: Open during daylight hours. Keep to marked paths. Dogs allowed in some areas, on leads at all times. Car park suitable for coaches.
Facilities: Education centre with disabled toilet. Firm path around part of the marsh, including easy access gates. Disabled access route along the river wall from Oulton Broad to Carlton Marshes. Free car park.
Public transport: Bus and train in walking distance.
Habitat: 120 acres of grazing marsh, peat pools and fen.
Key birds: Wide range of wetland and Broadland birds, including Reed, Sedge and Cetti's Warblers, Bearded Tit, Hobby and Marsh Harrier.
Other notable flora and fauna: Water vole, 15 species of dragonfly including Norfolk hawker, rare water soldier and raft spider. Plants include common spotted and southern marsh orchids.
Contact: Reserve warden, e-mail: carlton.reserve@ suffolkwildlifetrust.org www.suffolkwildlifetrust.org Education centre - 01502 564 250.

4. DINGLE MARSHES

Suffolk Wildlife Trust
Location: Sat nav: IP17 3EN. TM 479 708 (Dunwich beach car park). Eight miles from Saxmundham. Follow brown signs from A12 to Minsmere and continue to Dunwich. Forest car park (hide) TM 467 710. The reserve forms part of the Suffolk Coast NNR.
Access: Open at all times. Access via public rights of way and permissive path along beach. Dogs on lead in breeding season. Coaches can park on beach car park.
Facilities: Toilets at beach car park, Dunwich. Hide in Dunwich Forest overlooking reedbed, accessed via Forest car park. Circular trail marked from car park.
Public transport: Via Coastlink, Dial-a-ride service to Dingle (01728 833 546) links to buses and trains.
Habitat: Grazing marsh, reedbed, shingle beach, fresh and saline lagoons with forest and heath.
Key birds: *All year:* In reedbed, breeding Bittern, Marsh Harrier, Bearded Tit. *Winter:* Hen Harrier, White-fronted Goose, Wigeon, Snipe, Teal on grazing marsh, Twite. *Summer:* Lapwing, Avocet, Snipe, Black-tailed Godwit, Hobby. Good for passage waders.

Other notable flora and fauna: Site is internationally important for starlet sea anemone — the rarest sea anemone in Britain. Otter and water vole.
Contact: Alan Miller, Suffolk Wildlife Trust; e-mail: alan.miller@suffolkwildlifetrust.org www.suffolkwildlifetrust.org

5. HAVERGATE ISLAND

RSPB (Eastern England Office).
Location: Sat nav: IP12 2NU (Orford quay). TM 425 495. Part of the Orfordness-Havergate Island NNR on the Alde/Ore estuary. Orford is 17km NE of Woodbridge, signposted off the A12.
Access: Pre-booked boat crossings only on first Saturday of every month (10am) and special event weekends (see website). Book in advance through Minsmere RSPB visitor centre, (see below). RSPB members £12, non-members £19. Park in Orford's pay-and-display car park next to quay. Guide dogs only.
Facilities: Toilets, picnic area, five birdwatching hides, viewing platform, visitor trail (approx 2km).
Public transport: Local bus (route 160) from Ipswich to Orford. For timetable info call 0870 608 2608. Bus stop is 0.25 miles from quay.
Habitat: Shallow brackish water, lagoons with islands, Mudflats, saltmarsh.
Key birds: *Summer:* Breeding gulls, terns, Avocet, Shelduck and Oystercatcher. A flock of Spoonbills is present from mid July onwards. *Winter:* Wildfowl and waders including Wigeon, Teal, Pintail, Shoveler, Avocet, Lapwing and Black-tailed Godwit. Also, Short-eared Owl, Marsh Harrier and Barn Owl.
Other notable fauna: Brown hare.
Contact: RSPB Havergate Reserves 01394 450 732; e-mail:Kieren.Alexander@rspb.org.uk

6. HEN REEDBED NNR

Suffolk Wildlife Trust.
Location: Sat nav: IP18 6SQ. TM 471 771. Three miles from Southwold. Turn off A12 at Blythburgh and follow A1095 for two miles to sign-posted car park. The reserve forms part of the Suffolk Coast NNR.
Access: Open at all times. No dogs in hides.
Facilities: Two hides overlook Wolsey Creek marsh and two viewing platforms on waymarked trails.
Public transport: Bus service between Halesworth and Southwold.
Habitat: Reedbed, grazing marsh, scrape and estuary.
Key birds: *Spring/summer:* Marsh Harrier, Bittern, Bearded Tit, Hobby, Lapwing, Snipe, Avocet, Black-tailed and Bar-tailed Godwits, Reed and Sedge warblers. *Passage:* Wood and Green Sandpipers. *Winter:* Large flocks of waders on estuary, inc Golden and Grey Plovers, Bar and Black-tailed Godwits, Avocet and Dunlin.
Other notable flora and fauna: Otters and water voles frequently seen. Four-spot chaser and hairy dragonfly, occasional Norfolk hawker. Brown argus butterfly colony close to car park.
Contact: As Dingle Marshes.

7. LACKFORD LAKES NATURE RESERVE

Suffolk Wildlife Trust.
Location: Sat nav : IP28 6HX. TL 803 708. Via track off N side of A1101 (Bury St Edmunds to Mildenhall road), between Lackford and Flempton. Five miles from Bury.
Access: Reserve and hides open dawn to dusk every day. Visitor centre open winter (10am-4pm), summer (10am-5pm) Wed to Sun (closed Mon and Tues). Tea and coffee facilities, toilets. Visitor centre, Kingfisher Trail and 4 hides good for wheelchair access.
Facilities: Visitor centre with viewing area upstairs. Tea and coffee facilities, toilets. Eight hides. Coaches should pre-book.
Public transport: Bus to Lackford village (Bury St Edmunds to Mildenhall service) — walk from church.
Habitat: Restored gravel pit with open water, lagoons, islands, willow scrub, reedbeds.
Key birds: *Winter*: Bittern, Water Rail, Bearded Tit. Large gull roost (20,000+). Wide range of waders and wildfowl (inc. Goosander, Pochard, Tufted Duck, Shoveler). *Spring/autumn*: Migrants, inc. raptors. Breeding Shelduck, Little Ringed Plover and reedbed warblers. Nightingale, Turtle Dove, Hobby in summer and Osprey on passage.
Other notable flora and fauna: Otter. 17 species of dragonfly including hairy and emperor. Early marsh and southern orchid.
Contact: Lackford Lakes Visitor Centre, Lackford, Bury St Edmunds, Suffolk, IP28 6HX. 01284 728 706; e-mail: lackford.reserve@suffolkwildlifetrust.org

8. LAKENHEATH FEN

RSPB (Eastern England Office).
Location: Sat nav: IP27 9AD. TL722 864. W of Thetford, straddling the Norfolk/Suffolk border. From A11, head N on B1112 to Lakenheath and then two miles further. Entrance is 200 metres after level crossing.
Access: Dawn to dusk, year round. Group bookings welcome. Visitor centre accessible to wheelchair users and a few points on the reserve. £2 car park fee for non-RSPB members.
Facilities: Visitor centre, toilets (inc disabled). Coach parking (must book). Hard and grass paths. Viewpoints. Picnic area with tables. Events programme.
Public transport: On-demand Brecks Bus (Mon to Fri) can be used to reach the reserve from Brandon and Thetford. To book, phone Brecks Bus on 01638 664 304 by noon the weekday before travel. Weekend-only trains on Norwich-Ely service stop in Lakenheath.
Habitat: Reedbed, riverside pools, poplar woods.
Key birds: Principally a site for nesting migrants but ducks and some wild swans in winter. *Spring*: Bittern, Marsh Harrier, Crane. *Summer*: Golden Oriole, Hobby, Reed and Sedge Warblers. *Autumn*: Harriers, Bearded Tit. *Winter*: Ducks, swans, Peregrine.
Other notable flora and fauna: More than 15 species of dragonflies and damselflies, inc hairy dragonfly and scarce chaser. Range of fenland plants e.g. water violet, common meadow rue and fen ragwort. Roe

deer, otter and water vole.
Contact: David White (Information Officer), Visitor Centre, RSPB Lakenheath Fen, Lakenheath, Norfolk IP27 9AD. 01842 863 400; www.rspb.org.uk/reserves e-mail: lakenheath@rspb.org.uk

9. LANDGUARD BIRD OBERVATORY

Landguard Conservation Trust
Location: Sat nav: IP11 3TW. TM 283 317. On Landguard peninsula, off View Point Road S of Felixstowe town centre. Housed in wartime emplacements near Felixstowe Museum.
Access: Visiting by appointment — call 01394 673 782 well in advance to check a volunteer will be available.
Facilities: Migration watch point and ringing station.
Public transport: Buses and trains to Felixstowe centre (1.5 miles away).
Habitat: Adjoining Local Nature Reserve (common land) composed of close grazed turf, raised banks with holm oak, tamarisk, etc.
Key birds: Unusual species and common migrants, especially in spring and autumn. Mediterranean Gull regular on beach. In summer and autumn check for seabird and wildfowl movements offshore. Purple Sandpiper and Rock Pipit at Point in winter.
Other notable flora and fauna: 18 species of dragonfly and 29 species of butterfly have been recorded on the site. Several small mammal species plus sightings of cetaceans and seals off-shore. Nationally rare stinking goosefoot.
Contact: Landguard Bird Observatory, View Point Road, Felixstowe IP11 3TW. 01394 673 782; e.mail: landguardbo@yahoo.co.uk www.lbo.co.uk

10. MINSMERE

RSPB (Eastern England Regional Office)
Location: Sat nav: IP17 3BY. TM 452 680. Six miles NE of Saxmundham. From A12 at Yoxford or Blythburgh. Follow brown tourist signs via Westleton village. Car park is two miles from village.
Access: Car park and hides open dawn to dusk every day except Dec 25/26. Visitor centre open 9am-5pm (9am-4pm Nov-Jan). Shop and tea-room open from 10am. Charge for entry to reserve, except RSPB members. Free entry to visitor centre.
Facilities: Car park, hides, toilets (inc disabled and nappy changing), visitor centre with RSPB shop and cafe. Volunteer guides. Guided walks and family events (see website for details). Coaches by appointment only.
Public transport: Train to Saxmundham or Darsham (5 miles) then Suffolk Coastlink bus (book in advance on 01728 833 526.
Habitat: Coastal lagoons, 'the scrape', freshwater reedbed, grazing marsh, vegetated dunes, heathland, arable reversion and woodland.
Key birds: *All year*: Marsh Harrier, Bearded Tit, Bittern, Cetti's and Dartford Warblers, Little Egret, Green and Great Spotted Woodpeckers. *Summer*: Breeding Hobby, Avocet, Lapwing, Redshank, Common, Sandwich and Little Terns, Mediterranean

Gull, Sand Martin, warblers, Nightingale, Nightjar, Woodlark, Stone Curlew (sometimes visible). *Winter:* Wildfowl inc White-fronted Goose, Bewick's Swan, Smew, Hen Harrier (scarce), Water Pipit, Siskin. *Autumn/spring*: Passage waders inc Black-tailed Godwit, Spotted Redshank, Ruff. Regular Wryneck, Red-backed Shrike, Yellow-browed Warbler. **Other notable flora and fauna:** Red and muntjac deer, otter, water vole, badger. Dragonflies inc emperor, Norfolk hawker and small red-eyed damselfly. 27 species of butterflies inc purple and green hairstreaks and brown argus. Adder. Antlion. Marsh mallow, southern marsh orchid. **Contact:** Reserve Manager, RSPB Minsmere NR, 01728 648 281; e-mail: minsmere@rspb.org.uk

11. NORTH WARREN

RSPB (Eastern England Office).
Location: Sat nav: IP15 5BH. TM 467 575. Directly N of Aldeburgh on Suffolk coast. Take A1094 to Aldeburgh then follow Thorpe Road towards Thorpeness. Use signposted main car park on beach.
Access: Open at all times. Pay-and-display car park on thorpe Road. Please keep dogs on leads. Beach area suitable for disabled.
Facilities: Three nature trails, leaflet available from Minsmere RSPB. Toilets in Aldeburgh and Thorpeness. Three spaces for coaches at Thorpeness beach car park.
Public transport: Bus service to Aldeburgh. First Eastern Counties (08456 020 121). Nearest train station is Saxmundham (six miles away).
Habitat: Grazing marsh, lowland heath, reedbed, woodland.
Key birds: *Winter*: White-fronted Goose, Tundra Bean Goose, Wigeon, Shoveler, Teal, Gadwall, Pintail, Snow Bunting. *Spring/summer*: Breeding Bittern, Marsh Harrier, Hobby, Nightjar, Woodlark, Nightingale, Dartford Warbler.
Other notable flora and fauna: Hairy dragonfly, Norfolk hawker and red-eyed damselfly, green and purple hairstreak butterflies and southern marsh orchid.
Contact: As Minsmere above.

12. REDGRAVE & LOPHAM FENS

Suffolk Wildlife Trust.
Location: Sat nav: IP22 2HX. TM 052 803. Five miles from Diss, signposted and easily accessed from A1066 and A143.
Access: Reserve open all year (10am to 5pm summer, 10am to 4pm winter). Dogs on short leads. Visitor centre is fully accessible. Five waymarked circular trails (wheelchair-accessible gates on 'spider' trail). Trails can be muddy after heavy rain (not wheelchair accessible).
Facilities: Education centre with café, gift shop and light refreshments, toilets, including disabled, car park with coach space. Bike parking area, boardwalk and viewing platform/short boardwalk.
Public transport: Buses and trains to Diss — Coaches

to local villages of Redgrave and South Lopham from Diss. Simonds Coaches 01379 647 300 and Galloway Coaches 01449 766 323.
Habitat: Calcareous fen with open water areas, wet acid heath, river corridor, scrub and woodland.
Key birds: *All year:* Water Rail, Snipe, Teal, Shelduck, Gadwall, Woodcock, Sparrowhawk, Kestrel, Great Spotted and Green Woodpeckers, Tawny, Little and Barn Owls, Kingfisher, Reed Bunting, Bearded Tit, Willow and Marsh Tits, Linnet. *Summer:* Hobby, Blackcap, Chiffchaff, Willow, Reed, Sedge and Grasshopper Warblers, Spotted Flycatcher, Whitethroat, Hobby plus large Swallow and Starling roosts. *Winter/ occcasionals on passage:* Marsh Harrier, Greenshank, Green Sandpiper, Shoveler, Pintail, Garganey, Jack Snipe, Bittern, Little Ringed Plover, Oystercatcher, Wheatear, Stonechat and Whinchat.
Other notable flora and fauna: Otter, water vole, roe, muntjac and Chinese water deer, stoat, pipistrelle and natterer's bats. Great crested newt, grass snake, adder, slow worm, common lizard. More than 300 flowering plants. 27 species of butterflies inc purple and green hairstreaks and brown argus. More than 20 species of dragonfly inc emperor, hairy dragonfly, black-tailed skimmer and scarce emerald damselfly. Fen raft spider population on site.
Contact: Redgrave and Lopham Fens, 01379 688 333; e-mail: redgrave.centre@suffolkwildlifetrust.org www.suffolkwildlifetrust.org

13. WALBERSWICK NNR

Natural England (Suffolk Team)
Location: Sat nav: IP19 9NB (Westwood Lodge). TM 475 733. From A12 take B1387 (signposted to Walberswick). Good views from lane running W from Walberswick towards Westwood Lodge; elsewhere keep to public footpaths, open access heathland or shingle beach.
Access: Parties and coach parking by prior arrangement. Pay-and-display car parking in Walberswick free at Hoist and Westwood Lodge.
Facilities: Three hides (one on S side of Blyth estuary close to White Hart pub; one at East Hill and one in Dunwich Forest overlooking Westwood reedbed).
Public transport: Anglian Buses 601 Halesworth to Lowestoft service stops at Blythburgh and Southwold.
Habitat: Tidal estuary, shingle and saline shore pools, fen, freshwater marsh and reedbeds, heath, mixed woodland, carr.
Key birds: More than 280 bird species recorded. *Spring/summer:* Marsh Harrier, Bearded Tit, Water Rail, Bittern, Nightjar. Avocet and Ringed Plover on shingle. *Passage/winter:* Wildfowl, waders and raptors.
Other notable flora and fauna: Five species of deer, ant-lion, silver-studded blue and white admiral butterflies. Natterjack toad reintroduced.
Contact: Natural England, The Barn, Frostenden Hall Farm, Church Lane, Frostenden, Beccles, Suffolk NR34 7HS. 01502 676 171; e-mail:enquiries.east@naturalengland.org.uk

Northern England

Cheshire

FROM THE FELLS and forests bordering the Peak District to the wader-rich coastal sites along the Dee and Mersey estuaries, Cheshire has much to interest birdwatchers, while the Wildlife Trust's 40-plus reserves cover a broad range of habitats of value to flora and fauna.

1. DEE ESTUARY (BURTON MERE WETLANDS)

RSPB Dee Estuary Office, (formerly known as Inner Marsh Farm).
Location: CH64 5SF. SJ 31927 73914 Located on the Wirral. From Chester High Road (A540) follow signs for Burton Mere Wetlands. Turning down Puddington Lane, the reserve's entrance is just outside Burton Village.
Access: Reserve open between 9am and 9pm (or dusk if earlier) each day; visitor centre opens 9.30am to 5pm. £4 admission for non-RSPB members. Guide dogs only.
Facilities: Visitor centre and café. Large car park, not suitable for coaches. Two major hides (one in reception building) overlooking pools and wetland area, plus viewing screens. Wheelchair access to much of the footpaths and hides. Toilets including disabled facilities. Picnic tables. Guided walks and binocular hire available.
Public transport: Buses between Neston and Hooton stop at Burton post office (600m walk to reserve entrance). Contact Traveline on 0871 200 2233.
Habitat: Former farm and fishery now converted to wetland and meadow habitats.
Key birds: All year: Little Egret. Great Spotted and Green Woodpecker Spring/summer: Avocet, Grasshopper Warbler, Lesser Whitethroat and other commoner warblers, passage Black-tailed Godwit, Spotted Redshank and regular Mediterranean Gull. Hobby, Marsh Harrier, Spoonbill. Autumn: Passage waders (inc Little Stint, Ruff, Spotted Redshank, Green, Curlew and Wood Sandpipers). Winter: Linnet, Brambling, Fieldfare, Redwing, Whooper and Bewick's Swans, Teal, Water Rail, Hen Harrier.
Other notable flora and fauna: Extensive butterfly list. Pipistrelle, noctule, Daubenton's bats, water vole, wide array of orchids. Red-eyed damselfly.
Contact: Burton Point Farm, Station Road, Burton, Nr Neston CH64 5SB. 0151 353 8478; e-mail: deeestuary@rspb.org.uk

2. DEE ESTUARY (PARKGATE)

RSPB Dee Estuary Office.
Location: Sat nav: CH64 6RN. SJ 273 789. On W side of Wirral, S of Birkenhead. View high tide activity from Old Baths car park near Boathouse pub, Parkgate, off B5135.
Access: Open at all times. Viewing from public footpaths and car parks. Don't walk on saltmarsh — the tides are dangerous and nesting birds should not be disturbed. Dogs allowed only on footpaths.
Facilities: Shared car park (closes at 5pm in winter and 8pm in summer), picnic area, group bookings, guided walks, special events, wheelchair access. Toilets at Parkgate village opposite the Square.
Public transport: Bus to Parkgate every hour. Rail station at Neston, two miles from reserve.
Habitat: Estuary, saltmarsh, pools, mud, sand.
Key birds: Spring/summer/autumn: Little Egret, Greenshank, Spotted Redshank, Curlew Sandpiper, Skylark, Reed Bunting. Winter: Pink-footed Goose, Shelduck, Teal, Wigeon, Pintail, Oystercatcher, Black-tailed Godwit, Curlew, Redshank, Merlin, Peregrine, Water Rail, Short-eared Owl, Hen Harrier.
Other notable flora and fauna: On very high tides, the incoming water displaces several mammal species inc pygmy shrew, water shrew, harvest mouse, weasel and stoat.
Contact: Burton Point Farm, Station Road, Burton, Nr Neston, Cheshire CH64 5SB, 0151 3367 681; e-mail: deeestuary@rspb.org.uk

3. FRODSHAM MARSH

Manchester Ship Canal Company.
Location: Sat nav: WA6 7BN. SJ 512 779 (Marsh Lane), SJ 520 785 (Weaver Bend/Ship Street). Large area of mixed habitat lying alongside Manchester Ship Canal, SW of Runcorn. Follow Marsh Lane from Frodsham town centre over M56 motorway until it becomes a dirt track. Follow for three miles to small concrete bridge crossing Hoole Pool Gutter.
Access: Open at all times. Park just before concrete bridge and walk along grassy track to barrier gates and then towards vantage points overlooking Rivers Mersey and Weaver. Wheelchair access difficult.
Facilities: None. **Public transport:** None.
Habitat: Saltmarsh, mudflats, embanked tanks to hold river dredgings, reedbeds, farmland and river.
Key birds: More than 20 species of wader recorded, including large flocks of Black-tailed Godwit, Dunlin and Redshank. Winter: Wildfowl, inc Whooper Swan, Pinkfeet, Shelduck, Pochard, Pintail, Wigeon and other common species, Raven, Short-eared Owl, Hen Harrier, Peregrine. Passage migrants inc wagtails, pipits, terns, Garganey, Wheatear and Whinchat. Summer: Breeding Oystercatcher, Ringed and Little Ringed Plovers, Grasshopper, Sedge and Reed Warblers. Hobbies hunt in autumn.
Contact: None.

4. MOORE NATURE RESERVE

FCC Environment.

Location: Sat nav: WA4 6XE. SJ 577 854. SW of Warrington, via A56 Warrington-to-Chester road. At traffic lights at Higher Walton, follow signs for Moore. Take Moore Lane over swing bridge to reserve.

Access: Open all year. One hide suitable for wheelchairs, other parts of site unsurfaced or gravel paths.

Facilities: Car park, coaches by prior arrangement. Paths, ten bird hides, bird feeding area. Guided walks available on request. See website for wildlife events throughout the year.

Public transport: 62 and 66 buses from Warrington and Runcorn stop in Moore village, less than 1km from reserve. Call 0870 608 2608 for times.

Habitat: Almost 200 acres of wetland, woodland, grasslands, five pools.

Key birds: More than 130 species every year, inc. occasional rarities. *Spring/summer*: Breeding wildfowl and waders, warblers. *Autumn/winter*: Wide variety of wildfowl, Bittern. Also good for gulls, woodpeckers, owls (all five UK species recorded) and raptors. See website for list and latest sightings.

Other notable flora and fauna: Wildfowers including some rarities. Great crested newt.

Contact: The Site Manager, Moore Valley Nature Reserve, 01925 444 689; e-mail: paul.cassidy@wrg. co.uk – www.wrg.co.uk/moorenaturereserve

5. SANDBACH FLASHES

Privately owned.

Location: SJ 720 590. Series of flashes SW of Sandbach. Leave M6 at junction 17 for Sandbach, then head W on A533 before taking minor roads W of railway line. Main birding interest on Elton Hall and Pump House Flashes.

Access: No admittance to site – view from roadside and public footpaths. Elton Hall Flash from new road at SJ 716 595; The Moat (also known as Foden's Flash) from road at SJ 730 614; access Watch Lane Flash from car park at SJ 728 608.

Facilities: None.

Habitat: Fresh and brackish water, reedbed, carr woodland, inland saltmarsh.

Key birds: Wildfowl including Mallard, Teal, Shoveler, Wigeon, Gadwall, Barnacle Goose, Shelduck, occasional Garganey, Mandarin. Waders inc Black-tailed Godwit, Lapwing, Common Sandpiper, Dunlin, Green Sandpiper, Curlew, Snipe, Ringed and Little Ringed Plovers, Little Stint, Ruff, Oystercatcher, Greenshank, Spotted Redshank. Raptors inc Sparrowhawk, Kestrel, Buzzard, Hobby. Warblers: Lesser Whitethroat, Blackcap, Garden Warbler. Ravens, Water Rail, Kingfisher, Wheatear, Stonechat, Turtle Dove, Swift, Yellow Wagtail. Many rarities. Good for gulls due to nearby Maw Green refuse site.

Contact: None.

6. WOOLSTON EYES

Woolston Eyes Conservation Group.

Location: SJ 654 888. E of Warrington between the River Mersey and Manchester Ship Canal. Off Manchester Road down Weir Lane or from Latchford to end of Thelwall Lane. Do not park at the bottom end of Weir Lane.

Access: Open all year. Permits required from Chairman, £10 each, £20 per family (see address below).

Facilities: Toilets located at No 3 bed.

Public transport: Buses along A57 nearest stop to Weir Lane, or Thelwell Lane, Latchford. The bus to Weir Lane, Martinscroft (to access reserve from the N) is No3 from Central Station, Warrington. To access reserve from S take either No1 or No2 bus to Westy, Whitley Avenue and walk to the East end of Thelwall Lane. For further info go to www.warrington borough transport.co.uk

Habitat: Wetland, marsh, scrubland, wildflower meadow areas.

Key birds: Breeding Black-necked Grebe, warblers (including Grasshopper Warbler), all raptors (Merlin, Peregrine, Marsh Harrier). SSSI for wintering wildfowl, many duck species breed.

Other notable flora and fauna: 19 mammal species recorded, plus 241 species of lepidoptera, four species of bat. Wide variety of butterflies and 22 species of dragonfly. Notable plants include marsh and bee orchids, helleborine, snakeshead fritillary and cowslip.

Contact: BR Ankers, Chairman, 9 Lynton Gardens, Appleton, Cheshire, WA4 1PD. 01925 267 355. Please enclose A5 S.A.E. for reply. www.woolstoneyes.co.uk

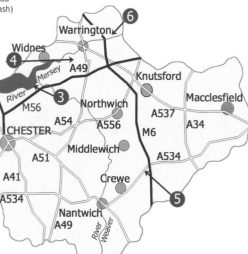

Cleveland /Co Durham

THE RECENTLY-PUBLISHED site guide by Brian Unwin (see page 88) underlines the tremendous birding potential of these two adjoining counties. While coastal sites such as Hartlepool Headland and Whitburn pull in rarities and regular migrants, there are many rewards in the unspoiled inland areas too.

1. BEACON HILL/HAWTHORN DENE MEADOW

Durham Wildlife Trust and National Trust
Location: NZ 427 458. Hawthorn Dene and Meadow located between Easington and Seaham on Durham coast. Leave A19 at Easington or Seaham and join B1432 to Hawthorn village. From N end of village, follow minor road E, signposted 'Quarry Traffic'. After quarter mile, road ends at two metal gates. Park on grass verge on opposite side to cottage. Access is by foot taking the right-hand path. Access to Beacon Hill (NZ 440 455) is along Coastal Footpath or through southern end of Hawthorn Dene.
Access: Open all year, dogs on leads in spring.
Facilities: Information point. Footpaths.
Public transport: Regular bus services from Durham to Hawthorn.
Habitat: Extensive area of semi-natural habitat situated on magnesian limestone escarpment. Steep-sided ravine woodland and limestone grassland.
Key birds: *Summer:* Skylark (important conservation site), Twite, Linnet, Yellowhammer, Goldfinch, Whitethroat, Blackcap, Wren, Long-tailed Tit, Grasshopper Warbler, Reed Bunting, Green Woodpecker, Kestrel, Sparrowhawk. *Winter:* Wide variety of waders inc Turnstone, Purple Sandpiper, Redshank, Curlew, Oystercatcher. Seabirds inc Red-throated Diver, Common Scoter, Guillemot, Cormorant and Great Crested Grebe. *Passage:* Wheatear, Fieldfare, Redwing, Waxwing, Buzzard, Ringed Plover, Dunlin, Knot, Lapwing.
Other notable flora and fauna: Good variety of butterflies. Snowdrops, bluebells and numerous species of orchid, including early purple, bird's nest, lesser butterfly and bee orchids. Grassland plants include bee, fragrant, common spotted and northern marsh orchids. Roe deer, badger and brown hare.
Contact: Durham Wildlife Trust, 0191 584 3112.
e-mail: mail@durhamwt.co.uk www.durhamwt.co.uk

2. DERWENT WALK COUNTRY PARK & DERWENTHAUGH PARK

Gateshead Council.
Location: Sat nav: NE39 1AU (Thornley Woodlands Centre). NZ 178 604. Along River Derwent, four miles SW of Newcastle and Gateshead. Several car parks along A694. Derwent Walk follows old railtrack bed for 11 miles from Swalwell to Consett.
Access: Site open all times. Thornley visitor centre near Rowlands Gill open Mon-Fri (10am-2pm), weekends and Bank Holidays (1pm-4pm). Keys for hides from Thornley Woodlands Centre. Swalwell

visitor centre open daily (9am-4pm). Both centres are closed on Bank Holidays and between Christmas and New Year. Derwent Walk and Derwenthaugh Parks both accessible to wheelchairs from Swalwell centre. Shopmobility scooters can be hired here.
Facilities: Toilets at Thornley and Swalwell visitor centres. Hides at Far Pasture Ponds and Thornley feeding station.
Public transport: 45, 46, 46A, 47/47A/47B buses from Newcastle/Gateshead to Swalwell/Rowlands Gill. Bus stop Thornley Woodlands Centre. (Regular bus service from Newcastle). Information from Nexus Travel Information, 0919 203 3333. www.nexus.org.uk
Habitat: Mixed woodland, river, ponds, meadows.
Key birds: *Summer:* Red Kite, Grasshopper Warbler, Lesser Whitethroat, Kingfisher, Dipper, Great Spotted and Green Woodpeckers, Blackcap, Garden Warbler, Nuthatch. *Winter:* Teal, Tufted Duck, Brambling, Marsh Tit, Bullfinch, Siskin, Great Spotted Woodpecker, Nuthatch, Goosander, Kingfisher.
Other notable flora and fauna: Otter, roe deer, badger, woodland flowers.
Contact: Thornley Woodlands Centre, 01207 545 212; e-mail: countryside@gateshead.gov.uk
www.gatesheadbirders.co.uk www.gateshead.gov.uk

3. HAMSTERLEY FOREST

Forestry Commission.
Location: Sat nav: DL13 3QL. NZ 067 298. Ten miles W of Bishop Auckland. Main entrance is five miles from A68, S of Witton-le-Wear and signposted through Hamsterley village and Bedburn.
Access: Open all year. £3 toll charge (£5 on Bank Holiday weekends). Forest drive and car park close 8pm (5pm in winter). Visitor centre open weekdays (10am-4pm) and weekends (11am-5pm). Visitors should not enter fenced farmland.
Facilities: Visitor centre, tea-room, toilets, shop, access for disabled. Cycles for hire.
Public transport: None.
Habitat: Commercial woodland, mixed and broadleaved trees.
Key birds: *Spring/summer:* Willow Warbler, Chiffchaff, Wood Warbler, Redstart, Pied Flycatcher. *Winter:* Crossbill, Redwing, Fieldfare. *All year:* Jay, Dipper, Green Woodpecker.
Other notable flora: Hay meadows have wide variety of plants including globe flower.
Contact: Forestry Commission, 01434 220 242; e-mail: enquiries.hamsterley@forestry.gsi.gov.uk

4. SALTHOLME

RSPB.
Location: Sat nav: TS2 1TU. NZ 506 231 N of River Tees between Middlesbrough and Billingham. From A19, take A689 north of Stockton and then A1185. After four miles join A178 at mini roundabout. Take third exit and reserve is 250 yards on right.
Access: Open every day except Dec 25. £3 per car for non-members. RSPB members, users of public transport and cyclists free. Opening hours: Apr 1 to Sept 30 (10am-5pm), Oct 1 to Mar 31 (10am-4pm).

NATURE RESERVES - NORTHERN ENGLAND

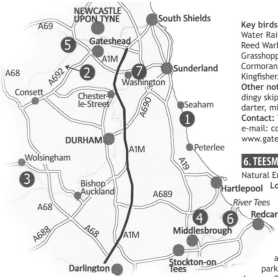

Key birds: *Winter*: Large numbers of wildfowl, Water Rail, occasional white-winged gulls. *Summer*: Reed Warbler, Sedge Warbler, Lesser Whitethroat, Grasshopper Warbler, Water Rail. Roosts of terns and Cormorants. *Autumn*: Passage waders and wildfowl, Kingfisher.
Other notable fauna: 17 species of butterfly, inc dingy skipper. Nine species of dragonflies inc ruddy darter, migrant hawker. Otter, great crested newt.
Contact: Thornley Woodlands Centre, 1209 545 212; e-mail: countryside@gateshead.gov.uk
www.gatesheadbirders.co.uk

6. TEESMOUTH NNR

Natural England (North East Region).
Location: Two components, centred on NZ 535 276 and NZ 530 260, three and five miles S of Hartlepool, E of A178. Access to northern component from car park at NZ 534 282, 0.5 miles E of A178. Access to southern part from A178 bridge over Greatham Creek at NZ 510 254. Car park adjacent to A178 at NZ 508 251. Both car parks can accommodate coaches.
Access: Open at all times. In northern component, no restrictions over most of dunes and North Gare Sands (avoid golf course, dogs must be kept under close control). In southern component, disabled access path to public hides at NZ 516 255 and NZ 516 252 (no other access).
Facilities: Nearest toilets at Seaton Carew, one mile to the N. Disabled access path and hides (see above), interpretive panels and leaflet. Teesmouth Field Centre (Tel: 01429 264 912).
Public transport: Half-hourly bus service (service 1) operates Mon-Sat between Middlesbrough and Hartlepool (hourly on Sundays), along A178, Stagecoach Hartlepool, Tel: 01429 267 082. Seaton Carew train station is 2km from North Gare car park.
Habitat: Grazing marsh, dunes, intertidal flats.
Key birds: Passage and winter wildfowl and waders. Passage terns and skuas in late summer. Scarce passerine migrants and rarities. *Spring/summer*: Breeding Little Ringed Plover, Lapwing, Oystercatcher and Snipe. *Winter*: Internationally important numbers of waterbirds, inc Cormorant, Curlew and Shelduck. Merlin, Peregrine, Snow Bunting, Twite, divers, grebes.
Other notable flora and fauna: Northern component has large marsh orchid populations in damp dune grassland. Colony of 70 common seals at Seal Sands.
Contact: Senior Reserve Manager: 01429 853 325/0300 060 1729; e-mail: northeast@naturalengland.org.uk; www.naturalengland.org.uk

7. WASHINGTON

The Wildfowl & Wetlands Trust.
Location: Sat nav: NE38 8LE. NZ 331 566. In Washington, on N bank of River Wear, W of Sunderland. Signposted from A195, A19, A1231 and A182.
Access: Open all year except Dec 25: 9.30am to

Dogs only allowed in small exercise area.
Facilities: Award-winning visitor centre with café (open to 4pm each day) and shop, large car park, including Blue Badge spaces and coach parking. Toilets (inc disabled), picnic area. Bound gravel surfaces to four nature trails ¬ wheelchair users may need assistance to reach the three bird hides. Walled garden designed by TV gardener Chris Beardshaw.
Public transport: Stagecoach No1 from Hartlepool stops outside reserve.
Habitat: Wet grasslands, reedbeds, pools with tern islands, wader scrapes.
Key birds: *All year*: Lapwing, Peregrine, Water Rail. *Spring/summer*: Breeding Great Crested Grebe, common wildfowl, Snipe, Skylark, Common Tern, Yellow Wagtail. *Autumn*: Varied waders inc Black-tailed Godwits and Green Sandpipers, occasional rarer species. *Winter*: Large numbers of wildfowl and waders, inc impressive flocks of Golden Plover and Lapwing.
Contact: The Warden, Saltholme, 01642 546 625; e-mail: saltholme@rspb.org.uk; www.rspb.org.uk/reserves

5. SHIBDON POND

Gateshead Council/ Durham Wildlife Trust.
Location: Sat nav: NE21 5NW. NZ 192 628. E of Blaydon, S of Scotswood Bridge, close to A1. Car park at Blaydon swimming baths. Open access from B6317 (Shibdon Road).
Access: Open at all times. Disabled access to hide.
Facilities: Hide in SW corner of pond. Free leaflet available.
Public transport: At least six buses per hour from Newcastle/Gateshead to Blaydon (bus stop Shibdon Road). Nexus Travel Line (0191 232 5325).
Habitat: Pond, marsh, scrub and damp grassland.

5.30pm (summer), 9.30am to 4.30pm (winter). Free to WWT members. Admission charge for non-members. Guide dogs only. Good access for people with disabilities.

Facilities: Visitor centre, toilets, parent and baby room, range of hides. Shop and café.

Public transport: Buses to Waterview Park (250 yards walk to Washington), from Sunderland, Newcastle-upon-Tyne, Durham and South Shields. Tel: 0845 6060 260 for details.

Habitat: Wetlands, woodland and meadows.

Key birds: *Spring/summer*: Nesting colony of Grey Heron, other breeders include Common Tern, Avocet, Oystercatcher, Lapwing. *Winter*: Bird-feeding station visited by Great Spotted Woodpecker, Bullfinch, Jay and Sparrowhawk. Goldeneye and other ducks.

Other notable flora and fauna: Wildflower meadows hold cuckoo flower, bee orchid and yellow rattle. Dragonfly and amphibian ponds.

Contact: Dean Heward (Conservation Manager), Wildfowl & Wetlands Trust, 01914 165 454 ext 231; e-mail: dean.heward@wwt.org.uk
www.wwt.org.uk

More detailed reports on 54 sites in Cleveland and Co. Durham in *Best Birdwatching Sites: North-East England*, available from Buckingham Press Ltd

Cumbria

SITES along the Solway coast tend to hog the limelight when it comes to bird sightings, but the Lake District can still offer a typical range of upland birds, plus one Golden Eagle still hanging on at Haweswater and an Osprey watchpoint at Lake Bassenthwaite. In all, the county's Wildlife Trust manages 43 reserves, of which 36 are open to visitors.

1. CAMPFIELD MARSH

RSPB (Northern England office)

Location: Sat nav: CA7 5AG. NY 197 615. At North Plain Farm, on S shore of Solway estuary, W of Bowness-on-Solway. Signposted on unclassified coast road from B5307 from Carlisle.

Access: Open at all times, no charge. Car park at North Plain Farm. Disabled visitors can drive to wheelchair-friendly hide to view high-tide roosts. Grassed paths can be muddy.

Facilities: Small visitor centre opened in 2013. One hide overlooking wetland areas, three viewing screens along nature trail (3 miles).

Public transport: Bus No 93 from Carlisle terminates at reserve's eastern end — 1.5 mile walk to North Plain Farm.

Habitat: Saltmarsh/intertidal areas, open water, peat bog, wet grassland.

Key birds: *Winter*: Waders and wildfowl include Barnacle and Pinkfooted Geese, Shoveler, Scaup, Grey Plover. *Spring/summer*: Breeding Lapwing, Curlew, Redshank, Snipe, Tree Sparrow and warblers. *Spring and autumn*: Passage waders such as Black-tailed Godwit, Whimbrel. Look for Pomarine, Arctic, Great and Long-tailed Skuas over the Solway. *Autumn/winter*: Up to 10,000 Oystercatchers among large roosting wader flocks. Hen Harrier.

Other notable flora and fauna: Roe deer, brown hare. Bog rosemary, bog asphodel, sundews and cot-ton grass. Large numbers of dragonflies (inc azure and emerald damselflies and four-spotted chaser).

Contact: North Plain Farm, Bowness-on-Solway, Wigton, Cumbria, CA7 5AG. 01697 351 330; e-mail: campfield.marsh@rspb.org.uk www.rspb.org.uk

2. DRUMBURGH MOSS NNR

Cumbria Wildlife Trust.

Location: Sat nav: CA7 5DW. NY 255 586 (OS Landranger 85). From Carlisle city centre, head W on B5307 to Kirkbride. After about one mile, turn R to Burgh by Sands. Follow road for 7.5 miles to Drum-burgh village. Turn L by post office, continue down track and park on R past Moss Cottage.

Access: Open all year. Difficult terrain, so it is best to walk on bunds built to re-wet the site.

Facilities: None.

Public transport: Bus service between Carlisle and Bowness-on-Solway stops in Drumburgh.

Habitat: One of four raised bogs south of Solway (rated best in England), woodland, grassland.

Key birds: *Summer*: Red Grouse, Curlew, Redshank and Grasshopper Warbler all breed. *Winter*: Geese from the Solway, plus Short-eared Owl.

Other notable flora and fauna: Large heath butterfly, emperor moth, adder and lizards, roe deer, brown hare. Specialist plants include 13 species of sphagnum moss, sundews, cotton grass and bog rosemary.

Contact: Trust HQ, 01539 816 300; e-mail: mail@cumbriawildlifetrust.org.uk www.cumbriawildlifetrust.org.uk

3. HAWESWATER

RSPB and United Utilities.

Location: Sat nav: CA10 2QT (Haweswater car park). NY 469 108. For the eagle viewpoint, go to Bampton village, 10 miles S of Penrith and five miles NW of Shap. From Bampton, head S towards Haweswater reservoir. Drive down unclassified road alongside Haweswater reservoir, the road ends at a car park.

From here you will need to walk.
Access: Visitors are asked not to go beyond the view-point, which is always open. There is no wheelchair access.
Facilities: Golden Eagle viewpoint, manned Sat/Sun, plus bank holidays, Apr to end Aug (11am-4pm), telescopes available. There is no coach parking.
Habitat: Fells with rocky streams, steep oak and birch woodlands.
Key birds: *Upland breeders:* Golden Eagle, Peregrine, Raven, Ring Ouzel, Curlew, Redshank, Snipe. *Woodlands:* Pied Flycatcher, Wood Warbler, Tree Pipit, Redstart, Buzzard, Sparrowhawk. Breeding Goosander on reservoir. Large gull roost in winter.
Other notable fauna: Red deer, red squirrel.
Contact: RSPB Office, 01931 713 376; e-mail: haweswater@rspb.org.uk

4. ST BEES HEAD

RSPB (Northern England).
Location: Sat nav: CA27 0ET. NX 959 118. S of White-haven via the B3545 road to St Bees village. Car park at end of Beach Road.
Access: Open at all times, no charge. Access via coast-to-coast footpath. The walk to the viewpoints is long and steep in parts. Dogs only on public footpaths.
Facilities: Copeland Council pay-and-display car park and toilets next to reserve. Three viewpoints overlooking seabird colony. Cliff-top path for nearly three miles.
Public transport: Nearest trains at St Bees (0.5 mile). No bus services.
Habitat: Three miles of sandstone cliffs up to 300 ft high.
Key birds: *Summer:* Largest seabird colony on W coast of England: Guillemot, Razorbill, Puffin, Kittiwake, Fulmar and England's only breeding pairs of Black Guillemot (around Fleswick Bay). Linnet, Stonechat, Whitethroat and Rock Pipit in cliff-top heath areas.
Contact: RSPB, North Plain Farm, Bowness-on-Solway, Wigton, Cumbria CA7 5AG. 01697 351 330; e-mail: stbees.head@rspb.org.uk www.rspb.org.uk

5. SMARDALE GILL NNR

Cumbria Wildlife Trust.
Location: Sat nav: CA17 4HG. NY 727 070. NNR occupies a 6km stretch of the disused railway between Tebay and Darlington. Approx 2.5 miles NE of Ravenstonedale on A685 or 0.5 miles S of Kirkby Stephen station. Take turning signed to Smardale. Cross over railway and turn L to junction, ignoring turn to Waitby. Cross over railway and turn L at junction ignoring sign for Smardale. Cross disused railway, turn L immediately and L again to car park.
Access: Railway line is open to all, non-members should obtain a permit before visiting other parts of the reserve.
Facilities: None.
Public transport: Train: nearest station Kirkby Stephen. Buses from here to Kendal, Brough and

Sedburgh.
Habitat: Limestone grassland, river, ancient semi-natural woodland, quarry.
Key birds: *Summer:* Redstart, Pied Flycatcher, Wood Warbler and commoner woodland species. *All year:* Usual woodland birds, Buzzard, Sparrowhawk.
Other notable flora and fauna: Scotch argus, northern brown argus, common blue and dark green fritillary butterflies. Fragrant orchid, common rockrose, bluebell and bloody cranesbill. Red squirrel.
Contact: Trust HQ, 01539 816 300; e-mail: mail@cumbriawildlifetrust.org.uk

6. SOUTH WALNEY

Cumbria Wildlife Trust.
Location: Sat nav: LA14 3YQ. SD 225 620. Six miles S of Barrow-in-Furness. From Barrow, cross Jubilee Bridge onto Walney Island, turn L at lights. Continue through Biggar village to South End Caravan Park. Follow road for 1 mile to reserve.
Access: Open daily (10am-5pm, 4pm in winter) plus Bank Holidays. No dogs except assistance dogs. Day permits: £2 adults, 50p children. Cumbria Wildlife Trust members free.
Facilities: Toilets, nature trails, eight hides (two are wheelchair accessible), 200m boardwalk, cottage available to rent – sleeps 10. Electric wheelchair for hire. Coach parking available. Small admission fee for non-Trust members.
Public transport: Bus service as far as Biggar.
Habitat: Shingle, lagoon, sand dune, saltmarsh.
Key birds: *Spring/autumn:* Passage migrants inc Wheatear, Redstart, Goldcrest

and Willow Warbler. *Summer*: 14,000 breeding pairs of Herring, Greater and Lesser Black-backed Gulls, Shelduck, Eider. *Winter*: Teal, Wigeon, Goldeneye, Redshank, Greenshank, Curlew, Oystercatcher, Knot, Dunlin, Merlin, Short-eared Owl, Twite.
Other notable flora and fauna: 450 species of flowering plants. Natterjack toad at North Walney.
Contact: The Warden, No 1 Coastguard Cottages, South Walney Nature Reserve, Walney Island, Barrow-in-Furness LA14 3YQ. 01229 471 066; e-mail: mail@cumbriawildlifetrust.org.uk

7. TALKIN TARN COUNTRY PARK

Carlisle City Council
Location: Sat nav: CA8 1HN. NY 544 591. Twelve miles E of Carlisle. From A69 E at Brampton, head S on B6413 for two miles. Talkin Tarn is on E just after level crossing.
Access: All year. Wheelchair access around tarn, two kissing gates accessible. Tearoom has lift. Coaches welcome.
Facilities: Tearoom open all year (10.30am-4pm). Mon - Wed, takeaway only, during winter. Dogs allowed. Angling by day permit (with closed season).
Public transport: Bus: infrequent. Tel: 0870 608 2608. Train: nearest station is Brampton Junction. Tel: 0845 748 4950. One mile away by footpath.
Habitat: Natural glacial tarn, mature oak/beech woodland, orchid meadow (traditionally managed), wet mire and farmland.
Key birds: *Spring/summer*: Pied Flycatcher, Spotted Flycatcher, Redstart, Chiffchaff, Wood Warbler. *Winter*: Grebes, Smew, Long-tailed Duck, Goosander, Gadwall, Wigeon, Brambling, swans.
Other notable flora and fauna: Common blue damselfly, common darter, small copper butterfly, otter, red squirrel.

Contact: Greenspaces Team, Carlisle City County, Civic Centre, Carlisle CA3 8QG. 01228 817 200; e-mail: parks@carlisle.gov.uk

8. WALNEY BIRD OBSERVATORY

Location: Sat nav: LA14 3YQ. Walney Island, south of Barrow-in-Furness.
Access: Several areas, notably the golf course and airfield, are restricted but the island's narrow width means most sites are viewable from the road or footpaths.
Facilities: Monitoring and ringing of breeding and migrant, with ringing opportunities for qualified visitors. For availability write to Walney Bird Observatory (address below).
Public transport: Barrow-in-Furness connects to the rail network and local bus routes serve Walney Island. Routes 1 and 1A cover the central area while 6 and 6A cover the north end of the island. No bus route to southern end.
Habitat: Estuarine, maritime, dunes, freshwater and brackish pools, scrub and farmland.
Key birds: Renowned Eider and gull colonies at south end. The winter months provide a wildfowl and wader spectacular across the island. Migrants aplenty appear during both passage periods — the island has a proven pedigree for attracting rare and unusual species.
Other notable flora and fauna: Famed for Walney geranium, but also important for coastal shingle species such as sea holly, sea rocket and sea kale. More than 500 species of moth recorded, inc sand dune specialities such as coast dart and sand dart.
Contact: Walney Bird Observatory, Coastguard Cottages, Walney Island, Barrow-in-Furness, Cumbria LA14 3YQ.

Lancashire

THE COUNTY'S mosses attract huge numbers of wintering Pink-footed Geese, Bewick's and Whooper Swans, while tens of thousands of waders winter in Morecambe Bay. A series of estuaries are attractive to wildfowl and waders. Inland, Pendle Hill attracts regular Dotterel on spring passage.

1. BROCKHOLES

Lancashire Wildlife Trust.
Location: Sat nav: PR5 0UJ. SD 579 300. Site in Preston New Road, Samlesbury, which first opened in 2011, is adjacent to junction 31 of the M6. From S take A59 towards Blackburn and then first exit, signposted to reserve, and follow under the southbound slip road north of River Ribble.
Access: Open 10am to 5pm (April to Oct), 4pm for rest of year. Most paths are surfaced and wheelchair-friendly. £10 refundable deposit for keys to access gates bypassing kissing gates. 16 blue badge parking spaces. Car park charges, but free coach parking.

Guided tours need to be booked. No dogs.
Facilities: Floating World is a cluster of buildings made from sustainable materials and housing a village store and gift shop, restaurant (free wi-fi access), and adapted toilets. Bird hides.
Public transport: Stagecoach No59 or Transdev Lancashire United X80/280 buses between Preston, Blackburn and Accrington stop at Tickled Trout Motel by M6.
Habitat: Created from disused gravel pits, the site alongside the River Ribble now features open water, reedbeds, wet grassland and woodland.
Key birds: *Spring/summer*: Breeding Great Crested Grebe, Lapwing, Redshank, Reed and Sedge Warblers, Reed Bunting, Skylark. *Winter*: Good for wildfowl, inc Pochard, Pintail, Goldeneye and Teal. Passage waders inc Turnstone, Grey Plover, Greenshank, Whimbrel, Curlew, Wood, Green and Curlew Sandpipers and Black-tailed Godwit.
Other notable flora and fauna: Brown hawker and emperor dragonflies.
Contact: info@brockholes.org or phone 01772 872 000.

2. HEYSHAM NR & BIRD OBSERVATORY

Wildlife Trust for Lancashire, Manchester and North Merseyside/British Energy Estates.
Location: Sat nav: LA3 2UP (Duke of Rothesay pub). SD 407 601 W of Lancaster. Take A683 to Heysham port. Turn L at traffic lights by Duke of Rothesay pub, then first R after 300m.
Access: Gate to reserve car park open 10am to 6pm (dusk in winter). Pedestrian access at all times. Dogs on lead. Limited disabled access.
Facilities: Hide overlooking Power Station outfalls. Map giving access details at the reserve car park. No manned visitor centre or toilet access, but someone usually in reserve office, next to the main car park, in the morning. Latest sightings board can be viewed through the window if office is closed.
Public transport: Train services connect with nearby Isle of Man ferry terminal. Plenty of buses to Lancaster from various Heysham sites within walking distance (ask for nearest stop to the harbour).
Habitat: Varied: wetland, acid grassland, alkaline grassland, foreshore.
Key birds: Passerine migrants in the correct conditions. Good passage of seabirds in spring, especially Arctic Tern. Storm Petrel and Leach's Petrel during strong onshore (SW-WNW) winds in midsummer and autumn respectively. Good variety of breeding birds (e.g. eight species of warbler on the reserve itself). Two-three scarce land-birds each year, most frequent being Yellow-browed Warbler.
Other notable flora and fauna: Notable area for dragonflies: red-veined darter breeds at nearby Middleton Community Woodland main pond SD 418 592 (mid June to mid July). Bee orchid.

Contact: Reserve Warden, Heysham Nature Reserve. 01524 855 030. Annual report from Leighton Moss RSPB reserve shop.
www.lancswt.org.uk
http://heyshamobservatory.blogspot.com

3. LEIGHTON MOSS

RSPB (Northern England).
Location: Sat nav: LA5 0SW. SD 478 750. Four miles NW of Carnforth, Lancs. Leave M6 at J35. Take the A6 N towards Kendal and follow brown signs for Leighton Moss off A6.
Access: Nature trail open daily dawn-dusk. Visitor centre open 9.30am-5pm (4.30pm Dec-Jan inclusive except dec 25). Free for RSPB members or those arriving by public transport or bike (you also get 10% off in cafe if you come by public transport or bike).
Facilities: Visitor centre, shop, cafe and toilets, disabled toilet. Nature trails and seven hides (four have wheelchair access), plus two hides at saltmarsh pools. Stairlift to café for those with mobility issues. Binoculars for hire.
Public transport: Silverdale train station (on Manchester Airport to Barrow line) is 250 metres from reserve. Shuttle bus service meets trains and takes passengers to Silverdale village. Call Traveline on 0871 200 2233, or visit http://www.lancashire.gov.uk
Habitat: Reedbed, shallow meres and woodland. Saltmarsh pools approx 1 mile.
Key birds: *All year:* Bittern, Bearded Tit, Water Rail, Shoveler, Gadwall, Marsh Tit, Little Egret. *Summer:* Breeding Marsh Harrier, Reed and Sedge Warbler. Avocet at saltmarsh pools. *Passage:* Good numbers of Black-tailed Godwits in spring with Greenshank, Ruff and godwits in autumn.*Winter:* Large flocks of Starlings roosting, hunting Peregrine and Merlin terrorise overwintering wildfowl.
Other notable flora and fauna: Common reed, otter, red deer.
Contact: RSPB Leighton Moss Nature Reserve, Myers Farm, Silverdale, Carnforth, LA5 0SW. 01524 701 601; e-mail: leighton.moss@rspb.org.uk
www.rspb.org.uk/leightonmoss

4. MARTIN MERE

The Wildfowl & Wetlands Trust
Location: Sat nav: L40 0TA. SD 428 145. Off Fish Lane, Burscough, six miles N of Ormskirk via Burscough Bridge (A59). 20 miles from Liverpool and Preston.
Access: Closed on Dec 25. Opening times: 9.30am-5pm (Oct 27 to Feb); 9.30am-5.30pm (rest of year). Special dawn and evening events. Guide dogs only. Admission charge for non-WWT members. Special rates for coach parties. Fully accessible to disabled, all hides suitable for wheelchairs. Coach park available.
Facilities: Visitor centre with toilets, gift shop, new Mere Side Café, education centre, play area, nature reserve and nature trails, hides, waterfowl collection and sustainable garden.
Public transport: Bus service to WWT Martin Mere

from Ormskirk. Train to Burscough Bridge or New Lane Stations (both 1.5 miles from reserve). For bus times contact Traveline 0870 608 2608.
Habitat: Open water, wet grassland, moss, copses, reedbed, parkland.
Key birds: *Winter*: Whooper and Bewick's Swans, Pink-footed Goose, various ducks, Ruff, Black-tailed Godwit, Peregrine, Hen Harrier, Tree Sparrow. *Spring*: Ruff, Shelduck, Little Ringed and Ringed Plovers, Lapwing, Redshank. *Summer*: Marsh Harrier, Garganey, hirundines, Tree Sparrow. Breeding Avocet, Lapwing, Redshank, Shelduck. *Autumn*: Pink-footed Goose, waders on passage.
Other notable flora and fauna: Whorled caraway, golden dock, tubular dropwort, 300 species of moth.
Contact: WWT Martin Mere Wetland Centre, 01704 895 181; e-mail: info.martinmere@wwt.org.uk

5. MERE SANDS WOOD

Wildlife Trust for Lancashire, Manchester and North Merseyside.
Location: Sat nav: L40 1TL. SD 447 157. 12 miles by road from Southport, 0.5 miles off A59 Preston – Liverpool road, in Rufford along B5246 (Holmeswood Road).
Access: Public footpaths open at all times. Visitor centre open 9am to 5pm. No admission charge but £2 donation encouraged. Car park open until 8pm in summer. Three miles of wheelchair-accessible footpaths. All hides accessible to wheelchairs. Guided walks for bird/wildlife groups can be arranged.
Facilities: Visitor centre with toilets (disabled), six viewing hides, three trails, exhibition room, latest sightings board. Feeding stations. Booking essential for two motorised buggies.
Public transport: Bus: Southport-Chorley 347 and Preston-Ormskirk 2B stop in Rufford, 0.5 mile walk. Train: Preston-Ormskirk train stops at Rufford station, one mile walk.
Habitat: 40h inc freshwater lakes, mixed woodland, sandy grassland/heath.
Key birds: 170 species recorded, with 60 known to have bred. *Winter*: Regionally important for Teal and Gadwall, good range of waterfowl inc Mandarin and Goosander, Kingfisher. Feeding stations attract Tree Sparrow, Bullfinch, Reed Bunting, Water Rail. *Woodland*: Lesser Spotted Woodpecker, Willow Tit, Treecreeper, Nuthatch. *Summer*: Kingfisher. *Passage*: Most years, Osprey, Crossbill, Green Sandpiper, Greenshank.
Other notable flora and fauna: 18 species of dragonfly recorded annually, broad bucker fern, plus more than 200 species of fungi.
Contact: Reserve Manager, Mere Sands Wood Nature Reserve, 01704 821 809; e-mail: meresandswood@lancswt.org.uk www.lancswt.org.uk

6. MORECAMBE BAY (HEST BANK)

RSPB (Northern England).
Location: Sat nav: LA2 6HN. SD 467 666. Two miles N of Morecambe at Hest Bank. Access car park from Hest Bank level crossing off A5105.
Access: Open at all times. Do not venture onto saltmarsh or intertidal area, as there are dangerous channels and quicksands. Paths from car park too rough for wheelchairs.
Facilities: Viewpoint and toilets at local council car park.
Public transport: No 5 bus runs between Carnforth and Morecambe. Tel: 0870 608 2608. Nearest rail station is Morecambe (three miles from reserve).
Habitat: Saltmarsh, estuary.
Key birds: 250,000 waders and wildfowl spend winter on Britain's second-most important estuary site. *Winter*: Wildfowl (Pintail, Shelduck, Wigeon) and waders. This is an important high tide roost for Oystercatcher, Curlew, Redshank, Dunlin and Bar-tailed Godwit.
Contact: RSPB Leighton Moss & Morecambe Bay Nature Reserves, 01524 701601; e-mail: leighton.moss@rspb.org.uk www.rspb.org.uk/morecambebay

7. RIBBLE ESTUARY

Natural England (NNR North Team).
Location: SD 380 240. Lies 7km W of Preston, stretching on both sides of River Ribble as far as Lytham and Crossens. Take A584 and minor roads for north bank and A59 and minor roads for the southern side.
Access: Public footpaths open at all times, but no access to saltmarsh itself.
Facilities: No formal visiting facilities. Ribble Discovery Centre is at Fairhaven Lake (5km W of Lytham).
Public transport: For bus service information visit: www.stagecoachbus.com
Habitat: Ramsar and SPA designation for one of England's largest areas of saltmarsh, and mudflats.
Key birds: High water wader roosts (of Knot, Dunlin, Black-tailed Godwit, Oystercatcher and Grey Plover) are best viewed from Southport, Marshside, Lytham and St Annes. Pink-footed Geese and wintering swans are present in large numbers from Oct-Feb on Banks Marsh and along River Douglas respectively. Banks Marsh can be viewed from the public footpath which runs along the sea defence embankment from Crossens Pumping Station to Hundred End. The large flocks of Wigeon, for which the site is renowned, can be seen on high tides from Marshside but feed on saltmarsh areas at night. Good numbers of raptors also present in winter.
Contact: Senior Reserve Manager, Natural England, Ribble Estuary NNR, 01704 578 774; e-mail: alice.kimpton@naturalengland.org.uk

Manchester, Greater

FOR A largely urban area, there are good places for birdwatching. Pennington Flash is the area's best all-round birding site, while Peregrines and Black Redstarts breed in the city centre and urban regeneration has cleaned up the water to such an extent that increasing numbers of ducks are wintering in Salford Docks. Etherow CP holds Dipper, Grey Wagtail, Pied Flycatcher and all three woodpeckers.

BROAD EES DOLE (SALE WATER PARK)

Mersey Valley Countryside Warden Service
Location: Sat nav: M32 9UP. SJ 799 933. Local Nature Reserve located close to visitor centre in Sale Water Park, Trafford. Access from Junction 6 of M60, following signs for Trafford Water Sports Centre.
Access: No paths within the reserve so view from perimeter paths. Sale Water Park visitor centre car park off Rifle Road. Walk to reserve by following track behind visitor centre.
Facilities: Small concrete bird hide overlooks site.
Habitat: Wetland site with water levels managed to provide feeding and breeding opportunities for a variety of birds such as herons, Kingfisher, Little Ringed Plover and Lapwing.
Key birds: Important site for migratory species and waders inc Snipe and Jack Snipe. Winter wildfowl inc Mallard, Gadwall, Teal, Coot, Moorhen in LNR, wider variety on main lake of Water Park.
Other notable flora and fauna: Spotted orchid, smooth and great crested newts. Variety of fish on main lake in Sale Water Park.
Contact: MVCWS, 0161 881 5639; e-mail: info@merseyvalley.org.uk www.merseyvalley.org.uk

ETHEROW COUNTRY PARK

Stockport Metropolitan Borough Council.
Location: Sat nav: SK6 5JD. SJ 965 908. Site lies at the halfway point on the 12-mile Valley Way Footpath which links Stockport and Woolley Bridge. Situated at Compstall on B6104 near Romiley, Stockport.
Access: Open at all times; permit required for conservation area. Keep to paths.
Facilities: Reserve area has SSSI status. One bird hide, nature trail, visitor centre, café and toilets, scooters for disabled.
Public transport: None.
Habitat: River Etherow, woodlands, marshy area.
Key birds: More than 100 species recorded, inc Sparrowhawk, Buzzard, Dipper, all three woodpeckers, Pied Flycatcher, warblers. *Winter*: Brambling, Siskin, Water Rail. Frequent sightings of Merlin and Raven over hills.
Other notable flora and fauna: 200 species of plant.
Contact: Wayne Bardsley, Etherow Country Park, Compstall, Stockport, Cheshire SK6 5JD. 01614 276 937; e-mail: parks@stockport.gov.uk

HOLLINGWORTH LAKE

Hollingworth Lake/Rochdale MBC.
Location: Sat nav: OL15 0AQ. SD 939 153 (visitor centre). On outskirts of Littleborough, 4 miles NE of Rochdale, signed from A58 Halifax Road and J21 of M62 – B6225 to Littleborough.
Access: Open access to lake and surroundings.
Facilities: Cafes, hide, trails and education service, car parks, coach park by prior arrangement. Free wheelchair hire, disabled toilets and baby changing facilities, fishing. Visitor centre open 10.30am to 4.45pm each day. Toilets and café open at 9.30am.
Public transport: Bus Nos 452, 450. Train to Littleborough or Smithy Bridge.
Habitat: Lake (116 acres, includes 20 acre nature reserve), woodland, streams, marsh, willow scrub.
Key birds: *All year*: Great Crested Grebe, Kingfisher, Lapwing, Little Owl, Bullfinch, Cormorant. Occasional Peregrine, Sedge Warbler, Water Rail, Snipe. *Spring/ autumn*: Passage waders, wildfowl, Kittiwake. *Summer*: Reed Bunting, Dipper, Common Sandpiper, Curlew, Oystercatcher, Black Tern, 'Commic' Tern, Grey Partridge, Blackcap. *Winter*: Goosander, Goldeneye, Siskin, Redpoll, Golden Plover.
Contact: The Ranger, Hollingworth Lake Visitor Centre, Rakewood Road. 01706 373 421. www.rochdale.gov.uk

PENNINGTON FLASH COUNTRY PARK

Wigan Leisure and Culture Trust
Location: Sat nav: WN7 3PA. SJ 640 990. One mile from Leigh town centre and well signposted from A580 East Lancashire Road. Main entrance on A572 (St Helens Road).
Access: Park is permanently open. Five largest hides, toilets and information point open 9am-dusk (except Christmas Day). Main paths flat and suitable for disabled. Main car park pay & display with coach parking available if booked in advance.
Facilities: Toilets (including disabled) and information point. Total of eight bird hides. Site leaflet available and Rangers based on site. Group visits welcome but please book in advance.
Public transport: Only 1 mile from Leigh bus station. Several services stop on St Helens Road near entrance to park. Tel: 01942 883 501 for more details.
Habitat: Lowland lake, ponds and scrapes, fringed with reeds, rough grassland and young woodland.
Key birds: Waterfowl all year, waders (14-plus species) and terns (4-plus species) mainly on passage in both spring and autumn. Breeding birds include nine species of warbler. Feeding station attracts Willow Tit, Stock Dove and up to 40 Bullfinches all year. Large gull roost in winter. More than 240 species recorded, including seven county firsts in the last decade alone.
Other notable flora and fauna: Several species of orchid including bee orchid. Wide variety of butterflies and dragonflies.
Contact: Site Manager, Pennington Flash CP. 01942 605 253; e-mail: pfcp@wlct.org; www.wlct.org/open-spaces/parks/park-information.htm

WIGAN FLASHES

Lancashire Wildlife Trust/Wigan Council.
Location: Sat nav: WN3 5NY (Hawkley Hall school). D 580 035. Leave M6 at J25 head N on A49, turn R on to Poolstock Lane (B5238). There are several entrances to the site; at end of Carr Lane near Hawkley Hall School; one off Poolstock Lane; two on Warrington Road (A573). Also accessible from banks of Leeds and Liverpool Canal.
Access: Free access, open at all times. Areas suitable for wheelchairs. Paths (10km in total) being upgraded. Access for coaches contact reserve manager for details.
Facilities: Six hide screens. Poolstock Lane car park has 300 spaces.
Public transport: 610 bus (Hawkley Hall Circular). Local timetable info - call 0161 228 7811.

Habitat: Open water (eight flashes) with reedbed, wet woodland and rough grassland.
Key birds: More than 200 species recorded. Black Tern on migration. *Summer:* Nationally important for Reed Warbler and breeding Common Tern. Willow Tit, Cetti's and Grasshopper Warblers, Kingfisher. *Winter:* Wildfowl, especially diving duck and Gadwall. Bittern (especially winter).
Other notable flora and fauna: Interesting orchids, with the six species including marsh and dune helleborine. One of the UK's largest feeding assemblage of noctule bats. Water vole. Eighteen species of dragonfly which has included red-veined darter.
Contact: Mark Champion, Lancashire Wildlife Trust, Highfield Grange, Wigan, Lancs WN3 6SU. 01942 233 976; e-mail: wiganflashes@lancswt.org.uk

Merseyside

S EAFORTH DOCKS has a good reputation for rare gulls, while north-westerly gales in autumn bring Leach's Petrels to the tip of the Wirral peninsula, probably the best place in Britain to see them away from their breeding sites.

1. DEE ESTUARY

Metropolitan Borough of Wirral.
Location: Sat nav: CH60 9JS. SJ 255 815. Leave A540 Chester to Hoylake road at Heswall and head downhill (one mile) to the free car park at the shore end of Banks Road. Heswall is 30 mins from South Liverpool and Chester by car.
Access: Open at all times. Best viewpoint 600 yards along shore N of Banks Road. No disabled access along shore, but good birdwatching from

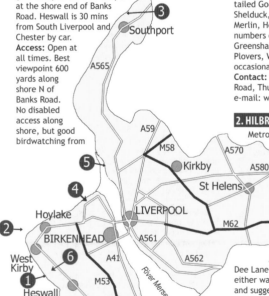

bottom of Banks Road. Arrive 2.5 hours before high tide. Coach parking available.
Facilities: Information board. No toilets in car park. Wirral Country Park Centre three miles N, off A540 has toilets, hide, café, kiosk (all accessible to wheelchairs). Sheldrakes Restaurant at the end of Banks Road with an outside terrace overlooking the foreshore. tel 0151 342 1556.
Public transport: Bus service to Banks Road car park from Heswall bus station, or bus to Irby village then walk one mile. Mersey Travel (0151 236 7676).
Habitat: Saltmarsh and mudflats.
Key birds: *Autumn/winter:* Large passage and winter wader roosts – Redshank, Curlew, Black-tailed Godwit, Oystercatcher, Golden Plover, Knot, Shelduck, Teal, Red-breasted Merganser, Peregrine, Merlin, Hen Harrier, Short-eared Owl. Smaller numbers of Pintail, Wigeon, Bar-tailed Godwit, Greenshank, Spotted Redshank, Grey and Ringed Plovers, Whimbrel, Curlew Sandpiper, Little Stint, occasional Scaup and Little Egret.
Contact: Wirral Country Park Visitors Centre, Station Road, Thustaston, Wirral CH61 0HN. 0151 648 4371; e-mail: wirralcountrypark@wirral.gov.uk

2. HILBRE ISLAND LNR

Metropolitan Borough of Wirral.
Location: Sat nav: CH48 0QA (Dee Lane, West Kirby). SJ 184 880. Three tidal islands in the mouth of the Dee Estuary. Park in West Kirby on A540 Chester-to-Hoylake road – 30 minutes from Liverpool, 45 minutes from Chester. Follow the brown Marine Lake signs to Dee Lane pay & display car park or free parking along the promenade. Coach parking available at West Kirby.
Access: Two mile walk across sands from Dee Lane slipway. No disabled access. Do not cross either way within 3.5 hours of high water – tide times and suggested safe route on noticeboard at slipway.

Call 0151 632 4455 for advice on tide times. Permit required for groups of six and above (apply to Wirral Visitor Centre).
Facilities: Hilbre Bird Observatory by prior appointment only. Composting toilets on the main island (Hilbre) and at Wirral Sailing Centre (end of Dee Lane, West Kirby). Leaflets and tide times from Thurstaston Visitor Centre.
Public transport: Bus and train station (from Liverpool) within 0.5 mile of Dee Lane slipway. Contact Mersey Travel, 0151 236 7676.
Habitat: Sandflats, rocky shore and open sea.
Key birds: *Late summer/autumn:* Seabird passage – Gannets, terns, skuas, shearwaters and after NW gales good numbers of Leach's Petrel. *Winter:* Wader roosts at high tide, Purple Sandpiper, Turnstone, sea ducks, divers, grebes. Passage migrants.
Other notable flora and fauna: Nationally scarce rock sea-lavender and sea spleenwort. Field vole, grey seal. Whales and dolphins seen offshore.
Contact: As Dee Estuary (above).

3. MARSHSIDE

RSPB (Northern England).
Location: SD 353 205. From Southport, follow minor coast road Marine Drive N (1.5 miles from Southport Pier) to small car park by sand works.
Access: Open 8.30am-5pm (dusk in winter) all year. Guide dogs only. Coach parties please book in advance. No charges but donations welcomed. Park in Sefton Council car park along Marine Drive.
Facilities: Information centre, toilets (inc disabled), two hides (one heated) and trails accessible to wheelchairs. Two viewing screens and a viewing platform.
Public transport: Bus service to Elswick Road/Marshside Road half-hourly, bus No 44, from Lord Street. Contact Traveline (0870 608 2608).
Habitat: Coastal grazing marsh and lagoons.
Key birds: *Winter:* Pink-footed Goose, wildfowl, waders, raptors. *Spring:* Breeding waders, inc. Avocet and wildfowl, Garganey, migrants. *Autumn:* Migrants. *All year:* Black-tailed Godwit.
Other notable flora and fauna: Hares, various plants including marsh orchid, migrant hawker dragonfly.
Contact: Marshside RSPB Reserve, 01704 226 190.

4. NORTH WIRRAL COASTAL PARK

Friends of North Wirral Coastal Park
Location: Sat nav: CH46 4TA. SJ 241 909. Located between the outer Dee and Mersey Estuaries. From Moreton take A553 E then A551 N. Turn left onto Tarran Way South then R onto Lingham Lane. Parking available by lighthouse. Foreshore can be viewed from footpath which runs alongside.
Access: Open at all times.
Facilities: Visitor centre, eight car parks, three toilet blocks (one summer-only), extensive footpath network and public bridleways, four picnic areas.
Public transport: The area being served by Grove Road (Wallasey), Leasowe, Moreton, and Meols Merseyrail Stations, and with bus routes along

Leasowe Road, Pasture Road and Harrison Drive.
Habitat: Saltmarsh.
Key birds: Important as a feeding and roosting site for passage and wintering flocks of waders, wildfowl, terns and gulls. Wintering populations of Knot (20,000+), Bar-tailed Godwit (2,000+) and Dunlin (10,000). Redshank (1,000+) and Turnstone (500+) feed on the rocky shore at Perch Rock and on the rocky sea walls. Oystercatcher (500+), Curlew, Grey Plover and Black-tailed Godwit also regularly roost here in relatively high numbers. Small populations of wildfowl, including Common Scoter, Scaup and Goldeneye, Red-throated Divers and Great Crested Grebes also frequently winter on this site.
Other notable flora and fauna: Sea holly, marram grass, storksbill, burnet rose and rarities like the Isle of Man cabbage can be found. One of two known sites in the world for the very rare British sub-species of the belted beauty moth.
Contact: Friends of North Wirral Coastal Park 01516 785 488;
e-mail: info@friendsofnorthwiralcoastalpark.co.uk

5. SEAFORTH NATURE RESERVE

Wildlife Trust for Lancs, Manchester and N Merseyside
Location: Sat nav: L21 1JD. SJ 318 971. Five miles from Liverpool city centre. From M57/M58 take A5036 to docks. Enter via Liverpool Freeport entrance in Crosby Road South.
Access: Organised groups must contact reserve office (see below) at least seven days in advance of their planned trip. Coaches welcome. Wildlife Trust members can apply for two-year permits from the Trust (£10 admin cost) but must pick them up in person from Port Police.
Facilities: Toilets at visitor centre when open, three hides.
Public transport: Train to Waterloo or Seaforth stations from Liverpool. Buses to dock gates from Liverpool.
Habitat: Saltwater and freshwater lagoons, scrub grassland and small reedbed.
Key birds: Noted site for Little Gull on passage (Apr), plus Roseate, Little and Black Terns. Breeding and passage Common Tern (Apr-Sept). Passage and winter waders and gulls - 15 species of gull recorded, with Ring-billed annual and Mediterranean seen almost daily. Passage passerines, especially White Wagtail, pipits and Wheatear, plus a sprinkling of vagrants.
Contact: Seaforth Nature Reserve, Port of Liverpool, L21 1JD. 0151 9203 769; www.lancswt.org.uk

6. WIRRAL COUNTRY PARK

Metropolitan Borough of Wirral.
Location: Sat nav: CH61 0HN. SJ 237 835. SW of Birkenhead. Take coast road E off A540 at Thurstaton (Station Road), visitor centre and parking is at end of road. Other car parking available at West Kirby and Caldy or close to the park at Banks Road or Riverbank Road (Lower Heswall).
Access: Visitor Centre open all year (10am - 4.45pm) except Dec 25.

Facilities: Visitor centre with toilets, bird hide, café, kiosk (all accessible to wheelchairs). Wirral Way footpath runs for 12 miles through park.
Public transport: No public transport to Thurstaston Centre. (Buses stop on A540 by Thurstaston Village 0.75 miles away. Train stations at West Kirby or Heswall.
Habitat: Hedgerows, fields and woodland overlooking large open estuary and shoreline.
Key birds: Common hedgerows and grassland species are joined by summer warblers and winter thrushes. Skylarks, Barn Owls over grassland with Kestrels along

cliff edge. Nearby Dee Estuary is feeding area for migrating birds like Knot, Dunlin and Oystercatcher. Redshank, Shelduck, Lapwing and terns and, particularly at high spring-tides, possible raptors like Peregrine, Hen Harrier and daytime-hunting Short-eared Owls.
Other notable flora and fauna: Up to 10 species of butterfly recorded, locally rare grassland wildflowers along the Dee Cliffs SSSI. Ragworm, Lugworm, cockles, shrimp-like creatures and tiny spire-shells in the adjacent Dee Estuary.
Contact: As Dee Estuary (above).

Northumberland

THIS IS A STUNNING county, with a fantastic range of habitats. The seabird colonies on the Farne Islands are world famous, while Holy Island (Lindisfarne) attracts a range of migrants in spring and autumn, plus huge numbers of wintering birds. Kielder Forest is good for Crossbills and raptors, including Goshawk. The nearby moors hold a good selection of upland species.

1. DRURIDGE POOLS – CRESSWELL POND

Northumberland Wildlife Trust.
Location: Two sites lying on coast between Newbiggin and Amble, off A1068. Sat nav: NE61 5EG for Druridge Pools (NZ 275 963). Roadside parking next to NT's Druridge Links site. 2: Cresswell Pond (NZ 283 944) . Park at bottom of track to Blakemoor Farm. Half mile N of Cresswell.
Access: Day permits needed for both reserves. Wheelchair users can view northern part of Cresswell Pond from public footpath or roadside. Dogs on leads.
Facilities: 1. Three hides. 2. Hide.
Public transport: Arriva No 420 (to within 2 miles).
Habitat: 1: Deep lake and two wet meadows with pools behind dunes. 2: Shallow brackish lagoon behind dunes fringed by saltmarsh and reedbed, some mudflats.
Key birds: 1: Especially good in spring. Winter and breeding wildfowl (mostly Wigeon and Teal); passage and breeding waders. 2: Good for waders, esp. on passage. Most northly recorded of breeding Avocets in 2011. Pinkfooted Geese in winter, plus wildfowl.
Other notable flora and fauna: The sheltered sunny banks are good for a range of butterflies and dragonflies in summer at Druridge Pools. Otters are often seen by the lakes.
Contact: Northumberland Wildlife Trust, 01912 846 884; e-mail: mail@northwt.org.uk www.nwt.org.uk

2. EAST CHEVINGTON

Northumberland Wildlife Trust.
Location: Sat nav: NE61 5BX. NZ 270 990. Near Red Row, overlooking Druridge Bay, off A 1068 between Hauxley and Cresswell.
Access: Main access from overflow car park at

Druridge Bay Country Park (signed from main road). **Facilities:** Four public hides, café, toilets and information at Country Park (County Council). ID boards for coastal plants.
Public transport: Arriva 420 and 423 bus services.
Habitat: Ponds and reedbeds created from former open cast coal mine. Areas of scrub and grassland.
Key birds: Large numbers of wildfowl, including Greylag and Pinkfooted Geese in winter. Breeding Skylark, Stonechat, Reed Bunting, plus Reed, Sedge and Grasshopper Warblers. Capable of attracting rarities at any time of year. Marsh Harriers bred in 2009 (first county record for 130 years).
Other notable flora and fauna: Coastal wildflowers and in grassland, dyer's greenweed.
Contact: Northumberland Wildlife Trust, 01912 846 884; e-mail: mail@northwt.org.uk www.nwt.org.uk

3. FARNE ISLANDS

The National Trust.
Location: Sat nav: NE68 7SS (Seahouses). NU 230 370. Access by boat from Seahouses Harbour, which is reached from A1.
Access: Apr, Aug-Oct: Inner Farne and Staple 10.30am-6pm (majority of boats land at Inner Farne when conditions are calm). May-Jul: Staple Island 10.30am-1.30pm, Inner Farne: 1.30pm-5pm. Disabled access possible on Inner Farne, telephone Property Manager for details. Dogs allowed on boats but not on islands. NT fees for visiting islands do not include boatmens' fees.
Facilities: Toilets on Inner Farne.
Public transport: Nearest rail stations at Alnmouth and Berwick. Hourly Travelsure buses between Budle and Beadnell Bays (Mon-Sat). Call 01665 720 955.
Habitat: Maritime islands — between 15-28 depending on height of tide.
Key birds: 18 species of seabirds/waders, four species of tern (including Roseate), 40,000-plus pairs of Puffin, 33,000 pairs of Guillemots, 800 Eider, Rock Pipit, Pied Wagtail etc.
Contact: David Steel, Farne Islands, Seahouses NE68 7SR. 01665 720 651.
e-mail: farneislands@nationaltrust.org.uk

4. KIELDER FOREST PARK

Forestry Commission
Location: Sat nav: NE48 1ER (Kielder Castle). NY 632 934. Kielder Castle is situated at N end of Kielder Water, NW of Bellingham, 20 miles from Hexham.
Access: Forest open all year. Toll charge on 12-mile forest drive (rough surface) and £4 car park charge applies. Visitor centre has limited opening in winter.
Facilities: Visitor centre, exhibition, toilets, shop, access for disabled, licensed café. Local facilities include youth hostel, camp site, pub and garage. Red squirrel hides at Leaplish Waterside Park and Kielder Castle. Nature reserve at Bakethin.
Public transport: 880 bus service runs Tuesdays, Fridays and Saturdays from Hexham. Following the same route but from Bellingham on Mondays and Thursdays is the 693.
Habitat: Commercial woodland, mixed and broadleaved trees.
Key birds: Breeding Ospreys since 2009. *Spring/summer*: Goshawk, Chiffchaff, Willow Warbler, Redstart, Siskin. *Winter*: Crossbill, Siskin and winter thrushes. *Resident*: Jay, Dipper, Great Spotted Woodpecker, Tawny Owl, Song Thrush, Goldcrest.
Other notable flora and fauna: Impressive display of northern marsh orchids at entrance to Kielder Castle. Red squirrel, badger, otter, roe deer, seven species of bat.
Contact: Forestry Commission, 01434 220 242.
e-mail: kieldercastle@forestry.gsi.gov.uk

5. LINDISFARNE ISLAND

Natural England (Northumbria Team).
Location: Sat nav: TD15 2SS. NU 090 430. Island access lies two miles E of A1 at Beal, 10 miles S of Berwick-on-Tweed.
Access: Causeway floods at high tide, so check when it is safe to cross. Some restricted access (bird refuges). Coach parking available on Holy Island.
Facilities: Toilets, visitor centre in village. Hide on island (new hide with disabled access at Fenham-le-Moor). Self-guided trail on island.
Public transport: Irregular bus service to Holy Island, mainly in summer. Main bus route follows mainland boundary of site north-south.
Habitat: Dunes, sand, mudflats and saltmarsh.
Key birds: *Passage and winter*: Wildfowl and waders, including pale-bellied Brent Goose, Long-tailed Duck and Whooper Swan. Rare migrants.
Other notable flora and fauna: Butterflies include dark green fritillary (July) and grayling (August). Guided walks advertised for nine species of orchid including coralroot and Lindisfarne helleborine.
Contact: Reserve Manager, Beal Station, Berwick-on-Tweed, TD15 2PB. 01289 381 470.

6. PRESTWICK CARR

Northumberland Wildlife Trust.
Location: Sat nav: NE20 9UD (Prestwick). NZ 192 733. Seven miles NW of Newcastle city centre between Dinnington and Ponteland. Take A696 from A1 western bypass for three miles and take minor road to Prestwick hamlet. Park on minor roads north of Prestwick and Dinnington.
Access: Restricted to minor roads and a bridleway across the carr. No access to northern section when military firing range between Prestwick Mill Farm and Berwick Hill is in use.
Facilities: None.
Habitat: SSSI designation for section of lowland raised mire, woodland, farmland.
Public transport: Bus service 45 runs between Newcastle Haymarket and Dinnington (0.75 mile walk to carr's eastern end).
Key birds: A noted raptor watchpoint: 2010's White-tailed Eagle became 14th bird of prey species recorded since 1990s. Hen Harriers are regular between Oct and Jan, along with Merlin and Peregrine. Barn, Little, Tawny and Long-eared Owls all nest and Short-eared Owls hunt in winter. Waders occur in large numbers at passage times if carr is flooded. Water Rail, Kingfisher, Stonechat, Whinchat and Willow Tit are resident with a good range of summer migrants, including Grasshopper Warbler.
Contact: Trust HQ, 01912 846 884;
e-mail: mail@northwt.org.uk www.nwt.org.uk

7. WHITELEE MOOR

Northumberland Wildlife Trust.
Location: Sat nav: TD8 6PT (Carter Bar). NT 690 065. Reserve located at head of Redesdale, south of A68 Newcastle to Jedburgh road where it crosses Scottish Border at Carter Bar.
Access: Park at tourist car park at Carter Bar and on lay-bys on forest track at reservoir end. A public footpath along old track to Whitelee Limeworks and

then southwards extends to site's southern boundary and eastwards to link up with a bridleway from White Kielder Burn to Chattlehope Burn. Additionally there is access on foot via Forest Enterprise road near eastern corner of reserve. Reserve is remote and wild, so hill-walking experience needed if attempting long walks.

Facilities: Car park and lay-bys.
Habitat: Active blanket bog and heather heath.
Key birds: The River Rede and its tributaries add to the habitat and bird diversity. Notable breeding birds include Merlin and Stonechat. Black Grouse, Skylark, Meadow Pipit, Dunlin, Curlew, Golden Plover, Grey Wagtail, Dipper and Ring Ouzel regularly visit the reserve.

Other notable flora and fauna: Otters often hunt along the Rede and a herd of feral goats may be seen.
Contact: Trust HQ, 01912 846 884;
e-mail: mail@northwt.org.uk www.nwt.org.uk

Yorkshire, East Riding

COASTAL birding dominates here, with Bempton Cliffs probably the best seabird colony in England, with Puffins in front of your face and a Gannetry to boot. Two headlands — Flamborough Head and Spurn Point — attract migrants, including scarce vagrants, in autumn. Book a boat trip from Bridlington to see shearwaters and skuas in autumn.

1. BEMPTON CLIFFS

RSPB (Northern England).
Location: Sat nav: YO15 1JF. TA 197 738. Near Bridlington. Take Cliff Lane N from Bempton village off B1229 to car park and visitor centre.
Access: Visitor centre open year round. 9.30am to 5pm Mar - Oct; 9.30am to 4pm Nov - Feb. Car parking fee for non-RSPB members. Cliff-top public footpath with two observation points accessible for wheelchair users. Dogs on leads.
Facilities: Visitor centre, toilets inc disabled, light refreshments, five cliff-top observation points, picnic area, limited coach parking. Four miles of stunning chalk cliffs, highest in county. Binoculars for hire.
Public transport: Bempton railway station (limited service) 1.5 miles — irregular bus service to village 1.25 miles from reserve.
Habitat: Seabird

nesting cliffs, farmland, grassland, coastal scrub.
Key birds: Largest mainland seabird colony in UK; only Gannet colony in England. Birds present January to October with numbers peaking in excess of 200,000 between Apr - Jun. Includes Kittiwake, Gannet, Puffin, Guillemot, Razorbill and Fulmar. Nesting Tree Sparrow and Corn Bunting. Passage skuas, shearwaters, terns and passerine migrants.
Other notable flora and fauna: Harbour porpoise and grey seal regularly offshore. Bee and northern marsh orchids can occur.
Contact: RSPB Bempton Cliffs Nature Reserve, Cliff Lane, Bempton YO15 1JF. 01262 851 179;
e-mail: bempton.cliffs@rspb.org.uk

2. BLACKTOFT SANDS

RSPB (Northern England).
Location: Sat nav: DN14 8HL. SE 843 232. Eight miles E of Goole. Follow brown tourist signs on minor road between Ousefleet and Adlingfleet.
Access: Reserve open 9am-9pm or dusk if earlier throughout year. Reception hide open daily 9am to 4pm (April to Oct) and at weekends and selected weekdays outside this period. RSPB members free, £4 permit for non-members, £2 concessionary, £1 under-16s, £7 family. Guide dogs only.
Facilities: Car park, toilets, visitor centre, six hides with wheelchair spaces, footpaths suitable for wheelchairs. Binoculars for hire.
Public transport: Goole/Scunthorpe bus 357 (Sweynes' Coaches) stops outside reserve entrance). Visit: www.sweyne.co.uk for details.
Habitat: Reedbed, saline lagoons, lowland wet grassland, willow scrub.
Key birds: 270 species recorded. *Summer*: Breeding Avocet, Marsh Harrier, Bittern, Bearded Tit, passage waders (exceptional list inc many rarities). *Winter*: Hen Harrier, Merlin, Peregrine, wildfowl.
Other notable flora and fauna: Good place to see water vole. Small number of dragonflies and damselflies including black-tailed skimmer, four-spotted chaser, large red damselfly. Marsh sow thistle easily seen from footpaths in summer.

Map showing locations: Bridlington, Flamborough Head, Driffield, Hornsea, Market Weighton, Beverley, Withernsea, HULL, Goole, Spurn Head, with roads A166, A164, A1079, A165, A614, M62, A63, A1033, M18 and River Hull, River Humber.

NATURE RESERVES - NORTHERN ENGLAND

Contact: Visitor Development Officer, Blacktoft Sands RSPB reserve, Hillcrest, Whitgift, Nr Goole DN14 8HL. 01405 704 665; e-mail: blacktoft.sands@rspb.org.uk

3. FLAMBOROUGH CLIFFS

Yorkshire Wildlife Trust.
Location: Sat nav: YO15 1BJ. TA 239 720. The reserve is part of Flamborough headland, approx 4 miles NE of Bridlington. From Bridlington take B1255 to Flamborough and follow the signs for the North Landing.
Access: Open all year. Car park at North Landing gives access to both parts of the reserve. Paths not suitable for wheelchairs.
Facilities: Car park (pay and display), trails, refreshments available at café at North Landing (open Apr-Oct 10am-5pm), toilets.
Public transport: Flamborough is served by buses from Bridlington and Bempton. Phone 01482 222 222 for details.
Habitat: Coastal cliffs, species-rich rough grassland and scrub, farmland. Spectacular views of this chalk coastline and living seas beyond.
Key birds: *Summer:* Nesting Puffin, Guillemot, Razorbill, Kittiwake, Shag, Fulmar, Skylark, Meadow Pipit, Linnet, Whitethroat, Yellowhammer, Tree Sparrow, occasional Corn Bunting. Thornwick reedbeds hold Reed and Sedge Warblers and Reed Buntings. *Passage migrants:* Fieldfare, Redwing and occasional rarities such as Wryneck and Red-backed Shrike. *Autumn:* Passage divers, grebes and seaduck.
Other notable flora and fauna: Pyramidal and northern marsh orchids, harebell, thrift on cliff tops. Migrant butterflies such as small skipper and painted lady.
Contact: Yorkshire Wildlife Trust, 01904 659 570; e-mail: info@ywt.org.uk www.ywt.org.uk

4. HORNSEA MERE

Wassand Hall.
Location: Sat nav: HU18 1AX. Hornsea lies 12 miles E of Beverley on B1244. Enter town, onto Southgate then take signposted road to car park at Kirkholme Point.
Access: Mere is owned by the nearby Wassand Hall estate., which opens to the public on selected days throughout the year. Mere footpath open all year during the day (see notices for closing times). View from footpath along southern edge. Dogs on leads.
Facilities: Café on site (limited opening in winter), toilets.
Habitat: Yorkshire's largest body of freshwater, located 1km inland from the coast. Edged by reedbeds and woodland.
Key birds: Common wildfowl throughout the year, but in winter there is always the chance of divers, grebes, Long-tailed Duck, Goosander and Pintail. *Spring and autumn passage:* Marsh Harrier, Osprey, Little Gull, terns, White and Yellow Wagtails, Wheatear, plus rarer species.
Contact: www.wassand.co.uk

5. LOWER DERWENT VALLEY NNR

Natural England/Yorkshire Wildlife Trust/Countryside Trust.
Location: Sat nav: YO8 5DG (North Duffield Carrs). Six miles SE of York, stretching 12 miles S along River Derwent from Newton-on-Derwent to Wressle and along Pocklington Canal. Visitor facilities at Bank Island (SE 691 448), Wheldrake Ings YWT (SE 691 444 see separate entry — page 74), Thorganby (SE 692 418) and North Duffield Carrs (SE 697 367).
Access: Open all year. No dogs. Disabled access at North Duffield Carrs.
Facilities: Bank Island — two hides, viewing tower. Wheldrake Ings — four hides. Thorganby — viewing platform. North Duffield Carrs — two hides and wheelchair access. Car parks at all sites, height restriction of 2.1m at Bank Island and North Duffield Carrs. Bicycle stands in car parks at Bank Island and North Duffield Carrs.
Public transport: Bus from York/Selby — contact First (01904 622 992). Train station at Wressle.
Habitat: SPA and Ramsar site composed of flood and hay meadows, swamp, open water and alder/willow woodland.
Key birds: More than 80 species recorded in recent times. *Spring/summer:* Breeding wildfowl and waders, incl. Garganey, Snipe and Ruff, plus Corncrake and Spotted Crake. Barn Owl and warblers. *Winter/spring:* Bittern, 20,000-plus waterfowl including Whooper Swan, wild geese, Teal and Wigeon. Large gull roost, incl. white-winged gulls. Also passage waders, incl. Whimbrel.
Other notable flora and fauna: Pocklington Canal is particularly good for a wide range of aquatic plants and animals. Noctule, Daubenton's and pipistrelle bats regularly recorded. Water vole, pygmy shrew and brown hare.
Contact: Senior Reserve Manager, Natural England Yorkshire and Humber Region, 01904 435 500; e-mail: york@naturalengland.org.uk
www.naturalengland.org.uk
Pocklington Canal: www.pocklington.gov.uk/pcas

6. NORTH CAVE WETLANDS

Yorkshire Wildlife Trust.
Location: Sat nav: HU15 2LY. SE 888 328. NW of North Cave village, approx 10 miles W of Hull (SE 886 328). From junction 28 of M62, follow signs to North Cave on B1230. In village, turn L and follow road to next crossroads, then go L, then and park in Dryham Lane.
Access: Open all year with car parking on Dryham Lane. Part of circular footpath is suitable for all abilities. No dogs in reserve.
Facilities: Five bird-viewing hides including unique straw bale constructions, four are accessible to wheelchair users. Portaloo available on site and Wild Bird Café open each day on Dryham Lane, adjacent to reserve.
Public transport: Buses serve North Cave from Hull and Goole: telephone 01482 222 222 for details.
Habitat: Former gravel pits have been converted

into various lagoons for wetland birds, including one reedbed. There are also, scrub and hedgerows, and since 2010 a large area of wet grassland.
Key birds: More than 200 species recorded. Breeding birds inc Great Crested Grebe, Gadwall, Pochard, Sparrowhawk, Avocet, Little Ringed and Ringed Plover, Oystercatcher, Sedge Warbler and Reed Bunting. Large numbers of Sand Martins feed over reserve in summer. Wintering wildfowl and waders include Golden Plover, Dunlin, Ruff and Redshank. Tree Sparrow.
Other notable flora and fauna: Water vole, dragon and damselflies, several butterfly species inc small colony of brown argus.
Contact: Yorkshire Wildlife Trust, 01904 659 570; e-mail: info@ywt.org.uk

7. SPURN NNR

Yorkshire Wildlife Trust.
Location: Sat nav HU12 0UH. Entrance Gate TA 419 149. 26 miles from Hull. Take A1033 from Hull to Patrington then B1445 from Patrington to Easington and unclassified roads on to Kilnsea and Spurn Point.
Access: Normally open at all times. Vehicle admission fee. No charge for pedestrians. No dogs allowed under any circumstances, not even in cars. Coaches by permit only (must be in advance).
Facilities: Reserve open all year Blue Bell café open daily. Visitor centre, four hides. Public toilets in Blue Bell car park.
Public transport: Nearest bus service is at Easington (3.5 miles away). 2011 Sunday service to the Point, hail and ride, Easter to last weekend of October.
Habitat: Sand dunes with marram and sea buckthorn scrub. Mudflats around Humber Estuary.
Key birds: *Spring:* Many migrants on passage and often rare birds such as Red-backed Shrike, Bluethroat etc. *Summer:* Little Terns feed offshore. *Autumn:* Passage migrants and rarities such as Wryneck, Pallas's Warbler. *Winter:* Large numbers of waders, Shelduck and Brent Geese, plus Merlin and Peregrine.
Other notable flora and fauna: Unique habitats and geographical position makes Spurn a very interesting site in Yorkshire for butterflies (25 species recorded) and moths.
Contact: Outer Humber Officer, Spurn NNR, Blue Bell, Kilnsea, Hull HU12 0UB; e-mail: info@ywt.org.uk

8. TOPHILL LOW NATURE RESERVE

Yorkshire Water.
Location: Sat nav: YO25 9RH. TA 071 482. Located SE of Driffield and signposted from village of Watton on A164.
Access: Open daily (9am-6pm). Charges: £2.80 per person. £1.20 concessions. No dogs. Provision for disabled visitors (paths, ramps, hides, toilet etc). Coaches welcome.

Facilities: Visitor Centre with toilets open every weekend/ most week days. Disabled toilet open at all times. 12 hides (five with wheelchair access), paths and sightings board.
Public transport: None.
Habitat: Open water (two reservoirs), marshes, wader scrapes, woodland and thorn scrub.
Key birds: 160 species annually. *Winter:* SSSI for wildfowl, plus one of the UK's largest Black-headed and Common Gull roosts. Regular wintering Bittern and Smew. Active feeding station with Brambling and Woodcock. *Spring/early summer:* Hirundines, Black Tern and Black-necked Grebe. Breeding Little Ringed Plover, Common Tern, Kingfisher and Barn Owl with variety of warblers. *Late summer/autumn:* Up to 20 species of passage wader.
Other notable flora and fauna: 400+ Sp. flora, 365+ Sp. fungi 16 Sp.odonata inc. hairy hawker. Grass snake, otter, water vole, great crested newt and roe deer.
Contact: Richard Hampshire, Tophill Low Nature Reserve, Hutton Cranswick, Driffield, East Yorkshire YO25 9RH. 01377 270 690. e-mail:richard.hampshire@yorkshirewater.co.uk, www.tophilllow.blogspot.com

9. WHELDRAKE INGS

Yorkshire Wildlife Trust.
Location: Sat nav: Y019 6AS (Ings Lane car park). SE 693 443. From York by-pass (A64) head S on A19 towards Selby for 1.2 miles, then turn left on Wheldrake Lane. Drive through Wheldrake village and turn sharp right to reach Natural England's Bank Island car park.
Access: Open at all times, but entrance road to YWT Wheldrake car park (Ings Lane) can be flooded in winter. Free admission and parking. Paths and hides not suitable for wheelchairs. No dogs allowed.
Facilities: Four hides. Sightings board in Bank Island car park. RADAR key toilets at Bank Island car park.
Public transport: York to Selby buses stop 25 metres from entrance road on Thorganby Road.
Habitat: Flooded meadows and pools, riverside vegetation.
Key birds: A noted site for large numbers of wintering wildfowl, inc Shelduck, Pintail and Goldeneye among the commoner species. Records of Hen Harrier, Whooper and Bewick's Swans, Little Egret. *Spring passage:* Garganey, Little Gull, terns and Wheatear. *Summer:* Breeding waders, plus Turtle Dove, Yellow Wagtail, hirundines and migrant warblers. *Autumn:* Passage waders, Hobby and wildfowl. Kingfisher, Little and Barn Owl are among a long list of resident species.
Other notable flora and fauna: Internationally important community of meadow plants.
Contact: Yorkshire Wildlife Trust 01904 659 570; e-mail: info@ywt.org.uk

Yorkshire, North

SEAWATCHING in autumn from Filey Brigg can produce a range of skuas and shearwaters, with divers and grebes becoming more noticeable as the season progresses. The North York Moors hold breeding waders, chats, raptors and Red Grouse. There are several areas to explore in the Lower Derwent Valley, with first class birding throughout the year.

1. COATHAM MARSH

Tees Valley Wildlife Trust.
Location: Sat nav TS10 5BQ (Tod Point Road). NZ 586 247 for car park. Located on W edge of Redcar. Access from minor road to Warrenby from A1085/A1042.
Access: Reserve is open throughout daylight hours. Please keep to permissive footpaths only.
Facilities: Good footpaths around site, but section along The Fleet prone to winter flooding. Nearest toilets on Redcar seafront.
Public transport: Very frequent bus service between Middlesbrough and Redcar. Nearest stops are in Coatham 0.25 mile from reserve (Arriva tel 0871 200 2233). Redcar Central Station one mile from site. Frequent trains from Middlesbrough and Darlington.
Habitat: Freshwater wetlands, lakes, reedbeds.
Key birds: *Spring/autumn:* Wader passage (including Wood Sandpiper and Greenshank). *Summer:* Passerines (including Sedge Warbler, Yellow Wagtail). *Winter:* Large numbers of common ducks (plus Smew). *Occasional rarities:* Water Rail, Great White Egret, Avocet, Bearded Tit and Bittern.
Other notable flora and fauna: The lime-rich soil allows wildflowers to grow around the site, including northern marsh orchid. Also good for insects including migrant hawker dragonfly.
Contact: Steve Ashton, Tees Valley Wildlife Trust, 01287 636 382; e-mail: info@teeswildlife.org www.teeswildlife.org

2. FILEY BRIGG BIRD OBSERVATORY / THE DAMS

FBOG/Yorkshire Wildlife Trust (The Dams).
Location: Sat nav: YO14 0DR (The Dams). TA 106 807. Two access roads into Filey from A165 (Scarborough to Bridlington road). Filey Dams is a nature reserve within the Observatory's recording area.
Access: Opening times – no restrictions. Dogs only in Parish Wood and The Old Tip (on lead). Coaches welcome. Park in the North Cliff Country Park.
Facilities: No provisions for disabled at present. Two hides at The Dams, one on The Brigg (open most weekends from late Jul-Oct, key for hire from Country Park café). Toilets in Country Park (Apr-Nov 1) and town centre. Nature trails at The Dams, Parish Wood/Old Tip. Cliff top walk for seabirds along Cleveland Way.
Public transport: All areas within a mile of Filey railway station. Trains into Filey tel. 08457 484 950; buses into Filey tel. 01723 503 020
Habitat: The Dams – two freshwater lakes, fringed with some tree cover and small reedbeds. Parish Wood – a newly planted wood which leads to the Old Tip, the latter has been fenced (for stock and crop strips) though there is a public trail. Carr Naze has a pond and can produce newly arrived migrants.
Key birds: *The Dams:* Breeding and wintering water birds, breeding Sedge Warbler, Reed Warbler and Tree Sparrow. *The Tip:* Important for breeding Skylark, Meadow Pipit, common warblers and Grey Partridge. *Winter:* Buntings, including Lapland. *Seawatch Hide:* (Jul-Oct). All four skuas, shearwaters, terns. *Winter:* Divers and grebes. *Rocket Pole Field:* A new project should encourage breeding species and wintering larks, buntings etc. Many sub-rare/rare migrants possible at all sites.
Contact: e-mail: secretary@fbog.co.uk www.fbog.co.uk

3. FYLINGDALES MOOR CONSERVATION AREA

Hawk and Owl Trust /Strickland Estate/Fylingdales Moor ESS Co Ltd.
Location: Sat nav: YO22 4UL (car park). NZ 947 003. Conservation area covers 6,800 acres within the National Park off A171 S of Whitby, stretching between Sneaton High Moor (Newton House Plantation) and the coast at Ravenscar.
Access: Open access. Parking (inc coaches) available at Jugger Howe lay-by (NZ 947 003) on A171.
Facilities: Numerous footpaths including Jugger Howe Nature Trail, Lyke Wake Walk and Robin Hood's Bay Road.
Public transport: Half-hourly Arriva buses (No. 93 and X93) between Scarborough and Whitby, nearest stop at Flask Inn (approx. 1 mile N of Jugger Howe lay-by). Call 0191 281 1313 for timetable information or visit: www.arrivabus.co.uk
Habitat: Heather moorland (former grouse moor), with scattered trees, wooded valleys and gulleys. Managed exclusively for wildlife and archaeological remains, the moor is an SSSI and SPA (Merlin and Golden Plover) and a Special Area of Conservation.
Key birds: More than 80 more common moor species, plus rare and endangered breeding birds such as harriers, Merlin, Golden Plover, Red Grouse, Curlew, Wheatear, Stonechat, Whinchat, Skylark, Marsh Tit, Willow Tit, Linnet, Bullfinch, Reed Bunting and Yellowhammer. The moor is also home to Kestrel, Lapwing, Snipe, Cuckoo, Meadow Pipit, Grey Wagtail and Wood Warbler and visited by Peregrine.
Other notable flora and fauna: Otter, roe deer, brown hare, stoat, weasel and badger. Important for water vole. Three species of heather, plus cranberry, cowberry, moonwort and, in wetter parts, bog myrtle, lesser twayblade, bog asphodel, butterwort, marsh helleborine, and sundews can be found. Also rare orchids and sedges. Insect species include large heath and small pearl-bordered fritillary butterflies and emperor moth.
Contact: Professor John Edwards, The Hawk and Owl Trust 01751 417 398; www.hawkandowl.org e-mail: john.edwards@wildfylingdales.co.uk

NATURE RESERVES - NORTHERN ENGLAND

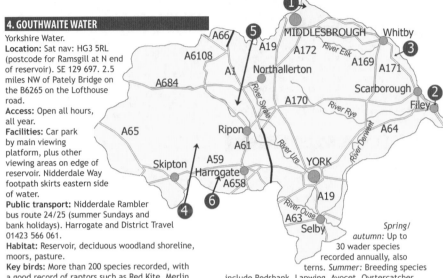

4. GOUTHWAITE WATER

Yorkshire Water.
Location: Sat nav: HG3 5RL (postcode for Ramsgill at N end of reservoir). SE 129 697. 2.5 miles NW of Pately Bridge on the B6265 on the Lofthouse road.
Access: Open all hours, all year.
Facilities: Car park by main viewing platform, plus other viewing areas on edge of reservoir. Nidderdale Way footpath skirts eastern side of water.
Public transport: Nidderdale Rambler bus route 24/25 (summer Sundays and bank holidays). Harrogate and District Travel 01423 566 061.
Habitat: Reservoir, deciduous woodland shoreline, moors, pasture.
Key birds: More than 200 species recorded, with a good selection of raptors such as Red Kite, Merlin and Buzzard all year. Green Woodpecker, Nuthatch, Dipper (on river) and Kingfisher resident. *Spring/ summer:* Migrant warblers, breeding Little Ringed Plover, with passage Osprey and terns. *Winter:* Hen Harrier, Short-eared Owl, Goosander, Goldeneye and Whooper Swan. Waders including Oystercatcher, Curlew, Redshank, Lapwing and waterfowl.
Contact: Recreation Officer, Yorkshire Water
e-mail:Geoff.D.Lomas@yorkshirewater.co.uk
www.yorkshirewater.co.uk (turn to recreation page).

5. NOSTERFIELD LNR

Lower Ure Conservation Trust.
Location: Sat nav: DL8 2QZ. SE 278 795. Six miles N of Ripon, between West Tanfield and Nosterfield E of A6108 (Ripon to Masham road) and approx 4 miles W of A1.
Access: Open all year. Lower viewing area beyond car park permits viewing from cars only. Please keep to footpath. Dogs (on short leads) on most of permissive footpath network. Footpath from Main Hide to Tanfield Hide (500 m) is disabled-friendly. Terrain is more uneven from car park to northern viewing screen (1,000 m). Coaches: book in advance.
Facilities: Two disabled-friendly hides, interpretation panels (main hide), comfortable 'woolly' seats, lowered windows for wheelchair users. No other on-site facilities.
Public transport: Irregular buses from Ripon and Masham stop at West Tanfield (half mile walk to reserve).
Habitat: Wetland grassland and open water. Also Magnesian limestone grassland, gravel banks, hedgerows and scrub.
Key species: Annually 150 species recorded — more than 225 species recorded overall (including rarities).

Spring/ autumn: Up to 30 wader species recorded annually, also terns. *Summer:* Breeding species include Redshank, Lapwing, Avocet, Oystercatcher, Curlew, Ringed Plover, Shoveler, Gadwall, Barn Owl, Skylark, Lesser Whitethroat, Tree Sparrow, Linnet, Reed Bunting. *Autumn:* Passage waders including regular Pectoral Sandpiper. *Winter:* Wildfowl (Wigeon, Teal, Greylag and rarer geese), waders (Golden Plover, Lapwing, Curlew) and Peregrine.
Other notable flora and fauna: Specialist grassland and wetland flora, including seven species of orchid, mudwort, yellow rattle, golden dock. Butterflies include white-letter hairstreak, brown argus, wall and large colony of common blue. Dragonflies include emperor, black-tailed skimmer, red-veined darter (has bred). At least 450 species of moths have now been recorded. Also, brown hare and water shrew.
Contact: e-mail:luct@luct.org.uk www.luct.org.uk

6. TIMBLE INGS

Yorkshire Water.
Location: Sat nav: LS21 2PP. SE 15 53. Large area of upland woodland west of Harrogate, north of Otley. Off the A59 south of Blubberhouses, near Timble village.
Access: Open at all times, all year.
Facilities: Toilets, cafes, pubs, coach parking all nearby. Hard forest tracks.
Public transport: None.
Habitat: Woodland and nearby reservoir.
Key birds: Bradford OG species list stands at 134. Habitat management work by Yorkshire Water makes site attractive to Long-eared and Tawny Owls, Nightjars and Tree Pipits. Buzzards now nest and Red Kites seen regularly. Goshawk numbers in decline. *Summer:* Breeding species inc Redpoll, Siskin, Crossbill, Woodcock, Redstart and Grasshopper Warbler. Short-eared Owls hunt adjacent moorland. *Winter:* Fieldfare, Redwing, Brambling, occasional

Waxwings and Hawfinches.
Other notable flora and fauna: Roe deer, badger, brown hare, shrew, vole and mouse species (all detected from owl pellets). Ponds attractive to

amphibians and dragonflies, inc broad-bodied chaser, emperor and black darter.
Contact: As Gouthwaite Reservoir above.

Yorkshire South & West

CONSIDERING the number of industrial towns in the area, such as Sheffield, Barnsley and Doncaster, South Yorkshire still manages to offer birdwatchers a surprising number of interesting wildlife sites. Places such as RSPB Fairburn Ings (right next to the A1), Potteric Carr, RSPB Old Moor reserve and its near neighbour, Bolton Ings, all have year-round interest.

1. BOLTON INGS (DEARNE VALLEY)

RSPB (Northern England)
Location: Sat nav: S73 0YF. SE 425 020. Park at RSPB Old Moor and walk east along Trans-Pennine Trail to Bolton Ings. By car, Old Moor is just off Manvers Way (A633). From the M1, take junction 36 then follow the A6195. From the A1M, take junction 37 then follow the A635 towards the A6195.
Access: Open all year round. Dearne Way footpath and Trans-Pennine Trail open at all times, but not suitable for wheelchair users.
Facilities: Cormorant View hide. More facilities at RSPB Old Moor.
Public transport: Wombwell and Swinton train stations approximately 3 miles from reserve. Buses run to Old Moor reserve from Barnsley, Doncaster and Meadowhall — call Traveline on 01709 515 151 for details. Trans-Pennine Trail runs along southern edge of reserve.
Habitat: 43 hectares of reedbed and scrub. Excellent warbler habitat.
Key birds: *All year:* Kingfisher, Grey Heron. *Winter:* Stonechat. *Spring/summer:* Reed Bunting. breeding waders and warblers, Cuckoo, Garganey. *Autumn:* Passage waders including Greenshank, Green Sandpiper, Golden Plover. *Winter:* Wildfowl, including Goosander, Wigeon and Teal.
Other notable flora and fauna: Dragonflies inc. banded demoiselle, brown hare.
Contact: RSPB Old Moor, Old Moor Lane, Wombwell, Barnsley, South Yorkshire, S73 0YF. 01226 751 593; e-mail: old.moor@rspb.org.uk www.rspb.org.uk

2. DENABY INGS

Yorkshire Wildlife Trust.
Location: Sat nav: S64 0JJ (Pastures Rd, off A6023 near Mexborough). SE 496 008. Proceed along Pastures Road for 0.5 miles and watch for a sign on R marking entrance to car park. Climb flight of concrete steps to enter reserve.
Access: Open all year. No dogs allowed. Field centre open only on Saturdays.
Facilities: Car park, visitor centre, two hides, interpretation panels, circular trail.

Public transport: None.
Habitat: Riverside and dry meadows, deciduous woodland, marsh, willows.
Key birds: *Spring/summer:* Waterfowl, Barn Owl, Tawny Owl, Sand Martin, Swallow, Whinchat, Grasshopper Warbler, Lesser Whitethroat, Whitethroat, other warblers, Kingfisher. *Passage:* Waders, Common, Arctic and Black Terns, Redstart, Wheatear. *Winter:* Whooper Swan, wildfowl, Jack Snipe and other waders, Grey Wagtail, Fieldfare, Redwing, Brambling, Siskin. *All year:* Corn Bunting, Yellowhammer, all three woodpeckers, common woodland birds, possible Willow Tit.
Contact: Yorkshire Wildlife Trust 01904 659 570; e-mail:info@ywt.org.uk; www.ywt.org.

3. FAIRBURN INGS

RSPB (Northern England).
Location: Sat nav: WF10 2BH. SE 452 277. 12 miles from Leeds, six miles from Pontefract, 3 miles from Castleford, situated next to A1246 from J42 of A1.
Access: Reserve and hides open every day except Dec 25/26. Centre and shop open each day (9am-5pm). Dogs on leads welcome. Boardwalks leading to Pickup Pool, feeding station and Kingfisher viewpoint are all wheelchair-friendly.
Facilities: Five hides open at all times. Toilets open 9am-5pm. Disabled toilets and baby-changing facilities. Hot and cold drinks, snacks available. Wildlife garden, pond-dipping and mini beast areas, plus duck feeding platform. Coach parking for club visits.
Public transport: Nearest train stations are Castleford, Micklefield and Garforth. No bus service.
Habitat: Open water, wet grassland, marsh and fen scrub, reedbed, reclaimed colliery spoil heaps.
Key birds: *All year:* Tree Sparrow, Kingfisher, Willow Tit, Green Woodpecker, Bullfinch. *Winter:* Smew, Goldeneye, Goosander, Wigeon, Peregrine. *Spring:* Osprey, Little Gull, Wheatear, five species of tern inc annual Black Tern. *Summer:* Nine species of breeding warbler, Grey Heron, Gadwall, Little Ringed Plover. *Autumn:* Thousands of waders on passage inc Green Sandpiper, Little Ringed Plover and Black-tailed Godwit.
Other notable flora and fauna: Brown hare, harvest mouse, roe deer, Leisler's and Daubenton's bats, 28 species of butterfly and 20 species of dragonfly.
Contact: Laura Bentley, Visitor Services Manager, Fairburn Ings Visitor Centre, 01977 628 191; e-mail: fairburnings@rspb.org.uk

4. HARDCASTLE CRAGS

National Trust.
Location: Sat nav: HX7 7AA (Midgehole car park).

SD 988 291. From Hebden Bridge follow National Trust signs to A6033 Keighley Road. Follow for 0.75 miles. Turn L at the National Trust sign to car parks. Alternate pay-and-display car park at Clough Hole on Widdop Road, Heptonstall.
Access: Open all year. NT car park charges.
Admission: no charge for NT members and disabled badge holders. Non-members: £3.60, child £1.60, family £9.
Facilities: Two small car parks, cycle racks and several way-marked trails. Gibson Mill visitor centre (not NT property) has toilets, café, exhibitions. No mains services — in extreme conditions mill may be closed for health and safety reasons.
Public transport: Trains to Hebden Bridge from Manchester or Leeds every 30 minutes. Call 08457 484 950. Weekday buses every 30 minutes to Keighley Road, then 1 mile walk to Midgehole. Summer weekend bus 906 Widdop-Hardcastle Crags: 0113 245 7676.
Habitat: 400 acres of unspoilt wooded valleys, ravines, streams, hay meadows and moorland edge.
Key birds: *Spring/summer:* Cuckoo, Redstart, Lesser Whitethroat, Garden Warbler, Blackcap, Wood Warbler, Chiffchaff, Spotted Flycatcher, Pied Flycatcher, Curlew, Lapwing, Meadow Pipit. *All year:* Sparrowhawk, Kestrel, Green and Greater Spotted Woodpeckers, Lesser Spotted Woodpecker, Tawny Owl, Barn Owl, Little Owl, Jay, Coal Tit, Dipper, Grey Wagtail and other woodland species. Goshawk in Crimsworth Dean.
Other notable flora and fauna: Northern hairy wood ant, moss carder bee, tree bumble bee, killarney fern, brittle bladder fern, roe deer and eight species of bat.
Contact: National Trust, Hardcastle Crags, 01422 844 518; www.nationaltrust.org.uk

5. INGBIRCHWORTH RESERVOIR

Yorkshire Water.
Location: Sat nav: S36 7GN. SE 217 058. Leave M1 at junction 37 and take A628 towards Manchester. After five miles turn R at roundabout onto A629 Huddersfield road. Drive 2.5 miles to Ingbirchworth and at The Fountain Inn, turn L, then bear L to cross the dam, proceed straight forward onto the track leading to the car park.
Access: Open all year. One of the few reservoirs in the area with footpath access.
Facilities: Car park, picnic tables.
Public transport: None.
Habitat: Reservoir, small strip of deciduous woodland.
Key birds: *Spring/summer:* Whinchat, warblers, woodland birds, House Martin. *Spring/autumn passage:* Little Ringed Plover, Ringed Plover, Dotterel, other waders, Common Tern, Arctic Tern, Black Tern, Yellow Wagtail, Wheatear. *Winter:* Wildfowl, Golden Plover, waders, occasional rare gull such as Iceland or Glaucous, Grey Wagtail, Fieldfare, Redwing, Brambling, Redpoll.
Other notable flora: Woodland wildflowers, inc bluebells.
Contact: e-mail: Geoff.D.Lomas@ yorkshirewater.co.uk
www.yorkshirewater.co.uk (turn to recreation page).

6. OLD MOOR (DEARNE VALLEY)

RSPB (Northern England).
Location: Sat nav: S73 0YF. SE 422 022. By car, Old Moor is just off Manvers Way (A633). From the M1, take junction 36 then follow the A6195. From the A1M, take junction 37 then follow the A635 towards the A6195.
Access: Visitor centre and cafe open daily, except Dec 25/26 (9.30am to 5pm from Feb to end of Oct), (9.30am to 4pm Nov to end of Jan). Reserve is open until 8pm from April to Oct. RSPB Members free, adult non-members £4, family £8, children £2, concessions £2.50. Guide dogs only.
Facilities: Visitor centre, café, shop, education and meeting rooms. Accessible toilets. Two trails with seven hides, all suitable for wheelchair users. Two viewing screens. Free electric scooters available on request.
Public transport: Buses run to Old Moor reserve from Barnsley, Doncaster and Meadowhall — Traveline (01709 515 151).
Habitat: Lakes and flood meadows, wader scrape and reedbeds.
Key birds: *All year:* Kingfisher, Little Owl. *Winter:* Large numbers of wildfowl, spectacular flocks of Lapwing and Golden Plover, Peregrine, Tree Sparrow in garden feeding area. *Summer:* Breeding Bittern, Sand Martin waders, inc Little Ringed Plover and drumming Snipe, migrant warblers and wildfowl.
Other notable flora and fauna: Water

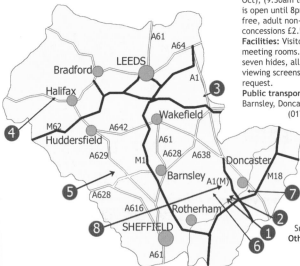

vole, brown hare, weasel, pygmy shrew, wildflowers including orchids and adders tongue fern.
Contact: RSPB Old Moor, 01226 751 593; e-mail: old. moor@rspb.org.uk www.rspb.org.uk

7. POTTERIC CARR

Yorkshire Wildlife Trust.
Location: Sat nav: DN4 8DB. SE 589 007. From M18 junction 3 take A6182 (Doncaster) and at first roundabout take third exit. Entrance and car park are on R after 50m.
Access: Open daily 9am-5pm. Obtain ticket on arrival, YWT members free; Single £4; family £7.50 (up to two adults / three children); concession £2.50; child £2. Groups of ten or more should book in advance. Guide dogs only.
Facilities: Around 8 km of paths (5 km accessible to wheelchairs, unassisted), 14 viewing hides (10 suitable for disabled) and a Field Centre with café, open daily (10am-4pm) with hot and cold drinks, snacks and meals. Toilets at entrance reception, in Field Centre (during café opening times) and outside.
Public transport: Nearest railway station is Doncaster. From Frenchgate Interchange, take bus number 72 or 75, and alight at B&Q on Woodfield Way. Cross White Rose Way, walk down Mallard Way. Cross car park to reserve entrance in Sedum House.
Habitat: Flood plain of River Tome, with reed fen, subsidence ponds, artificial pools, grassland, woodland.
Key birds: 102 of recorded 230 species have bred on site. Nesting waterfowl (inc. Shoveler, Gadwall, Pochard), Water Rail, Kingfisher, all three woodpeckers, Lesser Whitethroat, Reed and Sedge Warblers, Willow Tit. *Passage/winter:* Bittern, Marsh Harrier, Black Tern, waders, wildfowl.
Other notable flora and fauna: 20 species of

dragonfly recorded, 28 species of butterfly including purple hairstreak and dingy skipper. Palmate and great crested newt. Common spotted and bee orchids.
Contact: Potteric Carr Nature Reserve, 01302 570 077. e-mail: potteric.carr@ywt.org.uk www.potteric-carr.org.uk

8. SPROTBOROUGH FLASH/DON GORGE

Yorkshire Wildlife Trust.
Location: Sat nav: DN5 7NB (postcode for Boat Inn). SE 530 077. Leave A1(M) at junction 36 onto A630 towards Rotherham. After 0.8km, turn R at traffic lights to Sprotborough. After approx 1.6km the road drops down into Don Gorge. Cross a bridge over river, then another over a canal, turn immediately L. Public car park on left next to toll house in Nursery Lane.
Access: Open all year.
Facilities: Three hides (two accessible to wheelchairs), footpaths, interpretation panels. Café with toilets.
Public transport: River bus from Doncaster in summer months. Bus service from Doncaster to Sprotbrough village (10 minute walk to reserve).
Habitat: Limestone gorge, woodland, limestone grassland on plateau.
Key birds: *Summer:* Hirundines, Lesser Whitethroat, Whitethroat, Garden Warbler, Blackcap, Chiffchaff, Willow Warbler, Cuckoo. *Spring/autumn passage:* Little Ringed Plover, Dunlin, Greenshank, Green Sandpiper, waders, Yellow Wagtail. *Winter/all year:* Wildfowl, Water Rail, Snipe, Little Owl, Tawny Owl, all three woodpeckers, thrushes, Siskin, possible Corn Bunting.
Contact: Trust HQ . 01904 659 570; e-mail:info@ ywt.org.uk www.ywt.org.uk

South East England

Berkshire, Buckinghamshire, Hampshire, Kent, London (Greater), Surrey, East Sussex, West Sussex .

Berkshire

DESPITE its proximity to London, Berkshire offers a surprisingly wide range of habitats including heathland and downland. It is the gravel pits that attract the widest range of bird species though, including good numbers of wintering Smew. Increasingly wide areas along the Thames are good for Ring-necked Parakeets.

1. DINTON PASTURES COUNTRY PARK

Wokingham District Council.
Location: Sat nav: RG10 0TH. SU 784 718. From M4's

junction 10 head towards Reading, then follow sign to Winnersh on A329. Park is sign-posted off B3030 between Hurst and Winnersh.
Access: Open all year, dawn to dusk. Car parking charges apply 8am to 6.30pm each day. Dogs allowed. Electric buggies available for disabled visitors.
Facilities: Three hides (one adapted for wheelchairs), information centre, car park, café (open from 8.30am each day), toilets (suitable for wheelchairs). Electric buggies for hire. Various trails between one and three miles in length. Walks leaflet at café.
Public transport: Buses 128 and 129 between Reading and Wokingham stop near main entrance, roughly one an hour. Winnersh rail station is a 15 minute walk.

Habitat: 335 acres of mature gravel pits and banks of River Loddon. Sandford Lake managed for wildfowl, Lavell's Lake best for waders and scrub species. **Key birds:** All year: Kingfisher, Water Rail, Barn Owl. Spring/summer: Hobby, Little Ringed Plover, Common Tern, Nightingale, common warblers. Winter: Bittern, wildfowl (inc. Goldeneye, Wigeon, Teal, Gadwall), thrushes. Waders include Green and Common Sandpipers, Snipe, Redshank. **Other notable flora and fauna:** Water vole, harvest mouse, great crested newt, Loddon pondweed and Loddon lily. 18 species of dragonflies inc emperor, black-tailed skimmer, migrant hawker, white-legged and banded agrion damselfies. **Contact:** Dinton Pastures Country Park, 01189 342 016; e-mail: countryside@wokingham.gov.uk www.wokingham.gov.uk/parks/parks/countryparks/dintonpastures/

2. HUNGERFORD MARSH

Berks, Bucks & Oxon Wildlife Trust.
Location: Sat nav: RG17 0JB. SU 333 687. On W side of Hungerford, beside the Kennet and Avon Canal. From town centre, go along Church Street past the town hall. Turn R under the railway. Follow public footpath over swing bridge on the canal near the church. The reserve is separated from Freeman's Marsh by a line of willows and bushes.
Access: Open all year. Please keep to the footpath. Dogs on leads please.
Facilities: Car park.
Public transport: Hungerford railway station half mile from reserve.
Habitat: An idyllic waterside site with chalk stream, water meadows, unimproved rough grazing and reedbed.
Key birds: 120 species recorded. Spring/summer: Reed and Grasshopper Warblers. Winter: Siskin and Water Rail. All year: Common wildfowl, Grey Heron, Kingfisher, Mute Swan, Little Grebe, Reed Bunting, Bullfinch.
Other notable flora and fauna: Water vole, otter and grass snake. Southern marsh orchid, fen bedstraw.
Contact: Berks, Bucks & Oxon Wildlife Trust, 01865 775 476; e-mail: wendytobbitt@bbowt.org.uk www.bbowt.org.ukreserves/Hungerford-Marsh

3. LAVELL'S LAKE

Wokingham District Council.
Location: SU 785 727. Via Sandford Lane off B3030 between Hurst and Winnersh E of Reading or from Dinton Pastures..
Access: Dawn to dusk. No permit required. Dogs on leads all year.
Facilities: Car park (open 9am to 5pm), two public hides, one with disabled access, one members-only hide (see below), viewing screen.
Public transport: Thames Travel bus services 128/129 run between Reading and Wokingham, stopping outside Dinton Pastures main entrance. Nearest train

services are at either Winnersh, or Winnersh Triangle. **Habitat:** Ten hectare site composed of gravel pits, two wader scrapes, reed beds, rough grassland, marshy area, sand martin banks, between River Loddon & Emm Brook. To N of Lavell's Lake gravel pits are being restored to attract birds. The lake at Lea Farm is viewable walking N along the River Loddon from Lavell's Lake over small green bridge. It is on R and can be seen through a viewing screen and a members-only hide for Friends of Lavell's Lake (see www.foll.org.uk). No access.
Key birds: All year: Great Crested Grebe, Gadwall, Sparrowhawk, Kingfisher, Red Kite, Buzzard, Cetti's Warbler. Summer: Common Tern, Redshank, Lapwing, Hobby, warblers include Reed, Sedge, Whitethroat. Passage: Garganey, Little-Ringed Plover, Common and Green Sandpiper and Greenshank. Winter: Water Rail, Bittern, Little Egret, Teal, Shoveler, Pochard, Goldeneye, occasional Smew and Goosander. Along River Loddon — Siskin, Lesser Redpoll, Fieldfare and Redwing.
Contact: As for Dinton Pastures, 0118 934 2 016.

4. MOOR GREEN LAKES

Blackwater Valley Countryside Partnership/ Moor Green Lakes Group
Location: Sat nav: RG40 3TF (car park in Lower Sandhurst Road). SU 805 628. Main access and parking off Lower Sandhurst Road, Finchampstead (Sat nav: RG40 3TH). Alternatively, Rambler's car park, Chandlers Lane, Yateley near junction with Mill Lane (SU 820 619).
Access: Car parks open dawn-dusk (no charge). Dogs on leads. Site can be used by wheelchairs, though surface not particularly suitable.
Facilities: Two bird hides open to MGLG members (see website for details), two viewing screens. Feeder station viewable from bench on adjacent path. Footpaths along western, southern and eastern perimeter of site: Blackwater Valley long distance footpath passes alongside site.
Public transport: Nearest railway station, Crowthorne (South West Trains).
Habitat: Thirty-six hectares (90 acres) in total. Three lakes with gravel islands, beaches and scrapes. River Blackwater, grassland, surrounded by willow, ash, hazel and thorn hedgerows.
Key birds: More than 200 species recorded, with 60 breeding on a regular basis. Spring/summer: Redshank, Little Ringed Plover, Willow Warbler. Also Whitethroat, Sedge Warbler, Common Sandpiper, Common Tern. Mandarin Duck, Lapwing and Barn Owl breed on site. Dunlin and Green Sandpiper on passage. Winter: Wigeon, Teal, Gadwall and of particular interest, a roost of Goosander on Grove Lake. Little Egret regular, Snipe, Lapwing and Green Sandpiper. Gull roost includes up to 1,000 Lesser Black-backeds.
Other notable flora and fauna: 27 species of butterfly and 15 species of dragonfly have been recorded. See www.mglg.org.uk for more details.

NATURE RESERVES - SOUTH EAST ENGLAND

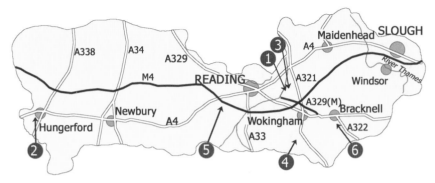

Contact: Blackwater Valley Countryside Partnership, 01252 331 353; www.blackwater-valley.org.uk
e-mail: blackwater.valley@hants.gov.uk

5. THEALE GRAVEL PITS

Theale Area Bird Conservation Group.
Location: Sat nav: RG7 4AP. SU 656 703 (main pit). Group of pits situated between junctions 11 and 12 of the M4, south of Reading. Includes Hosehill Lake LNR (SU 648 696). From Theale town centre head S on Station Road and Hanger Road and park in lay-bys in Dean Copse Road.
Access: Open at all times. Parking for a few vehicles in lay-bys near Fox & Hounds pub.
Facilities: Tern rafts, Sand Martin bank and wildflower meadow in Hosehill Lake LNR, together with information boards and benches on a mile-long circular walk.
Public transport: Theale railway station within walking distance of nearest pits.
Habitat: Flooded fields, Kennet & Avon Canal, scrub and worked-out gravel pits.
Key birds: *Spring/summer:* Migrant warblers, breeding Nightingale and Common Tern, passage Arctic and Black Terns, large number of hirundines, resident Peregrine favours pylon area. *Autumn:* Dunlin, Common Sandpiper and other waders on passage. Little Gulls recorded along with terns on passage, plus Osprey. *Winter:* Large numbers of wildfowl, including Goldeneye and Goosander. Thousands of gulls on nearby Moatlands pit. Bitterns sometimes recorded in Hosehill reedbed.
Other notable flora and fauna: Good range of

dragonflies and butterflies.
Contact: TABCC membership secretary Roger Stansfield, 01189 873 906;
e-mail: rogerstansfield@btinternet.com

6. WILDMOOR HEATH

Berks, Bucks & Oxon Wildlife Trust.
Location: Sat nav: GU47 8PD. SU 843 628. Between Bracknell and Sandhurst. From Sandhurst shopping area, take the A321 NW towards Wokingham. Turn E at the mini-roundabout on to Crowthorne Road. Continue for about one mile through one set of traffic lights. Car park is on the R at the bottom of the hill.
Access: Open all year. No access to woodland N of Rackstraw Road at Broadmoor Bottom. Dogs on a lead. Not suitable for wheelchairs due to slope of site and muddy, uneven terrain.
Facilities: Car park.
Public transport: The reserve is one mile north of Sandhurst railway station.
Habitat: 99-hectares of wet and dry lowland heath, bog, mixed woodland and mature Scots pine plantation.
Key birds: *Spring/summer:* Wood Lark, Tree Pipit, Nightjar, Dartford Warbler, Hobby, Reed Bunting and Stonechat among 55 species recorded at this site.
Other notable flora and fauna: Dragonflies (20 species recorded), slow worm, adder, grass snake, lizard, roe deer. Bog plants inc sundews.
Contact: Trust HQ, 01865 775 476;
e-mail:wendytobbitt@bbowt.org.uk
www.bbowt.org.uk/reserves/Wildmoor-Heath

Buckinghamshire

BORDERED by the River Thames to the south and River Ouse to the north, Buckinghamshire offers a good selection of woods, lakes and gravel pits. The high ground of the Chiltern escarpment is an excellent place to watch Red Kites. There is a good breeding population of Firecrests in the county.

1. BURNHAM BEECHES NNR

City of London Corporation.
Location: Sat nav: SL1 8PN. SU 950 850. Four kilometres N of Slough and on W side of A355, running between J2 of the M40 and J6 of M4. Entry from A355 via Beeches Road. Also smaller parking areas in Hawthorn Lane and Pumpkin Hill to the S and Park Lane to the W.
Access: Open all year, except Dec 25. Main Lord

NATURE RESERVES - SOUTH EAST ENGLAND

Mayor's Drive open from 8am-dusk. Beeches Café, public toilets and information point open 10am to 5pm. Motorised buggy available for hire. Network of wheelchair accessible roads and paths.
Facilities: Car parks, toilets, café, visitor information centre. Easy access path network, suitable for wheelchairs, most start at Victory Cross. Coach parking.
Public transport: Train - nearest station is Slough on main line from Paddington. Arriva, First and Jason Tours bus numbers 74 and 40, tel 0871 200 22 33 (Traveline).
Habitat: Ancient woodland, streams, pools, heathland (Stoke Common), grassland, scrub.
Key birds: *Spring/summer*: Cuckoo, possible Turtle Dove. *Winter*: Siskin, Crossbill, regular large flocks c100 Brambling. Possible Woodcock. *All year*: Mandarin (good population), all three woodpeckers, Sparrowhawk, Marsh Tit, possible Willow Tit, Red Kite and Buzzard.
Other notable flora and fauna: Ancient beech and oak pollards with associated wildlife. Rich array of fungi.
Contact: City of London Corporation, Burnham Beeches Office, Hawthorn Lane, Farnham Common, SL2 3TE. 01753 647 358; e-mail: burnham.beeches@cityoflondon.gov.uk www.cityoflondon.gov.uk

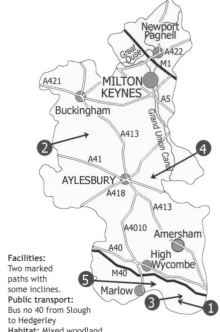

2. CALVERT JUBILEE

Berks, Bucks & Oxon Wildlife Trust.
Location: Sat nav: MK18 2FQ. SP 683 250. Near Steeple Claydon, 6.5 miles E of Bicester. Park opposite Greatmoor Sailing Club.
Access: Access by permit (free) only. Apply to Trust which provides map and information with permit. Please keep to network of paths. Surfaced path to bird hide. Guide dogs only.
Facilities: Two hides, small car park.
Public transport: None.
Habitat: Ex-clay pit, railway and landfill site. Now with deep lake, marginal reedbed and scrub habitat.
Key birds: *Summer*: Nesting Common Tern on rafts, Kingfisher, Hobby, warblers and occasional Nightingale. *Passage migrants*: Black Tern and fly-over waders. *Winter*: Large numbers of over-wintering waders and wildfowl. Bittern, Water Rail and large gull roost with occasional Glaucous and Iceland Gulls. Rarer birds turn up regularly.
Other notable flora and fauna: Rare butterflies, including dingy and grizzled skippers and black hairstreak. Bee and common spotted orchids.
Contact: Wildlife Trust HQ, 01865 775 476; e-mail: wendytobbitt@bbowt.org.uk www.bbowt.org.uk/reserves/Calvert-Jubilee

3. CHURCH WOOD

RSPB (Midlands Regional Office).
Location: Sat nav: SL2 3XB. SU 971 872. Reserve lies three miles from J2 of M40 in Hedgerley. Park in village, walk down small track beside pond for approx 200m. Reserve entrance is on L.
Access: Open all year. Not suitable for wheelchairs.

Facilities: Two marked paths with some inclines.
Public transport: Bus no 40 from Slough to Hedgerley
Habitat: Mixed woodland.
Key birds: *Spring/summer*: Red Kite, Buzzard, Blackcap, Garden Warbler, Swallow. *Winter*: Redpoll, Siskin. *All year*: Marsh Tit, Willow Tit, Nuthatch, Treecreeper, Great Spotted and Green Woodpeckers.
Other notable flora and fauna: Wood anenome, wood sorrel, bluebell and other woodland plants. Brimstone, comma, white admiral and peacock butterflies. Good range of fungi species.
Contact: RSPB central England office, 01865 351 163. www.rspb.org.uk/wildlife/reserves

4. COLLEGE LAKE

Berks, Bucks & Oxon Wildlife Trust.
Location: Sat nav: HP23 5QG. SU 931 143. Two miles N of Tring on B488, quarter mile N of canal bridge at Bulbourne turn L into gated entrance. Marked with brown tourist signs.
Access: Open Apr-Oct (9.30am-5pm); Nov-Mar (9.30am-4pm), seven days a week. Wheelchair access to some hides and disabled toilets. Electric tramper available for disabled visitors, please phone to book.
Facilities: Large car park, coach park, 11 bird hides, interpretive buildings. Network of wheelchair-friendly paths, visitor centre/gift shop, toilets. Café open 10am to 4pm (Feb to Oct) and 10am to 3pm for rest of year.
Public transport: Tring railway station, two miles walk mostly on canal towpath.
Habitat: Deep lake in former chalk pit, shallow pools, wet, chalk and rough grasslands, scrub.
Key birds: *Spring/summer*: Breeding Lapwing, Redshank, Little Ringed Plover, Sand Martin, Hobby,

Common Tern, Skylark. Kestrel and Barm Owl frequent scrub areas. *Winter:* Wildfowl (Wigeon, Shoveler, Teal, Gadwall), waders, inc. Snipe, Peregrine Falcon. Rarer birds turn up regularly.
Other notable flora and fauna: Chalk grassland flowers, including displays of cornflowers in June/July. Butterflies include small blue and green hairstreak. Good numbers of dragonflies (16 species). Brown hare.
Contact: The Warden, College Lake. 01442 826 7740 ext 208; (M)07711 821 303; www.bbowt.org.uk e-mail:collegelake@bbowt.org.uk
08 604 810; e-mail: friendsofhesc@gmail.com.

5. LITTLE MARLOW GRAVEL PITS

Lefarge Redland Aggregates.
Location: Sat nav: SL8 5PT. SU 880 880. NE of Marlow from J4 of M40. Use permissive path from Coldmoorholm Lane to Little Marlow village.

Follow path over a wooden bridge to N end of lake. Permissive path ends just past the cottages where it joins a concrete road to sewage treatment works. Be careful at all times when walking round the lake.
Access: Open all year. Do not enter the gravel works and watch for heavy traffic when crossing site's entrance road.
Facilities: Permissive footpath.
Habitat: Gravel pit with sand spit (best viewed from west bank), lake, scrub.
Key birds: *Spring*: Passage migrants including Whimbrel, Wheatear, Whinchat, Sand Martin, Garganey, Hobby. *Summer:* Reed warblers, Kingfisher, wildfowl. *Autumn:* Passage migrants. *Winter:* Wildfowl, possible Smew, Goldeneye, Water Rail, Yellow-legged Gull among large gull flocks, Lapwing, Snipe.
Contact: Ranger Service, Wycombe District Council, 01494 421 825.

Hampshire

DOMINATED by the New Forest, this huge county holds many scarce breeding birds including Honey Buzzard, Goshawk, Red Kite (north of the county), Firecrest, Hawfinch, Dartford Warbler and Nightjar, with Great Grey Shrikes regular in winter. Keyhaven and Farlington Marshes are the best sites for migrants. Blashford Lakes holds a good selection of waterbirds including wintering Bitterns.

1. BLASHFORD LAKES

Hampshire & Isle of Wight Wildlife Trust/Wessex Water.
Location: Sat nav: BH24 3PJ. SU 151 083. From Ringwood take A338 for two miles towards Fordingbridge/Salisbury, pass Ivy Lane R and take next R at Ellingham Cross, into Ellingham Drove. The main car park for hides is first L (entrance shared with Hanson works) after 400 yards.
Access: Car park, hides and visitor centre (with toilets) open daily (9am to 4.30pm) except Dec 25. Paths accessible outside these hours but without vehicle access. Dogs not allowed. Groups should book in advance. RADAR keys needed to open kissing gates for wheelchairs.
Facilities: Parking, footpaths, six hides, viewing screens, toilets and information including recent sightings board, webcams. Coach parking by arrangement.
Public transport: The X3 bus Bournemouth-Salisbury service stops at Ellingham Cross, 500yds W of the main reserve entrance.
Habitat: Flooded gravel pits, areas of wet ancient woodland, also dry grassland and lichen heath.
Key birds: *Winter:* Up to 5,000 over-wintering wildfowl, inc. internationally important numbers of Gadwall. Grey Heron, Little Egret and Bittern. Also a large gull roost on Ibsley Water. *Spring/summer:* Breeding birds include Common Tern, Sand Martin (in

artificial bank), Lapwing, Redshank, Oystercatcher, Kingfisher, Garden Warblers are especially common. *Autumn:* Waders on migration including Green and Common Sandpipers and Greenshank, also Hobby, Black Tern and passerines.
Other notable flora and fauna: Dragonflies (25 species recorded) including brown hawker, scarce chaser and large and small red-eyed damselfly. Roe deer, badgers, otters, foxes, reptiles include adders and grass snakes.
Contact: Blashford Lakes Centre, 01425 472 760 or 07917 616 695; e-mail: feedback@hwt.org.uk

2. FARLINGTON MARSHES

Hants & Isle of Wight Wildlife Trust.
Location: Sat nav: PO6 1RN. SU 685 045. North of Langstone Harbour. Main entrance off roundabout junction A2030/A27 is a small lane between the A27 westbound and the A2030 leading to Portsmouth.
Access: Open at all times, no charge or permits, but donations welcome. Dogs on leads at all times. Wheelchair access via RADAR gates. Short slopes up to sea wall. Paths are mostly level but the main path running along the sea wall can be uneven in places and muddy in wet weather.
Facilities: 2.5 mile circular walk around sea wall with benches every 300m. Information at entrance and shelter. No toilets. Height barriers on car parks.
Public transport: The 21 service from Portsmouth Harbour to Havant stops by Farlington Sainsbury's (north of A27), a 15 + min walk to the reserve. Contact First bus service on 023 8058 4321. By train: Hilsea station is 1.5 miles from reserve. Contact South West Trains on 0845 6000 650.
Habitat: Coastal grazing marsh with pools and reedbed within reserve. Views over intertidal mudflats/saltmarshes of Langstone Harbour.
Key birds: *Summer:* Breeding waders and wildfowl (including Lapwing, Redshank and Shelduck) also breeding Cetti's, Sedge and Reed Warbler, Bearded

NATURE RESERVES - SOUTH EAST ENGLAND

Tit. *Late summer:* Passage migrants (Yellow Wagtail, Whimbrel, etc) and returning waders, chance of rarities such as Spotted Crake, Curlew Sandpiper, stints. *Autumn/winter:* Waders and wildfowl, good numbers of Teal, Wigeon, Pintail, Marsh Harrier, Short-eared Owl regular visitors. Internationally-important numbers of Dark-bellied Brent Goose and Bar-tailed Godwit. Important high tide roost site best viewed over spring high tide.
Other notable flora and fauna: Corky fruited waterdropwort, slender hares-ear, southern marsh and early marsh orchids. Water vole in ditches.
Contact: Jamie Marsh, Solent Reserves Officer. 01489 774 429. www.hwt.org.uk - go to 'Reserves' and then 'news' for sightings, etc

3. FLEET POND LNR

Hart District Council Service/Fleet Pond Society.
Location: Sat nav: GU51 3QY (for Fleet rail station). SY 85. Located in Fleet, W of Farnborough. From the B3013, head to Fleet Station and park in the long-stay car park. Parking also available off Cove Road, Chestnut Grove and Wellington Avenue in Fleet. Pond car park off B3013.
Access: Open all year.
Facilities: Some surfaced paths, boardwalks in wet areas.
Public transport: Fleet railway station lies N of site.
Habitat: Largest freshwater lake in Hampshire, marshes, reedbeds, heathland, wet and dry woodland.
Key birds: Up to 180 species recorded. *Spring/autumn:* Migrant waders incl. Little Ringed Plover, Dunlin, Greenshank, Little Gull, Lesser Spotted Woodpecker, occasional Kittiwake, terns, Wood Lark, Skylark, occasional Ring Ouzel, Firecrest, Pied Flycatcher. *Summer:* Hobby, Common Tern, Tree Pipit, occasional Red Kite and Osprey. *Winter:* Bittern, wildfowl, occasional Smew, Snipe, occasional Jack Snipe, Siskin, Redpoll.
Other notable flora and fauna: Dragonflies and damselflies in wet areas of marshes and heathlands (21 species recorded). Butterflies (26 species recorded), roe deer. More than 400 plant species include ling and bell heather, phragmites reeds.
Contact: Hart District Council, 01252 623 443; e-mail: countryside@hart.gov.uk

4. LOWER TEST MARSHES

Hampshire & Isle of Wight Wildlife Trust.
Location: Sat nav: SO40 3BR. SU 364 150. Area bounded by M27, M271 and A35 west of Southampton. Limited on-road parking near Salmon Leap pub, Testwood Lane, Totton.
Access: Open at all times. No coach parking facilities. Disabled access limited. Dogs allowed only on Test Way footpath.
Facilities: One hide and two screens, all

accessible on foot from Compton Road. Hide open 9am-4pm every day, screens open at all times. Boardwalk over wetter areas of site. Another viewpoint at Old Redbridges, an unsurfaced lay-by off A36.
Public transport: Totton train station and bus stops within easy walking distance. Tel 01983 827 005 for bus details.
Habitat: Saltmarsh, brackish grassland, wet meadows, reedbed, scrapes, meres, estuary.
Key birds: *Summer/breeding:* Kingfisher, Oystercatcher, Reed Warbler, Cetti's Warbler, Sedge Warbler, Reed Bunting. *Autumn/winter waders:* Green Sandpiper, Common Sandpiper, Oystercatcher, Redshank, Curlew, Black-tailed Godwit, Lapwing. *Winter wildfowl:* Wigeon, Teal, Mallard, Shelduck. *Other notable species:* Peregrine, Water Pipit. *On passage:* Osprey, Marsh Harrier, Wood Sandpiper, Garganey.
Other notable flora and fauna: Good range of common butterflies. Dragonflies including scarce chaser, emperor and migrant hawker. Early marsh, green-winged, southern marsh orchids and green-flowered helleborine.
Contact: Reserves Officer, Hampshire and Isle of Wight Wildlife Trust, 02380 667 919; e-mail: clareb@hwt.org.uk www.hwt.org.uk

5. LYMINGTON REEDBEDS

Hampshire & Isle of Wight Wildlife Trust.
Location: Sat nav: SO41 9EW. SZ 323 963. From Lyndhurst in New Forest take A337 to Lymington. Turn L after railway bridge into Marsh Lane. Park in the lay-by next to allotments. The reserve entrance is

on opposite side, to R of the house and over railway crossing. The footpath exits the reserve near the Old Ampress Works, leading to a minor road between the A337 and Boldre.
Access: Open all year. The best viewpoint over the reedbeds is from Bridge Road or from the Undershore leading from the B3054. Dogs on leads please.
Facilities: None.
Public transport: Bus: at either end of the footpath through site, Marsh Lane and on the A337 (route 112). Five minutes walk from train station.
Habitat: At 31 hectares, this is one of largest reedbeds on S coast, fringed by alder and willow woodland.
Key birds: One of highest concentrations of Water Rail in the country; resident but most evident in winter. *Spring/summer*: Cetti's Warbler, Bearded Tit, Yellow Wagtail, Swallow, martins, Reed Warbler. *Passage*: Snipe, ducks.
Other notable fauna: Otters are in the area.
Contact: Trust HQ, 01489 774 400;
e-mail: jamiem@hwt.org.uk www.hwt.org.uk

6. MARTIN DOWN

Natural England (Wiltshire Team).
Location: Sat nav: SP6 3LS. SU 060 201. Fourteen miles SW of Salisbury, 1km W of Martin village. The N part of the site is crossed by the A354. A car park is on the A354 and another at the end of Sillens Lane, a minor road from Martin village.
Access: Open access, organised groups of 10+ should book in advance. Car park height barrier of 7ft 6 ins. Coaches only by prior arrangement. Hard flat track from A354 car park suitable for wheelchairs.
Facilities: Two car parks, interpretative boards.
Public transport: One bus Salisbury/Blandford. Call 01722 336 855 or visit www.wdbus.co.uk
Habitat: Unimproved chalk downland and scrub.
Key birds: *Spring/summer*: Cuckoo, Grey Partridge, Turtle Dove, warblers, Nightingale. *Winter*: Occasional Merlin, Hen Harrier. *All year*: Yellowhammer, Skylark.
Other notable flora and fauna: Species-rich chalk downland with a variety of orchids, plus pasqueflower and milkwort. More than 30 species of butterfly.
Contact: South Wiltshire NNR Office, 01980 620 485, www.naturalengland.org.uk
e-mail: wiltshire@naturalengland.org.uk

7. SWANWICK LAKES NATURE RESERVE

Hampshire & Isle of Wight Wildlife Trust.
Location: Sat nav: SO31 7AY. SU 505 098. SE from Southampton. About 2 miles from Bursledon and 7 miles from Fareham. From M27 J8, follow signs to A3024 Southampton and Hamble and then Park Gate A27. At lights by 'The Spinnaker' pub turn L onto Swanwick Lane. Cross motorway then L onto Sopwith Way. Turn R at mini roundabout. From J9 follow signs for Southampton A27 up to Park Gate. Take road to Botley. At Elm Tree pub turn L onto Swanwick Lane. After about a mile, turn R onto Sopwith Way. Turn R at mini roundabout by security

gates.
Access: Some surfaced paths for wheelchairs, plenty of benches.
Facilities: Network of surfaced and unsurfaced paths, 3 waymarked trails of varying lengths, frequent benches, fantastic viewpoints, reserve leaflet including a trail guide available.
Public transport: *By train*: About 30 mins walk from Swanwick. From station turn R at end of access road then continue to Elm Tree Pub. Turn L onto Swanwick Lane then continue as above. *By bus*: Several First Group buses stop on A27, at the bottom of Swanwick Lane. www.firstgroup.com/ukbus/hampshire/
Habitat: Mixed woodland, flower-rich meadows and deep lakes.
Key birds: Good range of birds including Little Grebe, Gadwall, Buzzard, Kingfisher, Great Spotted and Green Woodpecker, Nuthatch, Treecreeper, finches and tits.
Other notable flora and fauna: Common butterflies, with occasional silver-washed fritillary and purple emperor, common dragonflies and damselflies and other insects including mining bees. Great crested newts. Common spotted orchid. Rich variety of different fungi. Roe deer.
Contact: Trust HQ, 01489 774 400 or Swanwick Lakes Education Officer, 01489 570 240;
e-mail: dawnp@hwt.org.uk; www.hwt.org.uk

8. TESTWOOD LAKES

Southern Water/ HIOW Wildlife Trust.
Location: Sat nav: SO40 3XP. SU 347 155. Take M271 West J2 towards Totton. L at first roundabout, then left onto A36. L at next roundabout onto Brunel Rd. Entrance on L after ¼ mile.
Access: Car parks open 8am to 4pm, winter and 8am to 6pm summer. Surfaced paths around lakes and to hides are relatively flat. Dogs not allowed in conservation and education areas. RADAR key (available at centre) needed for wheelchair users to get through gates. Mobility vehicle available (please book in advance).
Facilities: Testwood Lakes Centre open 10am to 4pm (Mon to Fri) and 1pm to 4pm on Sundays and most Saturdays in summer. Closes 3pm in winter. Weekday access may not be possible if school groups are in attendance. Two hides and two screens. Hides open 10am-4pm daily. Disabled toilet in Education Centre.
Public transport: Totton rail station is 1.5 miles from the reserve. Bluestar and Wilts & Dorset buses stop ¼ mile from entrance. Tel 01983 827 005.
Habitat: Flooded gravel pits, scrapes, wet and dry grasslands, woodland and hedgerows.
Key birds: *Winter*: Various wildfowl (inc. Tufted Duck, Wigeon, Pochard, Teal, Gadwall, Goosander), Siskin, Hawfinch, Meadow Pipit, Common Sandpiper, Green Sandpiper, Pochard, Redwing, Fieldfare. *Spring*: Shelduck, Sand Martin, Little Ringed Plover, Willow Warbler. *Summer*: Swift, Swallow, Blackcap, Whitethroat. *Autumn*: Wheatear, Yellow Wagtail, Goldfinch.
Other notable flora and fauna: Good range of

butterflies. Dragonflies including emperor, scarce chaser, southern and migrant hawker and golden ring.
Contact: Clare Bishop, Trust HQ, 02380 424 206; e-mail: clareb@hwt.org.uk www.hwt.org.uk

9. TITCHFIELD HAVEN

Hampshire County Council.
Location: Sat nav: PO14 3JT. SU 535 025. Located on Cliff Road, Hill Head in Fareham. Reach from A27 and B3334 W of Fareham. Car park adjacent to Hill Head Sailing Club (free for blue badge holders).
Access: Free admission to visitor centre, charge applied for reserve. Open Wed-Sun all year (9.30am to 5pm summer, 9.30am to 4pm winter), plus Bank Hols, except Dec 25 & 26. Public footpath follows derelict canal along W of reserve and road skirts S edge. Guide dogs only.
Facilities: Centre has information desk, toilets, tea room and shop. Eight hides.
Public transport: Bus stops in Solent Road are within 150 yards of reserve.
Habitat: Covers 369 acres of Lower Meon valley. Shoreline, reedbeds, freshwater scrapes, wet grazing meadows.
Key birds: More than 200 species recorded. *Spring/ summer:* Waders (inc. Avocet and Black-tailed Godwit), wildfowl, Common Tern, breeding Cetti's Warbler, Water Rail. *Autumn/winter:* Bittern, Bearded Tit, Brent Geese, Wigeon, Teal, Shoveler and Snipe.
Other notable flora and fauna: Six species of nationally rare plant, roe deer, badger and pipistrelle bat. Dragonflies (19 species recorded) and more than 30 species of butterfly.
Contact: Reserve Manager, Titchfield Haven, 01329 662 145; e-mail:countryside@hants.gov.uk

Kent

THIS IS A FABULOUS county for birders. Being so close to France, the shingle spit at Dungeness offers excellent seawatching, an RSPB reserve and bird observatory. There is another observatory at Sandwich Bay, marshes all along the north coast and reedbeds at Stodmarsh. The Isle of Sheppey holds a wide selection and good numbers of birds of prey in winter.

1. BOUGH BEECH RESERVOIR

Kent Wildlife Trust.
Location: Sat nav: TN14 6LD. TQ 496 494. Lying SW of Sevenoaks, Bough Beech is situated 3.5 miles S of Ide Hill, sign-posted off B2042.
Access: Visitor centre in Winkhurst Green, Ide Hill open on Weds, Sat, Sun and Bank Holidays between 10am and 5pm and Sundays (10am to 4pm) between November and March.

Dogs on leads at all times. Roadside parking.
Facilities: Visitor centre offers hot and cold drinks, gift shop, picnic facilities, toilets (inc disabled). Paths are uneven and can be muddy. Hide overlooks wader scrape.
Public transport: Rail service to Penshurst Station (two miles south).
Habitat: Reserve occupies northern end of the reservoir and adjacent woodland and farmland.
Key birds: Approx 60 species of birds breed in and around the reserve annually, with Tufted Duck, Mandarin and Great Crested Grebe notable among the waterfowl. Little Ringed Plover nest most years. *Autumn:* Good for numbers of waders like Green and Common Sandpipers and Greenshank. Many rarities have been recorded. Ospreys recorded most years. Winter wildfowl numbers are much higher than summer and include Goldeneye and Goosander.
Other notable flora and fauna: Great crested newt, toad, dragonflies (black-tailed skimmer, ruddy darter, emperor, southern aeshna, migrant hawker, red-eyed damselfly), common lizard, Roesel's bush cricket, long-winged conehead, dormouse, water shrew, white admiral butterfly, glow-worm, bats (pipistrelle, Daubenton, noctule, brown long-eared).
Contact: Visitor Centre Manager Peter Bassett (01732 750 624), Reserve Manager Paul Glanfield (01732 456 407); e-mail: info@ kentwildlife.org.uk www.kentwildlifetrust.org.uk

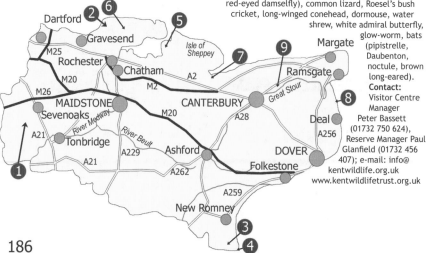

NATURE RESERVES - SOUTH EAST ENGLAND

2. CLIFFE POOLS

RSPB (South East Region Office).
Location: Sat nav: Salt Lane, Cliffe. TQ 722 757.
From coastbound A2, take A289 near Strood. From A289 follow signs for Wainscott and Cliffe onto B2000. At T-junction turn L to Cliffe. At crossroads, turn L to Higham. Before you enter Cliffe, take 2nd L after Cliffe sign. Turn L at next T-junction and L again into Salt Road. Car park is on L just past a sharp R bend.
Access: Free admission at all times. Group bookings welcome. Car park open daily from 8.30am-5pm, except Dec 25. Monthly guided walks available. Dogs only on public footpaths.
Facilities: Six viewing points. Public rights of way encircle reserve and bisect it. Pushchair friendly. Secure parking for 40 vehicles.
Public transport: Bus 133 from Chatham, Rochester and Strood stops at Six Bells pub in Cliffe.
Habitat: A mix of saline lagoons, freshwater pools, grassland, saltmarsh and scrub.
Key birds: Massed flocks of waders in winter (more than 10,000 Black-tailed Godwits reported in winter 2013), plus a wide range of wildfowl. A great variety of passage birds in spring and autumn. Breeding species include Lapwing, Redshank, Avocet, Ringed Plover, Shelduck. Also look out for Nightingale, Hobby and Turtle Dove.
Other notable flora and fauna: Good range of insects (rare bees include shrill carder bee, brown-banded carder bee). Butterflies, inc. marbled white, common blue, Essex skipper and the migrant clouded yellow, grasshoppers and bush crickets, including Roesel's.
Contact: Reserve Manager, 01634 222 480; e-mail:northkentmarshes@rspb.org.uk

3. DUNGENESS NATURE RESERVE

RSPB (South East Region Office).
Location: Sat nav: TN29 9PN. TR 062 197. One mile out of Lydd on the Dungeness Road, turn R for main site. Visitor centre and car park are one mile along entrance track. Entrance to Hanson ARC site and car park is opposite main reserve entrance on L of Dungeness Road.
Access: Open daily (9am to 9pm or sunset when earlier). Visitor centre open (10am to 5pm, or 4pm Nov-Feb). Parties over 12 by prior arrangement. Closed Dec 25 & 26. Charge for non-RSPB members. Only guide dogs allowed on site.
Facilities: Visitor centre, toilets (including disabled access), six hides (all wheelchair-accessible), viewing screen, two nature trails. Fully equipped classroom/ meeting room. Coach parking available. Hide and viewing screen at Hanson ARC site.
Public transport: Limited service. Bus 11 from Ashford stops at reserve entrance on request – one mile walk to visitor centre.
Habitat: Shingle, 90 flooded gravel pits, sallow scrub, newly-extended reedbed, wet grassland.
Key birds: *All year:* Bittern, Marsh Harrier, Bearded Tit. *Spring:* Little Ringed Plover, Wheatear, Yellow Wagtail, Lesser Whitethroat. *Autumn:* Migrant waders

and passerines. *Winter:* Smew, Goldeneye, Slavonian Grebe, Wigeon, Goosander and Bewick's Swan.
Other notable flora and fauna: Jersey cudweed, Nottingham catchfly, brown hare.
Contact: Reserve Manager, 01797 320 588; e-mail: dungeness@rspb.org.uk www.rspb.org.uk

4. DUNGENESS BIRD OBSERVATORY

Dungeness Bird Observatory Trust.
Location: Sat nav: TN29 9NA. TR 085 173. Three miles SE of Lydd. Turn south off Dungeness Road at TR 087 185 and continue to end of road, past two lighthouses.
Access: Observatory open throughout the year. No wheelchair access.
Facilities: Accommodation available for up to nine people (£15 a night for non-members, £10 for members). Apply in writing to the warden or by phone. Bring own sleeping bag/sheets and toiletries. Shared facilities including fully-equipped kitchen. Coach parking available at railway station.
Public transport: Bus service between Rye and Folkestone, numbers 11, 12. Alight at the Pilot Inn, Lydd-on-Sea, a short walk from Observatory. Tel: 01227 472 082.
Habitat: Shingle promontory with scrub and gravel pits.
Key birds: Breeding birds include Raven, Wheatear and Black Redstart and seabirds on RSPB Reserve. Important migration site. Excellent seawatching when weather conditions are suitable. Power station outfall, 'The Patch' good for gulls and terns.
Other notable flora and fauna: Long Pits are excellent for dragonflies, including small red-eyed damselfly. Moth trapping throughout the year.
Contact: David Walker, Dungeness Bird Observatory, 11 RNSSS Cottages, Dungeness, Romnet Marsh Kent TN29 9NA. 01797 321 309; e-mail: dungeness.obs@tinyonline.co.uk www.dungenessbirdobs.org.uk

5. ELMLEY MARSHES NNR

Elmley Conservation Trust.
Location: Sat nav: ME12 3RW. TQ 924 698. From J5 on the M2, follow A249 towards Sheerness. Reserve sign-posted from the exit for Iwade and Ridham Dock, immediately before the Sheppey bridge. At the roundabout, take second exit onto the old road bridge. On the Isle of Sheppey, after 1.25 miles (2 km), turn R following reserve sign. Follow the rough track for approximately 2 miles (3 km) to the car park at Kingshill Farm.
Access: Open every day (9am-9pm or dusk if earlier) except Tuesdays and Dec 25/26. Free to enter. Only guide dogs allowed on reserve. Less mobile visitors may drive closer to the hides.
Facilities: Five hides. Disabled access to Wellmarsh hide. No visitor centre, but owners Philip and Corinne Merricks have pledged to create an extra walk route and more hides. Toilets located in car park 1.25 miles from hides. Pushchair friendly.

Public transport: Swale Halt nearest railway station on Sittingbourne to Sheerness line. From there it is a three mile walk to reserve.
Habitat: Coastal grazing marsh, ditches and pools alongside the Swale Estuary with extensive intertidal mudflats and saltmarsh.
Key birds: *Spring/summer:* Breeding waders — Redshank, Lapwing, Avocet, Yellow Wagtail, passage waders, Hobby. *Autumn:* Passage waders. *Winter:* Spectacular numbers of wildfowl, especially Wigeon and White-fronted Goose. Waders. Hunting raptors — Peregrine, Merlin, Hen Harrier and Short-eared Owl.
Other notable flora and fauna: Water vole.
Contact: 01795 666014/07873 305 368;
e-mail: ect1@live.co.uk

6. NORTHWARD HILL

RSPB (South East Region Office).
Location: Sat nav: ME3 8DS. TQ 781 757. Leave M2 at junction 1 and join A228, sign-posted to Grain. Reserve is in Cooling Road, adjacent to High Halstow approx four miles NE of Rochester.
Access: Open all year, dawn to dusk, free access, trails in public area of wood joining Saxon Shoreway link to grazing marsh. Dogs only allowed on Saxon Shoreway. Trails often steep and not suitable for wheelchair users.
Facilities: Four trails vary in length from 0.5 to 4km. The Toddler trail is surfaced and suitable for 'off-road' push-chairs. Four viewpoints with benches. Rough surface in car park, where toilets are located.
Public transport: Infrequent buses to village of High Halstow, 1.5 miles from reserve. Contact Arriva buses (01634 283 600).
Habitat: Ancient and scrub woodland (approximately 130 acres), grazing marsh (approximately 350 acres).
Key birds: *Spring/summer:* Wood holds UK's largest heronry, with c.150 pairs of Grey Heron and c.50 pairs of Little Egret, breeding Nightingale (1% of UK population), Turtle Dove, scrub warblers and woodpeckers. Marshes — breeding Lapwing, Redshank, Avocet, Marsh Harrier, Shoveler, Pochard. *Winter:* Wigeon, Teal, Shoveler. Passage waders (ie Black-tailed Godwit), raptors, Corn Bunting. Long-eared Owl.
Other notable flora and fauna: Good range of dragonflies over the marsh, white-letter hairstreak butterfly in the woods.
Contact: Jason Mitchell, RSPB North Kent Marshes, 01634 222 480;
e-mail: northkentmarshes@rspb.org.uk

7. OARE MARSHES LNR

Kent Wildlife Trust.
Location: Sat nav: ME13 0QA. TR 01 36 48 (car park). Off Church Road, Oare, two miles N of Faversham. From A2 follow signs to Oare and Harty Ferry.
Access: Open at all times. Car parking opposite the Watch House near seawall. Disabled-only car park 300m from East Flood hide. Access along marked paths only. Dogs on leads.
Facilities: Three hides. Roadside viewpoint of East

Hide accessible to wheelchair users. Those with pneumatic tyres can reach seawall path and hide. Small car park, restricted turning space, not suitable for coaches.
Public transport: 333 bus from Feversham, Sittingbourne and Maidstone to Oare Village one mile from reserve. Arriva service (Mon-Sat), Jaycrest (Sun) — call Traveline on 0870 608 2608. Train: Faversham (two miles distance).
Habitat: Ramsar, SPA, ESA and SSSI designated site with grazing marsh, freshwater dykes, open water scrapes, reedbed, mudflats/Swale Sea Channel.
Key birds: *All year:* Waders and wildfowl, Little Egret, Marsh Harrier, Water Rail, Barn and Little Owls. *Winter:* Brent Goose, Red-breasted Merganser, Hen Harrier, Merlin, Peregrine, Short-eared Owl, Bittern, Stonechat. Divers, grebes and sea ducks on Swale. *Spring/summer:* Avocet, Garganey, Green, Wood and Curlew Sandpipers, Little Stint, Black-tailed Godwit, Little Tern. Site has a good record for attracting rarities.
Contact: Tony Swandale, Kent Wildlife Trust, 01622 662 012; e-mail: info@kentwildlife.org.uk
www.kentwildlifetrust.org.uk

8. SANDWICH BAY BIRD OBSERVATORY

Sandwich Bay Bird Observatory Trust.
Location: Sat nav: CT13 9PF. TR 355 575. 2.5 miles from Sandwich, five miles from Deal. A256 to Sandwich from Dover or Ramsgate. Follow signs to Sandwich Station and then Sandwich Bay.
Access: Open daily. Disabled access.
Facilities: New Field Study Centre. Visitor centre, toilets, refreshments, hostel-type accommodation, plus self-contained flat.
Public transport: Sandwich train station two miles from Observatory.
Habitat: Coastal, dune land, farmland, marsh, two small scrapes.
Key birds: *Spring/autumn passage:* Good variety of migrants and waders, specially Corn Bunting. Annual Golden Oriole. Firecrest and Yellow-browed Warbler occur in The Elms. *Winter:* Golden Plover. Breeding residents include Grey Partridge, Stonechat, Stock Dove, Little Owl, Oystercatcher, Littled Ringed Plover.
Other notable flora and fauna: Sand dune plants such as lady's bedstraw and sand sedge. Small heath butterfly, red-veined darter.
Contact: The Secretary, Sandwich Bay Bird Observatory, 01304 617 341; www.sbbot.co.uk
e-mail: sbbot@talk21.co.uk

9. STODMARSH NNR

Natural England (Kent Team).
Location: Sat nav: CT3 4BA (Red Lion, Stodmarsh). TR 222 618. Lies alongside River Stour and A28, five miles NE of Canterbury. Car park in Stodmarsh village.
Access: Open at all times. Keep to paths. No dogs.
Facilities: Fully accessible toilets at the Stodmarsh entrance car park. Five hides (one fully accessible), easy access nature trail, footpaths and information

panels. Car park, picnic area and toilets adjoining the Grove Ferry entrance with easily accessible path, viewing mound and two wheelchair-accessible hides.
Public transport: There is a regular Stagecoach East Kent bus service from Canterbury to Margate/Ramsgate. Alight at Upstreet for Grove Ferry. Hourly on Sun.
Habitat: Internationally-important mix of open water, reedbed (largest in SE England), wet meadows, dry meadows, woodland.

Key birds: *Spring/summer:* Breeding Marsh Harrier, Bearded Tit, Cetti's Warbler, Garganey, Reed, Sedge and Willow Warblers, Nightingale. Migrant Black Tern, Hobby, Osprey, Little Egret. *Autumn:* Large roosts of Swallows, martins and Starlings. *Winter:* Wildfowl, Hen Harrier, Bittern.
Other notable flora and fauna: Nationally rare plants and invertebrates, including shining ram's horn snail.
Contact: David Feast, Natural England, 07767 321 058 (mobile).

London, Greater

PEREGRINES are happily colonising tall city structures such as Tate Modern, Battersea Power Station and the O2 Arena to name but a few. Black Redstarts are present too. Recent attentions have been devoted to impressive visible migration over the city. There are many parks to explore and Common Terns now fish along the cleaned-up Thames.

BEDFONT LAKES COUNTRY PARK

Friends of BLCP/Continental Landscapes Ltd.
Location: Sat nav: TW14 8QA (Clockhouse Lane). TQ 080 728. From M25 take junction 13 (A30) towards central London. Continue through Crooked Billet traffic light complex, past Ashford Hospital and take B3003 (Clockhouse Lane) from the Clockhouse roundabout.
Access: Park open (8am to 9pm or dusk, whichever is earlier), all days except Dec 25. Disabled friendly. Dogs on leads. Main nature reserve only open Sun (2pm-4pm). Keyholder membership available (£12 annually) to access reserve at any time.
Facilities: Toilets, information centre, several hides, nature trail, free parking, up-to-date information.
Public transport: Train to Feltham and Ashford. Bus — H26 (Feltham to Hatton Cross) and 116 from Hounslow to Ashford Hospital.
Habitat: North side nature reserve consists of 180 acres of lakes, reedbed, wildflower meadows, wet woodland, scrub.
Key birds: 140 species recorded. *Winter:* Water Rail, Bittern, Smew and other wildfowl, Meadow Pipit. *Summer:* Common Tern, Willow, Garden, Reed and Sedge Warblers, Whitethroat, Lesser Whitethroat, hirundines, Hobby, Blackcap, Chiffchaff, Skylark. *Passage:* Wheatear, Wood Warbler, Spotted Flycatcher, Ring Ouzel, Redstart, Yellow Wagtail.
Other notable flora and fauna: 140 plant species inc bee and pyramidal orchid. Nathusius pipistrelle bat, emperor dragonfly plus other butterflies and dragonflies.
Contact: James Herd, Ranger, BLCP, Clockhouse Lane, Bedfont, Middx, TW14 8QA. 0845 456 2796.
e-mail: bedfont.lakes@continental-landscapes.co.uk

BRENT (WELSH HARP) RESERVOIR

Welsh Harp Conservation Group/British Waterways.
Location: Sat nav: NW9 7BH. In NW london close

to junction 1 of M1. A% (Edgeware Road) runs along eastern edge of site. From A5 turn into Cool Oak Lane and park just behind the bridge separating northern and eastern marshes.
Access: Open access at all times, but key needed to use Main and Heron hides overlooking the eastern marsh (apply to Conservation Group), unless a member is already in situ. Park in Birchen Grove to access Welsh Harp Open Space nature reserve. WHCG and North-East London RSPB Group organises regular Sunday birdwalks.
Facilities: Raised viewing platform and permanently open public hide overlooks northern marsh. Circular walk.
Public transport: Hendon station (Thameslink) is a short walk away take Station Road and West Hendon Broadway to Cool Oak Lane).
Habitat: Reservoir surrounded by marshland, woodland, unimproved grassland and playing fields.
Key birds: More than 250 species recorded. *Spring/summer:* Breeding Great Crested Grebe, Gadwall, Shoveler, Pochard, Common Tern, woodland species and up to eight species of warbler. A long history of rare birds includes London's first Great White Egret in 1997 and the UK's first Iberian Chiffchaff in 1972. *Winter:* A wide range of wildfowl and gull species.
Other notable flora and fauna: 28 species of butterfly recorded, including marbled white and ringlet, plus 15 species of dragonfly. A noted site for bat species.
Contact: WHCG telephone 0208 4471 810.

DAGENHAM CHASE LNR

Barking & Dagenham Parks Ranger Service.
Location: Sat nav: RM7 0SS (Millenium Centre). TQ 515 860. Lies in the Dagenham Corridor, an area of green belt between the London Boroughs of Barking & Dagenham and Havering.
Access: Open throughout the year and at all times. Reserve not suitable for wheelchair access. Eastbrookend Country Park which borders The Chase LNR has surfaced footpaths for wheelchair use.
Facilities: Millennium visitor centre in Eastbrookend CP, toilets, ample car parking, Timberland Trail walk.
Public transport: Rail: Dagenham East (District Line) 15 minute walk. Bus: 174 from Romford or Dagenham five minute walk.
Habitat: Shallow wetlands, reedbeds, horse-grazed pasture, scrub and wetland. These harbour an impressive range of animals and plants, including the nationally rare black poplar tree.

Key birds: A haven for birds, with approx 190 different species recorded. *Summer*: Breeding Reed Warbler, Lapwing, Water Rail, Lesser Whitethroat, Little Grebe, Kingfisher, Reed Bunting. *Winter*: Significant numbers of Teal, Shoveler, Redwing, Fieldfare and Snipe dominate the scene. *Spring/autumn migration*: Yellow Wagtail, Wheatear, Ruff, Wood Sandpiper, Sand Martin, Ring Ouzel, Black Redstart and Hobby regularly seen. **Other notable flora and fauna:** 140 plant species, wasp spider, butterflies and dragonflies. **Contact:** Ranger service 020 8227 2332

LONDON WETLAND CENTRE

Wildfowl & Wetlands Trust.
Location: Sat nav: SW13 9WT. TQ 228 770. In Queen Elizabeth's Walk, Barnes, less than 1 mile from South Circular (A205). In London Zone 2/3, one mile from Hammersmith.
Access: Winter (9.30am to 5pm: last admission 4pm), summer (9.30am to 6pm: last admission 5pm). Charge for admission for non-WWT members. Coach parking by arrangement.
Facilities: Visitor centre, hides, nature trails, discovery centre and children's adventure area, restaurant (hot and cold food), cinema, shop, observatory building, six hides (all wheelchair accessible), sustainable gardens, interactive pond zone, three interpretative buildings.
Public transport: Train: Barnes. Tube: Hammersmith then bus 283 (comes into centre). Other buses from Hammersmith are 33, 72, 209; from Richmond, 33.
Habitat: Main lake, reedbeds, wader scrape, open water lakes, wet woodland, grazing marsh.
Key birds: Nationally important numbers of wintering waterfowl, including Gadwall and Shoveler. Important numbers of wetland breeding birds, including grebes, swans, a range of duck species such as Pochard, plus Lapwing, Little Ringed Plover, Redshank, warblers, Reed Bunting and Bittern. Cetti's Warblers remain on site all year round and bred for the first time in 2010.

Artifical nesting bank for Sand Martins and rafts for nesting terns. Peregrines which nest on Charing Cross Hospital sighted regularly. **Other notable flora and fauna:** Water voles, slow worm, grass snake, common lizard. Seven species of bat, 22 species of dragonfly and 25 of butterfly. Notable plants inc snake's head fritillaries, cowslip, pyramidal and bee orchids. **Contact:** London Wetland Centre 020 8409 4400; e-mail: info.london@wwt.org.uk www.wwt.org.uk/london Twitter:@wwtlondon.

SYDENHAM HILL WOOD

London Wildlife Trust.
Location: Sat nav: SE26 6RU. TQ 342 722. Forest Hill, SE London, SE26, between Forest Hill and Crystal Palace, just off South Circular (A205). Entrances at Crescent Wood Road and Coxs Walk.
Access: Open at all times, no permits required. Some steep slopes, so wheelchair access is difficult.
Facilities: Nature trail, information boards. No toilets.
Public transport: Train stations: Forest Hill (from London Bridge) or Sydenham Hill (from Victoria). Buses 363, 202, 356, 185, 312, 176, P4. Call Transport for London 0207 5657 299 for details.
Habitat: Ancient woodland, reclaimed Victorian gardens, meadow and small pond.
Key birds: Woodland and gardens species all year round. *All year*: All three woodpeckers, Tawny Owl, Kestrel, Sparrowhawk, Goldcrest, Nuthatch, Treecreeper, Stock Dove. *Summer*: Blackcap, Chiffchaff, Willow Warbler. *Winter*: Fieldfare, Redwing.
Other notable flora and fauna: Five species of bat, including noctule and brown long-eared. Bluebell, wood anemone, dog violet and primrose. Oak and hornbeam. Speckled wood, comma, painted lady and orange-tip butterflies.
Contact: Centre for Wildlife Gardening 020 7252 9186.

Surrey

LONDON'S urban sprawl has now enveloped much of northern Surrey, but reservoirs and the sewage farm at Beddington offer opportunities for birders. To the west of the county, heathland at Thursley Common and around Frensham are good for the likes of Nightjar, Hobby, Woodlark and Dartford Warbler.

1. CHOBHAM COMMON NNR

Surrey Wildlife Trust.
Location: Sat nav: GU24 8TU. SU 971 647 (Staple Hill car park). From J3 of M3 head N on A322 and A30 in direction of Sunningdale. Car park in Staple Hill Road leading off from B383 Windsor Road.

Access: Open at all times.
Facilities: Three self-guided trails, six car parks with information boards. Site leaflet available from rangers.
Public transport: Hourly buses from Woking to Chobham, stopping in Bowling Green Road, just S of Common. Also services to Sunningdale from Ascot, Windsor, Camberley and Staines. Sunningdale railway station is 600 metres from NW cortner of Common.
Habitat: Largest NNR in southern England. Lowland wet and dry heath, with 30 pools, mixed broadleaf and pine woodlands.
Key birds: More than 115 species recorded, including nationally rare Dartford Warbler, Hobby and Nightjar. Other notable birds include Yellowhammer, Stonechat, Linnet and Skylark.
Other notable flora and fauna: More than 350

flowering plants, 25 species of mammal, 29 species of butterfly inc silver-studded blue and 22 species of dragonfly all recorded.

Contact: Surrey Wildlife Trust 01483 795 440 or e-mail: info@surreywt.org.uk

2. FARNHAM HEATH

RSPB (South East Region Office).

Location: Sat nav: GU10 2DL. SU 859 433. Take B3001 SE from Farnham. Take the R hand fork, signposted Tilford, immediately past level crossing. Keep to that road. Just outside Tilford village it is signed to the Rural Life Centre. Follow those signs. Entrance is on the R after 0.5 mile.

Access: Reserve open at all times. Car park opens 9.30 am weekdays and 10.30 am weekends. Park in lay-bys on adjacent roads outside those hours. Rural Life Centre open Wed-Fri and Sundays all year. Open on Saturdays April-Sept. Tea room opens at 11 am.

Facilities: Large grass car park, shared with Rural Life Centre. No height barrier, but gates may be locked outside opening hours. No bike racks. Toilets (including disabled), picnic area, refreshments. Group bookings accepted, guided walks available. Good for walking, pushchair friendly. Three way-marked trails.

Public transport: Bus 19 (Farnham to Hindhead service) stops in Millbridge village, outside entrance to Pierrepont House. Reserve is a mile away, along Reeds Road (follow signs to the Rural Life Centre).

Habitat: Heathland and pine woodland.

Key birds: Spring: Blackcap, Tree Pipit, Woodcock, Woodlark. Summer: Woodcock and Nightjar, woodland birds, including Stock Dove and Great and Great Spotted Woodpeckers. Winter: Crossbills in pine woods, winter finches, including Brambling around the feeders, winter thrushes.

Other notable flora and fauna: Fungi − more than 150 species. Bats in summer.

Contact: Mike Coates, c/o The Rural Life Centre, 01252 795 632; e-mail: farnham.heath@rspb.org.uk

3. FRENSHAM COMMON & COUNTRY PARK

Waverley BC and National Trust.

Location: Sat nav: GU10 3BT (Frensham main car park SU 857 418) or Bacon Lane car park, Churt (SU 843 403). Common (1,000 acres in area) lies on either side of A287 between Farnham and Hindhead.

Access: Open at all times. Car park (locked 9pm-9am). Keep to paths. Dogs on leads during breeding season.

Facilities: Car parks at Great and Little Ponds (free on weekdays). Information rooms, toilets (inc disabled) and refreshment kiosk at Great Pond.

Public transport: Stagecoach bus 19 from Farnham to Haslemere stops at Frensham Pond Lane (no Sunday service).

Habitat: Dry and humid heath, woodland, two large ponds, reedbeds.

Key birds: Summer: Dartford Warbler, Woodlark, Hobby, Nightjar, Common Tern, Stonechat, Spotted Flycatcher, Sedge and Reed Warblers, Reed Bunting. Winter: Wildfowl (inc. occasional Smew), Bittern, Great Grey Shrike.

Other notable flora and fauna: Tiger beetle, purple hairstreak and silver-studded blue butterflies, sand lizard, smooth snake.

Contact: The Rangers Office, 01252 792 416.

4. LIGHTWATER COUNTRY PARK

Surreyheath Council.

Location: Sat nav: GU18 5RG. SU 921 622. From J3 of M3, take the A322 and follow brown Country Park signs. From Guildford Road in Lightwater, turn into The Avenue. Entrance to the park is at the bottom of the road.

Access: Open all year, dawn-dusk. Check opening times for Heathland Visitor Centre.

Facilities: Car park, toilets, waymarked trails with leaflets available.

Public transport: Train: Bagshot two miles. Tel SW Trains 0845 6000 650. Arriva Bus: No 34 stops at Lightwater village Tel: 01483 306 397.

Habitat: Heathland, woodland, three ponds and meadows.

Key birds: All year: All three woodpeckers, Goldcrest in woods, Coot, Moorhen, Grey Heron and Kingfisher on ponds. Summer: Nightjar, Willow Warbler, Chiffchaff, Blackcap, Whitethroat. Winter: Fieldfare, Redwing, Siskin.

Other notable flora and fauna: Ox-eye daisies, knapweed and common spotted orchid in meadow, heathers and gorse species on heath. Wood ant nests in woodlands. Range of dragonflies and butterflies.

Contact: Surreyheath Ranger Service, Lightwater Country Park 01276 707 166; e-mail: rangers@surreyheath.gov.uk; www.surreyheath.gov.uk

5. THURSLEY COMMON NNR

Natural England (NNR Delivery Team South East).

Location: Sat nav: GU8 6LN. SU 900 417. From Guildford, take A3 SW to B3001 (Elstead/Churt

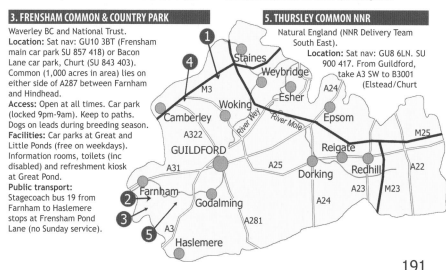

road). Use the Moat car park, S of Elstead village.
Access: Open access. Parties must obtain prior
permission.
Facilities: Boardwalk in wetter areas along the Heath
Trail (2.25 miles in length).
Public transport: None.
Habitat: Wet and dry heathland, woodland, bog.
Key birds: *Winter*: Hen/Marsh Harriers, Great Grey
Shrike and passage/migrant waders such as Redshank,
Greenshank, Wood and Common Sandpipers. *Summer*:
Hobby, Woodlark, Lapwing, Stonechat, Curlew, Snipe,
Nightjar, Spotted Flycatcher, Redstart, Crossbill.

Other notable flora and fauna: Large populations
of silver-studded blue, grayling and purple emperor
butterflies can be seen here, alongside 26 recorded
dragonfly species. Sandier sites on the reserve
provide homes for many species of solitary bees
and wasps and tiger beetles. Damp areas support
carnivorous sundews and a large population (in the
thousands) of early marsh orchid.
Contact: James Giles, Natural England, T01483 307
703; e-mail: james.giles@naturalengland.org.uk
www.naturalengland.org.uk

Sussex, East

THE AREA around Rye Harbour and nearby Pett
Level guarantees a good day's birdwatching,
with an interesting mix of wildfowl, waders,
raptors, terns and Bitterns, depending on the
season. If you enjoy finding your own migrants,
then a spring or autumn visit to Beachy Head is a
must. Ashdown Forest offers a fine mix of woodland
heathland birds.

important numbers, such as Shoveler and
Sanderling in the winter and breeding Little Tern
and Mediterranean Gull. Nesting Black-headed Gull
colony, Common and Sandwich Terns and a good range
of waders and ducks. Barn and Short-eared Owls.
Other notable flora and fauna: The saltmarsh
supports such unusual plants as sea-heath and marsh
mallow, and even highly specialised insects including
the star-wort moth and saltmarsh bee.
Contact: Sussex Wildlife Trust, 01273 492 630; e-mail:
enquiries@sussexwt.org.uk - www.sussexwt.org.uk

1. CASTLE WATER, RYE HARBOUR

Sussex Wildlife Trust.
Location: Sat nav: TN31 7TU. TQ 942 189. Reserve is
one mile SE of Rye along Harbour Road.
Access: Open at all times, entry is free. Information
centre at Limekiln Cottage open every day 10am-
4pm. Site is flat with some wheelchair access to all
four hides, although there are stiles where the sheep
are grazing the fields.
Facilities: Information centre, large car park at Rye
Harbour with nearby toilets. Replacement wader pool
hide now open.
Habitat: Large area of intertidal saltmarsh, marsh,
drainage ditches, shingle ridges, pits, sand, scrub,
woodland.
Key birds: Many birds occur here in nationally

2. LULLINGTON HEATH NNR

Natural England (NNR Delivery Team South East).
Location: TQ 525 026. Seven miles NW of Eastbourne,
between Jevington and Litlington, on northern edge
of Friston Forest.
Access: Via footpaths and bridleways. Site open for
access on foot.
Facilities: None. Nearest toilets/refreshments at
pubs in Jevington, Litlington or Seven Sisters CP, 2km
to S.
Public transport: Nearest bus stop is Seven Sisters
Country Park. Phone Brighton & Hove services on
01273 886 200 or visit: www.buses.co.uk/bustimes/
Habitat: Grazed chalk downland and heath, with
mixed scrub and gorse.
Key birds: *Summer*: Breeding Nightingale, Turtle
Dove, Nightjar and diverse range of grassland/scrub-
nesting species.Passage migrants include Wheatear,
Redstart, Ring Ouzel. *Winter*: Raptors (inc. Hen
Harrier), Woodcock.
Other notable flora and fauna: Bell
heather, ling and gorse
on chalk heath; orchid
species in grassland.
Contact: East Sussex
NNRs, Natural
England, 07971
974 401 or reserve
manager 07825 386
620; e-mail: malcolm.
emery@naturalengland.
org.uk
www.naturalengland.org.uk

NATURE RESERVES - SOUTH EAST ENGLAND

3. OLD LODGE RESERVE

Sussex Wildlife Trust.
Location: Sat nav: TN22 3JD. TQ 469 306 A Local Nature Reserve within the much larger Ashdown Forest on W side of B2026 between Maresfield and Hartfield, about 0.75 miles N of junction with B2188 at Kings Standing.
Access: Open all year on well-marked nature trail leading from car park. Dogs must be kept on leads between Jan-end Sept and when livestock is present.
Facilities: Car park, nature trail. Steep paths.
Public transport: None.
Habitat: Heath, pine and deciduous woodlands.
Key birds: *All year:* Heathland specialists inc Dartford Warbler. *Spring/summer:* Breeding Nightjar, Woodcock, Redstart, Woodlark, Tree Pipit, Stonechat. *Autumn/winter:* Raven, Crossbill.
Other notable flora and fauna: Good for dragonflies including black darter, golden ringed and small red damselfly. Small colony of silver-studded blue butterflies.
Contact: Sussex Wildlife Trust, 01273 492 630; e-mail: enquiries@sussexwt.org.uk - ww.sussexwt.org.uk

4. RYE HARBOUR

Rye Harbour LNR Management Committee.
Location: Sat nav: TN31 7TU. TQ 941 188. One mile from Rye off A259 signed Rye Harbour. From J10 of M20 take A2070 until it joins A259.

Access: Open at all times by footpaths. Organised groups please book.
Facilities: Car park in Rye Harbour village. Information kiosk in car park. Shop, two pubs, toilets and disabled facilities near car park, four hides (wheelchair access), information centre open most days (10am-4pm) by volunteers.
Public transport: Train stations at Rye and Winchelsea, (08457 484 950), bus (0870 608 2608), tourist information (tel: 01797 226 696).
Habitat: Sea, sand, shingle, pits, saltmarsh and grassland.
Key birds: Seventy of the 279 recorded species have bred on the reserve. *Spring:* Passage waders, especially roosting Whimbrel. *Summer:* Turtle Dove, Breeding terns (3 species), waders (7 species), gulls (6 species inc Mediterranean), Garganey, Shoveler, Cetti's Warbler, Bearded Tit, Wheatear. *Winter:* Wildfowl, inc Smew and nationally important numbers of Shoveler, Water Rail, Bittern.
Other notable flora and fauna: Good shingle flora including endangered least lettuce and stinging hawksbeard. Excellent range of dragonflies including breeding red-veined darter and scarce emerald damselfly.
Contact: Barry Yates, (Manager), 01797 227 784; e-mail: rhnr.office@eastsussex.gov.uk
www.wildrye.info

Sussex, West

PAGHAM HARBOUR is worth a visit at any time of year. Nearby Selsey Bill is good for migrants and there is a noticeable skua passage in the spring. The WWT reserve at Arundel is good for Mandarins and Cetti's Warblers, while further inland, RSPB Pulborough Brooks holds important numbers of wintering wildfowl including the chance of Bewick's Swans.

1. ADUR ESTUARY

RSPB (South East Region Office).
Location: Sat nav: BN43 5EE. TQ 215 049. On W side of Shoreham-on-Sea: view from Coronation Green, situated near town centre or footbridge linking High Street and Riverside Road.
Access: No direct access to reserve areas, but good views from riverside paths between footbridge in Shoreham town centre and A259 Norfolk bridge (car park). Free public car park at the Council's recreational field on N side of A259.
Facilities: None.
Public transport: Trains: Shoreham-by-Sea. Bus: Shoreham-by-Sea town centre. Brighton and Hove buses (01273 886 200) less than one mile away.
Habitat: Mudflats and saltmarsh.
Key birds: A small area but a haven for waders and

wildfowl. *Spring/summer:* Little Egret, Turnstone, Ringed Plover, Dunlin, Redshank, Common and Sandwich terns. *All year:* Oystercatcher. *Winter:* Good range of gulls, Kingfisher and several wader species.
Contact: RSPB, 01273 775 333;
e-mail: pulborough.brooks@rspb.org.uk
www.rspb.org.uk/adurestuary

2. ARUNDEL WETLAND CENTRE

Wildfowl and Wetland Trust.
Location: Sat nav: BN18 9PB. TQ 020 081. Centre clearly sign-posted from Arundel, just N of A27.
Access: Summer (9.30am-5.30pm) winter (9.30am-4.30pm). Closed Dec 25. Approx 1.5 miles of level footpaths, suitable for wheelchairs. Guide dogs only. Admission charges for non-WWT members.
Facilities: Visitor centre, restaurant, shop, hides, picnic area, seasonal nature trails. Eye of The Wind Wildlife Gallery. Corporate hire facilities. Electric boat safaris.
Public transport: Arundel station, 15-20 minute walk. Tel: 01903 882 131.
Habitat: Site covers 65 acres with lakes, wader scrapes, reedbed.
Key birds: *All year:* All three woodpeckers, Kingfisher. *Summer:* Nesting Redshank, Lapwing, Oystercatcher, Common Tern, Sedge, Reed and Cetti's Warblers, Peregrine, Hobby. *Winter:* Teal, Wigeon, Reed

Bunting, Water Rail, Cetti's Warbler and occasionally roosting Bewick's Swan.
Other notable flora and fauna: Bee orchid, water shrew, palmate and smooth newt, grass snake, six species of bat.
Contact: WWT Arundel Wetland Centre, Mill Road, Arundel. 01903 883 355; www.wwt.org.uk
e-mail: info.arundel@wwt.org.uk

3. CHICHESTER HARBOUR

Chichester Harbour Conservancy.
Location: West of Chichester, with various viewing points along 47 miles of coastline to Hayling Island. East Head/ West Wittering good places for birding from A27 S of Chichester, follow brown signs for West Wittering Beach.
Access: Five paths suitable for wheelchairs: Cobnor Point/ Itchenor/ Prinsted/ North Common, Northney/ Sandy Point, Hayling Island. All-terrain wheelchair can be hired (call 01243 514 143).
Facilities: Wheelchair-accessible viewing platform and toilet at Itchenor. RADAR-key tilet at Dell Quay.
Public transport: Contact Stagecoach South on 0871 200 2233 for information on services.
Habitat: Deep saltwater channels, mud banks, sand dunes and shingle.
Key birds: Internationally-important for birds, with an estimated 55,000 birds a year residing or passing through the harbour each year. *Autumn/ winter:* Waders inc Golden Plover, Lapwing, Curlew, Whimbrel, Black- and Bar-tailed Godwits, Oystercatcher, Turnstone, Snipe, Dunlin and Sanderling. Up to 10,000 Brent Geese, Red-breasted Merganser and common wildfowl species. Kingfisher, Short-eared owl, Hen Harrier, Linnet and Skylark. *Spring/summer:* Little, Sandwich and Common Terns all breed.
Other notable flora and fauna: Harbour seal, marsh samphire, sea purslane, sea lavender and sea aster.
Contact: Friends of Chichester Harbour, Harbour Office, Itchenor, PO20 7AW. 01243 512 301; e-mail: secretary@friendsch.org; www.friendsch.org

4. KINGLEY VALE NNR

Natural England (Sussex & Surrey Team).
Location: Part of South Downs National Park. Sat nav: PO18 9B. SU 825 088 (West Stoke car park, 1.2Km from reserve entrance). Approx five miles NW of Chichester town centre (as the crow flies). Travel N from Chichester on A286 to Lavant, then turn L (W) by the church on to Downs Road. Follow to West Stoke. Turn R at the junction after the church to West Stoke car park.
Access: Always open, no permits, no disabled access. All dogs on a lead please – grazing stock.
Facilities: There is a nature trail (posts 1-24) and an unmanned information centre – no toilets, but plenty of trees and bushes!
Public transport: Nearest railway station approx five miles walking distance. Nearest main bus route just over one mile on A286 at Mid Lavant. No 60 from

Chichester Bus Station next to the Rail Station.
Habitat: Greatest yew forest in Europe (more than 30,000 trees). Chalk grassland, mixed oak/ash woodland and scrub. Chalk heath.
Key birds: *Spring/summer:* Nightingale, Whitethroat, Blackcap, Lesser Whitethroat. *Autumn/winter:* Hen Harrier, Buzzard, Hobby on migration, Red Kite. Barn and Tawny Owls, Hawfinch, Ravens, Goldcrest, Firecrest, Redwing, Fieldfare, Osprey (passing over on migration), Green Woodpecker, Nuthatch.
Other notable flora and fauna: Yellow meadow ant, 39 recorded species of butterfly inc brown argus and chalkhill blue, 11 species of orchid.
Contact: Natural England, 01243 575 353; e-mail: enquiries.southeast@naturalengland.org.uk www.naturalengland.org.uk;

5. PAGHAM HARBOUR

West Sussex County Council/RSPB.
Location: Sat nav: PO20 7NE. SZ 857 966. Five miles S of Chichester on B2145 towards Selsey. After 0.5miles turn R at first roundabout still following Selsey. Look for entrance just after leaving Sidlesham after speed limit increases to 50mph.
Access: Car parks open at all times. Dogs must be on leads, disabled trail with accessible hide. All groups and coach parties must book in advance.
Facilities: Visitor Centre open most of the week throughout the year (10am-4pm) but check first (closed Dec 25 and 26). Toilets (including disabled), three hides and several other viewpoints, one nature trail.
Public transport: Bus 51 (Chichester to Selsey) stops by visitor centre.
Habitat: Mudflats, intertidal saltmarsh, shingle beaches, lagoons and farmland.
Key birds: *Spring:* Passage migrants (warblers, hirundines, Wheatear). *Summer:* Breeding Little and Common Terns. *Autumn:* Passage waders inc Curlew Sandpiper, Ruff and Little Stint, other migrants, inc Pied and Spotted Flycatchers, incoming wildfowl species. *Winter:* 20,000 birds inc Brent Goose, Slavonian Grebe, wildfowl and waders. *All year:* Little Egret.
Other notable flora and fauna: Wide range of grasses, butterflies and dragonflies (inc emperor, broad-bodied chaser and hairy dragonfly).
Contact: Reserve Manager 01243 641 508; e-mail: pagham.harbour@rspb.org.uk

6. PILSEY AND THORNEY ISLANDS

RSPB (South East Region Office).
Location: SU 766 051.W of Chichester. Take A259 and park in Prinstead, near Emsworth. Walk over sea walls to view both Thorney and Pilsey islands.
Access: No vehicle access to Thorney Island, viewing from footpaths only. Pilsey Island can be viewed from 5.5.mile coastal path (the Sussex Border Path) that runs around the Thorney Island MoD base. Long, exposed walk.
Facilities: Footpath.

NATURE RESERVES - SOUTH EAST ENGLAND

Habitat: Intertidal sandflats and mudflats, fore dunes and yellow dunes, bare and vegetated shingle and saltmarsh.
Key birds: The reserve, together with the adjacent area of Pilsey Sand, forms one of the most important pre-roost and roost site for passage and wintering waders in the area. Brent Geese in winter, plus Merlin and Peregrine possible. *Summer:* Breeding Sandwich and Common Terns. Ringed Plovers and Osprey possible.
Contact: Site Warden, 01798 875 851; e-mail: pilsey.island@rspb.org.uk

7. PULBOROUGH BROOKS

RSPB (South East Region Office).
Location: Sat nav: RH20 2EL. TQ 058 164. Part of South Downs National Park, sign-posted on A283 between Pulborough (via A29) and Storrington (via A24). Two miles SE of Pulborough.
Access: Open daily. Visitor centre open 9.30am-5pm (tea-room 4.30pm), closed Dec 25/26. Nature trail and hides (sunrise to sunset), closed Dec 25. Admission fee for nature trail (free to RSPB members). No dogs. All hides accessible to wheelchair users, though strong helper is needed.
Facilities: Visitor centre (incl RSPB shop, tea room with terrace, displays, toilets). Nature trail, four hides and additional viewpoints. Large car park including coach area. Play and picnic areas. An electric buggy is available for free hire,.
Public transport: Two miles from Pulborough train station. Connecting bus service regularly passes reserve entrance (not Sun). Compass Travel (01903 690 025). Cycle stands.
Habitat: Lowland wet grassland (wet meadows and ditches). Restored heathland, hedgerows, scrub and woodland.
Key birds: *Winter:* Thousands of wintering wildfowl and waterbirds, Bewick's Swan. Peregrine, Hen Harrier, Merlin and Short-eared Owl hunt regularly. *Spring/summer:* Breeding wading birds and songbirds (inc Lapwing and Nightingale), Nightjar, Woodlark, Lesser-spotted Woodpecker, Barn Owl. *Autumn:* Passage wading birds, Redstart, Whinchat, Yellow Wagtail, incoming wildfowl species.
Other notable flora and fauna: Good range of butterflies and dragonflies.
Contact: The Administrator, Pulborough Brooks NR, 01798 875 851;
e-mail: pulborough.brooks@rspb.org.uk
www.rspb.org.uk/pulboroughbrooks

8. WARNHAM LNR

Horsham District Council.
Location: Sat nav: RH12 2RA. TQ 167 324. One mile

NW from Horsham town centre on B2237, just off A24 'Robin Hood' roundabout.
Access: Open all year (except Dec 25 and 26) Mar - Oct (10am-6pm), Nov-Feb (10am-5pm). Day permits: Adults £1.50, children under 16 free. Annual permits also available. No dogs or cycling allowed. Good wheelchair access over most of the Reserve.
Facilities: Free access to visitor centre and café. Stag beetle loggery. Ample car park – coaches by request. Toilets (including disabled), two hides, reserve leaflets, millpond nature trail, bird feeding station, boardwalks, benches and hardstanding paths.
Public transport: One mile from Horsham Railway Station, along Hurst Road, with a R turn onto Warnham Road. Buses from 'CarFax' in Horsham Centre stop within 150 yards of the reserve. Travel line, 0870 608 2608.
Habitat: Site of 92 acres includes 17 acre millpond, reedbeds, marsh, meadow and woodland (deciduous and coniferous).
Key birds: *Summer:* Common Tern, Kingfisher, woodpeckers, Mandarin Duck, Marsh Tit, Goldcrest, hirundines, Hobby, warblers. *Winter:* Cormorant, gulls, Little Grebe, Water Rail, Brambling, Siskin, Lesser Redpoll, thrushes and wildfowl. *Passage:* Waders, pipits, terns and hirundines.
Other notable flora and fauna: Extensive invertebrate interest, including 33 species of butterfly and 25 species of dragonfly. Mammals including harvest mouse, water vole and badger. More than 450 species of plant, including broad-leaved helleborine and common spotted orchid.
Contact: The site manager, 01403 256 890;
e-mail:leisure@horsham.gov.uk
www.visithorsham.co.uk
www.friendsofwarnhamlnr.org.uk

South West England

Cornwall, Devon, Dorset, Somerset, Wiltshire

Cornwall

LOCATION, location, location.... Cornwall is ideally placed to attract overflying migrants in both spring and, particularly, autumn. For full coverage of migrant hotspots near Land's End such as Cot and Nanquidno Valleys see *Best Birdwatching Sites: Cornwall & Scilly*. Headlands at St Ives and Porthgwarra are ideal for autumn seawatching, while Choughs have recently started recolonizing the Lizard.

1. CROWDY RESERVOIR

South West Lakes Trust.
Location: SX 147 840. Follow signs from A39 at Camelford to Davidstow Airfield and pick up signs to reservoir. On edge of forestry plantation, park in pull-in spot near cattle grid. A track leads to a hide via stiles. Main car park located a little further down the lane.
Access: Open all year. No wheelchair access on tracks.
Facilities: Hide accessed from car park along rough track. **Public transport:** None.
Habitat: Reservoir, bog, moorland, forestry.
Key birds: *Spring*: Passage migrants, inc Wheatear, Whimbrel, Ruff. *Summer*: Black-headed Gull, Grasshopper, Reed and Sedge Warblers, returning waders. *Autumn*: Waders, raptors possible inc Peregrine, Goshawk, Merlin. *Winter*: Wild swans, wildfowl, possible Smew. Golden Plover, Woodcock, Fieldfare, Redwing.
Other notable flora: Mire floral communities.
Contact: South West Lakes Trust, 01566 771 930.
www.swlakestrust.org.uk

2. HAYLE ESTUARY

RSPB (South West England Office).
Location: Sat nav: TR27 6JF. SW 550 370. In town of Hayle. Follow signs to Hayle from A30. Take B3301 through Hayle past the Tempest factory, turn L into Chenells Rd and R into Ryans Field.
Access: Open at all times. No permits required. No admission charges. Not suitable for wheelchair users. Dogs on leads restricted to public footpaths. Sorry – no coaches.
Facilities: Eric Grace Memorial Hide at Ryan's Field has parking and viewing, but birds here only at high tide. Nearest toilets in town of Hayle. No visitor centre but information board at hide.
Public transport: Western Greyhound bus services 501 (summer only, not Saturdays) or 515 (not Sundays). Nearest bus stop for Carnsew Pool is in Foundry Square, Hayle (450 metres away). Call 0871 200 2233 for details. Nearest rail station at St Erth (one mile away).
Habitat: Intertidal mudflats, saltmarsh, lagoon and islands, sandy beaches and sand dunes.
Key birds: *Winter*: Large numbers of wildfowl and waders. Top UK site for over-wintering Ring-billed Gull, but they don't visit every year. Range of gulls, Kingfisher, Great Northern Diver. *Spring/summer*: Migrant waders, breeding Shelduck. *Autumn*: Rare waders, often from N America. Terns, gulls (inc Mediterranean).
Contact: RSPB South West Regional Office, 01736 360 624; e-mail: hayle.estuary@rspb.org.uk

3. HELMAN TOR NATURE RESERVE

Cornwall Wildlife Trust.
Location: Sat nav: PL30 5DU. SX 054 610 (The Barn, Lower Gurtla). Large wetland complex incorporating Breney Common and Red Moor Memorial Reserve. 2.5 miles S of Bodmin. From A30/A391 (Innis Downs) roundabout south of Bodmin, turn N to Lanivet and take first right under A30 bridge. For Breney Common entrance, turn R at Reperry Cross, then L fork to Trebell Green and on towards Gurtla. The entrance track is on the left in Gurtla, after the Methodist church, opposite The Barn.
Access: Open at all times but please keep to paths. Disabled access from small car park at Breney. Small car park at Helman Tor.
Facilities: Wilderness trail from Helman Tor. Boardwalk sections the only suitable surface for wheelchairs, but can be slippery when wet.
Public transport: None.
Habitat: Huge site (536 acres) includes wetland, grassland, heath and scrub.
Key birds: Willow Tit, Nightjar, Tree Pipit, Sparrowhawk, Lesser Whitethroat, Curlew.
Other notable flora and fauna: Royal fern, sundews and other bog plants. Butterflies (inc marsh and small pearl-bordered fritillaries, silver-studded blue).
Contact: Sean O'Hea, Cornwall Wildlife Trust, 01872 273 939; e-mail: info@cornwt.demon.co.uk
www.cornwallwildlifetrust.org.uk

4. MARAZION MARSHES

RSPB (South West England Office).
Location: Sat nav: TR17 0AA. SW 510 315. Reserve is one mile E of Penzance, 500 yards W of Marazion. Entrance off seafront road near Marazion.
Access: Open at all times. No permits required. No admission charges. Not suitable for wheelchair users. Dogs on leads please. Sorry — no coaches.
Facilities: No toilets or visitor centre. Nearest toilets in Marazion and seafront car park.
Public transport: First Group Nos 2, 7 and 8, plus Sunset Bay2Bay service 340 from Penzance. Call 0871 200 2233 for details.
Habitat: Wet reedbed, willow carr.
Key birds: *Winter*: Wildfowl, Snipe, occasional Bittern. *Spring/summer*: Breeding Reed, Sedge and

Cetti's Warblers, herons, swans. *Autumn*: Large roost of Swallows and martins in reedbeds, migrant warblers and Water Rail.
Other notable flora and fauna: Up to 22 species of dragonfly, plus 500 species of vascular plants, inc lawn camomile and yellow flag.
Contact: RSPB 01736 711 682;
e-mail: marazion.marsh@rspb.org.uk

5. NARE HEAD

National Trust.
Location: Part of the NT's Roseland estate. Sat nav: TR2 5PH. SW 922 379. Approx ten miles SE of Truro. from A390 head S on A307 to two miles S of Tregony just past the garage. Follow signs to Veryan then L sign-posted to Carne. Go straight over at crossroad, following Carne and Pendower. Turn L on a bend following NT signs for Nare Head. Bearing R, cross over a cattle grid to the car park. From the garage, Nare Head is about four miles.
Access: Open all year.
Facilities: Car park.
Habitat: Headland.
Key birds: *Spring/summer*: Razorbill, Guillemot, Sandwich, Common and Arctic Terns, possible Whimbrel, Fulmar. *Winter*: Black-throated and Great Northern Divers. Red-throated Diver possible. Common Scoter, Velvet Scoter, Slavonian, Black-necked and Red-necked Grebes.
Contact: National Trust, Lanhydrock House, Lanhydrock, Cornwall, PL30 4DE. 01208 432 691.

6. STITHIANS RESERVOIR

South West Lakes Trust.
Location: Sat nav: TR16 6NW (Golden Lion Inn). SS 715 365. Sign-posted from B3297 S of Redruth.
Access: Good viewing from causeway.
Facilities: New hide near main centre (opposite the Golden Lion Inn) open to all. Two other hides for members of CBWPS. Footpath around reservoir.
Habitat: Open water, marshland.
Key birds: County's best open water site for winter wildfowl. Winter gull flocks inc Mediterranean. Good for waders such as Common, Green and Wood Sandpipers, plus rarities, eg. Pectoral and Semipalmated Sandpipers, Lesser Yellowlegs. Passage birds can inc Osprey, Black Tern, Garganey. Good track record for rarities — records inc Wilson's Phalarope, Caspian Tern, White-rumped Sandpiper, and Black Kite.
Contact: South West Lakes Trust, Centre Manager, 01209 860 301. www.swlakestrust.org.uk

7. TAMAR ESTUARY

Cornwall Wildlife Trust.
Location: Sat nav: PL12 6LJ (China Fleet Club). SX 431 614 (Landulph section). SX 436 627 (Cargreen). From Plymouth head W on A38. Access parking at Cargreen and Landulph from minor roads off A388.

Access: Open at all times. Footpath from Cargreen to Landulph. Access two bird hides from China Fleet Club car park, Saltash. Follow path alongside golf course — do not walk on course itself. Combination number for hide locks available at club reception.
Facilities: Two hides on foreshore, first (0.25 miles from car park) overlooks estuary, second (0.5 miles) has excellent views across Kingsmill Lake.
Habitat: 269 acres of tidal mudflat with some saltmarsh.
Key birds: *Winter*: Large number of Avocet (Oct to March), Snipe, Black-tailed Godwit, Redshank, Dunlin, Curlew, Whimbrel, Spotted Redshank, Green Sandpiper, Golden Plover, Kingfisher. *Spring/summer*: Breeding Shelduck.
Contact: Reserves manager 07866 430 086;
e-mail: peter@cornwt.demon.co.uk
www.cornwallwildlifetrust.org.uk

8. TAMAR LAKES

South West Lakes Trust.
Location: SS 295 115. Site lies E of A39, N of Bude. Follow brown tourist signs from Holsworthy or Kilkhampton.
Access: Open all year. Limited wheelchair access. Pay-and-display car parks. Sailing and other watersports means Upper lake not good for birding. Nature reserve is located on Lower lake.
Facilities: Bird hide on Lower lake. Café (limited opening) at Upper Tamar. Toilets at Upper open all year, those at Lower only open in summer. Trail leaflet available from café.
Public transport: None.
Habitat: Two freshwater lakes, plus swamp, scrub and grassland.
Key birds: *All year*: Great Crested Grebe, Black-headed Gull, Kingfisher, Willow Tit, Reed Bunting. *Spring*: Black Tern. *Summer*: Breeding Sedge, Reed and Willow Warblers and House Martin. *Winter*: Moderate numbers of wildfowl, inc

Wigeon and Teal and gulls.
Other notable flora and fauna: Badger, roe deer, otter, southern marsh orchid, wood white butterfly, grass snake.

Contact: Conservation Officer, Upper Tamar Lakes Visitor Centre, 01288 321 262.

Devon

EXMOOR is the prettier of the county's two National Parks, with wonderful wooded valleys attractive to birds, whereas Dartmoor is much bleaker. Red-backed Shrikes are attempting to re-establish themselves on Exmoor. The island of Lundy in the Bristol Channel is good for vagrants. Look for waders around Exminster Marshes while the southern coast holds localised but increasing pockets of Cirl Buntings.

1. AYLESBEARE COMMON

RSPB (South West England Office).
Location: Sat nav: EX10 0DF. SY 057 898. Five miles E of J30 of M5 at Exeter, 0.5 miles past Halfway Inn on B3052. Turn R to Hawkerland, car park is on L. The reserve is on the opposite side of the main road.
Access: Open all year. One track suitable for wheelchairs and pushchairs.
Facilities: Car park, two nature trails, picnic area, group bookings, guided walks and special events. Disabled access via metalled track to private farm.
Public transport: Buses (Exeter to Sidmouth, 52a, 52b). Request stop at Joneys Cross (reserve entrance). Tel: 01392 427 711.
Habitat: Heathland, wood fringes, streams and ponds.
Key birds: *All year:* Dartford Warbler, Buzzard, Yellowhammer. *Spring/summer:* Hobby, Nightjar, Tree Pipit, Stonechat. *Winter:* Possible Hen Harrier.
Other notable flora and fauna: Good range of dragonflies and butterflies.
Contact: Toby Taylor, Hawkerland Brake Barn, Exmouth Road, Aylesbeare, Nr Exeter, Devon EX5 2JS. 01395 233 655;
e-mail: aylesbeare.common@rspb.org.uk

2. BERRY HEAD NNR

Torbay Coast & Countryside Trust.
Location: Sat nav: TQ5 9AP (Berry Head car park). Sign-posted from Brixham on minor roads from A3022 and A379. Located at end of Gillard Road, past Landscove Holiday Village.
Access: Open all year. Guardhouse visitor centre open Easter to Oct (Tues to Sun 10am to 4pm; Mon 1pm to 4pm). Sundays only for rest of year. Wheelchair-friendly 300m path from car park to visitor centre and café.
Facilities: Pay-and-display car park. Visitor centre (CCTV images of nesting seabirds), café and toilets. Two mobility vehicles for hire (pre-book). Bird hide overlooking cliffs.
Public transport: Bus 17 from Brixham to Victoria Road (Half mile walk to Berry Head: some steep

sections). Torbay Coastpath runs from Torquay.
Habitat: Limestone cliffs (200ft), grassland, quarry.
Key birds: *All year:* Cirl Buntings (in flocks in autumn), Peregrine (hunting in quarry area), Fulmar, Greenfinch. *Spring/summer:* Up to 1,000 nesting Guillemots on cliffs below Southern Fort. Wellknown as a migrant watchpoint.
Other notable flora and fauna: Limestone flora inc eight species of orchid, small hare's-ear. Harbour porpoise, common dolphin, greater and lesser horseshoe bats (walks arranged), bloody nose beetle and range of butterflies.
Contact: Tel: 01803 882 619; e-mail: berryhead@countryside-trust.org.uk

3. BOVEY HEATHFIELD

Devon Wildlife Trust.
Location: Sat nav: TQ12 6TU. SX 823 765. On the outskirts of Bovey Tracey on SE edge of Dartmoor. From A382 Bovey Straight take Battle Road into Heathfield Industrial estate. Turn L into Cavalier Road, then Dragoon Close – the reserve is along a gravel path.
Access: Open all year. Dogs allowed on leads. Please keep to paths. Rough paths not suitable for wheelchairs. No coach access.
Facilities: Information hut open when warden is on site. Circular way-marked path and viewpoint.
Public transport: Exeter to Plymouth buses stop at Drum Bridge, a 20 min walk to reserve.
Habitat: Mix of wet and dry lowland heath, surrounding by secondary woodland. Contains numerous ponds.
Key birds: Breeding Nightjar, Tree Pipit, Stonechat and Dartford Warbler, plus commoner species such as Skylark, Linnet and Yellowhammer.
Other notable flora and fauna: Heathers, wet and dry heathland plants, more than 60 endangered insect species, plus grayling and green hairstreak butterflies, slow worm, adder.
Contact: Devon Wildlife Trust, Cricklepit Mill, Commercial Road, Exeter, EX1 4AB. 01392 279 244; e-mail: devonwt@cix.co.uk

4. BOWLING GREEN MARSH

RSPB (South West England Office).
Location: Sat nav: EX3 0EN (Holman Rd car park). SX 971 875. On the E side of River Exe, four miles SE of Exeter in Bowling Green Road, Topsham.
Access: Open at all times. Please park at the Holman Way or The Quay public car parks in Topsham village, not in the lane by the reserve. Blue Badge parking space near hide.
Facilities: RSPB shop at Darts Farm, 1.5km from reserve, east of Topsham across River Clyst. Weekly

guided walks from Darts Farm, Topsham. Nearest RADAR toilets at The Quay car park. Wheelchair-friendly bird hide and viewing platform.
Public transport: Exeter to Exmouth railway has regular (every 30 mins) service to Topsham station (one mile from reserve). Stagecoach Devon 57 (Mon-Sat every 12 mins, Sun every half-hour) from Exeter to Topsham stops at Elm Grove Road (1km from reserve). Call Traveline 0871 200 2233.
Habitat: Coastal grassland, open water/marsh.
Key birds: *Winter:* Wigeon, Shoveler, Teal, Black-tailed Godwit, Curlew, Golden Plover. *Spring:* Shelduck, passage waders, Whimbrel, passage Garganey and Yellow Wagtail. *Summer:* Gull/tern roosts, high tide wader roosts contain many passage birds. *Autumn:* Wildfowl, Peregrine, wader roosts.
Other notable fauna: Hairy dragonfly, wasp spider.
Contact: RSPB, Darts Farm Shopping Village, Clyst St. George, Exeter EX3 0QH. 01392 879 438 or the reserve on 01392 824 614; www.rspb.org.uk

5. BURRATOR RESERVOIR

South West Lakes Trust.
Location: Sat nav: PL20 6PE. SX 551 681. On south side of Dartmoor, 10 miles NE of Plymouth, off A386 (Tavistock road). At Yelverton take B3212 towards Princeton. Turn R at Burrator Inn and follow signs to reservoir.
Access: Open all year. Free parking areas around reservoir. Main route, though suitable for disabled, is also used by motorists and cyclists. There are about 25 stiles on minor routes.
Facilities: Toilets (including disabled at Burrator Lodge). Snacks and ice-creams available during summer.
Public transport: Bus: daily from Plymouth to Dousland (a short walk from the reservoir). No 82 Western National or No 48 (Sun). Tel: 01752 402 060. Train: nearest station is Plymouth. 08457 484 950.
Habitat: Pine forests, wooded streams, open moorland scrub.
Key birds: *Winter:* Goosander, Dipper, Grey Wagtail, Green Sandpiper, Brambling, Crossbill, Siskin, Redpoll. *All year:* All three woodpeckers, Buzzard, Sparrowhawk, Kestrel, Barn Owl, Tree Sparrow.
Other notable flora and fauna: Marsh fritillary butterfly, dragonflies and damselflies, particularly in the arboretum, bats (various species), otter.
Contact: South West Lakes Trust, Lidn Park, Quarry Crescent, Pennygillam Industrial Estate, Launceston, Cornwall PL15 7PF. 01822 855 700.
www.swlakestrust.org.uk

6. DAWLISH WARREN NNR

Teignbridge District Council.
Location: Sat nav: EX7 0NF. SX 983 788. At Dawlish Warren on S side of Exe estuary mouth. Turn off A379 at sign to Warren Golf Club, between Cockwood and Dawlish. Turn into car park adjacent to Lea Cliff Holiday Park. Pass under tunnel and turn L away from amusements. Park at far end of car park and pass through two pedestrian gates.

Access: Open public access, but avoid mudflats. Also avoid beach beyond groyne nine around high tide due to roosting birds. Parking charges apply. Restricted access for dogs (none allowed in hide).
Facilities: Visitor centre (tel 01626 863 980) open most weekends (1pm to 4pm in winter, 2pm-to 5pm in summer). In summer also open Wed to Fri (2pm to 5pm). Toilets at entrance tunnel and in resort area only. Bird hide one mile NE of visitor centre open at all times — best around high tide.
Public transport: Train station at site, also regular bus service operated by Stagecoach.
Habitat: High tide roost site for wildfowl and waders of Exe estuary on mudflats and shore. Dunes, dune grassland, woodland, scrub, ponds.
Key birds: *Winter:* Waders and wildfowl in large numbers. Also good for divers and Slavonian Grebe offshore. *Summer:* Particularly good for terns. Excellent variety of birds all year, especially on migration.
Contact: Visitor centre: 01626 863 980. Teignbridge District Council: 01626 215 884 (answerphone). www.dawlishwarren.co.uk

7. EAST DARTMOOR NNR

Natural England.
Location: Sat nav: TQ13 9LJ (Yarner Wood). SX 778 787. The NNR is two miles from Bovey Tracey on road to Becky Falls and Manaton. Road continues across Trendlebere Down, where there are roadside car parks and adjacent paths.
Access: Yarner Wood car park open from 8.30am-7pm or dusk if earlier. Outside these hours, access on foot from Trendlebere Down. Dogs welcome under close control.
Facilities: Information/interpretation display and self-guided trails available in Yarner Wood car park also hide with feeding station (Nov-Mar).
Public transport: Carmel Coaches No 671 (Okehampton to Newton Abbot) stops at Manaton.
Habitat: The reserve consists of three connected sites (Yarner Wood, Trendlebere Down and Bovey Valley Woodlands) totalling 365 hectares of upland oakwood and heathland.
Key birds: *All year:* Raven, Buzzard, Goshawk, Sparrowhawk, Lesser Spotted, Great Spotted and Green Woodpeckers, Grey Wagtail and Dartford Warbler (on Trendlebere Down). *Spring/summer:* Pied Flycatcher, Wood Warbler, Redstart, Tree Pipit, Linnet, Stonechat, Cuckoo, Whitethroat, Skylark. *Autumn/winter:* Good range of birds with feeding at hide, inc Siskin, Redpoll, plus Hen Harrier on Trendlebere Down.
Contact: Site Manager, Natural England, Yarner Wood, 01626 832 330; www.natural-england.org.uk

8. EXMINSTER & POWDERHAM MARSHES

RSPB (South West England Office).
Location: Sat nav: EX6 8DZ (Swan's Nest Inn). SX 954 872. Five miles S of Exeter on W bank of River Exe.

NATURE RESERVES - SOUTH WEST ENGLAND

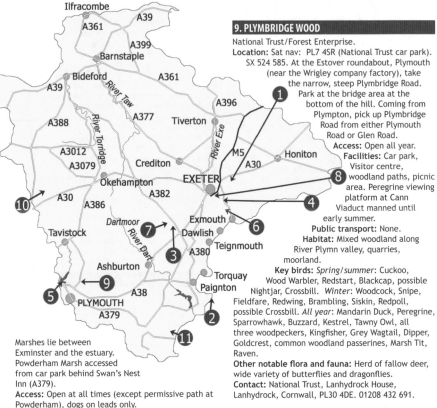

National Trust/Forest Enterprise.
Location: Sat nav: PL7 4SR (National Trust car park). SX 524 585. At the Estover roundabout, Plymouth (near the Wrigley company factory), take the narrow, steep Plymbridge Road. Park at the bridge area at the bottom of the hill. Coming from Plympton, pick up Plymbridge Road from either Plymouth Road or Glen Road.
Access: Open all year.
Facilities: Car park, Visitor centre, woodland paths, picnic area. Peregrine viewing platform at Cann Viaduct manned until early summer.
Public transport: None.
Habitat: Mixed woodland along River Plymn valley, quarries, moorland.
Key birds: *Spring/summer*: Cuckoo, Wood Warbler, Redstart, Blackcap, possible Nightjar, Crossbill. *Winter*: Woodcock, Snipe, Fieldfare, Redwing, Brambling, Siskin, Redpoll, possible Crossbill. *All year*: Mandarin Duck, Peregrine, Sparrowhawk, Buzzard, Kestrel, Tawny Owl, all three woodpeckers, Kingfisher, Grey Wagtail, Dipper, Goldcrest, common woodland passerines, Marsh Tit, Raven.
Other notable flora and fauna: Herd of fallow deer, wide variety of butterflies and dragonflies.
Contact: National Trust, Lanhydrock House, Lanhydrock, Cornwall, PL30 4DE. 01208 432 691.

Marshes lie between Exminster and the estuary. Powderham Marsh accessed from car park behind Swan's Nest Inn (A379).
Access: Open at all times (except permissive path at Powderham), dogs on leads only.
Facilities: No toilets or visitor centre. Information in RSPB car park (Exminster site) and marked footpaths across reserve. Exminster circular walk takes 90 minutes. Three viewing screens.
Public transport: Exeter to Newton Abbot No2 bus stop at Swan's Nest roundabout is 400 yds from reserve car park. Traveline 0871 200 2233.
Habitat: Coastal grazing marsh with freshwater ditches and pools, reeds, scrub-covered canal banks, winter stubbles and crops managed for farmland birds.
Key birds: *Winter*: Brent Goose, Wigeon, Water Rail, Short-eared Owl. *Spring*: Redshank and wildfowl breed, Cetti's Warbler on canal banks. Devon's final breeding site for Lapwing. *Summer*: Gull roosts, passage waders, hirundines, Hobby.. *Autumn*: Peregrine, Short-eared Owl, winter wildfowl, finch flocks. There are also records of Cirl Bunting and Woodlark.
Other notable flora and fauna: 23 species of dragonfly, including hairy and scarce chaser.
Contact: RSPB, 01392 824 614; www.rspb.org.uk

South West Lakes Trust.
Location: Sat nav: PL16 0JL. SX 421 900. Resevoir lies eight miles E of Launceston, sign-posted from A30.
Access: Two bird hides, several walks and cycleway. For disabled access to Bill Oddie Hide park in lay-by at SX 435 929.
Facilities: Visitor centre, cafe and toilets. Two bird hides. Pay-and-display car parks.
Public transport: Carmel Coaches' Friday-only service from Halwill Junction to Tavistock stops as Broadwoodwidger (short walk to lake).
Habitat: Reservoir of 295ha (northern third designated Special Protection Zone to benefit birds), surrounded by marsh, scrub and fields.
Key birds: County's top inland site for wildfowl (up to 2,000 birds in winter). Small wader passage in autumn depending on water levels. Internationally important site for Lesser Black-backed Gulls. Good record of attracting rarities.
Other notable flora and fauna: Hazel dormouse, various bat species.
Contact: Friends of South West Lakes Trust 01566 771 930.

11. SLAPTON LEY NNR

Field Studies Council/ Natural England
Location: Sat nav: TQ7 2QP (field centre). SX 825 440. The largest freshwater lake in SW England, which lies S of Dartmouth on the south coast, is separated from Start Bay by a shingle bank which carries A379.
Access: Pay-and-display car parks off A379 at Torcross and Slapton Sands. Higher ley is closed to the public, but can be viewed from public footpath.
Facilities: Hides overlooking Torcross and Stokely Bay areas of the lagoon and surrounding backdrops. Beach trailer with information in Memorial car park in school holiday (Sat to Thurs).
Public transport: First Group 93 bus from Plymouth and Kingsbridge to Slapton stops outside field centre.

Slapton Field Centre offers residential courses.
Habitat: Freshwater lake, reedbeds, marsh and woodland.
Key birds: Good seawatching in favourable conditions in spring and autumn, plus migrants on passage. Large gathering of Swallows in autumn roosts. *Winter:* Divers and grebes on sea, Bittern at Higher Ley. Diving ducks and grebes on Lower ley. *Spring/summer:* Migrant warblers. *All year:* Up to four pairs of Cirl Bunting, Cetti's Warbler (around 40 singing males each year). Most south-westerly population of Great Crested Grebe.
Other notable flora and fauna: UK's only site for strapwort. Badger, otter, dormouse, 2,000 species of fungi.
Contact: 01548 580 466;
e-mail: enquiries.sl@field-studies-council.org

Dorset

DORSET is established as one of England's top six birding counties. Weymouth makes a splendid base, with two RSPB reserves — Lodmoor and Radipole — in the town itself. From there you can visit the bird observatory and migration hotspot of Portland and The Fleet and Jurassic coast to the west. To the east, heathland such as Arne RSPB is good for Dartford Warblers and Nightjars. Studland Bay holds all three divers and five grebes species in winter.

1. ARNE

RSPB (South West England Office).
Location: Sat nav: BH20 5BJ. SY 971 876. Head S from Wareham over the causeway, turn off A351 at Stoborough.
Access: Open 8.30am to dusk. Car park (free for RSPB members) at beginning of Stoborough village. Shipstal Point and Coombe Birdwatchers' trails open all year. Coombe birdwatchers' screen on Middlebere Channel overlooks estuary. Visitor centre open all year except Dec 25/26. Limited wheelchair access on trails. Coaches and escorted parties by prior arrangement.
Facilities: Toilets in car park. Five sign-posted trails for different abilities. Two hides, one viewpoint and two viewing screens. Visitor hut (no toilets).
Public transport: None to reserve. Nearest train station is Wareham (4 miles from reserve), but 10% discount on cycle hire for RSPB members (call Purbeck Cycle Hire, based at station, on 01929 556 601).
Habitat: Lowland heath, woodland, reedbed and saltmarsh, extensive mudflats of Poole Harbour.
Key birds: *All year:* Dartford Warbler, Little Egret, Stonechat. *Winter:* Brent Goose flocks part of the 30,000 birds which use the harbour, including grebes, divers, Long-tailed Duck, Eider and Scaup. Hen Harrier, Marsh Harrier, Black-tailed Godwit, winter thrushes and finches. *Summer:* Nightjar, Sandwich

and Common Terns, Barn Owl, hirundines, warblers. *Passage:* Hobby, Spotted Redshank, Whimbrel, Greenshank, Osprey.
Other notable flora and fauna: Sika deer, all six species of UK reptile, silver-studded blue and 32 other butterflies, 23 dragonflies, 850 moths and 500 flowering plants.
Contact: Arne Nature Reserve, RSPB Work Centre, 01929 553 360: e-mail: arne@rspb.org.uk
www.rspb.org.uk/reserves/guide/a/arne/

2. BROWNSEA ISLAND NATURE RESERVE

Dorset Wildlife Trust/ National Trust.
Location: Sat nav: PH15 1HP (Poole Quay). SZ 026 883. Half hour boat rides from Poole Quay with Greenslade Pleasure Boats (01202 631 828) and Brownsea Island Ferries (01929 462 383). Ten minutes from Sandbanks Quay (next to Studland chain-ferry).
Access: Island open March 16 to Nov 3 (10am to 5pm). Free admission to nature reserve for DWT members (show card to NT staff), but landing fee must be paid if visiting rest of island. Assistance dogs only.
Facilities: Toilets, information centre, café, gift shop secondhand book shop, five hides, nature trail. Red squirrel CCTV coverage.
Public transport: Poole rail/bus station for access to Poole Quay and boats. Tel: 01202 673 555.
Habitat: Saline lagoon, reedbed, lakes, coniferous and mixed woodland.
Key birds: *Spring:* Avocet, Black-tailed Godwit and other waders, Water Rail, gulls and wildfowl. *Summer:* Common and Sandwich Terns, Yellow-legged Gull, Little Egret, Little Grebe, Golden Pheasant. *Autumn:* Curlew Sandpiper, Little Stint.
Other notable flora and fauna: Red squirrel (up to 200 on island), water vole, Bechstein's bat found 2007. Good range of butterflies and dragonflies.
Contact: Dorset Wildlife Trust, 01202 709 445;
e-mail: brownseaisland@dorsetwildlife.co.uk
www.wildlifetrust.org/dorset

NATURE RESERVES - SOUTH WEST ENGLAND

3. DURLSTON NNR & COUNTRY PARK

Dorset County Council.
Location: Sat nav: BH19 2JL. SZ 032 774. Located in Lighthouse Road, Swanage, one mile S of town centre (sign-posted).
Access: Open between sunrise and sunset. Visitor centre open weekends and holidays during winter and daily in other seasons.
Facilities: Guided walks, new visitor centre located in Durlston Castle features café, toilets, exhibitions, art displays and shop. hide, waymarked trails.
Public transport: Durlston shuttle bus runs between May 27 and September 30 (half-hourly from Swanage railway station and pier).
Habitat: 208 acres of sea cliffs, woodland, grassland, hedges, cliff, meadows.
Key birds: Cliff-nesting seabird colonies including Guillemot, Fulmar, Razorbill and Shag; good variety of scrub and woodland breeding species; spring and autumn migrants and seabirds on passage; seawatching esp. Apr/May and Aug/Nov. *All year*: Peregrine, Raven, woodland species.
Other notable flora and fauna: 34 species of butterfly and 500-plus species of flowering plants, inc nine species of orchid. Bottle-nose dolphin.
Contact: The Ranger, Durlston Country Park, 01929 424 443, e-mail: info@durlston.co.uk www.durlston.co.uk

4. GARSTON WOOD

RSPB (South West England Office).
Location: Sat nav: SP5 5PA (postcode for Dean Lane). SU 003 194. SW from Salisbury. From A354 take turn to Sixpenny Handley then take Bowerchalke road (Dean Lane). Proceed for approximately 1.5 miles on single-track road (with passing places). Garston Wood car park on L of road.
Access: Open at all times. Two nature trails accessible to pushchairs but terrain is best in dry weather. Dogs on leads only on public footpaths and bridleways.
Facilities: Car park, reserve leaflet, picnic area, group bookings accepted, guided walks available, remote location, good for walking, pushchair friendly. No toilets or catering facilities.
Public transport: From Salisbury bus station, take Wilts and Dorset 184 service to Sixpenny Handley (Roebuck Inn). One mile walk to reserve.
Habitat: Actively-managed ancient woodland includes large area of coppiced hazel and maple. Other habitats include oak woodland, scrub and mixed plantation, with important features such as glades, rides and dead wood.

Key birds: Common woodland birds plus Turtle Dove and migrant warblers including Blackcap, Willow Warbler, Garden Warbler and Nightingale. Spotted Flycatcher. Raptors include Buzzard, Sparrowhawk and Goshawk. Winter thrushes.
Other notable flora and fauna: Bluebells and spring flowers. Butterflies, including silver-washed fritillary and elusive white admiral. Adders can be seen on the ride side. Good range of fungi. Fallow deer.
Contact: Phone RSPB on 01929 553 360; e-mail: garston.wood@rspb.org.uk

5. HAM COMMON LNR

Poole Borough Council.
Location: Sat nav: BH15 4L (for Hamworthy Pier). SY 980 902. W of Poole. In Hamworthy, take the Blandford Road S along Lake Road, W along Lake Drive and Napier Road, leading to Rockley Park. Park in the beach car park by Hamworthy Pier or Rockley Viewpoint car park, off Napier Road, opposite the entrance to Gorse Hill Central Park.
Access: Open all year. Not suitable for coaches.
Facilities: None.
Habitat: 32-acre LNR consisting of damp and dry heathland, scrub, reedbeds, freshwater lake. Views over Wareham Channel and Poole Harbour.
Key birds: *Spring/summer*: Stonechat, Dartford Warbler. *Winter*: Brent Goose, Red-breasted Merganser, occasional divers, rarer grebes, Scaup. Waders inc Whimbrel, Greenshank and Common Sandpiper. *All year*: Little Egret.
Other notable flora and fauna: Up to 34 species of butterfly, 25 dragonflies and all six British reptile species.
Contact: Poole Borough Council, 01202 633 633; e-mail: information@poole.gov.uk www.hamcommonlnr.webs.com

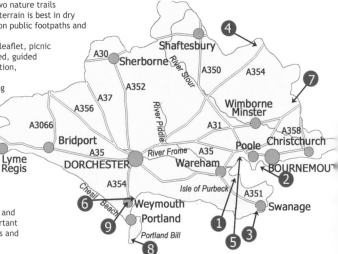

202

NATURE RESERVES - SOUTH WEST ENGLAND

6. LODMOOR NATURE RESERVE

RSPB (South West England Office). **Location:** Sat nav: DT4 7SX (Country Park). SY 688 809. Adjacent Lodmoor Country Park, NE of Weymouth, off A353 to Wareham.
Access: Free entry at all times.
Facilities: One viewing shelter, Three nature trails mostly accessible to wheelchairs. No visitor centre or toilets. Three pay-and-display car parks. Blue Badge spaces at Country Park.
Public transport: Nearest bus stop (without shelter) Preston Beach Road, 300 m away. Buses 4/4b, 31 and X53. Details from First Buses: 0870 0106 022.
Habitat: Marsh, shallow pools, large reedbed and scrub, remnant saltmarsh.
Key birds: *All year*: Little Egret, Kingfisher, Cetti's Warbler, Bearded Tit. *Spring/summer*: Large tern colony, warblers (including Reed, Sedge, Grasshopper), Hobby. *Winter*: Wildfowl, waders, Bittern, Marsh Harrier. *Passage*: Waders (inc Black-tailed Godwit, Green and Wood Sandpipers) and other migrants.
Contact: Nick Tomlinson, RSPB Visitor Centre, Swannery Car Park, 01305 778 313; www.rspb.org.uk e-mail:weymouth.reserves@rspb.org.uk

7. MOORS VALLEY CP & RINGWOOD FOREST

East Dorset District Council/Forestry Commission.
Location: Sat nav: BH24 2ET. Two miles W of Ringwood, well-sign-posted from Ashley Heath roundabout (junction of A31 and A338) between Ringwood and St Leonards.
Access: Open every day (except Dec 25) 8am-8pm (June to Aug), 5pm close Sept to March. Visitor centre open 9am to 4.30pm daily. Many trails wheelchair friendly.
Facilities: Visitor centre, toilets, tea-room, country shop. Coach parking. Way-marked trails are in good condition. Pay-and-display car parks (free for Blue Badge holders).
Public transport: Wilts and Dorset No 38 bus service stops at Castleman Trailway - one mile walk to visitor centre (01988 827 005) or visit: www.wdbus.co.uk
Habitat: River, wet meadow, lakes, scrub, broad-leaved woodland, large coniferous forest, golf course.
Key birds: *Spring/summer*: Cuckoo, Nightjar, Sand Martin, Tree Pipit, Whitethroat. Occasional Woodlark, Sedge Warbler. *Winter*: Teal, Pochard, Gadwall, Snipe, Redpoll. Occasional Brambling, Goosander. *Passage*: Whimbrel, Common Sandpiper, waders. *All year*: Buzzard, Lapwing, Woodcock, Little Owl, Grey Wagtail, Kingfisher, Dartford Warbler, Crossbill, usual woodland species.
Other notable flora and fauna: 20 species of dragonfly. Good numbers of butterflies and other

invertebrates. Roe deer, muntjac, badger, fox, rabbit, grey squirrel, adder, slow worm.
Contact: Moors Valley Country Park, 01425 470 721, e-mail: moorsvalley@eastdorset.gov.uk www.moors-valley.co.uk

8. PORTLAND BIRD OBSERVATORY

Portland Bird Observatory (registered charity).
Location: Sat nav: DT5 2JT. SY 681 690. Six miles S of Weymouth beside the road to Portland Bill.
Access: Open at all times. Parking only for members of Portland Bird Observatory. Self-catering accommodation for up to 20. Take own towels, sheets, sleeping bags.
Facilities: Displays and information, toilets, natural history bookshop, equipped kitchen.
Public transport: Bus service from Weymouth (First Dorset Transit Route 1).
Habitat: World famous migration watchpoint. Scrub and ponds.
Key birds: *Spring/autumn*: Migrants, including many rarities. *Summer*: Breeding auks, Puffin. Large numbers of Mediterranean Gulls at Ferrybridge, plus wide range of seabirds. A total of 355 species recorded.
Contact: Martin Cade, 01305 820 553; e-mail: obs@btinternet.com www.portlandbirdobs.org.uk

9. RADIPOLE LAKE

RSPB (South West England Office).
Location: Sat nav: DT4 7TZ. SY 671 804. In Radipole Park Drive, Weymouth. Enter from Swannery car park (pay-and-display) on footpaths.
Access: Visitor centre and nature trail open every day, summer (9am-5pm), winter (9am-4pm). Hide open (8.30am-4.30pm). Permit (available from visitor centre) required by non-RSPB members. Dogs on leads.
Facilities: Network of paths, one hide, one viewing shelter (both wheelchair-friendly). Information centre contains café and disabled toilets.
Public transport: reserve is 400m from train station serving London and Bristol.
Habitat: Lake, reedbeds.
Key birds: *Winter*: Wildfowl (many Pochard), Water Rail, Bittern, pre-roost gatherings of Pied Wagtails. *Spring/summer*: Hirundines arrive. Breeding reedbed warblers (including Cetti's), Bearded Tit, passage waders and other migrants. Garganey regular in spring while Hobbies hunt later in season. Good for rarer gulls.
Contact: Nick Tomlinson, RSPB Visitor Centre, Swannery Car Park, Weymouth, DT4 7TZ. 01305 778 313; e-mail: weymouth.reserves@rspb.org.uk www.rspb.org.uk

Somerset

EXTENSIVE habitat restoration work since the 1980s has boosted bird breeding success in the Somerset Levels and Common Cranes hatched at Slimbridge are being released in the area. Somerset is attractive to wildfowl and waders in autumn and winter thanks to a mild climate and its link to the Bristol Channel.

1. BREAN DOWN

National Trust (North Somerset).
Location: Sat nav: TA8 2RR. ST 290 590. 182 map. 100m high promontory jutting into Bristol Channel five miles N of Burnham-on-Sea. From junction 22 of M5, head for Weston-super-Mare on A370 and then head for Brean at Lympsham.
Access: Open all year (free of charge). Dogs on lead. Steep slope – not suitable for wheelchair-users.
Facilities: Café/shop at bottom of Brean Down. Toilet (disabled) at café.
Public transport: Call Tourist Information Centre for details 01934 888 800 (bus services differ in winter/ summer).
Habitat: Extension of the Mendips' hard limestone, featuring neutral grassland, scrub and steep cliffs.
Key birds: *All year:* Peregrine, Raven. *Summer:* Blackcap, Garden Warbler, Whitethroat, Stonechat. *Winter:* Curlew, Shelduck, Dunlin on mudflats. *Passage:* Skuas, shearwaters, divers, Gannet, gulls, waders and passerines.
Other notable flora and fauna: Chalkhill blue, marbled white and commoner butterflies. Extremely rare white rock rose in June. Somerset hair grass, dwarf sedge.
Contact: The National Trust, 01643 862 452; breandown@nationaltrust.org.uk

2. BRIDGWATER BAY NNR

Natural England (Dorset and Somerset Team).
Location: ST 270 470. Five kilometres N of Bridgwater and extends to Burnham-on-Sea. Take junction 23 or 24 off M5. Turn N off A39 at Cannington and take minor roads to Steart. **Access:** Hides open every day except Dec 25. Permits needed for Steart Island (by boat only). Dogs on leads. Disabled access to hides only by arrangement, other areas accessible.
Facilities: Car park, interpretive panels and leaflet dispenser at Steart – follow footpath approx 0.5 miles to tower hide and five other hides. No toilets within reserve.
Public transport: Train and bus stations in Bridgwater. First Group buses on A39 stop at Stockland Bristol, 2km SW of Steart. www.firstgroup.com
Habitat: Parratt River estuary, intertidal mudflats, saltmarsh totalling 2,559ha.
Key birds: *All year:* Approx 190 species recorded on this Ramsar and SPA site. Wildfowl includes large population of Shelduck and nationally important numbers of Wigeon. Internationally important numbers of Whimbrel and Black-tailed Godwit. Resident Curlews and Oystercatchers joined by many other waders on passage. Good for birds of prey. *Spring/autumn:* Passage migrants, including occasional vagrants.
Other notable flora and fauna: Saltmarsh flora. Rare invertebrates include great silver water beetle, aquatic snail and hairy dragonfly.
Contact: Senior Reserves Manager, Natural England, 0300 060 2570, www.naturalengland.org.uk

3. CATCOTT COMPLEX NATURE RESERVES

Somerset Wildlife Trust.
Location: Five reserves – Catcott Lows, North, Heath, South and Fen now managed together. ST 400 415. Access Catcott Lows from Catcott Broad Drove (sat nav TA7 8NQ), approx one mile N of Catcott village (off A39 from junction 23 of M5).
Access: Open at all times.
Facilities: River Parrett Trail passes through reserve. Two hides at Catcott Lows.
Public transport: None.
Habitat: Wet meadows with winter flooding and summer grazing.
Key birds: *Winter:* Wigeon, Teal, Pintail, Shoveler, Gadwall, Bewick's Swan, Peregrine and other raptors. Siskins and Redpolls in alders. *Spring:* Nationally important numbers of roosting Whimbrels, plus passage Greenshank, Ruff and Black-tailed Godwits. *Summer:* Breeding Lapwing, Snipe, Redshank, Yellow Wagtail, warblers. *All year:* Little Egret, Kingfisher, Cetti's Warbler, Reed Bunting.
Other notable flora and fauna: Otter, roe deer, great crested newt, rare dragonflies, threatened saw sedge.
Contact: Somerset Wildlife Trust. 01823 652 400; e-mail: enquires@somersetwildlife.org www.somersetwildlife.org

4. CHEW VALLEY LAKE

Avon Wildlife Trust/Bristol Water Plc.
Location: Sat nav: BS40 6HN (AWT reserve at Herriott's Pool). ST 570 600. Nine miles S of Bristol. Take B3114 south from Chew Stoke, bear L for West Harptree and head NE on A368. View reserve from causeway at Herriott's Bridge where there is car parking.
Access: Roadside viewing at Herons Green Bay. Permit needed for access to hides (five at Chew, two at Blagdon) – apply to Bristol Water, Recreation Department, Woodford Lodge, Chew Stoke, Bristol BS18 8SH. Tel/Fax 01275 332 339. Parking for coaches available.
Facilities: Grebe Trail (1.2km long) has hard surface suitable for wheelchairs. Unsurfaced Bittern Trail (1.5km) leads to hide but can be muddy. No dogs on this section. Chew tea-shop open 10.30am to 5.30pm (mid-March to Oct 31. 4.30pm close for rest of year).
Public transport: Traveline, 0870 6082 608.
Habitat: Largest artificial lake in SW England with important reedbed.

Key birds: More than 270 species recorded – often attracts rarities. *Winter and passage:* Wildfowl include important numbers of Shoveler, Gadwall, Teal and Tufted Duck. Large numbers of Goosander, Great Crested Grebe and Cormorant, with the grebe numbers often the highest in Britain in autumn. Plus Bewick's Swan, Goldeneye, Smew, Ruddy Duck. Huge winter gull roost (up to 50,000+), mostly Black-headed, Common and Mediterranean Gull. *Summer:* Breeding Great Crested and Little Grebe, Gadwall, Tufted Duck, Shoveler, Pochard, Reed Warbler. Hobbies hunt in late summer. When the water level low, mud can attract waders such as Dunlin, Ringed Plover and Green Sandpiper.
Other notable flora and fauna: Ruddy darter and migrant hawker dragonflies.
Contact: Avon Wildlife Trust HQ or Bristol Water Recreation Dept, 01275 332 339;
e-mail: mail@avonwildlifetrust.org.uk
www.avonwildlifetrust.org.uk

5. DUNKERY & HORNER WOOD NNR

National Trust.
Location: Sat nav: TA24 8HY. SS 920 469 (Horner Wood). On northern boundary of Exmoor, 7km south of Minehead. Take A39 W to a minor road 0.8km E of Porlock signed to Horner. Park in village car park.
Access: Open all year. Car parking in Horner village, West Luccombe and Webber's Post, 150 miles of footpaths. Webber's Post circular walk suitable for wheelchairs. Rugged terrain to reach Dunkery Beacon.
Facilities: Tea-room and toilets. Walks leaflets available from Holnicote Estate office and Porlock visitor centre. Interpretation boards in car parks.
Public transport: First Group bus between Porlock and Minehead passes close to reserve.
Habitat: Ancient oak woodland, moorland covering 1,604ha.
Key birds: *Spring/summer:* Wood Warbler, Pied Flycatcher, Redstart, Stonechat, Whinchat, Tree Pipit, Dartford Warbler possible. *All year:* Dipper, Grey Wagtail, woodpeckers, Buzzard, Sparrowhawk.
Other notable flora and fauna: Woodland holds 14 or the UK's species of bat. Silver-washed and heath fritillary butterflies.
Contact: National Trust, 01823 451 587;
e-mail: holnicote@nationaltrust.org.uk
www.nationaltrust.org.uk

6. GREYLAKE

RSPB (South West England Office).
Location: Sat nav: TA7 0JD (Othery). ST 399 346. Off A361 Taunton to Glastonbury road, between Othery and Greinton.
Access: Open all year, dawn to dusk, free admission. Guide-dogs only. Wheelchair users can access a 700 metre-long boardwalk and viewing hide.

Facilities: Information centre, but no toilets or catering facilities. Two nature trails (only one surfaced), interpretive signs. Hide on easy-access trail, viewing screen on reedbed loop trail. No toilets.
Public transport: Bus No 29 (First Group) stops one mile along main road at Greinton phone box, but drivers may stop at reserve on request. Hatch Green No 16 bus from Bridgewater makes request stops.
Habitat: A large wet grassland reserve bought by RSPB in 2003. Formerly arable farmland.
Key birds: *Spring/summer:* Kingfisher, Grey Heron, Little Egret and breeding Snipe, Lapwing, Redshank, Skylark, Meadow Pipit, Yellow Wagtail. *Autumn:* Green Sandpiper, waders on passage. *Winter:* Waders, wildfowl (including Lapwing, Golden Plover, Shoveler, Pintail, Teal and Wigeon). Peregrine, Hen Harrier.
Other notable fauna: Roe deer, water vole, stoat, otter, dragonflies including four-spotted chaser.
Contact: Site Manager, 01458 252 805;
e-mail: greylake@rspb.org.uk
www.rspb.org.uk/reserves/guide/g/greylake

7. HAM WALL

RSPB (South West England Office).
Location: Sat nav: BA6 9SX. ST 449 397. W of Glastonbury. From A39 turn N in Ashcott and follow road onto the moor. After three miles pass Church Farm Horticultural building. Shortly after, at metal bridge, reserve is opposite side of road to Shapwick Heath NNR.
Access: Open all year. 2m height restriction on car park. Coach parking available at Avalon Marshes Centre, Shapwick Road. Dogs restricted to public footpaths and disused railway line. Wheelchair users can access viewing areas from main track (use RADAR key). Other rougher tracks cover 3.8 miles.
Facilities: Two open-air viewing platforms, four roofed viewing screens. Height-restricted car park. Two nature trails.

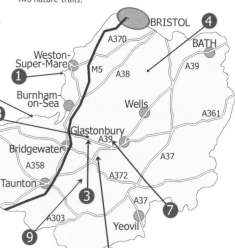

NATURE RESERVES - SOUTH WEST ENGLAND

Public transport: By bus: Service to St Mary's Road, Meare (approx 1.2 miles from reserve entrance).
Habitat: 200-plus hectare wetland, including region's largest reedbed.
Key birds: *All year:* Bittern (first breeding in county for 40 years), Cetti's Warbler, Water Rail, Barn Owl. Spring/summer: Migrant warblers, Hobby, *Autumn:* Migrant thrushes, Lesser Redpoll, Siskin, Kingfisher, Bearded Tit. *Winter:* Million-plus Starling roost, plus large flocks of ducks, Bittern, Little Egret, Peregrine, Merlin, Short-eared Owl.
Other notable flora and fauna: Otter, water vole, dragonflies, butterflies.
Contact: RSPB Ham Wall 1458 860 494; e-mail: ham. wall@rspb.org.uk

8. SHAPWICK MOOR

Hawk and Owl Trust.
Location: Sat nav: BA6 9TT (Peat Moors Centre). ST 417 398. On Somerset Levels. From J23 on M5 take A39 towards Glastonbury, after 6 miles turn N onto minor road, signed Shapwick. Continue straight over crossroads, through Shapwick village, towards Westhay, turn L at T-junction following signs for Peat Moors Centre, park here. Reserve is about half way between centre and Shapwick village.
Access: Open all year (except Dec 25). Access only along public footpaths and permissive path. Dogs on leads only.
Facilities: Information panels. Public toilets at nearby Avalon Marshes Centre (ST 425 414), none on site.
Public transport: Train to Bridgwater, then First Bus (01278 434 574) No 375 Bridgwater-Glastonbury, to Shapwick village. Sustrans National Route 3 passes through Shapwick village.
Habitat: A wet grassland reserve covering 134 acres. Grazing pasture, hay meadows with rough grass edges, fen, open ditches, pollard willows and hedges.
Key birds: *Spring/summer:* Hobby, Barn Owl, Reed Bunting and Cetti's Warbler. Whimbrel and other waders on passage. Passerines such as Skylark, Bullfinch, Greenfinch and Yellowhammer. *Autumn/winter:* Flocks of finches, Snipe, Shoveler, Gadwall, Stonechat, Brambling. Peregrine and harriers may

fly over. *All year:* Buzzard, Kestrel, Sparrowhawk, Kingfisher, Lapwing, Grey Heron, Mute Swan.
Other notable fauna: Roe deer, brown hare, stoat, badger, otter and water vole.
Contact: Hawk and Owl Trust, 0844 984 2824; e-mail: enquiries@hawkandowl.org
www.hawkandowl.org

9. SWELL WOOD

RSPB South West England Office).
Location: Sat nav: TA3 6PX. ST 360 238. Reserve lies 11 mile E of Taunton. From A378 Langport road, take minor road one mile E of Fivehead.
Access: Swell Wood car park and heronry hide open all year (dawn to dusk). Coach parking in lay-by across main road. Heronry hide and part of woodland trail are wheelchair accessible.
Facilities: Heronry hide, two nature trails: Scarp Trail links to public footpaths, disabled parking area.
Public transport: First Group Somerset & Avon bus 54 from Taunton stops at Swell — take Scarp Trail to reserve. WebberBus 38/37 accessible to wheelchairs and will make request stop.
Habitat: Semi-natural ancient oak woodland and views across wet grassland from woodland trails. Part of the Somerset Levels and Moors.
Key birds: Largest heronry in SW England with up to 100 pairs of Grey Herons and small number of Little Egrets. *Spring/summer:* Breeding Buzzard, Bullfinch, Spotted Flycatcher, Song Thrush, warblers such as Chiffchaff, Blackcap and Garden Warbler. *On escorted walks:* Curlew, Snipe, Sedge Warbler, Yellow Wagtail, Skylark, Nightingale. *Autumn:* Green Woodpecker, Robin, Wren, Coal Tit. *Winter:* Long-tailed Tit, Treecreeper, Great Spotted Woodpecker, Nuthatch.
Other notable flora and fauna: Roe deer, woodland flora such as bluebells, wood anemone, lesser celandine, plus dragonflies, damselflies, butterflies.
Contact: Site Manager, 01458 252 805; e-mail: swell.wood@rspb.org.uk
www.rspb.org.uk/reserves/guide/s/swellwood/

Wiltshire

WILTSHIRE'S position away from the coast limits its range of birds but the Wildlife Trust maintains more than 40 reserves throughout the county. The chalk downlands of Marlborough Downs and the extensive Salisbury Plain are internationally threatened habitats. The Army's use of Salisbury Plain limits human access which helps birds, and for this reason the area has been selected for the experiment to re-introduce Great Bustards to Britain.

LANGFORD LAKES

Wiltshire Wildlife Trust.
Location: Sat nav: SP3 4PA. SU 037 370. Nr Steeple Langford, S of A36, approx eight miles W of Salisbury. In centre of village, turn S into Duck Street, sign-posted Hanging Langford. Langford Lakes is first L just after a small bridge.
Access: Opened to the public in Sept 2002. Main gates open during the day — ample parking. Advance notice required for coaches. No dogs.
Facilities: Visitor centre, toilets, education centre.

NATURE RESERVES - SOUTH WEST ENGLAND

Four hides, all accessible to wheelchairs. Cycle stands provided (250m from Wiltshire Cycleway between Great Wishford and Hanging Langford).
Public transport: Nearest bus stop 500m - X4 Service between Salisbury and Warminster.
Habitat: Four former gravel pits, with newly created islands and developing reed fringes. 12 ha (29 acres) of open water; also wet woodland, scrub, chalk river. Great Meadow wetland opened in 2012.
Key birds: More than 150 species recorded. *Summer:* Breeding Coot, Moorhen, Tufted Duck, Pochard, Gadwall, Little Grebe, Great Crested Grebe. Also Kingfisher, Common Sandpiper, Grey Wagtail, warblers (8 species). *Winter:* Common wildfowl, sometimes also Bittern, Wigeon, Shoveler, Teal, Water Rail, Little Egret, Bittern. *Passage:* Sand Martin, Green Sandpiper and other waders, Black Tern.
Other notable flora and fauna: Otter, water vole, water shrew. Spawning salmon and trout in river.
Contact: Wiltshire Wildlife Trust, Langford Lakes, 01722 790 770; e-mail: info@wiltshirewildlife.org

RAVENSROOST WOOD COMPLEX

Wiltshire Wildlife Trust.
Location: Sat nav: SN16 9RL. SU 023 877 (Ravensroost Wood car park). NW of Swindon. Take B4696 Ashton Keynes road N from Wootton Bassett. After two miles take second turn L to Minety. Go straight on when main road turns R. Go straight over next crossroads and car park is on R after quarter mile.
Access: Wood connects to Ravensroost and Avis Meadows, Distillery and Warbler Meadows and all sites are open at all times.
Facilities: Small car park, small shelter.
Habitat: Woodland, both coppice and high oak forest, and ponds. Surrounding meadows rich in wildflowers.
Key birds: Breeding Willow Warblers, Blackcap, Chiffchaff and Garden Warblers. In winter mixed flocks of Nuthatches, tits and Treecreepers move noisily through the wood and Woodcock can be flushed from wet, muddy areas.
Other notable flora and fauna: Butterflies include silver-washed fritillary and white admiral. Good display of spring bluebells, wood anemone, wood sorrel, sanicle, violet and primrose. In summer, common spotted, early purple and greater butterfly orchids, hemp agrimony and betony.
Contact: Wiltshire Wildlife Trust, Langford Lakes, 01722 790 770.
e-mail: info@wiltshirewildlife.org www. wiltshirewildlife.or

SAVERNAKE FOREST

Savernake Estate Trustees.
Location: Sat nav: SN8 3HP. From Marlborough the A4 Hungerford road runs along side of forest. Two

pillars mark Forest Hill entrance, 1.5 miles E of A346/ A4 junction. The Grand Avenue leads straight through the middle of the woodland to join a minor road from Stibb.
Access: Privately owned but open all year to public. Visitors can drive along main avenues, but all roads are closed on first working day of the year.
Facilities: Car park, picnic site at NW end by A346. Only enter fenced-off areas if there is a footpath.
Habitat: Ancient woodland, with one of the largest collections of veteran trees in Britain. Beech avenue (4 miles in length) longest in UK. Designated SSSI for its lichens and fungi.
Key birds: *Spring/summer:* Garden Warbler, Blackcap, Willow Warbler, Chiffchaff, Wood Warbler, Redstart, occasional Nightingale, Tree Pipit, Spotted Flycatcher. *Winter:* Finch flocks possibly inc Siskin, Redpoll, Brambling and Hawfinch. *All year:* Sparrowhawk, Buzzard, Red Kite, Woodcock, owls, all three woodpeckers, Marsh Tit, Willow Tit, Jay and other woodland birds.
Other notable flora and fauna: Rare lichens and fungi, all main deer species, badgers, foxes.
Contact: Savernake Estate, Estate Foreman: 01672 512 161; savernakeestate@hotmail.com
www.savernakeestate.co.uk

SWILLBROOK LAKES

Lower Mill Estate.
Location: Sat nav: SN16 9QA. SU 018 934. NW of Swindon. Also known as Lakes 46 and 48 of Cotswold Water Park. From A419 Swindon to Cirencester road, turn L onto Cotswold Water Park Spine Road. Cross B4696 South Cerney/Ashton Keynes road, take next L, Minety Lane, after about 1.5 miles. Park in gateway either side of road, after about 0.5 miles. Swillbrook Lakes nature reserve and information board is on E side of road.
Access: Open at all times. Adjacent to Clattinger Farm, a Wilts Wildlife Trust reserve.
Facilities: Footpath along N and E sides of lakes.
Habitat: Gravel pits with shallow pools, rough grassland and scrub around edges.
Key birds: *Winter:* Wildfowl (inc. Gadwall, Pochard, Smew, Goosander, Goldeneye). *Summer:* Breeding Nightingale, Garden, Reed and Sedge Warblers, Blackcap, Cetti's Warbler, Sand and House Martin, Swallow. One of the best sites for Hobby and Nightingale in Cotswold WP.
Other notable flora and fauna: 13 species of dragonfly including downy emerald and lesser emperor in recent years.
Contact: www.waterpark.org

207

Scottish Border Counties

Borders, Dumfries and Galloway

Borders

OFTEN overlooked as birders head for the Highlands, counties in the Borders do have many good sites for birds. St Abb's Head holds a large summer seabird colony, while migrants move past in spring and autumn. Ospreys have recently moved into the area and can often be seen fishing at Duns Castle. Water Rails breed at Yetholm Loch, which is also good for wildfowl.

1. BEMERSYDE MOSS

Scottish Wildlife Trust.
Location: NT 614 340. Located eight miles E of Melrose. From here head S on A48 to St Boswells, then take B6404 across the Tweed into minor road to Maidenhall. At T-junction turn right and reserve is half mile ahead.
Access: Open at all times. Limited parking in lay-by on southern edge of loch.
Facilities: Boardwalk leads to wheelchair-friendly bird hide.
Habitat: Long narrow strip of marsh, willow scrub and open water.
Key birds: Breeding birds include Black-necked Grebe, Lapwing, Curlew, Spotted Flycatcher, Tree Sparrow, Yellowhammer, Reed Bunting, Grasshopper Warbler and thousands of Black-headed Gulls. Good range of wintering wildfowl including good numbers of Wigeon and Greylag Goose.
Other notable flora and fauna: Otter, water vole.
Contact: SWT headquarters, 01313 127 765.
www.scottishwildlifetrust.org.uk

2. DUNS CASTLE RESERVE

Scottish Wildlife Trust.
Location: Sat nav: TD11 3NW. NT 778 550. Duns lies W of Berwick-upon-Tweed. From town centre head N on Castle Street and North Castle Street. Alternatively drive N on A6112 for one mile and turn left on B6365 to car park on northern edge of reserve.
Access: Reserve covering 190 acres open all year.
Facilities: Network of well-marked paths, some suitable for wheelchair access.
Habitat: Two man-made lochs (Hen Poo and Mill Dam) and woodland.
Key birds: Woodland birds such as Green and Great Spotted Woodpeckers, Goldcrest and Redstart (Summer), waterfowl.
Other notable fauna: Red squirrel, roe deer, occasional otter. Woodland rich in wild flowers.
Contact: SWT headquarters, 01313 127 765.
www.scottishwildlifetrust.org.uk

3. ETTRICK MARSHES

Forestry Commission/
Borders Forest Trust.
Location: Sat nav: TD7 5HU
(Honey Cottage caravan park).

Sited in Ettrick Valley, off B7009, approx 16 miles SW from Selkirk.
Access: Open at all times. Best access from Honey Cottage car park.
Facilities: Three car parks, network of footpaths and board walk. Can be flooded after heavy rain.
Habitat: Floodplain mosaic of woodland, wetland, grass and open water of national conservation importance covering 125ha.
Key birds: Eighty species recorded. Goosander, Kingfisher, Buzzard, Crossbill and Dipper seen all year, with occasional Goshawk and Osprey. Summer species include Redstart, Sedge Warbler and Sand Martin.
Other notable flora and fauna: Red squirrel, otter. Moths and plants at northern edge of range.
Contacts: Borders Forest Trust 01835 830 750; enquiries@bordersforesttrust.org

4. GUNKNOWE LOCH AND PARK

Scottish Borders Council.
Location: Sat nav: TD1 3RP. NT 518 345. At Tweedbank, 3.2km from Galashiels on the A6091. Park at Gunknowe Loch or Abbotsford House visitor centre.
Access: Open all year. Surfaced paths suitable for wheelchair use.
Facilities: Car park, information boards, paths in park. Visitor centre, café and toilets at Abbotsford House.
Public transport: Tweedbank is on the Melrose-to-Peebles bus route.
Habitat: River, man-made loch, parkland, scrub, woodland.
Key birds: *Spring/summer:* Grey Wagtail, Kingfisher, Sand Martin, Blackcap, Sedge and Grasshopper Warblers. *Passage:* Yellow Wagtail, Whinchat, Wheatear. *Winter:* Thrushes, Brambling, Wigeon, Tufted Duck, Pochard, Goldeneye. *All year:* Great Spotted and Green Woodpeckers, Redpoll, Goosander, possible Marsh Tit.
Contact: Ranger Service 01835 825 060.
www.scotborders.gov.uk

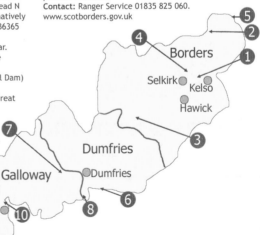

5. ST ABBS HEAD

National Trust for Scotland.
Location: Sat nav: TD14 5QF. NT 914 693 for car park and bus stop. Lies five miles N of Eyemouth. Follow A1107 from A1.
Access: Reserve open all year. All-ability path to viewpoint at Starney Bay. Well behaved dogs welcome; keep dogs under close control and droppings taken home. Coach parking at Northfield Farm by prior arrangement.
Facilities: Visitor centre and toilets (inc disabled) open daily Apr-Oct.
Public transport: Nearest rail station is Berwick-upon-Tweed, bus service from Berwick.
Habitat: Cliffs, coastal grasslands and freshwater loch.
Key birds: *Apr-Aug*: Seabird colonies with large numbers of Guillemot and Kittiwake; also Shag, Razorbill, Fulmar. *Apr-May and Sept-Oct*: Good autumn seawatching.
Other notable flora and fauna: Common rock-rose, purple milk-vetch, spring sandwort. Northern brown argus butterfly.
Contact: Liza Cole, Ranger's Office, 01890 771 443. www.nts.org.uk, www.stabbrangers.blotspot.com and St Abb's Head NNR page on Facebook

Dumfries and Galloway

THE SOLWAY holds nationally important numbers of wintering Barnacle Geese, with Caerlaverock WWT and RSPB Mersehead being prime sites. Ospreys and Red Kites are colonising and there is a chance of a Golden Eagle over upland areas or Hen Harrier on moorland. The Mull of Galloway has fine seabird cliffs. The Ken/Dee Marshes hold Willow Tit and Nuthatch.

6. CAERLAVEROCK WETLAND CENTRE

The Wildfowl & Wetlands Trust.
Location: Sat nav: DG1 4RS. NY 051 656. Overlooks the Solway. From St Michael's church in Dumfries take B725 towards Bankend, following tourist signs. Also sign-posted from A75 W of Annan.
Access: Open daily (10am-5pm), except Dec 25. Charge for non-WWT members. Assistance dogs only.
Facilities: 20 hides, heated observatory, four towers, Salcot Merse Observatory, sheltered picnic area. Self-catering accommodation and camping facilities. Nature trails in summer. Old Granary visitor building; coffee shop serving light meals and snacks; bookshop; optics for sale. Theatre/conference room. Binoculars for hire. Parking for coaches.
Public transport: Bus 6A from Dumfries stops 30 mins walk from reserve. Stagecoach 01387 253 496.
Habitat: Saltmarsh, grassland, wetland.
Key birds: *Winter*: Wildfowl esp. Barnacle Geese (max 40,000), Pink-footed Geese and Whooper Swans. *Summer*: Osprey (web-cam on nest), Barn Owl, Skylark, Tree Sparrow, migrant warblers.
Other notable flora and fauna: Natterjack toads, badger, tadpole shrimp, bats. Northern marsh,

common spotted and twayblade orchids.
Contact: WWT Caerlaverock, 01387 770 200; e-mail: info.caerlaverock@wwt.org.uk; wwt.org.uk

7. KEN-DEE MARSHES

RSPB (South & West Scotland Office).
Location: Sat nav: DG7 2NJ. NX 699 684. Six miles from Castle Douglas. Off the A762 (N of Laurieston) or B795 road (at Glenlochar), parking at the Mains of Duchrae.
Access: From car park at entrance to Mains of Duchrae farm. Open during daylight hours. No dogs.
Facilities: Two hides, viewing platform, nature trails. Three miles of trails available, nearer parking for elderly and disabled, but phone warden first. Part of Red Kite trail.
Public transport: None. **Habitat:** Marshes, woodlands, open water.
Key birds: *All year*: Mallard, Grey Heron, Buzzard, Nuthatch, Willow Tit. *Spring/summer*: Lapwing and Curlew nest on farmland. Pied Flycatcher, Redstart, Tree Pipit, Sedge Warbler. *Winter*: Greenland White-fronted and Greylag Geese, raptors (Hen Harrier, Peregrine, Merlin, Red Kite).
Other notable flora and fauna: Red squirrel, roe deer, otter.
Contact: RSPB Ken-Dee Marshes, 01556 670 464. www.gallowaykitetrail.com

8. MERSEHEAD

RSPB (South & West Scotland Office).
Location: Sat nav: DG2 8AH. NX 928 566. From Dumfries take A710 S for about 16 miles. Reserve is signposted on L just before Caulkerbush village. Single track road with passing places runs for a mile to car park, adjacent to visitor centre. From Castle Douglas, take A745, then A711 to Dalbeattie before joining A710.
Access: Wheelchair-friendly hides and trails open at all times. **Facilities:** Visitor centre with viewing room, refreshments and toilets (open 10am to 5pm). Blue Badge parking spaces within 400m of hides and 20m from visitor centre.
Public transport: None.
Habitat: Wet grassland, arable farmland, saltmarsh, inter-tidal mudflats.
Key birds: *Winter*: Up to 9,500 Barnacle Geese, 4,000 Teal, 2,000 Wigeon, 1,000 Pintail, waders (inc. Dunlin, Knot, Oystercatcher). *Summer*: Breeding birds include Lapwing, Redshank, Skylark.
Contact: RSPB Mersehead, 01387 780 579; e-mail: mersehead@rspb.org.uk

9. MULL OF GALLOWAY

RSPB (South & West Scotland Office).
Location: Sat nav: DG9 9HP. NX 156 305. Most southerly tip of Scotland - follow brown signs for five miles from village of Drummore, S of Stranraer.
Access: Open at all times. Blue Badge parking by centre. No wheelchair access to foghorn viewing platform overlooking seabird colonies or circular trail. Centre open summer only (Apr-Oct).

Facilities: Visitor centre, toilets, nature trails, CCTV on cliffs. Small shop at neighbouring Gallie Craig café (not RSPB).
Public transport: None.
Habitat: Sea cliffs, coastal heath.
Key birds: *Spring/summer*: Guillemot, Razorbill, Kittiwake, Black Guillemot, Puffin, Fulmar, Raven, Wheatear, Rock Pipit, Twite. Migrating Manx Shearwater. *All year*: Peregrine.
Contact: RSPB Mull of Galloway, 01988 402 130; e-mail: mullofgalloway@rspb.org.uk

10. WIGTOWN BAY LNR

Dumfries & Galloway Council.
Location: Sat nav: DG8 9JH. NX 465 545. Between Wigtown and Creetown, S of Newton Stewart The A75 runs along E side, with A714 S to Wigtown and B7004 providing superb views of the LNR.
Access: Reserve open at all times. The hide is disabled-friendly. Main accesses: Roadside lay-bys on A75 near Creetown and parking at Martyr's Stake and Wigtown Harbour. All suitable for coaches. Visitor Centre in Wigtown County Building has coach parking plus full disabled access, including lift and toilets.
Facilities: Hide at Wigtown Harbour overlooking River Bladnoch, saltmarsh and fresh water wetland has disabled access from harbour car park. Another hide at Martyr's Stake car park. CCTV of Ospreys breeding in Galloway during summer and wetland birds in winter. Open Mon-Sat 10am-5pm, later some days; Sun 2pm-5pm.
Public transport: Travel Information Line 08457 090 510 (local rate 9am-5pm Mon-Fri). Bus No 415 for Wigtown and W side. Bus No 431 or 500 X75 for Creetown and E side.
Habitat: The largest LNR in Britain at 2,845hr features an estuary with extensive saltmarsh/merse

and mudflats plus a freshwater wetland at Wigtown Harbour.
Key birds: *Winter*: Internationally important for Pink-footed Goose, nationally important for Curlew, Whooper Swan and Pintail, with major gull roost and other migratory coastal birds. Small Twite flock. *Summer*: Breeding Osprey, Peregrine, waders and duck.
Other notable flora and fauna: Fish including smelt and shad. Lax-flowered sea-lavender, sea aster.
Contact: Visitor Centre 01988 402 673, Keith Kirk, Countryside Ranger, 01556 505 479, (M)07850 157 661; e-mail:keith.kirk@dumgal.gov.uk
www.dgcommunity.net/wblr

11. WOOD OF CREE

RSPB (South & West Scotland Office).
Location: NX 382 708. Four miles N of Newton Stewart on minor road from Minnigaff, parallel to A714. Turn left past Minigaff church and continue along minor C50 for a further 3 miles to car park.
Access: Open during daylight hours. Dogs on lead. Not suitable for disabled.
Facilities: Car parks at Wood of Cree and Barclye Wood (3 miles from Newton Stewart). Nature trails rough in places.
Public transport: None. **Habitat:** Oak woodland, marshes, river.
Key birds: *Spring/summer*: Pied Flycatcher, Wood Warbler, Tree Pipit, Redstart, Buzzard, Great Spotted Woodpecker.
Other notable flora and fauna: Red squirrel, otter, Leisler's bat, carpet of bluebells and other spring wildflowers.
Contact: Wood of Cree, 01988 402 130; e-mail: wood.cree@rspb.org.uk

Central Scotland

Argyll, Ayrshire, Clyde, Fife, Forth, Lothian

Argyll

TWO ISLANDS take the birding honours for this region. Islay is renowned for its wintering wildfowl, including huge numbers of Barnacle and White-fronted Geese. Choughs, raptors and Corncrakes are other island specialities. The island of Mull is home to the highest breeding densities of Golden Eagle and White-tailed Eagles in Britain.

1. COLL RESERVE

RSPB (South & West Scotland Office).
Location: Sat nav: PA34 4LW (Oban harbour). NM 167 563. By ferry from Oban to island of Coll. Take the B8070 W from Arinagour for five miles. Turn R at Arileod. Continue for about one mile. Park at end of

the road. Reception point at Totronald.
Access: Open all year. A natural site with unimproved paths not suitable for wheelchairs. Please avoid walking through fields and crops.
Facilities: Car park, information bothy at Totronald, guided walks in summer. Corncrake viewing bench.
Public transport: None.
Habitat: Sand dunes, beaches, machair grassland, moorland, farmland.
Key birds: *Spring*: Great Northern Diver offshore. Corncrakes arrive in late April. Displaying waders, inc Redshank, Lapwing, Snipe. *Summer*: Auks offshore, plus Gannet, shearwaters and terns. *Autumn*: Barnacle and Greenland White-fronted Geese arrive, thrushes on passage. Waders inc Purple Sandpiper. *Winter*: Long-tailed Duck, divers offshore. Hunting Hen Harrier and Merlin. Twite.

Other notable flora and fauna: Good for ceteceans and basking shark. Otter, 300-plus machair wildflowers inc rare orchids, great yellow bumblebee.
Contact: RSPB Coll Nature Reserve, 01879 230 301; www.rspb.org.uk

2. LOCH GRUINART, ISLAY

RSPB (South & West Scotland Office).
Location: Sat nav: PA44 7PR. NR 275 672. Sea loch on N coast of Islay, seven miles NW from Bridgend.
Access: Hide open all hours, visitor centre open (10am-5pm), disabled access to hide, viewing area and toilets. Assistance required for wheelchair users. Coach parking at visitor centre only. No dogs in hides.
Facilities: Toilets (inc disabled), visitor centre (offers hot drinks), hide, trail. Two car parks — the one opposite the viewpoint is level and made from rolled stone. Group bookings accepted. Weekly guided walks every Thursday at 10am (April to Oct)
Public transport: Nearest bus stops 3 miles from reserve.
Habitat: Lowland wet grasslands, sea loch, moorland.
Key birds: *Oct-Apr:* Large numbers of Barnacle and White-fronted Geese, plus other wildfowl and waders. *May-Aug:* Breeding and displaying waders and Corncrake. *Sept-Nov:* Many passage migrants and arriving wildfowl. Birds of prey are present all year, esp Hen Harrier and Peregrine, while Chough can be seen feeding in nearby fields. *Spring:* Displaying Snipe, Lapwing, Curlew and Redshank.
Other notable flora and fauna: Otter, red and roe deer. Marsh fritillary butterflies during May and June.
Contact: RSPB Scotland, 01496 850 505: e-mail: loch.gruinart@rspb.org.uk; www.rspb.org.uk/scotland

3. MACHRIHANISH SEABIRD OBSERVATORY

Nancie Smith/ Eddie Maguire (sponsored by SNH).
Location: Sat nav: PA28 6PY. NR 628 209. Southwest Kintyre, Argyll. Six miles W of Campbeltown on A83, then B843.
Access: Daily April-Oct. Wheelchair access. Dogs welcome. Parking for three cars. Digiscoping facilities include electricity and monitor.
Facilities: Seawatching hide, toilets in nearby village. Coach parking.
Public transport: Regular buses from Campbeltown (West Coast Motors, tel 01586 552 319).
Habitat: Marine, rocky shore and upland habitats.
Key birds: *Summer:* Golden Eagle, Peregrine, Storm Petrel and Twite. *Autumn:* Passage seabirds and waders. On-shore gales often produce inshore movements of Leach's Petrel and more scarce seabirds, including Balearic Shearwater, Sabine's Gull and Grey Phalarope. *Winter:* Great Northern Diver, Purple Sandpiper, Ruddy Turnstone with occasional Glaucous and Iceland Gulls.
Other notable flora and fauna: Grey and common seals, otter, wild goat.
Contact: Eddie Maguire, Warden, 07919 660 292; e-mail: machrihanishbirds@btinternet.com www.machrihanishbirdobservatory.org.uk/

4. MULL EAGLE WATCH

RSPB Scotland/Forestry Commission Scotland
Location: NM 480 303 (rendezvous point). New watchpoint on northern shore of Loch Scridain, in the western part of Mull.
Access: Visitors will follow ranger in own cars from rendezvous point roughly 0.5km up the Forestry Commission Scotland track at Glen Seilisdeir off B8035 Salen/Kinloch scenic route. Booking places on trips is essential. Charge for all adults except Mull residents, under-16s half price. Trips run at 10am and 1pm Monday to Friday (March 25 to autumn).
Facilities: Purpose-built hide for observing nesting White-tailed Eagles. No toilet facilities.
Habitat: Large sea loch with tidal mudflats at its head (Loch Beg).
Key birds: White-tailed Eagles which bred regularly at Loch Frisa failed in 2010 and 2011, so it was decided to move the Eagle Hide to the northern shore of Loch Scridain. Other raptors in the area include Golden Eagle, Hen Harrier and Buzzard. In winter and early spring it is possible to see three species of diver, Slavonian Grebe, Red-breasted Merganser and Eider in the loch. Otter sightings common here. Waders can be seen on muddy areas at any time of year.
Contact: To book a trip call the Visit Scotland Information Centre, Craignure on 01680 812 556.

Ayrshire

A RUGGED coastline, combined with river valleys and inland woodland means Ayrshire has many potentially good birding opportunities, though its best known site is the island of Ailsa Craig, which boasts a huge gannetry, together with plenty of other breeding seabirds. Don't miss Martnaham Loch (good for wildfowl and a range of common species) or Turnberry Point (seawatching, plus Twite). The shore at Barassie and Troon sees a large build-up of waders in autumn, plus white-winged gulls in winter.

5. AILSA CRAIG

RSPB (South & West Scotland Office).
Location: NX 020 998. Island is nine miles offshore, nearest town on mainland is Girvan.
Access: Accessible only by boat: MFV Glorious (tel: 01465 713 219) or Kintyre Express (tel: 01294 270 160) from Girvan during summer. Also from Campbeltown by Mull of Kintyre Seatours' fast rib (07785 542 811).
Facilities: None
Public transport: None.
Habitat: Volcanic plug (338metres high) provides nest sites for seabirds.
Key birds: Ailsa Craig hosts the third largest gannetry in the UK and supports 73,000 breeding seabirds, including Guillemot, Razorbill, Puffin, Black Guillemot, Kittiwake and up to 36,000 pairs of Gannets. Twite can also be found here.
Other notable flora and fauna: Slow worm.
Contact: RSPB, 0141 331 0993; e-mail: glasgow@rspb.org.uk

6. CULZEAN CASTLE COUNTRY PARK

National Trust for Scotland.
Location: Sat nav: KA19 8LE. NS 234 103. 12 miles SW of Ayr on A719.
Access: Country Park open all year 9am to dusk. Restaurant/shops open daily (Apr-Oct) and weekends Nov-March. Access leaflet available. Admission charges for Country Park.
Facilities: Car park, visitor centre, children's playground, picnic areas, 21 miles of footpath and estate tracks, ranging from unsurfaced woodland paths to metalled roads.
Public transport: Stagecoach bus No 60 (Ayr to Girvan) stops at site entrance. One mile walk downhill to visitor centre and castle.
Habitat: Shoreline, parkland, woodland, gardens, streams, ponds.
Key birds: *All year:* Good populations of common woodland species, inc Jay, Great Spotted Woodpecker and thrushes. *Spring/summer:* Arriving migrants, esp Blackcap, Chiffchaff and Willow Warbler. Nesting Raven and Gannet on cliffs, Gannet and terns offshore. *Autumn/winter:* Regular flocks of Redwing and Fieldfare, Waxwing, crossbills. Wildfowl on pond inc Little Grebe, Tufted Duck, Goldeneye. Offshore divers and Eider.
Other notable fauna: Roe deer, otter, water vole, several species of bat. Shoreline SSSI rich in rock pool life.
Contact: Culzean Ranger Service 0844 493 2148; e-mail: culzean@nts.org.uk

7. GARNOCK FLOODS

Scottish Wildlife Trust.
Location: Sat nav: KA13 6PR. NS 306 417. On N edge of Kilwinning. Take B779 off the westbound A78 between Irvine and Kilwinning and park in the lay-by just past the bridge over the River Irvine.
Access: Open all year. No paths on reserve – site is best viewed from bridge or river embankment. Wheelchair users restricted to viewing through roadside hedges. No dogs.
Facilities: Parking.
Habitat: Low-lying floodplain of River Garnock, with ponds, rush pasture.
Key birds: *Spring/summer:* Sedge and Willow Warblers, Lesser Whitethroat, Sand Martin., occasional Garganey. *Winter:* Wildfowl inc Shoveler, Wigeon, Teal, Goldeneye, Tufted Duck, Little Grebe, Mute Swan, waders on pond edges including Ruff and Snipe.
Contact: SWT headquarters 01313 127 765.
www.scottishwildlifetrust.org.uk/garnock-floods

Clyde

THE FALLS OF CLYDE Scottish Wildlife Trust reserve has a well-known Peregrine watchpoint, with Dippers and Kingfishers along the river. Whinchats and several species of warbler breed at Baron's Haugh, with a good autumn passage of waders there. RSPB Lochwinnoch offers a good selection of commoner species throughout the year.

8. BARON'S HAUGH

RSPB (South & West Scotland Office).
Location: Sat nav: ML1 2PZ. NS 756 553. On SW edge of Motherwell, overlooking River Clyde. Via Adele Street, then lane off North Lodge Avenue.
Access: Open all year. Most paths suitable for wheelchairs, except circular nature trail, which has some steep sections.
Facilities: Four hides, information board in car park. Disabled access along some of the Clyde walkway but it is difficult due to erosion – ring for details.
Public transport: Airbles train station, with frequent services from Glasgow Central is about 15 minutes' walk. Buses 2 and 245 from Motherwell stop in Adele Street (half mile from reserve).
Habitat: Marshland, flooded areas, woodland, parkland, meadows, scrub, river.
Key birds: *Summer:* Breeding Gadwall, warblers (inc. Garden, Grasshopper); Whinchat, Common Sandpiper, Kingfisher, Sand Martin. *Autumn:* Excellent for waders (22 species). *Winter:* Whooper Swan, Pochard, Wigeon, Sparrowhawk.
Contact: RSPB, 0141 331 0993; e-mail: baronshaugh@rspb.org.uk

9. FALLS OF CLYDE

Scottish Wildlife Trust.
Location: Sat nav: ML11 9DB (visitor centre). NS 881 423. Approx one mile S of Lanark. Directions from Glasgow - travel S on M74 until junction 7 then along A72, following brown signs for New Lanark.
Access: Reserve open daily. From New Lanark car park, walk into village, through the iron gates and down steps to the right of the New Lanark Visitor Centre. Follow road to the Falls of Clyde Visitor Centre. Reserve terrain too steep for wheelchairs, but visitor centre is wheelchair friendly, inc toilet facilities.
Facilities: Visitor centre open daily 10am-4pm. Admission charge for non-SWT members. Peregrine watch site open from Mar-Jun. Woodland trails and a range of guided walks inc self-guided, wildflower trail and badger watches.
Public transport: Scotrail trains run to Lanark. Local bus service from Lanark to New Lanark.
Habitat: Reserve stretches along both sides of an ancient gorge, with waterfalls, meadow and wet woodland.
Key birds: Over 100 species of birds, unrivalled views of breeding Peregrines. Others inc Kingfisher, Dipper, Jay, Spotted Flycatcher and Goosander.
Other notable flora and fauna: Badgers, otters, bats and wildflowers.
Contact: Falls of Clyde Visitor Centre 01555 665 262; e-mail: fallsofclyde@swt.co.uk; www.swt.org.uk

10. LOCHWINNOCH

RSPB (South & West Scotland Office).
Location: Sat nav: PA12 4JF. NS 358 582. 18 miles SW of Glasgow, adjacent to A760 Largs Road, off the A737 (Irvine Road). Leave M8 at junction 28A.
Access: Open every day except Christmas and Boxing

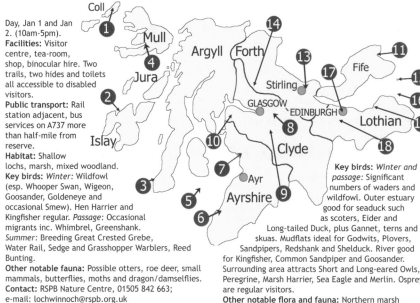

Day, Jan 1 and Jan 2. (10am-5pm).
Facilities: Visitor centre, tea-room, shop, binocular hire. Two trails, two hides and toilets all accessible to disabled visitors.
Public transport: Rail station adjacent, bus services on A737 more than half-mile from reserve.
Habitat: Shallow lochs, marsh, mixed woodland.
Key birds: *Winter:* Wildfowl (esp. Whooper Swan, Wigeon, Goosander, Goldeneye and occasional Smew). Hen Harrier and Kingfisher regular. *Passage:* Occasional migrants inc. Whimbrel, Greenshank. *Summer:* Breeding Great Crested Grebe, Water Rail, Sedge and Grasshopper Warblers, Reed Bunting.
Other notable fauna: Possible otters, roe deer, small mammals, butterflies, moths and dragon/damselflies.
Contact: RSPB Nature Centre, 01505 842 663; e-mail: lochwinnoch@rspb.org.uk
www.rspb.org.uk/lochwinnoch

Fife

WINTERING flocks of seaducks off Ruddons Point often hold a few Surf Scoters among the more numerous Common and Velvet Scoters, while Fife Ness is good for seawatching and autumn migrants. The Eden Estuary holds good numbers of wildfowl and waders throughout the year but especially in winter. Tentsmuir offers an unusual mix of woodland and coastal habitats.

11. EDEN ESTUARY LNR

Fife Coast and Countryside Trust
Location: Sat nav: KY16. 470 195 (centre of site). Reserve centre off main street in Guardbridge, two miles from St Andrews on A91, and from Leuchars via Tentsmuir Forest off A919 (4 miles). Use Outhead at St Andrews off West Sands beach, to access Balgove Bay.
Access: Eden Estuary Centre, Guardbridge (keypad number available from ranger service) open 9am- to 5pm all days except Dec 25, 26, 31 and Jan 1. Evans Hide: at GR 483 183, parking at Pilmuir Links golf course car park. Combination number required from ranger service.
Facilities: Visitor centre at Guardbridge. Viewing platform and picnic area at Outhead. Evans Hide at Balgove Bay (number from Ranger Service).
Public transport: Leuchars train station (1.5 miles), regular bus service from Cupar and Dundee. Tel 08457 484 950.
Habitat: Intertidal mudflats, saltmarsh, river, reed, sand dunes and wetland covering 891ha. Scotland's third oldest reserve.

Key birds: *Winter and passage:* Significant numbers of waders and wildfowl. Outer estuary good for seaduck such as scoters, Eider and Long-tailed Duck, plus Gannet, terns and skuas. Mudflats ideal for Godwits, Plovers, Sandpipers, Redshank and Shelduck. River good for Kingfisher, Common Sandpiper and Goosander. Surrounding area attracts Short and Long-eared Owls, Peregrine, Marsh Harrier, Sea Eagle and Merlin. Osprey are regular visitors.
Other notable flora and fauna: Northern marsh orchid, dune grasses and herbs. Harbour and grey seal, bottle-nosed dolphin, porpoise, brown hare, stoat and otter. Butterflies include comma, grayling, small pearl-bordered, dark green fritilliary, painted lady and orange tip.
Contact: Ranald Strachan, Fife Ranger Service, 01592 656 080, 07985 707 593.
e-mail: Ranald.Strachan@fifecountryside.co.uk

12. ISLE OF MAY NNR

Scottish Natural Heritage.
Location: NT 655 995. Small island lying six miles off Fife Ness in the Firth of Forth.
Access: Boats run from Anstruther and North Berwick. Contact SNH for details on 01334 654 038. Keep to paths. Those using Observatory accommodation should note delays are possible, both arriving and leaving, because of weather.
Facilities: No dogs; no camping; no fires. Prior permission required if scientific work, photography or filming is to be carried out.
Public transport: Regular bus service to Anstruther and North Berwick harbour.
Habitat: Sea cliffs, rocky shoreline.
Key birds: *Early summer:* Breeding auks, gulls and terns, Kittiwake, Shag, Eider, Fulmar. Over 45,000 pairs of Puffins. *Autumn/spring:* Weather-related migrations include rarities each year.
Contact: For accomodation: www.isleofmaybirdsobs.org or contact Jonathan Osbourne, The Shieling, Halcombe Crescent, Earlston, Berwickshire TD4 6DA; e-mail: jonathan@osbourn108.fsnet.co.uk.
For all other enquiries: SNH, 01463 725 000;
www.nnr-scotland.org

Forth

CAMBUS POOLS attracts passage waders and winter wildfowl, while high tide at Kinneil produces good numbers of waders in spring and autumn. The RSPB reserve at Inversnaid is good for Black Grouse, Twite, Redstart, Wood Warbler and Pied Flycatcher. There are large movements of finches and thrushes in autumn. A Red Kite feeding station at Argaty provides visitors with close-up views.

13. CAMBUS POOLS

Scottish Wildlife Trust.
Location: Sat nav: FK10 2PG. NS 846 937. Take A907 from Stirling towards Alloa, then Station Road to Cambus village. Park by river in village.
Access: Cross River Devon by bridge at NS 853 940 and walk down stream on R bank past bonded warehouses. Open all year.
Facilities: Bench on S side of western pool.
Public transport: None.
Habitat: Wet grassland with two salty pools.
Key birds: Used extensively by migrants in spring and autumn, inc. wildfowl and waders such as Black-tailed Godwit and Greenshank. Gadwall have bred here and Kingfisher is seen regularly.
Other notable flora and fauna: Brown hare, stoat, short-tailed vole, 115 species of vascular plants. Harbour porpoise seen in Forth.
Contact: SWT headquarters, 01313 127 765. www.scottishwildlifetrust.org.uk/reserve/cambus-pools

14. INVERSNAID

RSPB (South and West Scotland Office).
Location: Sat nav: FK8 3TU (Garrison Farm). NN 337 088. Lies within Loch Lomond & Trossachs National Park on E side of the loch. Via B829 W from Aberfoyle, then along minor road to car park by Inversnaid Hotel.
Access: Open all year. Three trails, all too rough for wheelchairs.
Facilities: New car park and trail at Garrison Farm (NN 348 095) for reserve's upland areas. No visitor centre, but accessible toilets now installed.
Habitat: Deciduous woodland (90ha) rises to craggy ridge and moorland (727ha).
Key birds: *Summer:* Breeding Black Grouse on moor, Snipe, Cuckoo, Wheatear and Twite. Raven, Grey Wagtail, Dipper, Wood Warbler, Redstart, Pied Flycatcher, Tree Pipit. The loch is on a migration route, especially for wildfowl and waders. Look for Red-throated and Black-throated Divers in spring. *Winter:* Hen Harrier and thrushes.
Other notable flora and fauna: Pine marten, slow worm, 17 species of butterfly inc small pearl-bordered fritillary on nature trail at Inversnaid. Wilson's and Tunbridge filmy ferns on boulders through woodland.
Contact: RSPB South and West Scotland Office, 01413 310 993; e-mail: inversnaid@rspb.org.uk

Lothian

THOUGH coastal locations usually grab the headlines, the Lammermuir Hills hold a range of upland species. More than 250 species have been recorded at Aberlady Bay, including many thousands of geese in winter. The Seabird Centre at North Berwick is a great place to take young children, or take a boat out to the gannetry at Bass Rock, while Ferny Ness sees a build-up of Red-necked Grebes in late summer.

15. ABERLADY BAY LNR

East Lothian Council.
Location: Sat nav: EH32 0QB. NT 472 806. From Edinburgh take A198 E to Aberlady. Reserve car park is 1.5 miles E of Aberlady village.
Access: Britain's first ever Local Nature Reserve is open at all times. Please stay on footpaths to avoid disturbance. Disabled access from reserve car park. No dogs please.
Facilities: Small car park and toilets. Notice board with recent sightings at end of footbridge. SOC HQ, Waterston House, located W of Aberlady village. Includes shop, library, hot and cold drinks.
Public transport: First Bus (Edinburgh to N Berwick services 124 X24 and X25 stop close to reserve (request). Nearest train station 4 miles away at Longniddry.
Habitat: Tidal mudflats, saltmarsh, freshwater marsh, dune grassland, scrub, open sea.
Key birds: *Summer:* Breeding birds include Shelduck, Eider, Reed Bunting and up to eight species of warbler. Passage waders inc. Green, Wood and Curlew Sandpipers, Little Stint, Greenshank, Whimbrel, Black-tailed Godwit. *Winter:* Divers (esp. Red-throated), Red-necked and Slavonian Grebes and geese (up to 15,000 Pinkfeet roost); sea-ducks, waders.
Contact: John Harrison, Reserve Warden – e-mail: jharrison@eastlothian.gov.uk; www.aberlady.org

16. BASS ROCK/ SCOTTISH SEABIRD CENTRE

Location: NT 605 875. Island NE of North Berwick. Scottish Seabird Centre is located in North Berwick Harbour (EH39 4SS).
Access: Island is private property. Regular daily sailings from N Berwick or Dunbar around Rock between April and September; local boatman has owner's permission to land individuals or parties by prior arrangement (3 hours on island). Cheaper non-landing trips by boat or RIB (rigid inflatable boat) around Bass Rock and Craigleath run from Mar 29-Oct.
Facilities: Café, shop, aquaria, telescope deck and toilets at Seabird Centre. No facilities on Bass Rock.
Habitat: Sea cliffs.
Key birds: The spectacular cliffs hold a massive Gannet colony, (with up to 150,000 birds it's the largest in the world), plus Puffin, Guillemot, Razorbill, Kittiwake, Shag, Arctic Tern and Fulmar.
Contact: For details of boat trips call 01620 892 838 or The Scottish Seabird Centre 01620 890 202; e-mail: info@seabird.org; www.seabird.org

17. BAWSINCH RESERVE & DUDDINGSTON LOCH

Scottish Wildlife Trust.
Location: Sat nav: EH15 3PX. NT 284 725. Two miles from centre of Edinburgh, below Arthur's Seat. Use car park on Duddingston Road West and Holyrood Park Gate.
Access: Open access to north shore of loch and cavalry ground to SE – best views from Hangman's Rock. Remainder of site and hide open to SWT members who need to apply for gate keys.
Facilities: Hide (SWT members only) with bird and plant lists.
Public transport: Call SWT on 0131 312 7765 for advice.
Habitat: Edinburgh's only natural freshwater loch. Reedbed, marsh, ponds, mixed woodland, flower meadow and scrub. Bawsinch reserve developed from former industrial wasteland.
Key birds: Heronry. Important site for breeding swans, geese, ducks and grebes. Summer migrants, inc Spotted Flycatcher, hirundines, warblers, inc occasional Grasshopper Warbler. Winter-roosting wildfowl, gulls and Bittern.
Other notable flora and fauna: Fox, water vole and otter. Damselfly, four species of amphibian.

Contact: SWT headquarters, 01313 127 765.
www.scottishwildlifetrust.org.uk/reserve/bawsinch-and-duddingston

18. GLADHOUSE RESERVOIR LNR

Scottish Water.
Location: Sat nav: EH23 4SY. NT 295 535. Lies 5 miles S of Penicuik in the Moorfoot Hills off the A703.
Access: Open all year although there is no access to the reservoir itself. Most viewing can be done from the road (telescope required).
Facilities: Small car park on north side. Not suitable for coaches.
Habitat: Reservoir, grassland, farmland.
Key birds: *Spring/summer*: Breeding Oystercatcher, Lapwing, Curlew. Possible Black Grouse. *Autumn*: Waders inc Greenshank, Oystercatcher and Whimbrel. *Winter*: Important site for roosting geese, including Pinkfeet (up to 3,000 birds) and Greylags (approx 600). Twite, finch flocks, Brambling, Hen Harrier.
Contact: Scottish Water, PO Box 8855, Edinburgh, EH10 6YQ, 084 6 018 855.
e-mail: customer.service@scottishwater.co.uk
www.scottishwater.co.uk

Eastern Scotland

Angus & Dundee, Moray & Nairn, NE Scotland, Perth & Kinross

Angus & Dundee

THE ANGUS glens hold a typical range of upland species, including Ring Ouzel, grouse, chats and Golden Eagle. Ospreys fish regularly at RSPB Loch of Kinnordy, while Montreathmont Forest is a mix of coniferous and broadleaved woodland. Montrose Basin is a flagship Scottish Wildlife Trust reserve, with a good selection of wildfowl ever present and waders on passage.

1. LOCH OF LINTRATHEN

Scottish Wildlife Trust.
Location: Sat nav: DD8 5JH. NO 278 550. Located next to Bridgend of Lintrathen, seven miles W of Kirriemuir. Take B951 and choose circular route on unclassified roads round loch.
Access: Two public hides (one on eastern side of loch is wheelchair-accessible) open 24 hours a day. Rest of reserve is private, but good views possible from unclassified roads.
Facilities: Viewpoint can accommodate five cars.
Public transport: None.
Habitat: Mesotrophic loch designated a Ramsar site because of its value to waterbirds. Surrounded by mainly coniferous woodland in the foothills of Braes of Angus.

Key birds: *Summer*: Grey Heron, Great Crested Grebe and other water birds. Osprey seen occasionally. *Winter*: Internationally-important numbers of Icelandic Greylag Geese, plus Pink-footed Goose, Goosander, Whooper Swan, Wigeon, Teal and other wildfowl.
Other notable flora and fauna: Red squirrel.
Contact: Robert Potter, Reserves Manager North East, SWT, 01575 540 396; (M)07920 468 568.
e-mail: rpotter@swt.org.uk

2. MONTROSE BASIN

Scottish Wildlife Trust/Angus Council.
Location: Sat nav: DD10 9TA. NO 702 565 (Wildlife SWT Centre on A92). 1.5 miles from centre of Montrose. Main car park for western end at the Old Mill, Mains of Dun (NN 669 591).
Access: Visitor Centre open March 1 to Oct 31 (10.30am to 5pm, 7 days per week) and from Nov 1 to Feb 28 (10.30am-4pm, Fri, Sat and Sun only). Admission: £4 Adults, £3 Concessions, £7.50 families, SWT members free. Several hides open at all times.
Facilities: Visitor centre, gift shop, fair-trade tea, coffee and snacks, toilets, disabled access to centre, two hides on western half of reserve.
Public transport: Train 1.5 miles in Montrose. Bus stop outside Visitor Centre.
Habitat: Estuary, saltmarsh, reedbeds, farmland.

Key birds: Pink-footed Goose — up to 65,000 arrive Oct. Wintering wildfowl and waders (Curlews at peak numbers in Aug, Dunlin in Feb). Breeding terns, gulls, Shelduck, Goldeneye, Eider Duck. Nationally important moulting site for Mute Swan.
Contact: Montrose Basin Wildlife Centre, 01674 676 336; e-mail: montrosebasin@swt.org.uk

Moray & Nairn

YEAR-ROUND variety is on offer here, with Lochindorb the best area of moorland to explore, with grouse, raptors, divers and waders all breeding. Roseisle Forest holds Crested Tits and opens out onto Burghead Bay which is superb in winter for seaducks, divers and grebes. Spey Bay can be explored from either side of the river and attracts passage waders, terns, Ospreys, seabirds and wildfowl.

3. CULBIN SANDS

RSPB (North Scotland Office).
Location: Sat nav: IV12 5LF. NH 900 576. Approx 1.5 miles NE of Nairn, overlooking Moray Firth. Access to parking at East Beach car park, signed off A96.
Access: Open at all times. 750m path to Minster's Pool suitable for all abilities.
Facilities: Toilets (inc disabled) and bike racks at car park. Track along dunes and saltmarsh.
Public transport: Buses stop in St Ninian's Road, Nairn, one mile W of site. Call Rapsons on 0870 608 2608 or Stagecoach on 01862 892 683. Train station in Nairn 2 miles W of reserve.
Habitat: Saltmarsh, sandflats, dunes.
Key birds: *Winter:* Flocks of Common Scoter, Long-tailed Duck, Knot, Bar-tailed Godwit, Red-breasted Merganser. Raptors including Peregrine, Merlin and Hen Harrier attracted by wader flocks. Roosting geese, Snow Bunting flocks. *Spring:* Tern flock, esp Sandwich, passage waders. *Summer:* Breeding Eider, Ringed Plover, Oystercatcher. Osprey on passage.
Other notable fauna: Dolphins in Firth. Otters sometimes seen.
Contact: RSPB North Scotland Office, 01463 715 000; e-mail:nsro@rspb.org.uk www.rspb.org.uk

4. SPEY BAY

Scottish Wildlife Trust.
Location: Sat nav: IV32 7NW. NJ 335 657. Eight miles NE of Elgin. From Elgin take A96 and B9015 to Kingston. Reserve is immediately E of village. Car parks at Kingston and Tugnet.
Access: Open all year.
Facilities: Car park, information board. Circular walk at Tugnet.
Public transport: None.
Habitat: Shingle, rivermouth and coastal habitats.
Key birds: *Summer:* Osprey, waders, wildfowl. *Winter:* Seaduck and divers offshore, esp. Long-tailed Duck, Common and Velvet Scoters, Red-throated Diver.
Other notable fauna: Otter, plus dolphin offshore.

Good range of dragonflies.
Contact: Robert Potter, SWT, The Kennels, 07920 468 568; e-mail: rpotter@swt.org.uk

NE Scotland

SCOTLAND'S only mainland gannetry is at Troup Head, while RSPB Loch of Strathbeg is the main UK arrival point for Pink-footed Geese and Whooper Swans every autumn. The Ythan Estuary is good for breeding terns, Eiders, and passage and wintering waders. The interior holds typical Highlands species, with the notable exception of Crested Tit.

5. FORVIE NNR

Scottish Natural Heritage.
Location: Sat nav: AB41 8RU (visitor centre). NK 034 289. On the Ythan Estuary, 12 miles N of Aberdeen. Waterside car park one mile N or Newburgh; visitor centre three miles N of Newburgh.
Access: Reserve open at all times but ternery closed Apr 1 to end of Aug annually. Stevenson Forvie Centre open every day (Apr-Sept) and, outside these months when staff are available. Centre, short trail and hide are wheelchair-accessible.
Facilities: Interpretive display and toilets at Stevenson Forvie Centre. Bird hide, waymarked trails. Coach parking at Waterside car park and Stevenson Forvie Centre.
Public transport: Bluebird No 263 to Cruden Bay. Ask for the Newburgh or Collieston Crossroads stop. Tel: 01224 591 381.
Habitat: Estuary, dunes, coastal heath.
Key birds: *Spring/summer:* Breeding Eider and terns. Migrant waders and seabirds offshore. *Autumn:* Pink-

footed Goose, migrant seabirds, waders and passerines inc occasional scarce species or rarity. *Winter:* Waders and wildfowl, inc Whooper Swan, Long-tailed Duck and Golden Plover.
Other notable flora and fauna: Occasional ceteceans offshore, esp in summer.
Contact: Annabel Drysdale (Reserve Manager), 01358 751 330. www.nnr-scotland.org

6. FOWLSHEUGH

RSPB.
Location: Sat nav: AB39 2TP. NO 879 808. Reserve is three miles S of Stonehaven. From A92 take minor road sign-posted Crawton. Car park justb before end of this road.
Access: Unrestricted. Not suitable for wheelchair users. Only assistance dogs allowed.
Facilities: Car park with 12 spaces, 200 yards from reserve. New stone-built viewing shelter at end of footpath. Nearest toilets in Stonehaven.
Public transport: Request bus stop (Stonehaven to Johnshaven route). Mile walk to reserve entrance.
Habitat: Sea cliffs.
Key birds: Spectacular 130,000-strong seabird colony, mainly Kittiwake and Guillemot plus Razorbill, Fulmar and Puffin. Gannet, Eider and skuas offshore, Peregrine regular throughout year. *Autumn:* Red-throated Diver on sea, terns on passage.
Other notable flora and fauna: Grey and common seals, bottle-nosed dolphin regular, white-beaked dolphin and minke whale occasional in summer. Spring flowers, common butterflies and moths.
Contact: RSPB Fowlsheugh Warden, 01346 532 017; e-mail: strathbeg@rspb.org.uk www.rspb.org.uk/fowlsheugh

7. HADDO COUNTRY PARK

Aberdeenshire Council.
Location: Sat nav: AB41 7EQ. NJ 875 345. On the A90 Aberdeen-Peterhead road. After Bridge of Don, turn on to the B999. Continue to Tarves for about 20km and pick up signs for Haddo House.
Access: Grounds open during daylight hours all year. Car park charges April to September.
Facilities: Car parks, display boards, more than 5,000m of surfaced paths, toilets open all year (inc disabled) and bird hides with wheelchair access. Coach parking.
Public transport: Bus: Aberdeen-Tarves stop 3.2km from house. Call Stagecoach on 01224 212 266.
Habitat: Parkland, woodland, wetland, loch, ponds.
Key birds: *Spring/summer:* Osprey, Sedge Warbler, Blackcap, Chiffchaff, Lapwing. *Winter:* Canada and Greylag geese, Teal, Wigeon, Goldeneye, Goosander, Brambling. *All year:* Buzzard, Sparrowhawk, Grey Partridge, Great Spotted Woodpecker, Goosander, Grey Wagtail, Tawny Owl, herons, Cormorant.
Other notable flora and fauna: Meadow brown, ringlet and common blue butterflies, burnet moths, blue damselfly. Plants include eyebright, yellow rattle, meadow cranesbill, meadowsweet, angelica, pignut,

devils' bit scabious, green alkanet, betony, rock rose, valerian, tansy and bird's foot trefoil. Fauna includes red squirrels, otters and pipistrelle and Daubenton's bats.
Contact: David Brown, Aberdeenshire Council Ranger Service, 01358 726 417.
e-mail: formartine.ranger@aberdeeshire.gov.uk

8. LOCH OF STRATHBEG

RSPB.
Location: Sat nav: AB43 8QN. NK 057 581. Britain's largest dune loch is near Crimond on the A90, nine miles S of Fraserburgh. Reserve sign-posted from village.
Access: Visitor Centre open daily 8am-6pm, dusk if earlier.
Facilities: Visitor centre, with toilets and coffee machine. New Willow Hide short walk from centre. Tower Pool hide accessible via 700 metre footpath. Two hides overlooking loch accessed via drive to airfield. Wildlife garden, indoor children's area. Long beach walks from St Combs.
Public transport: Access to whole reserve difficult without vehicle. Buses from Fraserburgh and Peterhead to Crimond, one mile from centre. Details at www.travelinescotland.com.
Habitat: Dune loch with surrounding marshes, reedbeds, grasslands and dunes.
Key birds: Breeding wetland species, passage waders, internationally important numbers of wintering wildfowl. Scarcities year round. *Winter:* Pink-footed and Barnacle Geese, Whooper Swan, large numbers of duck. Snow Goose and Smew annual. Raptors including Hen and Marsh Harriers. Great Northern Diver offshore. *Summer:* Common Tern, Water Rail, Corn Bunting. *Spring/autumn:* Spoonbill, Avocet, Marsh Harrier, Garganey, Little Gull, regular Pectoral Sandpiper, Osprey (seen almost daily), Common Crane (now annual on reserve).
Other notable flora and fauna: Otter, badger, stoat, roe deer. Early purple, butterfly and northern marsh orchids, dark green fritillary butterfly.
Contact: RSPB Loch of Strathbeg, 01346 532 017.
e-mail: strathbeg@rspb.org.uk www.rspb.org.uk

9. TROUP HEAD

RSPB (East Scotland).
Location: Sat nav: AB45 3JN. NJ 822 665. Troup Head is between Pennan and Gardenstown on B9031, E along coast from Macduff. It is signposted off B9031. Look for small RSPB signs which direct you to car park past the farm buildings.
Access: Unrestricted, not suitable for wheelchairs.
Facilities: Parking for small number of cars. Not suitable for coaches. Live pictures are beamed from the reserve to the Macduff Marine Aquarium during the summer. Boat trips run from Macduff and Banff or Gardenstown (contact North 580 01261 819 900).
Public transport: None.
Habitat: Sea cliffs, farmland.
Key birds: Spectacular seabird colony, including

Scotland's only mainland nesting Gannets. Bonxies linger in summer. Migrants occur during spring/autumn.
Other notable flora and fauna: Impressive common flower assemblage in spring. Ceteceans possible offshore in summer including minke whale. Brown hare common.
Contact: RSPB Troup Head Warden, 01346 532 017; e-mail: strathbeg@rspb.org.uk

Perth & Kinross

RSPB LOCH LEVEN (formerly known as Vane Farm) is the region's best known reserve and holds huge numbers of wintering geese, ducks and swans. Ospreys fish there too but the well-known watchpoint of Loch of the Lowes offers better views of birds on the nest than RSPB Loch Garten. The Hermitage at Dunkeld is good for woodland species, Dippers and raptors, possibly including Goshawk.

10. DOUNE PONDS

Stirling Council.
Location: Sat nav: FK16 6DY. NN 726 019. Doune lies midway between Stirling and Callander. Take A820 Dunblane road E from the junction with the A84 and first left turn into Station Wynd. Car park is second turn on the right. Argaty Red Kite feeding station two miles N from Doune.
Access: Wheelchair access to both hides though paths may be muddy. Open all year. Car parks open 9am to 5pm.
Facilities: Information board, paths, hides. Leaflet from local tourist information offices, local library. Circular walk through woodland.
Public transport: Bus: from Stirling and Callander to Doune. Traveline 0870 608 2608.
Habitat: Pools, scrape, birch and willow woodlands in former sand quarry.
Key birds: *All year:* Grey Heron, Buzzard, Snipe, Goldcrest, Siskin, Red Kite. *Spring/summer:* Common Sandpiper, Whitethroat, warblers.
Other notable flora: Red deer, red squirrel. Excellent site for fungi.
Contact: Stirling Council Ranger Service, 08452 777 000; e-mail: birdc@stirling.gov.uk
www.facebook.com/stirlingcouncilrangers

11. LOCH OF THE LOWES

Scottish Wildlife Trust.
Location: Sat nav: PH8 0ES. NO 041 435. Sixteen miles N of Perth, two miles NE of Dunkeld, just off A923 (signposted).
Access: Admission charge for non-members of SWT. Visitor centre open daily March 1 to October 31 (10am-5pm) and Fri-Sun only for rest of year (10.30am-4pm).

Observation hide open all year during daylight hours. Crannog hide accessible during visitor centre opening hours. No dogs allowed. Full access for wheelchairs.
Facilities: Visitor centre with exhibition, shop and toilets. Two hides overlooking loch.
Public transport: Railway station at Birnam and Dunkeld, three miles from reserve. Buses to Dunkeld, two miles from reserve.
Habitat: Freshwater loch fringed by areas of fen, reedbeds and semi-natural woodland.
Key birds: Breeding Ospreys (Apr-end Aug) nest 200 metres from hide. Wildfowl and woodland birds.
Other notable fauna: Red squirrels.
Contact: Caroline Hendry, (Manager), Loch of the Lowes, Visitor Centre, 01350 727 337; e-mail: lochofthelowes@swt.org.uk; www.swt.org.uk

12. VANE FARM (LOCH LEVEN)

RSPB Scotland.
Location: Sat nav: KY13 9LX. NT 160 990. Part of Loch Leven NNR. Seven miles from Cowdenbeath, signposted two miles E of junction 5 from M90 onto B9097. Drive for approx two miles. Car park on R.
Access: Reserve open at all times. Visitor centre open daily (10am-5pm) except Dec 25, 26, Jan 1 and 2. Cost £5 adults, £3 concessions, £1 children, £10 family. Free to RSPB members. Disabled access to shop, coffee shop, observation room area and toilets. Coach parking available. Free car parking.
Facilities: Shop, coffee shop and observation room with five telescopes overlooking Loch Leven and the reserve. There is a 1.25 mile hill trail through woodland and moorland. Wetland trail with three observation hides. Toilets, including disabled. binoculars can be hired from shop.
Public transport: Limited bus service (Stagecoach Fife 204) runs to the reserve from Kinross (4 miles) on Wednesdays, Saturdays and Sundays. Contact Stagecoach Fife on 01592 610 686 for further details. Eight-mile cycle path around loch.
Habitat: Wet grassland and flooded areas by Loch Leven. Arable farmland. Native woodland and heath moorland.
Key birds: *Spring/summer:* Breeding and passage waders (including Lapwing, Redshank, Snipe, Curlew), hirundines, Great Crested Grebe, Osprey. Farmland birds (including Skylark and Yellowhammer), Tree Pipit. *Autumn:* Migrating waders on exposed mud. *Winter:* Major fuelling stop for Pink-footed Geese (around 20,000 in late autmn). Also Whooper Swan (6% of Scotland's wintering population), Bewick's Swan, White-tailed Eagle, finch and tit flocks.
Other notable flora and fauna: 237 butterfly and moth species. 25 mammal species including pipstrelle bat and roe deer.
Contact: RSPB Loch Leven, 01577 862 355; e-mail: lochleven@rspb.co.uk

Highlands & Islands

Highlands Orkney, Outer Hebrides, Shetland

Highlands

HABITATS found nowhere else in Britain hold a range of scarce species: Dotterel, Ptarmigan and Snow Buntings on the tops, plus Crested Tit, the endemic Scottish Crossbill and Capercaillie are in the Caledonian pine forests. The boggy Flow Country of Caithness and Sutherland attracts breeding Greenshank, Common Scoter and Red- and Black-throated Divers.

1. BEINN EIGHE

Scottish Natural Heritage.
Location: NG 990 620. Complex mountain massif by Kinlochewe, Wester Ross, 50 miles from Inverness and 20 miles from Gairloch on A832.
Access: Reserve (UK's oldest NNR) open at all times, no charge. Visitor centre just outside Kinlochewe open Easter-Oct (9am to 5pm).
Facilities: Visitor centre, toilets, woodland, rhyming and mountain trails (self-guided with leaflets from visitor centre). Two trails suitable for all abilities.
Public transport: Very limited.
Habitat: Caledonian pine forest, dwarf shrub heath, mountain tops, freshwater loch shore.
Key birds: *All year:* Golden Eagle, Scottish Crossbill, Ptarmigan, Red Grouse, Siskin. *Summer:* Black-throated Diver, Redwing, Snow Bunting. Golden Plover breed on moorland.
Other notable flora and fauna: Wide range of dragonflies, including northern emerald, golden ringed and common hawker. Red deer, pine marten, mountain hare.
Contact: Eoghain Maclean, Reserve Manager, 01445 760 254; e-mail: eoghain.maclean@snh.gov.uk

2. CORRIMONY

RSPB (North Scotland Office).
Location: Sat nav: IV63 6TW (Corrimony village). NH 383 302. Lies 22 miles SW of Inverness between Glen Affric and Loch Ness, off A 831. Park in Corrimony Cairns car park.
Access: Open at all times. Waymarked trail suitable for wheelchairs. Unimproved paths, so terrain may not be suitable for disabled visitors.
Facilities: Way-marked trail (8.5 miles long) passes through farm. Please leave gates as you find them. Guided minibus safaris to see Black Grouse leks in April and May.
Public transport: No 17 bus from Inverness to Cannich stops 1.5 miles from reserve.
Habitat: Pine woodland, moorland, blanket bog.
Key birds: Black Grouse, Crested Tit, crossbill species, occasional Golden Eagle and Osprey. Breeding Greenshank, Red Grouse, Black-throated Diver. *Autumn:* Whooper Swan, Pinkfooted Goose, Woodcock.

Other notable flora and fauna: Red deer, pine marten. Many orchids in July.
Contact: RSPB North Scotland Office, 01463 715 000; e-mail: nsro@rspb.org.uk

3. FORSINARD FLOWS

RSPB (North Scotland Region).
Location: NC 891 425. 30 miles SW of Thurso on A897. From S turn off at Helmsdale (24 miles) or from N coast road (A836) turn 2 miles E of Melvich (14 miles).
Access: Open at all times. Contact reserve office during breeding season (mid-Apr to end Jul) and during deerstalking season (Jul 1 to Feb 15) for advice. Families welcome. Two self-guided trails open all year, disabled viewpoint accessed via farm track on Forsinain Trail. No dogs.
Facilities: Visitor centre situated in Forsinaid station open Apr 1 to Oct 31 (9am-5.30pm, seven days a week). Hen Harrier nest CCTV. Wheelchair access to centre and toilet. Guided walks Tue and Thu afternoon, May-Aug. Accommodation available locally. Viewpoint on Lochan Trail (not wheelchair accessible).
Public transport: Train from Inverness and Thurso (08457 484 950).
Habitat: Blanket bog, upland hill farm.
Key birds: The best time to visit for birds is May-July. Join a guided walk for the best chance of views of Red-throated Diver, Golden Plover, Greenshank, Dunlin, Hen Harrier, Merlin, Short-eared Owl, Dipper. Few birds between Sept-Feb apart from Red Grouse, Golden Eagle, Raven and Buzzard.

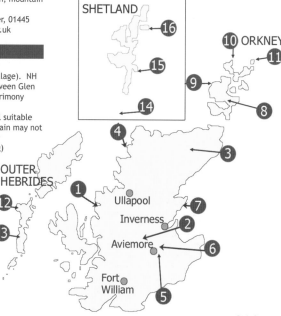

219

Other notable fauna: Red deer, otter, azure hawker dragonfly, emperor moth, bog plants including sundews.
Contact: RSPB, Forsinard Flows Reserve, 01641 571 225; e-mail: forsinard@rspb.org.uk; www.rspb.org.uk

4. HANDA

Scottish Wildlife Trust.
Location: NC 138 480. Island accessible by boat from Tarbet, near Scourie – follow A894 N from Ullapool for 40 miles. Continue another three miles, turn L down single track road another three miles to Tarbet.
Access: Open April-Sept. Boats leave 9.30am-2pm (last boat back 5pm). Dogs not allowed. Visitors are asked for a contribution of £2 towards costs. Not suitable for disabled due to uneven terrain.
Facilities: Three mile circular path, shelter (no toilets on island – use those in Tarbet car park). Visitors are given introductory talk and a leaflet with map on arrival.
Public transport: Post bus to Scourie (tel 01549 402 357 Lairg Post Office). Train to Lairg (tel 0845 484 950 National Train enquiries). No connecting public transport between Scourie and Tarbet.
Habitat: Sea cliffs, blanket bog.
Key birds: *Spring/summer:* Biggest Guillemot and Razorbill colony in Britain and Ireland. Also nationally important for Kittiwake, Arctic and Great Skuas. Puffin, Shag, Fulmar and Common and Arctic Terns also present.
Contact: Handa Ranger, 07920 468 572; e-mail: handaranger@swt.org.uk
Ferry operators – Roger (07780 967 800) or Paul (07775 625 890).

5. INSH MARSHES

RSPB (North Scotland Office).
Location: Sat nav: PH21 1NS. NN 775 998. In Spey Valley. From A9 take exit to Kingussie. Follow B970 S from village and then beyond Ruthven Barracks. Entrance to reserve is 1km further on.
Access: Open at all times. Disabled access to the information viewpoint. Coach parking available at car park.
Facilities: Unmanned information viewpoint, two hides, three nature trails. Access for disabled to Information Viewpoint only. No toilets.
Public transport: Nearest rail station and bus stop at Kingussie (one mile).
Habitat: Marshes, woodland, river, open water.
Key birds: *Spring/summer:* Waders (Lapwing, Curlew, Redshank, Snipe), wildfowl (including Goldeneye and Wigeon), Osprey, Wood Warbler, Redstart, Tree Pipit. *Winter:* Hen Harrier, Whooper Swan, Greylag Goose, Teal, Wigeon, other wildfowl.
Other notable flora and fauna: Black darter dragonflies along Invertromie trail plus northern brown argus butterflies. Five species of orchid in Tromie Meadow. Roe deer.
Contact: Pete Moore, 01540 661 518; e-mail: pete.moore@rspb.org.uk; www.visitkincraig.com

6. LOCH GARTEN-ABERNETHY FOREST

RSPB (North Scotland Office).
Location: Sat nav: PH25 3HA. NH 978 183. 2.5 miles from Boat of Garten, eight miles from Aviemore. Off B970, follow 'RSPB Ospreys' road signs (between April 1- Aug 31 only).
Access: Osprey Centre open daily 10am-6pm (Apr to end Aug). Disabled access. Guide dogs only. RSPB members free. Non-members: adults £4, senior citizens £2.50, children £1.00. Family ticket £8 (up to 2 adults and four children).
Facilities: Osprey Centre overlooking nesting Ospreys, toilets, optics and CCTV live pictures, shop, toilets. Three way-marked trails.
Public transport: Bus service to Boat of Garten from Aviemore, 2.5 mile footpath to Osprey Centre. Steam railway to Boat of Garten from Aviemore.
Habitat: Caledonian pine wood.
Key birds: *Spring/summer:* Ospreys nesting from Apr to Aug, Crested Tit, Redstart, Spotted Flycatcher, Tree Pipit, crossbills. Possible views of lekking Capercaillies from the Osprey Centre, Apr to mid-May. *Autumn:* Pinkfeet and Greylag Geese roost on loch, Whooper Swan and various duck species.
Other notable flora and fauna: Red squirrel, roe deer, otter, woodland plants and fungi.
Contact: The Warden, 01479 831 476; e-mail: abernethy@rspb.co.uk

7. UDALE BAY

RSPB (North Scotland Office).
Location: Sat nav: IV7 8LU. NH 712 651. On the Black Isle, one mile W of Jemimaville on the B9163.
Access: Open all year. View wader roost from lay-by. Nearest adapted unisex toilet in Allen Street, Cromarty (one mile away).
Facilities: Hide, lay-by. No coach parking.
Public transport: No 26 bus stops in Jemimaville six times a day (approx 5 min walk). contact Rapsons, 0870 608 2608 or Stagecoach on 01862 892 683.
Habitat: Mudflat, saltmarsh and wet grassland.
Key birds: *Spring/summer:* 10,000 Pinkfeet on passage each year, other wildfowl, Oystercatcher, Redshank, waders. Possible Osprey. *Autumn/winter:* Large flocks of wildfowl (approx 10,000 Wigeon), geese, waders.
Contact: RSPB North Scotland Office, 01463 715 000; e-mail: nsro@rspb.org.uk

Orkney

A LACK of managed grouse moors means that Hen Harriers breed here in excellent numbers. Other scarce breeders include Whimbrels, Great and Arctic Skuas and Red-throated Divers. There are excellent seabird colonies such as the one at Marwick Head. North Ronaldsay attracts good numbers of migrants.

8. HOBBISTER

RSPB (East Scotland).
Location: Sat nav: KW17 2RA. HY 396 070 or HY 381 068. Overlooking Scarpa Flow W of Kirkwall on A964.
Access: Open access between A964 and the sea. Dogs

on leads please.
Facilities: A council-maintained footpath to Waulkmill Bay, two car parks. New circular walk from RSPB car park along cliff top and Scapa Flow.
Public transport: Stagecoach 01856 878 014.
Habitat: Orkney moorland, bog, fen, saltmarsh, coastal cliffs, scrub.
Key birds: *Summer:* Breeding Hen Harrier, Merlin, Short-eared Owl, Red Grouse, Red-throated Diver, Eider, Red-breasted Merganser, Black Guillemot. Wildfowl and waders at Waulkmill Bay. *Autumn/winter:* Waulkmill for sea ducks, divers, auks and grebes (Long-tailed Duck, Red-throated, Black-throated and Great Northern Divers, Slavonian Grebe).
Other notable fauna: Otter occasionally seen from Scapa trail. Grey and common seal both possible from footpath looking towards Scapa Flow.
Contact: The Warden, 01856 850 176;
e-mail: orkney@rspb.org.uk; www.rspb.co.uk

9. MARWICK HEAD

RSPB (East Scotland).
Location: Sat nav: KW17 2NB. HY 229 240. Orkney's largest cliffside seabird colony lies 4 miles N of Skara Brae on W coast of mainland Orkney, near Dounby. Path N from Marwick Bay, or from council car park at Cumlaquoy at HY 232 252 (best for Kitchener Memorial).
Access: Open all year. Rough terrain not suitable for wheelchairs.
Facilities: Cliff top path.
Public transport: OCTO bus (tel: 01856 871 536) operates a 'by request' service to all parts of the west mainland of Orkney.
Habitat: Rocky bay, sandstone cliffs.
Key birds: May-July best for up to 25,000 seabirds. Huge numbers of Kittiwakes and auks, inc. Puffins, also nesting Fulmar, Rock Dove, Raven, Rock Pipit, Short-eared owl.
Other notable fauna: Cetaceans are a possibility from Marwick with porpoise and minke whale occasionally seen. Beach path good place for great yellow bumblebee in Aug.
Contact: The Warden 01856 850 176; e-mail: orkney@rspb.org.uk; www.rspb.co.uk

10. NORTH HILL, PAPA WESTRAY

RSPB (East Scotland).
Location: Sat nav: KW17 2BU. HY 495 538. From pier or airfield travel N along main road. From shop/hostel, take road to the junction at Holland Farm and turn R onto main road. Continue past Rose Cottage to reserve entrance.
Access: Access at all times. During breeding season report to summer warden at Rose Cottage, 650 yards S of reserve entrance (01857 644 240) or use trail guide.
Facilities: Nature trails, hide/info hut. Limited parking. Not suitable for wheelchairs or pushchairs.
Public transport: Orkney Ferries (01856 872 044), Loganair (01856 872 494).
Habitat: Sea cliffs, maritime heath.
Key birds: *Summer:* Close views of colony of Puffin, Guillemot, Razorbill and Kittiwake. Black Guillemot

nest under flagstones around reserve's coastline. One of UK's largest colonies of Arctic Tern, also Arctic Skua.
Other notable flora and fauna: One of the best areas to see Scottish primrose (*primula scotica*), with two flowering periods that just overlap (May-Aug).
Contact: The Warden at Rose Cottage, Papay Westray DW17 2BU. 01857 644 240 (Apr-Aug only); e-mail: orkney@rspb.org.uk; www.rspb.co.uk

11. NORTH RONALDSAY BIRD OBSERVATORY

Location: Sat nav: KW17 2BE. HY 64 52. 35 miles from Kirkwall, Orkney mainland.
Access: Open all year except Christmas.
Facilities: Three star guest house and hostel accommodation, restaurant, cafe, fully licenced, croft walk.
Public transport: Daily subsidised Loganair flights from Kirkwall from Mainland Orkney to North Ronaldsay. 15 minute flight gives stunning views of several islands. See Loganair website (www.loganair. co.uk/reservations/) for full information.
Habitat: Crofting island with a number of eutrophic and oligotrophic wetlands. Coastline has both sandy bays and rocky shore. Walled gardens concentrate passerines.
Key birds: *Spring/autumn:* Prime migration site including regular BBRC species. Wide variety of breeding seabirds, wildfowl and waders. *Winter:* Waders and wildfowl include Whooper Swan and hard weather movements occur.
Contact: Alison Duncan, North Ronaldsay Bird Observatory, 01857 633 200;
e-mail: alison@nrbo.prestel.co.uk; www.nrbo.co.uk

Outer Hebrides

THESE ISLANDS are the Corncrake stronghold of Britain, though having large numbers of birds doesn't make them any easier to see! There is a strong passage of Long-tailed and Pomarine Skuas past RSPB Balranald in May. The area's ability to attract rare migrants is only just being discovered with recent autumnal trips to Barra turning up trumps.

12. BALRANALD

RSPB (North Scotland Office).
Location: Sat nav: HS6 5DL. NF 705 707. On W coast of North Uist. From Skye take ferry to Lochmaddy, North Uist. Drive W on A865 for 20 miles to reserve. Turn off main road three miles NW of Bayhead at signpost to Houghharry.
Access: Reserve open at all times, no charge. Visitor centre open April to August (9am to 6pm). Dogs on leads. Circular walk not suitable for wheelchairs.
Facilities: Visitor Centre and toilets (disabled access). Marked circular nature trail (three miles). Group bookings welcome.
Public transport: Post bus service (01876 560 244).
Habitat: Freshwater loch, machair, coast and crofts.
Key birds: *Spring:* Skuas and divers at sea, Purple

Sandpiper and other waders on shore. Dotterel. *Summer*: Corncrake, Corn Bunting, Lapwing, Oystercatcher, Dunlin, Ringed Plover, Redshank, Snipe, terns. *Autumn*: Hen Harrier, Peregrine, Greylag Goose. *Winter*: Twite, Snow Bunting, Whooper Swan, Greylag Goose, Wigeon, Teal, Shoveler, sightings of Golden and White-tailed Eagles becoming commoner. *Passage*: Barnacle Goose, Pomarine Skua, Long-tailed Skua. **Other notable flora:** Blanket bog and machair plants reach their peak in July.
Contact: The Warden, 01463 715 000; e-mail: nsro@rspb.org.uk; www.rspb.org.uk

13. LOCH DRUIDIBEG NNR

SNH (Western Isles Area).
Location: Sat nav: HS8 5RS. NF 782 378. Lies just N of Kildonan on South Uist. Turn off A865 in Stillgarry at B890 road for Loch Sgioport. Track is 1.5 miles further on — park at side of road.
Access: Open all year. Several tracks and one walk covering a range of habitats — most not suitable for wheelchairs. Stout footwear essential. Observe Scottish Outdoor Access Code in all areas with livestock. View E part of reserve from public roads but parking and turning areas for coaches is limited.
Facilities: None.
Public transport: Bus stops at reserve. Hebridean Coaches 01870 620 345, MacDonald Coaches 01870 620 288.
Habitat: Covering 1,677ha, the NNR contains freshwater lochs, marshes, machair, coast and moorland.
Key birds: *Summer*: Breeding waders, Corncrake, Black-throated Diver, Greylag Goose, wildfowl, terns and raptors. *Spring autumn*: Migrant waders and wildfowl. *Winter*: Waders, wildfowl and raptors including Golden Eagle and Hen Harrier.
Contact: SNH Area Officer, 01870 620 238; e-mail: western.isles@snh.gov.uk

Shetland

BRITAIN'S most northerly archipelago is always going to attract large numbers of vagrants, with the observatory on Fair Isle boasting a phenomenal list of species. Seabird colonies here are spectacular and include such unusual species as Leach's Petrels; an overnight stay on Mousa is the best way to catch up with this largely nocturnal species.

14. FAIR ISLE BIRD OBSERVATORY

Fair Isle Bird Observatory.
Location: HZ 2172. Famous island for rarities located SE of mainland Shetland. Regular flights to Sumburgh, Shetland. Daily Direct Flight plane between Tingwell (near Lerwick) and Fair Isle. Enquiries: 01595 840 246. Good Shepherd ferry between Shetland and Fair Isle travels on Tues, Thurs and Sat. 01595 760 363.
Access: Open from end Apr-end Oct. No access restrictions.
Facilities: Public toilets at airstrip and Stackhoull Stores (shop). Accommodation at Fair Isle Bird

Observatory includes one room with wheelchair access (phone/e-mail for brochure/details). Guests can join in observatory work and see birds in the hand. Slide shows, guided walks through Ranger Service.
Public transport: Tue, Thurs, Sat — ferry (12 passengers) from Grutness, Shetland. Tel: Neil or Pat Thomson on 01595 760 363. Mon, Wed, Fri, Sat — air (7 seater) from Tingwall, Shetland. Tel: Direct Flight 01595 840 246.
Habitat: Heather moor and lowland pasture/crofting land.
Key birds: Large breeding seabird colonies (auks, Gannet, Arctic Tern, Kittiwake, Shag, Arctic Skua and Great Skua). Many common and rare migrants Apr/May/early Jun, late Aug-Nov.
Other notable flora and fauna: Northern marsh, heath spotted and frog orchid, lesser twayblade, small adders tongue, oyster plant. Orca, minke whale, white-backed, white-sided and Risso's dolphins. Endemic field mouse.
Contact: Fair Isle Bird Obs, 01595 760 258; e-mail: fibo@btconnect.com; www.fairislebirdobs.co.uk

15. FETLAR

RSPB Scotland.
Location: HU 603 917. Small island lying E of Yell. Take car ferry from Gutcher on Yell to Hamarsness, then drive 6 miles E. Ferry booking advised (01957 722 259).
Access: Apart from the footpath to Hjaltadance circle, Vord Hill, the Special Protection Area is closed mid May to end July. Entry during this period is only by arrangement with warden. Rest of site open at all times. Loch of Funzie can be observed from road.
Facilities: Hide at Mires of Funzie open Apr-Nov. Toilets and payphone at ferry terminal, interpretive centre at Houbie, campsite, shop.
Public transport: None.
Habitat: Serpentine heath, rough hill lane, upland mire.
Key birds: *Summer*: Breeding Red-throated Diver, Eider, Shag, Whimbrel, Golden Plover, Dunlin, Arctic and Great Skuas, Manx Shearwater, Storm Petrel. Red-necked Phalarope on Loch of Funzie (HU 655 899) viewed from road or RSPB hide overlooking Mires of Funzie.
Other notable flora and fauna: Heath spotted orchid and autumn gentian. Otters are common, harbour and grey seals breed.
Contact: RSPB North Isles Warden, 01957 733 246; e-mail: fetlar@rspb.org.uk

16. NOSS NNR

Scottish Natural Heritage (Shetland Office).
Location: HU 531 410. Take car ferry to Bressay from Lerwick and follow signs for Noss (5km). At end of road walk to shore (600 mtrs) where inflatable ferry (passenger only) to island will collect you. If red flag is flying, island is closed due to sea conditions. Information updated daily in season on 0800 107 7818.
Access: Open Tue, Wed, Fri, Sat, Sun (10am-5pm) between late Apr-late Aug. Access by zodiac inflatable.

No dogs on ferry. Steep rough track down to ferry. Commercial boat trips around island — call tourist office on 01595 693 434.
Facilities: Visitor centre, toilets. Bike rack/car park on Bressay side. Parking for small coaches.
Habitat: Dune and coastal grassland, moorland, heath, blanket bog, sea cliffs.
Key birds: *Spring/summer:* Breeding Fulmar, Shag,

Gannet, Arctic Tern, Kittiwake, Herring and Great Black-backed Gull, Great Skua, Arctic Skua, Guillemot, Razorbill, Puffin, Black Guillemot, Eider, Lapwing, Dunlin, Snipe, Wheatear, Twite plus migrant birds.
Other notable fauna: Grey and common seals, otter, porpoise regularly seen, killer whales annual.
Contact: Glen Tyler, SNH, 01595 693 345; e-mail:noss_nnr@snh.gov.uk www.nnr-scotland.org

Eastern Wales

Breconshire, Montgomeryshire, Radnorshire

POWYS, formed from the old counties of Breconshire, Radnorshire and Montgomeryshire, is a largely upland rural area with a limited but interesting community of birds. Raptors are prominent, with Hen Harrier, Merlin, Red Kite and Peregrine all well established, while Cors Dyfi reserve became the site for Wales' first Osprey breeding of the current era.

1. BRECHFA POOL

Brecknock Wildlife Trust.
Location: Sat nav: LD3 0NL (Llyswen). SO 118 377. Travelling NE from Brecon look for lane off A470, 1.5 miles SW of Llyswen; on Brechfa Common, pool is on R after cattle grid.
Access: Open dawn to dusk. Road runs around three-quarters of pool, giving good access.
Facilities: None.
Public transport: None.
Habitat: Marshy grassland, large shallow lake located at a height of 900ft.
Key birds: Good numbers of wintering wildfowl are replaced by breeding gulls and commoner waterfowl. Species recorded inc Teal, Gadwall, Tufted Duck, Shoveler, Wigeon, Little Grebe, Black-headed Gull, Lapwing, Dunlin, Redshank, Kestrel.
Other notable flora: Rare pillwort around pond margins, crowfoot, penny royal and orange foxtail.
Contact: Trust HQ, 01874 625 708;
e-mail: enquiries@brecknockwildlifetrust.org.uk
www.brecknockwildlifetrust.org.uk

2. CORS DYFI NATURE RESERVE

Montgomeryshire Wildlife Trust.
Location: Sat nav: SY20 8SR. SN701 985. Lies 3.5 miles SW of Machynlleth on the A487 Abersytwyth road. Approx 2.5 miles S of Derwenlas, turn right after caravan park. Head
Access: Open 10am to 6pm between April and Sept and at weekends for rest of year. Programme of special events in winter. Donations welcome to help fund reserve and the Dyfi Osprey Project. Site is wheelchair-accessible apart from elevated bird hide.
Facilities: Visitor centre, small café, elevated hide and toilets (inc disabled). Extensive boardwalk. £1.37

million 360 degree observatory opened in 2013.
Public transport: Nearest bus stop at Llyfnant Valley Bridge is half-mile from reserve.
Habitat: Bog, wet woodland and scrub.
Key birds: Site sprang to national prominence in 2011 when Ospreys bred successfully. *Spring/summer:* Nightjar, Grasshopper, Sedge and Reed Warblers, Snipe, Stonechat, Reed Bunting.
Other notable flora and fauna: Common lizard, four-spotted chaser dragonfly.
Contact: Trust HQ 01938 555 654;
e-mail: janine@montwt.co.uk (for Osprey enquiries).

3. ELAN VALLEY

Dwr Cymru /Welsh Water.
Location: Sat nav: LD6 5HP. SN 928 646 (visitor centre). Three miles SW of Rhayader, off B4518.
Access: Mostly open access. Pay-and-display car park with Blue Badge spaces.
Facilities: Visitor centre, cafe and toilets (open every day except Christmas Day). 10am-5.30pm (1st Mar-31st Oct), 10am-4pm (1st Nov-28th Feb). Nature trails all year and hide at SN 905 617.
Public transport: None.
Habitat: 45,000 acres of moorland, woodland, river and reservoir.
Key birds: *Spring/summer:* Upland birds including Golden Plover and Dunlin. Red Kite, Buzzard, Sparrowhawk, Peregrine, Raven, Green Woodpecker, Grey Wagtail and Marsh Tit are joined in the summer by Pied Flycatcher, Spotted Flycatcher, Wood Warbler, Redstart, Tree Pipit and Cuckoo. *Autumn/winter:* Fieldfare, Redwing, Ring Ouzel, woodpeckers and woodland species.
Other notable flora and fauna: Internationally important oak woodlands. More than 3,000 species of flora and fauna recorded.
Contact: Rangers office, 01597 810 880.
www.elanvalley.org.uk

4. GIGRIN FARM

Location: Sat nav: LD6 5BL. Farm lies half a mile south of Rhayader, Powys off A470.
Access: Open for kite feeding sessions from 1pm each day, except Dec 25. Feeding at 2pm (winter) and

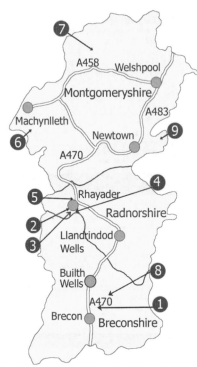

at Marteg Bridge, three miles N of Rhayader.
Access: Open every day, all year. Disabled access possible to centre, toilets and purpose-built trail. Full programme of activities – check website for details.
Facilities: Visitor centre usually open during summer holidays and some weekends, but this depends on availability of volunteers. Nestboxes fitted with cameras, plus pre-recorded footage of badgers and other mammals. Circular nature trail, short easy-access trail. Wye Valley Walk and Gwastedyn Church Trail also pass through reserve.
Public transport: None.
Habitat: Working organic hill farm covering 410 acres, river, oak woods, meadows, hill-land.
Key birds: Of 73 species recorded, 55 breed regularly. These include Common Sandpiper, Dipper, Grey Wagtail, Pied and Spotted Flycatchers, Redstart, Wood Warbler, Tree Pipit, Whinchat, Stonechat, Linnet, Yellowhammer, Siskin, Redpoll, Marsh and Willow Tit, Stock Dove, Wheatear, Barn Owl, Raven. Other visitors include: Curlew, Merlin, Red Kite, Goshawk, Sparrowhawk, Peregrine, Goosander, Kingfisher, Reed Bunting.
Other notable flora and fauna: Green hairstreak, wall brown and ringlet butterflies, mountain pansy, bloody-nosed beetle. Welsh clearwing moth first record for Radnorshire.
Contact: Reserve manager, 01597 870 301.
e-mail: info@rwtwales.org
www.radnorshirewildlifetrust.org.uk

6. LAKE VYRNWY
RSPB Mid-Wales Office.
Location: SJ 020 193. Located WSW of Oswestry. Nearest village is Llanfyllin on A490. Take B4393 to Llanwddyn and at dam, turn left and left again.
Access: Reserve open all year. Severn Trent's visitor centre open Apr-Oct (10.30am-5pm), Nov-March (10.30am-4pm).
Facilities: Toilets, visitor centre, five colour-coded nature trails, coffee shop, RSPB shop (open 10am to 5pm April to Oct, 4pm rest of year), craft workshops. Three bird hides, one accessible to wheelchair users.
Public transport: Infrequent bus service to dam.
Habitat: Heather moorland, woodland, meadows, rocky streams and large reservoir.
Key birds: *All year:* Siskin, Great Spotted Woodpecker, Buzzard, Raven. *Spring/summer:* Hen Harrier, Curlew, Cuckoo, Whinchat, Dipper, Kingfisher, Pied Flycatcher, Wood Warbler, Redstart, hirundines, Peregrine and Hobby.
Other notable flora and fauna: Mammals include otter, polecat, brown hare. Golden-ringed dragonflies frequent in summer.
Contact: Centre Manager, 1691 870 278; e-mail: vyrnwy@rspb.org.uk

3pm (summer). No booking required. See website for admission charges. Dogs on leads welcome.
Facilities: Red Kite Shop, five hides (three with disabled access), plus specialist photography hides.
Habitat: 200-acre upland sheep farm rising to 1,200 feet above sea level.
Details: Brilliant views of Red Kites. For the past 19 years, Gigrin has been the official Red Kite feeding station for Wales, helping young birds survive in winter. By attracting large numbers of birdwatchers it relieves pressure on other nest sites in summer.
Key birds: Daily feeds attract a wide range of species including Carrion Crow, Raven, Jackdaw, Buzzard and Red Kite. Kite numbers vary from a few dozen to around 400 when weather is bad. Other feeding stations attract smaller birds such as Brambling, Yellowhammer and Siskin. A 1.5ml trail links to the RSPB Dyffryn reserve while a wetland area attracts wild ducks, Grey Heron and wagtails.
Contact: Chris Powell, Gigrin Farm, South Street, Rhayader, Powys LD6 5BL. 01597 810 243; www.gigrinfarm.co.uk

5. GILFACH FARM RESERVE
Radnorshire Wildlife Trust.
Location: Sat nav: LD6 5LF (visitor centre). SN 965 717. Gilfach is just off the A470, seven miles from Llangurig. Follow the brown Nature Reserve signs. The Visitor Centre is one mile across the Reserve. Parking

7. PWLL-Y-WRACH
Brecknock Wildlife Trust.
Location: Sat nav: LD3 0DS (Talgarth). SO 165 326. From Talgarth town centre cross over River Enig, then take Bell Street and Hospital Road. After 1.5 miles, reserve is on the right.

Access: Reserve open all year. Please keep to footpaths. Level wheelchair-friendly path runs half way into site. Elsewhere, paths can be muddy and there are steps in places. Dogs on leads.
Facilities: Information panel in car park.
Public transport: No local services.
Habitat: 17.5 hectares of ancient woodland, river and spectacular Witches Pool waterfall.
Key birds: Large variety of resident woodland birds, with migrant boost in spring. Dipper, Kingfisher, Pied Wagtail, Great Spotted Woodpecker, Chiffchaff, Wood Warbler, Pied Flycatcher, Mistle and Song Thrushes, Nuthatch.
Other notable flora and fauna: Otter, dormouse, bats, common lizard. Early purple and birds' nest orchids, herb paris, bluebell, wood anenome.
Contact: Brecknock Wildlife Trust, 01874 625 708; e-mail: enquiries@brecknockwildlifetrust.org.uk www.brecknockwildlifetrust.org.uk

8. ROUNDTON HILL NNR

Montgomeryshire Wildlife Trust.
Location: Sat nav: SY15 6EL. SO 293 947. SE of Montgomery. Follow brown duck signs from Churchstoke on A489, taking minor road towards Old Churchstoke. After one mile turn R at phone box, then first R.
Access: Open access. Tracks rough in places. Dogs on lead at all times. Uneven tracks not suitable for wheelchairs.
Facilities: Car park. Waymarked trails.
Public transport: Buses to Old Churchstoke, 600 metres from reserve.
Habitat: Ancient hill grassland, woodland, streamside wet flushes, scree, rock outcrops.
Key birds: *All year:* Buzzard, Red Kite, Raven, all three woodpeckers, Tawny Owl, Linnet, Goldfinch. *Spring/summer:* Wheatear, Redstart, Whitethroat.
Contact: Trust HQ, 01938 555 654; www.montwt.co.uk

Northern Wales

Anglesey, Caernarfonshire, Denbighshire, Flintshire, Merioneth

HIGHLIGHTS on Anglesey include a seabird colony and Choughs at South Stack, terns at Cemlyn Bay and waders at Malltraeth. RSPB Valley Lakes, Newborough Warren and Llyn Alaw are all worth exploring too, while Conwy is one of the RSPB's flagship reserves. Smaller inland sites offer a good range of birds.

1. BARDSEY BIRD OBSERVATORY

Bardsey Bird Observatory.
Location: SH 11 21. Private 444 acre island. Twenty minute boat journey from Aberdaron 15 miles SW of Pwllheli.
Access: Open Mar-Nov. No dogs. Visitor accommodation in 150-year-old farmhouse (two single, two double, two x four bed dorm). To stay at the Observatory contact Alicia Normand (tel 01626 773 908; e-mail; stay@bbfo.org.uk). Day visitors by Bardsey Ferries (07971 760 895).
Facilities: Public toilets available for day visitors. Three hides, one on small bay, two seawatching. Gift shops and payphone.
Public transport: Trains from Birmingham to Pwllheli. Tel: 0345 484 950. Arriva bus from Bangor to Pwllheli. Tel: 0870 6082 608.
Habitat: Sea-birds cliffs viewable from boat only. Farm and scrubland, Spruce plantation, willow copses and gorse-covered hillside.
Key birds: *All year:* Chough, Peregrine. *Spring/ summer:* Night walks to see Manx Shearwaters (16,000 pairs). other seabirds. Migrant warblers, chats, Redstart, thrushes. *Autumn:* Masses of common migrants, plus many rarities (in past: Eye-browed

Thrush, Lanceolated Warbler, American Robin, Yellowthroat, Summer Tanager).
Other notable flora: Autumn ladies' tresses.
Contact: Steven Stansfield, 07855 264 151; e-mail: info@bbfo.org.uk; www.bbfo.org.uk

2. CEMLYN

North Wales Wildlife Trust.
Location: SH 332 936. Cemlyn on north coast of Anglesey is signposted from Tregele on A5025 between Valley and Amlwch.
Access: Open all year. Dogs on leads. No wheelchair access. During summer months walk on seaward side of ridge and follow signs.
Facilities: Car parks at either end of reserve.
Public transport: None within a mile.
Habitat: Brackish lagoon, shingle ridge, salt marsh, mixed scrub.
Key birds: Wintering wildfowl and waders, breeding terns, gulls and warblers, pipits and passing migrants. *Spring:* Wheatear, Whitethroat, Sedge Warbler, Manx Shearwater, Whimbrel, Dunlin, Knot and Black-tailed Godwit. *Summer:* Breeding Arctic, Common and Sandwich Terns, Black-headed Gull, Oystercatcher and Ringed Plover. *Autumn:* Golden Plover, Lapwing, Curlew, Manx Shearwater, Gannet, Kittiwake, Guillemot. *Winter:* Little and Great Crested Grebes, Shoveler, Shelduck, Wigeon, Red-breasted Merganser, Coot, Turnstone, Purple Sandpiper.
Other notable flora and fauna: 20 species of butterfly recorded. Sea kale, yellow horned poppy, sea purslane, sea beet, glasswort. Grey seal, harbour porpoise, bottlenose dolphin.

NATURE RESERVES - NORTHERN WALES

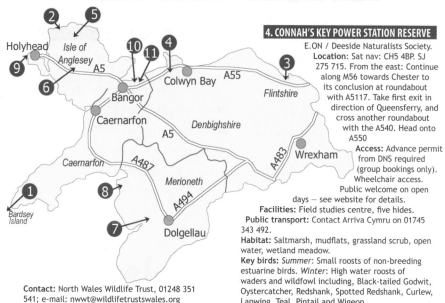

4. CONNAH'S KEY POWER STATION RESERVE

E.ON / Deeside Naturalists Society.
Location: Sat nav: CH5 4BP. SJ 275 715. From the east: Continue along M56 towards Chester to its conclusion at roundabout with A5117. Take first exit in direction of Queensferry, and cross another roundabout with the A540. Head onto A550
Access: Advance permit from DNS required (group bookings only). Wheelchair access. Public welcome on open days — see website for details.
Facilities: Field studies centre, five hides.
Public transport: Contact Arriva Cymru on 01745 343 492.
Habitat: Saltmarsh, mudflats, grassland scrub, open water, wetland meadow.
Key birds: *Summer:* Small roosts of non-breeding estuarine birds. *Winter:* High water roosts of waders and wildfowl including, Black-tailed Godwit, Oystercatcher, Redshank, Spotted Redshank, Curlew, Lapwing, Teal, Pintail and Wigeon.
Other notable fauna: Seventeen species of butterfly.
Contact: Pauline Moulton, Secretary, 01244 313 404; e-mail: secretary@deesidenaturalists.org.uk www.deesidenaturalists.org.uk

5. CONWY

RSPB (North Wales Office).
Location: Sat nav: LL31 9XZ. SH 797 773. On E bank of Conwy Estuary. Access from A55 at exit 18 signed to Conwy and Deganwy. Footpath and cycleway accessed from Conway Cob.
Access: Open daily (9.30am-5pm). Closed for Christmas Day. Ample parking for coaches. Toilets, buildings and trails accessible to pushchairs and wheelchairs.
Facilities: Visitor centre, gift shop, coffee shop, toilets including disabled. Three hides (accessible to wheelchairs) and three viewing screens. Three trails firm and level, though a little rough in places and wet in winter.
Public transport: Train service to Llandudno Junction, 10 minute walk. Bus service to Tesco supermarket, Llandudno Junction 5 minutes walk. 0871 200 2233.
Habitat: Lagoons, islands, reedbed, scrub, estuary.
Key birds: Wildfowl and waders in winter, warblers and wetland breeding birds in summer. *Spring:* Passage waders, hirundines and wagtails. *Summer:* Lapwing, waterbirds and warblers. *Autumn:* Black-tailed Godwit and other passage waders. *Winter:* Kingfisher, Goldeneye, Water Rail, Red-breasted Merganser, wildfowl, huge Starling roost.
Other notable flora and fauna: Common butterflies through summer, especially common blues. Great display of cowslips in March, bee orchids in summer. Otters seen early mornings.

Contact: North Wales Wildlife Trust, 01248 351 541; e-mail: nwwt@wildlifetrustswales.org www.northwaleswildlifetrust.org.uk

3. COED GARTH GELL

RSPB (North Wales Office).
Location: Sat nav: LL40 2TU (village of Taicynhaeaf). SH 683 192. Adjacent to main Dolgellau-to-Barmouth road (A496) near Taicynhaeaf. Use lay-bys close to the reserve's entrances. Nearby Arthog Bog (SH 630 138) is off Dolgellau-to-Tywyn road (A493) west of Arthog. Park at Morfa Mawddach station.
Access: Nature trails are open at all times. Dogs on leads.
Facilities: Nature trails at both sites in Mawddach Valley, plus information boards.
Public transport: Nearest bus stop is Taicynhaeaf on Dolgellau to Barmouth X94 route. Half mile walk to Coed Garth Gell.
Habitat: Oak woodland, bracken and heathland at Coed Garth Gell. Willow and alder scrub and raised bog at Arthog Bog.
Key birds: *At Coed Garth Gell:* Buzzard, Sparrowhawk, Peregrine, Raven, Lesser Spotted Woodpecker, Grey Wagtail, Dipper and Hawfinch are joined in the summer by Pied Flycatcher, Spotted Flycatcher, Wood Warbler, Redstart, Tree Pipit and Cuckoo. *At Arthog Bog:* Buzzard, Sparrowhawk, Peregrine, Raven are resident. Summer migrants include Tree Pipit, Grasshopper Warbler and Cuckoo. In winter flocks of Redpoll and Siskin are common and Red-breasted Merganser, Pintail and Little Egret are on the nearby estuary.
Other notable flora and fauna: Coed Garth Gell has Tunbridge filmy and beech ferns and a wide variety of butterflies. Golden-ringed dragonflies are regular.
Contact: Coed Garth Gell Reserve, 01654 700 222; e-mail: mawddach@rspb.org.uk

226

NATURE RESERVES - NORTHERN WALES

Contact: Conwy RSPB Nature Reserve, 01492 584 091;
e-mail: conwy@rspb.org.uk www.rspb.org.uk/conwy

6. LLYN ALAW

Welsh Water/United Utilities.
Location: SH 390 865. North Anglesey, SW of Amlwch.
Signposted from J5 of A55 along B5112. Main car park
at SH 375 856.
Access: Open all year. No dogs to hides or sanctuary
area but dogs allowed (maximum two per adult) in
other areas. Limited wheelchair access. Coach parking
in main car park.
Facilities: Visitor centre, Toilets (including disabled),
earth paths, boardwalks. Two hides, car parks,
network of mapped walks, picnic sites, information
boards. Coach parking at main car park.
Public transport: Not to within a mile.
Habitat: At 777 acres, Llyn Alaw is Anglesey's largest
body of fresh water, with shallow reedy bays, hedges,
scrub, woodland, marsh, grassland.
Key birds: *Winter*: Wildfowl and thrushes, breeding
warblers/waterfowl. *Summer*: Lesser Whitethroat,
Sedge and Grasshopper Warblers, Little and Great
Crested Grebes, Tawny Owl, Barn Owl, Buzzard.
Winter: Whooper Swan, Goldeneye, Hen Harrier,
Short-eared Owl, Redwing, Fieldfare, Peregrine,
Raven. *All year*: Bullfinch, Siskin, Redpoll, Goldfinch,
Stonechat. *Passage waders*: Ruff, Spotted Redshank,
Curlew Sandpiper, Green Sandpiper.
Other notable flora and fauna: Bee and northern
marsh orchid, royal fern, skullcap, needle spikerush.
Migrant hawker, hairy, four-spotted chaser dragonflies,
banded demoiselle, wall brown, gatekeeper, clouded
yellow and orange tip butterflies. Brown hare, water
vole.
Contact: The Warden, 01407 730 762.

7. LLYN CEFNI

Welsh Water/ Hamdden Ltd.
Location: Sat nav: LL77 7RQ (Rhosmeirch car park). A
reservoir located two miles NW of Llangefni, in central
Anglesey. NE section of reservoir managed as nature
reserve – entrance at Rhosmeirch SH 451 783. Follow
B5111 or B5109 from the village.
Access: Open at all times. Dogs allowed except in
sanctuary area. Good footpath (wheelchair accessible)
for most of the site, bridges over streams. Walkers can
reach reservoir from Dingle nature reserve, Llangefni,
on boardwalks and cycle route (one mile).
Facilities: Two picnic sites, good footpath, coach
parking at Rhosmeirch car park.
Public transport: Bus 32, 4 (44 Sun only, 52 Thu only).
Tel 0871 200 2233 for information.
Habitat: Large area of open water, reedy bays,
coniferous woodland, scrub, carr.
Key birds: *Summer*: Sedge and Grasshopper Warblers,
Whitethroat, Buzzard, Tawny Owl, Little Grebe,
Gadwall, Shoveler, Kingfisher. *Winter*: Waterfowl
(Whooper Swan, Goldeneye), Crossbill, Redpoll, Siskin,
Redwing. *All year*: Stonechat, Treecreeper, Song
Thrush.
Other notable flora and fauna: Northern marsh
orchid, rustyback fern, needle spikerush. Banded

demoiselle, migrant hawker, golden ringed dragonfly,
emerald damselfly. Ringlet, gatekeeper, clouded
yellow and wall butterflies. Bloody nose beetle.
Contact: The Warden, 01407 730 762.

8. SOUTH STACK CLIFFS

RSPB (North Wales Office).
Location: Sat nav: LL65 1YH. RSPB visitor centre SH
218 818, Ellin's Tower information centre SH 206 820.
Follow A55 to W end in Holyhead, proceed straight on
at roundabout, continue straight on through traffic
lights. After another half mile turn L and follow the
brown tourist signs for RSPB South Stack.
Access: RSPB car park (no charge) with Blue Badge
parking. 'Access for all' track to viewing area
overlooking the lighthouse. Access to Ellin's Tower
Seabird Centre gained via staircase. Reserve covered
by an extensive network of paths, some of which are
not accessible via wheelchair.
Facilities: Free access to RSPB Visitor Centre (open
10am to 5pm daily except Dec 25) and Ellin's Tower
which has windows overlooking main auk colony open
daily (10am-5pm Easter-Sep). RSPB café closes at
3pm each day. Network of footpaths over coastal and
heathland terrain.
Public transport: None.
Habitat: Sea cliffs, maritime grassland, maritime
heath, lowland heath.
Key birds: Peregrine, Chough, Fulmar, Puffin,
Guillemot, Razorbill, Rock Pipit, Skylark, Stonechat,
Linnet, Shag, migrant warblers and passage seabirds.
Other notable flora and fauna: Spathulate fleawort,
endemic to South Stack, adders, lizards, porpoise.
Contact: South Stack Visitor Centre, 01407 762 100;
e-mail: south.stack@rspb.org.uk
www.rspb.org.uk/southstackcliffs

9. SPINNIES ABER OGWEN

North Wales Wildlife Trust.
Location: Sat nav: LL57 3YH. SH 613 721. From
Bangor follow the Tal-y-Bont road from roundabout
on A5122 near Penrhyn Castle entrance. Road to
reserve is signposted on L after 1km. Reserve can also
be approached from a road at Junction 12 off A55.
Minor road leads to car park where reserve entrance
is signposted
Access: Open all year. Dogs on leads. Keep to the
paths. Wheelchair accessible to the main hide.
Facilities: Two hides clearly signposted from the car
park, main hide is wheelchair accessible and offers
views of Traeth Lafan sands and the Spinnies lagoon.
There is a drop-off point at the main entrance.
Footpaths are good throughout.
Public transport: Take the 5 or 5X bus from Bangor or
Llandudno.
Habitat: Woodland, scrub, grassland, shingle beach
mudflats, reed swamp and open water.
Key birds: *Autumn/winter:* Large numbers of
wintering wildfowl and waders such as Redshank,
Greenshank, Wigeon and Teal. Kingfisher can be seen
from Sep-Mar. *Spring/summer*: Merganser, Sandwich
Tern, large numbers of Mute Swans, Little Grebe,
Blackcap and Sedge Warbler.

Other notable flora and fauna: Broad-leaved helleborine, snowdrops, dog's mercury, bluebells. Red admiral, Speckled wood, holly blue, orange tip and small copper butterflies.

Contact: Chris Wynne, Conservation Officer, 01248 351 541; e-mail: ChrisWynne@wildlifetrustswales.org
www.wildlifetrust.org.uk/northwales

10. TRAETH LAFAN LNR

Gwynedd Council.

Location: NE of Bangor, stretching 9.5k to Llanfairfechan. 1: For Traeth Lafan, take minor road from old A55 near Tal-y-Bont (SH 610 710) to Aberogwen car park by coast (SH 614 723). 2: For nearby Morfa Aber Reserve (SH 646 731) follow brown signs from junction 13 of A55.
3: Access to Morfa Madryn Reserve is on foot 1 mile W from Llanfairfechan promenade (SH 679 754).

Access: Open access from 1, 2, and 3. All sites are wheelchair accessible.

Facilities: Public paths. 1: Car park, hides 200m away at Spinnies Reserve. 2: Car park and hide. 3: Car and coach park with toilets and café, hides at reserve.

Public transport: For local bus and train timetables call 0870 60 82 608 or log on to www.gwynedd.gov.uk

Habitat: Intertidal sands and mudflats (2,500ha), wetlands, streams. SPA SAC SSSI and LNR.

Key birds: Third most important area in Wales for wintering waders; of national importance for moulting Great Crested Grebe and Red-breasted Merganser; internationally important for Oystercatcher and Curlew; passage waders; winter concentrations of Goldeneye and Greenshank, and of regional significance for wintering populations of Black-throated, Red-throated and Great Northern Divers and Black-necked and Slavonian Grebes and breeding Lapwings at Morfa Madryn.

Contact: Countryside and Access Unit, 01286 679 827.

Southern Wales

Glamorgan, Gower, Gwent

SUMMER along the Gower coastline will produce breeding seabirds, Peregrines and thousands of Manx Shearwaters offshore. Cardiff Bay is good for passage and wintering waders. The best wetlands are Kenfig Pools — half way between and Cardiff and Swansea — and the Newport Wetlands Reserve. Both are worth visiting at any time of year.

1. CWM CLYDACH

RSPB Wales

Location: Sat nav: SA6 5TL. SN 684 026. N of Swansea. Three miles N of J45 on M4, through the village of Clydach on B4291, follow the signs for Craig-cefn-Parc. Car park is close to the New Inn pub.

Access: Open at all times along public footpaths and waymarked trails. Not suitable for wheelchairs. Coach parking not available. Dogs on leads.

Facilities: Two nature trails link to network of public footpaths, car park, information boards.

Public transport: Hourly buses from Swansea stop at reserve entrance.

Habitat: Oak and beech woodland on steep slopes along the banks of the fast-flowing Lower Clydach River.

Key birds: Red Kite, Sparrowhawk, Buzzard, Raven, Green Woodpecker, Dipper and Grey Wagtail are joined in the summer by Spotted Flycatcher, Garden Warbler, Wood Warbler and Cuckoo. In winter Siskin, Lesser Redpoll and Woodcock are regular.

Other notable flora and fauna: Wood sorrel, silver-washed fritillary and speckled wood butterflies. Fungi.

Contact: Reserve warden, 029 2035 3000; e-mail: cymru@rspb.org.uk

2. CWM COL-HUW

The Wildlife Trust of South and West Wales.

Location: Sat nav: CF61 1RF (Cwm Col-Huw car park). SS 957 674. SE from Bridgend, site includes Iron Age fort, overlooking Bristol Channel. From Bridgend take B4265 S to Llanwit Major. Follow beach road from village.

Access: Park in seafront car park. Climb steps. Open all year.

Facilities: All year toilets and café. Information boards.

Habitat: Unimproved calcerous grassland, woodland, scrub and Jurassic blue lias cliff. Iron Age promontory fort on site.

Key birds: Cliff-nesting House Martin colony, breeding Fulmar, Grasshopper Warbler. Large autumn passerine passage. Peregrine. Seawatching vantage point. Occasional Chough.

Other notable fauna: Hedgehog, slow worm, butterflies.

Contact: Trust HQ, 01656 724 100; e-mail: info@welshwildlife.org
www.welshwildlife.org

3. KENFIG NNR

Bridgend County Borough Council.

Location: Sat nav: CF33 4PT. SS 802 811. Seven miles W of Bridgend. From J37 on M4, drive towards Porthcawl, then North Cornelly, then follow signs.

Access: Open at all times. Unsurfaced sandy paths, not suitable for wheelchairs. Flooding possible in

winter and spring. Coach parking available.
Facilities: Toilets, hides, free car parking and sign-posted paths.
Public transport: Local bus service stops at reserve. Call Traveline Cymru for details on 0871 200 2233.
Habitat: 1,300 acre sand dune system, freshwater lake with reeds, numerous wet dune slacks, sandy coastline with some rocky outcrops.
Key birds: *Summer:* Warblers including Cetti's, Grasshopper, Sedge, Reed and Willow Warbler, Blackcap and Whitethroat. *Winter:* Wildfowl, Water Rail, Bittern, grebes.
Other notable flora and fauna: 16 species of orchid, hairy dragonfly, red-veined and ruddy darters, small blue, dark green fritillary, grayling, brown argus butterflies.
Contact: David Carrington, Ton Kenfig, Bridgend, CF33 4PT. 01656 743 386.
e-mail: david.carrington@bridgend.gov.uk

4. MAGOR MARSH

Gwent Wildlife Trust.
Location: Sat nav: NP26 3DD (Redwick Road). ST 428 866. Reserve lies to S of Magor. Leave M4 at exit 23, turning R onto B4245. Follow signs for Redwick in Magor village. Take first L after railway bridge. Reserve entrance is half mile further on R.
Access: Open all year. Keep to path. Wheelchair access to bird hide. No dogs please.
Facilities: Hide. Car park, footpaths and boardwalks.
Public transport: Bus no 61 from Newport stops outside reserve.
Habitat: 90 acres of sedge fen, reedswamp, willow carr, damp hay meadows and open water.
Key birds: Important for wetland birds. *Spring:* Reed, Sedge and Grasshopper Warblers, occasional Garganey and Green Sandpiper on passage, Hobby. *Winter:* Teal, Peregrine, Jack Snipe, Snipe, occasional Shoveler and Gadwall, Bittern records in two recent years. *All year:* Little Egret, Little Grebe, Reed Bunting, Cetti's Warbler and Water Rail.
Contact: Gwent Wildlife Trust, 01600 740 600; e-mail: info@gwentwildlife.co.uk www.gwentwildlife.org

5. NEWPORT WETLANDS NNR

CCW/ RSPB/ Newport City Council.
Location: Sat nav: NP18 2BZ. ST 334 834. SW of Newport. Reserve car park on West Nash Road, just before entrance

to Uskmouth power station. From M4 junction 24 take the A48 to Newport Retail Park, turn towards steelworks and follow brown 'duck' signs to the reserve car park.
Access: Free entry 9am to 5pm each day, except Dec 25. Six disabled parking bays. All nature trails are accessible by wheelchair. Dogs only on perimeter footpath.
Facilities: Information centre, tea-rooms (open 10am to 4pm), shop, toilets (inc disabled), viewing screens.
Public transport: The 63 service runs from Newport Bus Station to the reserve daily (exc bank hols).
Habitat: 438 hectares of wet meadows, saline lagoons, reedbed, scrub and mudflats on Severn estuary.
Key birds: *Spring/summer:* Breeding waders such as Lapwing and Oystercatcher, Bearded Tit, Cetti's Warbler, Cuckoo and regular migrants on passage. *Autumn:* Large numbers of migrating wildfowl and waders arrive at the reserve — regulars include Curlew, Dunlin, Ringed Plover, Shoveler. *Winter:* Massive Starling roost (up to 50,000 birds). Bittern, nationally important numbers of Black-tailed Godwit, Shoveler and Dunlin.
Other notable flora and fauna: Badger, wood mouse, otter. Great crested newt. Orchids in spring, 16 species of dragonfly, 23 species of butterfly and around 200 species of moth.
Contact: Newport Wetlands Reserve (CCW) 0845 1306 229; RSPB visitor centre 01633 636 363;
e-mail: newport-wetlands@rspb.org.uk

6. OXWICH NNR

CCW (Swansea Office).
Location: Sat nav: SA3 1LS. SS 512 874. From Swansea take A4118 Gower road towards Killay, Parkmill and continue through Nicholaston Oxwich village.
Access: Most of NNR open at all times. Groups can visit some restricted areas by arrangement. No permit required for access to foreshore, dunes, woodlands and facilities.
Facilities: Private car park, summer only. Toilets summer only. Marsh boardwalk and marsh lookout. No visitor centre, no facilities for disabled visitors.
Public transport: Bus service Swansea/ Oxwich. First Cymru, tel 01792 580 580.
Habitat: Freshwater marsh, saltmarsh, foreshore, dunes, woodlands.
Key birds: *Summer:* Breeding Reed, Sedge and Cetti's Warblers, Treecreeper, Nuthatch, woodpeckers. *Winter:* Wildfowl.
Contact: Countryside Council for Wales, 0845 1306 229; e-mail: enquiries@ccw.gov.uk
www.ccw.gov.uk

7. PARC SLIP NATURE PARK

The Wildlife Trust of South and West Wales.
Location: Sat nav: CF32 0EH. SS 880 840. 1km W of Aberkenfig. From junction 36 of M4 take A4063 towards Maesteg, then B4281 (signposted Aberkenfig and Pyle) and follow brown signs to visitor centre in Fountain Road.
Access: Open dawn to dusk. Space for coach parking.
Facilities: Revamped visitor centre opened in 2013 (open 10am to 4pm each day except Mondays). Four hides, nature trail, interpretation centre. Free car park off Fountain Road. Good access for wheelchairs throughout the site.
Public transport: On Route No 4 of the National Cycle Network. Bus No 63 from Bridgend bus station stops outside the Fountain Inn at the bottom of Fountain Road. Train station at Tondu.
Habitat: Restored opencast mining site, wader scrape, lagoons, grassland, woodland.
Key birds: *Summer*: Breeding Tufted Duck, Lapwing, Skylark. Migrant waders (inc. Little Ringed Plover, Green Sandpiper), Little Gull. Kingfisher, Green Woodpecker. *Winter*: Snipe, Water Rail, Red-breasted Merganser.
Other notable flora and fauna: Twenty species of dragonfly recorded, inc emperor and scarce blue-tailed damselfly. Seven species of orchid, twayblade and broad-leaved helleborine. Great crested newt, harvest mouse
Contact: Trust HQ, 01656 724 100; e-mail: info@welshwildlife.org; www.welshwildlife.org

Western Wales

Carmarthenshire, Ceredigion, Pembrokeshire

A SUMMER boat trip to either Skomer or Skokholm to see the huge seabird colonies, is a must-do outing in summer, but inland, steep wooded valleys are good for Redstarts, Pied Flycatchers, Wood Warblers and Red Kites in spring and summer. For good winter birds head for the National Wetland Centre for Wales in Llanelli.

1. CASTLE WOODS

The Wildlife Trust of South and West Wales.
Location: Sat nav: SA19 6RT (Dinefwr Park). SN 615 217. About 60 acres of woodland overlooking River Tywi, 2km W of Llandeilo town centre, adjacent to Dinefwr Park.
Access: Open all year by footpath from Tywi Bridge, Llandeilo (SN 627 221) or park next to fire station off A40 and walk down Dinefwr Park Drive.
Facilities: Footpaths, mostly too steep for wheelchairs.
Public transport: Buses X13 from Swansea and 280 from Carmarthen to Llandovery. Train station in Llandeilo.
Habitat: Old mixed deciduous woodlands, castle and quarry.
Key birds: All three woodpeckers, Buzzard, Raven, Sparrowhawk. *Summer*: Pied and Spotted Flycatchers, Redstart, Wood Warbler. *Winter*: On water meadows look for Teal, Wigeon, Goosander, Shoveler, Tufted Duck and Pochard.
Other notable flora and fauna: Fallow deer, badger, butterflies inc silver-washed fritillary.
Contact: Welsh Wildlife Centre, 01239 621 600; e-mail: info@welshwildlife.org
www.welshwildlife.org

2. CORS CARON NNR

CCW (West Wales Area).
Location: Sat nav: SY25 6JF (car park). SN 690 642. On B4343 two miles N of Tregaron, Ceredigion, NE of Lampeter.
Access: Open access from new car park on B4343. Circular 4 mile Riverside Walk, shut at times due to flooding/management requirements. Dogs under control on Old Railway Walk, on leads on boardwalk, but not allowed on Riverside Walk.
Facilities: Coach accessible car park with toilets and picnic space. Bird hide on boardwalk, 2nd hide on Old Railway Walk 1.5 miles from car park. Footpath through reserve part of Ystwyth Trail.
Public transport: Infrequent buses (nos T21 and T29) pass Cors Caron.
Habitat: Raised bog, river, fen, wet grassland, willow woodland, reedbed.
Key birds: *Summer*: Lapwing, Redshank, Curlew, Red Kite, Hobby, Grasshopper Warbler, Whinchat, Redpoll, Reed Bunting. *Winter*: Teal, Wigeon, Whooper Swan, Hen Harrier, Red Kite.
Other notable flora and fauna: Small red damselfy among the abundant dragonflies which can be seen from boardwalk. Also adder and common lizard.
Contact: CCW, 0845 1306 229; www.ccw.gov.uk

3. DYFI NNR

CCW (West Wales Area).
Location: Sat nav: SY24 5JZ (Ynyslas visitor centre). SN 640 955. Extensive reserve midway between Machynlleth and Aberystwyth and seaward side of A487, incorporating part of Dyfi estuary, Ynyslas dunes and Borth Bog.

Access: Ynyslas dunes and the estuary have unrestricted access. No access to Borth Bog (Cors Fochno) for casual birdwatching; permit required for study and research purposes. Good views over the bog and Aberleri marshes from W bank of Afon Leri. Public footpaths off A493 E of Aberdyfi, and off B4353 (S of river); minor road from B4353 at Ynyslas to dunes and parking area.
Facilities: CCW visitor centre/shop/toilets at Ynyslas (open 9.30am to 5pm between Easter and end of Sept). No refreshments. Public hide overlooking marshes beside footpath at SN 611 911.
Public transport: Aberystwyth to Tre'r-ddol bus service stops at Borth and Ynyslas.
Habitat: Sandflats, mudflats, saltmarsh, creeks, dunes, raised bog, grazing marsh.
Key birds: *Winter*: Greenland White-fronted Goose, wildfowl, waders and raptors. *Summer*: Breeding wildfowl and waders (inc. Teal, Shoveler, Merganser, Lapwing, Curlew, Redshank).
Contact: CCW 0845 1306 229;
e-mail: enquiries@ccw.gov.uk; www.ccw.gov.uk

4. GWYNFFRWD-DINAS

RSPB Wales
Location: SN 788 471. North of Llandovery.From A483 take B road sign-posted to Llyn Brianne Reservoir and then follow signs to reserve, which lies between Cynghordy and llanwrda.
Access: Public nature trail at Dinas open dawn to dusk. Donation (£1) for parking appreciated.
Facilities: Nature trail including a board walk and four benches. Other parts of the trail are rugged. Car park and information board at start of trail. Coach parking can be arranged.
Public transport: None.
Habitat: Hillside oak woods, streams and bracken slopes. Spectacular upland scenery.
Key birds: Upland species such as Red Kite, Buzzard, Peregrine, Raven, Goosander, Dipper and Grey Wagtail are joined in the summer by Pied Flycatcher, Spotted Flycatcher, Wood Warbler, Redstart, Tree Pipit, Common Sandpiper and Cuckoo. Marsh Tit and all three woodpecker species are present.
Other notable flora and fauna: Golden-ringed dragonfly, purple hairstreak, silver-washed fritillary and Wilson's filmy fern.
Contact: Reserve Warden, 01654 700 222;
e-mail: gwenffrwd.dinas@rspb.org.uk

5. NATIONAL WETLANDS CENTRE, WALES

The Wildfowl & Wetlands Trust.
Location: Sat nav: SA14 9SH. SS 533 984. Overlooks the Burry Inlet near Llanelli. Leave M4 at junction 48. Signposted from A484, E of Llanelli.
Access: Open daily 9.30am-5pm, except Dec 24 and 25. Grounds open until 6pm in summer. Centre is fully accessible with disabled toilets. Mobility scooters and wheelchairs are free to hire.
Facilities: Visitor centre with toilets, hides, restaurant, shop, education facilities, free car and coach parking. The centre has level access and hard-surfaced paths.
Public transport: Bus from Llanelli to Lllwydhendy, approx 1 mile from the centre. Telephone Traveline Cymru 0871 200 2233 (7am-10pm daily).
Habitat: Inter-tidal mudflats, reedbeds, pools, marsh, waterfowl collection.
Key birds: Large flocks of Curlew, Oystercatcher, Redshank on saltmarsh. *Winter*: Up to 50,000 waterbirds, including Pintail, Wigeon, Teal. Also Little Egret, Short-eared Owl, Barn Owl, Peregrine.
Other notable flora and fauna: Bee and southern marsh orchids, yellow bartisa. Damselflies and dragonflies, water voles and otters.
Contact: Centre Manager, WWT National Wetlands Centre Wales, 01554 741 087;
e-mail: info.llanelli@wwt.org.uk
www.wwt.org.uk

6. RAMSEY ISLAND

RSPB Wales
Location: Sat nav: SA62 6PY. SM 706 237. One mile offshore from lifeboat station at St Justinians, two miles west of St Davids, Pembrokeshire.
Access: Open every day, weather permitting, April 1 to-Oct 31. RSPB landing fees for non-members, in addition to boat fare.No wheelchair access. Coach and car parking available at St Justinians. For boat bookings (sailings at 10am and 12 noon), contact: Thousand Island Expeditions, 01437 721 721; e-mail. sales@thousandislands.co.uk
Facilities: Small RSPB visitor centre/shop selling snacks and hot and cold drinks in St Justinian's harbour. Toilets a five minute walk uphill. Self-guiding circular trail on island (rugged in parts) with introduction from resident wardens. Guided walks are also available.
Public transport: Trains to Haverfordwest Station. Hourly buses from Hverfordwest to St Davids and then Celtic Coaster shuttle bus to boat embarkation point (Tel 01348 840 539).
Habitat: Acid grassland, maritime heath, seacliffs.
Key birds: *Spring/ summer*: Cliff-nesting auks

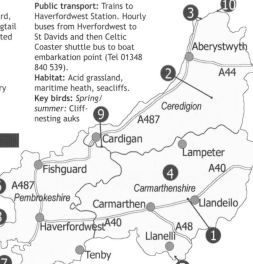

(Guillemot, Razorbill), Kittiwake, Fulmar, Lesser, Great Black-backed and Herring Gulls, Shag, Stonechat, Wheatear, Skylark, Linnet, Lapwing, plus passage migrants. *All year*: Peregrine, Raven, Chough.
Other notable fauna: Largest grey seal colony is southern Britain, red deer, harbour porpoise.
Contact: The Warden, 07836 535 733; e-mail:ramsey. island@rspb.org.uk; www.rspb.org.uk/ramseyisland

7. SKOKHOLM NNR

The Wildlife Trust of South and West Wales.
Location: Sat nav: SA62 3AZ (Marloes). SM 735 050. Island lying S of Skomer. Boats embark from Martin's Haven.
Access: Occasional day visits, also 3 or 4 night stays available. Weekly accomm. Apr-Sep, tel 01239 621 600 for details and booking. Booking for 2014 opened in Oct 2013.
Facilities: Upgraded self-catering accommodation for up to 20 people. Small shop selling basic foodstuffs.
Public transport: None.
Habitat: Cliffs, bays and inlets.
Key birds: *Spring*: Manx Shearwaters arrive at end of March. *Summer*: Internationally important colonies of Razorbill, Puffin, Guillemot, Storm Petrel (up to 5,000 pairs), Lesser Black-backed Gull. Migrants inc. rare species.
Other notable fauna: Grey seals, harbour porpoise, occasional common, bottlenose and Risso's dolphins, nationally rare moths.
Contact: 01239 621 600; www.welshwildlife.org e-mail: islands@welshwildlife.org

8. SKOMER

The Wildlife Trust of South and West Wales.
Location: Sat nav: SA62 3AZ (Marloes). SM 725 095. Fifteen miles from Haverfordwest. Take B4327 turn-off for Marloes, embarkation point at Martin's Haven, two miles past village. National Trust car park at Martin's Haven.
Access: Open between April 1 and Oct 31. Closed two days in May for seabird counts. Not suitable for infirm (steep landing steps and rough ground). Boats sail at 10am, 11am and noon every day except Mon (Bank Holidays excluded). Check (www.welshwildlife. org/2011/access-to-skomer-island) for more details. Island landing fees (for non-WTSWW members) payable at Lockley Lodge visitor centre.
Facilities: Information centre, toilets, two hides, wardens, booklets, guides, nature trails. Visitors need to take water/food.
Public transport: None.
Habitat: Maritime cliff, heathland, freshwater ponds.
Key birds: Largest colony of Manx Shearwater in the world (overnight). Puffin, Guillemot, Razorbill (Apr-end Jul). Kittiwake (until end Aug), Fulmar (absent Oct), Short-eared Owl (during day Jun and Jul), Chough, Peregrine, Buzzard (all year), migrants.
Contact: Reserve Warden, 07971 114 302; e-mail: skomer@wtww.co.uk; www.welshwildlife.org

9. WELSH WILDLIFE CENTRE

The Wildlife Trust of South and West Wales.
Location: Sat nav: SA43 2TB. SN 188 451. Centre based in Teifi Marshes Nature Reserve, Cilgerran, two miles SE of Cardigan. River Teifi is N boundary. Signposted from A478 Cardigan to Fishguard road.
Access: Open 10.30am-5pm all year. Free parking for WTSWW members, £3 non-members. Dogs on leads welcome. Disabled access to visitor centre, paths, four hides.
Facilities: Visitor centre, restaurant, network of four nature trails and seven hides. Binoculars for hire.
Public transport: Train station, Haverfordwest (23 miles). Bus station in Cardigan. Access on foot from Cardigan centre, ten mins.
Habitat: Wetlands, marsh, swamp, reedbed, open water, creek (tidal), river, saltmarsh, woodland.
Key birds: Extensive flooding in winter attracts large numbers of wildfowl, notably Teal, Wigeon and Mallard. Other winter regulars are Water Rail, Curlew, Snipe, Lapwing and Peregrine. Breeding birds include Cetti's Warbler, Kingfisher, Greater Spotted Woodpecker, Dipper, gulls, Marsh Harrier, Sand Martin, Hobby, Redstart. Occasional Bittern and Red Kite.
Other notable flora and fauna: Otter, water shrew, sika and red deer, good range of dragonflies.
Contact: Welsh Wildlife Centre, 01239 621 600; e-mail: info@welshwildlife.org; www.welshwildlife.org

10. YNYS-HIR

RSPB Wales.
Location: Sat nav: SY20 8TA. SN 682 961. Car park is one mile from Eglwys-fach village, off A487, six miles SW of Machynlleth.
Access: Entrance charge for non-RSPB members. Open every day (9am-9pm or dusk if earlier) except Dec 25. Visitor centre open daily Apr-Oct (10am-5pm), Wed-Sun Nov-Mar (10am-4pm). Coaches welcome but please call for parking information. No dogs allowed.
Facilities: Visitor centre and toilets. Two main circular trails (not suitable for wheelchairs), seven hides, two viewpoints, drinks machine.
Public transport: Bus service to Eglwys-fach from either Machynlleth or Aberystwyth, tel. 01970 617 951. Rail service to Machynlleth.
Habitat: Estuary, freshwater pools, woodland and wet grassland.
Key birds: Large numbers of wintering waders, wildfowl and birds of prey on the estuary are replaced with breeding woodland birds in spring and summer. *All year*: Red Kite, Buzzard, Little Egret, Lapwing, Teal. *Spring*: Wood Warbler, Redstart, Pied Flycatcher, nine species of warbler. *Winter*: Greenland Whitefronted Goose, Barnacle Goose, Wigeon, Hen Harrier.
Other notable fauna: Sixteen species of dragonfly and damselfly include small red damselfly and goldenringed dragonfly. Butterflies include dark green fritillary, brimstone and speckled wood. Otters (rarely seen) and brown hares are resident.
Contact: RSPB Ynys-Hir Reserve, 01654 700 222; e-mail: ynyshir@rspb.org.uk

COUNTY DIRECTORY

David Cromack

Like to contribute some time to monitoring wildfowl populations? Your local WeBS organiser (listed county-by-county) will be glad to hear from you.

England	234	Channel Islands	284
Scotland	271	Northern Ireland	285
Wales	279	Republic of Ireland	286
Isle of Man	283		

ENGLAND

THE INFORMATION in the directory has been obtained either from the persons listed or from the appropriate national or other bodies. In some cases, where it has not proved possible to verify the details directly, alternative responsible sources have been relied upon. When no satisfactory record was available, previously included entries have sometimes had to be deleted. Readers are requested to advise the editor of any errors or omissions.

AVON

See Somerset.

BEDFORDSHIRE

Bird Atlas/Avifauna
An Atlas of the Breeding Birds of Bedfordshire 1988-92 by R A Dazley and P Trodd (Bedfordshire Natural History Society, 1994).

Bird Recorders
Steve Blain, 9 Devon Drive, Biggleswade, Bedfordshire SG18 0FJ. 07979 606 300;
E-mail: recorder@bedsbirdclub.org.uk

Bird Report
BEDFORDSHIRE BIRD REPORT (1946-), from Mary Sheridan, 28 Chestnut Hill, Linslade, Leighton Buzzard, Beds LU7 2TR. 01525 378 245;
E-mail: membership@bnhs.org.uk

BTO Regional Representative
RR. Nigel Willits, Orchard Cottage, 68 High Street, Wilden, Beds MK44 2QD. 01234 771 948;
E-mail: btoinbeds@gmail.com

Club
BEDFORDSHIRE BIRD CLUB. (1992; 300). Miss Sheila Alliez, Flat 61 Adamson Court, Adamson Walk, Kempston, Bedford MK42 8QZ.
E-mail: sjalliez12@btinternet.com
www.bedsbirdclub.org.uk
Meetings: 8.00pm, last Tuesday of the month (Sep-Mar), Maulden Village Hall, Maulden, Beds.

Ringing Groups
IVEL RG. Graham Buss, 11 Northall Close, Eaton Bray, Dunstable LU6 2EB. 01525 221 023; E-mail: g1j2buss@yahoo.co.uk

RSPB. WB Kirby, The Lodge, Sandy, Bedfordshire SG19 2DL. 01767 680 551; E-mail: will.kirby@rspb.org.uk

RSPB Local Groups
BEDFORD. (1970; 80). Bob Montgomery, 36 Princes Road, Bromham, Beds MK43 8QD. 01234 822 035;
E-mail: montgomery5471@hotmail.co.uk
www.rspb.org.uk/groups/bedford/
Meetings: 7.30pm, 3rd Thursday of the month, A.R.A. Manton Lane, Bedford.

LUTON AND SOUTH BEDFORDSHIRE. (1973; 120+). Allyn Hill. 01582 666 297;
E-mail: cah_halfmoon@yahoo.com
www.rspb.org.uk/groups/luton
Meetings: 7.45pm, 2nd Wednesday of the month, Houghton Regis Social Centre, Parkside Drive, Houghton Regis, LU5 5QN.

Wetland Bird Survey Organiser
BEDFORDSHIRE. Mr R I Bashford, 6 Brook Road, Eaton Ford, St Neots, Cambridgeshire PE19 7AX.
E-mail: richard.bashford@rspb.org.uk

Wildlife Trust
See Cambridgeshire.

BERKSHIRE

BirdAtlas/Avifauna
The Birds of Berkshire 2nd Edition by Neil Bucknell, Brian Clews, Renton Righelato and Chris Robinson (Berkshire Atlas Group/Berkshire Ornithological Club 2013).

Bird Recorder
RECORDER (Records Committee and rarity records). Chris DR Heard, 3 Waterside Lodge, Ray Mead Road, Maidenhead, Berkshire SL6 8NP. 01628 633 828;
E-mail: chris.heard@virgin.net

Bird Reports
BERKSHIRE BIRD BULLETIN (Monthly, 1986-), from Brian Clews, 118 Broomhill, Cookham, Berks SL6 9LQ. 01628 525314; E-mail: brian.clews@btconnect.com

THE BIRDS OF BERKSHIRE (1974-), from Secretary of the Berkshire Ornithological Club.
E-mail: mike.turton@berksoc.org.uk
www.berksoc.org.uk

BIRDS OF THE THEALE AREA (1988-), from Secretary, Theale Area Bird Conservation Group.

NEWBURY DISTRICT BIRD REPORT (1959-), covering West Berkshire (approx 12 miles from centre of Newbury), plus parts of north Hants, south Oxon, from the Secretary, Newbury District Ornithological Club.

BTO Regional Representatives
RR. Sarah Priest and Kent White. 01635 268 442;
E-mail: btoberks.ken.sarah@googlemail.com

Clubs
BERKSHIRE BIRD BULLETIN GROUP. (1986; 100). Berkshire Bird Bulletin Group, PO Box 680, Maidenhead, Berks SL6 9ST. 01628 525 314;
E-mail: brian.clews@btconnect.com

NEWBURY DISTRICT ORNITHOLOGICAL CLUB. (1959; 110). John L Swallow, Yew Tree House, High Street, Kintbury, Hungerford, Berkshire RG17 9TN. 07795 027 490; E-mail: info1@ndoc.org.uk - www.ndoc.org.uk
Meetings: Indoor lectures from October to March and regular bird watching days around Newbury, throughout the summer and winter. Please see website for details.

BERKSHIRE ORNITHOLOGICAL CLUB. (1947; 320). Mike Turton, 7, Fawcett Crescent, Woodley, Reading RG5 3HX. 07815 644 385; E-mail: mike.turton@berksoc.org.uk www.berksoc.org.uk
Meetings: 8pm, alternate Wednesdays (Oct-Mar). University of Reading.

THEALE AREA BIRD CONSERVATION GROUP. (1988; 75). Catherine McEwan, Secretary. 01189 415 792; E-mail: catherine_j_mcewan@fsmail.net www.freewebs.com/tabcg/index.htm
Meetings: 8pm, 1st Tuesday of the month, Englefield Social Club, RG7 5ES.

Ringing Groups
NEWBURY RG. D Lond, 6 St Marks Close, Thatcham, Berks RG19 3SZ. E-mail: duncanflong@aol.com www.newburyrg.co.uk

RUNNYMEDE RG. D G Harris, 22 Blossom Waye, Hounslow, TW5 9HD.
E-mail: daveharris@tinyonline.co.uk www.rmxrg.org.uk

RSPB Local Groups
EAST BERKSHIRE. (1974; 200). Michael Huddy. 01844 690 571; E-mail: mmikehuddy@aol.com www.eastberksrspb.org.uk
Meetings: 7.30pm, Thursdays (Sept-April), Methodist Church Hall, King Street, Maidenhead, SL6 1EA.

READING. (1986; 130). Carl Feltham. 0118 941 1713; E-mail: carl.feltham@virginmedia.com www.reading-rspb.org.uk;
Meetings: 8.00 pm, 2nd Tuesday of the month (Sep-Jun), Pangbourne Village Hall, Pangbourne RG8 7AN.

WOKINGHAM & BRACKNELL. (1979; 200). Les Blundell, Folly Cottage, Buckle Lane, Warfield RG42 5SB. 01344 861 964; E-mail: lesrblundell@gmail.com www.rspb.org.uk/groups/wokinghamandbracknell
Meetings: 8.00pm, 2nd Tuesday of the month (Sep-Jun), Finchampstead Memorial Hall, Wokingham, RG40 4JU.

Wetland Bird Survey Organiser
BERKSHIRE. Mr & Mrs White, c/o WeBS Office; E-mail: white.zoothera@gmail.com

Wildlife Hospitals
LIFELINE. Wendy Hermon, Treatment Centre Co-ordinator, Swan Treatment Centre, Cuckoo Weir Island, South Meadow Lane, Eton, Windsor, Berks SL4 6SS. 01753 859 397 (fax) 01753 622 709; E-mail: wendyhermon@swanlifeline.org.uk www.swanlifeline.org.uk Registered charity. Thames

Valley 24-hour swan rescue and treatment service. Veterinary support and hospital unit. Operates membership scheme.

Wildlife Trust
See Oxfordshire,

BUCKINGHAMSHIRE

BirdAtlas/Avifauna
The Birds of Buckinghamshire ed by P Lack and D Ferguson (Buckinghamshire Bird Club, 1993). Now out of print.

Bird Recorder
Andy Harding, 93 Deanshanger Lane, Old Stratford, Milton Keynes MK19 6AX. 01908 565 896; E-mail: andyh444@sky.com

Bird Reports
AMERSHAM BIRDWATCHING CLUB ANNUAL REPORT (1975-), from Secretary.

BUCKINGHAMSHIRE BIRD REPORT (1980-), only some reports since 1990 are available, from John Gearing, Valentines, Dinton, Aylesbury, Bucks HP17 8UW. E-mail: john_gearing@hotmail.com

NORTH BUCKS BIRD REPORT (12 pa), from John Gearing. 01296 748 245; E-mail: clubrecorder@bucksbirdclub.co.uk

BTO Regional Representatives
RR. Roger Warren. 01491 638 691; E-mail: rcwarren@btinternet.com

Clubs
BUCKINGHAMSHIRE BIRD CLUB. (1981; 340). Rob Andrew, 01442 827 925; E-mail: Secretary@bucksbirdclub.co.uk www.bucksbirdclub.co.uk

NORTH BUCKS BIRDERS. (1977; N/A). Ted Reed, c/o AACS, The Open University, Walton Hall, Milton Keynes MK7 6AA.; E-mail: nbbr@yahoogroups.com
Meetings: No meetings. Contact is via North Bucks e-mail group. To join contact the Group Administrator, Simon Nichols (si.nich@yahoo.com)

RSPB Local Groups
See also Herts: Chorleywood.

AYLESBURY. (1981; 220). Brian Fisher. 01844 215 924; E-mail: brian.fisher45@yahoo.co.uk www.rspb.org.uk/groups/aylesburyPrebendal
Meetings: 7.30pm, Farm Community Centre, Fowler Road, Aylesbury HP19 7QW.

NORTH BUCKINGHAMSHIRE. (1976; 440). Chris Ward, 41 William Smith Close, Woolstone, Milton Keynes MK15 0AN. 01908 669 448; E-mail: northbucksrspb@hotmail.com www.rspb.org.uk/groups/northbucks
Meetings: 7.45pm, 2nd Thursday of the month, Cruck Barn, City Discovery Centre, Bradwell Abbey, MK13 9AP.

ENGLAND

Wetland Bird Survey Organiser
BUCKINGHAMSHIRE. Mr R S Warren, c/o WeBS Office, BTO, The Nunnery, Thetford, Norfolk IP24 2PU. 01491 638 691; E-mail: rcwarren@btinternet.com

Wildlife Hospitals
WILDLIFE HOSPITAL TRUST. St Tiggywinkles, Aston Road, Haddenham, Aylesbury, Bucks HP17 8AF. 01844 292 292 (24hr helpline);
E-mail: mail@sttiggywinkles.org.uk
www.sttiggywinkles.org.uk
Registered charity. All British species. Veterinary referrals and helpline for vets and others on wild bird treatments. Full veterinary unit and staff. Pub: *Bright Eyes* (free to members - sae).

Wildlife Trust
Director, See Oxfordshire,

CAMBRIDGESHIRE

BirdAtlas/Avifauna
Cambridgeshire Bird Atlas 2007-2011 by Louise Bacon, Alison Cooper and Hugh Venables (Cambridgeshire Bird Club).

Bird Recorders
CAMBRIDGESHIRE. Louise Bacon;
e-mail: recorder@cambridgebirdclub.org.uk
www.cambridgeshirebirdclub.org.uk

Bird Reports
CAMBRIDGESHIRE BIRD REPORT (1925-), from Bruce Martin, 178 Nuns Way, Cambridge, CB4 2NS. (H)01223 700 656; E-mail: bruce.s.martin@btinternet.com

PETERBOROUGH BIRD CLUB REPORT (1999-), from Secretary, Peterborough Bird Club.

BTO Regional Representatives
CAMBRIDGESHIRE RR. Mark Welch.
E-mail: m.welch@nhm.ac.uk

HUNTINGDON & PETERBOROUGH RR. Derek Langslow. 01733 232 153;
E-mail: derek.langslow@btinternet.com

Clubs
CAMBRIDGESHIRE BIRD CLUB. (1925; 350). Michael Holdsworth, 4a Cavendish Avenue, Cambridge, Cambs CB1 7US. E-mail: secretary@cambridgebirdclub.org.uk
www.cambridgebirdclub.org.uk
Meetings: 2nd Friday of the month, St John's Church Hall, Hills Road, Cambridge/Cottenham Village College.

PETERBOROUGH BIRD CLUB. (1999; 210). Keith Stapleford, 15 Derby Drive, Peterborough Pe1 4NG. 01733 555 793; e-mail: keith.stapleford@ talktalk.net
www.peterboroughbirdclub.co.uk
Meetings: Indoor last Tuesday of each month from Sep-Apr inclusive at 7.30pm at PO Social Club, Bourges Boulevard, Peterborough. Outdoor meetings monthly.

Ringing Group
WICKEN FEN RG. Dr C J R Thorne, 17 The Footpath, Coton, Cambs CB23 7PX. 01954 210 566;
E-mail: cjrt@cam.ac.uk

RSPB Local Groups
CAMBRIDGE. (1977; 100). Melvyn Smith. 01954 202 354; E-mail: mel_brensmith@hotmail.co.uk
www.rspb.org.uk/groups/cambridge
Meetings: 7.30pm, 3rd Wednesday of every month Jan-May and Sept-Dec. The Wilkinson Room, St John's the Evangelist, Hills Road, Cambridge, CB2 8RN

HUNTINGDONSHIRE. (1982; 180). Ursula Bulpitt. 01487 814 414; E-mail: ujbulpitt@btinternet.com
www.rspb.org.uk/groups/huntingdonshire
Meetings: 7.30pm, last Wednesday of the month (Sep-Apr), Free Church, St Ives.

Wetland Bird Survey Organisers
CAMBRIDGESHIRE (including Huntingdonshire). Bruce Martin, 178 Nuns Way, Cambridge, Cambs CB4 2NS. 01223 700 656; 07977 381 625;
E-mail: bruce.s.martin@ntlworld.com

NENE WASHES. Mr C E F Kitchin, RSPB Nene Washes Nature Reserve, 21a East Delph, Whittlesey, Cambridgeshire PE7 1RH. 01733 205 140; 01733 350 978; 07711 157 859;
E-mail: Charlie.kitchin@rspb.org.uk

OUSE WASHES. Mr P Harrington, Ouse Washes RSPB Reserve, Welches Dam, Manea, March PE15 0NF.
E-mail: paul.harrington@rspb.org.uk

SOUTH LINCOLNSHIRE/PETERBOROUGH (inland). Mr R C E Titman, 28 Eastgate Deeping St James, Peterborough PE6 8HJ. 01733 583 254; 01778 380 695; E-mail: bob.titman@gmail.com

Wildlife Trust
THE WILDLIFE TRUST FOR BEDFORDSHIRE, CAMBRIDGESHIRE, NORTHAMPTONSHIRE AND PETERBOROUGH. (1990; 36,000). The Manor House, Broad Street, Great Cambourne, Cambridgeshire CB23 6DH. 01954 713 500 (fax) 01954 710 051;
E-mail: cambridgeshire@wildlifebcnp.org
www.wildlifebcnp.org

CHESHIRE

BirdAtlas/Avifauna
Birds in Cheshire and Wirral - A Breeding and Wintering Atlas 2004-2007 by Professor David Norman, Liverpool University Press, Autumn 2008.

The Birds of Sandbach Flashes 1935-1999 by Andrew Goodwin and Colin Lythgoe (The Printing House, Crewe, 2000).

Bird Recorder (inc Wirral)
CHESHIRE & WIRRAL. Hugh Pulsford, 6 Buttermere Drive, Great Warford, Alderley Edge, Cheshire SK9 7WA. 01565 880 171; E-mail: countyrec@cawos.org

Bird Report
CHESHIRE & WIRRAL BIRD REPORT (1969-), from
Andrew Duncalf, 25 Monarch Drive, Northwich,
Cheshire CW9 8UN. 07771 774 5210;
E-mail: andrewduncalf@cawos.org
www.cawos.org

SOUTH EAST CHESHIRE ORNITHOLOGICAL SOCIETY
BIRD REPORT (1985-), from Secretary, South East
Cheshire OS. 01270 582 642.

BTO Regional Representatives
MID RR. Paul Miller. 01928 787 535;
E-mail: paulandhilarymiller@live.co.uk

NORTH & EAST RR. Mark Eddowes, 59 Westfield
Drive, Knutsford, Cheshire WA16 0BH. 01565 621 683;
E-mail: mark@eddowesaviationsafety.com

SOUTH RR. Mark Eddowes, 59 Westfield Drive,
Knutsford, Cheshire WA16 0BH. 01565 621 683;
E-mail: mark@eddowesaviationsafety.com

Clubs
CHESHIRE & WIRRAL ORNITHOLOGICAL SOCIETY.
 (2012; 311). Dr Ted Lock, 2 Bourne
Street, Wilmslow, Cheshire SK9
5HD. 01625 540 466;
E-mail: info@cawos.org
www.cawos.org

CAWOS Meetings: 7.45pm, 1st Friday of the
month, St Vincent's Church Hall,
Tatton Street, Knutsford.

CHESTER & DISTRICT ORNITHOLOGICAL SOCIETY.
(1967; 50). David King, 13 Bennett Close, Willaston,
South Wirral CH64 2XF. 0151 327 7212.
Meetings: 7.30pm, 1st Thursday of the month (Oct-
Mar), Caldy Valley Community Centre.

KNUTSFORD ORNITHOLOGICAL SOCIETY. (1974; 55).
Derek A Pike, 2 Lilac Avenue, Knutsford, Cheshire
WA16 0AZ. 01565 653 811;
E-mail: tony@mobberley.eu www.10X50.com
Meetings: 7.30pm, 4th Friday of the month (not Dec),
Jubilee Hall, Stanley Road, Knutsford.

LANCASHIRE & CHESHIRE FAUNA SOCIETY. (1914;
140). Dave Bickerton, 64 Petre Crescent, Rishton,
Blackburn, Lancs BB1 4RB. 01254 886 257;
E-mail: bickertond@aol.com www.lacfs.org.uk

LYMM ORNITHOLOGY GROUP. (1975; 60). Anne Ledden.
01514 240 441; E-mail: mandy.tonge@zetnet.co.uk
www.users.zetnet.co.uk/lymmog/
Meetings: 8.00pm, last Friday of the month (Aug-
May), Lymm Village Hall, Pepper Street WA13 0JB.

MID-CHESHIRE ORNITHOLOGICAL SOCIETY. (1963; 80).
John Drake, 17 Wisenholme Close, Beechwood West,
Runcorn, Cheshire WA7 2RU. 01928 561 133;
E-mail: contact@midcheshireos.co.uk
www.midcheshireos.co.uk
Meetings: 7:30pm, 2nd Friday of the month (Oct-
Mar), Cuddington and Sandiway Village Hall,near
Northwich CW8 2LB.

SOUTH EAST CHESHIRE ORNITHOLOGICAL SOCIETY.
(1964; 140). Derek Owen (Chairman),
E-mail: derek_owen07@tiscali.co.uk
www.secos.org.uk
Meetings: 2nd Friday (Sept-Apr), 7.30pm, Ettiley
Heath Church Community Centre, Sandbach.
South East Cheshire Ornithological Society celebrates
its Golden Anniversary in 2014.

WILMSLOW GUILD BIRDWATCHING GROUP. (1965;
67). Judith Rees, 15 Seymour Grove, Timperley,
Altrincham, Cheshire. 0161 980 5034.
http://wgbw.wikidot.com
Meetings: 7.30pm last Friday of the month, Wilmslow
Guild, Bourne St, Wilmslow SK9 5HD.

Ringing Groups
CHESHIRE SWAN RINGING GROUP. David Cookson.
01270 567 526; E-mail: Cheshireswans@aol.com
http://cheshireswanstudygroup.wordpress.com (blog
for Swan news, weather records, bird reports and
photos).

MERSEYSIDE RG. Bob Harris, 3 Mossleigh, Whixall,
Whitchurch, Shropshire SY13 2SA. 0151 706 4397;
E-mail: harris@liv.ac.uk

SOUTH MANCHESTER RG. Mr N.B. Powell,
e-mail: neville.powell@tiscali.co.uk

RSPB Local Groups
CHESTER. (1988; 220). Norman Sadler. 01244 335 670;
E-mail: chester1RSPB@btinternet.com
www.rspb.org.uk/groups/chester
Meetings: 7.30pm, 3rd Wednesday of the month (Sep-
Apr), St Mary's Centre, Chester CH1 2DW.

MACCLESFIELD. (1979; 250). Daryll Bailey. 01625 430
311; E-mail: daryll_96@hotmail.com
www.macclesfieldrspb.org.uk
Meetings: 7.45pm, 2nd Tuesday of the month (Sept-
May), Senior Citizens Hall, Duke Street, Macclesfield,
Cheshire, SK11 6UR

NORTH CHESHIRE. (1976; 100). Paul Grimmett. 01925
268 770; E-mail: paulwtwitcher@hotmail.com
www.rspb.org.uk/groups/north_cheshire
Meetings: 7.45pm, 3rd Friday (Jan-April and Sept-
Nov), Appleton Parish Hall, Dudlow Green Road,
Appleton, Warrington WA4 5EQ.

Wetland Bird Survey Organisers
CHESHIRE NORTH Mr K Brides, c/o WeBS Office, BTO,
The Nunnery, Thetford, Norfolk IP24 2PU. 01842 750
050; e-mail: webs@bto.org.

CHESHIRE SOUTH. Mr D.A. Cookson, 70 Rope Lane,
Rope, Crewe, Cheshire CW2 6RD. 01270 567 526;
07976 725 031; E-mail: cheshireswans@aol.com

Wildlife Hospitals
RSPCA STAPELEY GRANGE WILDLIFE CENTRE. London
Road, Stapeley, Nantwich, Cheshire, CW5 7JW. 0300
123 0722. All wild birds. Oiled bird wash facilities and
pools. Veterinary support.

ENGLAND

Wildlife Trust
CHESHIRE WILDLIFE TRUST. (1962; 13,100). Bickley Hall Farm, Bickley, Malpas, Cheshire SY14 8EF. 01948 820 728; e-mail: info@cheshirewt.org.uk
www.cheshirewildlifetrust.co.uk

CLEVELAND & CO. DURHAM

Bird Atlas/Avifauna
The Birds of Durham, edited by Keith Bowey and Mark Newsome (Durham Bird Club, 2012).

A Summer Atlas of Breeding Birds of County Durham by Stephen Westerberg/Kieth Bowey. (Durham Bird Club, 2000)

The Breeding Birds of Cleveland. Teesmouth Bird Club, 2008.

Bird Recorder
CLEVELAND. Tom Francis.
E-mail: mot.francis@ntlworld.com

DURHAM. Mark Newsome, 69 Cedar Drive, Jarrow, NE32 4BF. 07834 978 255;
E-mail: mvnewsome@hotmail.com

Bird Report
CLEVELAND BIRD REPORT (1974-), from Mr J Fletcher, 43 Glaisdale Avenue, Middlesbrough TS5 7PF. 01642 818 825.

BIRDS IN DURHAM (1971-), from D Sowerbutts, 9 Prebends Fields, Gilesgate, Durham DH1 1HH. 0191 386 7201; david.sowerbutts@dunelm.org.uk

BTO Regional Representative
CLEVELAND RR. Vic Fairbrother, 8, Whitby Avenue, Guisborough, Cleveland TS14 7AP. 01287 633 744;
E-mail: vic.fairbrother@ntlworld.com

DURHAM: David L Sowerbutts, 9 Prebends Field, Gilesgate Moor, Durham DH1 1HH. 0191 386 7201;
E-mail: david.sowerbutts@dunelm.org.uk

Club
DURHAM BIRD CLUB. (1975; 320). Paul Anderson, Chairman, 2 Hawsker Close, Tunstall Village, Sunderland SR3 2YD. 0191 523 6236;
E-mail: paulandcath29@aol.com
www.durhambirdclub.org
Meetings: Monthly indoor meetings (Sept-Apr), Durham Wildlife Trust HQ at Rainton Meadows, Houghton le Spring.

TEESMOUTH BIRD CLUB. (1960; 425). Chris Sharp (Hon Sec.), 45 Endeavour Close, Seaton Carew, Hartlepool TS25 1EY. 01429 865 163. www.teesmouthbc.com
Meetings: 7.30pm, 1st Monday of the month (Sep-Apr), Stockton Library, Church Road, Stockton.

Ringing Groups
DURHAM DALES RG. J R Hawes, Fairways, 5 Raby Terrace, Willington, Crook, Durham DL15 0HR.

NORTHUMBRIA RG. Richard Barnes, 12 Thorp Cottages, Bar Moor, Ryton, Tyne & Wear NE40 3AU. 0191 413 3846.

TEES RG. E Wood, Southfields, 16 Marton Moor Road, Nunthorpe, Middlesbrough, Cleveland TS7 0BH. 01642 323 563.

SOUTH CLEVELAND RG. W Norman, 2 Station Cottages, Grosmont, Whitby, N Yorks YO22 5PB. 01947 895 226; E-mail: wilfgros@btinternet.com

RSPB Local Group
CLEVELAND. (1974; 150). Terry Reeve. 01642 512 693;
E-mail: ClevelandRSPB@googlemail.com
www.rspb.org.uk/groups/cleveland
Meetings: 7.00 for 7.30pm, 2nd Monday of each month (Sep-Apr), Nature's World, Ladgate Lane, Middlesbrough, TS5 7YN.

DARLINGTON. (2005). Clifford Evans. 01325 466 471;
E-mail: cgevans1@virginmedia.com
www.communigate.co.uk/ne/darlingtonrspbgroup/index.phtml
Meetings: 1st Thursday of the month (Sept-July), Cockerton Methodist Church, Cockerton Green, Darlington.

DURHAM. (1974; 125). Richard Cowen. 0191 377 2061;
E-mail: richard.cowen313@gmail.com
www.durham-rspb.org.uk
Meetings: 7.30pm, 2nd Tuesday of the month (Oct-Mar), Room CG83, adjacent to Scarborough Lecture Theatre, University Science Site, Stockton Road entrance.

Wetland Bird Survey Organisers
CLEVELAND (excl. Tees Estuary). Mr C Sharp, 45 Endeavour Close, Seaton Carew, Hartlepool TS25 1EY. 01429 865 163;
E-mail: chrisandlucia@ntlworld.com

TEES ESTUARY. Mike Leakey, c/o EDF Energy, Tees Road, Hartlepool, Cleveland TS25 2BZ;
E-mail: mike.leakey@naturalengland.org.uk

Wildlife Trust
DURHAM WILDLIFE TRUST. (1971; 4,000). Rainton Meadows, Chilton Moor, Houghton-le-Spring, Tyne & Wear, DH4 6PU. 0191 584 3112 (fax) 0191 584 3934;
E-mail: mail@durhamwt.co.uk
www.durhamwt.co.uk

TEES VALLEY WILDLIFE TRUST. (1979; 5,000). Margrove Heritage Centre, Margrove Park, Boosbeck, Saltburn-by-the-Sea, TS12 3BZ. 01287 636 382, (fax) 01287 636 383; E-mail: info@teeswildlife.org
www.teeswildlife.org

CORNWALL

Bird Atlas/Avifauna
The Essential Guide to Birds of The Isles of Scilly 2007 by RL Flood, N Hudson and B Thomas, published by authors.

ENGLAND

Bird Recorders
CORNWALL. Dave Parker,
E-mail: recorder@cbwps.org.uk

ISLES OF SCILLY. Will Wagstaff, 42 Sally Port, St
Mary's, Isles of Scilly TR21 0JE. 01720 422 212;
E-mail: will@islandwildlifetours.co.uk
www.carnithen.co.uk

Bird Reports
BIRDS IN CORNWALL (1931-), by e-mail from
secretary@cbwps.org.uk www.cbwps.org.uk

*ISLES OF SCILLY BIRD REPORT and NATURAL HISTORY
REVIEW 2000 (1969-)*, from website;
www.scilly-birding.co.uk

BTO Regional Representatives
CORNWALL. Peter Kent, 01822 833 782;
E-mail: peter.kent@tesco.net

ISLES OF SCILLY RR & RDO. Will Wagstaff, 42 Sally
Port, St Mary's, Isles of Scilly TR21 0JE. 01720 422
212; E-mail: will@islandwildlifetours.co.uk

Clubs
CORNWALL BIRDWATCHING
& PRESERVATION SOCIETY.
(1931;1105). Cait Hutchings,
24 Kernick Road, Penryn,
Cornwall TR10 8NT. 01326 375
593; (M)07896 353 601; E-mail:
secretary@cbwps.org.uk
www.cbwps.org.uk

CORNWALL WILDLIFE TRUST PHOTOGRAPHIC GROUP.
(40). David Chapman, 41 Bosence Road, Townshend,
Nr Hayle, Cornwall TR27 6AL. 01736 850 287;
E-mail: david@ruralimages.freeserve.co.uk
www.ruralimages.freeserve.co.uk
Meetings: Mixture of indoor and outdoor meetings,
please phone for details.

ISLES OF SCILLY BIRD GROUP. (2000; 510). Membership
Secretary, 32 Sallyport, St Mary's, Isles of Scilly TR21
0JE. E-mail: isbgmembership@btinternet.com
www.scilly-birding.co.uk

Ringing Group
SCILLONIA SEABIRD GROUP. Peter Robinson, Secretary,
19 Pine Park Road, Honiton, Devon EX14 2HR. (Tel/
(fax) 01404 549 873 (M)07768 538 132;
E-mail: pjrobinson2@aol.com
www.birdexpertuk.com

RSPB Local Group
CORNWALL. (1972; 420). Roger Hooper. 01209 820
610; E-mail: rogerwhooper@btinternet.com
www.rspb.org.uk/groups/cornwall
Meetings: Indoor meetings (Oct-Apr), mainly in Truro
area, plus outdoor events throughout the year.

Wetland Bird Survey Organisers
CORNWALL (excl. Tamar Complex). Mr S Taylor, 42
Pendarves Street, Troon, Camborne, Cornwall TR14
9EG. 01209 614 857;
E-mail: simon.taylor@ap-group.co.uk

TAMAR COMPLEX. Gladys Grant, 18 Orchard Crescent,
Oreston, Plymouth, Devon PL9 7NF. 01752 406 287;
E-mail: gladysgrant@talktalk.net

Wildlife Hospital
MOUSEHOLE WILD BIRD HOSPITAL & SANCTUARY
ASSOCIATION LTD. Raginnis Hill, Mousehole, Penzance,
Cornwall, TR19 6SR. 01736 731 386. All species. No
ringing.

Wildlife Trust
CORNWALL WILDLIFE TRUST. (1962; 14,000). Five
Acres, Allet, Truro, Cornwall, TR4 9DJ. 01872 273 939
(fax) 01872 225 476;
E-mail: info@cornwallwildlifetrust.org.uk
www.cornwallwildlifetrust.org.uk

THE ISLES OF SCILLY WILDLIFE TRUST. (1984: 324)
Trenoweth,St Marys, Isles of Scilly TR21 0NS. 01720
422 153; E-mail: enquiries@ios-wildlifetrust.org.uk
www.ios-wildlifetrust.org.uk

CUMBRIA

BirdAtlas/Avifauna
The Breeding Birds of Cumbria by Stott, Callion,
Kinley, Raven and Roberts (Cumbria Bird Club, 2002).

Bird Recorders
CUMBRIA. Stephen Westerberg, 8 Beckside Gardens,
Brampton, Cumbria CA8 1US. 01697 742 652;
E-mail: stephen.westerberg@rspb.org.uk

NORTH EAST. Chris Hind, 01697 746 379:
E-mail: chris.m.hind@gmail.com

NORTH WEST (Allerdale & Copeland). Derek McAlone,
88 Whinlatter Road, Mirehouse, Whitehaven, Cumbria
CA28 8DQ. 01946 691 370;
E-mail: derek@derekmcalone3.wanadoo.co.uk

SOUTH (South Lakeland & Furness). Ronnie Irving, 24
Birchwood Close, Vicarage Park, Kendal, Cumbria LA9
5BJ. E-mail: ronnie@fenella.fslife.co.uk

Bird Reports
BIRDS AND WILDLIFE IN CUMBRIA (1970-), from
Dave Piercy, Secretary, Derwentwater Youth Hostel,
Borrowdale, Keswick CA12 5UR. 01768 777 909;
E-mail: daveandkathypiercy@tiscali.co.uk
www.cumbriabirdclub.org.uk

WALNEY BIRD OBSERVATORY REPORT, from Warden,
see Reserves.

BTO Regional Representatives
CUMBRIA. Clive Hartley, Undercragg, Charney Well
Lane, Grange-Over-Sands LA11 6DB. 01539 536 824;
E-mail: clive.hartley304@btinternet.com

Clubs
ARNSIDE & DISTRICT NATURAL HISTORY SOCIETY.
(1967; 219). Jennifer Rae, 01524 736 211.
http://www.arnsidesilverdaleaonb.org.uk/AONB/
Support/Local-societies-and-groups/Arnside-Natural-
History-Society.html

239

ENGLAND

Meetings: 7.30pm, 2nd Tuesday of the month (Sept-Apr). Arnside WI Hall, Orchard Road, Carnforth LA5 0DP. (Also summer walks).

CUMBRIA BIRD CLUB. (1989; 330). Dave Piercy, Secretary, Derwentwater Youth Hostel, Borrowdale, Keswick CA12 5UR. 01768 777 246; www.cumbriabirdclub.org.uk E-mail: daveandkathypiercy@tiscali.co.uk
Meetings: Various evenings and venues (Oct-Mar) check on website for further details.

Ringing Groups
EDEN RG. G Longrigg, 1 Spring Cottage, Heights, Appleby-in-Westmorland, Cumbria CA16 6EP.

MORECAMBE BAY WADER RG. J Sheldon, 140 Oxford Street, Barrow-in-Furness, Cumbria LA14 5PJ.

WALNEY BIRD OBSERVATORY. K Parkes, 176 Harrogate Street, Barrow-in-Furness, Cumbria LA14 5NA. 01229 824 219.

RSPB Local Groups
CARLISLE. (1974; 400). Richard Dixon. 01697 473 544; E-mail: sunzeco@hotmail.co.uk www.rspb.org.uk/groups/carlisle
Meetings: 7.30pm, Wednesday monthly (Sep-Mar), Tithe Barn, (Behind Marks And Spencer's), West Walls, Carlisle, Cumbria, CA3. Also monthly field trips except August.

SOUTH LAKELAND. (1973; 305). Richard Evans, 01539 722 221; www.rspb.org.uk/groups/southlakeland E-mail: RSPBsouthlakelandlocalgroup@gmail.com www.rspb.org.uk/groups/southlakeland/
Meetings: Evening meetings at 7:30pm in Kendal (LA9 4BH), Ulverston (LA12 7LZ), Ambleside (LA22 9DH) or Arnside (LA5 0DP), check website for details.

WEST CUMBRIA. (1986; 270). Marjorie Hutchin. 01900 825 231; E-mail: majorie.hutchin@btinternet.com www.rspb.org.uk/groups/westcumbria
Meetings: 7.30pm, 1st Tuesday (Sept-Apr), United Reformed Church, Main St, Cockermouth.

Wetland Bird Survey Organiser
CUMBRIA (excl. estuaries). Mr D Shackleton, 8 Burnbanks, Bampton, Penrith, Cumbria CA10 2RW. 01931 713693; e-mail: d.shackleton@btinternet.com

DUDDON ESTUARY. Mr C Gay, 8 Victoria Street, Millom, Cumbria LA18 5AS. 01229 773 820; 07759 589 702; E-mail: colinathodbarrow@btinternet.com

IRT/MITE/ESK ESTUARY. Mr P Jones, c/o WeBS Office, BTO, The Nunnery, Thetford Norfolk IP24 2PU. 01842 750 050; E-mail: webs@bto.org

SOLWAY ESTUARY INNER SOUTH. Mr N Holton, North Plain Farm, Bowness on Solway, Carlisle Cumbria CA7 5AG; E-mail: norman.holton@rspb.org.uk

CUMBRIA OUTER SOUTH. Mr D Shackleton, 8 Burnbanks, Bampton, Penrith, Cumbria CA10 2RW.

01931 713 693; E-mail: d.shackleton@btinternet.com

SOLWAY ESTUARY NORTH. Mr A C Riches, c/o WeBS Office, BTO, The Nunnery, Thetford, Norfolk IP24 2PU. 01683 300 393; 07792 142 446; E-mail: slioch69@aol.com

Wildlife Trust
CUMBRIA WILDLIFE TRUST. (1962; 15,000). Plumgarths, Crook Road, Kendal, Cumbria LA8 8LX. 01539 816 300 (fax) 01539 816 301; E-mail: mail@cumbriawildlifetrust.org.uk www.cumbriawildlifetrust.org.uk

DERBYSHIRE

BirdAtlas/Avifauna
The Birds of Derbyshire, ed. RA Frost (in preparation)

Bird Recorders
1. JOINT RECORDER. Roy A Frost, 66 St Lawrence Road, North Wingfield, Chesterfield, Derbyshire S42 5LL. 01246 850 037; E-mail: frostra66@btinternet.com

2. RECORDS COMMITTEE & RARITY RECORDS. Rodney W Key/Richard James. 01332 678 571; E-mail: r_key@sky.com/rmrjames@yahoo.co.uk

3. JOINT RECORDER. Richard M R James, 10 Eastbrae Road, Littleover, Derby DE23 1WA. 01332 771 787; E-mail: rmrjames@yahoo.co.uk

Bird Reports
CARSINGTON BIRD CLUB ANNUAL REPORT, from The Secretary.

DERBYSHIRE BIRD REPORT (1954- 2011). 2011 will become 2012 in mid-Nov 2013, from Bryan Barnacle, Mays, Meadow Lane, Froggatt, Hope Valley, Derbyshire S32 3ZA. 01433 630 726; E-mail: barney@mays1.demon.co.uk

OGSTON BIRD CLUB REPORT (1970-), records now published online; www.ogstonbirdclub.co.uk

BTO Regional Representatives
NORTH and SOUTH RR. Dave Budworth, 121 Wood Lane, Newhall, Swadlincote, Derbys DE11 0LX. 01283 215 188; E-mail: dbud01@aol.com

Clubs
BAKEWELL BIRD STUDY GROUP. (1987; 80).Irene Hayward, 14 Daysmill Close, Matlock, Derbys DE4 3NP. 01629 57918; E-mail: irene@daysmill.freeserve.co.uk www.bakewellbirdstudygroup.co.uk
Meetings: 7.30pm, 2nd Monday of the month, Friends Meeting House, Bakewell DE45 1EL.

BUXTON FIELD CLUB. (1946; 68). Rosemary Furness. 01246 582 213; E-mail: rosemary.furness@virgin.net
Meetings: 7.30pm, every three weeks in winter, Methodist Church Hall, Buxton.

CARSINGTON BIRD CLUB. (1992; 257). Peter Gibbon; E-mail: peter.gibbon@w3z.co.uk www.carsingtonbirdclub.co.uk

ENGLAND

Meetings: 7.30pm, 3rd Tuesday of the month (Sep-Mar), the Henmore Room, Carsington Water's main centre.

DERBYSHIRE ORNITHOLOGICAL SOCIETY. (1954; 550). Steve Shaw, 84 Moorland View Road, Walton, Chesterfield, Derbys S40 3DF. 01246 236090; E-mail: steveshaw84mvr@btinternet.com www.derbyshireOS.org.uk
Meetings: 7.30pm, last Friday of the winter months, various venues.

OGSTON BIRD CLUB. (1969; 1,126). Peter Birley, 35 Rosemary Drive, Alvaston, Derby DE24 0TA. 01332 753 078; E-mail: peter.birley@sky.com www.ogstonbirdclub.co.uk

SOUTH PEAK RAPTOR STUDY GROUP. (1998; 12). Trevor Grimshaw; e-mail: grimshaw758@btinternet.com

Ringing Groups
SORBY-BRECK RG. Dr Geoff P Mawson, Moonpenny Farm, Farwater Lane, Dronfield, Sheffield S18 1RA. E-mail: moonpenny@talktalk.net www.sorbybreckringinggroup.co.uk

SOUDER RG. Dave Budworth, 121 Wood Lane, Newhall, Swadlincote, Derbys DE11 0LX. E-mail: dbud01@aol.com

RSPB Local Groups
CHESTERFIELD. (1987; 274). Alan Goddard. 01246 230 244; (M)07764 895 657; E-mail: alangoddard100@gmail.com www.rspb.org.uk/groups/chesterfield
Meetings: 7.15pm, usually 3rd Monday of the month, Winding Wheel, New Exhibition Centre, 13 Holywell Street, Chesterfield.

DERBY. (1973; 500). Ray Worthy, 01332 232 748; E-mail: derbyrspblocalgroup@hotmail.co.uk www.rspb.org.uk/groups/derby
Meetings: 7.30pm, 2nd Wednesday of the month (Sep-Apr), Broughton Suite, Grange Banqueting Suite, 457 Burton Road, Littleover, Derby DE23 6FL.

HIGH PEAK. (1974; 110). Richard Stephenson. 0161 427 4187; E-mail: stephenson3rj@gmail.com www.rspb.org.uk/groups/highpeak
Meetings: 7.30pm, 3rd Monday of the month (Sep-May), Marple Senior Citizens Hall, Memorial Park, Marple, Stockport SK6 6BA.

Wetland Bird Survey Organiser
DERBYSHIRE. Mr P J Gibbon, 25 Church Street, Holloway Derbyshire DE4 5AY. 01629 534 173; e-mail: peter.gibbon@w3z.co.uk

Wildlife Trust
DERBYSHIRE WILDLIFE TRUST. (1962; 14,000). East Mill, Bridge Foot, Belper, Derbyshire DE56 1XH. 01773 881 188 (fax) 01773 821 826; E-mail: enquiries@derbyshirewt.co.uk www.derbyshirewildlifetrust.org.uk

DEVON

BirdAtlas/Avifauna
Birds of Devon by Michael Tyler (Devon Birdwatching & Preservation Society, 2010).

Tetrad Atlas of Breeding Birds of Devon by H P Sitters (Devon Birdwatching & Preservation Society, 1988).

The Birds of Lundy by Tim Davis and Tim Jones 2007. Available from R M Young (Bookseller) on 01769 573 350 (see www.birdsoflundy.org.uk for further details)

The **Birds** of **Devon**

Michael Tyler

Bird Recorder
Steve Waite, 46 Primrose Way, Seaton, Devon EX12 2XQ. 01297 792 339; www.devonbirds.org/ E-mail: recorder@devonbirds.org

Bird Reports
DEVON BIRD REPORT (1971). Previous annual reports since 1929, from the Secretary, Devon Bird Watching and Preservation Society; www.devonbirds.org

LUNDY FIELD SOCIETY ANNUAL REPORT (1946-). £3 each inc postage, check website for availability, from Frances Stuart, 3 Lower Linden Road, Clevedon, North Somerset BS21 7SU. E-mail: lfssec@hotmail.co.uk

BTO Regional Representative
RR. Stella Beavan. 07710 879 277; E-mail: stella@treedown.eclipse.co.uk

BTO Garden BirdWatch Ambassador
DEVON (south). Mr M K Overy. E-mail: martin@martin-overy.co.uk

Clubs
DEVON BIRD WATCHING & PRESERVATION SOCIETY. (1928; 1,200). Mr Mike Daniels, 1 Babbs Cottage, Princetown, Yelverton, Devon PL20 6QJ. 01822 890 899; E-mail: nellmegfly@gmail.com www.devonbirds.org

KINGSBRIDGE & DISTRICT NATURAL HISTORY SOCIETY. (1989; 130). Mike Hitch. E-mail: www.knhs.org.uk
Meeting:7.30pm 4th Monday of Sept-Apr, West Charleton Village Hall.

LUNDY FIELD SOCIETY. (1946; 450). Mr Michael Williams, 5 School Place, Oxford, Oxon OX1 4RG. E-mail: lfssec@hotmail.co.uk www.lundy.org.uk
Meeting: AGM 2nd Saturday of March in Crediton.

TOPSHAM BIRDWATCHING & NATURALISTS' SOCIETY. (1969; 140). Keith Chester (Membership Secretary). 01392 877 817; E-mail: tbns@talktalk.net http://topshambns.blogspot.com
Meetings: 7.30pm, 2nd Friday of the month (Sep-May), Matthews Hall, Topsham EX3 0HF.

ENGLAND

Ringing Groups

AXE ESTUARY RINGING GROUP. Mike Tyler, The Acorn, Shute Road, Kilmington, Axminster EX13 7ST. 01297 349 58; E-mail: mwtyler2@googlemail.com axeestuaryringinggroup.blogspot.co.uk

DEVON & CORNWALL WADER RG. R C Swinfen, 72 Dunraven Drive, Derriford, Plymouth PL6 6AT. 01752 704 184.

LUNDY FIELD SOCIETY. A M Taylor, 26 High Street, Spetisbury, Blandford, Dorset DT11 9DJ. 01258 857336; E-mail: ammataylor@yahoo.co.uk

SLAPTON BIRD OBSERVATORY. R C Swinfen, 72 Dunraven Drive, Derriford, Plymouth PL6 6AT. 01752 704 184.

RSPB Local Groups

EXETER & DISTRICT. (1974; 400). Roger Tucker. 01392 860 518; E-mail: r.345tucker@btinternet.com www.exeter-rspb.org.uk
Meetings: 7.30p, various evenings, Southernhay United Reformed Church Rooms, Dix's Field, Exeter.

PLYMOUTH. (1974; 600). Mrs Eileen Willey, 11 Beverstone Way, Roborough, Plymouth PL6 7DY. 01752 208 996; E-mail: edward.willey@sky.com

TORBAY AND SOUTH DEVON TEAM. John Allan. 01626 821 344; E-mail: john@morsey.f2s.com www.rspb.org.uk/groups/torbayandsouthdevon

Wetland Bird Survey Organisers

DEVON other sites. Dr P J Reay, Crooked Fir, Moorland Park, South Brent, Devon TQ10 9AS. 01364 73293; E-mail: peter.p.j.reay@btinternet.com

TAMAR COMPLEX. Gladys Grant, 18 Orchard Crescent, Oreston, Plymouth PL9 7NF. E-mail: gladysgrant@talktalk.net

TAW/TORRIDGE ESTUARY. Mr T Chaplin, c/o WeBS Office, BTO, The Nunnery, Thetford Norfolk IP24 2PU. 01271 342 590; 07810 757 451; E-mail: terry@chaplin.eclipse.co.uk

Wildlife Hospitals

BIRD OF PREY CASUALTY CENTRE. Mrs J E L Vinson, Crooked Meadow, Stidston Lane, South Brent, Devon TQ10 9JS. 01364 72174. Birds of prey, with emergency advice on other species. Aviaries, rehabilitation facilities. Veterinary support.

Wildlife Trust

DEVON WILDLIFE TRUST. (1962; 33,000). Cricklepit, Commercial Road, Exeter, EX2 4AB. 01392 279 244 (fax) 01392 433 221; E-mail: contactus@devonwildlifetrust.org www.devonwildlifetrust.org

DORSET

BirdAtlas/Avifauna

Dorset Breeding Bird Atlas (working title). In preparation.

The Birds of Dorset by Dr George Green (Christopher Helm 2004)

Bird Recorder

Kevin Lane. E-mail: kevin@ broadstoneheath.co.uk

Bird Reports

DORSET BIRDS (1977-), from Neil Gartshore, Moor Edge, 2 Bere Road, Wareham, Dorset BH20 4DD. 01929 552 560; E-mail: enquiries@ callunabooks.co.uk

THE BIRDS OF CHRISTCHURCH HARBOUR (1956-), from Ian Southworth, 1 Bodowen Road, Burton, Christchurch, Dorset BH23 7JL. E-mail: ianbirder@aol.com

PORTLAND BIRD OBSERVATORY REPORT, from Warden, (see Reserves).

BTO Regional Representatives

DORSET. Ieuan Evans (temporary). 01842 750 050; E-mail: ieuan.evans@bto.org

Clubs

CHRISTCHURCH HARBOUR ORNITHOLOGICAL GROUP. (1956; 290). Mr. I.H. Southworth, Membership Secretary, 1 Bodowen Road, Burton, Christchurch, Dorset BH23 7JL. 01202 478 093. www.chog.org.uk

DORSET BIRD CLUB. (1987; 525). Mrs Diana Dyer, The Cedars, 3 Osmay Road, Swanage, Dorset BH19 2JQ. 01929 421 402; www.dorsetbirds.org.uk E-mail: membership@dorsetbirds.org.uk

DORSET NATURAL HISTORY & ARCHAEOLOGICAL SOCIETY. (1845; 2188). Dorset County Museum, High West Street, Dorchester, Dorset DT1 1XA. 01305 262 735; E-mail: secretary@dorsetcountymuseum.org www.dorsetcountymuseum.org

Ringing Groups

CHRISTCHURCH HARBOUR RS. E C Brett, 3 Whitfield Park, St Ives, Ringwood, Hants BH24 2DX. E-mail: ed_brett@lineone.net

PORTLAND BIRD OBSERVATORY. Martin Cade, Old Lower Light, Portland Bill, Dorset DT5 2JT. 01305 820553; E-mail: obs@btinternet.com www.portlandbirdobs.org.uk

STOUR RG. R Gifford, 62 Beacon Park Road, Upton, Poole, Dorset BH16 5PE.

RSPB Local Groups

BLACKMOOR VALE. (1981; 130). Alison Rymell, Group Leader. 0782 574 7546; E-mail: rspb.bv@gmail.com www.rspb.org.uk/groups/blackmoorvale
Meetings: 7.30pm, 3rd Friday in the month, Gillingham Primary School, SP8 4QR.

EAST DORSET. (1974; 435). Hugh Clark. 01425 475 487; E-mail: hugh.clark@hotmail.co.uk

ENGLAND

www.rspb.org.uk/groups/eastdorset
Meetings: 7.30pm, 2nd Wednesday of the month, St Mark's Church Hall, Talbot Village, Wallisdown, Bournemouth.

POOLE. (1982; 305). Pam Hunt, 01929 553 338; E-mail: pam.hunt@talktalk.net
www.rspb.org.uk/groups/poole
Meetings: 7.30pm, Upton Community Centre, Poole Road, Upton BY16 5JA.

SOUTH DORSET. (1976; 422). For contact, please refer to the website.
www.rspb.org.uk/groups/southdorset
Meetings: 3rd Thursday of each month (Sep-April), St. Georges Church Hall, Fordington, Dorchester, Dorset DT1 1LB.

Wetland Bird Survey Organisers
DORSET (excl estuaries). Mr J M Jones, Blackbird Cottage, 14 Church Lane, Sutton Waldron, Nr Blandford, Dorset DT11 8PA. 01747 811 490; E-mail: blackbirdcott@tiscali.co.uk

POOLE HARBOUR. Mr P Morton, c/o WeBS Office, BTO, The Nunnery, Thetford, Norfolk IP24 2PU; E-mail: paulolua@yahoo.co.uk

THE FLEET & PORTLAND HARBOUR. Mr S Groves, 7 Grove Lane, Abbotsbury, Weymouth, Dorset DT3 4JH. 01305 871 684; 01305 871 562; 07531 939 081; E-mail: cygnusolor@yahoo.co.uk

RADIPOLE & LODMOOR. Mr T Branston, RSPB, Ryan House, Sandford Lane, Wareham, Dorset BH20 4DY; e-mail: toby.branston@rspb.org.uk

Wildlife Hospital
SWAN RESCUE SANCTUARY. Ken and Judy Merriman, The Wigeon, Crooked Withies, Holt, Wimborne, Dorset BH21 7LB. 01202 828 166.
www.swan-rescue.co.uk/
24 hr rescue service for swans. Large sanctuary of 40 ponds and lakes. Hospital and intensive care. Veterinary support. Free advice and help line. Three fully equipped rescue ambulances. Rescue water craft for all emergencies. Viewing by appointment only.

Wildlife Trust
DORSET WILDLIFE TRUST. (1961; 25,000). Brooklands Farm, Forston, Dorchester, Dorset, DT2 7AA. 01305 264 620 (fax) 01305 251 120; E-mail: enquiries@dorsetwildlifetrust.org.uk
www.dorsetwildlife.org.uk

DURHAM
See Cleveland & Co. Durham

ESSEX

Bird Atlas/Avifauna
The Birds of Essex by Simon Wood (A&C Black, August 2007).

The Breeding Birds of Essex by M K Dennis (Essex Birdwatching Society, 1996).

Bird Recorder
RECORDER. Les Steward, 6 Creek View, Basildon, Essex SS16 4RU. 01268 551 464, E-mail: les.steward@btinternet.com

Bird Report
ESSEX BIRD REPORT (inc Bradwell Bird Obs records) (1950-), from the Secretary, Essex Birdwatching Society.

BTO Regional Representatives & Regional Development Officer
NORTH-EAST RR & RDO. Ed Hutchings. 07557 096 401. E-mail: edhutchings@hotmail.co.uk

NORTH-WEST RR. Graham Smith. 01277 354 034; E-mail: silaum.silaus@tiscali.co.uk

SOUTH RR. Position vacant. 01842 750 050. E-mail: info@bto.org

Club
ESSEX BIRDWATCHING SOCIETY. (1949; 700). John and Louise Sykes, Joint General Secretary, 14 Acres End, Chelmsford, Essex CM1 2XR. 01245 355 132; E-mail: john.sykes@btinternet.com
www.ebws.org.uk
Meetings: 1st Friday of the month (Oct-Mar), Friends' Meeting House, Rainsford Road, Chelmsford CM1 2QL.

Ringing Groups
ABBERTON RG. C P Harris, Wyandotte, Seamer Road, Southminster, Essex CM0 7BX.

BRADWELL BIRD OBSERVATORY. C P Harris, Wyandotte, Seamer Road, Southminster, Essex CM0 7BX.

RSPB Local Groups
CHELMSFORD AND CENTRAL ESSEX. (1976; 1200). Viv Connett. 07985 796 657; E-mail: ivconnett@mail.com
www.rspb.org.uk/groups/chelmsford
Meetings: 8pm, Thursdays, eight times a year. The Cramphorn Theatre, Chelmsford CM1 2JG.

COLCHESTER. (1981; 220). Mr Russell Leavett, 10 Grove Road, Brantham, Manningtree, Essex CO11 1TX. 01206 399 059; E-mail: rleavett@btinternet.com
www.rspb.org.uk/groups/colchester
Meetings: 2nd Thursday of the month (Sep-Apr), Shrub End Community Hall, Shrub End Road, Colchester. Regular coach and car trips to local birding sites and those further afield.

SOUTH EAST ESSEX. (1983; 200). Graham Mee, 34 Park View Drive, Leigh-on-Sea, Essex SS9 4TU. 01702 525 152; E-mail: grahamm@southendrspb.co.uk
www.southeastrspb.org.uk
Meetings: 7.30pm, usually 1st Tuesday of the month (Sep-May), Belfairs School Hall, School Way, Leigh-on-Sea SS9 4HX.

Wetland Bird Survey Organisers
CROUCH/ROACH ESTUARY and SOUTH DENGIE. Canon Peter Mason, 8 Canuden Road, Chelmsford Essex CM1 2SX. 01245 351 465; E-mail: Petermason32@waitrose.com

243

ENGLAND

HAMFORD WATER. Mr J Novorol, The Brents, Harwich Road, Great Oakley, Harwich, Essex CO12 5AD. 01255 880 552.

LEE VALLEY. Miss C Patrick, Senior Conservation Officer, Myddelton House, Bulls Cross, Enfield, Middlesex EN2 9HG. 01992 709 882(direct)/01992 717 711; 07717 449 341; E-mail: cpatrick@leevalleypark.org.uk

NORTH BLACKWATER. Mr J Thorogood, 18 Smallwood Road, Colchester Essex CO2 9HA. 01206 768 771.

SOUTH BLACKWATER AND NORTH DENGIE. Mr A G Harbott, 5 Allnutts Road, Epping Essex CM16 7BD. 01992 575 213; E-mail: anthonyharbott@talktalk.net

STOUR ESTUARY. Mr R Vonk, RSPB, Unit 1 Brantham Mill, Bergholt Road, Brantham, Manningtree, Essex CO11 1QT. 01206 391 153; 07711 129 149; E-mail: rick.vonk@rspb.org.uk

THAMES ESTUARY - FOULNESS. Dr C P M Lewis, c/o WeBS Office, BTO, The Nunnery, Thetford, Norfolk IP24 2PU. E-mail: cpm.lewis@gmail.com

Wildlife Trust
ESSEX WILDLIFE TRUST. (1959; 36,000). The Joan Elliot Visitor Centre, Abbots Hall Farm, Great Wigborough, Colchester, CO5 7RZ. 01621 862 960 (fax) 01621 862 990; E-mail: admin@essexwt.org.uk www.essexwt.org.uk

GLOUCESTERSHIRE

Bird Atlas/Avifauna
Atlas of Breeding Birds of the North Cotswolds. (North Cotswold Ornithological Society, 1990).

Birds of The Cotswolds (Liverpool University Press 2009).

Bird Recorder
GLOUCESTERSHIRE EXCLUDING S.GLOS (AVON). Richard Baatsen. E-mail: baatsen@surfbirder.com

Bird Reports
CHELTENHAM BIRD CLUB BIRD REPORT (1998-2001) - no longer published, from Secretary.

GLOUCESTERSHIRE BIRD REPORT (1953-). £7.50 including postage, from David Cramp, 2 Ellenor Drive, Alderton, Tewkesbury GL20 8NZ. E-mail: djcramp@btinternet.com

NORTH COTSWOLD ORNITHOLOGICAL SOCIETY ANNUAL REPORT (1983-), from A Lewis, 41 Roman Way, Bourton-on-the-Water, Cheltenham, Glos GL54 2EW. E-mail: info@ncosbirds.org.uk www.ncosbirds.org.uk

BTO Regional Representative
Gordon Kirk. 01452 741 724; E-mail: gordonkirk@aol.com

Clubs
CHELTENHAM BIRD CLUB. (1976; 100). Membership

Secretary. 01451 850 385.
www.cheltenhambirdclub.org.uk
Meetings: 7.15pm, Mondays (Oct-Mar), Bournside School, Warden Hill Road, Cheltenham GL7 3EF.

DURSLEY BIRDWATCHING & PRESERVATION SOCIETY. (1953; 350). The Secretary, E-mail: dbwps@yahoo.com http://dursleybirdwatchers.btck.co.uk/ **Meetings:** 7.45pm, 2nd and 4th Monday (Sept-Mar), Dursley Community Centre.

GLOUCESTERSHIRE NATURALISTS' SOCIETY. (1948; 500). Mike Smart, 143 Cheltenham Road, Gloucester, GL2 0JH. 01452 421 131; www.glosnats.org E-mail: smartmike@btinternet.com **Meetings:** 7.30pm, 2nd Friday of the month (Oct-April), Watermoor Church Hall, Cirencester GL7 1JR.

NORTH COTSWOLD ORNITHOLOGICAL SOCIETY. (1982; 70). A Lewis, 41 Roman Way, Bourton-on-the-Water, Cheltenham, Glos GL54 2EW; www.ncosbirds.org.uk E-mail: info@ncosbirds.org.uk **Meetings:** Monthly field meetings, usually Sunday 9.30pm. **Additional notes:** We are a small surveying and recording group based in Cheltenham and the Cotswolds.

Ringing Groups
COTSWOLD WATER PARK RG. John Wells, 25 Pipers Grove, Highnam, Glos GL2 8NJ. E-mail: john.wells2@btinternet.com

SEVERN ESTUARY GULL GROUP. M E Durham, 6 Glebe Close, Frampton-on-Severn, Glos GL2 7EL. 01452 741 312.

WILDFOWL & WETLANDS TRUST. Richard Hearn, Wildfowl & Wetlands Trust, Slimbridge, Glos GL2 7BT. E-mail: richard.hearn@wwt.org.uk

RSPB Local Group
GLOUCESTERSHIRE. (1972; 600). David Cramp, 2 Ellenor Drive, Alderton, Tewkesbury GL20 8NZ. 01242 620 281; E-mail: djcramp@btinternet.com www.rspb.org.uk/groups/gloucestershire **Meetings:** 7.30pm, 3rd Tuesday of the month, Gala Club, Longford, Gloucester GL2 9EB.

Wildlife Hospital
VALE WILDLIFE RESCUE - WILDLIFE HOSPITAL & REHABILITATION CENTRE. Any staff member, Station Road, Beckford, Tewkesbury, Glos GL20 7AN. 01386 882 288; E-mail: info@valewildlife.org.uk www.valewildlife.org.uk All wild birds. Intensive care. Registered charity. Veterinary support.

Wetland Bird Survey Organisers
GLOUCESTERSHIRE. Mr M Smart, 143 Cheltenham Road, Gloucester, Glos GL2 0JH. 01452 421 131; 07816 14 0513; E-mail: smartmike@btinternet.com

COTSWOLD WATER PARK. Mr G O Harris, 28 Thurnham Court, Thomas Wyatt Road, Devizes, Wiltshire SN10

ENGLAND

5FL. 07868 427 916; 07868 42 7916;
E-mail: gharris_doh@hotmail.com

Wildlife Trust
GLOUCESTERSHIRE WILDLIFE TRUST. (1961; 27,800).
Conservation Centre, Robinswood Hill Country Park,
Reservoir Road, Gloucester, GL4 6SX. 01452 383 333
(fax) 01452 383334;
E-mail: info@gloucestershirewildlifetrust.co.uk
www.gloucestershirewildlifetrust.co.uk

HAMPSHIRE

Bird Atlas/Avifauna
Birds of Hampshire by J M Clark and J A Eyre
(Hampshire Ornithological Society, 1993).

Bird Recorder
RECORDER. Keith Betton, 8 Dukes Close, Folly Hill,
Farnham, Surrey GU9 0DR. 01252 724 068;
E-mail: keithbetton@hotmail.com

Bird Reports
HAMPSHIRE BIRD REPORT (1955-). 2011 now available.
Check for the 2012 edition which may be available
at the end of 2013, from Mr Bryan Coates, 8 Gardner
Way, Chandler's Ford, Eastleigh, Hants SO53 1JL. 023
80 252960; E-mail: sandyandbryan@tiscali.co.uk
www.hos.org.uk

BTO Regional Representatives
RR. Glynne C Evans, Waverley, Station Road,
Chilbolton, Stockbridge, Hants SO20 6AL. 01264 860
697; E-mail: hantsbto@hotmail.com

BTO Garden BirdWatch Ambassador
Prof A Jones. E-mail: gbwhants@btinternet.com

Clubs
HAMPSHIRE ORNITHOLOGICAL SOCIETY. (1979; 1,500).
John Shillitoe, Hon. Secretary, Westerly, Hundred
Acres Road, Wickham, Hampshire PO17 6HY. 01329
833 086; E-mail: john@shillitoe.freeserve.co.uk
www.hos.org.uk

Ringing Groups
FARLINGTON RG. D A Bell, 38 Holly Grove, Fareham,
Hants PO16 7UP.

ITCHEN RG. W F Simcox, 10 Holdaway Close,
Kingsworthy, Winchester SO23 7QH.
E-mail: wilfsimcox@gmx.com

RSPB Local Groups
BASINGSTOKE. (1979; 90). Peter Hutchins, 35
Woodlands, Overton, Whitchurch RG25 3HN. 01256
770 831; (M)07895 388 378;
E-mail: fieldfare@jaybry.gotadsl.co.uk
www.rspb.org.uk/groups/basingstoke
Meetings: 7.30pm 3rd Wednesday of the month (Sept-
May), The Barn, Church Cottage, St Michael's Church,
Church Square, Basingstoke.

NEW FOREST. Dane Thomas. 01452 615 171;
E-mail: RSPB@newmilton.org
www.rspb.org.uk/groups/newforest

Meetings: 7.30pm 2nd Wednesday of the month
(Sept-June) Lyndhurst Community Centre, High
Street, Lyndhurst SO43 7NY.

NORTH EAST HAMPSHIRE. (1976; 215). Sue Radbourne.
0127 629 434;
E-mail: Mailto@northeasthantsRSPB.org.uk
www.northeasthantsrspb.org.uk
Meetings: See website.

PORTSMOUTH. (1974; 210). Gordon Humby, 19
Charlesworth Gardens, Waterlooville, Hants PO7 6AU.
02392 353 949;
E-mail: PortsmouthRSPB@googlemail.com
www.rspb.org.uk/groups/portsmouth
Meetings: 7.30pm, 4th Saturday of every month.
St Andrews Church Hall, Havant Road, Farlington,
Portsmouth, PO6 1AA

WINCHESTER & DISTRICT LOCAL GROUP. (1974;
100). Pam Symes, 29A Maytree Close, Badger Farm,
Winchester SO22 4JE. 01962 851 821;
E-mail: psymes033@gmail.com
www.rspb.org.uk/groups/winchester
Meetings: 7.30pm, 1st Wednesday of the month (not
Jan or Aug), Shawford Parish Hall, Pearson Lane,
Shawford SO21 2AA.

Wetland Bird Survey Organisers
AVON VALLEY. John Clark, 4 Cygnet Court, Old Cove
Road, Fleet, Hants GU51 2RL;
E-mail: johnclark50@sky.com

HAMPSHIRE (estuaries/coastal). Mr J R D Shillitoe, c/o
WeBS Office, BTO, The Nunnery, Thetford, Norfolk
IP24 2PU; E-mail: john@shillitoe.freeserve.co.uk

HAMPSHIRE (Inland - excluding Avon Valley). Mr K
Wills, 51 Peabody Road, Farnborough, Hampshire
GU14 6EB. E-mail: kwills57@btinternet.com

ISLE OF WIGHT. Mr J R Baldwin, 21 Hillcrest Road,
Rookley, VentnorIsle of Wight PO38 3PB. 01983 202
223; 0779 342 1938;
E-mail: jimr.baldwin@tiscali.co.uk

Wildlife Trust
HAMPSHIRE & ISLE OF WIGHT WILDLIFE TRUST. (1960;
27,000). Beechcroft House, Vicarage Lane, Curdridge,
Hampshire SO32 2DP. 01489 774 400, (fax) 01489 774
401; E-mail: feedback@hwt.org.uk
www.hiwwt.org.uk

HEREFORDSHIRE

Bird Recorder
Steve Coney, 5 Springfield Road, Withington, Hereford
HR1 3RU. 01432 850 068;
E-mail: coney@bluecarrots.com

Bird Report
THE BIRDS OF HEREFORDSHIRE (2008 -), from Mr WJ
Marler, Cherry Tree House, Walford, Leintwardine,
Craven Arms, Shropshire SY7 0JT.

ENGLAND

HEREFORDSHIRE ORNITHOLOGICAL CLUB ANNUAL REPORT, from Mr J Wilkinson, Coughton Forge, Coughton, Ross-on-Wye HR9 5SF. 01989 763 182; E-mail: m.jim.wilkinson@googlemail.com

BTO Regional Representative
Chris Robinson, Rock Cottage, Newton St. Margarets, Hereford HR2 0QW. 01981 510 360; E-mail: herefordbtorep@btinternet.com

Club
HEREFORDSHIRE ORNITHOLOGICAL CLUB. (1950; 416). TM Weale, Foxholes, Bringsty Common, Worcester WR6 5UN. 01886 821 368; E-mail: weale@tinyworld.co.uk www.herefordshirebirds.org
Meetings: 7.30pm, 2nd Thursday of the month (autumn/winter), Holmer Parish Centre, Holmer, Hereford HR4 9RG.

Ringing Group
LLANCILLO RG. Dr G R Geen, Little Langthorns, High Cross Lane, Little Canfield, Dunmow, Essex CM6 1TD. 01371 878 095; E-mail: grahamgeen@btinternet.com

Wetland Bird Survey
HEREFORDSHIRE. Mr C M Robinson, Rock Cottage, Newton St Margarets, Hereford HR2 0QW. 01981 510360; 07717 831 577; E-mail: herefordbtorep@btinternet.com

Wildlife Trust
HEREFORDSHIRE NATURE TRUST. (1962; 2,535). Lower House Farm, Ledbury Road, Tupsley, Hereford, HR1 1UT. 01432 356 872 (fax) 01432 275 489; E-mail: enquiries@herefordshirewt.co.uk www.herefordshirewt.org

HERTFORDSHIRE

Bird Atlas/Avifauna
Birds at Tring Reservoirs by R Young et al (Hertfordshire Natural History Society, 1996).

Mammals, Amphibians and Reptiles of Hertfordshire by Hertfordshire NHS in association with Training Publications Ltd, 3 Finway Court, Whippendell Road, Watford WD18 7EN, (2001).

The Breeding Birds of Hertfordshire by K W Smith et al (Herts NHS, 1993). Purchase from HNHS at £5 plus postage.E-mail: herts.naturalhistorysociety@aol.com

Bird Recorder
Ken Smith, 24 Mandeville Rise, Welwyn Garden City, Herts AL8 7JU.01707 330 405; E-mail: birdrecorder@hnhs.org www.hnhs.org/birds

Bird Report
HERTFORDSHIRE BIRD REPORT 2011 (from 1878-2011), from Linda Smith, 24 Mandeville Rise, Welwyn Garden City, Herts AL8 7JU. 01707 330 405; E-mail: secretary@hnhs.org www.hnhs.org

BTO Regional Representative
Chris Dee, 26 Broadleaf Avenue, Thorley Park, Bishop's Stortford, Herts CM23 4JY. 01279 755 637; E-mail: hertsbto@hotmail.com website: http://hertsbto.blogspot.com

Clubs
FRIENDS OF TRING RESERVOIRS. (1993; 400). Membership Secretary, PO Box 1083, Tring HP23 5WU. 01442 822 471; E-mail: keith@fotr.org.uk www.fotr.org.uk
Meetings: See website.

HERTFORDSHIRE BIRD CLUB. (1971). Part of Hertfordshire Natural History Society. Linda Smith, 24 Mandeville Rise, Welwyn Garden City, Herts AL8 7JU. 01707 330 405; E-mail: secretary@hnhs.org www.hnhs.org/birds

HERTFORDSHIRE NATURAL HISTORY SOCIETY. (1875) Linda Smith, 24 Mandeville Rise, Welwyn Garden City, Herts AL8 7JU. 01707 330 405; E-mail: secretary@hnhs.org www.hertsbirdclub.org.uk
Meetings: Saturday afternoon in Mar and Oct/Nov (date varies) at Woolmer Green Hall, SG3 6XA.

Ringing Groups
MAPLE CROSS RG. P Delaloye. E-mail: pdelaloye@tiscali.co.uk

RYE MEADS RG. Chris Dee, 26 Broadleaf Avenue, Thorley Park, Bishop's Stortford, Herts CM23 4JY. H:01279 755637; www.rmrg.org.uk E-mail: ringingsecretary@rmrg.org.uk

RSPB Local Groups
CHORLEYWOOD & DISTRICT. (1977; 142). Carol Smith, 24 Beacon Way, Rickmansworth, Herts WD3 7PE. 01923 897 885; E-mail: carolsmithuk@hotmail.com www.rspb.org.uk/groups/chorleywood
Meetings: 8pm, 3rd Thursday of the month (Sept-Nov, Jan-May), 2nd Thursday (Dec), Russell School, Brushwood Drive, Chorleywood.

HARPENDEN. (1974; 1000). Geoff Horn, 41 Ridgewood Drive, Harpenden, Herts AL5 3LJ. 01582 765 443; E-mail: geoffrhorn@yahoo.co.uk www.rspb.org.uk/groups/harpenden
Meetings: 8pm, 2nd Thursday of the month (Sept-June), All Saint's Church Hall, Station Road, Harpenden.

HEMEL HEMPSTEAD. (1972; 150). Ian Wilson, 15 Seymour Crescent, Hemel Hempstead, Herts HP2 5DS. 01442 265 022; E-mail: ian.aeronautics@gmail.com www.hemelrspb.org.uk
Meetings: 8pm, 1st Monday of the month (Sep-Jun),The Cavendish School, Warners End Road, Hemel Hempstead HP1 3DW.

HITCHIN & LETCHWORTH. (1972; 113). Dr Martin Johnson, 1 Cartwright Road, Royston, Herts SG8 9ET.

01763 249459; E-mail: martinrjspc@hotmail.com
www.rspb.org.uk/groups/hitchinandletchworth
Meetings: 7.30pm, 1st Friday of the month, The
Settlement, Nevells Road, Letchworth SG6 4UB.

POTTERS BAR & BARNET. (1977; 1,400). Lesley
Causton, 57 Lakeside Crescent, East Barnet, Herts
EN4 8QH. 0208 440 2038;
E-mail: lesleycauston@talktalk.net
www.pottersbar-rspb.org.uk
Meetings: 2.00pm, 2nd Wednesday of the month,
St Johns URC Hall, Mowbray Road, Barnet. Evening
meetings, 3rd Friday of the month (not Jul, Aug or
Dec) 7.45pm, Potters Bar United Reform Church,
Tilbury Hall, Darkes Lane, Potters Bar EN6 1BZ.

ST ALBANS. (1979; 1,550 in catchment area). Peter
Antram, 6 Yule Close, Bricket Wood, St Albans, Herts
AL2 3XZ. 01923 678 534;
E-mail: st-albans-rspb@hotmail.co.uk
www.rspb.org.uk/groups/stalbans
Meetings: 7.30pm, 2nd Tuesday of the month (Sep-
May), St Saviours Church Hall, Sandpit Lane, St Albans
AL1 4DF.

SOUTH EAST HERTS. (1971; 2,400 in catchment area).
Terry Smith, 31 Marle Gardens, Waltham Abbey, Essex
EN9 2DZ. 01992 715 634;
E-mail: se_herts_rspb@yahoo.co.uk
www.rspb.org.uk/groups/southeasthertfordshire
Meetings: 7.30pm, usually last Tuesday of the month
(Sept-June), URC Church Hall, Mill Lane, Broxbourne
EN10 7BQ.

STEVENAGE. (1982; 1,300 in the catchment area). Mrs
Ann Collis, 16 Stevenage Road, Walkern, Herts. 01483
861 547; E-mail: p.collis672@btinternet.com
www.rspb.org.uk/groups/stevenage
Meetings: 7.30pm, 3rd Tuesday of the month, Friends
Meeting House, 21 Cuttys Lane, Stevenage SG1 1UP.

WATFORD. (1974; 590). Janet Reynolds. 01923 249
647; E-mail: janet.reynolds@whht.nhs.uk
www.rspb.org.uk/groups/watford
Meetings: 7.30pm, 2nd Wednesday of the month
(Sep-Jun), Stanborough Centre, 609 St Albans Rd,
Watford WD25 9JL.

Wetland Bird Survey Organisers
HERTFORDSHIRE (excl. Lee Valley). Mr J H Terry, 46
Manor Way, Borehamwood, Herts WD6 1QY. 02089 051
461; e-mail: jimjoypaddy@virginmedia.com

LEE VALLEY. Miss C Patrick, Senior Conservation
Officer, Myddelton House, Bulls Cross, Enfield
Middlesex EN2 9HG. 01992 709 882(direct)/01992 717
711; 07717 449 341;
E-mail: cpatrick@leevalleypark.org.uk

Wildlife Trust
HERTS & MIDDLESEX WILDLIFE TRUST. (1964; 18,500).
Grebe House, St Michael's Street, St Albans, Herts,
AL3 4SN. 01727 858 901 (fax) 01727 854 542;
E-mail: info@hmwt.org
www.wildlifetrust.org.uk/herts/

ISLE OF WIGHT

Bird Recorder
Robin Attrill, 17 Waterhouse Moor, Harlow, Essex CM18
6BA. 01279 423 467;
E-mail: robin@rpattrill.freeserve.co.uk

Bird Reports
*ISLE OF WIGHT BIRD REPORT (1986-) (Pre-1986 not
available),* from Mr DJ Hunnybun, 40 Churchill Road,
Cowes, Isle of Wight PO31 8HH. 01983 292 880;
E-mail: davehunnybun@hotmail.com

BTO Regional Representative
James C Gloyn, 3 School Close, Newchurch, Isle of
Wight PO36 0NL. 01983 865 567;
E-mail: gloynjc@yahoo.com

Clubs
ISLE OF WIGHT NATURAL HISTORY & ARCHAEOLOGICAL
SOCIETY. (1919; 500). The Secretary, Unit 16,
Prospect Business Centre, Prospect Business Centre,
West Cowes, Isle of Wight PO31 7HD.
E-mail: meetings@iwnhas.orgwww.iwnhas.org

ISLE OF WIGHT ORNITHOLOGICAL GROUP. (1986; 155).
Mr DJ Hunnybun, 40 Churchill Road, Cowes, Isle of
Wight PO31 8HH. 01983 292 880;
e-mail: davehunnybun@hotmail.com
http://iowbirds.awardspace.com/IWOG.htm

Wildlife Trust
Director, See Hampshire,

KENT

Bird Atlas/Avifauna
Birding in Kent by D W Taylor et al 1996. Pica Press

Bird Recorder
Barry Wright, 6 Hatton Close, Northfleet, Kent DA11
8SD. 01474 320 918 (M)07789 710 555;
E-mail: umbrellabirds66@gmail.com

Bird Reports
DUNGENESS BIRD OBSERVATORY REPORT (1989-), from
Warden, see Reserves.

KENT BIRD REPORT (1952-), from Chris Roome,
Rowland House, Station Road, Staplehurst, Kent TN12
0PY. 01580 891 686;
E-mail: chris.roome@zulogic.co.uk

SANDWICH BAY BIRD OBSERVATORY REPORT, from
Warden, see Reserves,

BTO Regional Representatives
RR. Geoff Orton, 07788 102 238;
e-mail: geofforton@hotmail.com

Club
KENT ORNITHOLOGICAL SOCIETY. (1952; 650). Mr
Martin Coath, 14A Mount Harry Road, Sevenoaks, Kent
TN13 3JH. 01732 460 710; www.kentos.org.uk
E-mail: crag_martin2000@yahoo.co.uk

ENGLAND

Meetings: Indoor: October-April at various venues; the AGM in April is at Grove Green Community Hall, Grovewood Drive, Maidstone ME14 5TQ. See website for details: www.kentos.org.uk

Ringing Groups
DARTFORD RG. R Taylor.
E-mail: dreolin@btopenworld.com

DUNGENESS BIRD OBSERVATORY. David Walker, Dungeness Bird Observatory, 01797 321 309; E-mail: dungeness.obs@tinyonline.co.uk www.dungenessbirdobs.org.uk

RECULVER RG. Chris Hindle, 42 Glenbervie Drive, Herne Bay, Kent CT6 6QL. 01227 373 070; E-mail: christopherhindle@hotmail.com

SANDWICH BAY BIRD OBSERVATORY. Mr KB Ellis, 6 Alderney Gardens, St Peters, Broadstairs, Kent CT10 2TN. 01304 617 341; E-mail: keithjulie@talktalk.net

SWALE WADER GROUP. Rod Smith, 67 York Avenue, Chatham, Kent ME5 9ES. 01634 865 836. www.swalewaders.co.uk

RSPB Local Groups
CANTERBURY. (1973; 216). Wendy Kennett. 01227 477 113; E-mail: wendywiffles@yahoo.co.uk www.rspb.org.uk/groups/canterbury
Meetings: 8.00pm, 2nd Tuesday of the month (Sept-Apr), Chaucer Social Club, Off Chaucer Drive, Canterbury, CT1 1YW.

GRAVESEND. (1977; 250). Paul Yetman. 01474 332 417; E-mail: Groupleader@RSPBgravesend.org.uk www.rspbgravesend.org.uk
Meetings: 7.45pm, 2nd Wednesday of the month (Sep-May), St Botolph's Hall, Northfleet, Gravesend DA11 9EX. 2.00pm 4th Tuesday of the month (Nov, Jan-Mar), Kent Room, Woodville Halls, Gravesend DA12 1AU

MAIDSTONE. (1973; 250). Jean Howland, E-mail: jean@imac.fsworld.co.uk http://maidstone.localrspb.org.uk/
Meetings: 7.30pm, 3rd Thursday of the month, Grove Green Community Hall, Penhurst Close, Grove Green, opposite Tesco's.

MEDWAY. (1974; 230). Marie Tilley. 01634 387 431; E-mail: marie.tilley@btinternet.com www.medway-rspb.pwp.blueyonder.co.uk
Meetings: 7.45pm 3rd Tuesday of the month (except Aug), Parkwood Community Centre, Parkwood Green, Gillingham ME8 9PN

SEVENOAKS. (1974; 265). Anne Chapman. 01732 456 459; E-mail: anneanddave.chapman@virgin.net www.rspb.org.uk/groups/sevenoaks
Meetings: 7.45pm 1st Thursday of the month, Otford Memorial Hall, High Street, Otford TN14 5PQ.

THANET. (1975; 119). Peter Radclyffe, Cottage of St

John, Caterbury Road, Sarre, Kent CT7 0JY. 01843 847 345; www.rspb.org.uk/groups/thanet
Meetings: 7.30pm last Tuesday of the month (Jan-Nov), Portland Centre, Hopeville Avenue, Broadstairs CT10 2TR.

TONBRIDGE. (1975; 150 reg attendees/1,700 in catchment). Martin Ellis. 01892 521 413;
E-mail: martin@ellismp.plus.com
www.rspb.org.uk/groups/tonbridge
Meetings: 7.45pm 3rd Wednesday of the month (Sept-Apr), St Phillips Church, Salisbury Road, Tonbridge TN10 4PA.

Wetland Bird Survey Organisers
DUNGENESS AREA. David Walker, Dungeness Bird Observatory, 01797 321 309; E-mail: dungeness.obs@tinyonline.co.uk www.dungenessbirdobs.org.uk

EAST KENT. Mr K W Lodge, 14 Gallwey Avenue, Birchington, Kent CT7 9PA. 01843 843 105; E-mail: lodge9pa@btinternet.com

NORTH KENT ESTUARIES. Mr G R Orton, c/o WeBS Office, BTO, The Nunnery, Thetford, Norfolk IP24 2PU. 07788 102 238; e-mail: geofforton@hotmail.com

PEGWELL BAY. Mr P W J Findley, 62 Elizabeth Carter Avenue, Deal, Kent CT14 9NT.
E-mail: pwjfindley@hotmail.com

Wildlife Hospital
RAPTOR CENTRE. Eddie Hare, Ivy Cottage, Groombridge Place, Groombridge, Tunbridge Wells, Kent TN3 9QG. 01892 861 175;
E-mail: raptorcentre@btconnect.com
www.raptorcentre.co.uk
Birds of prey. Veterinary support. 24hr rescue service for sick and injured birds of prey that covers the South-East.

Wildlife Trust
KENT WILDLIFE TRUST. (1958; 10,500). Tyland Barn, Sandling, Maidstone, Kent, ME14 3BD. 01622 662 012, (fax) 01622 671 390; E-mail: info@kentwildlife.org.uk www.kentwildlifetrust.org.uk

LANCASHIRE

Bird Atlas/Avifauna
An Atlas of Breeding Birds of Lancaster and District by Ken Harrison (Lancaster & District Birdwatching Society, 1995).

Birds of Lancashire and North Merseyside by White, McCarthy and Jones (Hobby Publications 2008).

Breeding Birds of Lancashire and North Merseyside (2001), sponsored by North West Water. Contact: Bob Pyefinch, 12 Bannistre Court, Tarleton, Preston PR4 6HA.

Bird Recorder
(See also Manchester).

ENGLAND

LANCASHIRE (Inc North Merseyside). Steve White, 102 Minster Court, Crown Street, Liverpool L7 3QD. 0151 707 2744; E-mail: stevewhite102@btinternet.com

Bird Reports
BIRDS OF LANCASTER & DISTRICT (1959-2012), (£8.00) from the Secretary, LDBWS (see website- www. lancasterbirdwatching.org.uk) and RSPB Leighton Moss shop. E-mail: peter.cook33@btinternet.com www.lancasterbirdwatching.org.uk

EAST LANCASHIRE ORNITHOLOGISTS' CLUB BIRD REPORT (1982-) Members £2.50, Non-members £5.50 from Tony Cooper, 28 Peel Park Ave, Clitheroe BB7 1ET; www.eastlancashireornithologists.org.uk

CHORLEY AND DISTRICT NATURAL HISTORY SOCIETY ANNUAL REPORT (1979 -), published on website www.chorleynats.org.uk

BLACKBURN & DISTRICT BIRD CLUB ANNUAL REPORT (1992-), from Doreen Bonner, 6 Winston Road, Blackburn, BB1 8BJ. 01254 261 480; E-mail: webmaster@blackburnbirdclub.co.uk www.blackburnbirdclub.co.uk

FYLDE BIRD REPORT (1983-), from Paul Ellis, 18 Staining Rise, Blackpool, FY3 0BU. 01253 891 281; E-mail: paul.ellis24@btopenworld.com or news@fyldebirdclub.org - www.fyldebirdclub.org

LANCASHIRE BIRD REPORT (1914-), from Dave Bickerton, 64 Petre Crescent, Rishton, Blackburn, Lancs BB1 4RB. 01254 886 257; E-mail: bickertond@aol.com

ROSSENDALE ORNITHOLOGISTS' CLUB BIRD REPORT (1977-).from Ian Brady. 01706 222 120; http://roc.wikispaces.com

BTO Regional Representatives
EAST RR. Tony Cooper, 28 Peel Park Avenue, Clitheroe, Lancs BB7 1ET. 01200 424 577; E-mail: anthony.cooper34@btinternet.com

NORTH & WEST RR. Jean Roberts. 01524 770 295; E-mail: JeanRbrts6@aol.com

SOUTH RR. Stuart Piner, 01524 751 987; E-mail: stuartpiner@hotmail.com

Clubs
BLACKBURN & DISTRICT BIRD CLUB. (1991; 100). Jim Bonner, 6 Winston Road, Blackburn, BB1 8BJ. 01254 261 480; E-mail: webmaster@blackburnbirdclub.co.uk www.blackburnbirdclub.co.uk
Meetings: Normally 7.30pm, 1st Monday of the month, (Sept-Apr), St Silas's Church Hall, Preston New Road. Check website for all meetings.

CHORLEY & DISTRICT NATURAL HISTORY SOCIETY. (1979; 170). Phil Kirk, Millend, Dawbers Lane, Euxton, Chorley, Lancs PR7 6EB. 01257 266783; E-mail: secretary@chorleynats.org.uk www.chorleynats.org.uk
Meetings: 7.30pm, 3rd Thursday of the month (Sept-Apr), St Mary's Parish Centre, Chorley PR7 2SR.

EAST LANCASHIRE ORNITHOLOGISTS' CLUB. (1955; 45). Dr J Plackett, 71 Walton Lane, Nelson, Lancs BB9 8BG. 01282 612 870; E-mail: j.plackett@eastlancsornithologists.org.uk www.eastlancsornithologists.org.uk
Meetings: 7.30pm, 1st Monday of the month (Check website or local press), St Anne's Church Hall, Fence-in-Pendle, Nr Burnley BB12 9EP.

FYLDE BIRD CLUB (Registered charity number 1102961). (1982; 150). Paul Ellis, 18 Staining Rise, Blackpool, FY3 0BU. 01253 891281; E-mail: paul. ellis24@btopenworld.com or KBeaver@uclan.ac.uk www.fyldebirdclub.org
Meetings: 7.45pm, 4th Tuesday of the month, River Wyre Hotel, Breck Road, Poulton-le-Fylde.

FYLDE NATURALISTS' SOCIETY. (1946; 140). Julie Clarke, 7 Cedar Avenue, Poulton-le-Fylde, Blackpool FY6 8DQ. 01253 883 785; www.fyldenaturalists.co.uk E-mail: secretary@fyldenaturalists.co.uk
Meetings: 7.30pm, fortnightly (Sep-Mar), Fylde Coast Alive, Church Hall, Raikes Parade, Blackpool unless otherwise stated in the Programme.

LANCASHIRE & CHESHIRE FAUNA SOCIETY. (1914; 150). Dave Bickerton, 64 Petre Crescent, Rishton, Lancs BB1 4RB. 01254 886257; E-mail: bickertond@aol.com www.lacfs.org.uk

LANCASTER & DISTRICT BIRD WATCHING SOCIETY. (1959; 200). Peter Cook (Secretary), 21 Threshfield Avenue, Heysham, Morecambe, Lancs LA3 2DU. 01524 851 454/(M) 07880 541 798; E-mail: peter.cook33@btinternet.com www.lancasterbirdwatching.org.uk
Meetings: 7.30pm, last Monday of the month (Sep-Nov, Jan-Mar) For details and venues see website.

PRESTON BIRD WATCHING & NATURAL HISTORY SOCIETY. (1876 as the Preston Scientific Society; 140). Stephen R. Halliwell, 3 Baillie Street, Williams Lane, Fulwood Park, Preston. 01772 705 468; E-mail: stephen.halliwell@prestonsociety.co.uk www.prestonsociety.co.uk
Meetings: Check website for details.

ROSSENDALE ORNITHOLOGISTS' CLUB. (1976; 35). Ian Brady. 01706 222 120; http://roc.wikispaces.com
Meetings: 7.30pm, 3rd Monday of the month, Weavers Cottage, Bacup Road, Rawtenstall.

Ringing Groups
FYLDE RG. G Barnes,17 Lomond Avenue, Marton, Blackpool FY3 9QL.

NORTH LANCS RG. John Wilson BEM, 40 Church Hill Avenue, Warton, Carnforth, Lancs LA5 9NU. E-mail: johnwilson711@btinternet.com

SOUTH WEST LANCASHIRE RG. I H Wolfenden, 35 Hartdale Road, Thornton, Liverpool, Merseyside L23 1TA. 01519 311 232.

RSPB Local Groups
BLACKPOOL. (1983; 170). Alan Stamford, 6 Kensington

ENGLAND

Road, Cleveleys, FY5 1ER. 01253 859 662;
E-mail: alanstamford140@msn.com
Meetings: 7.30pm, 2nd Friday of the month (Sept-
June), Cleveleys Community Centre, Beach Road,
Cleveleys FY5 1ER.

LANCASTER. (1972; 176). Michael Gardner. 01524 65
211; e-mail: RSPBlancaster@gmail.com
www.rspb.org.uk/localgroups/lancaster
Meetings: Indoors a Leighton Moss.

Wetland Bird Survey Organisers
EAST LANCASHIRE AND FYLDE. Miss H Hilton, 7
Swallow Close, Blackpool, Lancashire FY3 9NZ. 01253
588 164; 07754 193 096;
e-mail: edieandmax@live.co.uk

MORECAMBE BAY NORTH. Mr C Hartley, Undercragg,
Charney Well Lane, Grange-over-Sands LA11 6DB.
01539 536 824;
E-mail: clive.hartley304@btinternet.com

MORECAMBE BAY SOUTH. Mrs J Roberts, 3 Claughton
Terrace, Claughton, Lancaster LA2 9JZ. 01524 770
295; 07815 979 856; E-mail: Jeanrbrts6@aol.com

NORTH LANCASHIRE (Inland). Mr P J Marsh, Leck View
Cottage, Ashleys Farm, High Tatham, Lancaster LA2
8PH. 07989 866 487; E-mail: pmrsh123@aol.com

RIBBLE ESTUARY. Mr K Abram, 25 Schwarzman Drive,
Banks, Southport, Merseyside PR9 8BG.
E-mail: k.abram@btinternet.com

RIVER LUNE. Mrs J Roberts, 3 Claughton Terrace,
Claughton, Lancaster LA2 9JZ. 01524 770 295; 07815
979 856; E-mail: Jeanrbrts6@aol.com

WEST LANCASHIRE (INLAND). Mr T Clare, c/o WeBS
Office, BTO; E-mail: Tom.Clare@www.org.uk

Wildlife Trust
THE WILDLIFE TRUST FOR LANCASHIRE, MANCHESTER
AND NORTH MERSEYSIDE. (1962; 18,000). Mr James
Ellaby, Communications Officer, The Barn, Berkeley
Drive, Bamber Bridge, Preston PR5 6BY. 01772 324 129
(fax); 01772 628 849; E-mail: info@lancswt.org.uk
www.lancswt.org.uk

LEICESTERSHIRE & RUTLAND

The Birds of Leicestershire and Rutland, by Rob Fray
et al. (A&C Black).

Bird Recorder
Steve Lister, 6 Albert Promenade, Loughborough,
Leicestershire LE11 1RE. 01509 829 495;
E-mail: stevelister@surfbirder.com

Bird Reports
LEICESTERSHIRE & RUTLAND BIRD REPORT (1941-),
from Mrs S Graham, 5 Lychgate Close, Cropston,
Leicestershire LE7 7HU. 0116 236 6474;
E-mail: JSGraham83@aol.com
www.lros.org.uk

RUTLAND NAT HIST SOC ANNUAL REPORT (1965-),

from Secretary. 01572 747302.
BTO Regional Representative
LEICESTER & RUTLAND RR. David Wright, 01530 231
102; e-mail: davewrightbto@gmail.com

Clubs
BIRSTALL BIRDWATCHING CLUB. (1976; 50). Mr KJ
Goodrich, 6 Riversdale Close, Birstall, Leicester LE4
4EH. 0116 267 4813; E-mail: kjgood1532@aol.com
www.leicestershirevillages.com/rothley/
birdwatchingclub.html
Meetings: 7.30pm, 2nd Tuesday of the month (Oct-
Apr), The Rothley Centre, Mountsorrel Lane, Rothley,
Leics LE7 7PR.

LEICESTERSHIRE & RUTLAND
ORNITHOLOGICAL SOCIETY. (1941; 580).
Jennifer Thompson, 36 Burnside Road,
Leicester, LE12 6QD. 0116 233 0320;
E-mail: jennythompson1301@gmail.com
www.lros.org.uk
Meetings: 7.30pm, 1st Friday of the month (Oct-
May), Oadby Methodist Church, off Central Car Park,
alternating with The Rothley Centre, Mountsorrel
Lane, Rothley. Additional meeting at Rutland Water
Birdwatching Centre.

SOUTH LEICESTER BIRDWATCHERS. (2006; 60). Marion
Turner. 01455 282 854; (M)07852 782 002;
E-mail: graham.turner@btinternet.com
Meetings: 7.15 pm, 2nd Wednesday of the month
(Sep-Jun), All Saints Parish Centre, Wigston Road,
Blaby, Leicester, LE8 4FA.

RUTLAND NATURAL HISTORY SOCIETY. (1964; 256).
Mrs L Worrall, 6 Redland Close, Barrowden, Oakham,
Rutland LE15 8ES. 01572 747 302; www.rnhs.org.uk
E-mail: rnhscontact@btinternet.com
Meetings: 7.30pm, 1st Tuesday of the month (Oct-
Apr), Voluntary Action Rutland, Lands End Way,
Oakham LE15 6RB.

Ringing Groups
RUTLAND WATER RG. Tim Appleton, Reserve Manager,
Egleton, Oakham, Rutland LE15 8BT;
E-mail: awbc@rutland water.org.uk

STANFORD RG. John Cranfield, 41 Main Street,
Fleckney, Leicester LE8 8AP. 0116 240 4385;
E-mail: JacanaJohn@talktalk.net
www.stanfordrg.org.uk

RSPB Local Groups
LEICESTER. (1969; 1600 in catchment area). Graham
Heningham, 01455 616 098;
E-mail: grahamheninghem@waitrose.com
www.rspb.org.uk/groups/leicester
Meetings: 7.30pm, 3rd Friday of the month (Sep-
May), Trinity Methodist Hall, Harborough Road, Oadby,
Leicester LE2 4LA

LOUGHBOROUGH. (1970; 300). Robert Orton. 07961
249 625; E-mail: Lboro.RSPB@virgin.net
www.rspb.org.uk/groups/loughborough
Meetings: Monthly on Friday nights, Brockington
Building, Loughborough University.

ENGLAND

Wetland Bird Survey Organisers
LEICESTERSHIRE & RUTLAND (excl Rutland Water). Mr B Moore, 13 Swinford Avenue, Glen Parva, Leics LE2 9RW. E-mail: b_moore@ntlworld.com

RUTLAND WATER. Tim Appleton, Reserve Manager, Egleton, Oakham, Rutland LE15 8BT. 01572 770 651; E-mail: tim@rutlandwater.org.uk

Wildlife Trust
LEICESTERSHIRE & RUTLAND WILDLIFE TRUST. (1956; 14,000). Brocks Hill Environment Centre, Washbrook Lane, Oadby, Leicestershire LE2 5JJ. 0116 272 0444 (fax) 0116 272 0404; E-mail: info@lrwt.org.uk www.lrwt.org.uk

LINCOLNSHIRE

Bird Recorders
NORTH. John Clarkson.
E-mail: recorder_north@lincsbirdclub.co.uk

SOUTH. John Badley.
E-mail: recorder_south@lincsbirdclub.co.uk

Bird Reports
LINCOLNSHIRE BIRD REPORT (1979-). Several years sold out. 2011 is the latest report, £15 + £2 postage, from Bill Sterling, Newlyn, 5 Carlton Avenue, Healing, NE Lincs DN41 7PW. E-mail: wbsterling@hotmail.com

LINCOLNSHIRE RARE AND SCARCE BIRD REPORTS (1997-1999 & 2000-2002), £13.75 each including postage. Bill Sterling, Newlyn, 5 Carlton Avenue, Healing, NE Lincs DN41 7PW.
E-mail: wbsterling@hotmail.com

SCUNTHORPE & NORTH WEST LINCOLNSHIRE BIRD REPORT (1973-), from Secretary, Scunthorpe Museum Society, Ornithological Section, (Day)01724 402 871, (Eve)01724 734 261.

BTO Regional Representatives
EAST RR. Philip Espin. 01507 605 448;
E-mail: pmjespin@gmail.com

NORTH RR. Chris Gunn.
E-mail: donandchris@hotmail.co.uk

SOUTH RR. Hugh Dorrington. 01778 440 716;
E-mail: hdorrington@btconnect.com

WEST RR. Peter Overton, 01400 273 323;
E-mail: nyika@biosearch.org.uk
Sponsoring the Kestrel in the Bird Atlas through Biosearch Expeditions www.biosearch.org.uk

Club
LINCOLNSHIRE BIRD CLUB. (1979; 304). Robert Carr, 35 St Leonard's Close, Woodhall Spa, Lincs LN10 6SX. E-mail: secretary@lincsbirdclub.co.uk
www.lincsbirdclub.co.uk
Meetings: Local groups hold winter evening meetings (contact Secretary for details). AGM in March with a guest speaker.

LINCOLNSHIRE NATURALISTS' UNION. C/o Lincolnshire Wildlife Trust, Banovallum House, Manor House Street, Horncastle, Lincs LN9 5HF. Website: http://lnu.org/
Meetings: Monthly meetings (field trips between April and October and indoors November to March). Often bird elements to meetings, occasional joint meetings with the Lincolnshire Bird Club.

Ringing Groups
GIBRALTAR POINT BIRD OBSERVATORY. Mr M.R. Briggs.
E-mail: mbriggs@gibobs.fsworld.co.uk

MID LINCOLNSHIRE RG. J Mawer, 2 The Chestnuts, Owmby Road, Searby, Lincolnshire DN38 6EH. 01652 628583.

WASH WADER RG. P L Ireland, 27 Hainfield Drive, Solihull, W Midlands B91 2PL. 0121 704 1168;
E-mail: enquiries@wwrg.org.uk

RSPB Local Groups
GRIMSBY AND CLEETHORPES. (1986; 2,200 in catchment area). Terry Whalin. 01472 211 115;
E-mail: terence@terencewhalin.wanadoo.co.uk
www.rspb.org.uk/groups/grimsby
Meetings: 7.30pm, 1st Monday of the month (Sept-May), Corpus Christi Church Hall, Grimsby Road, Cleethorpes, DN35 7LJ.

LINCOLN. (1974; 250). Peter Skelson, 26 Parksgate Avenue, Lincoln, LN6 7HP. 01522 695747;
E-mail: peter.skelson@lincolnrspb.org.uk
www.lincolnrspb.org.uk
Meetings: 7.30pm, 2nd Thursday of the month (not Jun, Jul, Aug, Dec), The Robert Hardy Centre, Bishop Grosseteste University, Longdales Road, Lincoln.

SOUTH LINCOLNSHIRE. (1987; 350). Adrian Slater. 01205 360 858; E-mail: adrian.slater@btinternet.com www.southlincsrspb.org.uk
Meetings: Contact group for details.

Wetland Bird Survey Organisers
HUMBER ESTUARY - INNER SOUTH. Mr K Parker, 7 Ryedale Avenue, Winterton, Scunthorpe, Lincolnshire DN15 9BJ. E-mail: Keith.Parker@corusgroup.com

HUMBER ESTUARY - MID SOUTH. Mr R Barnard, RSPB Northern England, Westleigh Mews, Wakefield Road, Denby Dale, Huddersfield HD8 8QD. 01484 868 425;
E-mail: richard.barnard@rspb.org.uk

HUMBER ESTUARY - NORTH. Mr N Cutts, c/o WeBS Office, BTO, The Nunnery, Thetford, Norfolk IP24 2PU. 01842 750050; E-mail: webs@bto.org.uk

HUMBER ESTUARY - OUTER SOUTH. Mr J R Walker MBE, 3 Coastguard Cottage, Churchill Lane, Theddlethorpe, Mablethorpe, Lincs LN12 1PQ. 01507 338 038.

NORTH LINCOLNSHIRE. Ms C Gunn, c/o WeBS Office, BTO, The Nunnery, Thetford Norfolk IP24 2PU. 01777 707 888; E-mail: donandchris@hotmail.co.uk

251

ENGLAND

SOUTH LINCOLNSHIRE/PETERBOROUGH (inland).
Mr R C E Titman, 28 Eastgate, Deeping St James,
Peterborough PE6 8HJ. 01733 583 254; 01778 380 695;
E-mail: bob.titman@gmail.com

Wildlife Trust
LINCOLNSHIRE WILDLIFE TRUST. (1948; 26,000).
Banovallum House, Manor House Street, Horncastle,
Lincs, LN9 5HF. 01507 526 667 (fax) 01507 525 732;
E-mail: info@lincstrust.co.uk
www.lincstrust.org.uk

LONDON, GREATER

Bird Atlas/Avifauna
*The Breeding Birds Illustrated magazine of the
London Area, 2002.* ISBN 0901009 121 ed Jan Hewlett,
(London Natural History Society).

Two Centuries of Croydon's Birds by John Birkett
(RSPB Croydon Local Group 2007). £10 plus p&p.

Bird Recorder (see also Surrey)
Andrew Self, 16 Harp Island Close, Neasden, London
NW10 0DF. 07889 761 828; E-mail: a-self@sky.com
http://londonbirders.wikia.com

Bird Report
CROYDON BIRD SURVEY (1995), from Secretary,
Croydon RSPB Group, 020 8640 4578;
E-mail: johndavis.wine@care4free.net
www.croydon-rspb.org.uk

*LONDON BIRD REPORT (20-mile radius of St Paul's
Cathedral) (1936-),* from Catherine Schmitt,
Publications Sales, London Natural History Society, 4
Falkland Avenue, London N3 1QR. 020 8346 4359.

BTO Regional Representatives
LONDON, NORTH. Ian Woodward, 245 Larkshall Road,
Chingford, London E4 9HY. 02085 298 964; E-mail:
ianw_bto_nlon@hotmail.co.uk

LONDON, SOUTH. Richard Arnold. 0208 224 1135;
E-mail: bto@thomsonecology.com

Clubs
THE LONDON BIRD CLUB (formerly the Ornithological
Section of the London Natural History Society).
(1858; 1000). Mrs Angela Linnell, 20 Eleven Acre Rise,
Loughton, Essex IG10 1AN. 020 8508 2932;
E-mail: angela.linnell@phonecoop.coop
www.lnhs.org.uk
Meetings: See website.

MARYLEBONE BIRDWATCHING SOCIETY. (1981; 110).
Marion Hill, 20 Howitt Close, Howitt Road, London
NW3 4LX. E-mail: birdsmbs@yahoo.com
www.birdsmbs.org.uk; www.facebook.com/birdsmbs;
www.flickr.com/photos/mbsbirds
Meeting: 3rd Friday of month (Sept-May), 7.15pm
Gospel Oak Methodist Church, Lisburne Road, London
NW3 2NT. Weekly Tuesday walks on Hampstead Heath.

Ringing Groups
LONDON GULL STUDY GROUP - (SE including

Hampshire, Surrey, Sussex, Berkshire and
Oxfordshire). This group is no longer active but still
receiving sightings/recoveries of ringed birds. and
give information on gulls.
Mark Fletcher, 24 The Gowans, Sutton-on-the-Forest,
York YO61 1DJ. E-mail: m.fletcher48@btinternet.com

RUNNYMEDE RG. D G Harris, 22 Blossom Waye,
Hounslow, TW5 9HD. E-mail: daveharris@tinyonline.
co.ukhttp://rmxrg.org.uk

RSPB Local Groups
BEXLEY. Stuart Banks, 157 Garland Road, Plumstead,
London SE18 2PP0208 854 7251;
E-mail: stuartbans@hotmail.co.uk
Meetings: 7.30pm, 2nd Friday of the month,
Hurstmere School Hall, Hurst Road, Sidcup.

BROMLEY. (1972; 285). Des Garrahan, 0207 808 1240;
E-mail: des.garrahan@RSPB.org.uk
www.rspb.org.uk/groups/bromley
Meetings: 2nd Wednesday of the month (Sep-Jun),
4th floor, Central Library Building, Bromley High
Street.

CENTRAL LONDON. (1974; 250). Margaret Blackburn.
0208 866 5853;
E-mail: Graemehutchinson@hotmail.com
www.janja.dircon.co.uk/rspb
Meetings: 2nd Thursday of the month (Sep-May), St
Columba's Church Hall, Pont St, London SW1. See
website for details of field meetings.

CROYDON. (1973; 4,000 in catchment area). John
Davis, 9 Cricket Green, Mitcham, CR4 4LB. 020 8640
4578; E-mail: johndavis.wine@care4free.net
www.croydon-rspb.org.uk
Meetings: 2nd Monday of each month at 2pm-4pm
and again at 8pm-10pm at Old Whitgiftian Clubhouse,
Croham Manor Road, South Croydon.

ENFIELD. (1971; 2,700). Norman G Hudson, 125
Morley Hill, Enfield, Middx EN2 0BQ. 020 8363 1431
(daytime); E-mail: dorandnor@tiscali.co.uk
www.rspb.org.uk/groups/enfield
Meetings: 8pm, 1st Thursday of the month, St
Andrews Hall, 14 Silver Street, Enfield EN1 3EG.

HAVERING. (1972; 270). Martin Runchman. 01767 690
093; E-mail: mrunchman@yahoo.com
www.rspb.org.uk/groups/havering/
Meetings: 8pm, 2nd Friday of the month, Hornchurch
Library, North Street, Hornchurch.

NORTH EAST LONDON. David Littlejohns. 0208 989
4746; E-mail: NelondonRSPB@yahoo.co.uk
www.rspb.org.uk/groups/northeastlondon
Meetings: 7.30pm, 2nd Tuesday of every month,
Snaresbrook Primary School, Meadow Walk, South
Woodford, London, E18 2EN.

NW LONDON RSPB GROUP. (1983; 2000 in catchment
area). Bob Husband, The Firs, 49 Carson Road,
Cockfosters, Barnet, Herts EN4 9EN. 020 8441 8742;
E-mail: bobhusband@hotmail.co.uk
www.rspb.org.uk/groups/nwlondon. A full programme

of events can be downloaded from the site.
Meetings: 8pm, Usually last Tuesday of the month, (Sep-Mar), Wilberforce Centre, St Paul's Church, The Ridgeway, Mill Hill, London, NW7 1QU.

PINNER & DISTRICT. (1972; 300). Ian Jackson, 5 Oakfield Avenue, Kenton, Harrow, Middx HA3 8TH. 020 8907 3513; E-mail: imnme@btinternet.com www.rspb.org.uk/groups/pinner/
Meetings: 8pm, 2nd Thursday of the month (Sept-May), Church Hall, St John The Baptist Parish Church, Pinner HA5 3AS.

RICHMOND & TWICKENHAM. (1979; 215). Roger Theobald. 0208 977 6343;
E-mail: RichmondRSPB@yahoo.co.uk www.rspb.org.uk/groups/richmond
Meetings: 8.00pm, 1st Wednesday of the month and 2pm 2nd Tuesday of the month, both meetings held York House, Richmond Road, Twickenham TW1 3AA.

Wetland Bird Survey Organiser
GREATER LONDON (excl. Thames Estuary). Miss H Baker, 60 Townfield, Rickmansworth, Herts WD3 7DD. E-mail: helen.baker60@tiscali.co.uk

LEE VALLEY. Miss C Patrick, Senior Conservation Officer, Myddelton House, Bulls Cross, Enfield, Middlesex EN2 9HG. 01992 709 882(direct)/01992 717 711; 07717 449 341;
E-mail: cpatrick@leevalleypark.org.uk

Wildlife Trust
LONDON WILDLIFE TRUST. (1981; 7500). Skyline House, 200 Union Street, London, SE1 0LX. 0207 261 0447 (fax) 0207 633 0811;
E-mail: enquiries@wildlondon.org.uk www.wildlondon.org.uk

MANCHESTER, GREATER

Bird Atlas/Avifauna
Breeding Birds in Greater Manchester by Philip Holland et al (1984).

Bird Recorder
RECORDER. Ian McKerchar, 42 Green Ave, Astley, Manchester M29 7EH. 01942 701 758;
E-mail: ianmckerchar1@gmail.com www.manchesterbirding.com

Bird Reports
BIRDS IN GREATER MANCHESTER (1976-). 2006 sold out, Mrs M McCormick, 91 Sinderland Road, Altrincham WA14 5JJ (can only supply editions up to year 2000. Year 2001 onwards from County Recorder).

LEIGH ORNITHOLOGICAL SOCIETY BIRD REPORT (1971-), from Mr D Shallcross, 28 Surrey Avenue, Leigh, Lancs WN7 2NN. www.leighos.org.uk E-mail: leighos.chairman@gmail.com

BTO Regional Representatives
MANCHESTER. Steve Suttill, 01457 836 360;
E-mail: suttill.parkinson@virgin.net www.manchesterbirding.com

Clubs
ALTRINGHAM AND DISTRICT NATURAL HISTORY SOCIETY. Claire Joures (Secretary). 0161 928 4513.
Meetings: 7:30pm, Tuesdays, Hale Methodist Church Hall, Oak Road, off Hale Road, Hale. 50p charge includes refreshments.

GREATER MANCHESTER BIRD RECORDING GROUP. (2002: 61). Ian McKerchar.
E-mail: ianmckerchar1@gmail.com

LEIGH ORNITHOLOGICAL SOCIETY. (1971; 98). Mr D Shallcross, 28 Surrey Avenue, Leigh, Lancs WN7 2NN.
E-mail: leighos.chairman@gmail.com www.leighos.org.uk
L.O.S. Young Birders: www.losybc. blogspot.co.uk/
Meetings: 7.15pm, Fridays, Leigh Library, 150 Deansgate M3 3EH, (check website for details).

ROCHDALE FIELD NATURALISTS' SOCIETY. (1970; 90). Mrs D Francis, 20 Hillside Avenue, Shaw, Oldham OL2 8HR. 01706 843 685; E-mail: secretary@rochdalefieldnaturalistssociety.co.uk www.rochdalefieldnaturalistssociety.co.uk
Meetings: 7.30pm (Sept-Apr) at Cutgate Baptist Church, Edenfield Rd, Rochdale OL12 7SS. Yearly syllabus (out after AGM in Sept) states dates of lectures and outings.

STOCKPORT BIRDWATCHING SOCIETY. (1972; 80). Dave Evans, 36 Tatton Road South, Stockport, Cheshire SK4 4LU. 0161 432 9513;
E-mail: windhover1972@yahoo.co.uk
Meetings: 7.30pm, last Wednesday of the month (Sep-Apr), The Heatons Sports Club, Heaton Moor Stockport SK4 2NF.

Ringing Groups
LEIGH RG. A J Gramauskas, 21 Elliot Avenue, Golborne, Warrington WA3 3DU. 0151 929 215.

SOUTH MANCHESTER RG. Mr N.B. Powell.
E-mail: neville.powell@tiscali.co.uk

RSPB Local Groups
BOLTON. (1978; 320). Barrie Shore.
E-mail: b.shore@sky.com
http://boltonrspb.users.btopenworld.com
Meetings: 7.30pm, Thursdays (dates vary),Canon Slade School, Bradshaw Brow, Bolton BL2 3BP.

MANCHESTER. (1972; 3,600 in catchment area). Peter Wolstenholme, 31 South Park Road, Gatley, Cheshire SK8 4AL. 0161 428 2175;
E-mail: Conservation@RSPBmanchester.org.uk www.rspbmanchester.org.uk
Meetings: 7.30 pm, St James Parish Hall, Gatley Green, Church Road, Gatley, Cheadle.

STOCKPORT LOCAL GROUP. (1979; 120). Gay Crossley, 5 Broadhill Close, Bramhall, Stockport, Cheshire SK7 3BY. 0161 439 3210.
E-mail: StockportRSPB@googlemail.com www.rspb.org.uk/groups/stockport

ENGLAND

Meetings: 7.30pm, 2nd Monday of the month (Sep-Apr), Stockport College of Technology, Lecture Theatre B, Wellington Road SK1 3UQ.

WIGAN. (1973; 80). Neil Martin. 01695 624 860; E-mail: neimaz07@yahoo.co.uk www.rspb.org.uk/groups/wigan
Meetings: 7.45pm. St Anne's Parish Hall, Church Lane, Shevington, Wigan, Lancashire, WN6 8BD.

Wetland Bird Survey Organiser
GREATER MANCHESTER. Mr J Dunning, c/o WeBS Office, BTO, The Nunnery, Thetford, Norfolk IP24 2PU. 07984 237 822;
E-mail: jamiedunning8@googlemail.com

Wildlife Trust
See Lancashire,

MERSEYSIDE & WIRRAL

Bird Atlas see Cheshire

Bird Recorders see Cheshire; Lancashire

Bird Reports see also Cheshire
HILBRE BIRD OBSERVATORY REPORT, from Warden, see Reserves,

BTO Regional Representatives
MERSEYSIDE RR and RDO. Bob Harris, 3 Mossleigh, Whixall, Whitchurch, Shropshire SY13 2SA. 01948 880 112; E-mail: harris@liv.ac.uk

WIRRAL RR. Paul Miller. 01928 787 535;
E-mail: paulandhilarymiller@live.co.uk

BTO Garden BirdWatch Ambassador
Miss J Grant. E-mail: janet.grant1967@tiscali.co.uk

Clubs
MERSEYSIDE NATURALISTS' ASSOCIATION. (1938; 150). David Bryant, Chairman, 13, Strafford Drive, Bootle, Merseyside L20 9JN. 0151 523 5240;
E-mail: chairman@mnapage.info www.mnapage.info
Meetings: 2-4pm, Saturday afternoons (Feb, Oct and Nov), Bootle Cricket Club, Wadham Road, L20 2DD. Check website for details. 7-8 coach outings per year.

WIRRAL BIRD CLUB. (1977; 150). The Secretary. E-mail: wirralbirdclub@gmail.com www.wirralbirdclub.com
Meetings: 8pm, 4th Thursday of the month, (Sept-Nov and Jan-Jul), Kingsmead School Hall, Bertram Drive, Hoylake CH47 0LL.

Ringing Groups
MERSEYSIDE RG. Bob Harris, 3 Mossleigh, Whixalll, Whitchurch, Shropshire SY13 2SA. Work 0151 706 4397; E-mail: harris@liv.ac.uk

SOUTH WEST LANCASHIRE RG. I H Wolfenden, 35 Hartdale Road, Thornton, Liverpool, Merseyside L23 1TA. 01519 311 232.

RSPB Local Groups
LIVERPOOL. (1966; 180). Chris Tynan, 10 Barker Close, Huyton, Liverpool L36 0XU. 0151 480 7938, (M)07831 352 870; E-mail: christtynan@aol.com www.rspb.org.uk/groups/Liverpool/;
twitter @RSPBLiverpool
Meetings: Indoor meetings, 7 for 7.30pm, 3rd Monday of the month (Sep-Apr), Mossley Hill Parish Church, Junc. Rose Lane and Elmswood Rd L18 8DB. Outdoor meetings visiting sites across the north west.

SOUTHPORT. (1974; 240). Alan Toms. 01704 871 540; E-mail: tomsrspb@talktalk.net www.rspb.org.uk/groups/southport
Meetings: 7.45pm, 3rd Friday of the month, Lord Street West Church Hall, Duke Street, Southport PR8 2BH.

WIRRAL. (1982; 120). Jeremy Bradshaw. 0151 632 2364; E-mail: Info@wirralRSPB.org.uk www.rspb.org.uk/groups/wirral
Meetings: 7.30pm, 1st Thursday of the month, Bromborough Civic Centre, 2 Bromborough Village Road, Wirral CH62 7HR.

Wetland Bird Survey Organiser
ALT ESTUARY. Steve White, c/o WeBS Office, Thetford Norfolk IP24 2PU;
E-mail: stevewhite102@btinterncom

DEE ESTUARY. Mr C E Wells, The Cottage, 1 Well Lane, Ness, Neston, Wirral, Cheshire CH64 4AW;
E-mail: colin.wells@rspb.org.uk

MERSEY ESTUARY. Mr D J Smith, 71 Richmond Avenue, Grappenhall, Warrington, Cheshire WA4 2NX. 01925 542 745; 01925 602 397;
E-mail: dermot.smith@fsmail.net

Wildlife Trust
See Lancashire,

NORFOLK

Bird Atlas/Avifauna
The Birds of Norfolk by Moss Taylor, Michael Seago, Peter Allard & Don Dorling (Pica Press, 1999).

Bird Recorder
JOINT COUNTY RECORDERS. Dave and Jacquie Bridges, 27 Swann Close, Hempstead Road, Holt, Norfolk NR25 6DP. 01263 713 249;
E-mail: dnjnorfolkrec@btinternet.com

Bird Reports
CLEY BIRD CLUB 10-KM SQUARE BIRD REPORT (1987-), from the Secretary. 01263 577 354;
E-mail: cleybcnewsletter@gmail.com

NAR VALLEY ORNITHOLOGICAL SOCIETY ANNUAL REPORT (1976-), from The Chairman, Ian Black. www.narvos.org.uk

ENGLAND

NORFOLK BIRD & MAMMAL REPORT (1953-), from DL Paull, 8 Lindford Drive, Eaton, Norwich NR4 6LT. E-mail: info@nns.org.uk - www.NNNS.org.uk

NORFOLK ORNITHOLOGISTS' ASSOCN ANNUAL REPORT (1961-), from Holme Bird Observatory, 01485 525 406, or NOA, Broadwater Road, Holme-Next-the-Sea, Hunstanton, Norfolk, PE36 6LQ. E-mail: info@noa.org.uk

WENSUM VALLEY BIRDWATCHING SOCIETY (2003-), from E-mail: admin@wvbs.co.uk www.wvbs.co.uk

BTO Regional Representatives
NORTH-EAST RR. Chris Hudson, Cornerstones, 5 Ringland Road, Taverham, Norwich NR8 6TG. 01603 868 805, (M)07771 635 844; E-mail: Chris697@btinternet.com

NORTH-WEST RR. Bob Osborne. 01553 670 430; E-mail: rtoclass40@yahoo.co.uk

SOUTH-EAST RR. Rachel Warren. 01603 593 912; E-mail: campephilus@btinternet.com

SOUTH-WEST RR. Vince Matthews, Rose's Cottage, The Green, Merton, Thetford, Norfolk IP25 6QU. 01953 884 125; E-mail: norfolksouthwest@tiscali.co.uk

Clubs
CLEY BIRD CLUB. (1986; 500). John Dicks, Chairman, Cherry Tree House, Cherry Tree Road, Plumstead, Norfolk NR11 7LQ. 01263 577 354; E-mail: cleybcnewsletter@gmail.com www.cleybirdclub.org.uk/ Meetings: 8.00pm, Wednesdays, monthly (Dec-Feb), White Horse Hotel, Blakeney NR25 7AL.

GREAT YARMOUTH BIRD CLUB. (1989; 30). Keith R Dye, 104 Wolseley Road, Great Yarmouth, Norfolk NR31 0EJ. 01493 600 705.www.gybc.org.uk Meetings: 7.30pm, 4th Monday of the month, Rumbold Arms, Southtown Road NR31 0JX.

NAR VALLEY ORNITHOLOGICAL SOCIETY. (1976; 125). Ian Black, Three Chimneys, Tumbler Hill, Swaffham, Norfolk PE37 7JG. 01760 724092; E-mail: ian_a_black@hotmail.com www.narvos.org.uk Meetings: 7.30pm, last Tuesday of the month (Jul-Nov and Jan-May), Barn Theatre, Convent of The Sacred Heart, Mangate Street, Swaffham, PE37 7QW.

NORFOLK & NORWICH NATURALISTS' SOCIETY. (1869; 630). The Secretary, Woodhouse, Free Lane, Ditchingham, Bungay NR35 2DW. www.NNNS.org.uk Meetings: 7.30pm, 3rd Tuesday of the month (Oct-Mar), St Andrew's Church Hall, Church Lane, Norwich NR3 1AU.

NORFOLK ORNITHOLOGISTS' ASSOCIATION. (1962; 1,500). Sophie Barker, Broadwater Road, Holme-next-Sea, Hunstanton, Norfolk PE36 6LQ. 01485 525 406; E-mail: info@noa.org.uk - ww.noa.org.uk

WENSUM VALLEY BIRDWATCHING SOCIETY. (2003; 125). Lin Pateman (Secretary), E-mail: wvbs.secretary@gmail.com www.wvbs.co.uk Meetings: 7.30pm, 3rd Thursday of the month, Weston Longville village hall NR9 5JU.

Ringing Groups
BTO NUNNERY RG. Kate Risely, c/o BTO, The Nunnery, Thetford, Norfolk IP24 2PU. E-mail: kate.risely@bto.org

HOLME BIRD OBSERVATORY. Miss SA Barker. E-mail: info@noa.org.uk

NORTH NORFOLK FARMLAND STUDY & RINGING GROUP. Keith Herber, Laleham, 60 Dale End, Brancaster Staithe, King's Lynn PE31 8DA. 07785 920 044; E-mail: keith.herber@btinternet.com

NORTH WEST NORFOLK RG. Mr J L Middleton, 8 Back Lane, Burnham Market, Norfolk PE31 8EY. E-mail: johnmiddleton@bmarket.freeserve.co.uk

SHERINGHAM RG. D Sadler, 26 Abbey Road, Sheringham, Norfolk NR26 8NN. 01263 821 904.

WASH WADER RG. P L Ireland, 27 Hainfield Drive, Solihull, W Midlands B91 2PL. 0121 704 1168; E-mail: pli@blueyonder.co.uk

RSPB Local Groups
NORWICH. (1971; 360). David Porter. 01603 745 310; E-mail: RSPBnorwichgroup@virginmedia.com www.rspb.org.uk/groups/norwich Meetings: 7.30pm, 2nd Monday of the month (except Aug), Hellesdon Community Centre, Middletons Lane, Hellesdon, Norwich (entrance of Woodview Road) NR6 5SR.

WEST NORFOLK. (1977; 176). Neil Stephenson. 01553 828 752; E-mail: neilstephenson@onetel.com www.rspb.org.uk/groups/westnorfolk/ Meetings: 7.15pm, 3rd Wednesday of the month (Sep-Apr), South Wootton Village Hall, Church Lane, South Wootton, King's Lynn PE30 3LJ.

Wetland Bird Survey Organisers
BREYDON WATER. Jim Rowe, Ashtree Farm, Goodchild Marine, Butt Lane, Burgh Castle, Great Yarmouth NR31 9PZ; E-mail: jim.rowe@rspb.org.uk

NORTH NORFOLK COAST. Mr M Rooney, The Old Bakery, High Street, Docking, Norfolk PE31 8NH. E-mail: michael.rooney@naturalengland.org.uk

NORFOLK (excl. estuaries). Tim Strudwick, RSPB Strumpshaw Fen, Staithe Cottage, Low Road, Strumpshaw, Norfolk NR13 4HS. E-mail: tim.strudwick@rspb.org.uk

THE WASH. Mr J Scott, RSPB Snettisham Site Manager, Barn A, Home Farm Barns, Snettisham, Kings Lynn PE31 7PD. 01485 545 261; E-mail: jim.scott@rspb.org.uk

Wildlife Trust
NORFOLK WILDLIFE TRUST. (1926; 35,000). Bewick

255

ENGLAND

House, 22 Thorpe Road, Norwich, Norfolk NR1 1RY.
01603 625 540 (fax) 01603 598 300;
E-mail: info@norfolkwildlifetrust.org.uk
www.norfolkwildlifetrust.org.uk

NORTHAMPTONSHIRE

Bird Recorder
Mike Alibone, 25 Harrier Park, East Hunsbury,
Northampton, Northants NN4 0QG.
E-mail: northantsbirds@ntlworld.com

Bird Report
NORTHAMPTONSHIRE BIRD REPORT (1969-), from Mr
John Coleman, 2 Marsons Drive, Crick, Northants NN6
7TD. 01788 822 905.
http://northamptonshirebirdclub.ning.com

BTO Regional Representatives
RR. Barrie Galpin. 01780 444 351;
E-mail: barrie.galpin@zen.co.uk

Club
NORTHAMPTONSHIRE BIRD CLUB. (1973; 100). Eleanor
 McMahon (Secretary), 01604
880 009;
http://sites.google.com/site/
northantsbirdclub/
Meetings: 7.30pm, 1st
Wednesday of the month.
Moulton Community Sports
Centre, Pound Lane, Moulton,
Northants NN3 7SD.

Ringing Group
NORTHANTS RG. D M Francis, 2 Brittons Drive, Billing
Lane, Northampton NN3 5DP.

STANFORD RG. John Cranfield, 41 Main Street,
Fleckney, Leicester LE8 8AP. 0116 240 4385;
E-mail: JacanaJohn@talktalk.net

RSPB Local Groups
MID NENE. (1975; 350). Hilary Guy. 01536 516 422;
E-mail: hilary@snowdrop.demon.co.uk
www.rspb.org.uk/groups/midnene
Meetings: 7.30pm, 2nd or 3rd Thursday of the month
(Sep-Apr), The Saxon Hall, Thorpe Street/Brook
Street, Raunds NN9 6LT.

Wetland Bird Survey Organiser
Mr J Williams, Langsend, Newnham, Daventry,
Northants NN11 3HQ. 01203 402 121; 01327 871 395;
e-mail: jim.williams4@btinternet.com

Wildlife Trust
Director, See Cambridgeshire,

NORTHUMBERLAND

Bird Atlas/Avifauna
The Atlas of Breeding Birds in Northumbria edited
by J C Day et al (Northumberland and Tyneside Bird
Club, 1995).

Bird Recorder
Tim Dean, 2 Knocklaw Park, Rothbury,
Northumberland NE65 7PW. 01669 621460 (M)07766
263167; E-mail: t.r.dean@btinternet.com

Bird Reports
BIRDS IN NORTHUMBRIA (1970-), from Trevor Blake, 6
Glenside, Ellington, Morpeth, Northumberland NE61
5LS. 01670 862 635; E-mail: trevor.1958@live.co.uk

BIRDS ON THE FARNE ISLANDS (1971-), from Secretary,
Natural History Society of Northumbria. 0191 232
6386; E-mail: nhsn@ncl.ac.uk
www.nhsn.ncl.ac.uk

**BTO Regional Representative & Regional
Development Officer**
RR. Tom Cadwallender, 22 South View, Lesbury,
Alnwick, Northumberland NE66 3PZ. 01665 830 884;
E-mail: tomandmurielcadwallender@hotmail.com

RDO. Muriel Cadwallender, 22 South View, Lesbury,
Alnwick, Northumberland NE66 3PZ. 01665 830 884;
E-mail: tomandmurielcadwallender@hotmail.com

Clubs
NATURAL HISTORY SOCIETY OF NORTHUMBRIA. (1829;
about 950). James Littlewood, Natural History Society
of Northumbria, Great North Museum: Hancock,
Barras Bridge, Newcastle-upon-Tyne NE2 4PT. 0191
232 6386, (fax)0191 232 2177;
E-mail: nhsn@ncl.ac.uk www.nhsn.ncl.ac.uk
Meetings: Weekly indoor and outdoor meetings
throughout the year, details can be found at
www.nhsn.ncl.ac.uk

NORTH NORTHUMBERLAND BIRD CLUB. (1984;
210). Richard Narraway, Workshop Cottage, The
Friary, Bamburgh NE69 7AE. 01668 214 759; E-mail:
ringouzel@northnorthumberlandbirdclub.co.uk
www.northnorthumberlandbirdclub.co.uk
Meetings: 7.30pm, 1st Friday of the month (Sept),
2nd Friday (Oct-Jun), Bamburgh Pavilion (below
castle) NE69 7BP.

NORTHUMBERLAND & TYNESIDE BIRD CLUB. (1958;
270). Alan Tilmouth, 12 Stowe Gardens, Pegsworth,
Morpeth NE61 6TH. 01670 512 013;
E-mail: ntbcorg@gmail.com www.ntbc.org.uk
Meetings: 7.00pm, 2nd Thursday of the month (Sep-
Apr), Newcastle Falcons Rugby Club, Brunton Road,
Kenton Bank Foot, Newcastle-upon-Tyne NE13 8AF.

Ringing Group
NORTHUMBRIA RG. Secretary. B Galloway, 34 West
Meadows, Stamfordham Road, Westerhope, Newcastle
upon Tyne NE5 1LS. 0191 286 4850.

Wetland Bird Survey Organisers
LINDISFARNE. Mr A Craggs, Natural England,
Lindisfarne National Nature Reserve, Beal Station,
Beal, Berwick-upon-Tweed TD15 2SP. 01289 381 470;
E-mail: andrew.craggs@naturalengland.org.uk

NORTHUMBERL AND COAST. Mr D M Turner, 9 Haswell
Gardens, North Shields, Tyne & Wear NE3 2DY. 01912
576 680; E-mail: Dan.M.Turner@btopenworld.com

ENGLAND

NORTHUMBERLAND (Inland). Steve Holliday, 2 Larriston Place, Cramlington, Northumberland NE23 8ER. E-mail: steveholliday@hotmail.co.uk

Wildlife Hospitals
BERWICK SWAN & WILDLIFE TRUST. The Honorary Secretary, Windmill Way East, Ramparts Business Park, Berwick-upon-Tweed TD15 1TU. 01289 302 882; E-mail: swan-trust@hotmail.co.uk www.swan-trust.org Registered charity. All categories of wildlife. Pools for swans and other waterfowl. Veterinary support.

Wildlife Trust
NORTHUMBERLAND WILDLIFE TRUST. (1962; 13,000). The Garden House, St Nicholas Park, Jubilee Road, Gosforth, Newcastle-upon-Tyne, NE3 3XT. 0191 284 6884 (fax) 0191 284 6794; E-mail: mail@northwt.org.uk www.nwt.org.uk

NOTTINGHAMSHIRE

Bird Recorders
Andy Hall. E-mail: andy.h11@ntlworld.com

Bird Reports
LOUND BIRD REPORT (1990-) latest 2007 report £4, from Gary Hobson, 18 Barnes Avenue, Wrenthorpe, Wakefield WF1 2BH. 01924 384 419; E-mail: gary. lbc1@tiscali.co.uk

BIRDS OF NOTTINGHAMSHIRE (1943-) - £9 for 2011, £3 for previous issues, plus p&p. , from Ms Jenny Swindells, 21 Chaworth Road, West Bridgford, Nottingham NG2 7AE. 0115 9812 432; E-mail: j.swindells@btinternet.com www.nottsbirders.net; Twitter: @NottsBirders

NETHERFIELD WILDLIFE GROUP ANNUAL REPORT (1990-). £5 inc postage, from Mr N Matthews, 4 Shelburne Close, Heronridge, Nottingham NG5 9LL. www.netherfieldwildlife.org.uk

BTO Regional Representatives
RR. Mrs Lynda Milner, 6 Kirton Park, Kirton, Newark, Notts NG22 9LR. 01623 862 025; E-mail: milner.lynda@googlemail.com

Clubs
LOUND BIRD CLUB. (1991; 90).
Gary Hobson, 18 Barnes Avenue, Wrenthorpe, Wakefield WF1 2BH. 01924 384 419; E-mail: loundbirdclub@btinternet.com www.loundbirdclub.com
Meetings: See website for walks and talks throughout the year.

NETHERFIELD WILDLIFE GROUP. (1999; 130). Philip Burnham, 57 Tilford Road, Newstead Village, Nottingham NG15 0BU. 01623 401 980 (M)07765 369 590; E-mail: philb50@fastmail.fm www.netherfieldwildlife.org.uk

NOTTINGHAMSHIRE BIRDWATCHERS. (1935; 323). Ms Jenny Swindells, 21 Chaworth Road, West Bridgford, Nottingham NG2 7AE. 0115 9812 432; E-mail: j.swindells@btinternet.com www.nottsbirders.net; Twitter: @NottsBirders **Meetings and events:** Please see website for details.

WOLLATON NATURAL HISTORY SOCIETY. (1976; 86). Graham Birkett, 07528 753 470; E-mail: graham.birkett@ntlworld.com www.spanglefish.com/wollatonnaturalhistory/ **Meetings:** 7.30pm, 3rd Wednesday of the month, St Leonards Community Centre, Wollaton Village, HG8 2ND.

Ringing Groups
BIRKLANDS RG. A Ashley, 39 Winkburn Road, Mansfield, Notts NG19 6SJ. 07794 179 494; E-mail: alowe@nottswt.co.uk

Integrated Population Monitoring Group
TRESWELL WOOD INTEGRATED POPULATION MONITORING GROUP. Chris du Feu, 66 High Street, Beckingham, Notts DN10 4PF. E-mail: chris@chrisdufeu.force9.co.uk

NORTH NOTTS RG. Adrian Blackburn, Willows End, 27 Palmer Road, Retford, Notts DN22 6SS. 01777 706 516 (M)07718 766 873. E-mail: adrian.blackburn@sky.com

SOUTH NOTTINGHAMSHIRE RG. K J Hemsley, 8 Grange Farm Close, Toton, Beeston, Notts NG9 6EB. E-mail: k.hemsley@ntlworld.com

RSPB Local Groups
MANSFIELD LOCAL GROUP. (1986; 200). John Barlow, 240 Southwell Road West, Mansfield, Notts NG18 4LB. 01623 626 647; E-mail: Terri-Cumberland@supanet.com www.rspb.org.uk/groups/mansfield **Meetings:** 7pm, 1st Wednesday of the month (Sep-Jun), Bridge St Methodist Church, Rock Valley, Mansfield NG18 1AL.

NOTTINGHAM. (1974; 290). Penny Cross, 93 Hilton Road, Nottingham, NG3 6AQ. 0115 960 4205; E-mail: pennyguilbert@hotmail.com www.notts-rspb.org.uk **Meetings:** 7.30pm, 1st Wed of month (Sept - May). Nottingham Mechanics, North Sherwood St. Nottingham, NG1 4EZ.

Wetland Bird Survey Organiser
Mr G Hobson, 18 Barnes Avenue, Wrenthorpe, Wakefield WF1 2BH. 01924 384 419; 07712 244 469 (Evenings are prefered for telephone contact); E-mail: loundbirdclub@btinternet.com

Wildlife Trust
NOTTINGHAMSHIRE WILDLIFE TRUST. (1963; 4,300). The Old Ragged School, Brook Street, Nottingham, NG1 1EA. 0115 958 8242 (fax) 0115 924 3175; E-mail: info@nottswt.co.uk www.nottinghamshirewildlife.org.uk

ENGLAND

OXFORDSHIRE

Bird Atlas/Avifauna
Birds of Oxfordshire by J W Brucker et al (Oxford, Pisces, 1992).

The New Birds of the Banbury Area by T G Easterbrook (Banbury Ornithological Society, 1995).

Bird Recorder
Ian Lewington, 119 Brasenose Road, Didcot, Oxon OX11 7BP. 01235 819 792;
E-mail: ian@recorder.fsnet.co.uk

Bird Reports
BIRDS OF OXFORDSHIRE (1921-), from Barry Hudson, Pinfold, 4 Bushy Row, Bampton, Oxon OX18 2JU. 01865 775632.

BANBURY ORNITHOLOGICAL SOCIETY ANNUAL REPORT (1952-). £5 each including postage, from MJ Lewis, Old Mill Cottage, Avon Dassett, Southam, Warwickshire CV47 2AE. 01295 690 643; E-mail: mikelewisad@hotmail.com

BTO Regional Representatives & Regional Development Officer
NORTH. Frances Buckel, Witts End, Radbones Hill, Over Norton, Chipping Norton, Oxon OX7 5RA. 01608 644 425; E-mail: fran.buckel@btinternet.com

SOUTH RR. Mr John Melling, 17 Lime Grove, Southmoor, Nr Abingdon, Oxon OX13 5DN. 01865 820 867; E-mail: bto-rep@oos.org.uk

Clubs
BANBURY ORNITHOLOGICAL SOCIETY (includes parts of Northamptonshire, Oxfordshire and Warwickshire). (1952; 100). Frances Buckel, Witts End, Radbones Hill, Over Norton, Chipping Norton, Oxon OX7 5RA. 01608 644 425; E-mail: fran.buckel@btinternet.com www.banburyornithologicalsociety.org.uk
Meetings: 7.30pm, 2nd Monday of the month,The Banbury Cricket Club, White Post Road, Bodicote OX15 4BN.

OXFORD ORNITHOLOGICAL SOCIETY. (1921; 330). Barry Hudson, 07833 350 288;
E-mail: secretary@oos.org.uk
www.oos.org.uk
Meetings: 7.45pm, various dates, Stratfield Brake, Kidlington.

Ringing Group
EDWARD GREY INSTITUTE. Dr A G Gosler, c/o Edward Grey Institute, Department of Zoology, South Parks Road, Oxford OX1 3PS. 01865 271 158;
E-mail: andrew.gosler@zoo.ox.ac.uk

RSPB Local Groups
OXFORD. (1977; 100). Roy Grant, 23 St Christopher's Place, Cowley, Oxford OX4 2HS. 01865 774 659;
E-mail: roy.otters@hotmail.co.uk

www.rspb-oxford.org.uk
Meetings: 7.45pm, normally 1st Thursday of the month (Sept-May), Sandhills Primary School, Terret Avenue, Headington, Oxford (opposite Thornhill park and ride).

VALE OF WHITE HORSE. (1977; 330). Steve Bastow. 07900 213 698; E-mail: stevebastow@btinternet.com
www.rspb-vwh.org.uk
Meetings: 7.45pm, 3rd Monday of the month (Sep-May). Civic Hall, Britwell Road, DIDCOT, Oxfordshire, OX11 7HN.

Wetland Bird Survey Organiser
OXFORDSHIRE (North). Mrs S Bletchly, 11 Orchard Grove, Bloxham, Banbury, Oxfordshire OX15 4NZ. 01295 721 048;
E-mail: sandra.banornsoc@btinternet.com

OXFORDSHIRE (South). Mr I Lees, 16 Dove House Close, Upper Wolvercote, Oxford OX2 8BG. 01865 256 370; 01865 311 104; 07595 358 066;
E-mail: ianlees@me.com

Wildlife Trust
BBOWT. (1959; 24,000). The Lodge, 1 Armstrong Road, Littlemore, Oxford, OX4 4XT. 01865 775 476 (fax) 01865 711 301; E-mail: info@bbowt.org.uk
www.bbowt.org.uk

SHROPSHIRE

Bird Atlas/Avifauna
Atlas of the Breeding Birds of Shropshire (Shropshire Ornithological Society, 1995).

Bird Recorder
Geoff Holmes, 22 Tenbury Drive, Telford Estate, Shrewsbury SY2 5YF. 01743 364 621;
E-mail: geoff.holmes.4@btinternet.com

Bird Report
SHROPSHIRE BIRD REPORT (1956-) Annual, from Helen Griffiths (Hon Secretary), 104 Noel Hill Road, Cross Houses, Shrewsbury SY5 6LD. 01743 761 507;
E-mail: helen.griffiths@naturalengland.org.uk
www.shropshirebirds.com

BTO Regional Representative
Allan Dawes, 01691 654 245;
e-mail: allandawes@btinternet.com

Club
SHROPSHIRE ORNITHOLOGICAL SOCIETY. (1955; 800). Helen Griffiths, 104 Noel Hill Road, Cross Houses, Shrewsbury SY5 6LD. 01743 761 507;
E-mail: hjgriffiths104@btinternet.com
www.shropshirebirds.com
Meetings: 7.15pm, 1st Thursday of month (Oct-Apr), Shirehall, Shrewsbury SY2 6ND.

RSPB Local Group
SHROPSHIRE. (1992; 320). Anne Trigg. 01295 253 330;
E-mail: Anna.keen@RSPB.org.uk
www.rspb.org.uk/groups/shropshire

ENGLAND

Meetings: 7.30pm, 4th Wednesday of the month (Sep-Apr), Council Chamber, Shirehall, Shrewsbury. Also field trips, year round, 3rd Wednesday in the month (Oct-March) Secret Hills Centre Craven Arms SY7 9RS.

SOUTH SHROPSHIRE Sub Group - CRAVEN ARMS. (2004; c100). Alvin Botting. 01547 540 176; E-mail: Christinelbateman@yahoo.com www.rspbsouthshropshire.co.uk
Meetings: 7.30pm, 2nd Tuesday of the month (Sep-Apr), Culmington Village Hall, Culmington, Ludlow SY8 2DA.

Wetland Bird Survey Organiser
SHROPSHIRE. Mr M F Wallace, 75 Larkhill Road, Copthorne, Shrewsbury, Shropshire SY3 8XJ. 01743 369 035; E-mail: michaelwallace47@gmail.com

Wildlife Trust
SHROPSHIRE WILDLIFE TRUST. (1962; 10,000). 193 Abbey Foregate, Shrewsbury, Shropshire SY2 6AH. 01743 284 280 (fax) 01743 284281; E-mail: enquiries@shropshirewildlifetrust.org.uk www.shropshirewildlifetrust.org.uk

SOMERSET & BRISTOL

Bird Atlas/Avifauna
Atlas of Breeding Birds in Avon 1988-91 by R L Bland and John Tully (John Tully, 6 Falcondale Walk, Westbury-on-Trym, Bristol BS9 3JG, 1992).

The Birds of Exmoor and the Quantocks by DK Ballance and BD Gibbs. (Isabelline Books, 2 Highbury House, 8 Woodland Crescent, Falmouth TR11 4QS. 2003).

Bird Recorders
Brian D Gibbs, 23 Lyngford Road, Taunton, Somerset TA2 7EE. 01823 274 887; E-mail: brian.gibbs@virgin.net www.somersetbirds.net

BRISTOL, S GLOUCESTERSHIRE, BATH AND NE SOMERSET, NORTH SOMERSET. John Martin, 34 Cranmoor Green, Pilning, Bristol BS35 4QF. 01454 633 040; (M)07767 867 341; E-mail: avonbirdrecorder@googlemail.com www.boc-bristol.org.uk

Bird Reports
AVON BIRD REPORT (1977-), £9 plus postage, from Harvey Rose; E-mail: h.e.rose@bris.ac.uk

EXMOOR NATURALIST (1974-), from Secretary, Exmoor Natural History Society. E-mail: carol.enhs@virgin.net

SOMERSET BIRDS (1912-) £7.50 inc p&p, from Somerset Ornithological Society, c/o Flat 2, Dunboyne, Bratton Lane, Minehead, Somerset TA24 8SQ. 01643 706 820.

BTO Regional Representatives
AVON RR. Gordon Youdale, 36 Quedgeley, Yate, Bristol PS37 4JJ. 01454 881 690; E-mail: gordon.youdale@blueyonder.co.uk

SOMERSET RR. Eve Tigwell, Hawthorne Cottage, 3 Friggle Street, Frome, Somerset BA11 5LP. 01373 451 630; E-mail: eve.tigwell@zen.co.uk

Clubs
BRISTOL NATURALISTS' SOCIETY (Ornithological Section). (1862; 550). Hon. Secretary, Bristol Naturalists' Society, c/o City Museum & Art Gallery, Bristol BS8 1RL. 01179 243 352; E-mail: info@bristolnats.org.uk www.bristolnats.org.uk
Meetings: 7.30pm, 2nd Wednesday in the month (check for dates, Oct-Mar), Westmoreland Hall, Westmoreland Road, Bristol BS1 5TX.

BRISTOL ORNITHOLOGICAL CLUB. (1966; 620). Mrs Judy Copeland, 19 St George's Hill, Easton-in-Gordano, North Somerset BS20 0PS. 01275 373 554; E-mail: judy.copeland@tiscali.co.uk www.bristolornithologicalclub.co.uk
Meetings: 7.30pm, 3rd Thursday of the month, Newman Hall, Grange Court Road, Westbury-on-Trym.

CAM VALLEY WILDLIFE GROUP. (1994; 356). André Fournier, 1 Boomfield Lane, Paulton, Bristol BS39 7QU. 01761 418 153; E-mail: enquiries@cvwg.org.uk www.somersetmade.co.uk/cvwg/

EXMOOR NATURAL HISTORY SOCIETY. (1974; 480). The Secretary, 12 King George Road, Minehead, Somerset TA24 5JD. 01643 707 624; www.enhs.org.uk E-mail: carol.enhs@talktalk.net
Meetings: 7.30pm, 1st Wednesday of the month (Oct-Mar), Methodist Church Hall, The Avenue, Minehead.

SOMERSET ORNITHOLOGICAL SOCIETY. (1974; 475). Mr JA Hazell, Membership Secretary, 9 Hooper Road, Street, Somerset BA16 0NP. 01458 443 780; E-mail: jeff.hazell@somersetbirds.net www.somersetbirds.net
Meetings: Indoor meetings, with guest speaker, various Thursdays Oct to Apr; and field meetings, with leader, on 10 to 12 dates throughout the year.

Ringing Groups
CHEW VALLEY RS. Mr A Ashman. E-mail: alan.ashman@talktalk.net

GORDANO VALLEY RG. Lyndon Roberts, 20 Glebe Road, Long Ashton, Bristol BS41 9LH. 01275 392 722; E-mail: mail@lyndonroberts.com

RSPCA. Mr K Leighton. E-mail: kev.leighton@O2.co.uk

STEEP HOLM RS. A J Parsons, Barnfield, Tower Hill Road, Crewkerne, Somerset TA18 8BJ. 01460 736 40.

RSPB Local Groups
BATH AND DISTRICT. (1969; 260). Alan Barrett. 01225 310 905; E-mail: alan_w_h_barrett@yahoo.com www.rspb.org.uk/groups/bath
Meetings: 7.30pm, 3rd Wednesday of the month (Sep-Apr), First Floor, Green Park Station, Bath BA1 2DR.

259

SOUTH SOMERSET. (1979; 300). Denise Chamings, Daniels Farm, Lower Stratton, South Petherton, Somerset TA13 5LP. 01460 240 740; E-mail: denise.chamings@talktalk.net www.rspb.org.uk/groups/southsomerset Meetings: 7.30pm, 3rd Thursday of the month (Sep-May), The Millennium Hall, Seavington St. Mary, Ilminster, TA19 0QH.

TAUNTON. (1975; 148). Eric Luxton. 01823 283 033; E-mail: eric.luxton@btinternet.com www.rspb.org.uk/groups/taunton Meetings: 7.30pm, last Friday of the month, Trull Memorial Hall, Church Road, Trull, Taunton TA3 7JZ.

WESTON-SUPER-MARE (N SOMERSET). (1976; 215). Tony West. 01934 622 793; E-mail: tony.west34@yahoo.com www.rspb.org.uk/groups/westonsupermare Meetings: 7.45pm, 1st Thursday of the month (Sep-Apr), St Pauls Church Hall, Walliscote Road, Weston-Super-Mare BS23 1EF.

Wetland Bird Survey Organisers
AVON (other sites). Mr R Higgins, 28 Egerton Road, Bishopston, Bristol BS7 8HL. 0117 944 1034; E-mail: rupert@wessexeco.fsnet.co.uk

SEVERN ESTUARY - SOUTHERN COAST. Dr H E Rose, Arncliffe, Walton Bay, Clevedon. 0127 587 3407; E-mail: H.E.Rose@bristol.ac.uk

SOMERSET (other sites). Ms E M Tigwell, c/o WeBS Office, BTO, The Nunnery, Thetford, Norfolk IP27 0AB. 01373 451 630; E-mail: eve.tigwell@zen.co.uk

SOMERSET LEVELS. Steve Meen, RSPB West Sedgemoor, Dewlands Farm, Redhill, Curry Rivel, Langport Somerset TA10 0PH. 01458 252 805; 01458 252 820; E-mail: steve.meen@rspb.org.uk

Wildlife Trusts
AVON WILDLIFE TRUST. (1980; 17,000). 32 Jacobs Wells Road, Bristol, BS8 1DR. 0117 917 7270 (fax) 0117 929 7273; E-mail: mail@avonwildlifetrust.org.uk www.avonwildlifetrust.org.uk

SOMERSET WILDLIFE TRUST. (1964; 21,000). Tonedale Mill,Tonedale,Wellington,Somerset TA21 0AW. 01823 652 400 (fax) 01823 652 411; E-mail: enquiries@somersetwildlife.org www.somersetwildlife.org

STAFFORDSHIRE

Bird Recorder
Nick Pomiankowski, 22 The Villas, West End, Stoke ST4 5AQ. 01782 849 682; E-mail: staffs-recorder@westmidlandbirdclub.com

Bird Report See West Midlands

BTO Regional Representatives
RR. Scott Petrek; E-mail: scott.petrek@gmail.com

Clubs
SOUTH PEAK RAPTOR STUDY GROUP. (1998; 12). Trevor Grimshaw. e-mail: grimshaw758@btinternet.com

WEST MIDLAND BIRD CLUB (STAFFORD BRANCH). Scott Petrek (Branch Secretary). E-mail: stafford-secretary@westmidlandbirdclub.com www.westmidlandbirdclub.com/stafford Meetings: 7.30pm, 2nd Friday of the month (Oct-Mar), at Perkins Engines Sports & Social Club, Tixall Road, Stafford ST16 3UB.

WEST MIDLAND BIRD CLUB (TAMWORTH BRANCH). (1992). Barbara Stubbs, 19 Alfred Street, Tamworth, Staffs B79 7RL. 01827 57865; E-mail: tamworth@westmidlandbirdclub.com www.westmidlandbirdclub.com/tamworth Meetings: 7.30pm, 3rd Friday of the month (Sep-Apr), Carnegie Centre, Corporation Street, Tamworth B79 7DN.

RSPB Local Groups
BURTON-ON-TRENT AND SOUTH DERBYSHIRE. (1973; 50). Dave Lummis, 121 Wilmot Road, Swadlincote, Derbys DE11 9BN. 01283 219 902; E-mail: david.lummis@btinternet.com www.basd-rspb.co.uk Meetings: 7.30pm 1st Wednesday of the month, All Saint's Church, Branston Road, Burton.

LICHFIELD & DISTRICT. (1977; 1150). Bob Russon, 108 Walsall Road, Lichfield, Staffs WS13 8AF. 01543 252 547; E-mail: LichfieldRSPB@hotmail.co.uk www.rspb.org.uk/groups/lichfield Meetings: 7.30pm, 2nd Tuesday of the month (Jan-May, Sept-Dec), St Mary's Centre, Lichfield WS13 6LG.

NORTH STAFFS. (1982; 208). John Booth, 32 St Margaret Drive, Sneyd Green, Stoke-on-Trent ST1 6EW. 01782 262 082; E-mail: daylateuk@yahoo.co.uk www.rspb.org.uk/groups/northstaffordshire Meetings: 7.30pm, normally 3rd Wednesday of the month, North Staffs Conference Centre (Medical Institute), Hartshill Road, Stoke ST4 7NY.

SOUTH WEST STAFFORDSHIRE. (1972; 165). Mrs Theresa Dorrance, 39 Wilkes Road, Codsall, Wolverhampton WV8 1RZ. 01902 847 041; E-mail: stevedorrance@googlemail.com ww.rspb.org.uk/groups/southweststaffs Meetings: 8.00pm, 2nd Tuesday of the month (Sep-May), Codsall Village Hall WV8 1PW.

Wetland Bird Survey Organisers
STAFFORDSHIRE. Mr S Turner, c/o WeBS Office, BTO, The Nunnery, Thetford, Norfolk IP24 2PU. E-mail: sjturner76@btinternet.com

Wildlife Hospitals
BRITISH WILDLIFE RESCUE CENTRE. Alfred Hardy, Amerton Working Farm, Stowe-by-Chartley, Stafford ST18 0LA. 01889 271 308; E-mail: joyce.hardy351@ntlworld.com

ENGLAND

www.britishwildliferescue.co.uk
On A518 Stafford/Uttoxeter road. All species,
including imprints and permanently injured. Hospital,
large aviaries and caging. Open to the public every
day. Veterinary support.

GENTLESHAW BIRD OF PREY HOSPITAL. Jenny Smith,
Gentleshaw Wildlife Centre, Fletcher's Country
Garden Centre, Stone Road, Eccleshall, Staffs ST21
6JY. 01785 850 379;
E-mail: info@gentleshawwildlife.co.uk
www.gentleshawwildlife.co.uk
Registered charity. All birds of prey (inc. owls).
Hospital cages and aviaries; release sites. Veterinary
support. Also
GENTLESHAW BIRD OF PREY AND WILDLIFE CENTRE,
Fletchers Country Garden Centre, Stone Road,
Eccleshall, Stafford. 01785 850 379 (10am-5pm).

Wildlife Trust
STAFFORDSHIRE WILDLIFE TRUST. (1969; 14,000). The
Wolseley Centre, Wolseley Bridge, Stafford, ST17
0WT. 01889 880 100, (fax) 01889 880 101;
E-mail: info@staffs-wildlife.org.uk
www.staffs-wildlife.org.uk

SUFFOLK

Bird Atlas/Avifauna
Birds of Suffolk by Steve Piotrowski (April 2003) Helm
County Avifauna.

Bird Recorders
NORTH EAST. Andrew Green,
E-mail: andrew@waveney1.fsnet.co.uk

SOUTH EAST (inc. coastal region from Slaughden Quay
southwards). Scott Mason.
E-mail: smsuffolkbirder@gmail.com

WEST (whole of Suffolk W of Stowmarket, inc.
Breckland). Colin Jakes, 7 Maltward Avenue, Bury St
Edmunds, Suffolk IP33 3XN. 01284 702 215;
E-mail: colin@jakes.myzen.co.uk

Bird Report
*SUFFOLK BIRDS (inc Landguard Bird Observatory
Report) (1950-)*, from Ipswich Museum, High Street,
Ipswich, Suffolk.

BTO Regional Representative
Mick T Wright, 15 Avondale Road, Ipswich, IP3 9JT.
01473 721 486; E-mail: micktwright@btinternet.com

Clubs
LAVENHAM BIRD CLUB. (1972;
54). Mr G Pattrick, Brights
Farmhouse, Brights Lane,
Lavenham, Suffolk CO10 9PH.
01787 248 128.
Meetings: 7.30pm, normally 3rd
Saturday (Sep-Mar, except Dec),
Lavenham Guildhall, Lavenham
CO10 9QZ.

SUFFOLK ORNITHOLOGISTS' GROUP.
(1973; 650). Phil Whittaker, Oak Barn,
Pipps Ford, Needham Market, Ipswich,
Suffolk IP6 8LJ. 01449 76 0353;
E-mail: oakbarn@hotmail.com
www.sogonline.org.uk
Meetings: Last Thursday of the month
(Jan-Apr, Sep-Nov), London Road Holiday
Inn (IP2 0UA) on the SW side of Ipswich
near the A14/A12 Copdock roundabout.

Ringing Groups
DINGLE BIRD CLUB. Dr D Pearson, 4 Lupin Close,
Reydon, Southwold, Suffolk IP18 6NW. 01502 722348.

LACKFORD RG. Dr Peter Lack, 11 Holden Road,
Lackford, Bury St Edmunds, Suffolk IP28 6HZ.
E-mail: bee.eaters@btinternet.com

LANDGUARD RG. Landguard Ringing Group, Landguard
Bird Observatory, View Point Road, Felixstowe,
Suffolk, IP11 3TW. 01394 673782;
E-mail: landguardbo@yahoo.co.uk
www.lbo.co.uk

LITTLE OUSE RG (formerly MARKET WESTON RG). Dr
R H W Langston, Walnut Tree Farm, Thorpe Street,
Hinderclay, Diss, Norfolk IP22 1HT.
E-mail: rlangston@wntfarm.demon.co.uk

RSPB Local Groups
IPSWICH. (1975; 230). Mr Chris Courtney, St Elmo, 19
Marlborough Road, Ipswich, Suffolk IP4 5AT. 01473 423
213; E-mail: chrisc.courtney@yahoo.co.uk
www.rspb.org.uk/groups/ipswich
Meetings: 7.30pm, 2nd Thursday of the month (Sep-
Apr), Sidegate Lane Primary School, Sidegate Lane,
Ipswich IP4 4JD.

LOWESTOFT & DISTRICT. (1976; 85). Julie Martin, 19
The Boundaries, Geldeston Road, Gillingham, Beccles,
Suffolk NR34 0HT. 01502 714 950;
E-mail: swottouk@yahoo.co.uk
www.rspb.org.uk/groups/lowestoft
Meetings: 7.15pm 1st Friday in the month, St Marks
Church Centre, Oulton Broad NR33 9JX.

WOODBRIDGE. (1987; 390). Malcolm Key, Riverside,
Parham, Suffolk IP13 9LZ. 01728 723 155;
E-mail: malcolm.key@btopenworld.com
Meetings: 7.30pm, 1st Thursday of the month (Oct-
May), Woodbridge Community Hall IP12 4AU.

Wetland Bird Survey Organisers
ALDE COMPLEX. Mr I Castle, 5 Chapelfield, Orford,
Woodbridge, Suffolk IP12 2HW. 01394 450 188; 01394
450 181 (fax); E-mail: ian@castle-hamlett.co.uk

ALTON WATER. Mr J A Glazebrook, c/o WeBS Office,
e-mail: johnglazebrook@btopenworld.com

BLYTH ESTUARY (Suffolk). Mr A Burrows, c/o WeBS
Office, BTO, The Nunnery, Thetford, Norfolk IP24
2PU. 01842 750 050; e-mail: webs@bto.org

ENGLAND

DEBEN ESTUARY. Nick Mason, The Decoy, 8 Mallard Way, Hollesley, Nr Woodbridge, Ipswich IP12 3QU. 07876 086 039; 01394 411150; E-mail: nick.mason4@btinternet.com

ORWELL ESTUARY. Mick T Wright, 15 Avondale Road, Ipswich, Suffolk IP3 9JT. 01473 721 486; 07540 880 095; E-mail: micktwright@btinternet.com

STOUR ESTUARY. Mr R Vonk, RSPB, Unit 1 Brantham Mill, Bergholt Road, Brantham, Manningtree, Essex CO11 1QT. 01206 391 153; 07711 129 149; E-mail: rick.vonk@rspb.org.uk

SUFFOLK (other sites). Alan Miller, Suffolk Wildlife Trust, Moonrakers, Back Lane, Wenhaston, Halesworth, Suffolk, IP19 9DY. 01502 478 788; 00776 741 1778; E-mail: alan.miller@suffolkwildlifetrust.org

Wildlife Trust
SUFFOLK WILDLIFE TRUST. (1961; 25,000). Brooke House, The Green, Ashbocking, Ipswich, IP6 9JY. 01473 890 089, (fax) 01473 890 165; E-mail: info@suffolkwildlifetrust.org www.suffolkwildlifetrust.org

SURREY

Bird Atlas/Avifauna
Birds of Surrey by Jeffery Wheatley (Surrey Bird Club 2007).

Bird Recorder
SURREY (includes Greater London south of the Thames and east to the Surrey Docks, excludes Spelthorne).
Eric Soden, Ceres, Moushill Lane, Milford, Surrey GU8 5BQ. 01483 429 799; E-mail: eric.soden@talktalk.net

Bird Report
SURBITON AND DISTRICT BIRD WATCHING SOCIETY (1972-), from Thelma Caine, 21 More Lane, Esher, Surrey KT10 8AJ. E-mail: sdbws@encief.co.uk www.encief.co.uk/sdbws

SURREY BIRD REPORT (1952-), from J Gates, 5 Hillside Road, Weybourne, Farnham, Surrey GU9 9DW. 01252 315 047; E-mail: jeremygates@live.com

BTO Regional Representative
RR. Penny Williams, Bournbrook House, Sandpit Hall Lane, Chobham Surrey GU24 8HA. 01276 857 736; E-mail: penny@waxwing.plus.com

Clubs
SURBITON & DISTRICT BIRDWATCHING SOCIETY. (1954; 140). Gary Caine, 21 More Lane, Esher, Surrey KT10 8AJ. 01372 468 432; E-mail: gary.caine@royalmail.co.uk www.encief.co.uk/sdbws
Meetings: 7.30pm, 3rd Tuesday of the month, Surbiton Library Annex.

SURREY BIRD CLUB. (1957; 340). Penny Williams, Bournbrook House, Sandpit Hall Lane, Chobham Surrey GU24 8HA. 01276 857 736;

E-mail: penny@waxwing.plus.com www.surreybirdclub.org.uk
Meetings: See website for details.

Ringing Groups
HERSHAM RG. A J Beasley, 29 Selbourne Avenue, New Haw, Weybridge, Surrey KT15 3RB. E-mail: abeasley00@hotmail.com

RUNNYMEDE RG. D G Harris, 22 Blossom Waye, Hounslow, TW5 9HD. E-mail: daveharris@tinyonline.co.uk http://rmxrg.org.uk

RSPB Local Groups
DORKING & DISTRICT. (1982; 230). John Burge, Broughton Norrels Drive, East Horsley, Leatherhead KT24 5DR. 01483 283 803; E-mail: burgejs@gmail.com www.rspb.org.uk/groups/dorkinganddistrict
Meetings: 8.00pm, Fridays once a month (Sep-Apr), Christian Centre, next to St Martin's Church, Dorking RH4 1DW.

EAST SURREY. (1984; 2800 plus in catchment area). John Lawrence, 123 Chaldon Way, Coulsdon, Surrey CR5 1DN. 01737 553 316 (evenings); E-mail: jflawrence@gmail.com www.eastsurreyrspb.co.uk
Meetings: 8.00pm, 2nd Wednesday of the month (except August), White Hart Barn, Godstone, RH9 8DT.

EPSOM & EWELL. (1974; 102). Janet Gilbert, 78 Fairfax Avenue, Ewell, Epsom, Surrey KT17 2QQ. 0208 394 0405; E-mail: janetegilbert@btinternet.com www.rspb.org.uk/groups/epsom
Meetings: 7.45pm, 2nd Friday of the month, All Saints Church Hall, Fulford Road, West Ewell KT19 9QY.

GUILDFORD AND DISTRICT. (1974; 550). Michael Grimshaw. 01372 467 074; E-mail: michaelgrimshaw@btinternet.com www.rspb.org.uk/groups/guildford
Meetings: 2.15pm 2nd Thursday and 7.45pm 4th Wednesday (Oct-Apr), Onslow Village Hall, Guildford GU2 7QR.

NORTH WEST SURREY. (1973; 150). Dave Braddock, 20 Meadway Drive, New Haw, Surrey KT15 2DT. 01932 858 692; E-mail: dave.braddock@btinternet.com www.rspb.org.uk/groups/nwsurrey
Meetings: 7.45pm, 4th Wednesday of the month (not Dec, Jul, Aug), St James Parish Church Hall, Church Street, Weybridge, Surrey KT13 8DE.

Wetland Bird Survey Organiser
SURREY (includes Greater London south of the Thames and east to the Surrey Docks, excludes Spelthorne). Mrs P Williams, Bournbrook House, Sandpit Hall Road, Chobham, Surrey GU24 8HA. E-mail: penny@waxwing.plus.com

ENGLAND

Wildlife Hospitals
THE SWAN SANCTUARY. See National Directory.

THE WILDLIFE AID FOUNDATION. Randalls Farm House, Randalls Road, Leatherhead, Surrey, KT22 0AL. 24-hr Wildlife Help & Enquiries line: 09061 800 132 (50p/min), (fax) 01372 375 183;
E-mail: mail@wildlifeaid.org.uk
www.wildlifeaid.org.uk
Registered charity. Wildlife hospital and rehabilitation centre helping all native British species. Special housing for birds of prey. Membership scheme and fund raising activities. Veterinary support.

Wildlife Trust
SURREY WILDLIFE TRUST. (1959; 25,700). School Lane, Pirbright, Woking, Surrey, GU24 0JN. 01483 795 440, (fax) 01483 486 505; E-mail: info@surreywt.org.uk
www.surreywildlifetrust.org

SUSSEX

Bird Atlas/Avifauna
The Birds of Selsey Bill and the Selsey Peninsular (a checklist to year 2000) from: Mr O Mitchell, 21 Trundle View Close, Barnham, Bognor Regis, PO22 0JZ.

Birds of Sussex ed by Paul James (Sussex Ornithological Society, 1996).

Fifty Years of Birdwatching, a celebration of the achievements of the Shoreham District OS from 1953 onwards. £5 + P&P at current rates. Mrs Sue Miles, SDOS Hon.Secretary, 24 Chancellors Park, Hassocks, West Sussex BN6 8EZ. e-mail: secretary@sdos.org or through website www.sdos.org

Henfield Birdwatcher Reports 2000 and 2005 ed Mike Russell et al, Henfield Birdwatch

Bird Recorder
Mr David Howey, 2 Portobello Cottages, South Coast Road, Telscombe Cliffs, East Sussex BN10 7BD. 01273 300906; E-mail: recorder@sos.org.uk
www.sos.org.uk

Bird Reports
BIRDS OF RYE HARBOUR NR ANNUAL REPORT (1977- no longer printed, but available on www.WildRye.info), from Dr Barry Yates, see Clubs.

PAGHAM HARBOUR LOCAL NATURE RESERVE ANNUAL REPORT, from Warden, see Reserves,

SHOREHAM DISTRICT ORNITHOLOGICAL SOCIETY ANNUAL REPORT (1952-) - back issues available at £3.50 + P&P at current rates, from Mrs Sue Miles, 24 Chancellors Park, Hassocks, West Sussex BN6 8EZ. E-mail: secretary@sdos.orgor through website - www.sdos.org

SUSSEX BIRD REPORT (1963-), from J E Trowell, Lorrimer, Main Road, Icklesham, Winchelsea, E Sussex TN36 4BS. E-mail: membership@sos.org.uk
www.sos.org.uk

BTO Regional Representative
Dr Helen Crabtree. 01444 441 687;
E-mail: hcrabtree@gmail.com

Clubs
FRIENDS OF RYE HARBOUR NATURE RESERVE. (1973; 1900). Friends of Rye Harbour, Lime Kiln Cottage, Rye Harbour Road, Rye, E Sussex TN31 7TU. 01797 227 784; www.wildrye.info/reserve/friends/
Meetings: Monthly talks in winter, monthly walks all year.

HENFIELD BIRDWATCH. (1999; 135). Mike Russell, 31 Downsview, Small Dole, Henfield, West Sussex BN5 9YB. 01273 494 311;
E-mail: mikerussell@sussexwt.org.uk
http://henfieldbirdwatch.co.uk/

SHOREHAM DISTRICT ORNITHOLOGICAL SOCIETY. (1953; 200). Mrs Sue Miles (Hon. Secretary), 24 Chancellors Park, Hassocks, West Sussex BN6 8EZ. E-mail: secretary@sdos.org or through website - www.sdos.org
For membership enquiries contact the Membership Secretary (Sheena Maskell); e-mail: membership@sdos.org
Meetings: 7.30pm, 2nd Tuesday of the month (Oct-Apr), St Peter's Church Hall, Shoreham-by-Sea. (7 indoor meetings, 18+ field outings).

SUSSEX ORNITHOLOGICAL SOCIETY. (1962; 1700). Val Bentley, Chetsford, London Road, Henfield, West Sussex BN5 9JJ. 01273 494 723;
E-mail: secretary@sos.org.uk
www.sos.org.uk
Meetings: Annual conference in January (Haywards Heath), AGM in April, field outings throughout year.

Ringing Groups
BEACHY HEAD RS. R D M Edgar, 32 Hartfield Road, Seaford, E Sussex BN25 4PW.

CUCKMERE RG. Tim Parmenter, 18 Chapel Road, Plumpton Green, East Sussex BN7 3DD. 01273 891 881.

RYE BAY RG. P Jones, Elms Farm, Pett Lane, Icklesham, Winchelsea, E Sussex TN36 4AH. 01797 226374; E-mail: philjones@beamingbroadband.com

STEYNING RINGING GROUP. B R Clay, Meghana, Honeysuckle Lane, High Salvington, Worthing, West Sussex BN13 3BT. E-mail: brian.clay@ntlworld.com

RSPB Local Groups
BATTLE. (1973; 80). David Yates. 01424 773 826;
E-mail: familyatbattle@yahoo.co.uk
www.battlerspb.org.uk
Meetings: 7.30pm, 4th Tuesday of the month, Battle and Langton Primary School, Market Road, Battle TN33 0HQ.

263

ENGLAND

BRIGHTON & DISTRICT. (1974; 260). Mark Weston. 07802 293 417; E-mail: mark.weston@rspb.org.uk www.rspb.org.uk/groups/brighton
Meetings: 7.30pm, 4th Thursday of the month, All Saints Church Hall, Eaton Road, Hove BN3 3QE. Anyone is welcome, non-members should phone first as dates can vary.

CHICHESTER & SW SUSSEX. (1979; 245). Kerry Jackson. 01243 265 783; E-mail: chichesterrspb@aol.com www.rspb.org.uk/groups/chichester
Meetings: 7.30, 4th Thursday of month Sept to May (ex Dec), The Masonic Hall, 7 South Pallant, Chichester PO19 1SY. Three monthly walks all year.

CRAWLEY & HORSHAM. (1978; 148). Andrea Saxton, 104 Heath Way, Horsham, W Sussex RH12 5XS. 01403 242 218; E-mail: Andrea.saxton@sky.com www.rspb.org.uk/groups/crawley
Meetings: 8.00pm, 3rd Wednesday of the month (Sept-Apr), The Friary Hall, Crawley RH10 1HR.

EAST GRINSTEAD. (1998; 185). Nick Walker, 14 York Avenue, East Grinstead, W Sussex RH19 4TL. 01342 315 825; E-mail: nickwalker55@btinternet.com www.rspb.org.uk/groups/egrinstead
Meetings: 8.00pm, last Wednesday of the month, Large Parish Hall, De La Warr Road, East Grinstead RH19 3BP.

EASTBOURNE & DISTRICT. (1993; 320). David Jode. 01323 422 368 (daytime); E-mail: david@parkmove.com www.rspb.org.uk/groups/eastbourne
Meetings: 2.15 pm and 7.30 pm,1st Wednesday of the month (Sep-Jun), St. Wilfrid's Church Hall, Eastbourne Road, Pevensey Bay BN24 6HL.

HASTINGS & ST LEONARDS. (1983; 80). Richard Prebble. 01424 751 790; E-mail: Lynn.jenkins98@gmail.com www.rspb.org.uk/groups/hastings
Meetings: 7.30pm, 3rd Friday of the month, Taplin Centre, Upper Maze Hill, St Leonards TN38 0LQ.

Wetland Bird Survey Organiser
CHICHESTER HARBOUR. Mr E Rowsell, Field House, Bury Gate, Bury, Pulborough, West Sussex RH20 1NN. 01798 839 230; 07843 380 202; E-mail: edrowsell@gmail.com

OTHER SITES. Mr H R Bown, 49 Long Beach View, Sovereign Harbour North, Eastbourne, East Sussex BN23 5NB. 01323 479 569; E-mail: hr.bown@btinternet.com

Wildlife Hospital
BRENT LODGE BIRD & WILDLIFE TRUST. Penny Cooper, Brent Lodge, Cow Lane, Sidlesham, Chichester, West Sussex PO20 7LN. 01243 641 672 (emergency number) www.brentlodge.org
All species of wild birds and small mammals. Full surgical and medical facilities (inc. X-ray) in conjunction with veterinary support. Purpose-built oiled bird washing unit. Veterinary support.

Wildlife Trust
SUSSEX WILDLIFE TRUST. (1961; 33,000). Woods Mill, Shoreham Road, Henfield, W Sussex, BN5 9SD. 01273 492 630 (fax) 01273 494 500; E-mail: enquiries@sussexwt.org.uk www.sussexwildlifetrust.org.uk

TYNE & WEAR

Bird Recorders
See Durham; Northumberland.

Bird Report See Durham; Northumberland.

Clubs
NATURAL HISTORY SOCIETY OF NORTHUMBRIA. (1829; 900). The Natural History Society of Northumbria, Great North Museum: Hancock, Newcastle-upon-Tyne, NE2 4PT. 0191 232 6386; E-mail: nhsn@ncl.ac.uk www.NHSN.ncl.ac.uk
Meetings: Weekly indoor and outdoor meetings throughout the year, details can be found at www.nhsn.ncl.ac.uk

NORTHUMBERLAND & TYNESIDE BIRD CLUB. (1958; 250). Alan Tilmouth, 12 Stowe Gardens, Pegswood, Morpeth, Northumberland NE61 6TH. 07807 507 182; E-mail: ntbcorg@gmail.com www.ntbc.org.uk

RSPB Local Groups
NEWCASTLE-UPON-TYNE. (1969; 250). Marie Ollerenshaw. E-mail: NewcastleRSPBgroup@gmail.com www.rspb.org.uk/groups/newcastle
Meetings: 7pm, (Mar, Jun, Sep, Nov), Northumbria University, Ellison Place, Newcastle-upon-Tyne.

WARWICKSHIRE

Bird Recorder
Steven Haynes, E-mail: warks-recorder@westmidlandbirdclub.com

Bird Report See West Midlands.

BTO Regional Representative
WARWICKSHIRE. Mark Smith. 01926 735 398; E-mail: mark.smith36@ntlworld.com www.wildwarwickshire.co.uk

Club
NUNEATON & DISTRICT BIRDWATCHERS' CLUB. (1950; 78). Alvin K Burton, 23 Redruth Close, Horeston Grange, Nuneaton, Warwicks CV11 6FG. 024 7664 1591; http://ndbwc.webs.com/
Meetings: 7.30pm, 3rd Thursday of the month (Sep-Jun), Hatters Space Community Centre, Upper Abbey Street, Nuneaton CV11 5DN.

Ringing Groups
ARDEN RG. Roger J Juckes, 24 Croft Lane, Temple Grafton, Alcester, Warks B49 6PA. 01789 778 748.

ENGLAND

BRANDON RG. David Stone, Overbury, Wolverton, Stratford-on-Avon, Warks CV37 0HG. 01789 731 488.

RSPB Local Group
See West Midlands.

Wetland Bird Survey Organiser
Mr M Griffiths, 422 Tilehouse Lane, Tidbury Green, Solihull, West Midlands B90 1PX. 01564 826 685; 07837 138 815;
E-mail: matt_avesmaster@hotmail.com

Wildlife Trust
WARWICKSHIRE WILDLIFE TRUST. (1970; 13,000). Brandon Marsh Nature Centre, Brandon Lane, Coventry, CV3 3GW. 024 7630 2912 (fax) 024 7663 9556; E-mail: enquiries@wkwt.org.uk
www.warwickshire-wildlife-trust.org.uk

WEST MIDLANDS

Bird Atlas/Avifauna
The New Birds of the West Midlands edited by Graham and Janet Harrison (West Midland Bird Club, 2005). Available from 147 Worlds End Lane, Quinton, Birmingham B32 1JX.

Bird Recorder
Kevin Clements, 26 Hambrook Close, Dunstall Park, Wolverhampton, West Midlands WV6 0XA. 01902 568 997; E-mail: west-mids-recorder@ westmidlandbirdclub.com

Bird Reports
THE BIRDS OF SMESTOW VALLEY AND DUNSTALL PARK (1988-), from Secretary, Smestow Valley Bird Group.

WEST MIDLAND BIRD REPORT (inc Staffs, Warks, Worcs and W Midlands) (1934-), from Barbara Oakley, 147 Worlds End, Quinton, Birmingham B32 1JX.
E-mail: secretary@westmidlandbirdclub.com
www.westmidlandbirdclub.com

BTO Regional Representative
BIRMINGHAM & WEST MIDLANDS. Steve Davies. 07882 891 726; E-mail: stevedaviesbtorep@hotmail.co.uk

BTO Garden BirdWatch Ambassador
Mr M Hope-Urwin. E-mail: mandm@greenbee.net

Clubs
SMESTOW VALLEY BIRD GROUP. (1988; 46). http://smestowvalley.blogspot.co.uk/p/smestow-valley-bird-group.html

WEST MIDLAND BIRD CLUB - serving Ornithologists in Staffs, Warks, Worcs and the West Midlands County. (1929; 2,000). Mark Rickus, 27 Ringmere Avenue, Castle Bromwich, Birmingham B36 9AT. 0121 749 5348; E-mail: secretary@westmidlandbirdclub.com - www.westmidlandbirdclub.com
Meetings: Check website for details of the different branches and their events.

WEST MIDLAND BIRD CLUB (BIRMINGHAM BRANCH). (1995; 800). Andy Mabbett. E-mail: birmingham@

westmidlandbirdclub.com
www.westmidlandbirdclub.com/birmingham
Meetings: 7.30pm, usually last Tuesday (Oct-Apr), Unitarian New Meeting, 31 Ryland Street, Ladywood, Birmingham B16 8BL.

WEST MIDLAND BIRD CLUB (SOLIHULL BRANCH). (1973). Humphrey Miller, 29 Dorchester Court, Dorchester Road, Solihull B91 1LL. 0212 705 8507; E-mail: solihull@westmidlandbirdclub
www.westmidlandbirdclub.com/solihull
Meetings: 7.30 pm, Fridays (usually 1st of month), Guild House, Knowle, Solihull, West Midlands B93 0LN.

Ringing Groups
MERCIAN RG (Sutton Coldfield). Mr DJ Clifton, 59 Daisybank Crescent, Walsall, WS5 3BH. 01922 628 572.

RSPB Local Groups
BIRMINGHAM. (1975; 100). Sandra Bourne, 0121 382 7154 (Paul Hobbs); E-mail: BhamlocalRSPB@gmail.com www.rspb-birmingham.org.uk
Meetings: 7.30pm, 3rd Thursday of month (2nd Thursday in December), The Nautical Club, 5 Bishopsgate Street, Birmingham B15 1ET.

COVENTRY & WARWICKSHIRE. (1969; 130). Peter Worthy. 1926 497 967;
E-mail: pete@cpworthy.plus.com
www.rspb.org.uk/groups/coventryandwarwickshire
Meetings: 7.30pm, 4th Friday of the month, (Sep-May unless otherwise stated), Warwick Arts Centre or Baginton Village Hall.

SOLIHULL. (1983; 2,600). John Roberts, 115 Dovehouse Lane, Solihull, West Midlands B91 2EQ. 0121 707 3101; E-mail: johnbirder@care4free.net www.rspb.org.uk/groups/solihull
Meetings: 7.30pm, usually 2nd Tuesday of the month (Sep-Apr), Oliver Bird Hall, Church Hill Road, Solihull B91 3RQ.

STOURBRIDGE. (1978; 150). David Ackland. 01384 293 090; E-mail: davidackland@blueyonder.co.uk
www.rspb.org.uk/groups/stourbridge
Meetings: 2nd Wednesday of the month (Sep-May), Wollaston Suite, Stourbridge Town Hall, Crown Centre, Stourbridge, West Midlands, DY8 1YE.

SUTTON COLDFIELD. (1986; 250). Martin Fisher. 01295 253 330; E-mail: Anna.keen@RSPB.org.uk
www.rspb.org.uk/groups/suttoncoldfield
Meetings: 7.30pm, 1st Monday of the month, Bishop Vesey's Grammer School, Lichfield Road, Sutton Coldfield B74 2NH.

WALSALL. (1970). Mike Pittaway, 2 Kedleston Close, Bloxwich, Walsall WS3 3TW. 01922 710 568;
E-mail: michaelp@kedclose.freeserve.co.uk

ENGLAND

www.rspb-walsall.org.uk
Meetings: 7.30pm, 3rd Wednesday of the month, St Marys School, Jesson Road, Walsall WS1 3AY.

WOLVERHAMPTON. (1974; 100). Barry Proffitt. 01902 751 835; E-mail: RSPBwolverhampton@hotmail.co.uk
www.rspb.org.uk/groups/wolverhampton
Meetings: 7.30pm, 2nd Wednesday of the month (Sept-Apr), The Newman Centre, Haywood Drive, Tettenhall, Wolverhampton WV6 8RF. Also monthly field-trips (Sep-Jun).

Wetland Bird Survey Organiser
Mr N R Lewis, 99 Lyttelton Road, Stechford, Birmingham, West Midlands B33 8BN. 0121 783 0874; E-mail: nick.r.lewis@btinternet.com

Wildlife Trust
THE WILDLIFE TRUST FOR BIRMINGHAM AND THE BLACK COUNTRY. (1980; 5,500). 16 Greenfield Crescent, Edgbaston, Birmingham, B15 3AU. 0121 454 1199 (fax) 0121 454 6556;
E-mail: info@bbcwildlife.org.uk
www.bbcwildlife.org.uk

WILTSHIRE

Bird Atlas/Avifauna
Birds of Wiltshire by James Ferguson-Lees 2007, Wiltshire Ornithological Society

Bird Recorder
Rob Turner, 14 Ethendun, Bratton, Westbury, Wilts BA13 4RX. 01380 830 862;
E-mail: robt14@btopenworld.com

Bird Report
HOBBY (journal of the Wiltshire OS) (1975-), from John Osborne, 4 Fairdown Avenue, Westbury, Wiltshire BA13 3HS. 01373 8645 98;
E-mail: josb@talktalk.net
www.wiltshirebirds.co.uk

BTO Regional Representatives
NORTH & SOUTH. Bill Quantrill. 01225 866 245;
E-mail: william.quantrill@btinternet.com

Clubs
SALISBURY & DISTRICT NATURAL HISTORY SOCIETY. (1952; 146). Gail Baines, Membership Secretary, 01722 336 690;
www.salisburynaturalhistory.com
Meetings: 7.30pm, 3rd Thursday of the month (Sept-Apr), Salisbury Baptist Church, Brown Street, Salisbury SP1 2AS.

WILTSHIRE ORNITHOLOGICAL SOCIETY. (1974; 500). Main contact point is website -
www.wiltshirebirds.co.uk
Phil Deacon, 12 Rawston Close, Nythe, Swindon, Wilts SN3 3PW. 01793 528 930;
E-mail: phil.deacon@ntlworld.com
Meetings: See website for details.

Ringing Group
COTSWOLD WATER PARK RG. John Wells, 25 Pipers

Grove, Highnam, Glos GL2 8NJ.
E-mail: john.wells2@btinternet.com

WEST WILTSHIRE RG. Mr M.J. Hamzij, 13 Halfway Close , Trowbridge, Wilts BA14 7HQ.
E-mail: m.hamzij@btinternet.com

RSPB Local Groups
SOUTH WILTSHIRE. (1986; 650). Tony Goddard, 3 Forestry House, Livery Road, Farley, Salisbury SP5 1AG. 01722 712 713;
E-mail: goddard543@hotmail.com
www.rspb.org.uk/groups/southwiltshire
Meetings: 7.30pm, Tuesday evenings (monthly), Salisbury Arts Centre, Salisbury SP1 3UT.

Wetland Birds Survey Organiser
COTSWOLD WATER PARK. Mr G O Harris, 28 Thurnham Court, Thomas Wyatt Road, DevizesWiltshire SN10 5FL. 07868 427 916; 07868 42 7916;
E-mail: gharris_doh@hotmail.com

WILTSHIRE. Mr J C Rolls, c/o WeBS Office, BTO, The Nunnery, Thetford, Norfolk IP24 2PU. 01842 750 050;
www.webs@bto.org

Wildlife Trust
WILTSHIRE WILDLIFE TRUST. (1962; 18,500). Elm Tree Court, Long Street, Devizes, Wilts, SN10 1NJ. 01380 725 670 (fax) 01380 729 017;
E-mail: info@wiltshirewildlife.org
www.wiltshirewildlife.org

Wiltshire Wildlife Trust

WORCESTERSHIRE

Bird Recorder
Steven Payne, 6 Norbury Close, Redditch B98 8RP. 01527 60169;
E-mail: worcs-recorder@westmidlandbirdclub.com
www.westmidlandbirdclub.com

Bird Report
See West Midlands.

BTO Regional Representative
G Harry Green MBE, Windy Ridge, Pershore Road, Little Comberton, Pershore, Worcs WR10 3EW. 01386 710 377; E-mail: zen130501@zen.co.uk

Ringing Group
WYCHAVON RG. J R Hodson, 15 High Green, Severn Stoke, Worcester WR8 9JS. 01905 371 333;
E-mail: hodson77@btinternet.com

Club
WEST MIDLAND BIRD CLUB (KIDDERMINSTER BRANCH). Brian Rickett, 1 Russell Road, Kidderminster DY10 3HT. 01562 824 615;
E-mail: kidderminster@westmidlandbirdclub.com
www.westmidlandbirdclub.com
Meetings: 7.30pm, 4th Wednesday of the month (Sep-Apr), St Oswalds Church Centre, Broadwaters, Kidderminster DY10 2RY.

ENGLAND

RSPB Local Group
WORCESTER & MALVERN. (1980; 300). Frances Evans, 120 Bath Road, Worcester WR5 3EP. 01905 359 132; E-mail: francesevans@gmail.com
www.rspb.org.uk/groups/worcester
Meetings: 7.30pm, 2nd Wednesday in month (Sept-May), Powick Village Hall, Malvern Road, WR2 4RT.

Wetland Birds Survey Organiser
WORCESTERSHIRE. Mr A Warr, 14 Bromsgrove Street, Barbourne, Worcester WR3 8AR. 01905 28 281; E-mail: andrew.warr3@btopenworld.com

Wildlife Trust
WORCESTERSHIRE WILDLIFE TRUST. (1968; 9,000). Lower Smite Farm, Smite Hill, Hindlip, Worcester, WR3 8SZ. 01905 754 919 (fax) 01905 755868; E-mail: enquiries@worcestershirewildlifetrust.org
www.worcswildlifetrust.co.uk
Charity no. 256618.

YORKSHIRE

Bird Atlas/Avifauna
Atlas of Breeding Birds in the Leeds Area 1987-1991 by Richard Fuller et al (Leeds Birdwatchers' Club, 1994).

The Birds of Halifax by Nick Dawtrey (only 20 left), 14 Moorend Gardens, Pellon, Halifax, W Yorks, HX2 0SD.

The Birds of Yorkshire by John Mather (Croom Helm, 1986).

An Atlas of the Breeding Birds of the Huddersfield Area, 1987-1992, by Brian Armitage et al (2000) - very few copies left.

Birds of Barnsley by Nick Addey (Pub by author, 114 Everill Gate Lane, Broomhill, Barnsley S73 0YJ, 1998).

Birds of The Huddersfield Area by Paul and Betty Bray (Huddersfield Birdwatchers Club 2008).

Breeding Bird Atlas for Barnsley in preparation.

County Bird Recorders
YORKSHIRE. Craig Thomas, Sunnybank, Church Lane, Flamborough YO15 1PG. 01262 851 677; e-mail: craigcthomas@yahoo.co.uk

EAST YORKSHIRE AND EDITOR. Geoff Dobbs, 1 Priory Road, Beverley, East Yorkshire HU17 0EG. 07778 559 763; e-mail: geoffdobbs@aol.com

NORTH YORKSHIRE. Ian Court, 2 Burley Mews, Steeton, Keighley BT20 6TX. 01535 658 582; e-mail: ian.court@mypostoffice.co.uk

SOUTH YORKSHIRE. Martin Wells, 715 Manchester Road, Stocksbridge, Sheffield S36 1DQ. 0114 288 4211; E-mail: martinwells@barnsleybsg.plus.com

WEST YORKSHIRE. Covering all bird study groups and South and West Yorkshire and three reserves – Fairburn Ings, Old Moor (both RSPB) and Potteric Carr

(Yorkshire Wildlife Trust). John Wint, 9 Yew Tree Park, Whitley, Goole, East Yorkshire DN14 0NZ. 01977 662 826; e-mail: j.wint114@btinternet.com

Bird Reports
BARNSLEY & DISTRICT BIRD STUDY GROUP REPORT (1971-), from Waxwing Books, Sunnybank Cottage, Ruston Parva, Driffield YO25 4DG.

YORK ORNITHOLOGICAL CLUB REPORT (1966 -). The 2012 report is due to be published in Autumn 2013. Latest report and some back numbers can be ordered and paid for through the club website, from Linda Newton, 5 Fairfields Drive, Skelton, York YO30 1YP, 01904 471 446; E-mail: secretary@yorkbirding.org.uk
www.yorkbirding.org.uk

YORKSHIRE BIRD REPORT, published by the Yorkshire Naturalists' Union (1940-). 2011 edition £14 including postage, from Jill Warwick, Sharow Grange, Sharow, Ripon HG4 5BN. 01765 602 832; e-mail: jill@swland.co.uk

BRADFORD NATURALISTS' SOCIETY ANNUAL REPORT, from Mr I Hogg, 23 St Matthews Road, Bankfoot, Bradford BD5 9AB. 01274 727 902.

BRADFORD ORNITHOLOGICAL GROUP REPORT (1987-) - after the 2008 issue, this report will only be available to paid up members of the group, from Jenny Barker, 3 Chapel Fold, Slack Lane, Oakworth, Keighley BD22 0RQ.

DONCASTER BIRD REPORT (1955-), from Mr M Roberts, 8 Sandbeck Court, Rossington, Doncaster DN11 0FN. 01302 326 265.

FILEY BRIGG BIRD REPORT (1976-), from Colin and Rose Court. 01723 515 925; E-mail: colincourt@uwclub.net
www.fbog.co.uk

HARROGATE & DISTRICT NATURALISTS' SOCIETY BIRD REPORT (1996-) 2012 edition £6 including postage, from Jill Warwick, Sharow Grange, Sharow, Ripon HG4 5BN. 01765 602 832; e-mail: jill@swland.co.uk

HULL VALLEY WILDLIFE GROUP REPORT (2000-) covering Hull Valley. from
www.hullvalleywildlifegroup.co.uk

BIRDS IN HUDDERSFIELD (1966-), from Mr M Wainman, 2 Bankfield Avenue, Taylor Hill, Huddersfield HD4 7QY. 01484 305054; E-mail: brian.armitage@ntlworld.com

BIRDS OF ROTHERHAM (1975-) - cost £2.50 inc p&p, cheque payable to R.D.O.S., from The Secretary, Rotherham & District Bird Club.
E-mail: rdos@hotmail.co.uk
www.rotherhambirds.co.uk

BIRDS IN THE SHEFFIELD AREA (1973-), from Richard Hill, Honorary Secretary, 22 Ansell Road, Sheffield, South Yorkshire S11 7PE. E-mail: Secretary@sbsg.org
www.sbsg.org

267

ENGLAND

THE BIRDS OF SK58 (1993-), from Secretary, SK58 Birders. E-mail: recorder@sk58birders.com www.sk58birders.com

SORBY RECORD (1962-), from Ken Dorning, Sorby NHSoc, c/o Room C12i, Dainton Building, Brook Hill, Sheffield S3 7HF.

SPURN BIRD OBSERVATORY ANNUAL REPORT, from Warden, see Reserves.

SWILLINGTON INGS BIRD GROUP - ANNUAL REPORT AND TWENTY YEAR REVIEW - 2008, from Chris Robinson, 43 Northfield Road, Sprotbrough, Doncaster DN5 8AY. 07534 271 254; E-mail: GBFShrike@hotmail.com http://sibg1.wordpress.com

WINTERSETT AREA ANNUAL REPORT (1988-), from Steve Denny, 13 Rutland Drive, Crofton, Wakefield WF4 1SA. 01924 864 487.

BTO Regional Representatives & Regional Development Officers
BRADFORD RR & RDO. Mike L Denton, 77 Hawthorne Terrace, Crosland Moor, Huddersfield HD4 5RP. 01484 646 990.

EAST RR. Geoff Dobbs, 1 Priory Road, Beverley, East Yorkshire HU17 0EG. 07778 559 763; e-mail: geoffdobbs@aol.com

HULL RR. Geoff Dobbs, 1 Priory Road, Beverley, East Yorkshire HU17 0EG. 07778 559 763; e-mail: geoffdobbs@aol.com

LEEDS & WAKEFIELD RR. Position vacant. 01842 750 050; e-mail: info@bto.org

NORTH-EAST RR. Mick Carroll, 10 Crofts Avenue, Pickering, North Yorkshire YO18 7HP. 01751 476 550.

NORTH-WEST RR. Gerald Light. 01756 753 720; E-mail: gerald@uwlig.plus.com

RICHMOND RR. John Edwards, 7 Church Garth, Great Smeaton, Northallerton, N Yorks DL6 2HW. 01609 881 476; E-mail: john@jhedwards.plus.com

SOUTH-EAST AND SOUTH-WEST RR. Position vacant. 01842 750 050. E-mail: info@bto.org

YORK RR. Rob Chapman, 12 Moorland Road, York, YO10 4HF. 01904 633 558; E-mail: robert.chapman@tinyworld.co.uk

YORKSHIRE (HARROGATE) RR. Mike Brown, 48 Pannal Ash Drive, Harrogate, N Yorks HG2 0HU. 01423 567 382; E-mail: mikebtorep@gmail.com

Clubs
BARNSLEY BIRD STUDY GROUP. (1970; 35). Graham Speight, 58 Locke Avenue, Barnsley, South Yorkshire S70 1QH. 01226 321 300. http://barnsleybirds.blogspot.co.uk/
Meetings: 7.15pm, 1st Thursday in the month (Nov-Mar), RSPB Old Moor, Barnsley.

BRADFORD ORNITHOLOGICAL GROUP. (1987; 160). Shaun Radcliffe, Chairman, 8 Longwood Avenue, Bingley, W Yorks BD16 2RX. 01274 770 960; E-mail: shaun.radcliffe@btinternet.com www.bradfordbirding.org
Meetings: 1st Tuesday of the month - see website for details.

CASTLEFORD & DISTRICT NATURALISTS' SOCIETY. (1956; 16). Michael J Warrington, 31 Mount Avenue, Hemsworth, Pontefract, W Yorks WF9 4QE. 01977 614 954; E-mail: michaelwarrington@talktalk.net
Meetings: 7.30pm, Tuesdays monthly (Sep-Mar), Castleford Campus, Castleford WF10 4UA. Check contact name for dates.

FILEY BRIGG ORNITHOLOGICAL GROUP. (1977; 100). Dr Sue Hull, 32 West Road, Filey, N Yorkshire YO14 9LP. 01723 515 042; E-mail: secretary@fbog.co.uk www.fbog.co.uk

HARROGATE & DISTRICT NATURALISTS' SOCIETY. (1947; 230). Mrs S Coldwell, General Secretary, 4 Abbots Way, Knaresborough, North Yorkshire HG5 8EU. E-mail: gen.sechdns@yahoo.co.uk www.hdns.org.uk
Meetings: 7.30pm, St. Roberts Centre, 2/3 Robert Street, Harrogate. The programme of meetings is sent out to members in April.

HORNSEA BIRD CLUB. (1967; 35). John Eldret, 44 Rolston Road, Hornsea, HU18 1UH. 01964 532 854.
Meetings: 7.30pm, 3rd Friday of the month (Sep-Mar), Hornsea Library. Monthly visits to local bird reserves.

HUDDERSFIELD BIRDWATCHERS' CLUB. (1966; 90). Chris Abell, 57 Butterley Lane, New Mill, Holmfirth HD9 7EZ. 01484 681 499; E-mail: cdabell@gmail.com www.huddersfieldbirdwatchersclub.co.uk
Meetings: 7.30pm, Tuesday's fortnightly (Sep-May), The Old Court Room, Town Hall, Ramsden St, Huddersfield HD1 2TA.

HULL VALLEY WILDLIFE GROUP. (1997; 175). The Secretary, 29 Beech View, Cranswick, East Yorkshire YO25 9QQ. 01377 270 957. 01377 270 957. www.hullvalleywildlifegroup.co.uk

NORTH YORKSHIRE BIRD STUDY GROUP. Mick Carroll, 10 Crofts Avenue, Pickering, North Yorkshire YO18 7HP. 01751 476 550.

ROTHERHAM & DISTRICT ORNITHOLOGICAL SOCIETY. (1974; 80). Malcolm Taylor, 18 Maple Place, Chapeltown, Sheffield S35 1QW. 0114 246 1848; E-mail: rdos@hotmail.co.uk www.rotherhambirds.co.uk
Meetings: 7.30pm, 2nd Friday of the month, United Reform Church Hall, Herringthorpe S60 4JN.

SCARBOROUGH BIRDERS. (1993; 38). Steve Wignill, Flat 3, 101 Castle Road, Scarborough, N Yorkshire YO11 1HX. 07859 435 592;

ENGLAND

E-mail: steve.wignill@scarboroughbirding.co.uk
www.scarboroughbirding.co.uk
Meetings: 3rd Thursday of the month (Sep-Nov) and
(Jan-Apr). Check website for details.

SHEFFIELD BIRD STUDY GROUP. (1972; 227). Richard
Hill, Honorary Secretary, 22 Ansell Road, Sheffield,
South Yorkshire S11 7PE; E-mail: Secretary@sbsg.org
www.sbsg.org
Meetings: 7.15pm, 2nd Wednesday of the month
(Sep-May), Lecture Theatre 5, Sheffield University
Arts Tower S11 7PE.

SK58 BIRDERS. (1993; 66). Brian Chambers, 01909 770
816; E-mail: brianchambers101940@hotmail.com
www.sk58birders.com
Chair: Mick Clay, 2 High St, S.Anston, Sheffield. 01909
566 000.
Meetings: 7.30pm, last Wednesday of the month
(Sep-Nov and Jan-Jun), Anston Parish Hall, 15A
Ryton Road, North Anston, Sheffield S25 4DL.

SORBY NHS (ORNITHOLOGICAL SECTION). (1918; 400).
The Secretary, c/o 159 Bell Hagg Road, Sheffield S6
5DA; E-mail: secretary@sorby.org.uk
www.sorby.org.uk
Meetings: Indoor and field meetings held regularly as
advertised on the website and in the newsletter.

SOUTH PEAK RAPTOR STUDY GROUP. (1998; 12).
Trevor Grimshaw,
e-mail: grimshaw758@btinternet.com

SOUTH RYEDALE AND EAST YORKSHIRE RAPTOR
GROUP. Mick Carroll, 10 Crofts Avenue, Pickering,
North Yorkshire YO18 7HP. 01751 476 550.

SWILLINGTON INGS BIRD GROUP. (1989; 83). Chris
Robinson, 43 Northfield Road, Sprotbrough, Doncaster
DN5 8AY. 07534 271 254.
http://sibg1.wordpress.com
Meetings: 7.30pm, 1st Thursday of even months with
informal social evenings 1st Thursday of odd months
(please phone for details of venue).

WAKEFIELD NATURALISTS' SOCIETY. (1851; 32).
Michael Warrington, 31 Mount Avenue, Hemsworth,
Pontefract, W Yorks WF9 4QE. 01977 614 954;
E-mail: michaelwarrington@talktalk.net
http://wakefieldnaturalists.org/?tag=wakefield-
naturalists-society
Meetings: 7.30pm, 2nd Tuesday of the month (Sep-
Apr), Friends Meeting House, Thornhill Street,
Wakefield WF1 1NQ.

YORK ORNITHOLOGICAL CLUB. (1967; 80). Linda
Newton, 5 Fairfields Drive,
Skelton, York YO30 1YP, 01904
471 446; E-mail: secretary@
yorkbirding.org.uk
www.yorkbirding.org.uk
Meetings: 7.30pm, 1st Tuesday
of the month, St Olaves Church
Hall, Marygate Lane, Marygate,
York YO30 7BJ.

YORKSHIRE NATURALISTS' UNION (Bird Section).
(1875; 500). Mr John Wint (Vice Chairman). 01977 662
826; E-mail: j.wint114@btinternet.com
www.ynu.org.uk

Ringing Groups
BARNSLEY RG. M C Wells, 715 Manchester Road,
Stocksbridge, Sheffield S36 1DQ. 0114 288 4211;
E-mail: barnsleybsg.plus.com

DONCASTER RG. D Hazard, 41 Jossey Lane,
Scawthorpe, Doncaster, S Yorks DN5 9DB. 01302 788
044; E-mail: dave.hazard@tiscali.co.uk

EAST DALES RG. P. Bone, 11 Dorrington Close,
Pocklington, York YO42 2GS.
E-mail: philsarab@aol.co.uk

EAST YORKS RG. Peter J Dunn, 43 West Garth
Gardens, Cayton, Scarborough, N Yorks YO11 3SF.
01723 583149; E-mail: pjd@fbog.co.uk
www.eyrg.co.uk

SORBY-BRECK RG. Geoff P Mawson, Moonpenny Farm,
Farwater Lane, Dronfield, Sheffield S18 1RA.
E-mail: moonpenny@talktalk.net

SPURN BIRD OBSERVATORY. Paul Collins, Kew Villa,
Seaside Road, Kilnsea, Hull HU12 0UB. 01964 650 479;
E-mail: pcnfa@hotmail.com

WINTERSETT RG. P Smith, 16 Templar Street,
Wakefield, W Yorks WF1 5HB. 01924 375 082.

RSPB Local Groups
AIREDALE AND BRADFORD. (1972; 3500 in catchment
area). Paul Barrett. 01274 582 078;
E-mail: AbRSPB@blueyonder.co.uk
www.rspb.org.uk/groups/airedaleandbradford
Meetings: 7.30pm, monthly on Fridays, Room 3,
Shipley Library, 2 Well Croft BD18 3QH.

CRAVEN & PENDLE. (1986; 300). Colin Straker. 01756
751 888; E-mail: colin.straker@btinternet.com
www.cravenandpendlerspb.org
Meetings: 7.30pm 2nd Wednesday of the month (Sep-
May), Annexe Hall, Skipton Town Hall BD23 1AH.

DONCASTER. (1984; 86). Trevor Bonham, Willowford,
Melton Mill Lane, High Lane, High Melton, Doncaster
DN5 7TE. 01709 585 677;
E-mail: trevorbonham@yahoo.co.uk

EAST YORKSHIRE. (1986;120). Paul Leyland, 61 Muston
Road, Hunmanby, North Yorkshire YO14 0JY. 01723 891
507; E-mail: eastyorksrspb@yahoo.co.uk
www.rspb.org.uk/groups/eastyorkshire
Meetings: 7.30pm, North Bridlington Library,
Martongate, Bridlington (check website for details).

HARROGATE DISTRICT. (2005). Bill Sturman. 01423 870
883; E-mail: pam-bill@sturmanw.fsnet.co.uk
www.harrogaterspb.com
Meetings: 7.50pm, 3rd Monday of the month
(Oct-Mar). Christ Church Parish Centre, The Stray,
Harrogate HG1 4SW.

ENGLAND

HUDDERSFIELD & HALIFAX. (1981; 120). David Hemingway, 267 Long Lane, Dalton, Huddersfield HD5 9SH. 01484 301 920; E-mail: d.hemingway@ntlworld.com www.rspb.org.uk/groups/huddersfieldand halifax **Meetings:** 7.30pm, Huddersfield Methodist Mission, 3-13 Lord Street, Huddersfield HD1 1QA.

HULL & DISTRICT. (1983; 334). Betty Hilton. 01482 849 503; E-mail: betty9hilton@gmail.com www.rspb.org.uk/groups/hull **Meetings:** 7.30pm, Tuesdays (Sept-Apr), Christchurch United Reformed Church, South Ella Way, Kirk Ella, Hull. (£2 for Local Group Members and £2.50 for Non Members).

LEEDS. (1974; 560). Ian Willoughby. 0113 258 6555. E-mail: RSPBleeds@googlemail.comwww.rspb.org.uk/groups/leeds **Meetings:** 7.30pm, 3rd Wednesday of the month (Sep-Apr), Friends Meeting House, 188 Woodhouse Lane, Leeds, Yorkshire, LS2 9DX.

RICHMONDSHIRE & HAMBLETON. (2005). Grahame Bentley. 1748 824 776; E-mail: grahame@bentley000.plus.com www.rspb.org.uk/groups/richmondshireandhambleton **Meetings:** Check website.

SHEFFIELD. (1981; 500). Susan Bradshaw. 0114 239 9072; e-mail: suebradshaw135@talktalk.net www.rspb-sheffield.org.uk **Meetings:** 7.30pm 1st Thursday of the month (Sept-May), Central United Reformed Church, Norfolk St, Sheffield S1 2JB.

WAKEFIELD. (1987; 130). Duncan Stokoe, 12 New Road, Horbury, Wakefield, West Yorkshire WF4 5LR. E-mail: duncanstokoe@gmail.com www.rspb.org.uk/groups/wakefield **Meetings:** 7.30pm, 4th Thursday of the month (Sep-Apr), Ossett War Memorial Community Centre, Prospect Road, Ossett, WF5 8AN.

YORK. (1972; 600). Chris Lloyd, 7 School Lane, Upper Poppleton, York YO26 6JS. 01904 794 865; E-mail: rspb.calyork@btinternet.com www.yorkrspb.org.uk **Meetings:** 7.30pm, Tues, Wed or Thurs, Temple Hall, York St John University, Lord Mayors Walk, York. www.rspb.org.uk/groups/doncaster **Meetings:** 7.00pm on the second Wednesday of the month from 11th September 2013, at Castle Park Rugby Club, Armthorpe Road, Doncaster DN2 5QB.

Wetland Bird Survey Organiser
EAST YORKSHIRE AND SCARBOROUGH (excl. Humber). Mr J Morgan, 4 Rise Lane, Catwick, Beverley, North Humberside HU17 5PL. 01964 544947; 07951 075045; e-mail: jimmygpz@hotmail.com

HARROGATE AND YORKSHIRE DALES. Mr W G Haines, 3 Rosemount Road, Ealing, London W13 0HJ. 07870 828 978; E-mail: bill.haines@tiscali.co.uk

LEEDS AREA. Mr P R Morris, 10 The Grove, Alwoodley, Leeds LS17 7BW; E-mail: pmorris@wyjs.org.uk

WAKEFIELD AREA. c/o WeBS Office, BTO, The Nunnery, Thetford, Norfolk IP24 2PU. 01842 750 050; E-mail: webs@bto.org

Wildlife Hospital
ANIMAL HOUSE WILDLIFE WELFARE. Mr T Buckroyd, 14 Victoria Street, Scarborough, YO12 7SS. 01723 371 256 (please leave a message on the answer machine and callers will be contacted as soon as possible). All species of wild birds. Oiled birds given treatment before forwarding to cleaning stations. Incubators, hospital cages, heat pads, release sites. Birds ringed before release. Prior telephone call requested. Collection if required. Veterinary support. Charity shop at 127 Victoria Road.

Wildlife Trusts
THE WILDLIFE TRUST FOR SHEFFIELD AND ROTHERHAM. (1985; 5,613). 37 Stafford Road, Sheffield, S2 2SF. 0114 263 4335 (fax) 0114 263 4345; E-mail: mail@wildsheffield.com www.wildsheffield.com

YORKSHIRE WILDLIFE TRUST. (1946; 21,500). 1 St George's Place, Tadcaster Road, York YO24 1GN. 01904 659 570, (fax) 01904 613 467; E-mail: info@ywt.org.uk www.ywt.org.uk

SCOTLAND

Bird Report
SCOTTISH BIRD REPORT, from: The SOC, The Scottish Birdwatching Resource Centre, Waterston House, Aberlady, East Lothian, EH32 0PY

Club
See Scottish Ornithologists' Club in National Directory.

ANGUS & DUNDEE

Bird Recorder
ANGUS & DUNDEE. Jon Cook, 76 Torridon Road, Broughty Ferry, Dundee DD5 3JH. 01382 738 495; e-mail: 1301midget@tiscali.co.uk

Bird Report
ANGUS & DUNDEE BIRD REPORT (1974-), from the County Recorder, 01382 738 495;
e-mail: 1301midget@tiscali.co.uk

BTO Regional Representative
ANGUS RR. Position vacant.

Clubs
ANGUS & DUNDEE BIRD CLUB. (1997; 230). George Rodger (Club Chairman), 01382 816 107;
e-mail: curlew1@sky.com
www.angusbirding.com
Meetings: 7.30pm, Tuesdays, Panbride Church Hall, Carnoustie, Angus.

SOC TAYSIDE BRANCH. (145). Brian Brocklehurst. 01382 778 348; e-mail: brian.brocklehurst1@btinternet.com
www.the-soc.org.uk

Ringing Group
TAY RG. Ms S Millar, Edenvale Cottage, 1 Lydox Cottages, Dairsie, Fife, KY15 4RN;
e-mail: shirley@edenecology.co.uk

RSPB Members' Group
DUNDEE. (1972; 110). Graham Smith, 01382 532 461;
e-mail: grahamnjen@hotmail.com
www.RSPB.org.uk/groups/dundee
Meetings: 7.30 pm, monthly on a Wednesday (Sep-Mar), Methodist Church, 20, West Marketgait, Dundee. Admission £1.00 for all, including refreshments. outdoor meetings on Sunday leaving Crichton Street, Dundee at 9am.

Wetland Bird Survey Organisers
ANGUS (excl Montrose Basin). c/o WeBS Office, BTO, The Nunnery, Thetford, Norfolk IP24 2PU. 01842 750 050; e-mail: webs@bto.org

MONTROSE BASIN. Miss A Cheshier, Scottish Wildlife Trust, Montrose Basin Wildlife Centre, Rossie Braes, Montrose, Angus,DD10 9TA;
e-mail: acheshier@swt.org.uk

ARGYLL

Bird Atlas/Avifauna
Birds of Argyll (Argyll Bird Club 2007, £45 inc postage), available from Bob Furness, The Cnoc, Tarbert, Arrochar, Dunbartonshire G83 7DG. 01301 702 603.

Bird Recorders
ARGYLL (rare bird records). Jim Dickson, 11 Pipers Road, Cairnbaan, Lochgilphead, Argyll PA31 8UF. 01546 603 967; e-mail: meg@jdickson5.plus.com
Also for submission of rare bird records.

Assistant Recorder (non rare bird records). Malcolm Chattwood, 1 The Stances, Kilmichael Glassary, Lochgilphead, Argyll PA31 8QA. 01536 603 389;
e-mail: abcrecorder@outlook.com
For submission of all non-rare bird records.

Bird Reports
ARGYLL BIRD REPORT (1984-), From Dr Bob Furness, The Cnoc, Tarbet, Dunbartonshire G83 7DG.01301 702 603; e-mail: r.furness@bio.gla.ac.uk

ISLE OF MULL BIRD REPORT (2011), From Mr Alan Spellman, Maridon, Lochdon, Isle of Mull, Argyll. PA64 6AP. 01680 812 448; e-mail: mullbirds@btinternet.com
www.mullbirds.com

MACHRIHANISH SEABIRD OBSERVATORY REPORT (1992-), From the Observatory, see Reserves & Observatories.

BTO Regional Representatives
ARGYLL (MULL, COLL, TIREE AND MORVERN). Arthur Brown/ Rod Little, 01688 400 415/01688 400 315; e-mail: pamartbrown@btinternet.com/rltt@aol.com

ARGYLL MAINLAND, BUTE AND GIGHA. Position vacant, 01842 750 050; e-mail: info@bto.org

ISLAY, JURA, COLONSAY RR. John S Armitage, Airigh Sgallaidh, Portnahaven, Isle of Islay, PA47 7SZ. 01496 860 396; e-mail: jsa@ornquest.plus.com
www.birdingodyssey.blogspot.com

Clubs
ARGYLL BIRD CLUB. (1983; 270). Katie Pendreigh, The Whins, Farry Road, Tayinloan, Argyll PA37 1PT. 01631 710 630. www.argyllbirdclub.org
Meetings: All-day Indoor Meetings are held on a Saturday in early March and early November each year, see website for details.

ISLE OF MULL BIRD CLUB. (2001;160), Mrs Janet T Hall, Membership Secretary, Druim Mhor, Craignure, Isle of Mull, Argyll PA65 6AY.01680 812 441;
e-mail: j.phall142@gmail.com

SCOTLAND

www.mullbirdclub.org.uk
Meetings: 7 for 7.30pm start, 3rd Friday of the month (Oct-Apr), Craignure Village Hall.

Ringing Group
TRESHNISH ISLES AUK RG. Robin Ward, 15 Church Clost, Great Stukeley, Cambridgeshire PE28 4AP; e-mail: robin.ward2@virginmedia.com

RSPB Members' Group
HELENSBURGH. (1975; 62). John Clark, 01436 821 178; e-mail: johnclark@jcmc.demon.co.uk
www.rspb.org.uk/groups/helensburgh
Meetings: The Guide Halls, Lower John Street, Helensburgh.

Wildlife Hospital
WINGS OVER MULL. Richard and Sue Dewar, Auchnacroish House, Torosay, Craignure, Isle of Mull PA65 6AY. Tel/fax: 01680 812 594; e-mail: dewars@wingsovermull.com
www.wingsovermull.com

Wetland Bird Survey Organisers
ARGYLL MAINLAND. Mr P C Daw, Tigh-na-Tulloch, Minard, Inveraray, Argyll PA32 8YQ. 01546 886 260; e-mail: monedula@globalnet.co.uk01546 886 260

MULL. Mr P C Daw, Tigh-na-Tulloch, Minard, Inveraray, Argyll PA32 8YQ. 01546 886 260; e-mail: monedula@globalnet.co.uk

TIREE & COLL. Dr J Bowler, c/o WeBS Office, BTO, The Nunnery, Thetford, Norfolk IP24 2PU. 01879 220 748; e-mail: john.bowler@rspb.org.uk

AYRSHIRE

Bird Recorder
AYRSHIRE. Fraser Simpson, 4 Inchmurrin Drive, Kilmarnock, Ayrshire KA3 2JD.
e-mail: recorder@ayrshire-birding.org.uk -
www.ayrshire-birding.org.uk

Bird Reports
AYRSHIRE BIRD REPORT (1976-), From Dr RG Vernon, 29 Knoll Park, Ayr KA7 4RH. 01292 442 195; e-mail: rgv_mcv@tiscali.co.uk

BTO Regional Representatives
AYRSHIRE RR. Brian Broadley, 01290 424 241; e-mail: brianbroadley@onegreendoor.com

Club
SOC AYRSHIRE. (1962; 154). Anne Dick, Rowanmyle House,Tarbolton, Mauchline KA5 5LU. 01292 541 981. www.ayrshire-birding.org.uk
www.the-soc.org.uk
Meetings: 7.30pm, Tuesdays monthly, Monkton Community Church, Monkton by Prestwick KA9 2RN.

RSPB Members' Groups
CENTRAL AYRSHIRE LOCAL GROUP. (1978; 85). Ronnie Coombes (Group Leader), 01292 265 891; e-mail: ronnie.coombes@tesco.net

www.ayrshire-birding.org.uk
Meetings: 7.30pm 3rd Monday of the month (Sep-Apr), Newton Wallacetown Church Hall, 60 Main Street, Ayr.

NORTH AYRSHIRE. (1976; 180). John Tedd, 01294 823 434; e-mail: john.tedd@virgin.net
www.narspb.org.uk
Meetings: 7.30pm, various Fridays (Sep-Apr), Argyll Centre, Donaldson Avenue, Saltcoats, Ayrshire, KA21 5AG.

Wetland Bird Survey Organiser
AYRSHIRE. Mr D A Grant, c/o WeBS Office, BTO, The Nunnery, Thetford, Norfolk IP24 2PU; e-mail: daveg466@gmail.com

ARRAN. Mr J Cassels, Kilpatrick Kennels, Kilpatrick, Blackwaterfoot, Isle of Arran KA27 8EY. 01770 860 316; e-mail: james.cassels@virgin.net

Wildlife Hospital
HESSILHEAD WILDLIFE RESCUE CENTRE. Gay & Andy Christie, Gateside, Beith, Ayrshire, KA15 1HT. 01505 502 415; e-mail: info@hessilhead.org.uk
www.hessilhead.org.uk
All species. Releasing aviaries. Veterinary support. Visits only on open days please.

THE SCOTTISH BORDERS

Bird Atlas/Avifauna
The Breeding Birds of South-east Scotland, a Tetrad Atlas 1988-1994 by R D Murray et al. (Scottish Ornithologists' Club, 1998).

Bird Recorder
Ray Murray, 4 Bellfield Crescent, Eddleston, Peebles, EH45 8RQ. 01721 730 677;
e-mail: ray1murray@btinternet.com

Bird Report
BORDERS BIRD REPORT (1979-), from Malcolm Ross, Westfield Cottage, Smailholm, Kelso TD5 7PN.01573 460 699; e-mail: eliseandmalcolm@btinternet.com

BTO Regional Representative
RR. Graham Pyatt, The Schoolhouse, Manor, Peebles EH45 9JN. 01721 740 319;
e-mail: d.g.pyatt@btinternet.com

Club
SOC BORDERS BRANCH. (100). Graham Pyatt, The Schoolhouse, Manor, Peebles EH45 9JN. 01721 740 319e-mail: d.g.pyatt@btinternet.com
www.the-soc.org.uk
Meetings: 7.30pm, 2nd Monday of the month, George & Abbotsford Hotel, Melrose.

Ringing Group
BORDERS RG. (1991; 10) Dr T W Dougall, 38 Leamington Terrace, Edinburgh EH10 4JL. (Office) 0131 344 2600.

RSPB Members' Group
BORDERS. (1995; 94). John Marshall, 01896 850 564;

SCOTLAND

e-mail: ncmandjrm@btinternet.com
www.rspb.org.uk/groups/borders
Meetings: 7.30pm, 3rd Wednesday of the month, The
Corn Exchange, Market Square, Melrose TD6 9PN.

Wetland Bird Survey Organiser
BORDERS. Mr A T Bramhall, 2 Abbotsferry Road,
Tweedbank, Galashiels, Scottish Borders TD1 3RX;
01896 755 326;
e-mail: andrew@atbramhall.go-plus.net

CAITHNESS

Bird Recorders
CAITHNESS. Sinclair Manson, 01847 892 379;
e-mail: sinclairmanson@btinternet.com

Bird Report
CAITHNESS BIRD REPORT (1983-97). Now incorporated
into *The Highland Bird Report.*

BTO Regional Representative
CAITHNESS. Donald Omand, 9 Skiall, Shebster, Thurso,
Caithness KW14 7YD. 01847 811 403;
e-mail: achreamie@yahoo.co.uk

Club
SOC CAITHNESS BRANCH. (51). Angus McBay,
Schoolhouse, Weydale, Thurso, Caithness, KY14 8YJ.
01847 894 663; e-mail: angus.mcbay@btinternet.com
www.the-soc.org.uk

CLYDE

Bird Atlas/Avifauna
A Guide to Birdwatching in the Clyde Area (2001) by
Cliff Baister and Marin Osler (Scottish Ornithologists'
Club, Clyde branch).

Clyde Breeding Bird Atlas (working title). In
preparation.

Bird Recorders
CLYDE ISLANDS (ARRAN, BUTE & CUMBRAES). Bernard
Zonfrillo, 28 Brodie Road, Glasgow,G21 3SB.
e-mail: b.zonfrillo@bio.gla.ac.uk

CLYDE. Iain P Gibson, 8 Kenmure View, Howwood,
Johnstone, Renfrewshire, PA9 1DR. 01505 705 874;
e-mail: iaingibson.soc@btinternet.com

Bird Report
CLYDE BIRDS (1973-2006), From Valerie
Wilson, Flat 2/1, 12 Rawcliffe Gardens,
Glasgow, G41 3DA.
e-mail: val.wilson38@btinternet.com

BTO Regional Representative
LANARK, RENFREW, DUMBARTON. Andy
Winnington, Skelmorlie,
Ayrshire. 07946 724 440;
e-mail: andy.winnington@yahoo.com

Club
SOC CLYDE BRANCH. (300). Ian Fulton.

Clyde Birds

Clyde Bird Report 2005
Clyde Islands Bird Report 2005

e-mail: SOC.Clyde@btinternet.com
www.the-soc.org.uk

Ringing Group
CLYDE RG. (1976; 22). I Livingstone, 57 Strathview
Road, Bellshill, Lanarkshire ML4 2UY. 01698 749 844;
e-mail: iainlivcrg@googlemail.com

RSPB Members' Groups
GLASGOW. (1972;141). Ross Lennox. 0141 956 4175;
e-mail: Glasgowwex@gmail.com
www.rspb.org.uk/groups/glasgowwex
Meetings: 7.30pm, monthly on a Thursday (Sep-Apr),
Adelaides, 209 Bath Street, Glasgow G2 4HZ.

HAMILTON. (1976;90). Jim Lynch, 0141 583 1044;
e-mail: birder45a@yahoo.co.uk
www.baronshaugh.co.uk
Meetings: 7.00pm, 3rd Thursday of the month
(Sept-May), Watersports Centre, Motherwell (next to
Strathclyde Loch).

RENFREWSHIRE. (1984; 94). Iain Smeaton,
e-mail: RenfrewRSPB@hotmail.co.uk
www.rspb.org.uk/groups/renfrewshire
Meetings: 1st Friday of the month (Sep-Apr), except
Jan (2nd Friday), The McMaster Centre, 2a Donaldson
Drive, Renfrew PA4 8LX.

Wetland Bird Survey Organisers
CLYDE ESTUARY. Mr J Clark, Laighfield, Station Road,
Shandon, Helensburgh G84 8NX; 01436 821 178;
e-mail: johnclark@jcmc.demon.co.uk

GLASGOW/RENFREWSHIRE/LANARKSHIRE/
DUNBARTONSHIRE. Mr J Clark, Laighfield, Station
Road, Shandon, Helensburgh G84 8NX; 01436 821 178;
e-mail: johnclark@jcmc.demon.co.uk

BUTE. Mr I L Hopkins, 2 Eden Place, 179 High Street,
Rothesay, Isle of Bute PA20 9BS. 01700 504 042;
e-mail: ian@hopkins0079.freeserve.co.uk

DUMFRIES & GALLOWAY

Bird Recorder
Paul Collin, Gairland, Old Edinburgh Road, Minnigaff,
Newton Stewart, DG8 6PL. 01671 402 861;
e-mail: pncollin@live.co.uk

Bird Report
DUMFRIES & GALLOWAY REGION BIRD REPORT (1985-),
From Peter Swan, 3 Castle View, Castle Douglas DG7
1BG. 01556 502 144.

BTO Regional Representatives
DUMFRIES RR. Edmund Fellowes, 01387 262 094;
e-mail: edmundfellowes@aol.com

KIRKCUDBRIGHT RR and Atlas Co-ordinator. Andrew
Bielinski, 41 Main Street, St Johns Town of Dalry,
Castle Douglas, Kirkcudbright, DG7 3UP. 01644 430
418 (evening); e-mail: andrewb@bielinski.fsnet.co.uk

WIGTOWN RR. Geoff Sheppard, The Roddens, Leswalt,
Stranraer, Wigtownshire, DG9 0QR. 01776 870 685;
e-mail: geoff.roddens@btinternet.com

273

SCOTLAND

Clubs

SOC DUMFRIES BRANCH. (1961; 105). Mrs Pat Abery, East Daylesford, Colvend, Dalbeattie, Dumfries DG5 4QA. 01556 630 483.
www.the-soc.org.uk
Meetings: 7.30pm, 2nd Wednesday of the month (Sept-Apr), Cumberland St Day Centre, Dumfries DG1 2JX.

SOC STEWARTRY BRANCH. (1976; 80). Miss Joan Howie, 60 Main Street, St Johns Town of Dalry, Castle Douglas, Kirkcudbrightshire, DG7 3UW. 01644 430 226.
www.the-soc.org.uk
Meetings: 7.30pm, usually 2nd Thursday of the month (Sep-Apr), Kells School, New Galloway DG7 3RU.

SOC WEST GALLOWAY BRANCH. (1975; 50). Geoff Sheppard, The Roddens, Leswalt, Stranraer, Wigtownshire, DG9 0QR. 01776 870 685;
e-mail: geoff.roddens@btinternet.com
www.the-soc.org.uk
Meetings: 7.30pm, 2nd Tuesday of the month (Oct-Mar), Stranraer Library.

Ringing Group

NORTH SOLWAY RG. Geoff Sheppard, The Roddens, Leswalt, Stranraer, Wigtownshire, DG9 0QR. 01776 870 685; e-mail: geoff.roddens@btinternet.com

RSPB Members' Group

GALLOWAY. (1985;150). John Dewhurst, 01566 502 736; e-mail: johnsteph@mkcott.wanadoo.co.uk
www.rspb.org.uk/groups/galloway
Meetings: 7.30pm 3rd Tuesday in the month (Sep-Apr inc), Parish Church Hall, Queen Street, Castle Douglas.

Wetland Bird Survey Organisers

AUCHENCAIRN AND ORCHARDTON BAYS. Mr E A M MacAlpine, Auchenshore, Auchencairn, Castle Douglas, Galloway DG7 1QZ. 01556 640 244; e-mail: js.eamm@sky.com

DUMFRIES AND GALLOWAY (other sites). Mr A C Riches, c/o WeBS Office BTO, The Nunnery, Thetford, Norfolk IP24 2PU. 01683 300 393; 07792 142 446; e-mail: slioch69@aol.com

FLEET BAY. Mr D M Hawker, Windywalls, Upper Drumwall, Gatehouse of Fleet, Castle Douglas DG7 2DE0. 1557 814 249; 0774 859 0838; e-mail: hawker398@btinternet.com

LOCH RYAN. Mr P N Collin, Gairland, Old Edinburgh Road, Minnigaff, Newton Stewart DG8 6PL. 01671 402 861; e-mail: pncollin@live.co.uk

ROUGH FIRTH. Ms J Baxter, c/o WeBS OfficeBTO, The Nunnery, Thetford, Norfolk IP24 2PU. 01842 750 050; e-mail: jbaxter@nts.org.uk

SOLWAY ESTUARY - NORTH. Mr A C Riches, c/o WeBS Office, BTO, The Nunnery, Thetford, Norfolk IP24 2PU. 01683 300 393; 07792 142 446; e-mail: slioch69@aol.com

WIGTOWN BAY. Mr P N Collin, Gairland, Old Edinburgh Road, Minnigaff, Newton Stewart, DG8 6PL. 01671 402 861; e-mail: pncollin@live.co.uk

FIFE

Bird Atlas/Avifauna

The Fife Bird Atlas 2003 by Norman Elkins, Jim Reid, Allan Brown, Derek Robertson & Anne-Marie Smout. Available from Allan W. Brown (FOAG), 61 Watts Gardens, Cupar, Fife KY15 4UG, Tel. 01334 656804, email: swans@allanwbrown.co.uk

Bird Recorders

FIFE REGION INC OFFSHORE ISLANDS (NORTH FORTH). Mr Malcolm Ware, 80 Castland Road, Rosyth, Fife, KY11 2DH .e-mail: malcolm.ware12@talktalk.net

ISLE OF MAY BIRD OBSERVATORY. Iain English, 19 Nethan Gate, Hamilton, S Lanarks, ML3 8NH. e-mail: i.english@talk21.com

Bird Reports

FIFE BIRD REPORT (1988-) (FIFE & KINROSS BR 1980-87), From Mr Malcolm Ware, 80 Castland Road, Rosyth, Fife, KY11 2DH;
e-mail: malcolm.ware12@talktalk.net

ISLE OF MAY BIRD OBSERVATORY REPORT (1985-), From Iain English, 19 Nethan Gate, Hamilton, S Lanarks, ML3 8NH. e-mail: i.english@talk21.com

BTO Regional Representative

FIFE & KINROSS RR. Norman Elkins, 18 Scotstarvit View, Cupar, Fife, KY15 5DX. 01334 654 348; e-mail: jandnelkins@btinternet.com

Clubs

FIFE BIRD CLUB. (1985; 200). Keith Ballantyne (Chairperson); e-mail: chairman@fifebirdclub.org
www.fifebirdclub.org
Meetings: 7.30pm, (various evenings), Dean Park Hotel, Chapel Level, Kirkcaldy.

LOTHIANS AND FIFE SWAN & GOOSE STUDY GROUP. (1978; 12). Allan & Lyndesay Brown, 61 Watts Gardens, Cupar, Fife, KY15 4UG.
e-mail: swans@allanwbrown.co.uk

SOC FIFE BRANCH. (1950;170). Alison Creamer, 52 Balgarvie Crescent, Cupar, Fife, KY15 4EG; 01334 657 188; e-mail: alisonhcreamer@yahoo.co.uk
www.the-soc.org.uk
Meetings: 7.30pm, 2nd Wednesday of the month (Sep-Apr), Venue details available at www.the-soc.org.uk/branch-meetings.htm#fife

Ringing Groups

ISLE OF MAY BIRD OBSERVATORY. David Grieve, 50 Main Street, Symington, Biggar, South Lanarkshire ML12 6LJ. 01899 309 176.

SCOTLAND

TAY RG. Ms S Millar, Edenvale Cottage, 1 Lydox Cottages, Dairsie, Fife, KY15 4RN; e-mail: shirley@edenecology.co.uk

Wetland Bird Survey Organisers
FIFE (excluding estuaries). Grey Goose count organiser for Fife, Lothians and Borders. Mr A W Brown, 61 Watts Gardens, Cupar, Fife KY15 4UG. 01334 656 804; 07871 575 131; e-mail: swans@allanwbrown.co.uk

FORTH ESTUARY (North). Mr A Inglis, 5 Crowhill Road, Dalgety Bay, Fife KY11 5LJ. 01383 822 115; e-mail: aandjinglis@hotmail.com

TAY & EDEN ESTUARY. Mr N Elkins, 18 Scotstarvit View, Cupar, Fife KY15 5DX. 01334 654 348; e-mail: jandnelkins@btinternet.com

Wildlife Hospital
SCOTTISH SPCA WILD LIFE REHABILITATION CENTRE. Middlebank Farm, Masterton Road, Dunfermline, Fife, KY11 8QN. 01383 412 520.
All species. Open to visitors, groups and school parties. Illustrated talk on oiled bird cleaning and other aspects of wildlife rehabilitation available. Veterinary support.

FORTH

Bird Recorder
UPPER FORTH (Does not include parts of Stirling in Loch Lomondside/Clyde Basin). Chris Pendlebury, 3 Sinclair Street, Dunblane, FK5 0AH. 07798 711 134; e-mail: chrispendlebury@gmail.com

Bird Report
FORTH AREA BIRD REPORT (1975-) - enlarged report published annually in The Forth Naturalist and Historian, University of Stirling, from Dr Roy Sexton, Asst. Editor, Forth Naturalist and Historian, 22 Alexander Drive, Bridge of Allan, FK9 4QB. 01786 833 409; e-mail: RoyGravedigger@AOL.com www.fnh.stir.ac.uk

BTO Regional Representative
CENTRAL RR. Neil Bielby, 56 Ochiltree, Dunblane, Perthshire, FK15 0DF. 01786 823 830; e-mail: n.bielby@sky.com

Club
SOC CENTRAL SCOTLAND BRANCH. (1968; 101). Mr RL Gooch, The Red House, Dollarfield, Dollar, Clacks FK14 7LX. 01259 742 326; www.the-soc.org.uk
Meetings: 7.30pm, 1st Thursday of the month (Sep-Apr), The Smith Art Gallery and Museum, Dumbarton Road, Stirling.

RSPB Members' Group
CENTRAL, FORTH VALLEY. (1995; 111). Tam Craig, 01259 211 550; e-mail: tam_craig@btinternet.com www.rspb.org.uk/groups/forthvalley
Meetings: 7.30pm, 3rd Thursday of the month (Sept-Apr), Hillpark Centre, Stirling FK7 0HZ.

Wetland Bird Survey Organiser
CENTRAL (excl Forth Estuary). Mr N Bielby, 56 Ochiltree, Dunblane, Perthshire FK15 0DF. 01786 823 830; e-mail: n.bielby@sky.com

HIGHLAND

Bird Atlas/Avifauna
The Birds of Sutherland by Alan Vittery (Colin Baxter Photography Ltd, 1997).

Birds of Skye by Andrew Currie. In preparation.

Bird Recorder
ROSS-SHIRE, INVERNESS-SHIRE, SUTHERLAND, BADENOCH & STRATHSPEY, LOCHABER, LOCHALSH and SKYE. Peter Gordon, 2 Criagmore Crescent, Nethy Bridge, Highland PH25 3RA. 01479 821 339; e-mail: gordon890@btinternet.com

Bird Reports
HIGHLAND BIRD REPORT (1991-). 2008 edition £9.50 inc p&p.

BTO Regional Representatives & Regional Development Officers
INVERNESS & SPEYSIDE RR & RDO. Hugh Insley, 1 Drummond Place, Inverness,IV2 4JT. 01463 230 652; e-mail: hugh.insley@btinternet.com

RUM, EIGG, CANNA & MUCK RR & RDO. Bob Swann, 14 St Vincent Road, Tain, Ross-shire, IV19 1JR. 01862 894 329; e-mail: robert.swann@homecall.co.uk

ROSS-SHIRE RR. Simon Cohen, E-mail: saraandsimon@hotmail.com

SUTHERLAND. Position vacant.

SKYE. Position vacant.

Clubs
EAST SUTHERLAND BIRD GROUP. (1976; 120). Tony Mainwood, 13 Ben Bhraggie Drive, Golspie, Sutherland KW10 6SX. 01408 633 ; e-mail: tony.mainwood@btinterne
Meetings: 7.30pm, Last Monday o month (Oct, Nov, Jan, Feb, Mar), Golspie Community Centre.

SOC HIGHLAND BRANCH. (1955; 151). Kathy Bonniface, Alt Dubh, North End, Tomatin, IV13 7YP. 01808 511 740; e-mail: kathybonniface@aol.com www.the-soc.org.uk
Meetings: 7.45pm, 1st Tuesday of the month (Sep-Mar), Culloden Library, Keppoch Road IV2 7LL.

Ringing Groups
HIGHLAND RG. Bob Swann, 14 St Vincent Road, Tain, Ross-shire, IV19 1JR. e-mail: robert.swann@homecall.co.uk

RSPB Members' Group
HIGHLAND. (1987; 214). Doreen Manson, Muirton

SCOTLAND

Lodge, Urray, Muir of Ord, Ross-shire IV6. 01997 433 283; e-mail: john@jmanson2.wanadoo.co.uk www.rspb.org.uk/groups/highland
Meetings: 7.30pm, last Thursday of the month (Sep-Apr), Kingsmill Hotel, Culcabock Road, Inverness.

Wetland Bird Survey Organisers
BADENOCH AND STRATHSPEY. Mr K Duncan, c/o WeBS Office, BTO, The Nunnery, Thetford, Norfolk IP24 2PU. 01842 750 050; e-mail: webs@bto.org

CAITHNESS. Mr S A M Manson, 7 Duncan Street, Thurso, Caithness KW14 7HZ.
E-mail: sinclairmanson@btinternet.com

LOCHABER. Mr J Dye, Toad Hall, Dalnabreac, Acharacle, Argyll PH36 4JX;
e-mail: john.dye@virgin.net

SKYE & LOCHALSH. Mr R L McMillan, 11 Elgol, Nr Broadford, Isle of Skye IV49 9BL. 01471 866 305;
e-mail: bob@skye-birds.com

LOTHIAN

Bird Atlas/Avifauna
The Breeding Birds of South-east Scotland, a tetrad atlas 1988-1994 by R D Murray et al. (Scottish Ornithologists' Club, 1998).

Bird Recorder
Stephen Welch, 25 Douglas Road, Longniddry, EH32 0LQ; 01875 852 802;(M) 07931 524 963;
e-mail: lothianrecorder@the-soc.org.uk

Bird Report
LOTHIAN BIRD REPORT (1979-), from the Lothian SOC Branch Secretary.

BTO Regional Representative
RR. Alan Heavisides, 9 Addiston Crescent, Balerno, Edinburgh, EH14 7DB. 0131 449 3816;
e-mail: alanheavisides@yahoo.com

BTO Garden BirdWatch Ambassador
Prof J I B Wilson, e-mail: jib4wilson@o2.co.uk

Clubs
EDINBURGH NATURAL HISTORY SOCIETY. (1869; 200). The Secretary, e-mail: enquiries@ edinburghnaturalhistorysociety.org.uk www.edinburghnaturalhistorysociety.org.uk
Meetings: 7.30pm, 4th Wednesday of the month The Guide Hall, 33 Melville Street, Edinburgh.

LOTHIANS AND FIFE SWAN AND GOOSE STUDY GROUP. (1978; 12). Allan & Lyndesay Brown, 61 Watts Gardens, Cupar, Fife, KY15 4UG.
e-mail: swans@allanwbrown.co.uk

LOTHIAN SOC. (1936; 570).
Doreen Main; Seatoller, Gullane, East Lothian EH31 2DH. 01620 844 532; e-mail:
doreen.main@yahoo.com
www.the-soc.org.uk

Meetings: 7.30pm, 2nd Tuesday (Sep-Dec and Jan-Apr), Lounge 2, Meadowbank Sports Stadium - Oct & Mar), Waterston House, Aberlady.

Ringing Group
LOTHIAN RG. Mr M Cubitt, 12 Burgh Mills Lane, Linlithgow, West Lothian EH49 7TA.

RSPB Members' Group
EDINBURGH. (1974;480). Rosie Filipiak.
e-mail: rosie.birds1@gmail.com
www.rspb.org.uk/groups/edinburgh/
Meetings: 7.30pm, 3rd Tuesday or Wednesday of the month (Sep-Apr), Napier University, Craiglockhart Campus, Edinburgh. Outdoor meetings held year round (check group website for details).

Wetland Bird Survey Organisers
FORTH ESTUARY (Outer South). Mr D J Priddle, c/o WeBS Office, BTO, The Nunnery, Thetford, Norfolk IP24 2PU. 01620 827 459;
e-mail: dpriddle@eastlothian.gov.uk

LOTHIAN (excl estuaries). Miss J Wilcox, 18 Howdenhall Gardens, Edinburgh, Midlothian EH16 6UN. 0131 664 8893.

TYNINGHAME ESTUARY. Mr B Anderson, c/o WeBS Office, BTO, The Nunnery, Thetford, Norfolk IP24 2PU. 01620 827 318; e-mail: randerson@eastlothian.gov.uk

MORAY & NAIRN

Bird Atlas/Avifauna
The Birds of Moray and Nairn by Martin Cook (Mercat Press, 1992).

Bird Recorder
MORAY & NAIRN. Martin J H Cook, Rowanbrae, Clochan, Buckie, Banffshire, AB56 5EQ. 01542 850 296; e-mail: martin.cook99@btinternet.com

Bird Reports
BIRDS IN MORAY AND NAIRN (1988-), from The Moray & Nairn Recorder, 01542 850 296;
e-mail: martin.cook99@btinternet.com

MORAY & NAIRN BIRD REPORT (1985-1998), from The Moray & Nairn Recorder, 01542 850 296;
e-mail: martin.cook99@btinternet.com

BTO Regional Representative
MORAY & NAIRN RR. Bob Proctor, 78 Marleon Field, Elgin, Moray, IV30 4GE.
e-mail: bobandlouise@proctor8246.fsnet.co.uk

Wetland Bird Survey Organisers
LOSSIE ESTUARY. Mr R Proctor, 78 Marleon Field, Silvercrest, Bishopmill, Elgin, IV30 4GE; 07976 456 657; e-mail: bobandlouise@proctor8246.fsnet.co.uk

MORAY & NAIRN (Inland). Mr D Law, Hollybrae, South Darkland, Elgin, Moray IV30 8NTO. 1463 725 200; 01343 842 007; e-mail: jdavidlaw@btinternet.com

MORAY BASIN COAST. Mr R.L. Swann, 14 St Vincent Road, Tain , Ross-Shire IV19 1JR;
e-mail: robert.swann@homecall.co.uk

SCOTLAND

NORTH EAST SCOTLAND

Bird Atlas/Avifauna
The Birds of North East Scotland by S T Buckland, M V Bell & N Picozzi (North East Scotland Bird Club, 1990).

The Breeding Birds of North-East Scotland, edited by Ian Francis & Martin Cook (SOC 2011) www.the-soc.org.uk

Bird Recorder
NORTH-EAST SCOTLAND. Nick Littlewood, The James Hutton Institute, Craigiebuckler, Aberdeen AB15 8QH. 07748 965 920; e-mail: nesrecorder@yahoo.co.uk

Bird Reports
NORTH-EAST SCOTLAND BIRD REPORT (1974-), From Dave Gill, Drakemyre Croft, Cairnorrie, Methlick, Aberdeenshire, AB41 7JN. 01651 806 252; e-mail: david@gilldavid1.orangehome.co.uk

NORTH SEA BIRD CLUB ANNUAL REPORT (1979-), From Andrew Thorpe, Ocean Laboratory and Centre for Ecology, Aberdeen University, Newburgh, Ellon, Aberdeenshire, AB41 6AA01224 274428; e-mail: nsbc@abdn.ac.uk

BTO Regional Representatives
ABERDEEN. Paul Doyle, e-mail: paul@wildlifeweb.co.uk

KINCARDINE & DEESIDE. Graham Cooper, Westbank, Beltie Road, Torphins, Banchory, Aberdeen, AB31 4JT. 01339 882 706; e-mail: grm.cooper@btinternet.com

Club
SOC NORTH-EAST SCOTLAND BRANCH. (1956; 130). Hugh Addlesee, 31 Ashtree Road, Banchory, Kincardineshire AB31 5JB. 01330 829 949; e-mail: grampian.secretary@the-soc.org.uk
www.the-soc.org.uk
Meetings: 7.30pm, usually 1st Monday of the month (Oct-Apr), Sportsmans's Club, 11 Queens Road, Aberdeen AB15 4YL.

Ringing Group
GRAMPIAN RG. R Duncan, 86 Broadfold Drive, Bridge of Don, Aberdeen, AB23 8PP; e-mail: Raymond@waxwing.fsnet.co.uk

RSPB Members' Group
ABERDEEN & DISTRICT. (1975; 210). Mark Sullivan, 29 Earlswells Rd, Cults AB15 9NY. 01224 861 446; e-mail: geolbird_abz@btinternet.com
www.rspb.org.uk/groups/aberdeen
Meetings: 7.30pm, monthly in the winter, Lecture Theatre, Zoology Dept, Tillydrone Av, Aberdeen. Two birding trips monthly throughout the year.

Wildlife Hospital
GRAMPIAN WILDLIFE REHABILITATION TRUST. 40 High Street, New Deer, Turriff, Aberdeenshire, AB53 6SX. 01771 644 489; (M)07803 235 383; e-mail: laurence.brain@btconnect.com
Veterinary surgeon. Access to full practice facilities. Will care for all species of birds.

Wetland Bird Survey Organiser
ABERDEENSHIRE. Mr R Minshull, c/o WeBS Office, BTO, The Nunnery, Thetford, Norfolk IP24 2PU, 01842 750 050; e-mail: webs@bto.org

ORKNEY

Bird Atlas/Avifauna
The Birds of Orkney by CJ Booth et al (The Orkney Press, 1984).

Bird Recorder
Mr EJ Williams, Fairholm, Finstown, Orkney, KW17 2EQ. e-mail: jim@geniefea.freeserve.co.uk

Bird Report
ORKNEY BIRD REPORT (inc North Ronaldsay Bird Report) (1974-), From Mr EJ Williams, Fairholm, Finstown, Orkney, KW17 2EQ. e-mail: jim@geniefea.freeserve.co.uk

BTO Regional Representative
Colin Corse, Garrisdale, Lynn Park, Kirkwall, Orkney, KW15 1SL. 01856 874 484; e-mail: ccorse@btinternet.com

Club
SOC ORKNEY BRANCH. (1993; 15). Colin Corse, Garrisdale, Lynnpark Road, Kirkwall, Orkney, KW15 1SL. 01856 874 484; e-mail: ccorse@btinternet.com
www.the-soc.org.uk

Ringing Groups
NORTH RONALDSAY BIRD OBSERVATORY. Ms A E Duncan, Twingness, North Ronaldsay, Orkney, KW17 2BE; e-mail: alison@nrbo.prestel.co.uk
www.nrbo.co.uk

ORKNEY RG. Colin Corse, Garrisdale, Lynn Park, Kirkwall, Orkney, KW15 1SL. H: 01856 874 484; e-mail: ccorse@btinternet.com

SULE SKERRY RG. Dave Budworth, 121 Wood Lane, Newhall, Swadlincote, Derbys, DE11 0LX. 01283 215 188.

RSPB Members' Group
ORKNEY. (1985;300 in catchment area). Dick Matson 01856 751 426; e-mail: p.wilson410@btinternet.com
Meetings: Meetings advertised in newsletter and local press, held at St Magnus Centre, Kirkwall.

SCOTLAND

Wetland Bird Survey Organiser
ORKNEY. Mr ER Meek, Smyril, Stenness, Stromness, Orkney KW16 3JX. 01856 851 755; 07879 238 391; e-mail: erandammeek@gmail.com

OUTER HEBRIDES

Bird Recorder
OUTER HEBRIDES. Brian Rabbits. 6 Carinish, Isle of North Uist HS6 5HL. 01876 580 328; e-mail: rabbitts@hebrides.net

Bird Report
OUTER HEBRIDES BIRD REPORT (1989-91 and 1997-2007), From The Recorder. 6 Carinish, Isle of North Uist HS6 5HL. 01876 580 328; e-mail: rabbitts@hebrides.net

BTO Regional Representatives & Regional Development Officer
BENBECULA & THE UISTS RR & RDO. Yvonne Benting, 07501 332 803; e-mail: uistbto@gmail.com

LEWIS & HARRIS RR. Chris Reynolds, 11 Reef, Isle of Lewis, HS2 9HU. 01851 672 376; e-mail: cmreynolds@btinternet.com

Ringing Group
SHIANTS AUK RG. Mr J.J. Lennon, The Dovecote, Main Street, Flintham, Newark NG23 5LA. 01636 525 963. Group Secretary, Jim Lennon, The Dovecote, Main Street, Flintham, Newark NG23 5LA. 01636 525 963.

Wetland Bird Survey Organisers
HARRIS & LEWIS. Ms Y Benting, Suthainn, Askernish, Isle of South Uist, Western Isles HS8 5SY. 07837 253 698; e-mail: uistbto@gmail.com

UISTS AND BENBECULA. Ms Y Benting, Suthainn, Askernish, Isle of South Uist, Western Isles HS8 5SY. 07837 253 698; e-mail: uistbto@gmail.com

ISLAY, JURA AND COLONSAY. Mr J S Armitage, Airigh, Sgallaidh, Portnahaven, Isle of Islay PA47 7SZ. 01496 860 396; www.islaybirder.blogspot.com/

PERTH & KINROSS

Bird Recorder
PERTH & KINROSS. Scott Paterson, 12 Ochil View, Kinross, KY13 8TN. 01577 864 248, e-mail: scottpaterson12@yahoo.co.uk

Bird Report
PERTH & KINROSS BIRD REPORT (1974-). 1974 to 2006 available as PDF's. 2006 onwards in preparation. From The Recorder, 12 Ochil View, Kinross, KY13 8TN. 01577 864 248, e-mail: scottpaterson12@yahoo.co.uk

BTO Regional Representative
PERTHSHIRE RR. Richard Paul. 01882 632 212; e-mail: richard@rannoch.net

Club
PERTHSHIRE SOCIETY OF NATURAL SCIENCE (Ornithological Section). (1964; 25). Miss Esther Taylor, 23 Verena Terrace, Perth PH2 0BZ. 01738 621 986; e-mail: birdsatpsns@btinternet.com www.psns.org.uk
Meetings: 7.30pm, Wednesdays monthly (Oct-Mar), Perth Museum. Summer outings.

Wetland Bird Survey Organisers
LOCH LEVEN. Mr J Squire, c/o Scottish Natural Heritage, The Pier, Kinross, KY13 8UF. e-mail: jeremy.squire@snh.gov.uk

PERTH AND KINROSS (INLAND). Dr M V Bell, 48 Newton Crescent, Dunblane, Perthshire FK15 0DZ; e-mail: mvbell34@tiscali.co.uk

TAY & EDEN ESTUARY. Mr N Elkins, 18 Scotstarvit View, Cupar, Fife KY15 5DX. 01334 654 348; e-mail: jandnelkins@btinternet.com

SHETLAND

Bird Recorders
FAIR ISLE. David Parnaby, e-mail: fibo@btconnect.com

SHETLAND. Mark Chapman, 55 Leaside, Firth, Mossbank, Shetland ZE2 9TF. 01806 242 401; e-mail: msc.1@btinternet.com

Bird Reports
FAIR ISLE BIRD OBSERVATORY REPORT (1949-). From Scottish Ornithologists' Club, 21 Regent Terrace, Edinburgh, EH7 5BT. 0131 556 6042.

SHETLAND BIRD REPORT (1969-) £10 plus p&p, no pre 1973 available. From Rob Fray, Shetland Bird Club, Sunnydell, Virkie, Shetland ZE3 9JS; e-mail: robfray@btinternet.com

BTO Regional Representative
RR and RDO. Dave Okill, Heilinabretta, Trondra, Shetland, ZE1 0XL. 01595 880 450; e-mail: david@auroradesign.plus.com

Club
SHETLAND BIRD CLUB. (1973; 200). Helen Moncrieff, Scholland, Virkie, Shetland ZE3 9JL. 01950 460 249; e-mail: helen.moncrieff@btinternet.com www.nature-shetland.co.uk

Ringing Groups
FAIR ISLE BIRD OBSERVATORY. Deryk Shaw, Bird Observatory, Fair Isle, Shetland, ZE2 9JU. e-mail: fairisle.birdobs@zetnet.co.uk

SHETLAND RG. Dave Okill, Heilinabretta, Trondra, Shetland, ZE1 0XL. 01595 880 450

Wetland Bird Survey Organisers
SHETLAND. Mr P V Harvey, Headlands, Virkie, Shetland ZE3 9JS. 01595 694 688; 07879 444 612; e-mail: paul@shetlandamenity.org

278

WALES

Bird Report
See Welsh Ornithological Society in National Directory

BTO Honorary Wales Officer
BTO WALES OFFICER. John Lloyd, Cynghordy Hall, Cynghordy, Llandovery, Carms SA20 OLN.
e-mail: the_lloyds@dsl.pipex.com

Club
See Welsh Ornithological Society in National Directory.

EASTERN AREA OF WALES

Bird Atlas/Avifauna
The Birds of Radnorshire in preparation.

Bird Recorders
BRECONSHIRE. Andrew King, Heddfan, Pennorth, Brecon, Powys LD3 7EX. 01874 658 351;
e-mail: andrew.king53@virgin.net

MONTGOMERYSHIRE. Paul Leafe,
e-mail: paul_leafe@hotmail.co.uk

RADNORSHIRE (VC43). Pete Jennings, Park View, Staunton-on-Arrow, Leominster HR6 9HT. 01544 388 905; e-mail: radnorshirebirds@hotmail.com

Bird Reports
BRECONSHIRE BIRDS (1962-), from Brecknock Wildlife Trust.

MONTGOMERYSHIRE BIRD REPORT (1981-82-), from Montgomeryshire Wildlife Trust.

BTO Regional Representatives
BRECKNOCK RR. John Lloyd, Cynghordy Hall, Cynghordy, Llandovery, Carms, SA20 OLN. 01550 750 202; e-mail: the_lloyds@dsl.pipex.com

MONTGOMERY RR. Jane Kelsall, 01970 872 019; e-mail: janekelsall@phonecoop.coop

RADNOR RR. Carlton Parry, 01597 824 050; e-mail: cj.parry@tiscali.co.uk

Clubs
MONTGOMERYSHIRE WILDLIFE TRUST BIRD GROUP. (1997; 110). A M Puzey, Four Seasons, Arddleen, Llanymynech, Powys SY22 6RU. 01938 590 578.
www.montwt.co.uk/bird_group.html
Meetings: 7.30pm, 3rd Wednesday of the month (Jan-Mar) and (Sep-Dec), Welshpool Methodist Hall.

RADNORSHIRE BIRD GROUP. Pete Jennings, Park View, Staunton-on-Arrow, Leominster HR6 9HT. 01544 388 905; e-mail: radnorshirebirds@hotmail.com
Co-ordinates bird recording and surveys in the county through the county recorder

Ringing Groups
GOLDCLIFF RG. Mr Richard M Clarke.
e-mail: chykembro2@aol.com

LLANGORSE RG. (1987; 15). Jerry Lewis, Y Bwthyn Gwyn, Coldbrook, Abergavenny, Monmouthshire NP7 9TD. H:01873 855091; W:01633 644856

Wetland Bird Survey Organisers
BRECONSHIRE. Mr V A King, Heddfan, Pennorth, Brecon LD3 7EX. 01874 658 351; e-mail: andrew. king53@virgin.net

MONTGOMERYSHIRE. Ms J Kelsall, c/o WeBS Office, BTO, The Nunnery, Thetford, Norfolk IP24 2PU. 01970 872 019; e-mail:janekelsall@phonecoop.coop

RADNORSHIRE. Mr P P Jennings, Park View, Staunton-on-Arrow, Leominster, HR6 9HT. 01597 811 522; e-mail: radnorshirebirds@hotmail.com

Wildlife Trusts
BRECKNOCK WILDLIFE TRUST. (1963; 650). Lion House, Bethel Square, Brecon, Powys LD3 7AY. 01874 625 708; e-mail: enquiries@brecknockwildlifetrust.org.uk
www.brecknockwildlifetrust.org.uk

MONTGOMERYSHIRE WILDLIFE TRUST. (1982; 1000). 42 Broad Street, Welshpool, Powys, SY21 7RR. 01938 555 654; e-mail: info@montwt.co.uk
www.montwt.co.uk

RADNORSHIRE WILDLIFE TRUST. (1987; 878). Warwick House, High Street, Llandrindod Wells, Powys LD1 6AG. 01597 823 298; e-mail:info@rwtwales.org
www.radnorshirewildlifetrust.org.uk

NORTHERN AREA OF WALES

Bird Atlas/Avifauna
The Birds of Caernarfonshire by John Barnes (1998, from Lionel Pilling, 51 Brighton Close, Rhyl LL18 3HL.

The Birds of Meirionnydd by Rhion Pritchard (2013 Cambrian Ornithological Society), £7.50 from Geoff Gibbs. 01248 681 936;
e-mail: geoffkate.gibbs@care4free.net

Bird Recorders
ANGLESEY. Stephen Culley, 22 Cae Derwydd, Cemaes Bay, Anglesey, LL67 OLP. 01407 710 542;
e-mail: SteCul10@aol.com

CAERNARFONSHIRE. Rhion Pritchard, Pant Afonig, Hafod Lane, Bangor, Gwynedd LL57 4BU.
e-mail: rhion678pritchard@btinternet.com

DENBIGHSHIRE & FLINTSHIRE. Ian Spence, 43 Blackbrook, Sychdyn, Mold, Flintshire CH7 6LT. 01352 750118; e-mail: ianspence.cr1@btinternet.com
www.cbrg.org.uk

MEIRIONNYDD (Vice County Recorder). Jim Dustow, Afallon, 7 Glan y Don, Rhiwbryfdir, Blaenau Ffestiniog, Gwynedd LL41 3LW.
e-mail: Jim.Dustow@rspb.org.uk

279

WALES

Bird Reports

BARDSEY BIRD OBSERVATORY ANNUAL REPORT, from the Warden, see Reserves.

CAMBRIAN BIRD REPORT (sometime Gwynedd Bird Report) (1953-), from Geoff Gibbs. 01248 681 936; e-mail: geoffkate.gibbs@care4free.net www.welshos.org.uk/cambrian/

MEIRIONNYDD BIRD REPORT Published in Cambrian Bird Report (above).

NORTH-EAST WALES BIRD REPORT (2004-), formerly CLWYD BIRD REPORT (2002-2003), from Ian M Spence, 43 Blackbrook, Sychdyn, Mold, Flintshire CH7 6LT. 01352 750 118; e-mail: ianspence.cr@btinternet.com www.cbrg.org.uk

WREXHAM BIRDWATCHERS' SOCIETY ANNUAL REPORT (1982-), from The Secretary, Wrexham Birdwatchers' Society.

BTO Regional Representatives

ANGLESEY RR. Kelvin Jones. 01248 383285; e-mail: kelvin.jones@bto.org

CAERNARFON RR. Geoff Gibbs. 01248 681 936; e-mail: geoffkate.gibbs@care4free.net

CLWYD EAST RR. Dr Anne Brenchley, Ty'r Fawnog, 43 Black Brook, Sychdyn, Mold, Flints CH7 6LT. 01352 750 118; e-mail: anne.brenchley@btinternet.com

CLWYD WEST RR. Mel ab Owain, 31 Coed Bedw, Abergele, Conwy, LL22 7EH. 01745 826 528; e-mail: melabowain@btinternet.com

MEIRIONNYDD RR. Rob Morton. 01341 422 426; e-mail: r.morton1@btinternet.com

Clubs

BANGOR BIRD GROUP. (1947; 100). Jane Prosser, 15 Victoria Street, Bangor, Gwynedd LL57 2HD. 01248 364 632.
Meetings: 7.30pm every Wednesday, Semester terms, Brambell Building, University of Bangor.

CAMBRIAN ORNITHOLOGICAL SOCIETY. (1952; 190). Barry Jones, Hon. Secretary, 24 Tan y Bryn Road, Llandudno LL30 1UU. 01492 868 467; e-mail: barrypaneuro@aol.co.uk www.welshos.org.uk/cambrian/
Meetings: 7.30pm, 1st Friday of the month, Pensychnant Centre, Sychnant Pass.

CLWYD BIRD RECORDING GROUP (committee that produces the Bird Report). Julie Rogers, Hon. Secretary, e-mail: julierogers123@ gmail.com www.cbrg.org.uk

CLWYD ORNITHOLOGICAL SOCIETY. (1956; 45). Ms J Irving, 45, Plas Uchaf Avenue, Prestatyn, Denbighshire LL19 9NR. 01745 854 132; e-mail: jacqui970irving@btinternet.com
Meetings: 7.30pm (Sep-Apr), Farmers Arms, Waen, St. Asaph.

DEE ESTUARY CONSERVATION GROUP. (1973; 25 grps). Richard Smith, Secretary, e-mail: decg@deeestuary.co.uk www.deeestuary.co.uk/decg.htm

DEESIDE NATURALISTS' SOCIETY. (1973; 1,000). The Secretary, e-mail: secretary@ deesidenaturalists.org.uk www.deesidenaturalists.org.uk

WREXHAM BIRDWATCHERS' SOCIETY. (1974; 90). Miss Marian Williams, 10 Lake View, Gresford, Wrexham, Clwyd LL12 8PU. 01978 854 633.
Meetings: 7.30pm, 1st Friday of the month (Sep-Apr), Gresford Memorial Hall, Gresford.

Ringing Groups

BARDSEY BIRD OBSERVATORY. Steven Stansfield, Bardsey Island, off Aberdaron, Pwllheli, Gwynedd LL53 8DE. 07855 264151; e-mail: warden@bbfo.org.uk bbfo.org.uk; bbfo.blogspot.com

CHESHIRE SWAN GROUP. David Cookson, 01270 567 526; E-mail:Cheshireswans@aol.com http://cheshireswanstudygroup.wordpress.com (blog for Swan news, weather records, bird reports and photos).

MERSEYSIDE RG. Bob Harris, 3 Mossleigh, Whixall, Whitchurch, Shropshire SY13 2SA. Work 0151 706 4397; e-mail: harris@liv.ac.uk

SCAN RG. Dr D. Moss. e-mail: dorian@dorianmoss.com

RSPB Local Group

NORTH WALES. (1986; 80). John Beagan, 01492 531 409 (answerphone); e-mail: colwynbooks@waitrose.com www.rspb.org.uk/groups/northwales
Meetings: 7.30pm, 3rd Friday of the month (Sep-Apr), St Davids Church Hall, Penrhyn Bay, Llandudno, Gwynedd, LL30 3EJ.

Wetland Bird Survey Organisers

ANGLESEY (other sites). Ian Sims, RSPB Malltraeth Marsh, Tai'r Gors, Pentre Berw, Gaerwen, Anglesey, LL60 6LB; e-mail: ian.sims@rspb.org.uk

ARTRO/MAWDDACH/TRAETH BACH/DYSYNNI ESTUARY. Mr J Dustow, Warden, Lake Vyrnwy/ Llyn Efyrnwy RSPB, Llanwddyn, Oswestry, Shropshire SY10 OLZ. 01691 870 278; e-mail: Jim.Dustow@rspb.org.uk

CAERNARFONSHIRE. Rhion Pritchard, Pant Afonig, Hafod Lane, Bangor, Gwynedd LL57 4BU; e-mail: rhion678pritchard@btinternet.com

DEE ESTUARY. Mr C E Wells, The Cottage, 1 Well Lane, Ness, Neston, Wirral, Cheshire CH64 4AW. 0151 336 7681; e-mail: colin.wells@rspb.org.uk

FORYD BAY. Mr S Hugheston-Roberts, c/o WeBS Office, BTO, The Nunnery, Thetford, Norfolk IP24 2PU; e-mail: simon.hr@btinternet.com

MEIRIONNYDD (other sites). Mr TG Owen, Crochendy Twrog, Maentwrog, Blaenau Ffestiniog, Gwynedd LL41 3YU. 01766 590 302.

WALES

Wildlife Trust
NORTH WALES WILDLIFE TRUST. (1963; 6,450). 376 High Street, Bangor, Gwynedd, LL57 1YE. 01248 351 541; e-mail: nwwt@wildlifetrustswales.org www.northwaleswildlifetrust.org.uk

SOUTHERN AREA OF WALES

Bird Atlas/Avifauna
An Atlas of Breeding Birds in West Glamorgan by David M Hanford et al (Gower Ornithological Society, 1992).

Birds of Glamorgan by Clive Hurford and Peter Lansdown (Published by the authors, c/o National Museum of Wales, Cardiff, 1995).

The Birds of Gwent by Venables et al, published by Helm on behalf of Gwent Ornithological Society.

The Gwent Atlas of Breeding Birds by Tyler, Lewis, Venables & Walton (Gwent Ornithological Society, 1987).

Bird Recorders
GLAMORGAN (EAST). David RW Gilmore, 116, Donald Street, Roath, Cardiff, Glamorgan CF24 4TN. 7779 176 766; e-mail: d.gilmore2@ntlworld.com

GOWER (WEST GLAMORGAN). Robert Taylor, 285 Llangyfelach Road, Brynhyfryd, Swansea, SA5 9LB. 01792 464 780; (M) 07970 567 007; e-mail: rob@birding.freeserve.co.uk

Bird Reports
EAST GLAMORGAN BIRD REPORT (title varies 1963-95) 1996-2011 - 2012 should be published by end of 2013, from Mr John D Wilson, 122 Westbourne Road, Penarth, Vale of Glamorgan, CF64 3HH. 029 2033 9424; e-mail: johndw@ntlworld.com www.glamorganbirds.org.uk

GOWER BIRDS (1965-). Covers Swansea, Neath and Port Talbot counties, from Barry Stewart, 36 Pencaecrwn Road, Gorseinon, Swansea SA4 4FU. e-mail: gowerbirdsf@hotmail.co.uk www.glamorganbirds.org.uk

GWENT BIRD REPORT (1964-), from Jerry Lewis, Y Bwthyn Gwyn, Coldbrook, Abergavenny, Monmouthshire NP7 9TD. (H)01873 855 091; (W)01633 644 856.

BTO Regional Representatives
EAST GLAMORGAN (former Mid & South Glam) RR. Wayne Morris, 8 Hughes Street, Penygraig, Tonypandy, Rhondda Cynon Taf CF40 1LX. 01443 430 284; e-mail: eastglambto@gmail.com http://eastglambto.wordpress.com

GLAMORGAN (WEST) RR. Alastair Flannagan, 27 Llys Dol, Morriston, Swansea SA6 6LD. 01792 537 439; e-mail: alastair.flannagan@ntlworld.com

GWENT RR. Jerry Lewis, Y Bwthyn Gwyn, Coldbrook, Abergavenny, Monmouthshire NP7 9TD. 01873 855 091; e-mail: jmsl2587@yahoo.co.uk

Clubs
CARDIFF NATURALISTS' SOCIETY. (1867; 200). Stephen R Howe, Amgueddfa Cymru-National Museum Wales, Cathays Park,Cardiff CF10 3NP. 02920 573 363. e-mail: steve.howe@museumwales.ac.uk www.cardiffnaturalists.org.uk
Meetings: 7.30pm, various evenings, Cardiff Metropolitan University, Llandaff Campus, Western Avenue, Cardiff.

GLAMORGAN BIRD CLUB. (1990; 300). **Alan Rosney**, 10 Parc-y-Nant, Nantgarw, CF15 7TJ. 01443 841 555; e-mail: alan.rosney@glamorganbirds.org.uk www.glamorganbirds.org.uk
Meetings: 7.30pm, 2nd Tuesday of winter months, Kenfig Reserve Centre.

GOWER ORNITHOLOGICAL SOCIETY. (1956; 120). Jeremy Douglas-Jones, 14 Alder Way, West Cross, Swansea, SA3 5PD. 01792 551 331; e-mail: jeremy@douglas-jones.biz www.glamorganbirds.org.uk
Meetings: 7.15pm, last Friday of the month (Sep-Mar), The Environment Centre, Pier Street, Swansea.

THE GWENT ORNITHOLOGICAL SOCIETY. (1964; 420). T J Russell. 01600 716 266; e-mail: secretary@GwentBirds.org.uk www.gwentbirds.org.uk
Meetings: 7.30pm, alternate Saturdays (Sept-Apr), Goytre Village Hall.

Ringing Groups
KENFIG RG. Mr D.G. Carrington, Kenfig NNR, Ton Kenfig, Bridgend, CF33 4PT. 01656 743 386; (M) 07779 978 738; e-mail: david.carrington@bridgend.gov.uk kenfignnr.blogspot.com www.bridgendcountryside.com

RSPB Local Groups
CARDIFF & DISTRICT. (1973:). Huw Moody-Jones. 01446 760 757; e-mail: huwmoodyjones@hotmail.com www.RSPB.org.uk/groups/cardiff
Meetings: 7.30pm, various Fridays (Sept-May), Llandaff Parish Hall, Llandaff, Cardiff.

WEST GLAMORGAN. (1985; 346). Maggie Cornelius. 01792 229 244; e-mail: RSPBwglamgrp@googlemail.com www.rspb.org.uk/groups/westglamorgan
Meetings: 7.30pm, Environment Centre, Pier Street, SWANSEA, SA1 1RY

Wetland Bird Survey Organisers
BURRY INLET (NORTH). Mr A W Flannagan, c/o WeBS Office, BTO, The Nunnery, Thetford, Norfolk IP24 2PU. 01792 537439; e-mail: alastair.flannagan@ntlworld.com

EAST GLAMORGAN. Mr D Jenkins-Jones, 18 St. Margarets Road, Whitchurch, Cardiff, South

WALES

Glamorgan CF14 7AA. 0292 062 1394; 07828 093 613; e-mail: jenkinsjones@btinternet.com

GWENT (excl. Severn Estuary). Dr W A Venables, 111 Blackoak Road, Cyncoed, Cardiff CF23 6QW. 01222 874 000; 01222 756 697; e-mail: wa.venables@zen.co.uk

SEVERN ESTUARY. Dr W A Venables, 111 Blackoak Road, Cyncoed, Cardiff CF23 6QW. 01222 874 000; 01222 756 697; e-mail: wa.venables@zen.co.uk

WEST GLAMORGAN. Mr A W Flannagan, 27 Llys Dol, Morriston, Swansea SA6 6LD. 01792 459 287; 01792 537 439; e-mail: alastair.flannagan@ntlworld.com

Wildlife Hospital

GOWER BIRD HOSPITAL. Karen Kingsnorth and Simon Allen, Valetta, Sandy Lane, Pennard, Swansea, SA3 2EW. 01792 371 630; e-mail: admin@ gowerbirdhospital.org.uk www.gowerbirdhospital.org.uk All species of wild birds, also hedgehogs and small mammals. Prior phone call essential. Gower Bird Hospital cares for sick, injured and orphaned wild birds and animals with the sole intention of returning them to the wild. Post release radio tracking projects, ringing scheme. Contact us for more information.

Wildlife Trust

GWENT WILDLIFE TRUST. (1963; 9,950). Seddon House, Dingestow, Monmouth, NP25 4DY. 01600 740 600; e-mail: info@gwentwildlife.org www.gwentwildlife.org

WILDLIFE TRUST OF SOUTH AND WEST WALES. (2002; 4,000). Nature Centre, Parc Slip, Fountain Road, Tondu, Bridgend CF32 0EH. 01656 724 100; fax 01656 726 980; e-mail: info@welshwildlife.org www.welshwildlife.org

WESTERN AREA OF WALES

Bird Atlas/Avifauna
Birds of Ceredigion by Hywel Roderick and Peter Davis (2010).

Carmarthenshire Birds 2008/2009, by G. Harper, R. Hunt, J.V. Lloyd, Carmarthenshire Bird Club.

Birds of Pembrokeshire by Jack Donovan and Graham Rees (Dyfed Wildlife Trust, 1994).

Bird Recorders
CARMARTHENSHIRE. Owen Harris, 5 William Terrace, Burry Port, Carmarthenshire SA16 0PG. e-mail: Owenharris@aol.com

CEREDIGION. Russell Jones, Bron y Gan, Talybont, Ceredigion, SY24 5ER. 07753 774 891; e-mail: russell.jones@rspb.org.uk

PEMBROKESHIRE (Joint Recorder). Stephen Berry, The Old Mill, Llanychaer, Pembrokeshire SA65 9TB. 07772 869 730; e-mail: stephen.berry16@btinternet.com

PEMBROKESHIRE (Joint Recorder rarities). Jon Green, Crud Yr Awel, Bowls Road, Blaenporth, Ceredigion SA43 2AR. 01239 811 561; e-mail: jonrg@tiscali.co.uk

Bird Reports
CARMARTHENSHIRE BIRD REPORT (1982-) £6.80 by post or £6.30 online, available online at www.carmarthenshirebirds.co.uk.

CEREDIGION BIRD REPORT (biennial 1982-87; annual 1988-2012) - costs £9 and is available from RSPB Ynys-hir, Teifi Marshes Welsh Wildlife Centre and Ystwyth Bookshop (Aberystwyth). Also available by post (cheques for £10 to include p&p payable to The Wildlife Trust for South and West Wales), from John Davis, Pantllidiart, Tristant, Aberystwyth, SY23 4RQ

PEMBROKESHIRE BIRD REPORT (1981-) - £7, including postage, from Jon Green (County Recorder), Crud Yr Awel, Bowls Road, Blaenporth, Cardigan SA43 2AR. e-mail: jonrg@tiscali.co.uk

BTO Regional Representatives
CARDIGAN RR. Moira Convery, 41 Danycoed, Aberystwyth, SY23 2HD. 01970 612 998; e-mail: moira.convery@gmail.com

CARMARTHEN RR. Terry Wells, 01267 238 836; e-mail: terry@twells.me.uk

PEMBROKE RR. Bob and Annie Haycock, 1 Rushmoor, Martletwy, Narberth, Pembrokeshire SA67 8BB; e-mail: rushmoor1@tiscali.co.uk

Clubs
CARMARTHENSHIRE BIRD CLUB. (2003; 120).Owen Harris, 5 William Terrace, Burry Port, Carmarthenshire SA16 0PG. e-mail: Owenharris@aol.com www.carmarthenshirebirds. co.uk
Meetings: Winter evenings at WWT Penclacwydd (check website for details).

PEMBROKESHIRE BIRD GROUP. (1993; 60). Lyndon Lomax (Chairman), 17 Maes Y Dre, St David's, Pembrokeshire SA62 6QQ. 01437 721 859; e-mail: lplomax@btinternet.com http://pembrokeshirebirdgroup.blogspot.co.uk/ **Meetings:** 7.30pm, 1st Monday of the month (Oct-Apr), The Patch, Furzy Park, Haverfordwest SA61 1HT.

Ringing Group
PEMBROKESHIRE RG. J Hayes, 3 Wades Close, Holyland Road, Pembroke, SA71 4BN. 01646 687 036; e-mail: hayes313@btinternet.com

WALES

Wetland Bird Survey Organisers
CARDIGAN (incl Dyfi Estuary). Mr R Squires, c/o WeBS Office, BTO, The Nunnery, Thetford, Norfolk IP24 2PU; e-mail: caerberllan@talktalk.net

CARMARTHENSHIRE. Mr T Wells, 24 Heol Beca, Carmarthen, SA31 3LS. 01792 205 693; e-mail: bto@ twells.me.uk

PEMBROKESHIRE. Mrs A N Haycock, c/o WeBS Office, BTO, The Nunnery, Thetford, Norfolk IP24 2PU; e-mail: annie@rushmoorphotos.co.uk

Wildlife Hospital
NEW QUAY BIRD HOSPITAL. Jean Bryant, Penfoel, Cross Inn, Llandysul, Ceredigion, SA44 6NR. 01545 560 462. All species of birds. Fully equipped for cleansing oiled seabirds. Veterinary support.

Wildlife Trust
WILDLIFE TRUST OF SOUTH AND WEST WALES. (2002; 4,000). Nature Centre, Parc Slip, Fountain Road, Tondu, Bridgend CF32 0EH. 01656 724 100; fax 01656 726 980; e-mail: info@welshwildlife.org
www.welshwildlife.org

ISLE OF MAN

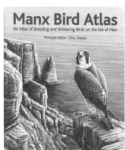

Manx Bird Atlas
An Atlas of Breeding and Wintering Birds on the Isle of Man
Principal Editor: Chris Sharpe

Bird Atlas/Avifauna
Manx Bird Atlas. 5-yr BBS and Winter Atlas research completed. (Liverpool University Press, 2007). Contact: Chris Sharpe (see below, BTO)

Bird Recorder
Chris Sharpe. E-mail:chris@manxbirdlife.im

Bird Reports
MANX BIRD REPORT (1947-), published in *Peregrine*. From Mrs A C Kaye, Cronk Ny Ollee, Glen Chass, Port St Mary, Isle of Man IM9 5PL. 01624 834 015.

CALF OF MAN BIRD OBSERVATORY ANNUAL REPORT, from Secretary, Manx National Heritage, Manx Museum, Douglas, Isle of Man, IM1 3LY.

BTO Regional Representatives
Dr Pat Cullen, as below. 01624 623 308; e-mail:bridgeen@mcb.net

Club
MANX ORNITHOLOGICAL SOCIETY. (1967; 150). Mrs A C Kaye, Cronk Ny Ollee, Glen Chass, Port St Mary, Isle of Man IM9 5PL. 01624 834 015. http:// manxbirdlife.im/manx-ornithological-society
Meetings: 1st Tues in month, 7.30pm, Union Mills Hall, IM4 4NP.

Ringing Group
MANX RINGING GROUP. Mr Kevin Scott; e-mail: manxrg@gmail.com
www.manxringer.blogspot.com

Wetland Bird Survey Organiser
Dr Pat Cullen, Troutbeck, Cronkbourne, Braddan, Isle of Man, IM4 4QA. Home: 01624 623 308, Work 01624 676 774; E-mail:bridgeen@mcb.net

Wildlife Trust
MANX WILDLIFE TRUST. (1973; 900). 7-8 Market Place, Peel, Isle of Man IM5 1AB. 01624 844 432; E-mail:enquiries@manxwt.org.uk
www.manxwt.org.uk

283

CHANNEL ISLANDS

Wetland Bird Survey Organisers
CHANNEL ISLANDS (inland). Glyn Young. 01534 860
000; e-mail:glyn.young@durrell.org

ALDERNEY

Atlas/Avifauna
The Birds of Alderney, by JG Sanders. (The Press at St
Anne, 2007).

Bird Recorder
Mark Atkinson; e-mail:atkinson@cwgsy.net

Bird Report
ALDERNEY SOCIETY AND COUNTY ORNITHOLOGICAL
REPORT (1992-), from Recorder;
e-mail: atkinson@cwgsy.net

BTO Regional Representative
See Guernsey.

Wetland Birds Survey Organiser
Trust Ecologist, Alderney Wildlife Trust Office, 51
Victoria Street, St Anne, Alderney GY9 3TA. 01481 822
935; e-mail:info@alderneywildlife.org

Wildlife Trust
ALDERNEY WILDLIFE TRUST. (2002; 460). Alderney
Wildlife Trust Office, 51 Victoria Street, St Anne,
Alderney GY9 3TA. 01481 822 935;
e-mail:info@alderneywildlife.org
www.alderneywildlife.org

GUERNSEY

Bird Atlas/Avifauna
Birds of the Bailiwick: Guernsey, Alderney, Sark and
Herm by Duncan Spencer & Paul Hillion, (Jill Vaudin
Publishing 2010).

Bird Recorder
Mark Lawlor; e-mail:mplawlor@cwgsy.net

Bird Report
REPORT & TRANSACTIONS OF LA SOCIETE
GUERNESIAISE (1882-), from Recorder.

BTO Regional Representative
Philip Alexander. 01481 726 173;
e-mail:alybru@cwgsy.net

Clubs
LA SOCIÉTÉ GUERNESIAISE (Ornithological Section).
(1882; 1,400). Secretary, La Société Guernesiaise,
Candie Gardens, St Peter Port, Port Guernsey GY1
1UG. 01481 725 093; e-mail:societe@cwgsy.net
www.societe.org.gg
Meetings: First Thurs of month, 8pm, Candie Gardens
lecture theatre, St Peter Port.

RSPB Local Group
GUERNSEY BAILIWICK. (1975; 350+). Donna Francis.

01481 232 632; e-mail:donna@cwgsy.net
www.rspbguernsey.co.uk
Meetings: 8pm, La Villette Hotel, St Martins,
Guernsey, GY4 6QG.

Wetland Bird Survey Organiser
GUERNSEY COAST. Mary Simmons, Les Maeures, Mont
d'Aval, Castel, Guernsey GY5 7UQ. 01481 256 016;
e-mail:msim@cwgsy.net

Wildlife Hospital
GUERNSEY. GSPCA ANIMAL
SHELTER. Mrs Jayne Le
Cras, Les Fiers Moutons, St
Andrews, Guernsey, Channel
Islands GY6 8UD. 01481 257 261; (emergency number
07781 104 082); e-mail:admin@gspca.org.gg
www.gspca.org.gg
All species. Modern cleansing unit for oiled seabirds.
24-hour emergency service. Veterinary support.

JERSEY

Bird Recorder
Tony Paintin, Cavok, 16 Quennevais Gardens, St
Brelade, Jersey, Channel Islands, JE3 8FQ. 01534 741
928; e-mail:cavokjersey@hotmail.com

Bird Report
JERSEY BIRD REPORT (1991-), from La Société
Jersiaise, 7 Pier Road, St Helier, Jersey JE2 4XW;
e-mail:societe@societe-jersiaise.org

BTO Regional Representative
Tony Paintin, Cavok, 16 Quennevais Gardens, St
Brelade, Jersey, Channel Islands, JE3 8FQ. 01534 741
928; e-mail:cavokjersey@hotmail.com

Club
SOCIÉTIÉ JERSIAISE (Ornithological Section). (1948;
40). La Société Jersiaise, 7 Pier Road, St Helier,
Jersey JE2 4XW. 01534 758 314;
e-mail:societe@societe-jersiaise.org
www.societe-jersiaise.org
Meetings: 8.00pm, alternate Thursdays throughout
the year, Museum in St.Helier.

Wetland Bird Survey Organiser
JERSEY COAST. Roger Noel.
e-mail:rogernoel1@googlemail.com

Wildlife Hospital
JERSEY. JSPCA ANIMALS' SHELTER. The Manager, 89 St
Saviour's Road, St Helier, Jersey, JE2 4GJ. 01534 724
331; e-mail:info@jspca.org.je
www.jspca.org.je
All species. Expert outside support for owls and
raptors. Oiled seabird unit. Veterinary surgeon on
site. Educational Centre.

NORTHERN IRELAND

Bird Recorder
George Gordon, 2 Brooklyn Avenue, Bangor, Co Down, BT20 5RB. 028 9145 5763; e-mail: gordon@ballyholme2.freeserve.co.uk

Bird Reports
NORTHERN IRELAND BIRD REPORT, from Secretary, Northern Ireland, Birdwatchers' Association (see National Directory).

IRISH BIRD REPORT, Included in Irish Birds, BirdWatch Ireland in National Directory.

COPELAND BIRD OBSERVATORY REPORT, from the Bookings Secretary: David Galbraith, 028 9338 2539 or 07885 834 398;
e-mail: davidgalbraith903@btinternet.com

BTO Regional Representatives
BTO IRELAND OFFICER. Shane Wolsey. 028 9146 7947; e-mail:shane@swolsey.biz

ANTRIM & BELFAST. Adam McClure. 028 2827 1875; e-mail:a.d.mcclure84@hotmail.co.uk

ARMAGH. Stephen Hewitt;
e-mail: sjameshewitt@hotmail.com

DOWN. Kerry Leonard. 028 9145 2602;
e-mail:kerrysleonard@hotmail.com

FERMANAGH. Michael Stinson. 07890 358 239;
e-mail:mick.stinston@hotmail.com

LONDONDERRY. Charles Stewart, Bravallen, 18 Duncrun Road, Bellarena, Limavady, Co Londonderry BT49 0JD. 028 7775 0468;
e-mail:charles.stewart2@btinternet.com

TYRONE. Michael Stinson. 07890 358 239;
E-mail:mick.stinston@hotmail.com

BTO Garden BirdWatch Ambassador
Pat Flowerday. E-mail: pflowerday@utvinternet.com

Clubs
NORTHERN IRELAND BIRDWATCHERS' ASSOCIATION
See National Directory.

NORTHERN IRELAND ORNITHOLOGISTS' CLUB
See National Directory.

CASTLE ESPIE BIRDWATCHING CLUB (COMBER). (1995; 60). Dot Blakely, 8 Rosemary Park, Bangor, Co Down, BT20 3EX. 028 9145 0784;
e-mail: dotbirdblakely@gmail.com

Ringing Groups
COPELAND BIRD OBSERVATORY. C Chris Acheson;
e-mail: CWA70@hotmail.com

NORTH DOWN RINGING GROUP. Mr D C Clarke. 07774 780 750; e-mail: declan.clarke@homecall.co.uk;

RSPB Local Groups
ANTRIM. (1977; 23). Brenda Campbell. 02893 323 657; e-mail:brendacampbell@supanet.com
www.rspb.org.uk/groups/antrim
Meetings: 8pm, 2nd Monday of the month, College of Agriculture Food & Rural Enterprise, 22 Greenmount Road, Antrim.

BANGOR. (1973; 25). Fulton Somerville;
e-mail: fultonsomerville@yahoo.co.uk
Meetings: Trinity Presbyterian Church Hall, Main Street, Bangor, County Down.

BELFAST. (1970; 130). Derek McLain. 028 9334 1488; e-mail: d.mclain@btinternet.com
Meetings: Cooke Centenary Church Hall, Park Road, Belfast BT7 2FW.

COLERAINE. (1978; 45). Peter Robinson, 34 Blackthorn Court, Coleraine, Co Londonderry, BT52 2EX. 028 7034 4361; e-mail: robinson493@btinternet.com
Meetings: 7.30pm, third Monday of the month (Sept-Apr), St Patricks Church, Minor Church Hall, Corner of Brook St and Circular Road, Coleraine.

FERMANAGH. (1977; 28). Doreen Brown. 028 6632 2479; e-mail: dbrown498@btinternet.com
Meetings: 8pm, Cathedral Hall, Halls Lane, Enniskillen BT74 7DR.

LARNE. (1974; 35). Jimmy Christie, 314 Coast Road, Ballygally, Co Antrim, BT40 2QZ. 028 2858 3223;
E-mail: candjchristie@btinternet.com
Meetings: 7.30pm, 1st Wednesday of the month, Larne Grammar School.

LISBURN. (1978; 30). Peter Galloway. 028 9266 1982; E-mail: pgalloway56@o2.co.uk
www.rspblisburn.com
Meetings: 7.30pm, 4th Monday of the month, Friends Meeting House, 4 Magheralave Road, Lisburn.

Wetland Bird Survey Organisers
BANN ESTUARY. Hill Dick. 02870 329 720;
e-mail: webs@bto.org

BELFAST LOUGH. Shane Wolsey, 25 Ballyholme Esplanade, Bangor, County Down, BT20 5LZ. 07831 697 371; e-mail:shane@swolsey.biz

DUNDRUM BAY. Malachy Martin, Murlough NNR, Keel Point, Dundrum, Co. Down BT33 0NQ. 028 4375 1467; e-mail: Malachy.Martin@nationaltrust.org.uk

LARNE LOUGH. Doreen Hilditch;
E-mail: mail18brae@btinternet.com

LOUGH FOYLE. Matthew Tickner. 02890 491 547;
e-mail:matthew.tickner@rspb.org.uk

STRANGFORD LOUGH. Kerry Mackie, WWT Castle Espie; 78 Ballydrain Road, Co Down. 02891 874 146; e-mail: kerry.mackie@wwt.org.uk

Wildlife Hospital
TACT WILDLIFE CENTRE. Mrs Patricia Nevines, 2 Crumlin Road, Crumlin, Co Antrim, BT29 4AD. 028 9442 2900; e-mail: tactwildlife@btinternet.com www.tactwildlifecentre.org.uk All categories of birds treated and rehabilitated; released where

practicable, otherwise given a home. Visitors (inc. school groups and organisations) welcome by prior arrangement. Veterinary support.

Wildlife Trust
ULSTER WILDLIFE TRUST. (1978; 7.500). 3 New Line, Crossgar, Co Down, BT30 9EP. 028 4483 0282 (fax) 028 4483 0888; e-mail: info@ulsterwildlifetrust.org www.ulsterwildlifetrust.org

---

REPUBLIC OF IRELAND

BirdWatch Ireland, Unit 20, Block D, Bullford Business Campus, Kilcoole, Co. Wicklow, Ireland 353 (0)1 281 9878 E-mail: info@ birdwatchireland.ie www.birdwatchireland.ie

BirdWatchIreland

Rarities. Paul Milne, 100 Dublin Road, Sutton, Dublin 13, +353 (0)1 832 5653; e-mail: paul.milne@oceanfree.net

CLARE. John Murphy, e-mail: jemurphy@esatclear.ie

CORK. Mark Shorten, e-mail: mshorten@indigo.ie

DONEGAL. Ralph Sheppard, e-mail: rsheppard@eircom.net

DUBLIN, LOUTH, MEATH AND WICKLOW. Declan Murphy & Dick Coombes, e-mail: dmurphy@birdwatchireland.ie or e-mail: rcoombes@birdwatchireland.ie

GALWAY. Chris Peppiatt, e-mail: chris.peppiatt@iol.ie

KERRY. Michael O'Clery & Jill Crosher, e-mail: moclery@tinet.ie

LIMERICK. Tony Mee, Ballyorgan, Kilfinane, Co. Limerick.

MAYO. Tony Murray, National Parks and Wildlife, Lagduff More, Ballycroy, Westport; e-mail: murraytony@hotmail.com

MID-SHANNON. Stephen Heery, e-mail: sheery@eircom.net

MONAGHAN. Joe Shannon, e-mail: joeshan@eircom.net

WATERFORD. Paul Walsh, 16 Castlepoint, Crosshaven, Co. Cork; e-mail: pmwalsh@waterfordbirds.com

WEXFORD. Tony Murray, Wexford Wildfowl Reserve, North Slob; e-mail: murraytony@hotmail.com

Bird Reports
IRISH BIRD REPORT, contact BirdWatch Ireland in National, Directory).

CAPE CLEAR BIRD OBSERVATORY ANNUAL REPORT, from the observatory.

CORK BIRD REPORT (1963-71; 1976-), Cork Bird Report Editorial Team, Long Strand, Castlefreke, Clonakilty, Co. Cork; e-mail: cbr@corkecology.net

EAST COAST BIRD REPORT (1980-), Contact BirdWatch Ireland.

BirdWatch Ireland Branches
Branches may be contacted in writing via BirdWatch Ireland HQ (see entry in National Directory).

Ringing Groups
CAPE CLEAR B.O, Steve Wing, e-mail: steve.ccbo@gmail.com

GREAT SALTEE RINGING STATION, Mr O J Merne, 20 Cuala Road, Bray, Co Wicklow, Ireland, e-mail: omerne@eircom.net

MUNSTER RG, Mr K.P.C. Collins, Ballygambon, Lisronagh, Clonmel, County Tipperary, e-mail: kcsk@eircom.net

NATIONAL DIRECTORY

David Cromack

Organisations such as the RSPB are keen to use volunteers to engage with the general public — as here at the Symonds Yat Peregrine watch.

National directory of organisations   288

National research projects   301

NATIONAL ORGANISATIONS

After the title of each organisation you will see (in brackets) the year the group was founded and, where known, the current membership figure.

ARMY ORNITHOLOGICAL SOCIETY (1960; 200)
Open to serving and retired MoD employees who have an interest in their local MoD estate. Activities include field meetings, expeditions, the preparation of checklists of birds on Ministry of Defence property, conservation advice and an annual bird count. Annual journal *Adjutant*.
Contact: Maj AJ Bray RLC, www.armybirdingng.com
e-mail: secretary@aos.org.uk

ASSOCIATION FOR THE PROTECTION OF RURAL SCOTLAND (1926)
Works to protect Scotland's countryside from unnecessary or inappropriate development, recognising the needs of those who live and work there and the necessity of reconciling these with the sometimes competing requirements of recreational use.
Contact: Association for the Protection Rural Scotland, Gladstone's Land, 3rd Floor, 483 Lawnmarket, Edinburgh EH1 2NT. 0131 225 7012;
e-mail: info@ruralscotland.org
www.ruralscotland.btck.com

ASSOCIATION OF COUNTY RECORDERS AND EDITORS (1993; 120)
The basic aim of ACRE is to promote best practice in the business of producing county bird reports, in the work of Recorders and in problems arising in managing record systems and archives. Organises periodic conferences and publishes *newsACRE*.
Contact: The Secretary; e-mail: countyrec@cawos.org

BARN OWL TRUST (1988)
A registered charity dedicated to conserving the Barn Owl and its environment. It is the main source of Barn Owl information in the UK. It carries out surveys of old buildings, due for development, and advises on Barn Owl mitigation measures. A booklet *Barn Owls on Site*, a guide for developers and planners, published by English Nature is widely used by local authorities and other official bodies. Trust members have erected more than 2,000 nestboxes and is closely involved in habitat creation both on its own land and through farm visits.
Contact: Barn Owl Trust, Waterleat, Ashburton, Devon TQ13 7HU. 01364 653 026;
www.barnowltrust.org.uk
e-mail: info@barnowltrust.org.uk

BIRDING FOR ALL (formerly The Disabled Birder's Association) (2000; 750)
Birding For All is a registered charity and international movement, which aims to promote access to reserves and other birding places and to a range of services, so that people with different needs can follow the birding obsession as freely as able-bodied people. Membership is currently free and new members are needed to help send a stronger message

to those who own and manage nature reserves to improve access when they are planning and improving facilities. DBA also seeks to influence those who provide birdwatching services and equipment. The DBA also runs overseas trips. Chairman, Bo Beolens.
Contact: Phil Gatley. Membership Secretary.
e-mail: BAnderson1550539@aol.com
www.birdingforall.com

BIRD OBSERVATORIES COUNCIL (1970)
Aims to provide a forum for establishing closer links and co-operation between individual observatories and to help co-ordinate the work carried out by them. All accredited bird observatories affiliated to the Council undertake a ringing programme and provide ringing experience to those interested. Most are also provide accommodation for visiting birdwatchers.
Contact: Peter Howlett, Bird Observatories Council, c/o Dept of BioSyB, National Museum Wales, Cardiff CF10 3NP. 0292 057 3233;
e-mail: info@birdobscouncil.org.uk
www.birdobscouncil.org.uk

BIRD STAMP SOCIETY (1986; 170)
Quarterly journal *Flight* contains philatelic and ornithological articles. Lists all new issues and identifies species. Runs a quarterly Postal Auction; number of lots range from 400 to 800 per auction. UK subs £14 per annum from 1st August.

Contact: Bob Wilks, Membership Secretary, 4 Curlew Road, Porthcawl, Mid-Glamorgan CF36 3QA; 01656 785055; e-mail: bobwilks581@btinternet.com
www.birdstampsociety.org

BIRDWATCH IRELAND (1968; 14,000 with a network of 20 branches)
The largest independent conservation organisation in Ireland. Its primary objective is the protection of wild birds and their habitats in Ireland through the efforts of its staff, members and volunteers alike. It carries out extensive research and survey work, operates applied conservation projects and manages a network of reserves nationwide. It publishes *Wings* magazine and an annual journal *Irish Birds*.
Contact: BirdWatch Ireland, Unit 20, Block D, Bullford Business Campus, Kilcoole, Co. Wicklow, Ireland. +353 (0)1 2819 878 353 (0)1 281 9878; Fax: +353 (0)1 281 0997; e-mail: info@birdwatchireland.org
www.birdwatchireland.ie

NATIONAL ORGANISATIONS

BRITISH BIRDS RARITIES COMMITTEE (1959, 16)

The Committee adjudicates records of species of rare occurrence in Britain (marked `R' in the Log Charts) and publishes its annual report in B*ritish Birds*. The BBRC also assesses records from the Channel Islands. In the case of rarities trapped for ringing, records should be sent to the Ringing Office of the British Trust for Ornithology, who will in turn forward them to the BBRC.

Contact: The Hon Secretary, British Birds Rarities Committee, e-mail: secretary@bbrc.org.uk www.bbrc.org.uk

BRITISH DECOY WILDFOWL CARVERS ASSOCIATION (1990)

The Association is a non-profitmaking organisation, run by carvers to promote all aspects of their art. Its aims are: to produce three annual *Wingspan* newsletters: to keep the members in touch with the art; to promote regional groups; to generate local interest; to organise competitions and exhibitions; and finally, to care generally for wildfowl carvers' interests. Each September the Association stages the Bakewell Festival of Bird Art in the Peak District, which includes the national carving championships.

Contact: Janet Nash (club secretary) e-mail: janet.nash@talk21.com www.bdwca.org.uk

BRITISH DRAGONFLY SOCIETY (1983; 1,500)

The BDS aims to promote the conservation and study of dragonflies. Members receive two issues of

Dragonfly News and *BDS Journal* each year. There are countrywide field trips, an annual members' day and training is available on aspects of dragonfly ecology. The BDS has published a booklet, *Dig a Pond for Dragonflies* containing advice on pond creation and maintenance to attract dragonflies. *Managing Habitats for Dragonflies* is aimed at countryside managers.

Contact: Mr H Curry, Hon Secretary, British Dragonfly Society, 23 Bowker Way, Whittlesey, Cambs PE7 1PY. e-mail: bdssecretary@dragonflysoc.org.uk www.dragonflysoc.org.uk

BRITISH FALCONERS' CLUB (1927; 1,200)

Largest falconry club in Europe, with regional branches. Its aim is to encourage responsible falconers and conserve birds of prey by breeding, holding educational meetings and providing facilities, guidance and advice to those wishing to take up the sport. Publishes *The Falconer* annually and newsletter twice yearly.

Contact: British Falconers' Club, Westfield, Meeting Hill, Worstead, North Walsham, Norfolk NR28 9LS. 01692 404 057; www.britishfalconersclub.co.uk e-mail: admin@britishfalconersclub.co.uk

BRITISH LIBRARY SOUND ARCHIVE - WILDLIFE SOUNDS (1969).

The most comprehensive collection of bird sound recordings in existence: over 150,000 recordings

of more than 8,000 species of birds worldwide, available for free listening. Copies or sonograms of most recordings can be supplied for private study or research and, subject to copyright clearance, for commercial uses. Contribution of new material and enquiries on all aspects of wildlife sounds and recording techniques are welcome. Publishes *Bioacoustics journal*, CD guides to bird songs and other wildlife, including ambience titles. Comprehensive catalogue available on-line at http://cadensa.bl.uk/uhtbin/cgisirsi/x/x/0/49/

Contact: Cheryl Tipp, Curator, Wildlife Sounds, The British Library Sound Archive, 96 Euston Road, London NW1 2DB. 020 7412 7403; (Fax) 020 7412 7441; e-mail: wildlifesound@bl.uk www.bl.uk/reshelp/findhelprestype/sound/wildsounds/wildlife.html

BRITISH NATURALISTS ASSOCIATION (1905)

The association was founded to promote the interests of nature lovers and bring them together. It encourages and supports schemes and legislation for the protection of the country`s natural resources. It organises meetings, field weeks, lectures and exhibitions to help popularise the study of nature. BNA publishes two magazines, *Countryside* (bi-annual) and *British Naturalist* (bi-annual).

Contact: General Secretary, BNA, BM 8129, London WC1N 3XX. 0844 892 1817; www.bna-naturalists.org e-mail: info@bna-naturalists.org

BRITISH ORNITHOLOGISTS' CLUB (1892; 450)

The Club's objects are 'the promotion of scientific discussion between members of the BOU, and others interested in ornithology, and to facilitate the publication of scientific information in connection with ornithology'. The Club maintains a special interest in avian systematics, taxonomy and distribution. About eight dinner meetings are held each year. Publishes the *Bulletin of the British Ornithologists' Club* quarterly, and a continuing series of occasional publications.

Contact: BOC Office, British Ornithologists' Club, PO Box 417, Peterborough, PE7 3FX. (Tel/Fax) 01733 844 820; e-mail: boc.admin@bou.org.uk www.boc-online.org

BRITISH ORNITHOLOGISTS' UNION (1858; 1,100)

The BOU is one of the world's oldest and most respected ornithological societies. It aims to promote ornithology within the scientific and birdwatching communities, both in Britain and around the world. This is largely achieved by the publication of its quarterly international journal, *Ibis*, featuring work at the cutting edge of our understanding of the world's birdlife. It also publishes an on-going series of country/island group 'checklists' (see website for details) and operates an active programme of meetings, seminars and conferences.

NATIONAL ORGANISATIONS

Work being undertaken around the world can include research projects that have received financial assistance from the BOU's on-going programme of Ornithological Research Grants. The BOU Records Committee maintains the official British List (see below)
Contact: Steve Dudley, British Ornithologists' Union, PO Box 417, Peterborough, PE7 3FX. (Tel/Fax) 01733 844 820; e-mail: bou@bou.org.uk www.bou.org.uk and www.ibis.ac.uk

BRITISH ORNITHOLOGISTS' UNION RECORDS COMMITTEE (11)

A standing committee of the British Ornithologists' Union, the BOURC's function is to maintain the British List, the official list of birds recorded in Great Britain. The up-to-date list can be viewed on the BOU website. Where vagrants are involved it is concerned only with those which relate to potential additions to the British List (ie first records). In this it differs from the British Birds Rarities Committee (qv).
It also examines, where necessary, important pre-1950 records, monitors introduced species for possible admission to, or deletion from, the List, and reviews taxonomy and nomenclature relating to the List. BOURC reports are published in *Ibis* and are also available via the BOU website.
Contact: Steve Dudley, BOURC, PO Box 417, Peterborough, PE7 3FX. (Tel/Fax) 01733 844 820; e-mail: bourc@bou.org www.bou.org.uk

BRITISH TRUST FOR ORNITHOLOGY (1933; 13,200)

A registered charity governed by an elected Council, BTO enjoys the support of a large number of county and local birdwatching clubs and societies through the BTO/Bird Clubs Partnership. Its aims are: 'To promote and encourage the wider understanding, appreciation and conservation of birds through scientific studies using the combined skills and enthusiasm of its members, other birdwatchers and staff.'

Through the fieldwork of its members and other birdwatchers, the BTO is responsible for the majority of the monitoring of British birds, British bird population and their habitats. BTO surveys include the National Ringing Scheme, the Nest Record Scheme, the Breeding Bird Survey (in collaboration with JNCC and RSPB), and the Waterways Breeding Bird Survey, which all contribute to an integrated programme of population monitoring.
The BTO also runs projects on the birds of farmland and woodland, also (in collaboration with WWT, RSPB and JNCC) the Wetland Bird Survey, in particular Low Tide Counts. Garden BirdWatch, now has more than 14,000 participants. The Trust has 140 voluntary regional representatives (see County Directory) who organise fieldworkers for the BTO's programme of national surveys in which members participate. The results of these co-operative efforts are communicated to government departments, local authorities, industry and conservation bodies for effective action.
For details of current activities see National Projects. Members receive *BTO News* six times a year and have the option of subscribing to the thrice-yearly journal, *Bird Study* and twice yearly *Ringing & Migration*. Local meetings are held in conjunction with bird clubs and societies; there are regional and national birdwatchers' conferences, and specialist courses in bird identification and modern censusing techniques. Grants are made for research, and members have the use of a lending and reference library at Thetford and the Alexander Library at the Edward Grey Institute of Field Ornithology (qv)
Contact: British Trust for Ornithology, The Nunnery, Thetford, Norfolk IP24 2PU. 01842 750 050; (Fax) 01842 750 030; e-mail: info@bto.org www.bto.org

BTO SCOTLAND (2000; 989)

BTO Scotland's main functions are to promote the work of the Trust and develop wider coverage for surveys in Scotland, by encouraging greater participation in survey work. It also seeks to develop contract research income within Scotland. BTO Scotland ensures that the Trust's work is not just related to the priorities of the UK as a whole but is also focused on the priorities of Scotland, with a landscape and wildlife so different from the rest of the UK.
Contact: BTO Scotland, British Trust for Ornithology, Biological and Environmental Sciences, University of Stirling, Stirling FK9 4LA. 01786 466 560 (Fax) 01786 466 561; e-mail: scot.info@bto.org www.bto.org

BRITISH WATERFOWL ASSOCIATION

The BWA is an association of enthusiasts interested in keeping, breeding and conserving all types of waterfowl, including wildfowl and domestic ducks and geese. It is a registered charity, without trade affiliations, dedicated to educating the public about waterfowl and the need for conservation as well as to raising the standards of keeping and breeding ducks, geese and swans in captivity. Publishes *Waterfowl* magazine for members three times a year
Contact: Mrs Sue Schubert, British Waterfowl Association, PO Box 163, Oxted, RH8 0WP. 01732 867 987; e-mail: info@waterfowl.org.uk www.waterfowl.org.uk

BRITISH WILDLIFE REHABILITATION COUNCIL (1987)

Promoting the care and rehabilitation of wildlife casualties through the exchange of information between people such as rehabilitators, zoologists and veterinary surgeons who are active in this field. Organises an annual symposium or workshop. Publishes a regular newsletter. Supported by many national bodies including the Zoological Society of

NATIONAL ORGANISATIONS

London, the British Veterinary Zoological Society, the RSPCA, the SSPCA, and the Vincent Wildlife Trust. **Contact:** To make a contribution - Janet Peto, BWRC, PO Box 8686, Grantham, Lincolnshire NG31 0AG; e-mail: admin@bwrc.org.uk www.bwrc.org.uk

BTCV (formerly British Trust for Conservation Volunteers) (1959)

BTCV's mission is to create a more sustainable future by inspiring people and improving places. It aims to enrich the lives of people, through volunteering opportunities, employment, improved health, and life skills development; to improve the biodiversity and local environment of 20,000 places and to support active citizenship in 5,000 community-based groups. BTCV currently supports 140,000 volunteers to take practical action to improve their urban and rural environments. Publishes a quarterly magazine, *Roots*, a series of practical handbooks and a wide range of other publications.
Contact: TCV, Sedum House, Mallard Way, Potteric Carr, Doncaster DN4 8DB. 01302 388 883; e-mail: Information@tcv.org.uk www.tcv.org.uk

BTCV CYMRU
Contact: The Conservation Centre, BTCV Cymru, Forest Farm Road, Whitchurch, Cardiff, CF14 7JJ. 029 2052 0990; Fax: 029 2052 2181; e-mail: wales@ttcv.org.uk www.btcvcymru.org

BTCV SCOTLAND
Runs 7-14 day Action Breaks in Scotland during which participants undertake conservation projects; weekend training courses in environmental skills; midweek projects in Edinburgh, Glasgow, Aberdeen, Stirling and Inverness.
Contact: BTCV Scotland, Balallan House, 24 Allan Park, Stirling FK8 2QG. 01786 479 697; (Fax) 01786 465359; e-mail: scotland@tcv.org.uk www2.btcv.org.uk/display/btcv_scotland

BTCV NORTHERN IRELAND (1983)
Contact: Conservation Volunteers Northern Ireland, Beech House, 159 Ravenhill Road, Belfast BT6 0BP. 028 9064 5169; (Fax) 028 9064 4409; e-mail: CVNI@btcv.org.uk www.cvni.org

BUGLIFE – THE INVERTEBRATE CONSERVATION TRUST (2000)
The first organisation in Europe devoted to the conservation of all invertebrates, actively engaged in halting the extinction of Britain's rarest slugs, snails, bees, wasps, ants, spiders, beetles and many more. It works to achieve this through practical conservation projects; promoting the environmental importance of invertebrates and raising awareness about the challenges to their survival; assisting in the development of helpful legislation and policy and encouraging and supporting invertebrate conservation initiatives by

other organisations in the UK, Europe and worldwide.
Contact: Buglife (ICT), 1st Floor, 90 Bridge Street, Peterborough PE1 1DY. 01733 201 210; e-mail: info@buglife.org.uk www.buglife.org.uk

CAMPAIGN FOR THE PROTECTION OF RURAL WALES (1928; 2,800)
Its aims are to help the conservation and enhancement of the landscape, environment and amenities of the countryside, towns and villages of rural Wales and to form and educate opinion to ensure the promotion of its objectives. It gives advice and information upon matters affecting protection, conservation and improvement of the visual environment.
Contact: Ty Gwyn, 31 High Street, Welshpool, Powys SY21 7YD. 01938 552 525 or 01938 556 212; e-mail: info@cprwmail.org.uk www.cprw.org.uk

CENTRE FOR ECOLOGY & HYDROLOGY (CEH)
The work of the CEH, a component body of the Natural Environment Research Council, includes a range of ornithological research, covering population studies, habitat management and work on the effects of pollution. The CEH has a long-term programme to monitor pesticide and pollutant residues in the corpses of predatory birds sent in by birdwatchers, and carries out detailed studies on affected species. The Biological Records Centre (BRC), which is part of the CEH, is responsible for the national biological data bank on plant and animal distributions (except birds).
Contact: Centre for Ecology & Hydrology, Maclean Building, Benson Lane, Crowmarsh Gifford, Wallingford, Oxfordshire OX10 8BB. 01491 692 371. E-mail: enquiries@ceh.ac.uk www.ceh.ac.uk

CONSERVATION FOUNDATION (1982)
Created by David Bellamy and David Shreeve, it provides a means for people in public, private and not-for-profit sectors to collaborate on environmental causes. Over the years its programme has included award schemes, conferences, promotions, special events, field studies, school programmes, media work, seminars and workshops etc. The Conservation Foundation has created and managed environmental award schemes of all kinds including the Ford European Awards, The Trust House Forte Community Chest, The PA Golden Leaf Awards, The Co-op Save Our Species Awards, the Pollution Abatement Technology Awards and many others. For information about how to apply for current award schemes visit the website.
Contact: Conservation Foundation, 1 Kensington Gore, London SW7 2AR. 020 7591 3111; e-mail: info@conservationfoundation.co.uk www.conservationfoundation.co.uk

COUNTRY LAND AND BUSINESS ASSOCIATION (Formerly Country Landowners Association) (1907; 36,000).
The CLA is at the heart of rural life and is the voice of the countryside for England and Wales, campaigning on issues which directly affect those who live and

work in rural communities. Its members, ranging from some of the largest landowners, with interests in forest, moorland, water and agriculture, to some with little more than a paddock or garden, together manage 50% of the countryside.
Contact: Country Land and Business Association, 16 Belgrave Square, London, SW1X 8PQ. 020 7235 0511; (Fax) 020 7235 4696; e-mail: mail@cla.org.uk www.cla.org.uk

CPRE (formerly Council for the Protection of Rural England) (1926; 60,000)

Patron HM The Queen. CPRE now has 43 county branches and 200 local groups. It highlights threats to the countryside and promotes positive solutions. In-depth research supports active campaigning, and through reasoned argument and lobbying, CPRE seeks to influence public opinion and decision-makers at every level. Membership is open to all.
Contact: CPRE National Office, 5-11 Lavington Street, London SE1 0NZ. 020 7981 2800; (Fax) 020 7981 2899; e-mail: info@cpre.org.uk www.cpre.org.uk

DEPARTMENT OF THE ENVIRONMENT FOR NORTHERN IRELAND

Responsible for the declaration and management of National Nature Reserves, the declaration of Areas of Special Scientific Interest, the administration of Wildlife Refuges, the classification of Special Protection Areas under the EC Birds Directive, the designation of Special Areas of Conservation under the EC Habitats Directive and the designation of Ramsar sites under the Ramsar Convention. It administers the Nature Conservation and Amenity Lands (Northern Ireland) Order 1985, the Wildlife (Northern Ireland) Order 1985, the Game Acts and the Conservation (Natural Habitats, etc) Regulations (NI) 1995 and the Environment (Northern Ireland) Order 2002.
Contact: Environment and Heritage Service, Klondyke Building, Cromac Avenue, Gasworks Business Park, Lower Ormeau Road, Belfast BT7 2JA. 0845 302 0008; (pollution hotline; 0800 807 060);
e-mail: nieainfo@doeni.gov.uk www.ehsni.gov.uk

EARTHWATCH INSTITUTE (1971)

Earthwatch developed the innovative idea of engaging the general public into the scientific process by bringing together individual volunteers and scientists on field research projects, thereby providing an alternative means of funding, as well as a dedicated labour force for field scientists. Last year, more than 3,500 volunteers had worked on Earthwatch projects, which have grown to 140 projects in more than 50 countries around the world.
Contact: Earthwatch Institute (Europe), Mayfield House, 256 Banbury Road, Oxford OX2 7DE. 01864 318 838; e-mail: info@earthwatch.co.uk www.earthwatch.org/europe

EDWARD GREY INSTITUTE OF FIELD ORNITHOLOGY (1938)

The EGI takes its name from Edward Grey, first Viscount Grey of Fallodon, a life-long lover of birds and former Chancellor of the University of Oxford. The Institute now has a permanent research staff of 12-15 research students, five or six senior visitors and post-doctoral research workers. Field research is carried out mainly in Wytham Woods near Oxford and on the island of Skomer in West Wales. In addition there are laboratory facilities and aviary space for experimental work.
The Institute houses the Alexander Library, one of the largest collections of 20th Century material on birds in the world, and which is supported by the British Ornithologists Union which provides much of the material. It also houses the British Falconers Club library. The Library is open to members of the BOU and Oxford Ornithological Society; other bona fide ornithologists may use the library by prior arrangement.
Contact: Claire Harvey, PA to Professor Sheldon, The EGI, Department of Zoology, South Parks Road, Oxford OX1 3PS; +44(0)1865 271 275; Fax: +44(0)1865 271 168. e-mail: claire.harvey@zoo.ox.ac.uk www.zoo.ox.ac.uk/egi/

ENVIRONMENT AGENCY

A non-departmental body which aims to protect and improve the environment and to contribute towards the delivery of sustainable development through the integrated management of air, land and water. Functions include pollution prevention and control, waste minimisation, management of water resources, flood defence, improvement of salmon and freshwater fisheries, conservation of aquatic species, navigation and use of inland and coastal waters for recreation. Sponsored by the Department of the Environment, Transport and the Regions, MAFF and the Welsh Office.
Contact: Environment Agency, National Customer Contact Centre, PO Box 544, Rotherham S60 1BY. General enquiries; 08708 506 506 (Mon-Fri, 8am - 6pm); pollution hotline 0800 807 060; floodline 0845 988 1188; www.environment-agency.gov.uk e-mail: enquiries@environment-agency.gov.uk

EURING

EURING is the co-ordinating organisation for European bird-ringing schemes. It aims to promote and encourage:
• Scientific and administrative co-operation between national ringing schemes.
• Development and maintenance of high standards in bird ringing.
• Scientific studies of birds, in particular those based on marked individuals.
• The use of data from bird ringing for the management and conservation of birds.
These objectives are achieved mainly through co-operative projects, the organisation of meetings and the collection of data in the EURING Data Bank.
Contact: www.euring.org/

FARMING AND WILDLIFE ADVISORY GROUP (FWAG) (1969 - 2012)
An independent UK-registered charity led by farmers and supported by government and leading countryside organisations — now in administration with individual groups setting up.

FIELD STUDIES COUNCIL (1943)

Manages Centres where students from schools, universities and colleges, as well as individuals of all ages, can stay to study various aspects of the environment under expert guidance. Courses include many for birdwatchers, providing opportunities to study birdlife on coasts, estuaries, mountains and islands. Others demonstrate bird ringing. Research workers and naturalists wishing to use the records and resources are welcome. There are centres in England, Scotland, Wales and Northern Ireland — see website for contacts and courses available.
Contact: Field Studies Council, Preston Montford, Montford Bridge, Shrewsbury SY4 1HW. 0845 345 4071; 01743 852 100; www.field-studies-council.org e-mail: enquiries@field-studies-council.org

FIELDFARE TRUST
Fieldfare works with people with disabilities and countryside managers to improve access to the countryside for everyone. It provides advice and training services to countryside management teams, supported by its research into national standards for accessibility under the BT Countryside for All Project. For members of the public, it runs projects which can enable them to take action locally, provide information on accessible places to visit and run events like the Fieldfare Kielder Challenge which encourages young people to get active in the countryside.
Contact: Fieldfare Trust, Volunteer House, 69 Crossgate, Cupar, Fife KY15 5AS. 01334 657 708; e-mail: info@fieldfare.org.uk www.fieldfare.org.uk

FORESTRY COMMISSION OF GREAT BRITAIN (1919)
The government department responsible for the protection and expansion of Britain's forests and woodlands, it runs from national offices in England, Wales and Scotland, working to targets set by Commissioners and Ministers in each of the three countries. Its objectives are to protect Britain's forests and resources, conserve and improve the biodiversity, landscape and cultural heritage of forests and woodlands, develop opportunities for woodland recreation and increase public understanding and community participation in forestry.
Contact: Forestry Commission England, England National Office, 620 Bristol Business Park, Coldharbour Lane, Bristol BS16 1EJ. 0117 906 6000: e-mail: fc.england@forestry.gsi.gov.uk

Forestry Commission Scotland, 231 Corstorphine Road, Edinburgh EH12 7AT. 0131 334 0303, (Fax) 0131 314 6152; e-mail: fscotland@forestry.gsi.gov.uk

Forestry Commission Wales, Welsh Assembly Government, Rhodfa Padarn, Llanbadarn Fawr, Aberystwyth, Ceredigion SY23 3UR. 0300 068 0300: e-mail: fcwenquiries@forestry.gsi.gov.uk

FRIENDS OF THE EARTH (1971; 100,000)
The largest international network of environmental groups in the world, represented in 68 countries. In the UK it has a unique network of campaigning local groups, working in 200 communities in England, Wales and Northern Ireland. It is largely funded by supporters with more than 90% of income coming from individual donations, the rest from special fundraising events, grants and trading.
Contact: Friends of the Earth, 26-28 Underwood Street, London, N1 7JQ. 020 7490 1555; e-mail: info@foe.co.uk www.foe.co.uk

GAME AND WILDLIFE CONSERVATION TRUST (formerly Game Conservancy Trust) (1933; 22,000)
A registered charity which researches the conservation of game and other wildlife in the British countryside. More than 60 scientists are engaged in detailed work on insects, pesticides, birds (30 species inc. raptors) mammals (inc. foxes), and habitats. The results are used to advise government, landowners, farmers and conservationists on practical management techniques which will benefit game species, their habitats, and wildlife. Each June the *Annual Review* lists about 50 papers published in the peer-reviewed scientific press.
Contact: Game & Wildlife Conservation Trust, Burgate Manor, Fordingbridge, Hampshire, SP6 1EF. 01425 652 381; (Fax) 01425 655 848; e-mail: info@gwct.org.uk www.gwct.org.uk

GAY BIRDERS CLUB (1994; 350+)
A voluntary society for lesbian, gay and bisexual birdwatchers, their friends and supporters, over the age of consent, in the UK and worldwide. The club has a network of regional contacts and organises day trips, weekends and longer events at notable birding locations in the UK and abroad; about 200+ events in a year. Members receive a quarterly newsletter Out Birding with details of all events. There is a Grand Get-Together every 18 months. Membership £12 waged and £5 unwaged.
Contact: Gay Birders Club, GeeBeeCee, BCM-Mono, London WC1N 3XX. e-mail: contact@gbc-online.org.uk www.gbc-online.org.uk

HAWK AND OWL TRUST (1969)
Registered charity dedicated to the conservation and appreciation of wild birds of prey and their habitats. Publishes a newsletter members' magazine, *Peregrine* and educational materials for all ages.

The Trust achieves its major aim of creating and enhancing nesting, roosting and feeding habitats for birds of prey through projects which involve practical research, creative conservation and education, both on its own reserves and in partnership with landowners, farmers and others. Members are invited to take part in fieldwork, population studies, surveys, etc. The Trust manages three main reserves: Sculthorpe Moor in Norfolk; Shapwick Moor on the Somerset Levels; and Fylingdales Moor conservation area in North Yorkshire. Its Sculthorpe reserve near Fakenham, Norfolk and National Conservation and Education Centre at Chiltern Open Air Museum near Chalfont St Giles, Buckinghamshire, offers schools and other groups cross-curricular environmental activities

Contact: Hawk and Owl Trust, PO Box 100400, Bishops Lydeard, Taunton TA4 2WX3WH. Tel: 0844 984 2824; e-mail: enquiries@hawkandowl.org www.hawkandowl.org

HELPWILDLIFE.CO.UK (2005)

HelpWildlife.co.uk is maintained by a very small team of people involved in British wildlife rehabilitation to fully utilise the internet to help with wildlife issues. The site aims to provide informed, unbiased advice about caring for sick or injured birds and animals. Volunteers trawl the internet for details of those who might be able to help so that assistance can be offered quickly in an emergency. Visitors to the site are invited to provide feedback on the listings published to ensure they are kept as up to date as possible. E-mail: info@helpwildlife.co.uk

INTERNATIONAL CENTRE FOR BIRDS OF PREY (1967)

The ICBP works for the conservation of birds of prey and their habitats through public education, captive breeding, treatment and rehabilitation of wild injured birds of prey. Education is on-going to visitors and specific groups and parties, from first schools to universities,

offering off-site lectures and teaching. The Centre continues its captive breeding aims; to research species; maintain the Collection and provide birds for demonstrations.

The Centre also works with many other groups and facilities to continue to support worldwide field research projects and international conservation programmes. It accepts, treats and rehabilitates injured wild birds of prey. Open all year 10.30am-5.30pm (or dusk if earlier). Closed Christmas and Boxing Day.

Contact: International Birds of Prey Centre, Boulsdon House, Newent, Gloucestershire, GL18 1JJ. 01531 820 286 or 01531 821 581; e-mail: jpj@icbp.org www.icbp.org

IRISH RARE BIRDS COMMITTEE (1985)

Assesses records of species of rare occurrence in the Republic of Ireland. Details of records accepted and rejected are incorporated in the *Irish Bird Report*, published annually in *Irish Birds*. In the case of rarities trapped for ringing, ringers in the Republic of Ireland are required to send their schedules initially to the National Parks and Wildlife Service, 51 St Stephen's Green, Dublin 2. A copy is then taken before the schedules are sent to the British Trust for Ornithology.

Contact: Secretary: Kieran Fahy, Silveracre, Yoletown, Tacumshin, County Wexford. e-mail: secretary@irbc.ie www.irbc.ie

JOINT NATURE CONSERVATION COMMITTEE (1990)

A committee of the three country agencies (English Nature, Scottish Natural Heritage and the Countryside Council for Wales), together with independent members and representatives from Northern Ireland and the Countryside Agency. Supported by specialist staff, its statutory responsibilities include the establishment of common standards for monitoring; the analysis of information and research; advising Ministers on the development and implementation of policies for or affecting nature conservation; and the undertaking and commissioning of research relevant to these functions. JNCC additionally has the UK responsibility for relevant European and wider international matters. The Species Team, located at the HQ address is responsible for terrestrial bird conservation.

Contact: Joint Nature Conservation Committee, Monkstone House, City Road, Peterborough PE1 1JY. 01733 562 626; e-mail: comment@jncc.gov.uk www.jncc.gov.uk

LINNEAN SOCIETY OF LONDON (1788: 2,000)

Named after Carl Linnaeus, the 18th Century Swedish biologist, who created the modern system of scientific biological nomenclature, the Society promotes all aspects of pure and applied biology. It houses Linnaeus' collection of plants, insects and fishes, library and correspondence. The Society has a major reference library of some 100,000 volumes. Publishes the *Biological*, *Botanical* and *Zoological* Journals, and the *Synopses of the British Fauna*.

Contact: Linnean Society of London, Burlington House, Piccadilly, London W1J 0BF. 020 7434 4479; e-mail: info@linnean.org www.linnean.org

MAMMAL SOCIETY (1954; 2,500)

The Mammal Society is the only organisation solely dedicated to the study and conservation of all British mammals. It seeks to raise awareness of mammal ecology and conservation needs, to survey British mammals and their habitats to identify the

threats they face and to promote mammal studies in the UK and overseas.

Contact: The Mammal Society, 3 The Carronades, New Road, Southampton SO14 0AA. 0238 0237 874;

NATIONAL ORGANISATIONS

e-mail: enquiries@mammal.org.uk
www.mammal.org.uk

MARINE CONSERVATION SOCIETY (1983)

MCS is the UK charity that campaigns for clean seas and beaches around the British coastline, sustainable fisheries, and protection for all marine life. MCS is consulted on a wide range of marine issues and provides advice primarily to government, but also to industry, on topics ranging from offshore wind, oil and gas, to marine strategies and fisheries reform. It provides advice to ensure that further action is taken to conserve our seas and reduce the effect of marine activities on marine habitats and species. It has an extensive programme for volunteers, ranging from fund-raising and an annual clean-up of UK beaches, to surveys of species such as basking shark.
Contact: Marine Conservation Society, Unit 3 Wolf Business Park, Alton Road, Ross-on-Wye, Herefordshire HR9 5NB. 01989 566 017
www.mcsuk.org

NATIONAL TRUST (1895; 3.5 million)

Charity that works for the preservation of places of historic interest or natural beauty in England, Wales and Northern Ireland. It relies on 3.5 million members, 49,000 volunteers, 500,000 school children and millions of visitors, donors and supporters. The Trust protects and opens to the public more than 300 historic houses and gardens, 49 industrial monuments and mills, plus more than 617,500 acres of land and 700 miles of coast. About 10% of SSSIs and ASSIs in England, Wales and Northern Ireland are wholly or partially owned by the Trust, as are 63 NNRs, 33% of Ramsar sites and 45% of SPAs. Central Office: Heelis, Kemble Drive, Swindon, Wiltshire SN2 2NA. Tel: 01793 817 400; (Fax) 01793 817 401.
Contact: National Trust, PO Box 39, Warrington, WA5 7WD. 0844 800 1895;
e-mail: enquiries@thenationaltrust.org.uk

NATIONAL TRUST FOR SCOTLAND (1931; 310,000)

The conservation charity that protects and promotes Scotland's natural and cultural heritage for present and future generations to enjoy. Its 128 properties open to the public are described in its annual *Scotland For You* guide.
Contact: National Trust for Scotland, Hermiston Quay, 5 Cultins Road, Edinburgh, EH11 4DF. 0844 493 2100; e-mail: information@nts.org.uk www.nts.org.uk

NATURAL ENGLAND

Natural England has been formed by bringing together English Nature, the landscape, access and recreation elements of the Countryside Agency and the environmental land management functions of the Rural Development Service. Natural England is working towards the delivery of four strategic outcomes: 1) A healthy natural environment through conservation and enhancement. 2) Encouraging more people to enjoy, understand and act to improve the natural environment. 3) Ensure the use and management of the natural environment is more sustainable. 4) A secure environmental future.

Contact: Natural England, Head Office – Foundry House, 3 Millsands, Riverside Exchange, Sheffield S3 8NH. 0845 600 3078;
e-mail: enquiries@naturalengland.org.uk
www.naturalengland.org.uk

NATURAL HISTORY MUSEUM AT TRING (1937)

Founded by Lord Rothschild, the Museum displays British and exotic birds (1,500 species) including many rarities and extinct species. Galleries open all year except Dec 24-26. Adjacent to the Bird Group of the Natural History Museum - with over a million specimens and an extensive ornithological library, an internationally important centre for bird research.
Contact: The Natural History Museum at Tring, Akeman Street, Tring, Herts HP23 6AP. 020 7942 6171;
e-mail: tring-enquiries@nhm.ac.uk
www.nhm.ac.uk/tring

NATURAL RESOURCES WALES

Natural Resources Wales brings together the work of the Countryside Council for Wales, Environment Agency Wales and Forestry Commission Wales, as well as some functions of Welsh Government. Its purpose is to ensure that the natural resources of Wales are sustainably maintained, enhanced and used, now and in the future.
Contact: Natural Resources Wales, Tŷ Cambria, 29 Newport Road, Cardiff CF24 0TP. 0300 065 3000 (Mon-Fri, 8am - 6pm). Incident hotline: 0800 807060 (Freephone, 24 hour service). Floodline: 0845 988 1188 (24 hour service)
E-mail: enquiries@naturalresourceswales.gov.uk
www.naturalresourceswales.gov.uk

NATURE PHOTOGRAPHERS' PORTFOLIO (1944; 71)

A society for photographers of wildlife, especially birds. Circulates postal portfolios of prints and transparencies, and an on-line folio.
Contact: A Winspear-Cundall, Hon Secretary, Nature Photographers' Portfolio, 8 Gig Bridge Lane, Pershore, Worcs WR10 1NH. 01386 552 103;
e-mail: arthurcundall@hotmail.co.uk
www.nature-photographers-portfolio.co.uk

NORTHERN IRELAND BIRDWATCHERS' ASSOCIATION (1991; 120)

The NIBA Records Committee, established in 1997, has full responsibility for the assessment of records in N Ireland. NIBA also publishes the Northern Ireland Bird Report and is responsible for Flightline, a local rate telephone hotline for rare bird sightings.
Contact: The Membership Secretary, Northern Ireland Birdwatchers' Assoc, 9 Ballymacash Rd, Lisburn, Co. Antrim, N Ireland BT28 3DX . 01247 467 408;
http://nibirds.blogspot.com

NORTHERN IRELAND ORNITHOLOGISTS' CLUB (1965; 150)

Formed to focus the interests of active birdwatchers in Northern Ireland, it operates Tree Sparrow and Barn Owl nestbox schemes and a winter feeding programme for Yellowhammers. Has a regular programme of lectures and field trips for members and organises a high quality annual photographic

competition. Publishes *The Harrier* quarterly.
Contact: The Honorary Secretary, C Gillespie, Northern Ireland Ornithologists Club, 4 Demesne Gate, Saintfield, Co. Down, BT24 7BE. 02897 519 371; e-mail: carolgillespie@btinternet.com; www.nioc.co.uk

NORTH SEA BIRD CLUB (1979; 200)
The Club aims to: provide a recreational pursuit for people employed offshore; obtain, collate and analyse observations of all birds seen offshore; produce reports of observations, including an annual report; promote the collection of data on other wildlife offshore. Currently it holds in excess of 100,000 records of birds, cetaceans and insects reported since 1979.
Contact: The North Sea Bird Club, Ocean Laboratory and Culterty Field Station, University of Aberdeen, Newburgh, Aberdeenshire AB41 6AA. 01224 274 428; e-mail: nsbc@abdn.ac.uk www.abdn.ac.uk/nsbc

PEOPLE'S DISPENSARY FOR SICK ANIMALS (1917)
Provides free veterinary treatment for sick and injured animals whose owners qualify for this charitable service.
Contact: PDSA, Whitechapel Way, Priorslee, Telford, Shropshire TF2 9PQ. 01952 290 999; e-mail: pr@pdsa.org.uk www.pdsa.org.uk

POND CONSERVATION

Pond Conservation is dedicated to creating and protecting ponds and the wildlife they support. It carries out research, surveys and practical conservation, working in partnership with others. It also works to protect the wildlife of other freshwaters. Key projects include: the Million Ponds Project; Garden ponds survey; Pond Habitat Action Plan, in conjunction with the Environment Agency.
Contact: Pond Conservation, 01865 483 249; e-mail: info@pondconservation.org.uk www.pondconservation.org.uk

RAPTOR FOUNDATION (1989)
Involved in the care of wild, disabled birds of prey, as well as raptors rescued from breeders. The foundation researches raptor ailments and assists veterinary schools. A full 24 hour rescue service is available for injured raptors and owls and the centre assists in breed-and-release schemes to rebuild populations across Europe. Centre is open to the public (200 birds of 40 different species on display) 10am to 5pm each day apart from Jan 1 and Dec 25/26.
Contact: The Raptor Foundation, The Heath, St Ives Road, Woodhurst, Cambs PE28 3BT. 01487 741 140; e-mail: info@raptorfoundation.org.uk www.raptorfoundation.org.uk

RAPTOR RESCUE (1978)
Since inauguration, Raptor Rescue has evolved into one of the UK's foremost organisations dedicated to ensuring all sick and injured birds of prey are cared for by suitably qualified people, and wherever possible, released back into the wild. Facilities include secluded aviaries, rehabilitation aviaries/flights, and foster birds for rearing young to avoid imprinting.
Contact: Raptor Rescue, Bird of Prey Rehabilitation, 0870 241 0609; www.raptorrescue.org.uk e-mail: secretary@raptorrescue.org.uk

RARE BREEDING BIRDS PANEL (1973; 7)
An independent body funded by the JNCC and RSPB, it collects all information on rare breeding birds in the United Kingdom, so that changes in status can be monitored as an aid to conservation and stored for posterity. Special forms are used (obtainable from the website) and records should be submitted via the county and regional recorders. Since 1996 the Panel also monitors breeding by scarcer non-native species and seeks records of these in the same way. Annual report is published in *British Birds*. For details of species covered by the Panel see Log Charts and the websites.
Contact: The Secretary, Rare Breeding Birds Panel, The Old Orchard, Grange Road, North Berwick, East Lothian EH39 4QT. 01620 894 037; e-mail: secretary@rbbp.org.uk www.rbbp.org.uk

ROYAL AIR FORCE ORNITHOLOGICAL SOCIETY (1965; 250)
RAFOS organises regular field meetings for members, carries out ornithological census work on MoD properties and mounts major expeditions annually to various UK and overseas locations. Publishes a Newsletter twice a year, a Journal annually, and reports on its expeditions and surveys.
Contact: General Secretary by e-mail: rafos_secretary@hotmail.com www.rafos.org.uk

ROYAL NAVAL BIRDWATCHING SOCIETY (1946; 250)
Covering all main ocean routes, the Society reports the positions and identity of seabirds and landbirds at sea by means of standard sea report forms. Maintains an extensive worldwide seabird database. Members are encouraged to photograph birds and a library of images is maintained. Publishes a Bulletin and an annual report entitled *The Sea Swallow*. The Simpson Scholarship provides assistance to embryonic ornithologists for studies regarding seabirds and landbirds at sea.
Contact: General Secretary, CPO Steve Copsey (temporary position) www.rnbws.org.uk

ROYAL PIGEON RACING ASSOCIATION (1897; 39,000)
Exists to promote the sport of pigeon racing and controls pigeon racing within the Association. Organises liberation sites, issues rings, calculates distances between liberation sites and home lofts, and assists in the return of strays. May be able to assist in identifying owners of ringed birds found.

Contact: Royal Pigeon Racing Association, The Reddings, Cheltenham, GL51 6RN. 01452 713 529; e-mail: gm@rpra.org www.rpra.org

ROYAL SOCIETY FOR THE PREVENTION OF CRUELTY TO ANIMALS (1824; 43,690)

In addition to its animal centres, the Society also runs a woodland study centre and nature reserve at Mallydams Wood in East Sussex, and specialist wildlife rehabilitation centres at West Hatch, Taunton, Somerset TA3 5RT (0870 0101 847), at Station Road, East Winch, King's Lynn, Norfolk PE32 1NR (0870 9061 420), and London Road, Stapeley, Nantwich, Cheshire CW5 7JW (not open to the public). Inspectors are contacted through their National Communication Centre, which can be reached via the Society's 24-hour national cruelty and advice line: 08705 555 999.
Contact: RSPCA Headquarters, Willberforce Way, Horsham, West Sussex RH13 9RS. 0300 1234 555; (Fax) 0303 123 0284. 24-hour cruelty and advice line: 0300 1234 999. www.rspca.org.uk

ROYAL SOCIETY FOR THE PROTECTION OF BIRDS (1899 1,000,000+)

UK Partner of BirdLife International, and Europe's largest voluntary wildlife conservation body. The RSPB, a registered charity, is governed by an elected body (see also RSPB Phoenix and RSPB Wildlife Explorers). Its work in the conservation of wild birds and habitats covers the acquisition and management of nature reserves; research and surveys; monitoring and responding to development proposals, land use practices and pollution which threaten wild birds and biodiversity; and the provision of an advisory service on wildlife law enforcement.

The RSPB currently manages 200 nature reserves in the UK, covering almost 130,00 hectares and home to 80% of Britain's rarest or most threatened bird species. The aim is to conserve a countrywide network of reserves with all examples of the main bird communities and with due regard to the conservation of plants and other animals. Current national projects include extensive work on agriculture, and conservation and campaigning for the conservation of the marine environment and to halt the illegal persecution of birds of prey. Increasingly, there is involvement with broader environmental concerns such as climate change and transport.
The RSPB's International Dept works closely with Birdlife International and its partners in other countries and is involved with numerous projects overseas, especially in Europe and Asia.
Contact: RSPB, The Lodge, Sandy, Beds SG19 2DL. Membership enquiries: 01767 693 680. Wildlife enquiries: 01767 693 690; www.rspb.org.uk e-mail: (firstname.name)@rspb.org.uk

Regional Offices:

ENGLAND
Eastern England, Stalham House, 65 Thorpe Road, Norwich NR1 1UD. 01603 661 662.
Covers: Beds, Cambs, Essex, Herts, Lincs, Norfolk, Suffolk.

London Office, RSPB London Office, 2nd Floor, 65 Petty France, London, SW1H 9EU. 0207 808 1240.

Midlands, 46 The Green, South Bar, Banbury, Oxfordshire, OX16 9AB. 01295 253 330.
Covers: Bucks, Derbys, Herefordshire, Leicestershire, Northants, Notts, Oxon, Rutland, Shropshire, Staffs, Warwickshire, West Midlands, Worcestershire.

Northern England, Denby Dale Office, Westleigh Mews, Wakefield Road, Denby Dale, Huddersfield, HD8 8QD. 01484 861 148.
Covers: Cheshire, Cleveland, Cumbria, East Riding of Yorkshire, Greater Manchester, Lancashire, Merseyside, Middlesbrough, North, South and West Yorkshire, North East and North Lincolnshire, Northumberland, Tyne and Wear.

South East, 2nd Floor, 42 Frederick Place, Brighton, East Sussex, BN1 4EA. 01273 775 333.
Covers: East Sussex, Hampshire, Isle of Wight, Kent, Surrey, West Berkshire, West Sussex.

South West, Keble House, Southernhay Gardens, Exeter EX1 1NT. 01392 432 691.
Covers: Bristol, Cornwall, Devon, Dorset, Somerset, Gloucs, Wiltshire.

SCOTLAND
Scotland Headquarters, Dunedin House, 25 Ravelston Terrace, Edinburgh, EH4 3TP. 0131 311 6500.
e-mail: rspb.scotland@rspb.org.uk

East Scotland, 10 Albyn Terrace, Aberdeen, Aberdeenshire, AB10 1YP. 01224 624 824.
Covers: Aberdeen, Aberdeenshire, Angus, Moray, Perth and Kinross.

North Scotland, Etive House, Beechwood Park, Inverness, IV2 3BW. 01463 715 000; e-mail: nsro@rspb.org.uk
Covers: Eilean Siar, Highland.

South and West Scotland, 10 Park Quadrant, Glasgow, G3 6BS. 0141 331 0993; e-mail: glasgow@rspb.org.uk
Covers: Argyll and Bute, Clackmannanshire, Dumfries and Galloway, East Ayrshire, East Lothian, East Dunbartonshire, East Renfrewshire, Midlothian, North Ayrshire, North Lanarkshire, Renfrewshire, Scottish borders, South Ayrshire, South Lanarkshire, Stirling, West Dunbartonshire, West Lothian.

WALES
RSPB Wales, Sutherland House, Castlebridge, Cowbridge Road East, Cardiff CF11 9AB. 029 2035 3000.

NORTHERN IRELAND
Northern Ireland Headquarters, Belvoir Park Forest, Belfast, BT8 7QT. 028 9049 1547.
Covers: County Antrim, County Armagh, County Down, County Fermanagh, County Londonderry, County Tyrone.

NATIONAL ORGANISATIONS

RSPB WILDLIFE EXPLORERS and RSPB PHOENIX (formerly YOC) (1965; 168,000)
Junior section of the RSPB. There are more than 100 groups run by 300 volunteers. Activities include projects, holidays, roadshows, competitions, and local events for children, families and teenagers. Phoenix members (13 years and over) receive *BirdLife* magazine every two months, plus *Wingbeat* — the only environmental magazine written by teenagers for teenagers — four times a year.
Contact: The Youth Manager, RSPB Youth and Education Dept, The Lodge, Sandy, Beds SG19 2DL. 01767 680 551; e-mail: explorers@rspb.org.uk and phoenix@rspb.org.uk www.rspb.org.uk/youth

SCOTTISH BIRDS RECORDS COMMITTEE (1984; 7 members, plus secretary)
Set up by the Scottish Ornithologists' Club to ensure that records of species not deemed rare enough to be considered by the British Birds Rarities Committee, but which are rare in Scotland, are fully assessed; also maintains the official list of Scottish birds.
Contact: Angus Hogg, Secretary, Scottish Birds Records Committee, 11 Kirkmichael Road, Crosshill, Maybole, Ayrshire KA19 7RJ. www.the-soc.org.uk e-mail: dcgos@globalnet.co.uk

SCOTTISH ORNITHOLOGISTS' CLUB (1936; 2,250)
The Club has 14 branches (see County Directory), each with a programme of winter meetings and field trips throughout the year. The SOC organises an annual weekend conference in the autumn and a joint SOC/BTO one-day birdwatchers' conference in spring. *Scottish Birds* is published quarterly and incorporates the *Scottish Bird News* and the scarce sightings journal *Birding Scotland*. The SOC is based in a large resource centre which offers panoramic views of Aberlady Bay and houses the George Waterston Library.
Contact: The Scottish Birdwatching Resource Centre, The SOC, Waterston House, Aberlady, East Lothian EH32 0PY. 01875 871 330; (Fax) 01875 871 035; e-mail: mail@the-soc.org.uk www.the-soc.org.uk

SCOTTISH NATURAL HERITAGE (1991)
SNH is the Scottish Executive's statutory advisor in respect to the conservation, enhancement, enjoyment, understanding and sustainable use of the natural heritage.
Contact: Scottish Natural Heritage, Great Glen House, Leachkin Road, Inverness IV3 8NW. 01463 725 000; e-mail: enquiries@snh.gov.uk www.snh.org.uk

SCOTTISH SOCIETY FOR THE PREVENTION OF CRUELTY TO ANIMALS (1839; 45,000 supporters)
Represents animal welfare interests to Government, local authorities and others. Educates young people to realise their responsibilities. Maintains an inspectorate to patrol and investigate and to advise owners about the welfare of animals and birds in their care. Maintains welfare centres, two of which include oiled bird cleaning centres. Bird species, including birds of prey, are rehabilitated and where possible released back into the wild.
Contact: Scottish SPCA, Braehead Mains, 603 Queensferry Road, Edinburgh EH4 6EA. 03000 999 999; (Fax) 0131 339 4777; www.scottishspca.org e-mail: enquiries@scottishspca.org

SCOTTISH WILDLIFE TRUST (1964; 35,000)
The Trust aims to re-establish: 'a network of healthy and resilient ecosystems supporting expanding communities of native species across large areas of Scotland's land, water and seas.' Its main activities focus on managing 123 wildlife reserves and undertaking practical conservation tasks; influencing and campaigning for better wildlife-related policy and action; inspiring people to enjoy and find out more about wildlife. Member of The Wildlife Trusts partnership and organises Scottish Wildlife Week. Publishes *Scottish Wildlife* three times a year.
Contact: Scottish Wildlife Trust, Harbourside House, 110 Commercial Street, Edinburgh EH6 6NF. 0131 312 7765; (Fax) 0131 312 8705; e-mail: enquiries@swt.org.uk www.swt.org.uk

SEABIRD GROUP (1966; 350)
Concerned with conservation issues affecting seabirds. Assists with co-ordination of census and monitoring work on breeding seabirds; has established and maintains the Seabird Colony Register in collaboration with the JNCC; organises regular conferences on seabird biology and conservation topics. Small grants available to assist with research and survey work on seabirds. Publishes the *Seabird Group Newsletter* every four months and the journal *Seabird* annually.
Contact: Linda Wilson, JNCC, Inverdee House, Baxter Street, Aberdeen, AB11 9QA; ww.seabirdgroup.org.uk e-mail: linda.wilson@jncc.gov.uk

SOCIETY FOR CONSERVATION IN AVICULTURE (1993)
The Society aims to promote and develop all species and varieties of birds kept by aviculturists, with special regard to threatened and endangered species both in the wild and in captivity. Officers play an active role in promoting responsible care and ownership of all birds. Members do not have to be bird keepers.
Contact: SCA, PO Box 208, Wirral CH29 9DD. Helpline: 0845 634 2193. www.thesca.org.uk

SOCIETY OF WILDLIFE ARTISTS (1964; 62 Members, 68 Associates)
Registered charity that seeks to generate an appreciation of the natural world through all forms of fine art. Annual exhibition held in Oct/Nov at the Mall Galleries, London. Through bursary schemes, the Society has been able to help young artists with awards of up to £1,000 towards travel, education or the cost of materials.
Contact: The Secretary, Society of Wildlife Artists, Federation of British Artists, 17 Carlton House Terrace, London SW1Y 5BD. 020 7930 6844; e-mail: info@mallgalleries.com www.swla.co.uk

NATIONAL ORGANISATIONS

SWAN SANCTUARY (2005)

Founded by Dorothy Beeson BEM, this registered charity operates nationally. Has a fully equipped swan hospital. New site has several nursing ponds and a four acre rehabilitation lake where around 4,000 swans and the same number of other forms of wildlife are treated. 24-hour service operated, with volunteer rescuers on hand to recover victims of oil spills, vandalism etc. **Contact:** The Swan Sanctuary, Felix Lane, Shepperton, Middlesex TW17 8NN. Emergency number: 01932 240 790; www.swanuk.org.uk e-mail: swans@swanuk. org.uk

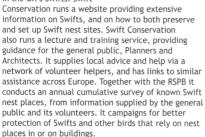

SWIFT CONSERVATION (2009)

An advice service which aims to reverse the decline in the UK's Swifts. Swift Conservation runs a website providing extensive information on Swifts, and on how to both preserve and set up Swift nest sites. Swift Conservation also runs a lecture and training service, providing guidance for the general public, Planners and Architects. It supplies local advice and help via a network of volunteer helpers, and has links to similar assistance across Europe. Together with the RSPB it conducts an annual cumulative survey of known Swift nest places, from information supplied by the general public and its volunteers. It campaigns for better protection of Swifts and other birds that rely on nest places in or on buildings.
Contact: Swift Conservation, 28 Yale Court, Honeybourne Road, London NW6 1JG, 020 7794 2098; e-mail@swift-conservation.org www.swift-conservation.org

UK400 CLUB (1981)

Serves to monitor the nation's leading twitchers and their life lists, and to keep under review contentious species occurrences. Publishes a bi-monthly magazine *Rare Birds*. Membership open to all.
Contact: LGR Evans, UK400 Club, 8 Sandycroft Road, Little Chalfont, Amersham, Bucks HP6 6QL. 01494 763 010; e-mail: LGREUK400@aol.com www.uk400clubonline.co.uk

WADER STUDY GROUP (1970; 600)

An association of wader enthusiasts, both amateur and professional, from all parts of the world, the Group aims to maintain contact between them, help organise co-operative studies, and provide a vehicle for the exchange of information. Publishes the *Wader Study Group Bulletin* three times a year and holds annual meetings throughout Europe.
Contact: The General Secretary, International Wader Study Group, The British Trust for Ornithology, The Nunnery, Thetford, Norfolk IP24 2PU. www.waderstudygroup.org

WELSH KITE TRUST (1996; 1,200)

A registered charity that undertakes the conservation and annual monitoring of Red Kites in Wales. It attempts to locate all the breeding birds, to compile data on population growth, productivity, range expansion etc. The Trust liaises with landowners, acts as consultant on planning issues and with regard to filming and photography, and represents Welsh interests on the UK Kite Steering Group. Provides a limited rescue service for injured kites and eggs or chicks at risk of desertion or starvation. Publishes a newsletter *Boda Wennol* twice a year, sent free to subscribing Friends of the Welsh Kite and to all landowners with nesting kites.
Contact: Tony Cross, Project Officer, Welsh Kite Trust, Samaria, Nantmel, Llandrindod Wells, Powys LD1 6EN. 01597 825 981; www.welshkitetrust.org; e-mail: info@welshkitetrust.org

WELSH ORNITHOLOGICAL SOCIETY (1988; 250)

Promotes the study, conservation and enjoyment of birds throughout Wales. Runs the Welsh Records Panel which adjudicates records of scarce species in Wales. Publishes the journal *Birds In Wales* and organises an annual conference.
Contact: Membership details from Welsh Ornithological Society, Alan Williams, Treasurer/Membership Secretary; e-mail: treasurer@birdsinwales.org.uk www.birdsinwales.org.uk

WETLAND TRUST

Set up to encourage conservation of wetlands and develop study of migratory birds, and to foster international relations in these fields. Destinations for recent expeditions inc. Brazil, Senegal, The Gambia, Guinea-Bissau, Nigeria, Kuwait, Thailand, Greece and Jordan. Large numbers of birds are ringed each year in Sussex and applications are invited from individuals to train in bird ringing or extend their experience.
Contact: Phil Jones, Wetland Trust, Elms Farm, Pett Lane, Icklesham, Winchelsea, E Sussex TN36 4AH. 01797 226374; e-mail: phil@wetlandtrust.org

WILDFOWL & WETLANDS TRUST (1946; 130,000 members)

Founded by Sir Peter Scott to conserve wetlands and their biodiversity, WWT has nine centres (see below). The centres are nationally, or internationally, important for wintering wildfowl. Programmes of walks and talks are available for visitors, and resources and programmes are provided for school groups. Centres, except Caerlaverock and Welney, have wildfowl from around the world, inc. endangered species. Research Department works on population dynamics, species management plans and wetland ecology. The Wetland Advisory Service (WAS) undertakes contracts,

NATIONAL ORGANISATIONS

and Wetland Link International promotes the role of wetland centres for education and public awareness.
Contact: Wildfowl and Wetlands Trust, Slimbridge, Glos, GL2 7BT. 01453 891 900; (Fax) 01453 890 827; e-mail: enquiries@wwt.org.uk www.wwt.org.uk

CENTRES:
WWT Arundel Wetland Centre, Mill Road, Arundel, Sussex BN18 9PB. 01903 883 355; (Fax) 01903 884834; e-mail: info.arundel@wwt.org.uk

WWT Caerlaverock Wetland Centre, Eastpark Farm, Caerlaverock, Dumfriesshire, Scotland DG1 4RS. 01387 770 200 (Fax) 01387 770 539; e-mail: info.caerlaverock@wwt.org.uk

WWT Castle Espie Wetland Centre, 78 Ballydrain Road, Comber, Co Down, N Ireland BT23 6EA. 028 9187 4146 (Fax) 028 9187 3857; e-mail: info.castleespie@wwt.org.uk

WWT London Wetland Centre, Queen Elizabeth's Walk, Barnes, London SW13 9WT. 020 8409 4400 (Fax) 020 8409 4401; e-mail: info.london@wwt.org.uk

WWT Martin Mere Wetland Centre, Fish Lane, Burscough, Lancashire L40 0TA. 01704 895 181 (Fax) 01704 892 343; e-mail: info.martinmere@wwt.org.uk

WWT National Wetland Centre Wales, Llwynhendy, Llanelli, Carmarthenshire SA14 9SH. 01554 741 087; (Fax) 01554 744 101; e-mail: info.llanelli@wwt.org.uk

WWT Slimbridge Wetland Centre, Slimbridge, Gloucestershire GL2 7BT. 01453 891 900; (Fax) 01453 890 827; e-mail: info.slimbridge@wwt.org.uk

WWT Washington Wetland Centre, Pattinson, Washington, Tyne and Wear NE38 8LE. 0191 416 5454; e-mail: info.washington@wwt.org.uk

WWT Welney Wetland Centre, Hundred Foot Bank, Welney, Nr. Wisbech, PE14 9TN. 01353 860 711; (Fax) 01353 863 524; e-mail: info.welney@wwt.org.uk

WILDLIFE SOUND RECORDING SOCIETY (1968; 327)
Works closely with the Wildlife Section of the National Sound Archive. Members carry out recording work for scientific purposes as well as for pleasure. A field weekend is held each spring, and members organise meetings locally. Four CD sound magazines of members' recordings are produced for members each year, and a journal, *Wildlife Sound*, is published twice a year.
Contact: Hon Membership Secretary, WSRS, Wildlife Sound Recording Society; www.wildlife-sound.org/ e-mail: enquiries@wildlife-sound.org

WILDLIFE TRUSTS (1995; 800,000)
Founded in 1912 and now the largest UK charity exclusively dedicated to conserving all habitats and species, with a membership of more than 800,000 people including 108,000 junior members in 47 individual county trusts.

Collectively, they manage more than 2,200 nature reserves spanning over 80,000 hectares. The Wildlife Trusts also lobby for better protection of the UK's natural heritage and are dedicated to protecting wildlife for the future. Members receive *Natural World* magazine three times a year.
Contact: The Wildlife Trusts, The Kiln, Waterside, Mather Road, Newark NG24 1WT. 01636 677 711; (Fax) 01636 670 001; e-mail: enquiry@wildlifetrusts.org www.wildlifetrusts.org

WILDLIFE WATCH (1977; 108.000)
The junior branch of The Wildlife Trusts. It supports 1,500 registered volunteer leaders running Watch groups across the UK. Publishes *Watchword* and *Wildlife Extra* for children, and activity books for adults working with young people.
Contact: Wildlife Watch, The Wildlife Trusts, The Kiln, Waterside, Mather Road, Newark NG24 1WT. 01636 677 711; (Fax) 01636 670 001; e-mail: watch@wildlifetrusts.org www.wildlifewatch.org.uk

WWF-UK (1961)
WWF is the world's largest independent conservation organisation, comprising 27 national organisations. It works to conserve and species, protect endangered spaces, and address global threats to nature by seeking long-term solutions with people in government and industry, education and civil society. Publishes *WWF News* (quarterly magazine)

Contact: WWF-UK (World Wide Fund for Nature), Panda House, Weyside Park, Catteshall Lane, Godalming, Surrey GU7 1XR. 01483 426 444; (Fax) 01483 426 409; www.wwf.org.uk

ZOOLOGICAL PHOTOGRAPHIC CLUB (1899)
Circulates black and white and colour prints of zoological interest via a series of postal portfolios.
Contact: Martin B Withers, Hon Secretary, Zoological Photographic Club, 93 Cross Lane, Mountsorrel, Loughborough, Leics LE12 7BX. 0116 229 6080.

ZOOLOGICAL SOCIETY OF LONDON (1826)
Carries out research, organises symposia and holds scientific meetings. Manages the Zoological Gardens in Regent's Park (first opened in 1828) and Whipsnade Wild Animal Park near Dunstable, Beds, each with extensive collections of birds. The Society's library has a large collection of ornithological books and journals. Publications include the *Journal of Zoology, Animal Conservation, Conservation Biology* book series, *The Symposia* and *The International Zoo Yearbook*.
Contact: Zoological Society of London, Regent's Park, London, NW1 4RY. 020 7722 3333; www.zsl.org

NATIONAL PROJECTS

National ornithological projects depend for their success on the active participation of amateur birdwatchers. In return they provide birdwatchers with an excellent opportunity to contribute in a positive and worthwhile way to the scientific study of birds and their habitats, which is the vital basis of all conservation programmes. The following entries provide a description of each particular project and a note of whom to contact for further information (full address details of project organisers are in the previous section).

BIG GARDEN BIRDWATCH
An RSPB Survey
The Big Garden Birdwatch has grown into fun for all the family. All you need to do is count the birds in your garden or a local park for one hour over the weekend of 25-26 January 2014 then tell us what you see.
Contact: RSPB, www.rspb.org.uk

BIRD CONSERVATION TARGETING PROJECT
An RSPB survey
The project has been developed to target management and resources towards important sites for scarce and declining farmland and woodland birds. Records are brought together from a wide range of sources, including individual birdwatchers, county bird clubs and national surveys.
The project produces distribution maps which are already being used to guide the spending of hundreds of millions of pounds to benefit birds through agri-environment and woodland grant schemes, and influencing woodland management to benefit birds on publicly owned woodland. The targeting maps help to ensure that government grant schemes are allocated to put the right conservation measures in the right places
Contact: RSPB, www.rspb.org.uk

BIRDTRACK
Organised by BTO on behalf of BTO, RSPB, BirdWatch Ireland and WOS
BirdTrack is a free, online bird recording system for birdwatchers to store and manage bird records from anywhere in Britain and Ireland. The idea is simple. Make a note of the birds seen or heard at each site visited, and then enter your observations on an easy-to-use web page (www. birdtrack.net). There's also a free App for Android and iPhone smartphones through which you can log your sightings whilst you're in the field and upload them at the click of a button. Exciting real-time outputs are generated by BirdTrack, including species reporting-rate graphs and animated maps of sightings, all freely-available online. The data collected are used by researchers to investigate migration movements and the distribution of scarce birds, and to support species conservation at local, national and international scales.
Contact: Nick Moran, BTO.
E-mail: birdtrack@bto.org

BREEDING BIRD SURVEY
Supported by BTO, JNCC and RSPB
Started in 1994, the BBS is designed to keep track of the changes in populations of our common breeding birds. It is dependent on volunteer birdwatchers throughout the country who make two visits, about five hours in total, to survey the breeding birds in a 1x1km square. Survey squares are picked at random by computer to ensure that all habitats and regions are covered.
Since its inception it has been a tremendous success, with more than 3,000 squares covered and more than 200 species recorded each year.
Contact: Kate Risely, e-mail: bbs@bto.org, or your local BTO Regional Representative (see County Directory).

CONSTANT EFFORT SITES (CES) SCHEME
Funded by a partnership between BTO, JNCC, The National Parks & Wildlife Service (Ireland) and ringers themselves
The CES scheme, run since 1983, coordinates standardised summer ringing at over 120 sites across Britain and Ireland. This allows the BTO to monitor trends in the numbers of 25 scrub and woodland species, while simultaneously providing annual estimates of breeding success and survival rates of adult birds.
Information from CES complements demographic information collected by other BTO surveys and feeds into the BTO's Integrated Population Monitoring, highlighting the causes of changes in bird populations. Results are updated annually and published on-line as part of the BirdTrends Report (www.bto.org/BirdTrends).
Contact: Allison Kew, BTO ces@bto.org and www.bto.org/ces

NATIONAL PROJECTS

GARDEN BIRD FEEDING SURVEY
A BTO project
The Garden Bird Feeding Survey is the longest-running study of garden birds in Britain. Each year, approximately 250 householders record the numbers and variety of birds using food supplements and water that they have provided in their garden. Observations are made on a weekly basis from October to March inclusive. Gardens are selected by region and type; from city flats to suburban semis, rural houses to outlying farms.
Contact: Clare Simm, BTO.
E-mail: clare.simm@bto.org

BTO GARDEN BIRDWATCH
A BTO project
Started in January 1995, this project is a year-round survey that monitors the use that birds and other types of wildlife make of gardens. Approximately 15,000 participants from all over the UK and Ireland keep a weekly log of species using their gardens. The data collected are used to monitor regional, seasonal and year-to-year changes in the garden populations of our commoner birds, mammals, butterflies, reptiles and amphibians. To cover running costs there is an annual subscription of £17. Participants receive a quarterly magazine and all new joiners receive a garden bird book. Results and more information are available online: www.bto.org/gbw
Contact: Garden Ecology Team, BTO.
E-mail: gbw@bto.org

GARDEN WILDLIFE HEALTH
A joint scheme of Institute of Zoology, BTO, Froglife & RSPB
This project aims to monitor the health of, and identify disease threats to, British wildlife. The particular focus is on garden birds, amphibians, reptiles and hedgehogs. Members of the public are asked to submit reports of sick or dead wildlife and to submit samples for analysis.
Contact: Garden Wildlife Health line 0207-449-6685; E-mail gwh@zsl.org
www.gardenwildlife.org

GOOSE AND SWAN MONITORING
A WWT project
Geese and swans are a cornerstone of the Wildfowl and Wetland Trust's conservation work. During winter, geese and swans from Canada to central Russia undertake arduous migrations to reach their wintering grounds in the UK. In order to safeguard them WWT tracks how many individuals are in each population, where they are found, and the overall trend of the population (whether it is increasing, decreasing, or remaining stable). Other demographic measures — most importantly, productivity (how many young are born each year) and survival (or mortality) rates — help to understand the reasons behind any increase or decrease. To get information like this WWT use a number of techniques and tools, including counts and capture and marking. A large amount of this work is carried out by volunteer birdwatchers who give their time to assist with data collection.
Contact: e-mail:enquiries@wwt.org.uk
http://monitoring.wwt.org.uk

HERONRIES CENSUS
A BTO project
This survey, started in 1928, has been carried out under the auspices of the BTO since 1934 and represents the longest continuous series of population data for any European breeding bird (Grey Heron). Counts of apparently occupied nests are made at as many UK heronries as possible each year, to provide an index of current population levels.
Data from Scotland and Wales are relatively scanty, and more contributions from these countries would be especially welcomed. Herons may be hit hard during periods of severe weather and are vulnerable to pesticides and pollution. Currently, population levels are suffering from the recent cold winters. Little Egret and other incoming species of colonial waterbird such as Cattle Egret are now fully included, whether nesting with Grey Herons, or on their own. Counts of Cormorant nests at heronries are also encouraged.
Contact: John Marchant, BTO.
E-mail: herons@bto.org

IRISH WETLAND BIRD SURVEY (I-WeBS)
A joint project of BirdWatch Ireland, the National Parks & Wildlife Service of the Dept of Arts, Culture & the Gaeltacht, and WWT, and supported by the Heritage Council and WWF-UK.
The Irish Wetland Bird Survey (I-WeBS) is the scheme that monitors wintering waterbirds in Ireland. The survey runs from September to March each winter. Wetlands of all types and sizes are monitored, including estuaries, coastlines,

bays, rivers, turloughs, lakes, streams and flooded fields. Each winter, more than 350 people take part. These counters go out and count waterbirds at over 800 wetlands throughout the country. The counts are done once-monthly by skilled volunteers, as well as by professional staff of the National Parks and Wildlife Service and BirdWatch Ireland.

Contact: Helen, I-WeBS Office, BirdWatch Ireland, 353 (0)1 281 9878; www.birdwatchireland.ie e-mail: hboland@birdwatchireland.ie

NATIONAL BEACHED BIRD SURVEY
An RSPB project
The results of the annual survey are used in conjunction with those from other European countries and aim to contribute to international monitoring efforts to document trends in chronic marine oil pollution and to promote adequate methods of controlling illegal oil discharge to help reduce seabird mortality.

Contact: Sabine Schmitt, Senior Research Assistant; E-mail: sabine.schmitt@rspb.org.uk

NEST BOX CHALLENGE
A BTO project
NBC is an on-line survey which aims to monitor the breeding success of birds in Britain's green spaces. Participants are asked to register one or more nests, or nest boxes, in their garden or local green space, monitoring their progress via regular nest inspections and recording the number of eggs and/or chicks present at each visit. Records of unused boxes are also valuable as they can be used to determine next box occupancy rates. Anyone who has a nest box or nest in their garden or local park can take part.

Contact: Hazel Evans, BTO. E-mail: nbc@bto.org and www.bto.org/nbc

NEST RECORD SCHEME
A BTO Project carried out with funding from the JNCC.
The scheme monitors changes in the nesting success and the timing of breeding of Britain's bird species by gathering information on nests found anywhere in the country, from a Blackbird in a garden to an Oystercatcher on a Scottish loch. Participants locate nests and monitor their progress over several visits, making counts of the number of eggs and/or chicks on each occasion and recording whether they are successful. Information from NRS complements demographic information collected by other BTO surveys and feeds into the BTO's Integrated Population Monitoring, highlighting the causes of changes in bird populations.

More than 40,000 nest records are submitted to the BTO each year by volunteer surveyors and the results are updated annually and published on-line as part of the BirdTrends Report (www. bto.org/BirdTrends). Guidance on how to become a BTO nest recorder, including best practice guidelines on minimising disturbance while visiting nests, is available online. A free starter pack is available on request.

Contact: Carl Barimore, BTO E-mail: nrs@bto.org and www.bto.org/nrs

RAPTOR AND OWL RESEARCH REGISTER
A BTO project
The Register has helped considerably over the past 30 years in encouraging and guiding research, and in the co-ordination of projects. There are currently almost 500 on-going projects. Barn Owls and Tawny Owls are currently receiving most attention. As to raptors, the most popular subjects are Kestrels, Buzzards, Sparrowhawks, Hobbies and Peregrines, with researchers showing increasing interest in Red Kites, and fewer large in-depth studies of Goshawks, Ospreys and harriers.

Contributing is a simple process and involves all raptor enthusiasts, whether it is to describe an amateur activity or professional study. The nature of research on record varies widely, and includes local pellet analyses, captive breeding and rehabilitation programmes, and national surveys of Peregrines, Buzzards and Golden Eagles. Birdwatchers, both in Britain and abroad, are encouraged to write for photocopies of cards relevant to the species or nature of their work. The effectiveness of the Register depends upon those running projects (however big or small) ensuring that their work is included.

Contact: David Glue, BTO.

RETRAPPING ADULTS FOR SURVIVAL (RAS) SCHEME
Funded by a partnership between BTO, JNCC, The National Parks & Wildlife Service (Ireland) and ringers themselves
The RAS scheme, started in 1998, gathers information on recaptures or re-sightings of adult birds. Ringers choose a target species, typically one that is poorly monitored by CES or general ringing, and aim to catch or re-sight as many of the breeding adults within their study area as possible on an annual basis. These data allow the BTO to monitor survival rates in adult birds, which helps us to understand the causes underlying changes in population sizes as part of the BTO's Integrated Population Monitoring framework.

Results are updated annually and published on-line as part of the BirdTrends Report (www.bto. org/BirdTrends).
Contact: Allison Kew, BTO. E-mail: ras@bto.org and www.bto.org/ras

RINGING SCHEME

Funded by a partnership between BTO, JNCC (on behalf of the Country Agencies), The National Parks & Wildlife Service (Ireland) and ringers themselves
Marking birds with individually numbered metal rings allows us to study survival, productivity and movements of British and Irish birds.
More than 2,700 trained and licensed ringers operate in Britain and Ireland, marking around one million birds annually. Training takes at least a year, but more often two or more years, depending on the aptitude of the trainee and the amount of ringing they do. A restricted permit can usually be obtained more quickly.
Anyone can contribute to the scheme by reporting any ringed or colour-marked birds they see or find. Reports can be submitted online at www. ring.ac or direct to BTO HQ. Anyone finding a ringed bird should note the ring number, species, when and where found and, if possible, what happened to it. If the bird is dead, it may also be possible to remove the ring, which should be kept in case there is a query. Anyone reporting a ringed bird will be sent details of where and when the bird was originally ringed. More info: www.bto. org/ringing/
The 'Demog Blog' for up to date news and stories is at: http://btoringing.blogspot.com
Contact: Jacquie Clark, BTO.
E-mail: Jacquie.clark@bto.org

TOOTH & CLAW

An independent project aimed at improving knowledge about Britain's predators and promoting discussion on the issues that surround them.
Tooth & Claw explores some of the complex issues surrounding our relationship with wild predators and questions how we really feel and why.
Through the web site, Tooth & Claw provides a meeting place between anecdotal input and scientific research and encourages constructive and imaginative dialogue on predator issues.
A series of case studies led by powerful imagery will provide insightful interviews and personal accounts of our lives alongside the likes of eagles and foxes with a glimpse into the future and the return of creatures we have not known for centuries.
Contact: Peter Cairns, Northshots, Ballintean, Glenfeshie, Kingussie, Scotland, PH21 1NX. (44) (0)1540 651 352;
e-mail: peter@wildmedia.org
www.wildmedia.org/our_projects_tooth_and_claw.asp

WATERWAYS BREEDING BIRD SURVEY

A BTO project, supported by the Environment Agency
WBBS uses transect methods like those of the Breeding Bird Survey to record bird populations along randomly chosen stretches of rivers and canals throughout the UK. Just two survey visits are needed during April-June. WBBS began in 1998 and in 2008 took over from the Waterways Bird Survey as the main monitoring scheme for birds in this habitat.
Contact: BTO Regional Representative (see County Directory) to enquire if any local stretches require coverage, otherwise John Marchant at BTO HQ. E-mail: wbbs@bto.org

WETLAND BIRD SURVEY (WeBS)

A joint scheme of BTO, RSPB, JNCC in association with WWT
The Wetland Bird Survey (WeBS) is the monitoring scheme for non-breeding waterbirds in the UK. The principal aims are:
1. To determine the population sizes of waterbirds.
2. To determine trends in numbers and distribution.
3. To identify important sites for waterbirds.
WeBS data are used to designate important waterbird sites and protect them against adverse development, for research into the causes of declines, for establishing conservation priorities and strategies and to formulate management plans for wetland sites and waterbirds.
Monthly, synchronised Core Counts are made at as many wetland sites as possible. Low Tide Counts are made on about 20 estuaries each winter to identify important feeding areas. Counts are relatively straightforward and can take from a few minutes up to a few hours, depending on the size of the site. The 3,000 participants receive an annual newsletter and a comprehensive annual report. New counters are always welcome.
Contact: General Webs Enquiries - Heidi Mellan - WeBS Office, BTO.
E-mail webs@bto.org   www.bto.org/webs

tooth&claw

INTERNATIONAL DIRECTORY

David Cromack

Black-chinned Honeyeater is part of a large family of birds found across Australia.

International organisations   306

Special interest organisations   312

BirdLife INTERNATIONAL

The BirdLife Partnership
BirdLife is a Partnership of non-governmental organisations (NGOs) with a special focus on conservation and birds. Each NGO Partner represents a unique geographic territory/country.

The BirdLife Network explained
Partners: Membership-based NGOs who represent BirdLife in their own territory. Vote holders and key implementing bodies for BirdLife's Strategy and Regional Programmes in their own territories.

Partners Designate: Membership-based NGOs who represent BirdLife in their own territory, in a transition stage to becoming full Partners. Non-vote holders.

Affiliates: Usually NGOs, but also individuals, foundations or governmental institutions when appropriate. Act as a BirdLife contact with the aim of developing into, or recruiting, a BirdLife Partner in their territory.

Secretariat: The co-ordinating and servicing body of BirdLife International.

SECRETARIAT ADDRESSES

BirdLife Global Office
BirdLife International
Wellbrook Court, Girton Road
Cambridge CB3 0NA
United Kingdom
Tel. +44 1 223 277 318
Fax +44 1 223 277 200
E-mail: birdlife@birdlife.org.uk
www.birdlife.org

Birdlife Africa Regional Office
c/o ICIPE Campus
Kasarani Road, off Thika Road
Nairobi, Kenya
Postal Address
PO Box 3502
00100 GPO
Nairobi, Kenya
Tel: +254 020 806 8314
Fax: +254 020 806 8315
E-mail: birdlife-africa@birdlife.org
www.birdlife.org

BirdLife Americas Regional Office
Birdlife International
Juan de Dios Martinez N35-76 y
Av Portugal
Quito Ecuador

Postal address
BirdLife International
Casilla 17-17-717
Quito, Equador
Tel. +593 (2) 2464 768
Fax +593 (2) 2469 838
E-mail: americas @birdlife.org
www.birdlife.org/regional/americas/
partnership

BirdLife Asia Regional Office
TM Suidobashi Building
4F, Misaki-cho 2-14-6
Chiyoda-ku
Tokyo 101-0061, Japan
Tel.+81 (3) 5213 0461
Fax.+81 (3) 5213 0422
E-mail: info@birdlife-asia.org
www.birdlife.org/regional/asia/
partnership

BirdLife Europe
Avenue de la Toison d'Or 67
(2nd floor), B-1060 Brussels
Belgium
Tel. +32 2280 08 30
Fax +32 2230 38 02
E-mail: europe@birdlife.org
www.birdlife.org/regional/europe/
partnership

BirdLife Middle East Regional Office
BirdLife International Middle East Division
P. O. Box 2295
Amman 11953
Jordan
Postal address
Amman
Khalda
Salameh El-Ma'aaytah Street
Building No 6. Jordan
Tel: +962 (6) 564-8173
Fax: +962 (6) 564-8172
E-mail: me@birdlife.org
www.birdlife.org/regional/
middle_east/partnership

BirdLife Pacific Regional Office
10 MacGregor Road
Suva, Fuji
Postal address
GPO Box 18332
Suva, Fuji
Tel: +679 331 3492
Fax: +679 331 9658
E-mail: don@birdlifepacific.org.fj

AFRICA

PARTNERS

Burkina Faso
La Fondation NATURAMA 01 B.P. 6133, Ouagadougou 01, Burkina Faso; e-mail: info@naturama.bf
www.naturama.bf

Ethiopia
Ethiopian Wildlife and Natural History Society, PO Box 13303, Addis Ababa, Pub: *Agazen; Ethiopian Wildl. and Nat. Hist. News. (& Annual Report); Ethiopian Wildl.*

and Nat. Hist. Soc. Quarterly News (WATCH); Walia (WATCH) (Ethiopia); www.ewnhs.org.ete-mail: ewnhs.ble@ethionet.et

Ghana
Ghana Wildlife Society, PO Box 13252, Accra, Pub: *Bongo News; NKO (The Parrots);*
e-mail: ghanawild@4u.co.gh
www.ghanawildlifesociety.org

Kenya
Nature Kenya, PO Box 44486, 00100 GPO. Nairobi. Pub: *Bulletin of the EANHS; Journal of East African Natural; Kenya Birds;* e-mail: office@naturekenya.org
www.naturekenya.org

INTERNATIONAL ORGANISATIONS

Seychelles
Nature Seychelles, Roche Caiman, Box 1310, Victoria, Mahe, Seychelles. Pub: *Zwazo - a BirdLife Seychelles Newsletter;* e-mail: nature@seychelles.net www.natureseychelles.org.

Sierra Leone
Conservation Society of Sierra Leone, PO Box 1292, Freetown. Pub: *Rockfowl Link, The.*
e-mail: cssl_03@yahoo.com http://conservationsl.org

South Africa
BirdLife South Africa, PO Box 515, Randburg, Johannesburg 2125, South Africa, Pub: *Newsletter of BirdLife South Africa; Ostrich;*
e-mail: secretary@birdlife.org.za www.birdlife.org.za

Tanzania
Wildlife Conservation Society of Tanzania, PO Box 70919, Dar es Salaam, Pub: *Miombo.*
e-mail: wcst@africaonline.co.tz
www.wcst@arusha.org

Tunisia
Association Les Amis des Oiseaux, Bureau des Projets, Ariana Centre – Bureau C 208/209, 2080 Ariana, Tunis. Pub: *Feuille de Liaison de l'AAO; Houbara, l'.*
e-mail: aao@topnet.tn www.aao.org.tn

Uganda
Nature Uganda, The EANHS, PO Box 27034, Kampala. Pub: *Naturalist - A Newsletter of the East Africa Nat. His. Soc;* e-mail: nature@natureuganda.org
www.natureuganda.org/

Zimbabwe
BirdLife Zimbabwe, P O Box RV 100, Runiville, Harare, Zimbabwe. Pub: *Babbler (WATCH) (Zimbabwe); Honeyguide;* e-mail: birds@zol.co.zw
www.birdlifezimbabwe.co.zw/

PARTNERS DESIGNATE

Botswana
Birdlife Botswana, PO Box 26691, Game City, Gaborone, Botswana; www.birdlifebotswana.org.bw
e-mail: blb@birdlifebotswana.org.bw

Burundi
Association Burundaise pour la Protection des Oiseaux, P O Box 7069, Bujumbura, Burundi;
e-mail: info@aboconservation.org
http://www.aboconservation.org/

Nigeria
Nigerian Conservation Foundation, PO Box 74638, Victoria Island, Lagos. Pub: *NCF Matters/News/ Newsletter; Nigerian Conservation Foundation Annual Report;* e-mail: info@ncf-nigeria

AFFILIATES

Cameroon
Cameroon Biodiversity Conservation Society (CBCS), PO Box 3055, Messa, Yaoundé; e-mail: cbcs_cam@yahoo.fr

Djibouti Nature
Djibouti (DN)
Djibouti Nature is the BirdLife Affiliate in Djibouti.
P. O. Box 3088-Djibouti
Djibouti; e-mail: naturedjibouti@gmail.com

Egypt
Nature Conservation Egypt, 10 Managem wa Mahager str, Mohandeseen, Giza.
e-mail: halabarakat2002@yahoo.com
https://sites.google.com/site/natconegy/
E-mail: Natureegypt@gmail.com

Ivory Coast
Cote d'Ivoire (SOS-FORETS), 22 BP 918 Abidjan 22.
E-mail: sosforets@hotmail.com

Liberia
Society for Conservation of Nature in Liberia, SCNL, Monrovia Zoo, Lakpazee, PO Box 2628, Monrovia.
E-mail: scnlliberia@yahoo.com www.scnlib.net

Madagascar
Asity Madagascar, Lot IIN 184 PH Ter Analamahitsy – 101 Antananarivio, Madagascar BP 1074;
e-mail: zicoma@birdlife-mada.org
http://asitymadagascar.org

Malawi
Wildlife & Environmental Socity of Malawi, Private Bag 578, Limbe. E-mail: wesm-hq@africa-online.net
www.wildlifemalawi.org

Rwanda
Association pour la Conservation de la Nature au Rwanda, P O Box 4290, Kigali, www.acnrwanda.org/
e-mail: conserverwanda@yahoo.fr

Zambia
Zambian Ornithological Society, Box 33944, Lusaka 10101, Pub: *Zambian Ornithological Society Newsletter;* e-mail: zos@zamnet.zm www.wattledcrane.com

---

AMERICAS

PARTNERS

Argentina
Aves Argentina (AOP), Matheu 1246/8, C1249AAB, Buenos Aires. Pub: *Hornero; Naturaleza & Conservacion; Nuestras Aves; Vuelo de Pajaro;*
e-mail: info@avesargentinas.org.ar
www.avesargentinas.org.ar

Belize
The Belize Audubon Society, PO Box 1001, 12 Fort Street, Belize City. Pub: *Belize Audubon Society Newsletter;* e-mail: base@btl.net
www.belizeaudubon.org

Bolivia
Asociacion Armonia, Avenidad Lomas de Arena 400, Casilla 3566, Santa Cruz. Pub: *Aves en Bolivia;*
e-mail: armonia@armonia-bo.org www.armonia-bo.org

Canada
Bird Studies Canada, PO Box/160, Port Rowan, Ontario N0E 1M0. Pub: *Bird Studies Canada - Annual Report; Birdwatch Canada;* e-mail: generalinfo@bsc-eoc.org
www.bsc-eoc.org

Canada
Nature Canada, 85 Albert Street,Suite 900, Ottawa, Ontario K1P 6A4. Pub: *Grass 'n Roots; IBA News Canada; Nature Canada; Nature Matters; Nature Watch News (CNF);* e-mail: info@naturecanada.ca
www.naturecanada.ca

INTERNATIONAL ORGANISATIONS

Ecuador
Aves & Conservación (Corporación Ornitológica del Ecuador, Pasaje Joaquin Tinajero E3-05 y Jorge Drom, Casilla 17-17-906, Quito; www.avesconservaccion.org e-mail: aves_direccion@avesconservacion.org

Falkland Islands
Falklands Conservation, PO Box 26, Stanley, Falklands or UK Office, 14 East Hatley, sandy, Bedfordshire SG19 3JA. UK. Pub: *Falklands Conservation.* e-mail: info@falklandsconservation.com www.falklandsconservation.com

Panama
Panama Audubon Society, Apartado 0843-03076, Balboa, Ancon. Pub: *Toucan;* e-mail: info@panamaaudubon.org www.panamaaudubon.org

United States
Audubon Society, 225 Varick Street, 7ᵗʰ Floor New York, NY, 10004. Pub: *American Birds; Audubon (USA); Audubon Field Notes; Audubon Bird Conservation Newsletter;* e-mail: international@audubon.org www.audubon.org

PARTNER DESIGNATE

Paraguay
Guyra Paraguay, Gaetano Martino 215 esq. Tte. Ross, Asunción. Pub: *Boletin Jara Kuera;* e-mail: guyra@guyra.org.py www.guyra.org.py/

AFFILIATES

Bahamas
Bahamas National Trust, PO Box 4105, Nassau. Pub: *Bahamas Naturalist; Currents; Grand Bahama Update.* e-mail: bnt@bnt.bs www.bnt.bs

Brazil
SAVE Brasil
Rua Fernão Dias, 219 conj 2 Pinheiros, São Paulo SP, Brasil 05427-010; http://www.savebrasil.org.br

Chile
Comite Nacional Pro defensa de la Flora y Fauna (CODEFF), Ernesto Reyes 035, Providencia, Santiago 21. Pub: *Boletin Chileno de Ornitologia; Boletin Informativo (WATCH)* (Chile). e-mail: administra@codeff.cl www.codeff.cl

Cuba
Centro Nacional de Áreas Protegidas (CNAP). Calle 18 a, No 1441, e/ 41 y 47, Playa, Ciudad Habana, Cuba. e-mail: cnap@snap.cu www.snap.co.cu/

Dominican Republic
Grupo Jaragua (GJI), Calle El Vergel No 33 Ensanche, El Vergel, Santo Domingo. E-mail: jaragua@tricom.net www.grupojaragua.org.do

El Salvador
SalvaNATURA, 33 Avenida Sur #640, Colonia Flor Blanca, San Salvador. e-mail: info@salvanatura.org www.salvanatura.org

Mexico
Pronatura, Chiapas, A.C. es: Calle Pedro Moreno # 1 esq. Benito Juárez, Barrio Santa Lucia C.P. 29200, San Cristobal de las Casas, Chiapas, México e-mail: pronatura@pronatura.org.mx www.pronatura.org.mx

Puerto Rico (to USA)
Sociedad Ornitológica Puertorriqueña, Inc. (SOPI), SOPI PO Box 195166, San Juan, Puerto Rico, 00919-5166 e-mail: directivasopi@yahoo.com www.avesdepuertorico.org

Suriname
Foundation for Nature Preservation in Suriname, Cornelis Jongbawstraat 14, PO Box 12252, Paramaribo e-mail: research@stinasu.sr www.stinasu.sr

Uruguay
Aves Uruguay (GUPECA), Canelones 1164, Montevideo, Uruguay. Pub: *Achara;* www.avesuruguay.org.uy/ e-mail: info@avesuruguay.org.uy

ASIA

PARTNERS

India
Bombay Natural History Society, Hornbill House, Shaheed Bhagat Singh Road, Mumbai-400 023. Pub: *Buceros; Hornbill; Journal of the Bombay Natural History Society;* e-mail: bnhs@bom4.vsnl.net.in www.bnhs.org

Japan
Wild Bird Society of Japan (WBSJ), Maruw Bldg, 3-9-23, Nishi-Gotanda, Shinagawa-ku, Tokyo 141-0031, Japan. Pub: *Strix; Wild Birds; Wing.* e-mail: hogo@wbsj.org www.wbsj.org

Malaysia
Malaysian Nature Society, PO Box 10750, Kuala Lumpur 50724. Pub: *Enggang; Suara Enggang; Malayan Nature Journal; Malaysian Naturalist.* e-mail: mns@mns.org.my www.mns.my

Philippines
Haribon Foundation, 2/F, Santos and Sons Building, 973 Aurora Blvd, Cubao, Quezon CIty 1109. Pub: *Haribon Foundation Annual Report; Haring Ibon; Philippine Biodiversity;* e-mail: act@haribon.org.ph www.haribon.org.ph

Singapore
Nature Society (Singapore), 510 Geylang Road, #02-05, The Sunflower, 398466. Pub: *Nature News; Nature Watch (Singapore);* e-mail: nss@nss.org.sg www.nss.org.sg

Taiwan
Chinese Wild Bird Federation (CWBF), 1F, No. 3, Lane 36 Jing-Long St., 116 Taipei, Taiwan. Pub: *Yuhina Post;* e-mail: mail@bird.org.tw www.bird.org.tw

Thailand
Bird Conservation Society of Thailand, 221 Moo 2, Soi Ngamwongwan 2, Tambol Bangkhen, Ampur Meung, Nontaburi 11000. Pub: *Bird Conservation Society of Thailand;* e-mail: bcst@bcst.or.th www.bcst.or.th

PARTNERS DESIGNATE

Hong Kong
The Hong Kong Birdwatching Society, 14/F Ruby Commercial Building, 480 Nathan Road, Kowloon, Hong Kong, People's Republic of China. Pub: *Hong Kong Bird Report;* e-mail: hkbws@hkbws.org.uk www.hkbws.org.hk

INTERNATIONAL ORGANISATIONS

Nepal
Bird Conservation Nepal, P.O.Box 12465, Kathmandu, Nepal. Pub: *Bird Conservation Nepal (Danphe); Ibisbill;* e-mail: bcn@mail.com.np www.birdlifenepal.org

AFFILIATES

Indonesia
Burung Indonesia (Perhimpunan Pelestari Burung dan Habitatnya), Jl. Dadali 32, Bogor 16161, PO. Box 310/ Boo, Bogor 16003, Indonesia; e-mail: birdlife@burung.org www.burung.org

Kazakhstan
Association for the Conservation of Biodiversity of Kazakhstan (ACBK), Office 406, 40 Beibitshilik Str, Astana 010000, Kazakhstan. E-mail: office@acbk.kz www.acbk.kz

Kyrgyzstan
NABS Public Association. www.wildlife.kg

Myanmar (Burma)
Biodiversity and Nature Conservation Association (BANCA), 145(B), Thirimingalar Lane, 8th Mile, Ward (4), Mayangone Township, Yangon, Myanmar +951 667 067; e-mail: banca@yangon.net.mm - www.banca-env.org

Sri Lanka
Field Ornithology Group of Sri Lanka, Dept of Zoology, University of Colombo, Colombo 03. Pub: *Malkoha - Newsletter of the Field Ornithology Group of Sri Lanka.* e-mail: fogsl@slt.lk www.fogsl.net

Uzbekistan
Uzbekistan Society for the Protection of Birds (UzSPB), Off.89, Institte of Zoology of Uzkek Academy of sciences, A. Niyazov str.1, Tashkent 100095. E-mail: roman.kashkarov@iba.uz www.uzspb.uz

UNAFFILIATED COUNTRIES

Cambodia
BirdLife International Cambodia Programme, ±9 Street 29, Tonie Basac, Chamkarmon, Phnom Penh. e-mail: admin@birdlifecambodia.org www.birdlifeindochina.org

Laos
BirdLife International in Indochina, No 4 Lane 209, Doi Can, Ba Dinh, Hanoi, Vietnam; e-mail: birdlife@birdlife.netnam.vn www.birdlifeindochina.org

Vietnam
BirdLife International in Indochina, PO Box 89 – 6 Dinh Le, Hanoi, Vietnam. e-mail: birdlife@birdlife.org.vn - www.birdlifeindochina.org

EUROPE

PARTNERS

Austria
BirdLife Austria, Museumplatz 1/10/8, AT-1070 Wien. Pub: *Egretta; Vogelschutz in Osterreich.* e-mail: office@birdlife.at www.birdlife.at/

Belarus
BirdLife Belarus (APB), PO Box 306, Minsk, 220050

Belarus. Pub: *Subbuteo - The Belarusian Ornithological Bulletin;* e-mail: apb@tut.by www.ptushki.org

Belgium
BirdLife Belgium (Natuurpunt-Natagora), Natuurpunt, Michiel Coxiestraat 11N 2800 Mechelen, Belgium. e-mail: wim.vandenbossche@natuurpunt.be www.natuurreservaten.be (Dutch) and Natagora, rue du Wisconsin 3, 5000 Namur, Belgium; e-mail (Natagora): Philippe.funcken@natagora. be - www.natagora.be (French)

Bulgaria
Bulgarian Society for the Protection of Birds (BSPB), PO Box 50, Yavorov Complex, Block 71, vh.4, ap 1, BG-1111, Sofia, Bulgaria. Pub: *Neophron (& UK);* e-mail: bspb_hq@bspb.org www.bspb.org

Czech Republic
Czech Society for Ornithology (CSO), Na Belidle 252/34, 150 00 Prague 5. Pub: *Ptaci Svet; Sylvia; Zpravy Ceske Spolecnosti Ornitologicke.* e-mail: cso@birdlife.cz www.birdlife.cz

Denmark
Dansk Ornitologisk Forening (DOF), Vesterbrogade 138-140, DK-1620, Copenhagen V, Denmark. Pub: *DAFIF - Dafifs Nyhedsbrev; Dansk Ornitologisk Forenings Tidsskrift; Fugle og Natur;* e-mail: dof@dof.dk www.dof.dk

Estonia
Estonian Ornithological Society (EOU), PO Box 227, Vesti Str. 4, EE-50002 Tartu, Estonia. Pub: *Hirundo Eesti Ornitoogiauhing;* e-mail: eoy@eoy.ee www.eoy.ee

Finland
BirdLife FINLAND, Annankatu 29 A 16, FI 00101, Helsinki. Pub: *Linnuston-Suojelu; Linnut; Tiira;* e-mail: office@birdlife.fi www.birdlife.fi

France
(also covers New Caledonia, Wallis & Futuna Islands) Ligue pour la Protection des Oiseaux (LPO), Fonderies Royale, 8-10 rue de Docteur Pujos, B.P. 90263, 17305 Rochefort Cedex. Pub: *Lettre Internationale; Ligue Francaise Pour La Protection des Oiseaux; Oiseau, L' (LPO); Outarde infos;* e-mail: lpo@lpo.fr www.lpo.fr/

Germany
Naturschutzbund Deutschland (NABU), Charitestr. 3, D-10117, Berlin. Pub: *Naturschutz Heute (NABU) Naturschutzbund Deutschland.* e-mail: nabu@nabu.de www.nabu.de

Gibraltar
Gibraltar Ornithological and Nat. History Society, Gibraltar Natural History Field Centre, Jew's Gate, Upper Rock Nature Reserve, PO Box 843, GI. Pub: *Alectoris; Gibraltar Nature News.* e-mail: gohns@gibnet.gi www.gonhs.org

Greece
Hellenic Ornithological Society (HOS), Themistokleous 80, 10861, Athens, Greece. Pub: *HOS Newsletter.* e-mail: info@ornithologiki.gr www.ornithologiki.gr

Hungary
Hungarian Orn. and Nature Cons. Society (MME), Kolto u. 21, 1121 Budapest. Pub: *Madartani Tajekoztato;*

INTERNATIONAL ORGANISATIONS

Madartavlat; Ornis Hungarica; Tuzok. e-mail: mme@mme.hu www.mme.hu

Ireland
BirdWatch Ireland, Unit 20, Block D, Bullford Business Campus, Kilcoole, Co Wicklow, Eire. Pub: Irish Birds; Wings (IWC Birdwatch Ireland); e-mail: info@birdwatchireland.org www.birdwatchireland.ie

Israel
Society for the Protection of Nature in Israel (SPNI), Hanagev 2 St, Tel-Aviv 66186. Pub: SPNI News. e-mail: ioc@netvision.net.il www.birds.org.il

Italy
Lega Italiana Protezione Uccelli (LIPU), Via Trento 49, 43100, Parma. Pub: Ali Giovani; Ali Notizie. e-mail: info@lipu.it www.lipu.it

Latvia
Latvijas Ornitologijas Biedriba (LOB), Kalnciema iela 27-18, Riga LV-1046. Pub: Putni Daba. e-mail: putni@lob.lv www.lob.lv

Luxembourg
Letzebuerger Natur-a Vulleschutzliga (LNVL), Kraizhaff, 5 Route de Luxembourg, L-1899 Kockelscheuer. Pub: Regulus (WATCH); Regulus Info (& Annual Report) (WATCH); Regulus Wissenschaftliche Berichte; e-mail: birgit.jacoby@luxnatur.lu www.lnvl.lu

Malta
BirdLife Malta, 57 /28, Triq Abate Rigord, Ta' Xbiex, XBX 1120, Malta. Pub: Bird Talk (WATCH) (Malta); Bird's Eye View (WATCH) (Malta); Il-Merill; e-mail: office@birdlifemalta.org www.birdlifemalta.org

Netherlands
Vogelbescherming Nederland (VBN), Boulevard 12, 3707, BM Zeist. Pub: Vogelniews; Vogels. e-mail: info@vogelbescherming.nl www.vogelbescherming.nl/

Norway
Norsk Ornitologisk Forening (NOF), Sandgata 30 B, N-7012 Trondheim, Norway. Pub: Fuglearet; Fuglefauna; Var; Ringmerkaren; e-mail: nof@birdlife.no www.birdlife.no

Poland
Ogólnopolskie Towarzystwo Ochrony Ptaków (OTOP), ul.Odrowaza 24, 05-270 Marki k. Warsaw, Poland. Pub: Ptaki; Ptasie Ostoje; e-mail: office@otop.most.org.pl www.otop.org.pl/

Portugal
Sociedade Portuguesa para o Estuda das, Aves (SPEA), Avenida João Crisóstomo, nº 18 – 4º Dir. | 1000-179 Lisboa | Portugal. Pub: Pardela; e-mail: spea@spea.pt www.spea.pt

Romania
Romanian Ornithological Society (SOR), Bd. M Kogalniceanu nr 49, sc. A, ap 8, 0150108 Sector 5, Bucharest. Pub: Alcedo; Buletin AIA; Buletin de Informare Societatea Ornitologica Romana; Milvus (Romania); e-mail: office@sor.ro www.sor.ro/

Slovakia
Slovak Ornithological Society (SOS), Mlynske Nivy 41, 821 09 Bratislava, Slovakia. Pub: Spravodaj SOVS;

Vtacie Spravy; e-mail: vtaky@vtaky.sk www.birdlife.sk

Slovenia
BirdLife Slovenia (DOPPS), Trzaska 2, PO Box 2990, SI-1000 Ljubljana, Slovenia. Pub: Acrocephalus; Svet Ptic; e-mail: dopps@dopps.si www.ptice.si

Spain
Sociedad Espanola de Ornitologia (SEO), Melquiades Biencinto 34, ES-28053, Madrid. Pub: Ardeola; Areas Importantes para las Aves. e-mail: seo@seo.org www.seo.org

Sweden
Sveriges Ornitologiska Forening (SOF), Stenhusa Gard, SE-380 62 Morbylanga. Pub: Fagelvarld; var; Ornis Svecica; e-mail: info@sofnet.org www.sofnet.org

Switzerland
SVS/BirdLife Switzerland, Wiedingstrasse 78, PO Box, CH-8036, Zurich, Switzerland. Pub: Oiwvos Ornis; Ornis Junior; Ornithologische Beobachter; Der Ornithos; Steinadler; e-mail: svs@birdlife.ch www.birdlife.ch

Turkey
Doga Dernegi (DD), PK: 640 06445, Yenisehir, Ankara, Turkey. Pub: Kelaynak; Kuscu Bulteni. e-mail: doga@dogadernegi.org www.dogadernegi.org

Ukraine
Ukrainian Union for Bird Conservation (UTOP), PO Box 33, Kiev, 1103, UA. Pub: Life of Birds. e-mail: uspb@birdlife.org.ua www.birdlife.org.ua

United Kingdom
Royal Society for the Protection of Birds, The Lodge, Sandy, Bedfordshire, SG19 2DL; e-mail: info@rspb.org.uk www.rspb.org.uk

PARTNERS DESIGNATE

Azerbaijan
Azerbaijan Ornithological Society (AOS), Mukhtarov str. 13, apt 16, AZ1001 Baku. e-mail: info@aos.az http://aos.az/eng/index.php

Georgia
Georgian Centre for the Conservation of Wildlife, Nature House (2nd Floor), Didi Digomi, 0131, Tbilisi, Georgia; e-mail: office@gccw.org http://gccw.bunebaprint.ge/

Iceland
Icelandic Society for the Protection of Birds (ISPB), Fuglaverndarfélag Islands, Skulatuni 6, , 105 Reykjavik, Simi 5620477. www.fuglavernd.is e-mail: fuglavernd@fuglavernd.is

AFFILIATES

Andorra
Associacio per a la Defensa de la Natura (AND), Apartado de Correus Espanyols No 96, Andorra La Vella, Principat d'Andorra. Pub: Aiguerola; e-mail: adn@andorra.ad www.adn-andorra.org/

Armenia
Armenian Society for the Protection of Birds (ASPB), Garaegin Njdeh 27/2, 10 Yerevan, 0026, Armenia. E-mail: armbirds@yahoo.com www.aspbirds.org

Cyprus
BirdLife Cyprus, PO Box 28076, 2090 Lefkosia, Cyprus.

e-mail: birdlifecyprus@birdlifecyprus.org.cy
www.birdlifecyprus.org

Faroe Islands
Føroya Fuglafrødifelag (Faroese Orginithological Society)
(FOS), Postssmoga 1230, FR-110 Torshavn, Faroe
Islands; e-mail: doreteb@ngs.fo
www.faroenature.net/foroya-fuglafrodifelag/kunning/
blog.html

Liechtenstein
Botanish-Zoologische Gesellschaft (ZG), Im Bretscha 22,
FL-9494 Schaan, Liechtenstein;
e-mail: bzg@bzg.li www.bzg.li

Lithuania
Lietuvos Ornitologu Draugija (LOD), Naugarduko St.
47-3, LT-2006, Vilnius, Lithuania. Pub: *Baltasis Gandras;*
e-mail: lod@birdlife.lt www.birdlife.lt

**Former Yugoslav Republic of Macedonia
(FYROM)**
Macedonia (MES)Macedonian Ecological Society, Blvd
"Kuzman Josifovski - Pitu" 28/3-7, 1000 Skopje
Macedonia; e-mail:contact@mes.org.mk -
www.mes.org.mk

MIDDLE EAST

PARTNERS

Jordan
Royal Society of the Conservation of Nature, PO Box
6354, Jubeiha-Abu-Nusseir Circle, Amman 11183. Pub:
Al Reem; e-mail: adminrscn@rscn.org.jo
www.rscn.org.jo

Lebanon
Society for the Protection of Nature in Lebanon, Awad
Bldg, 6th Floor, Abdel Aziz Street, P.O.Box: 11-5665,
Beirut, Lebanon; e-mail: spnlorg@cyberia.net.lb
www.spnlb.org

Palestinian Authority Territories
Palestine Wildlife Society (PWLS), Beit Sahour, PO Box
89, Palestine. Pub: *Palestine Wildlife Society - Annual
Report.*
e-mail: pwls@wildlife-pal.org www.wildlife-pal.org

AFFILIATES

Bahrain
Dr Saeed A. Mohamed, PO Box 1858, Manama, Bahrain.
e-mail: saeed@alreem.com http://bahrainwildlife.com

Iraq
Nature Iraq, House 25, Street 27, Qtr 104 Ashti,
Sulaimani, Kurdistan, Iraq. e-mail: info@natureiraq.org
www.natureiraq.org

Kuwait
Kuwait Environment Protection Society, PO Box 1896,
Safat 13019, Kuwait; e-mail: rasamhory@hotmail.com
www.keps.org.kw

Qatar
Friends of the Environment Centre, PO Box 1822, Doha,
Qatar. E-mail: cefdoha@qatar.net.qa
http:// my qatar.org

Saudi Arabia
Saudi Wildlife Commission (SWC), PO Box 61681, Riyadh
11575. Pub: *Phoenix; The.*
e-mail: ncwcd@zajil.net www.ncwcd.gov.sa/

Syria
Syrian Society ofr the Conservation of Wildlife (SSCW),
PO Box 9853, Damascus, Syria;
e-mail: sscw.syria@gmail.com www.sscw-syria.org/ar/

Yemen
Yemen Society for the Protection of Wildlife (YSPW), 29
Alger Street, PO Box 19759, Sana'a, Yemen.
e-mail: wildlife.yemen@y.net.ye

PACIFIC

PARTNER

Australia
**(also covers Christmas Island, Cocos Islands,
Norfolk Island, Heard & McDonald Islands,
Antarctica)**
Birds Australia, Suite 2-05, 60 Leicester Street, Carlton,
VIC 3053, Australia. Pub: *Australia Garcilla; Birds
Australia Annual Report; Eclectus; Emu; Wingspan*
(WATCH) (Australia); from wingspan@birdsaustralia.
com.au; e-mail: info@birdlife.org.au -
www.birdlife.org.au/

French Polynesia
Société d'Ornithologie de Polynésie 'Manu', B.P. 7023,
98719 Taravao, Tahiti, French Polynesia;
e-mail: sop@manu.pf www.manu.pf

New Zealand
(also covers Niue and Tokelau)
Forest & Bird, Level 1, 90 Ghunzee Street, PO Box 631,
Wellington 6140. Pub: *Forest & Bird; Forest & Bird
Annual Report; Forest & Bird Conservation News.*
e-mail: office@forestandbird.org.nz
www.forestandbird.org.nz/

Palau
Palau Conservation Society, PO Box 1811, Koror,
PW96940, Republic of Palau. Pub: *Ngerel a Biib;*
e-mail: pcs@palaunet.com www.palauconservation.org

AFFILIATES

Cook Islands
Te Ipukarea Society (TIS), PO Box 649, Rarotonga, Cook
Islands; e-mail: 2tis@oyster.net.ck

New Caledonia (to France)
Société Calédonienne d'Ornithologie (SCO)
BP 13641, 98 803 Nouméa Cedex, New Caledonia
e-mail: president@sco.asso.nc - www.sco.asso.nc

Samoa
O le Si'osi'omaga Society Incorporated (OLSSI), P O Box
2282, Apia, Western Samoa;
e-mail: ngo_siosiomaga@samoa.ws

311

SPECIAL INTEREST ORGANISATIONS

AFRICAN BIRD CLUB.

c/o Birdlife International as below. e-mail (general): contact@african-birdclub.org e-mail: (membership and sales): membership@africanbirdclub.org www.africanbirdclub.org
Pub: *Bulletin of the African Bird Club.*

BIRDLIFE INTERNATIONAL.
Wellbrook Court, Girton Road, Cambridge, CB3 ONA, +44 (0)1223 277 318; (Fax) +44 (0)1223 277 200; www.birdlife.org
e-mail: birdlife@birdlife.org
Pub:*World Birdwatch.*

EAST AFRICA NATURAL HISTORY SOCIETY see Kenya in preceding list.

EURING (European Union for Bird Ringing).
Euring Data Bank, c/o BTO, The Nunnery, Thetford, Norfolk IP24 2PU. 01842 750 050. www.euring.org

FAUNA AND FLORA INTERNATIONAL.
Jupiter House, 4th Floor, Station Road, Cambridge, CB1 2JD. Call on +44 (0)1223 571 000; (Fax) +44 (0)1223 461 481. www.fauna-flora.org
e-mail: info@fauna-flora.org
Pub: *Fauna & Flora News; Oryx.*

LIPU-UK
(the Italian League for the Protection of Birds).
David Lingard, Fernwood, Doddington Road, Whisby, Lincs, LN6 9BX, +44 (0)1522 689 030, e-mail: david@lipu-uk.org www.lipu-uk.org

Pub:*The Hoopoe,* annually, *Ali Notizie,* quarterly.

NEOTROPICAL BIRD CLUB.
(Central and South America and the Caribbean) c/o The Lodge, Sandy, Bedfordshire, SG19 2DL. Pub:*Cotinga.*
e-mail: secretary@neotropicalbirdclub.org www.neotropicalbirdclub.org

ORIENTAL BIRD CLUB.
P.O.Box 324, Bedford, MK42 0WG
Pub:*The Forktail; BirdingASIA.*
email: mail@orientalbirdclub.org www.orientalbirdclub.org

ORNITHOLOGICAL SOCIETY OF THE MIDDLE EAST (OSME).
c/o The Lodge, Sandy, Beds, SG19 2DL.
Pub: *Sandgrouse.* e-mail: secretary@osme.org www.osme.org

TRAFFIC International (formerly Wildlife Trade Monitoring Unit).
219a Huntingdon Road, Cambridge, CB3 ODL, +44 (0)1223 277 427; (Fax) +44 (0)1223 277 237.
Pub:*TRAFFIC Bulletin.*
e-mail: traffic@traffic.org www.traffic.org

WEST AFRICAN ORNITHOLOGICAL SOCIETY.
R E Sharland, 1 Fisher's Heron, East Mills, Hants, SP6 2JR. Pub: *Malimbus.*
http://malimbus.free.fr

WETLANDS INTERNATIONAL.
PO Box 471, 6700 AL Wageningen, Netherlands, +31 317 485 774; (Fax) +31 317 486 770, Pub:*Wetlands.*
e-mail: post@wetlands.org www.wetlands.org

WORLD OWL TRUST.
The World Owl Centre, Muncaster Castle, Ravenglass, Cumbria, CA18 1RQ, +44 (0)1229 717393; www.owls.org

WORLD PHEASANT ASSOCIATION.
7-9 Shaftesbury St, Fordingbridge, Hants SP6 1JF. 01425 657 129; (Fax) 01425 658 053. Pub:*WPA News.* e-mail: office@pheasant.org.uk www.pheasant.org.uk

WORLD WIDE FUND FOR NATURE.
Panda House, Weyside Park, Godalming United Kingdom. +44 1483 426 444; (Fax) +44 1483 426 409, e-mail: supporterrelations@wwf.org.uk www.panda.org

QUICK REFERENCE SECTION

David Cromack

When planning a trip to the coast, it is important to know when hide tide is going to occur, or you may miss the best of the birding. The Yearbook's Tide Table calculator allows you to plan up to 15 months in advance.

Tide tables — 314

Sunrise/set times — 320

Sea areas — 322

Schedule 1 species list — 323

Birdwatchers and twitchers take note! — 323

Birdline numbers — 325

Index to reserves — 326

TIDE TABLES: USEFUL INFORMATION

BRITISH SUMMER TIME

In 2013 BST applies from 01:00 on March 30 to 01:00 on October 26.
Note that all the times in the following tables are GMT.

During British Summer Time one hour should be added.

Shetland 42, 43
Orkney 44, 45

Predictions are given for the times of high water at Dover throughout the year.

The times of tides at the locations shown here may be obtained by adding or subtracting their 'tidal difference' as shown opposite (subtractions are indicated by a minus sign).

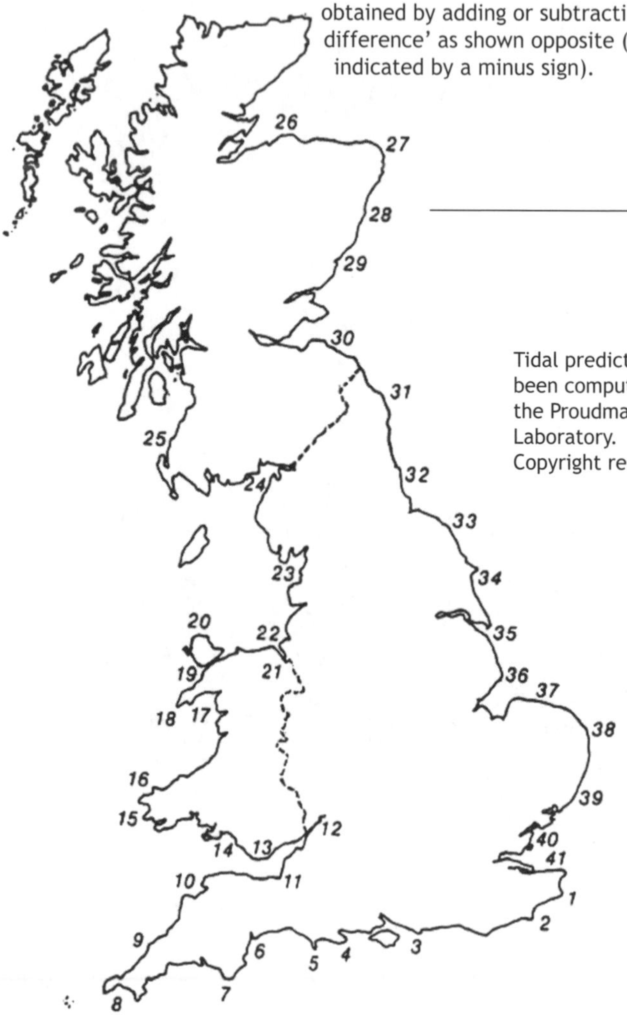

Tidal predictions for Dover have been computed by the Proudman Oceanographic Laboratory.
Copyright reserved.

Map showing locations for which tidal differences are given on facing page.

TIDE TABLES 2014

Example 1
To calculate the time of first high water at Girvan on February 9
1. Look up the time at Dover (06 27)* = 06:27 am
2. Add the tidal difference for Girvan = 0.54
3. Therefore the time of high water at Girvan = 07:21 am

Example 2
To calculate the time of second high water at Blakeney on June 22
1. Look up the time at Dover (19 05) = 19:05 pm
2. Add 1 hour for British Summer Time = 20:05 pm
3. Subtract the tidal difference for Blakeney = - 4.07
4. Therefore the time of second high water at Blakeney = 15.58 pm

NB: *All Dover times are shown on the 24-hour clock.
Following the time of each high water, the height of the tide is given in metres. This height only applies to the high water level at Dover and may be different in other areas around the country. (Tide tables beyond April 2015 are not available at the time of going to press.)

TIDAL DIFFERENCES

1	Dover	See pp 316-319		23	Morecambe	0	20
2	Dungeness	-0	12	24	Silloth	0	51
3	Selsey Bill	0	09	25	Girvan	0	54
4	Swanage (lst H.W.Springs)	-2	36	26	Lossiemouth	0	48
5	Portland	-4	23	27	Fraserburgh	1	20
6	Exmouth (Approaches)	-4	48	28	Aberdeen	2	30
7	Salcombe	-5	23	29	Montrose	3	30
8	Newlyn (Penzance)	5	59	30	Dunbar	3	42
9	Padstow	-5	47	31	Holy Island	3	58
10	Bideford	-5	17	32	Sunderland	4	38
11	Bridgwater	-4	23	33	Whitby	5	12
12	Sharpness Dock	-3	19	34	Bridlington	5	53
13	Cardiff (Penarth)	-4	16	35	Grimsby	-5	20
14	Swansea	-4	52	36	Skegness	-5	00
15	Skomer Island	-5	00	37	Blakeney	-4	07
16	Fishguard	-3	48	38	Gorleston	-2	08
17	Barmouth	-2	45	39	Aldeburgh	-0	13
18	Bardsey Island	-3	07	40	Bradwell Waterside	1	11
19	Caernarvon	-1	07	41	Herne Bay	1	28
20	Amlwch	-0	22	42	Sullom Voe	-1	34
21	Connahs Quay	0	20	43	Lerwick	0	01
22	Hilbre Island			44	Kirkwall	-0	26
	(Hoylake/West Kirby)	-0	05	45	Widewall Bay	-1	30

NB. Care should be taken when making calculations at the beginning and end of British Summer Time. See worked examples above.

TIDE TABLES 2014

Tidal Predictions : HIGH WATERS 2014

Datum of Predictions = Chart Datum : 3.67 metres below Ordnance Datum (Newlyn)

British Summer Time Dates for 2014 : 30th March to 26th October (data not adjusted)

DOVER — January

Day	Morning time	m	Afternoon time	m
1 W	10:22	6.8	22:52	6.8
2 Th	11:14	6.9	23:43	7.0
3 F	##:##	#.#	12:06	6.9
4 Sa	00:33	7.0	12:57	6.9
5 Su	01:21	7.0	13:47	6.7
6 M	02:06	6.9	14:35	6.5
7 Tu	02:53	6.6	15:24	6.2
8 W	03:43	6.4	16:19	5.9
9 Th	04:41	6.0	17:24	5.6
10 F	05:49	5.8	18:38	5.5
11 Sa	07:04	5.6	19:50	5.6
12 Su	08:12	5.7	20:51	5.8
13 M	09:10	5.9	21:39	6.0
14 Tu	09:57	6.0	22:21	6.2
15 W	10:36	6.2	22:57	6.4
16 Th	11:12	6.3	23:32	6.5
17 F	11:45	6.5	##:##	#.#
18 Sa	00:06	6.6	12:17	6.4
19 Su	00:38	6.6	12:47	6.3
20 M	01:08	6.4	13:16	6.3
21 Tu	01:36	6.4	13:46	6.2
22 W	02:06	6.3	14:21	6.1
23 Th	02:42	6.2	15:04	5.9
24 F	03:30	6.0	16:02	5.7
25 Sa	04:35	5.8	17:12	5.6
26 Su	05:49	5.7	18:30	5.6
27 M	07:07	5.8	19:48	5.8
28 Tu	08:19	6.1	20:56	6.1
29 W	09:20	6.4	21:52	6.5
30 Th	10:14	6.7	22:43	6.8
31 F	11:05	6.9	23:31	7.0

DOVER — February

Day	Morning time	m	Afternoon time	m
1 Sa	11:54	7.0	##:##	#.#
2 Su	00:18	7.1	12:42	6.9
3 M	01:01	7.1	13:26	6.8
4 Tu	01:43	7.0	14:09	6.6
5 W	02:25	6.8	14:51	6.3
6 Th	03:10	6.4	15:40	6.0
7 F	04:02	6.0	16:39	5.6
8 Sa	05:06	5.6	17:51	5.3
9 Su	06:27	5.4	19:14	5.3
10 M	07:46	5.4	20:24	5.5
11 Tu	08:51	5.6	21:18	5.8
12 W	09:41	5.8	22:01	6.1
13 Th	10:20	6.1	22:37	6.3
14 F	10:53	6.2	23:10	6.4
15 Sa	11:23	6.3	23:42	6.6
16 Su	11:52	6.4	##:##	#.#
17 M	00:12	6.6	12:21	6.4
18 Tu	00:41	6.6	12:49	6.4
19 W	01:08	6.6	13:19	6.4
20 Th	01:36	6.5	13:52	6.3
21 F	02:11	6.4	14:33	6.1
22 Sa	02:57	6.2	15:28	5.9
23 Su	04:00	5.9	16:39	5.6
24 M	05:20	5.6	18:06	5.5
25 Tu	06:50	5.6	19:35	5.7
26 W	08:10	5.9	20:46	6.1
27 Th	09:13	6.3	21:42	6.5
28 F	10:06	6.6	22:30	6.8

DOVER — March

Day	Morning time	m	Afternoon time	m
1 Sa	10:53	6.8	23:14	7.0
2 Su	11:38	6.9	23:57	7.1
3 M	##:##	#.#	12:21	6.9
4 Tu	00:39	7.0	13:02	6.8
5 W	01:18	7.0	13:41	6.6
6 Th	01:56	6.7	14:21	6.4
7 F	02:38	6.4	15:05	6.0
8 Sa	03:26	6.0	15:58	5.6
9 Su	04:27	5.5	17:07	5.3
10 M	05:48	5.2	18:33	5.1
11 Tu	07:16	5.2	19:51	5.3
12 W	08:25	5.4	20:49	5.6
13 Th	09:17	5.7	21:34	5.9
14 F	09:56	5.9	22:10	6.2
15 Sa	10:26	6.2	22:42	6.4
16 Su	10:54	6.3	23:12	6.5
17 M	11:22	6.4	23:42	6.6
18 Tu	11:52	6.5	##:##	#.#
19 W	00:11	6.6	12:23	6.6
20 Th	00:40	6.6	12:56	6.5
21 F	01:12	6.6	13:32	6.4
22 Sa	01:50	6.4	14:15	6.2
23 Su	02:38	6.2	15:12	6.0
24 M	03:44	5.9	16:25	5.7
25 Tu	05:09	5.6	17:53	5.5
26 W	06:43	5.6	19:23	5.7
27 Th	08:03	5.9	20:32	6.1
28 F	09:03	6.2	21:25	6.4
29 Sa	09:52	6.5	22:11	6.7
30 Su	10:36	6.7	22:53	6.9
31 M	11:18	6.8	23:34	7.0

DOVER — April

Day	Morning time	m	Afternoon time	m
1 Tu	11:59	6.8	##:##	#.#
2 W	00:15	7.0	12:38	6.7
3 Th	00:52	6.8	13:15	6.6
4 F	01:30	6.6	13:53	6.4
5 Sa	02:09	6.3	14:35	6.1
6 Su	02:54	5.9	15:24	5.7
7 M	03:50	5.5	16:25	5.4
8 Tu	05:05	5.1	17:45	5.1
9 W	06:33	5.1	19:06	5.2
10 Th	07:46	5.3	20:09	5.5
11 F	08:39	5.5	20:56	5.8
12 Sa	09:19	5.8	21:34	6.1
13 Su	09:50	6.1	22:06	6.3
14 M	10:19	6.3	22:37	6.5
15 Tu	10:50	6.5	23:09	6.6
16 W	11:24	6.6	23:42	6.7
17 Th	##:##	#.#	12:00	6.6
18 F	00:18	6.7	12:39	6.6
19 Sa	00:57	6.6	13:21	6.5
20 Su	01:42	6.4	14:11	6.3
21 M	02:36	6.2	15:11	6.1
22 Tu	03:45	5.9	16:21	5.8
23 W	05:06	5.7	17:41	5.7
24 Th	06:33	5.7	19:03	5.8
25 F	07:47	5.9	20:09	6.1
26 Sa	08:45	6.2	21:03	6.4
27 Su	09:33	6.4	21:48	6.6
28 M	10:16	6.5	22:30	6.7
29 Tu	10:57	6.6	23:12	6.8
30 W	11:37	6.7	23:52	6.7

National Oceanography Centre (www.noc.ac.uk)

TIDE TABLES 2014

Time Zone: GMT

Units: METRES

Tidal Predictions : HIGH WATERS 2014

Datum of Predictions = Chart Datum : 3.67 metres below Ordnance Datum (Newlyn)

British Summer Time Dates for 2014 : 30th March to 26th October (data not adjusted)

DOVER — May

Day	Morning time	m	Afternoon time	m
1 Th	##:##		12:16	6.6
2 F	00:31	6.6	12:54	6.5
3 Sa	01:08	6.4	13:31	6.4
4 Su	01:46	6.2	14:10	6.2
5 M	02:27	5.9	14:54	5.9
6 Tu	03:16	5.6	15:46	5.6
7 W	04:18	5.3	16:51	5.3
8 Th	05:35	5.1	18:06	5.3
9 F	06:48	5.2	19:13	5.4
10 Sa	07:45	5.7	20:06	5.7
11 Su	08:30	5.7	20:48	5.9
12 M	09:07	6.0	21:25	6.2
13 Tu	09:43	6.5	22:01	6.4
14 W	10:20	6.6	22:39	6.6
15 Th	11:00	6.6	23:19	6.7
16 F	11:43	6.7	##:##	
17 Sa	00:03	6.7	12:30	6.7
18 Su	00:51	6.6	13:21	6.6
19 M	01:45	6.5	14:15	6.5
20 Tu	02:43	6.3	15:11	6.3
21 W	03:46	6.0	16:11	6.1
22 Th	04:54	5.9	17:20	6.0
23 F	06:09	5.8	18:33	6.0
24 Sa	07:20	5.9	19:39	6.1
25 Su	08:19	6.0	20:36	6.2
26 M	09:10	6.2	21:24	6.4
27 Tu	09:56	6.5	22:10	6.5
28 W	10:38	6.4	22:53	6.5
29 Th	11:18	6.5	23:33	6.5
30 F	11:57	6.5	##:##	
31 Sa	00:12	6.4	12:36	6.5

DOVER — June

Day	Morning time	m	Afternoon time	m
1 Su	00:50	6.3	13:12	6.4
2 M	01:27	6.2	13:49	6.2
3 Tu	02:04	6.0	14:27	6.1
4 W	02:45	5.7	15:10	5.8
5 Th	03:33	5.5	16:01	5.6
6 F	04:32	5.3	17:01	5.5
7 Sa	05:37	5.3	18:06	5.5
8 Su	06:40	5.4	19:06	5.6
9 M	07:36	5.6	19:59	5.8
10 Tu	08:25	5.9	20:46	6.1
11 W	09:11	6.2	21:31	6.4
12 Th	09:56	6.4	22:16	6.6
13 F	10:42	6.6	23:03	6.7
14 Sa	11:32	6.8	23:53	6.8
15 Su	##:##		12:24	6.8
16 M	00:47	6.7	13:16	6.8
17 Tu	01:43	6.6	14:07	6.7
18 W	02:38	6.5	14:58	6.6
19 Th	03:33	6.3	15:51	6.4
20 F	04:30	6.0	16:50	6.2
21 Sa	05:35	5.9	17:57	6.0
22 Su	06:44	5.8	19:05	5.9
23 M	07:49	5.9	20:09	6.0
24 Tu	08:48	5.9	21:04	6.1
25 W	09:37	6.1	21:53	6.2
26 Th	10:21	6.3	22:36	6.3
27 F	11:00	6.4	23:17	6.3
28 Sa	11:39	6.5	23:54	6.3
29 Su	##:##		12:15	6.5
30 M	00:30	6.3	12:51	6.5

DOVER — July

Day	Morning time	m	Afternoon time	m
1 Tu	01:06	6.2	13:26	6.4
2 W	01:39	6.1	14:00	6.3
3 Th	02:12	5.9	14:34	6.1
4 F	02:50	5.8	15:13	5.9
5 Sa	03:36	5.6	16:02	5.7
6 Su	04:32	5.5	17:02	5.6
7 M	05:37	5.5	18:08	5.6
8 Tu	06:44	5.6	19:14	5.8
9 W	07:48	5.8	20:14	6.0
10 Th	08:46	6.1	21:09	6.3
11 F	09:39	6.4	22:00	6.6
12 Sa	10:30	6.7	22:51	6.8
13 Su	11:20	6.9	23:42	6.9
14 M	##:##		12:11	7.0
15 Tu	00:36	6.9	13:01	7.0
16 W	01:29	6.8	13:49	6.8
17 Th	02:19	6.6	14:36	6.6
18 F	03:07	6.4	15:23	6.4
19 Sa	03:57	6.1	16:16	6.3
20 Su	04:55	5.9	17:18	6.0
21 M	06:04	5.6	18:31	5.7
22 Tu	07:18	5.6	19:45	5.7
23 W	08:25	5.7	20:48	5.8
24 Th	09:19	6.0	21:39	6.0
25 F	10:03	6.1	22:21	6.2
26 Sa	10:42	6.3	22:59	6.3
27 Su	11:18	6.5	23:34	6.3
28 M	11:54	6.6	##:##	
29 Tu	00:08	6.4	12:27	6.6
30 W	00:39	6.3	12:59	6.5
31 Th	01:09	6.3	13:28	6.4

DOVER — August

Day	Morning time	m	Afternoon time	m
1 F	01:38	6.2	13:56	6.3
2 Sa	02:09	6.0	14:27	6.2
3 Su	02:47	5.9	15:09	6.0
4 M	03:38	5.7	16:07	5.8
5 Tu	04:45	5.6	17:20	5.7
6 W	06:01	5.7	18:39	5.9
7 Th	07:21	5.7	19:53	6.3
8 F	08:30	6.1	20:55	6.3
9 Sa	09:27	6.4	21:48	6.6
10 Su	10:18	6.8	22:39	6.8
11 M	11:06	7.0	23:27	7.0
12 Tu	11:53	7.1	##:##	
13 W	00:18	7.1	12:39	7.2
14 Th	01:06	6.9	13:24	7.1
15 F	01:51	6.7	14:07	6.9
16 Sa	02:35	6.5	14:51	6.6
17 Su	03:21	6.2	15:41	6.2
18 M	04:16	5.8	16:42	5.8
19 Tu	05:24	5.5	17:58	5.5
20 W	06:46	5.4	19:22	5.5
21 Th	08:02	5.6	20:31	5.6
22 F	09:00	5.8	21:24	5.9
23 Sa	09:44	6.1	22:05	6.1
24 Su	10:21	6.4	22:39	6.3
25 M	10:56	6.5	23:11	6.4
26 Tu	11:28	6.6	23:41	6.4
27 W	##:##		12:00	6.7
28 Th	00:09	6.5	12:28	6.6
29 F	00:37	6.6	12:54	6.6
30 Sa	01:05	6.4	13:20	6.5
31 Su	01:35	6.3	13:51	6.4

National Oceanography Centre (www.noc.ac.uk)

TIDE TABLES 2014

Time Zone: **GMT**

Units: **METRES**

Tidal Predictions : HIGH WATERS 2014

Datum of Predictions = Chart Datum : 3.67 metres below Ordnance Datum (Newlyn)

British Summer Time Dates for 2014 : 30th March to 26th October (data not adjusted)

DOVER — September

Date	Morning time	m	Afternoon time	m
1 M	02:11	6.2	14:31	6.2
2 Tu	03:00	5.9	15:27	5.9
3 W	04:07	5.7	16:45	5.7
4 Th	05:32	5.5	18:17	5.5
5 F	07:03	5.7	19:41	5.9
6 Sa	08:18	6.0	20:45	6.3
7 Su	09:14	6.5	21:38	6.6
8 M	10:02	6.8	22:24	6.9
9 Tu	10:47	7.1	23:10	7.0
10 W	11:31	7.2	23:55	7.0
11 Th	##:##	#.#	12:14	7.2
12 F	00:39	6.9	12:56	7.1
13 Sa	01:21	6.8	13:36	6.9
14 Su	02:02	6.5	14:18	6.5
15 M	02:46	6.2	15:06	6.1
16 Tu	03:39	5.8	16:06	5.7
17 W	04:44	5.4	17:24	5.3
18 Th	06:08	5.3	18:55	5.3
19 F	07:31	5.4	20:09	5.5
20 Sa	08:33	5.7	21:03	5.8
21 Su	09:18	6.1	21:43	6.1
22 M	09:56	6.3	22:15	6.3
23 Tu	10:29	6.5	22:43	6.4
24 W	10:59	6.6	23:10	6.5
25 Th	11:27	6.7	23:38	6.6
26 F	11:55	6.7	##:##	#.#
27 Sa	00:07	6.6	12:23	6.7
28 Su	00:37	6.6	12:51	6.6
29 M	01:10	6.6	13:25	6.5
30 Tu	01:48	6.3	14:08	6.2

DOVER — October

Date	Morning time	m	Afternoon time	m
1 W	02:38	6.1	15:06	5.9
2 Th	03:47	5.8	16:28	5.6
3 F	05:15	5.6	18:05	5.6
4 Sa	06:47	5.7	19:30	5.9
5 Su	08:01	6.1	20:34	6.2
6 M	08:57	6.5	21:24	6.6
7 Tu	09:43	6.8	22:08	6.8
8 W	10:26	7.0	22:51	6.9
9 Th	11:08	7.1	23:33	7.0
10 F	11:49	7.1	##:##	#.#
11 Sa	00:14	6.9	12:30	7.0
12 Su	00:54	6.8	13:09	6.7
13 M	01:33	6.5	13:50	6.4
14 Tu	02:16	6.3	14:35	6.1
15 W	03:04	5.9	15:30	5.6
16 Th	04:03	5.6	16:42	5.3
17 F	05:21	5.3	18:13	5.2
18 Sa	06:45	5.3	19:33	5.3
19 Su	07:53	5.6	20:29	5.6
20 M	08:43	5.9	21:11	5.9
21 Tu	09:23	6.2	21:43	6.2
22 W	09:56	6.4	22:11	6.4
23 Th	10:25	6.5	22:39	6.5
24 F	10:54	6.6	23:09	6.6
25 Sa	11:25	6.7	23:42	6.7
26 Su	11:57	6.7	##:##	#.#
27 M	00:17	6.7	12:33	6.6
28 Tu	00:56	6.6	13:12	6.5
29 W	01:39	6.4	14:00	6.3
30 Th	02:33	6.2	15:02	6.0
31 F	03:41	5.9	16:22	5.7

DOVER — November

Date	Morning time	m	Afternoon time	m
1 Sa	04:59	5.8	17:51	5.7
2 Su	06:24	5.8	19:12	5.9
3 M	07:36	6.1	20:15	6.2
4 Tu	08:33	6.4	21:06	6.4
5 W	09:21	6.7	21:51	6.6
6 Th	10:05	6.9	22:32	6.8
7 F	10:47	6.9	23:13	6.8
8 Sa	11:29	6.9	23:54	6.8
9 Su	##:##	#.#	12:09	6.8
10 M	00:33	6.7	12:48	6.6
11 Tu	01:12	6.6	13:27	6.4
12 W	01:52	6.3	14:09	6.1
13 Th	02:36	6.1	14:57	5.7
14 F	03:26	5.8	15:57	5.4
15 Sa	04:27	5.5	17:12	5.2
16 Su	05:44	5.3	18:33	5.2
17 M	06:57	5.4	19:37	5.4
18 Tu	07:54	5.7	20:25	5.7
19 W	08:39	5.9	21:03	6.0
20 Th	09:17	6.2	21:35	6.2
21 F	09:51	6.4	22:08	6.5
22 Sa	10:24	6.6	22:44	6.6
23 Su	11:00	6.7	23:23	6.7
24 M	11:40	6.8	##:##	#.#
25 Tu	00:06	6.8	12:23	6.6
26 W	00:51	6.7	13:10	6.6
27 Th	01:40	6.6	14:03	6.4
28 F	02:33	6.4	15:03	6.1
29 Sa	03:33	6.2	16:10	5.9
30 Su	04:38	6.0	17:24	5.8

DOVER — December

Date	Morning time	m	Afternoon time	m
1 M	05:51	6.0	18:40	5.8
2 Tu	07:03	6.1	19:47	6.0
3 W	08:05	6.2	20:44	6.2
4 Th	08:59	6.4	21:33	6.4
5 F	09:47	6.6	22:17	6.5
6 Sa	10:31	6.6	22:58	6.6
7 Su	11:13	6.7	23:38	6.7
8 M	11:53	6.6	##:##	#.#
9 Tu	00:17	6.7	12:31	6.5
10 W	00:54	6.6	13:09	6.3
11 Th	01:31	6.4	13:46	6.1
12 F	02:09	6.3	14:27	5.9
13 Sa	02:51	6.0	15:12	5.6
14 Su	03:38	5.8	16:06	5.4
15 M	04:36	5.5	17:12	5.2
16 Tu	05:42	5.4	18:22	5.2
17 W	06:48	5.5	19:23	5.4
18 Th	07:46	5.7	20:15	5.7
19 F	08:34	6.0	21:00	6.0
20 Sa	09:18	6.2	21:42	6.2
21 Su	10:00	6.5	22:25	6.6
22 M	10:42	6.7	23:09	6.8
23 Tu	11:28	6.8	23:57	6.9
24 W	##:##	#.#	12:16	6.8
25 Th	00:45	6.9	13:06	6.7
26 F	01:34	6.8	13:59	6.6
27 Sa	02:24	6.7	14:53	6.4
28 Su	03:15	6.5	15:48	6.1
29 M	04:11	6.2	16:50	5.9
30 Tu	05:14	6.1	18:00	5.8
31 W	06:25	5.9	19:12	5.7

National Oceanography Centre (www.noc.ac.uk)

TIDE TABLES 2015

Time Zone: GMT Units: METRES

Tidal Predictions : HIGH WATERS 2015

Datum of Predictions = Chart Datum : 3.67 metres below Ordnance Datum (Newlyn)

British Summer Time Dates for 2015 : 29th March to 25th October (data not adjusted)

DOVER — January

Day	Morning time	m	Afternoon time	m
1 Th	07:36	5.9	20:20	5.9
2 F	08:39	6.1	21:17	6.1
3 Sa	09:33	6.2	22:03	6.3
4 Su	10:19	6.3	22:45	6.4
5 M	11:00	6.4	23:23	6.6
6 Tu	11:39	6.5		
7 W	00:00	6.6	12:15	6.5
8 Th	00:36	6.6	12:50	6.4
9 F	01:10	6.6	13:24	6.3
10 Sa	01:44	6.4	13:57	6.1
11 Su	02:17	6.2	14:30	5.9
12 M	02:52	6.0	15:10	5.7
13 Tu	03:35	5.8	16:01	5.5
14 W	04:30	5.6	17:04	5.3
15 Th	05:38	5.4	18:16	5.3
16 F	06:49	5.5	19:27	5.5
17 Sa	07:54	5.7	20:28	5.8
18 Su	08:51	6.1	21:21	6.2
19 M	09:41	6.4	22:09	6.5
20 Tu	10:28	6.7	22:57	6.8
21 W	11:16	6.9	23:44	7.0
22 Th			12:05	6.9
23 F	00:32	7.1	12:55	6.9
24 Sa	01:19	7.1	13:45	6.8
25 Su	02:06	6.9	14:33	6.6
26 M	02:51	6.7	15:21	6.3
27 Tu	03:42	6.4	16:15	6.0
28 W	04:39	6.1	17:20	5.7
29 Th	05:50	5.8	18:37	5.5
30 F	07:09	5.6	19:56	5.6
31 Sa	08:23	5.7	21:00	5.8

DOVER — February

Day	Morning time	m	Afternoon time	m
1 Su	09:22	5.9	21:49	6.1
2 M	10:08	6.1	22:39	6.3
3 Tu	10:47	6.3	23:06	6.5
4 W	11:22	6.4	23:41	6.6
5 Th	11:56	6.4		
6 F	00:15	6.6	12:28	6.4
7 Sa	00:48	6.6	12:58	6.4
8 Su	01:17	6.5	13:26	6.3
9 M	01:43	6.4	13:53	6.1
10 Tu	02:10	6.2	14:26	6.0
11 W	02:45	6.0	15:08	5.8
12 Th	03:33	5.8	16:06	5.5
13 F	04:40	5.5	17:21	5.4
14 Sa	06:02	5.4	18:46	5.4
15 Su	07:23	5.6	20:03	5.7
16 M	08:30	6.0	21:03	6.1
17 Tu	09:25	6.3	21:54	6.5
18 W	10:14	6.7	22:41	6.8
19 Th	11:01	6.9	23:27	7.1
20 F	11:49	7.0		
21 Sa	00:13	7.2	12:37	7.0
22 Su	00:59	7.2	13:24	6.9
23 M	01:42	7.0	14:08	6.7
24 Tu	02:26	6.8	14:53	6.4
25 W	03:13	6.4	15:44	6.0
26 Th	04:09	6.1	16:45	5.7
27 F	05:18	5.6	18:03	5.4
28 Sa	06:44	5.4	19:29	5.4

DOVER — March

Day	Morning time	m	Afternoon time	m
1 Su	08:06	5.5	20:38	5.6
2 M	09:07	5.7	21:29	5.9
3 Tu	09:53	6.0	22:09	6.2
4 W	10:30	6.2	22:45	6.4
5 Th	11:02	6.3	23:18	6.5
6 F	11:33	6.4	23:51	6.6
7 Sa			12:03	6.4
8 Su	00:21	6.6	12:30	6.4
9 M	00:46	6.5	12:55	6.3
10 Tu	01:09	6.4	13:21	6.2
11 W	01:36	6.3	13:53	6.0
12 Th	02:09	6.2	14:33	5.8
13 F	02:55	5.9	15:28	5.7
14 Sa	04:02	5.6	16:45	5.5
15 Su	05:30	5.4	18:17	5.4
16 M	07:00	5.6	19:40	5.7
17 Tu	08:12	5.9	20:44	6.1
18 W	09:09	6.3	21:35	6.5
19 Th	09:57	6.7	22:21	6.9
20 F	10:43	6.9	23:06	7.1
21 Sa			23:51	7.2
22 Su	00:36	7.1	12:16	7.0
23 M	01:18	7.0	13:01	6.9
24 Tu	02:00	6.7	13:44	6.7
25 W	02:46	6.4	14:27	6.4
26 Th	03:40	6.1	15:15	6.1
27 F	04:48	5.5	16:14	5.7
28 Sa			17:28	5.4
29 Su	06:15	5.2	18:54	5.3
30 M	07:39	5.3	20:06	5.5
31 Tu	08:42	5.6	21:00	5.8

DOVER — April

Day	Morning time	m	Afternoon time	m
1 W	09:28	5.9	21:42	6.1
2 Th	10:05	6.1	22:18	6.3
3 F	10:36	6.2	22:51	6.4
4 Sa	11:06	6.3	23:21	6.5
5 Su	11:33	6.4	23:50	6.5
6 M			12:00	6.4
7 Tu	00:16	6.5	12:28	6.4
8 W	00:42	6.5	12:57	6.4
9 Th	01:12	6.4	13:32	6.3
10 F	01:48	6.2	14:14	6.1
11 Sa	02:36	6.0	15:11	5.9
12 Su	03:45	5.7	16:28	5.6
13 M	05:13	5.5	17:56	5.6
14 Tu	06:42	5.6	19:17	5.8
15 W	07:53	5.9	20:21	6.2
16 Th	08:49	6.3	21:12	6.5
17 F	09:38	6.6	21:59	6.8
18 Sa	10:24	6.8	22:45	7.0
19 Su	11:10	6.9	23:30	7.1
20 M	11:56	6.9		
21 Tu	00:14	7.0	12:40	6.8
22 W	00:57	6.8	13:22	6.6
23 Th	01:39	6.6	14:04	6.4
24 F	02:24	6.2	14:51	6.1
25 Sa	03:15	5.9	15:44	5.8
26 Su	04:17	5.5	16:50	5.5
27 M	05:36	5.2	18:09	5.3
28 Tu	06:58	5.3	19:23	5.5
29 W	08:03	5.5	20:21	5.7
30 Th	08:52	5.8	21:06	5.9

National Oceanography Centre (www.noc.ac.uk)

319

SUNRISE AND SUNSET TIMES FOR 2014

Predictions are given for the times of sunrise and sunset on every Sunday throughout the year. For places on the same latitude as the following, add 4 minutes for each degree of longitude west (subtract if east).

These times are in GMT, except between 01:00 on Mar 30 and 01:00 on Oct 26, when the times are in BST (1 hour in advance of GMT).

		London		Manchester		Edinburgh	
		Rise	Set	Rise	Set	Rise	Set
January	5	08 05	16 07	08 24	16 05	08 42	15 55
	12	08 02	16 16	08 20	16 15	08 37	16 06
	19	07 56	16 27	08 13	16 27	08 29	16 19
	26	07 48	16 39	08 04	16 40	08 18	16 33
February	2	07 38	16 52	07 53	16 53	08 06	16 48
	9	07 26	17 05	07 40	17 07	07 52	17 03
	16	07 13	17 17	07 26	17 21	07 36	17 19
	23	06 59	17 30	07 11	17 35	07 19	17 34
March	2	06 44	17 43	06 55	17 48	07 02	17 49
	9	06 29	17 55	06 38	18 02	06 44	18 04
	16	06 13	18 07	06 22	18 15	06 26	18 18
	23	05 57	18 19	06 05	18 28	06 08	18 32
	30	06 41	19 30	06 48	19 40	06 49	19 47
April	6	06 25	19 42	06 31	19 53	06 31	20 01
	13	06 10	19 54	06 14	20 06	06 13	20 15
	20	05 55	20 05	05 58	20 19	05 55	20 29
	27	05 41	20 17	05 43	20 32	05 39	20 44
	4	05 27	20 29	05 29	20 44	05 23	20 58
May	11	05 15	20 40	05 16	20 56	05 08	21 12
	18	05 05	20 50	05 04	21 08	04 55	21 25
	25	04 56	21 00	04 54	21 18	04 44	21 37
June	1	04 49	21 08	04 47	21 28	04 35	21 47
	8	04 45	21 15	04 42	21 35	04 29	21 55
	15	04 43	21 20	04 39	21 40	04 26	22 01
	22	04 43	21 22	04 40	21 42	04 27	22 03
	29	04 46	21 22	04 43	21 42	04 30	22 02

SUNRISE AND SUNSET TIMES

		London		Manchester		Edinburgh	
		Rise	Set	Rise	Set	Rise	Set
July	6	04 52	21 19	04 49	21 38	04 36	21 58
	13	04 59	21 14	04 56	21 32	04 45	21 51
	20	05 07	21 06	05 06	21 24	04 56	21 42
	27	05 17	20 57	05 16	21 14	05 08	21 30
August	3	05 27	20 46	05 28	21 02	05 21	21 16
	10	05 38	20 33	05 40	20 48	05 34	21 01
	17	05 49	20 19	05 52	20 33	05 48	20 45
	24	06 00	20 05	06 04	20 18	06 01	20 28
	31	06 11	19 50	06 16	20 01	06 15	20 10
September	6	06 21	19 36	06 27	19 47	06 27	19 55
	14	06 34	19 18	06 40	19 28	06 42	19 33
	21	06 45	19 02	06 53	19 10	06 56	19 15
	28	06 56	18 46	07 05	18 53	07 10	18 56
October	5	07 08	18 30	07 17	18 36	07 23	18 38
	12	07 19	18 14	07 30	18 20	07 38	18 20
	19	07 31	17 59	07 43	18 04	07 52	18 03
	26	06 43	16 45	06 56	16 49	07 07	16 46
November	2	06 56	16 32	07 10	16 35	07 21	16 31
	9	07 08	16 20	07 23	16 22	07 36	16 16
	16	07 20	16 10	07 36	16 11	07 51	16 04
	23	07 32	16 02	07 49	16 02	08 05	15 53
	30	07 42	15 56	08 00	15 55	08 17	15 45
December	7	07 52	15 52	08 10	15 51	08 28	15 40
	14	07 59	15 52	08 18	15 49	08 37	15 38
	21	08 04	15 54	08 23	15 51	08 42	15 40
	28	08 06	15 58	08 25	15 56	08 44	15 45

SEA AREAS

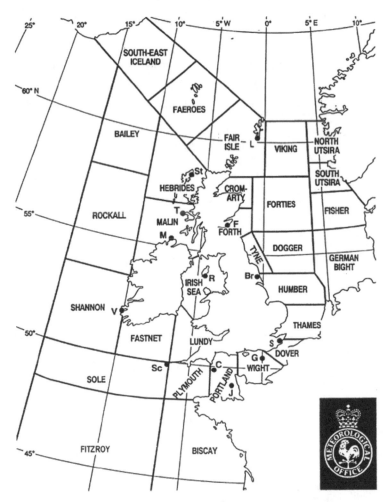

STATIONS WHOSE LATEST REPORTS ARE BROADCAST IN THE 5-MINUTE FORECASTS

Br Bridlington; C Channel Light-Vessel Automatic; F Fife Ness; G Greenwich Light-Vessel Automatic; J Jersey; L Lerwick; M Malin Head; R Ronaldsway; S Sandettie Light-Vessel Automatic; Sc Scilly Automatic; St Stornoway; T Tiree; V Valentia.

From information kindly supplied by the Meteorological Office

REVISION OF SEA AREAS

On 4 February 2002, the southern boundary of areas Plymouth and Sole, and the northern boundary of areas Biscay and Finisterre were realigned along the Metarea I/II boundary at 48°27′ North. At the same time, sea area Finisterre was renamed FitzRoy.

Did you know that the FitzRoy shipping area is named after the founder of the Met Office?

SCHEDULE 1 SPECIES

Under the provisions of the Wildlife and Countryside Act 1981 the
following bird species (listed in Schedule 1 - Part I of the Act) are
protected by special penalties at all times.

Avocet
Bee-eater
Bittern
Bittern, Little
Bluethroat
Brambling
Bunting, Cirl
Bunting, Lapland
Bunting, Snow
Buzzard, Honey
Chough
Corncrake
Crake, Spotted
Crossbills (all species)
Stone-curlew
Divers (all species)
Dotterel
Duck, Long-tailed
Eagle, Golden
Eagle, White-tailed

Falcon, Gyr
Fieldfare
Firecrest
Garganey
Godwit, Black-tailed
Goshawk
Grebe, Black-necked
Grebe, Slavonian
Greenshank
Gull, Little
Gull, Mediterranean
Harriers (all species)
Heron, Purple
Hobby
Hoopoe
Kingfisher
Kite, Red
Merlin
Oriole, Golden
Osprey

Owl, Barn
Owl, Snowy
Peregrine
Petrel, Leach's
Phalarope, Red-necked
Plover, Kentish
Plover, Little Ringed
Quail, Common
Redstart, Black
Redwing
Rosefinch, Scarlet
Ruff
Sandpiper, Green
Sandpiper, Purple
Sandpiper, Wood
Scaup
Scoter, Common
Scoter, Velvet
Serin
Shorelark

Shrike, Red-backed
Spoonbill
Stilt, Black-winged
Stint, Temminck's
Swan, Bewick's
Swan, Whooper
Tern, Black
Tern, Little
Tern, Roseate
Tit, Bearded
Tit, Crested
Treecreeper, Short-toed
Warbler, Cetti's
Warbler, Dartford
Warbler, Marsh
Warbler, Savi's
Whimbrel
Woodlark
Wryneck

The following birds and their eggs (listed in Schedule 1 - Part II of the Act) are protected by
special penalties during the close season, which is Feb 1 to Aug 31 (Feb 21 to Aug 31 below high
water mark), but may be killed outside this period - Goldeneye, Greylag Goose (in Outer Hebrides,
Caithness, Sutherland, and Wester Ross only), Pintail.

BIRDWATCHERS AND TWITCHERS TAKE NOTE!

Be tick-aware while enjoying the great outdoors

IF YOU'RE a keen birdwatcher, the following situations may be familiar: wandering through
bracken to spot nesting locations, walking through long grass to view wetland birds, and waiting
in scrubland, watching migratory birds fly overhead. What you might not be so familiar with,
however, is checking yourself for ticks afterwards.

Wherever you choose to enjoy birdwatching – be it forest, wetland or coast, UK or abroad –
spending prolonged periods outside and in among the bushes increases the chance of being bitten
by a tick which, if infected, can lead to the potential problem of Lyme disease.

Says Stella Huyshe-Shires, Chair of the charity Lyme Disease Action: "As a high-risk group,
birdwatchers need to be particularly tick-aware. The number of cases of Lyme disease in the UK
has risen over the last few years. It's important that awareness of potential problems associated
with tick bites increases too."

Ticks, which can be tiny (the size of a full stop on an A4 page) blood-sucking parasites, peak

BIRDWATCHERS AND TWITCHERS TAKE NOTE!

in population from April to October, and are found throughout the UK, North America and across Europe.

Lyme disease causes a range of unpleasant symptoms which may include a circular red rash, headaches, a stiff neck, extreme fatigue, muscle and joint pain, and disturbances of sight, hearing, digestive system and sleep. If left untreated it can progress to the joints, the heart and the nervous system.

To reduce the risk of being bitten by an infected tick, the charity Lyme Disease Action advises birdwatchers to take the following precautions:

- Wear long sleeves and trousers.
- Wear light-coloured clothing so ticks are easier to spot.
- Use an insect repellent effective against ticks (look for those containing the chemical DEET).
- Keep to pathways and try to avoid areas of overgrown vegetation.
- Check for ticks regularly during the day.
- Remove any ticks found attached as soon as possible.
- Pack a tick remover if birdwatching away from home.

Tick removal

Ticks should be removed immediately with a tick removal tool or fine pointed tweezers. Gently pull the tick's body away from your skin directly outwards, without jerking. Do not try to pull the tick out with your fingers, burn the tick or cover it with creams or chemicals. If you don't have a tick removal tool, use a thread of cotton wound round close to the skin and pull upwards or, alternatively, cut a slit in a plastic card and slide that under the tick's body.

Treatment

If you have been bitten by a tick and notice any of the above symptoms, seek medical help straight away. Diagnosed and treated early, Lyme disease can be treated successfully with antibiotics.

DOES AND DON'TS OF REMOVING A TICK

Your main aims are to remove all parts of the tick's body and to prevent it releasing additional saliva or regurgitating its stomach contents into your bite wound.

DO use a proprietary tick removal tool (available from www.lymediseaseaction.org.uk or many vets and pet shops), and follow the instructions provided, or a pair of tweezers.

If no tools are available, rather than delay use a cotton thread. Tie a single loop of cotton around the tick's mouthparts, as close to the skin as possible, then pull gently upwards and outwards.

DO commence by cleansing the tweezers with antiseptic. After tick removal, cleanse the bite site and the tweezers with antiseptic.

DO wash hands thoroughly afterwards.

DO save the tick in a container in case you develop symptoms later (label with date and location). The Health Protection Agency are currently running a scheme to investigate ticks, details available at www.lymediseaseaction.org.uk/information/tick. htm or from the HPA at www.hpa.org.uk.

DO NOT squeeze or twist the body of the tick, as this may cause the head and body to separate, leaving the head embedded in your skin.

DO NOT use your fingernails to remove a tick. Infection can enter via any breaks in your skin, e.g. Close to the fingernail.

DO NOT crush the tick's body, as this may cause it to regurgitate its infected stomach contents into the bite wound.

DO NOT try to burn the tick off, apply petroleum jelly, nail polish or any other chemical. Any of these methods can cause discomfort to the tick, resulting in regurgitation, or saliva release.

A detailed leaflet (free to download) is available from www.lymediseaseaction.org.uk

Leaflets are also available from:
Lyme Disease Action,
PO Box 235, Penryn. TR10 8WZ. UK
Including a donation/sae will help them in their work for people affected by Lyme disease.

Lyme Disease Action (www.lymediseaseaction.org.uk) is a charity striving for greater awareness of Lyme disease and associated tick-borne diseases.

THE COUNTRYSIDE CODE

Launched on 12 July 2004, this Code for England has been produced through a partnership between the Countryside Agency and Countryside Council for Wales.

The Countryside Code has been revised and re-launched to reflect the introduction of new open access rights (Countryside & Rights of Way Act 2000) and changes in society over the last 20 years.

● Be safe – plan ahead
Follow any signs, even when going out locally, it's best to get the latest information about where and when you can go; for example, your rights to go onto some areas of open land may be restricted while work is carried out, for safety reasons or during breeding seasons. Follow advice and local signs, and be prepared for the unexpected.

● Leave gates and property as you find them
Please respect the working life of the countryside, as our actions can affect people's livelihoods, our heritage, and the safety and welfare of animals and ourselves.

● Protect plants and animals, and take your litter home
We have a responsibility to protect our countryside now and for future generations, so make sure you don't harm animals, birds, plants, or trees.

● Keep dogs under close control
The countryside is a great place to exercise dogs, but it's every owner's duty to make sure their dog is not a danger or nuisance to farm animals, wildlife or other people.

● Consider other people
Showing consideration and respect for other people makes the countryside a pleasant Environment for everyone – at home, at work and at leisure.

RARE BIRD NETWORK
This is a new, free bird sightings service, which covers any sighting, not just rarities, that might be of interest to anyone who lives or may be visiting a county or birdwatching area. Rare Bird Network (RBN) uses the social networking site Twitter and works by using pre-defined hashtags for each county (or defined region) in the United Kingdom
Contact: E-mail: info@rarebirdnetwork.co.uk; Twitter: @rbnUK; Facebook: www.facebook.com/ RareBirdNetwork@rbnUK

BIRDLINE NUMBERS - National and Regional

Birdline name	To obtain information	To report sightings (hotlines)
National		
Bird Information Service	09068 700 222	
www.birdingworld.co.uk		
Flightline (Northern Ireland)	028 9146 7408	
Regional		
Northern Ireland	028 9146 7408	
Scotland	09068 700 234	01292 611 994
Wales	09068 700 248	01492 544 588
East Anglia	09068 700 245	07941 333 970
Midlands	09068 700 247	01905 754 154
North East	09068 700 246	07974 358 988
North West	09068 700 249	01492 544 588
South East	09068 700 240	01845 570 444
www.southeastbirdnews.co.uk		or 08000 377 240
South West	09068 700 241	0845 4567 938

Charges
At the time of compilation, calls to premium line numbers cost 60p per minute.

INDEX TO RESERVES

A

Abberton Reservoir	145
Abbotts Hall Farm	145
Aberlady Bay	214
Abernethy Forest Reserve	220
Adur Estuary	193
Ailsa Craig	211
Alkborough Flats	124
Amwell NR	148
Arne	201
Arundel	193
Aston Rowant NNR	130
Attenborough NR	128
Aylesbeare Common	198

B

Balranald	221
Bardsey Bird Observatory	225
Baron's Haugh	212
Bass Rock	214
Bawsinch Reserve	215
Beacon Hill	160
Bedfont Lakes CP	189
Beinn Eighe	219
Belvide Reservoir	133
Bemersyde Moss	208
Bempton Cliffs	172
Benacre Broad NNR	154
Berry Head NNR	198
Besthorpe NR	128
Bettisfield Mosses NNR	132
Blacktoft Sands	172
Blashford Lakes	183
Blithfield Reservoir	134
Blow's Downs	140
Bolton Ings (Dearne Valley)	177
Bough Beech Reservoir	186
Bovey Heathfield	198
Bowling Green Marsh	198
Boyton Marshes	154
Bradwell Bird Observatory	146
Brandon Marsh	135
Brean Down	204
Brechfa Pool	223
Brent (Welsh Harp) Reservoir	189
Bridgwater Bay NNR	204
Broad Ees Dole (Sale Water Park)	167
Brockholes	164
Brodgar	220
Brownsea Island	201
Burnham Beeches NNR	181
Burrator Reservoir	199
Burton Mere Wetlands	158

C

Caerlaverock Wetland Centre	209
Calvert Jubilee	182
Cambus Pools	214
Campfield Marsh	162
Carlton Marshes	155
Carr Vale	118
Carsington Water	118
Castle Water, Rye	192
Castle Woods	230
Catcott Complex	204
Cemlyn	225
Chew Valley Lake	204
Chichester Harbour	194
Chobham Common NNR	190
Church Wood	182
Cley Marshes NNR	150
Cliffe Pools	187
Clunton Coppice	132
Coatham Marsh	175
Coed Garth Gell	226
Coll Reserve	210
College Lake	182
Colwick CP	129
Connah's Key Power Station	226
Connahs Quay	226
Conwy	226
Coombe CP	135
Coombe Hill Canal and Meadows	120
Coombes Valley	134
Copinsay	220
Corrimony	219
Cors Caron NNR	230
Cors Dyfi	223
Cresswell Pond	170
Crowdy Reservoir	196
Croxhall Lakes	134
Culbin Sands	216
Culzean Castle CP	212
Cwm Clydach	228
Cwm Col-Huw	228

D

Dagenham Chase LNR	189
Dawlish Warren NNR	199
Dee Estuary (Burton Mere)	158
Dee Estuary (Parkgate)	158
Dee Estuary (Wirral)	168
Denaby Ings NR	177
Derwent Walk CP and Derwenthaugh Park	160
Dingle Marshes	155
Dinton Pastures	179
Ditchford Lakes	126
Donna Nook	124
Doune Ponds	218
Doxey Marshes	135
Drakelow NR	119
Draycote Water	136
Drumburgh Moss NNR	162
Druridge Pools	170
Duddingston Loch	215
Dungeness Bird Observatory	187
Dungeness NR	187
Dunkery & Horner Wood NNR	205
Duns Castle Reserve	208
Durlston NNR and CP	202
Dyfi NNR	230

E

Earl's Hill	132
East Chevington	170
East Dartmoor NNR	199
Eden Estuary LNR	213
Elan Valley	223
Elmley Marshes	187
Epworth Turbary	124
Etherow CP	167
Ettrick Marshes	208
Exminster Marshes	199
Eyebrook Reservoir	122

F

Fair Isle Bird Observatory	222
Fairburn Ings	177
Falls Of Clyde	212
Farlington Marshes	183
Farmoor Reservoir	131
Farne Islands	171
Farnham Heath	191
Fen Drayton	142
Fenn's Whixall Mosses NNR	132
Ferry Meadows CP	142
Fetlar	222
Filey Brigg Bird Observatory	175
Fingringhoe Wick	146

INDEX TO RESERVES

Flamborough Cliffs 173
Fleet Pond LNR 184
Flitwick Moor 140
Forsinard 219
Forvie NNR 216
Fowlmere 143
Fowlsheugh 217
Foxholes Reserve 131
Frampton Marsh 125
Freiston Shore 125
Frensham Common 191
Frodsham Marsh 158
Fylingdales Moor
Fylingdales Moor
Conservation Area 175

G

Garnock Floods 212
Garston Wood 202
Gibraltar Point NNR &
Bird Observatory 125
Gigrin Farm 223
Gilfach 224
Gladhouse Reservoir 215
Gouthwaite Reservoir 176
Goyt Valley 119
Grafham Water 143
Great Fen 143
Greylake 205
Gunknowe Loch and Park 208
Gwenffrwd - Dinas 231

H

Haddo CP 217
Haldon Forest Raptor
Ham Common LNR 202
Ham Wall 205
Hamsterley Forest 160
Handa 220
Hanningfield Reservoir 146
Hardcastle Crags 177
Havergate Island 155
Haweswater 162
Hayle Estuary 196
Helman Tor Nature Reserve 196
Hen Reedbed NNR 155
Heysham NR and Bird
Observatory 165
Hickling Broad NNR 150
Highgate Common 135
Highnam Woods 120
Hilbre Island LNR 168
Hilton Gravel Pits 119

Hobbister 220
Holkham NNR 151
Hollingworth Lake 167
Holme Bird Observatory 151
Hornsea Mere 173
Hungerford Marsh 180

I

Idle Valley
(Sutton & Lound Pits) 129
Ingbirchworth Reservoir 178
Insh Marshes 220
Inversnaid 214
Isle Of May NNR 213

K

Ken-Dee Marshes 209
Kenfig NNR 228
Kielder Forest Park 171
Killingholme Haven Pits 126
Kingley Vale 194
Kings Meads 148
Kingsbury Water Park 136
Knapp and Papermill 138

L

Lackford Lakes NR 156
Ladywalk Reserve 136
Lake Vyrnwy 224
Lakenheath Fen 156
Landguard Bird Observatory 156
Langford Lakes 206
Langford Lowlands 129
Lavell's Lake 180
Leighton Moss 165
Lemsford Springs 149
Lickey Hills CP 137
Lightwater CP 191
Lindisfarne NNR 171
Little Marlow Gravel Pits 183
Llyn Alaw 227
Llyn Cefni 227
Loch Druidibeg NNR 222
Loch Garten 220
Loch Gruinart, Islay 211
Loch Of Lintrathen 215
Loch Of Strathbeg 217
Loch Of The Lowes 218
Lochwinnoch 212
Lodge (The) 141
Lodmoor 203
London Wetland Centre 190
Lower Derwent Valley 173

Lower Test Marshes 184
Lullington Heath 192
Lymington Reedbeds 184

M

Machrihanish Seabird
Observatory 211
Magor Marsh 229
Malvern Hills 138
Maple Lodge NR 149
Marazion Marsh 196
Marshside 169
Marston Vale
Millennium CP 141
Martin Down 185
Martin Mere 165
Marwick Head 221
Mere Sands Wood 166
Mersehead 209
Middleton Lakes 137
Minsmere 156
Montrose Basin 215
Moor Green Lakes 180
Moore NR 159
Moors Valley CP 203
Morecambe Bay
(Hest Bank) 166
Mull Eagle Watch 211
Mull Of Galloway 209

N

Nagshead 120
Narborough Bog 122
Nare Head 197
National Wetlands
National Wetlands
Centre Wales 231
Nene Washes 144
Newport Wetlands NNR 229
North Cave Wetlands 173
North Hill, Papa Westray 221
North Ronaldsay Bird
Observatory 221
North Warren 157
North Wirral Coastal Park 169
Northward Hill 188
Noss NNR 222
Nosterfield Local NR 176
Nunnery Lakes 151

O

Oare Marshes LNR 188
Ogston Reservoir 119
Old Hall Marshes 146

INDEX TO RESERVES

Old Lodge Reserve 193
Old Moor
(Dearne Valley) 178
Otmoor NR 131
Ouse Washes 144
Oxwich 229

P
Padley Gorge 119
Pagham Harbour 194
Parc Slip Nature Park 230
Parkgate 158
Paxton Pits NR 144
Pegsdon Hill Reserve 141
Pennington Flash CP 167
Pensthorpe NR and
Gardens 152
Pilsey/Thorney Islands 194
Pitsford Water 126
Plymbridge Wood 200
Portland Bird
Observatory 203
Potteric Carr 179
Prestwick Carr 171
Priorslee Lake 132
Priory CP 142
Pulborough Brooks 195
Pwll-Y-Wrach 224

R
Radipole Lake 203
Rainham Marshes 147
Ramsey Island 231
Ravensroost Wood 207
Redgrave and
Lopham Fens 157
Ribble Estuary 166
Ringwood Forest 203
Roadford Lake CP 200
Rough Wood Chase LNR 137
Roundton Hill 225
Rutland Water 122
Rye Harbour 193
Rye Harbour (Castle Water) 192
Rye Meads 149

S
Saltfleetby-Theddlethorpe
Saltholme 160
Sandbach Flashes 159
Sandwell Valley (RSPB) 138

Sandwell Valley CP 137
Sandwich Bay Bird
Sandwich Bay Bird
Observatory 188
Savernake Forest 207
Sculthorpe Moor 152
Sculthorpe Moor
Seaforth NR 169
Sence Valley Forest Park 123
Shapwick Moor Reserve 206
Shibdon Pond 161
Shorncote Reedbed 121
Skokholm Island 232
Skomer 232
Slapton Ley NNR 201
Slimbridge 121
Smardale Gill NNR 163
Snettisham 152
South Stack Cliffs 227
South Walney 163
Spey Bay 216
Spinnies Aber Ogwen 227
Sprotborough Flash
Reserve 179
Spurn NNR 174
St Abb's Head 209
St Bees Head 163
Stanwick Lakes 127
Stithians Reservoir 197
Stodmarsh NNR 188
Strumpshaw Fen 153
Summer Leys LNR 127
Swanwick Lakes NR 185
Swell Wood 206
Swillbrook Lakes 207
Swithland Reservoir 123
Sydenham Hill Wood 190
Symond's Yat 121

T
Talkin Tarn CP 164
Tamar Estuary 197
Tamar Lakes 197
Teesmouth NNR 161
Testwood Lakes 185
Theale Gravel Pits 181
Therfield Heath LNR 149
Thrapston Gravel Pits/
Titchmarsh LNR 127
Thurrock Thameside
Nature Park 147

Thursley Common 191
Tiddesley Wood NR 138
Timble Ings 176
Titchfield Haven 186
Titchwell Marsh 153
Tollesbury Wick Marshes 147
Top Lodge-Fineshade
Wood 128
Tophill Low NR 174
Traeth Lafan 228
Tring Reservoirs 150
Troup Head 217

U
Udale Bay 220
Upton Warren 139

V
Vane Farm (Loch Leven) 218
Venus Pool 133

W
Walberswick NNR 157
Walney Bird Observatory 164
Warburg Reserve 131
Warnham LNR 195
Washington 161
Watermead Country Park 123
Weeting Heath 153
Welney 153
Welsh Wildlife Centre 232
Wheldrake Ings 174
Whelford Pools 122
Whitelee Moor 171
Wicken Fen 145
Wigan Flashes LNR 168
Wigtown Bay LNR 210
Wilden Marsh 139
Wildmoor Heath 181
Willington Gravel Pits 120
Wirral CP 169
Wollaton Park 130
Wood Lane 133
Wood Of Cree 210
Woolston Eyes 159
Wrabness Nature
Reserve & Marsh 148
Wyre Forest 139

Y
Ynys-Hir 232